Venice & the Veneto

"All you've got to do is decide to go and the hardest part is over.

So go!"

TONY WHEELER, COFOUNDER – LONELY PLANET

THIS EDITION WRITTEN AND RESEARCHED BY

Alison Bing

Robert Landon

Contents

Plan Your Trip 4

Explore Venice & the Veneto 46

Understand Venice & the Veneto 203

Survival Guide 249

Venice & the Veneto Maps 283

RUTH EASTHAM & MAX PAOLI / LONELY PLANET IMAGES ©

KIMBERLEY COOLE / LONELY PLANET IMAGES ©

Left: Carnevale (p20)

Above: Basilica di San Marco (p52)

Right: Murano glass (p92)

HOLGER LEUE / LONELY PLANET IMAGES ©

Welcome to Venice

Imagine the audacity of building a city of marble palaces on a lagoon – and that was only the start.

Epic Grandeur

Never was a thoroughfare so aptly named as the Grand Canal, reflecting the glories of Venetian architecture lining its banks. At the end of Venice's signature waterway, Palazzo Ducale and Basilica di San Marco add double exclamation points. But wait until you see what's hiding in narrow backstreets: neighbourhood churches lined with Veroneses and priceless marbles, Tiepolo's glimpses of heaven on homeless-shelter ceilings, and a tiny Titian that mysteriously lights up an entire cathedral.

Venetian Feasts

Garden islands and lagoon aquaculture yield speciality produce and seafood you won't find elsewhere – all highlighted in inventive Venetian cuisine, with tantalising traces of ancient spice routes. The city knows how to put on a royal spread, as France's King Henry III once found out when faced with 1200 dishes and 200 bonbons. Today such feasts are available in miniature at happy hour, when bars mount lavish spreads of *cicheti* (Venetian tapas). Save room and time for a proper sit-down Venetian meal, with lagoon seafood to match views at canalside bistros and toasts with Veneto's signature bubbly, *prosecco*.

Historic Firsts

The city built on water was never afraid to attempt the impossible. When plague struck, Venice consulted its brains trust of Mediterranean doctors, who recommended a precaution that has saved untold lives since: quarantine. Under attack by Genovese rivals, Venice's Arsenale shipyards innovated the assembly line, producing a new warship every day to defeat Genoa.

Eyeglasses, platform shoes and uncorseted dresses are outlandish Venetian fashions that continental critics sniffed would never be worn by respectable Europeans. When prolific Ghetto publishing houses circulated Renaissance ideas, Rome banned Venice from publishing books. Venice was excommunicated for ignoring such bans – but when savvy Venice withheld tithes, Rome recanted. Venice's artistic triumphs over censorship are now displayed in the Gallerie dell'Accademia.

Why I Love Venice

By Alison Bing, Author

In Italo Calvino's *Invisible Cities*, Venetian explorer Marco Polo describes the cities he's seen to Kublai Khan – only everywhere he describes is actually Venice. From the moment you arrive, you'll understand why. Venice floods the imagination with possibility, launching dreams like ships from its Istrian stone shores. Gothic palaces, glass-blowing studios, art biennials, masquerade parties: every seemingly permanent fixture of this floating landscape is the culmination of a thousand creative efforts, anchored by a thousand years of travellers' tales. Yet the city's glories cannot be exaggerated or repeated enough; Venice makes Marco Polos of us all.

For more about our authors, see p304.

Above: Gondolas on the Grand Canal (p66)

Venice's Top 10

1

DAVID TOMLINSON / LONELY PLANET IMAGES ©

Palazzo Ducale *(p55)*

1 Other cities have government buildings; Venice has Palazzo Ducale, a monumental propaganda campaign. To reach the halls of power, first you must pass the Stairs of the Censors and a staircase lined with 24-carat gold before waiting under a Tintoretto ceiling showing Venice wielding the sword of Justice. Venice is pictured as a dreamy blonde by Veronese, whose *Virtue Conquering Vice* graces an anteroom leading to the headquarters of the Council of Ten, Venice's CIA. There are no such rosy views upstairs in the Piombi, the attic prison where Casanova was confined in 1756 until his escape.

Sestiere di San Marco

Basilica di San Marco *(p52)*

2 Early risers insist you must arrive when morning sunlight bathes millions of tesserae with an otherworldly glow and jaws drop to the semiprecious stone floors. Sunset romantics lobby you to linger in Piazza San Marco until the fading sun shatters portal mosaics into golden shards and the Caffè Florian house band strikes up the tango. Yet no matter how you look at it, the Basilica is a marvel. Two eyes may seem insufficient to absorb 800 years of architecture and 8500 sq metres of mosaics – Basilica di San Marco will stretch your sense of wonder.

Sestiere di San Marco

KRZYSZTOF DYDYNSKI / LONELY PLANET IMAGES ©

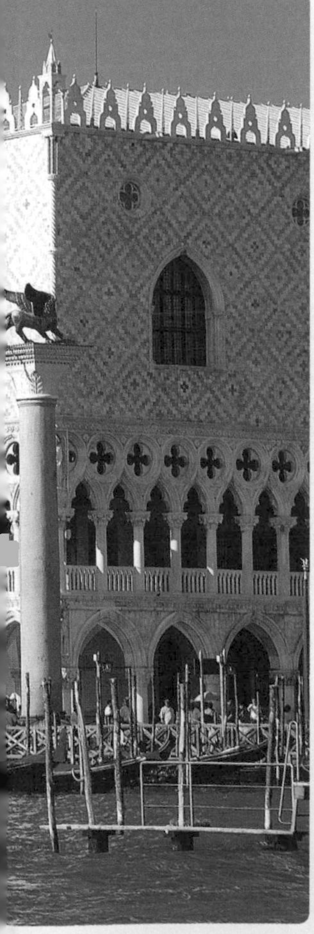

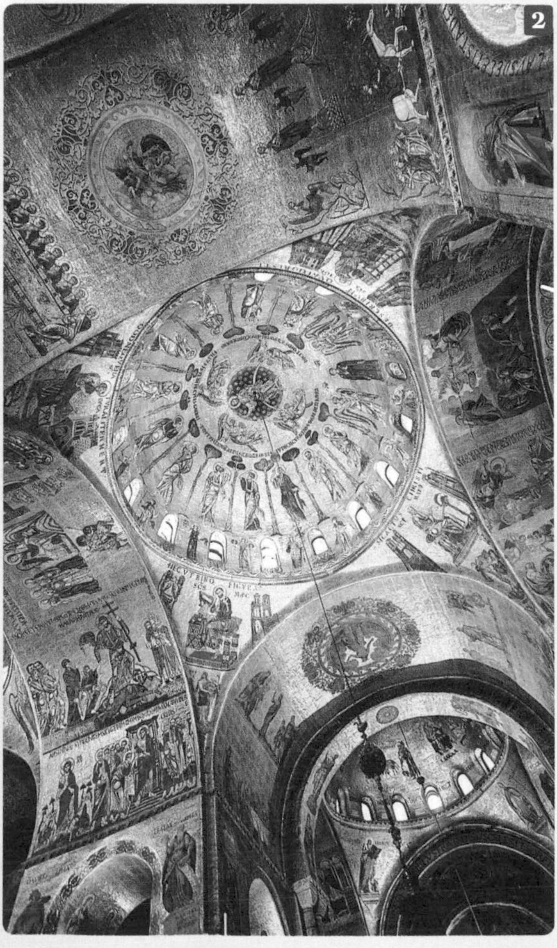

2

Gallerie dell'Accademia *(p79)*

3 They've been censored and stolen, raised eyebrows and inspired generosity – here you'll understand the fuss over Venetian paintings. The Inquisition did not appreciate earthy versions of Biblical stories – especially Veronese's *Last Supper* showing drunkards, dwarves, dogs, Turks and Germans alongside apostles in a wild dinner party. But Napoleon quite enjoyed Venetian paintings, warehousing them here as booty. Wars and floods took their toll, but Save Venice recently restored Sala Albergo's crowning glory: Titian's *Presentation in the Temple*, with a modest Madonna upstaged by a Venetian beauty.

Sestiere di Dorsoduro

Travel by Canal *(p26)*

4 Traffic never seemed so romantic as at sunset in Venice, when smooching echoes under the Bridge of Sighs from passing gondolas. Road rage is not an issue in a town with no actual roads, though boaters do sometimes call 'Oooooeeee!' around blind corners to avoid collisions with rookie rowers. Without honking or gunning engines, you might not initially recognise the sounds of morning rush hour: footsteps rushing to catch the *vaporetto* (water bus) and oars gently slapping canal waters.

Tours

Neighbouring Venetian Masters *(p98)*

5 In other cities you have to search to find artistic inspiration, but here you just cross a *campo* to get from one master painter to another. Titian is the master of the red-hot moment, and his altarpiece for I Frari (p100) fills the nave with the radiant warmth of the Madonna's red robes – her pale wrist revealed by a slipping sleeve has been known to make priests too hot and bothered to pray. Lightning bolts can scarcely keep up with Tintoretto's loaded paintbrush as it streaks across stormy scenes inside Scuola Grande di San Rocco (p98), offering a ray of light in the shadow of the plague that took Titian. SAN ROCCO IN GLORY BY JACOPO TINTORETTO

Sestieri di San Polo & Santa Croce

4

Palladian Vicenza *(p173)*

6 No wonder Unesco declared Palladio's work in Vicenza a World Heritage Site: the city packed with Palladios has a mood-altering neoclassical impact, leaving visitors simultaneously uplifted and grounded, rational and open to possibility. Palladio had a strong classical foundation to build on here in the historic Roman town of Vicenza, and stripped away baroque flourishes in favour of easy graces in its villas, town hall and theatre. PALAZZO BARBARAN DA PORTO

Day Trips from Venice

Opera at Teatro La Fenice *(p59)*

7 Before the curtain rises, the drama has already begun. Wraps shed in lower-tier boxes reveal jewels and Murano-glass baubles, while in top *loggie* (balconies), *loggione* (opera critics) predict which singers will be in good voice, and which understudies merit a promotion. Meanwhile, architecture aficionados debate whether the theatre's baroque reconstruction after its 1998 fire was worth the €90 million, or whether it should have been modernised. But when the overture begins, all voices hush. No one wants to miss a note of performances that could match premieres by Stravinsky, Rossini, Prokofiev and Britten.

Sestiere di San Marco

6

7

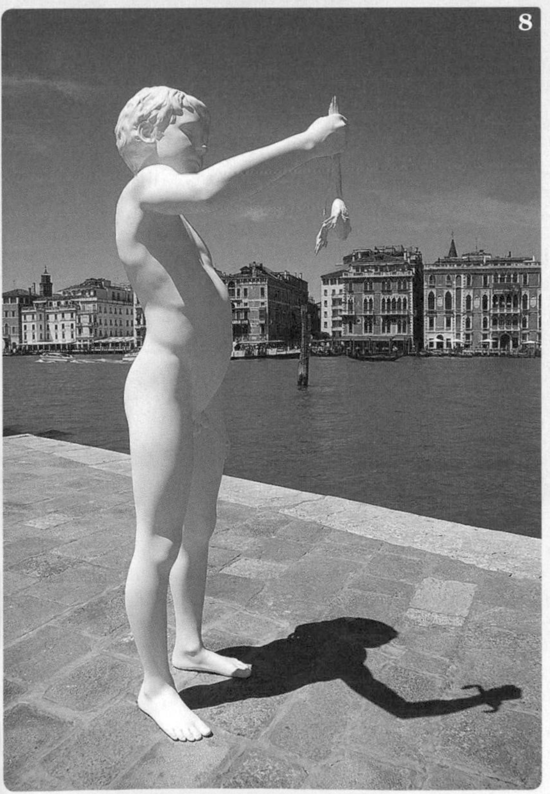

8

Punta Della Dogana

(p84)

8 Paris is still burning with indignation over French billionaire François Pinault's decision to showcase his world-class contemporary art installations not in the Parisian suburbs, but in Venice's abandoned 17th-century customs house. Minimalist architect Tadao Ando stripped down interior walls and inserted windows in watergates to let light and ideas flow through the galleries, inviting visitors to stay and reflect on provocative artworks. *BOY WITH FROG* BY CHARLES RAY

Sestiere di Dorsoduro

Artisans *(p43)*

9 In Venice, you're not only in good hands, you're in highly skilled hands. As they have for centuries, artisans here ply esoteric trades that don't involve a computer mouse: glass-blowing, paper marbling, oarlock carving. Yet while other craft traditions have fossilised into relics of bygone eras, Venetian artisans have kept their creations current. A modern Murano-glass chandelier morphs into an outer-space octopus, marbled paper makes splendid handbags, and oarlocks custom-made for the likes of Mick Jagger are mantelpiece sculptures that outclass marble busts.

GLASS-BLOWING

Shopping

Dolomites *(p185)*

10 Whether you're looking for your next mountaintop to conquer or need to stop and smell the flowers, the Dolomites will meet your desires and raise your expectations. This mountain range is Unesco-protected, from its steep snow-capped peaks to its valleys carpeted with spring wildflowers, and skiers and hikers can't speak more highly of it. There is a downside, though: Dolomites wildflower honey and fried Schiz cheese are highly addictive.

Day Trips from Venice

What's New

Creatively Repurposed Architecture

The cutting-edge trend is ancient history in Venice, where Basilica di San Marco was built with ancient marbles, erm, repurposed from Egypt, Greece and Syria. Minimalist master Tadao Ando revived the idea with his 2009 relaunch of Venice's triangular customs warehouses as contemporary art showcase Punta della Dogana (p84), and in 2010 Pritzker prize winner Renzo Piano reinvented ancient salt warehouses as longshoreman-chic public art galleries (p83).

Palazzo Grimani Reopening

After a 27-year restoration, this frescoed Renaissance palace is at last open to the public for tours, Veronese retrospectives and other blockbuster shows (p130).

Negozio Olivetti

Venetian architect Carlo Scarpa shocked Venice with his radical 1950s transformation of a Piazza San Marco souvenir shop into the high-modernist Negozio Olivetti showroom, now open as a museum (p61).

Venissa

With its secluded vineyard patio on sunny, sleepy Mazzorbo, Venissa seems like an idyllic hideaway – but the inspired cuisine draws international critical acclaim (p160).

Baroque-n-roll

Heading Italy's baroque music revival, Venice's leading classical musicians are playing on authentic period instruments *con brio* (with vigour), as though they might smash antique cellos any second (p39).

Gallerie dell'Accademia expansion

Grand Tour finales have never been grander: painstakingly restored Sala dell'Albergo elicits one last gasp in reorganised, expanded Gallerie dell'Accademia (p79).

Speciality enoteche (wine bars)

'No *spritz*' is the refrain at Venice's backstreet *enoteche*, bringing fresh bliss to happy hour with *ombre* (small glasses) of small-production vintages and inspired IGT blends from Veneto's renegade winemakers (p36).

Doge's Apartments

After much restoration, the home of Venice's most powerful leader is open to the public – secret passageways, hidden Titians, faulty maps and all – at Palazzo Ducale (p55).

Giudecca

Improved *vaporetto* service reveals attractions hiding in plain sight across Giudecca Canal: waterfront bistros, art galleries, spa-hotels and organic farmers markets run by a women's prison cooperative (p145).

Ponte di Calatrava

Over budget and years overdue, Venice's strikingly modern fish-tail bridge is unfinished – wheelchair access is underway – yet sparks spirited happy-hour debates (p119).

Al Pesador

At last, a romantic Grand Canal restaurant with food to equal the view. Pesador's creative *cicheti* inspire flirting, but the squid-ink gnocchi is proposal-worthy (p104).

For more recommendations and reviews, see **lonelyplanet.com/venice**

Need to Know

Currency
Euro (€)

Language
Italian, with some use of Venetian dialect.

Visas
EU citizens do not need a visa to enter Italy. Nationals of Australia, Brazil, Canada, Japan, New Zealand and the USA do not need visas for visits up to 90 days; see p261.

Money
ATMs widely available; credit cards accepted at most hotels, B&Bs and stores. Bars, gondolas and some restaurants are cash-only.

Mobile Phones
GSM and tri-band phones can be used in Italy with a local SIM card.

Time
GMT/UTC + one hour during winter and GMT/UTC + two hours during summer daylight savings.

Tourist Information
Azienda di Promozione Turistica (APT; ☎041 529 87 11; www.turismovenezia.it) is Venice's tourism office, providing information on events, attractions, day trips, transport and shows. For more, see p260.

Your Daily Budget

Budget under €120
- Dorm beds €22–30
- Basilica di San Marco free
- *Cicheti* at All'Arco €5–15
- *Traghetto* ride €0.50
- Chorus Pass €10
- Pizza at Antica Birreria della Corte €8–15
- Venice Jazz Club entry €20
- *Spritz* €1.50–2

Midrange €120–250
- B&B €50–150
- Civic Museum Pass €18
- Entry to Peggy Guggenheim Collection €12
- 12-hour *vaporetto* pass €16
- Happy hour in Piazza San Marco €8–12
- Interpreti Veneziani ticket €25
- *Osteria* meal €20–40

Top End over €250
- Boutique hotel €150+
- Gondola ride €80
- Palazzo Grassi & Punta della Dogana combined ticket €20
- Dinner at Met €60–100
- 72-hour *vaporetto* pass €33
- La Fenice ticket from €40

Advance Planning

Two months before Book accommodation for high season and snap up tickets to La Fenice operas, Venice film festival premieres, and Biennale openings.

Three weeks before Check special event calendars at www.aguestinvenice.com and www.veneziadavivere.com, and reserve boat trips (p26).

One week before Make restaurant reservations for a big night out; skip the queues by booking tickets to major attractions and events online at www.venetoinside.com or www.veniceconnected.com.

Useful Websites

- **Lonely Planet** (www.lonelyplanet.com) Expert travel advice.
- **Twitter** (www.twitter.com) Follow Venice insiders.
- **Venezia da Vivere** (www.veneziadavivere.com) The creative guide to Venice: music performances, art openings, nightlife, new designers.
- **Weekend a Venezia** (http://en.venezia.waf.it) Offers discounted and last-minute tickets to major tourist attractions.
- **Venice Connected** (www.veniceconnected.com) Official Venice tourism site with event listings, ticket sales and facilities info.

WHEN TO GO

Autumn has warmth, sparse crowds and lower rates. Winter has chilly, quiet days; warm, sociable nights; glorious snow. Spring is damp but lovely as ever indoors.

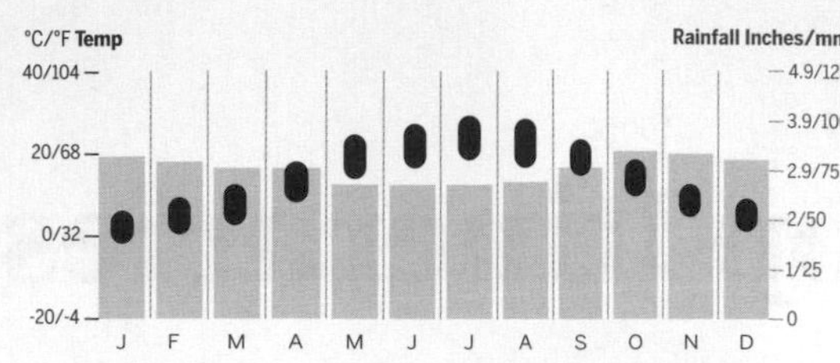

Arriving in Venice

Marco Polo Airport (VCE) Located on the mainland 12km from Venice, east of Mestre. Alilaguna operates ferry service (€13) to Venice from the airport ferry dock (an eight-minute walk from the terminal); expect it to take 45 to 90 minutes to reach most destinations. Water taxis to Venice from airport docks cost €90 to €100. ATVO buses (€5) depart from the airport every 30 minutes from 8am to midnight, and reach Venice's Piazzale Roma within an hour.

Piazzale Roma This car park is the only point within central Venice accessible by car or bus. *Vaporetto* (water-bus) lines to destinations throughout the city depart from Piazzale Roma docks.

Stazione Santa Lucia Venice's train station. *Vaporetto* lines depart from Ferrovia (Station) docks.

Stazione Venezia Mestre Mestre's mainland train station; transfer here to Stazione Santa Lucia.

For much more on **arrival**, see p250.

Getting Around

Vaporetto Slow and scenic, the *vaporetto* is Venice's main public transport. Single rides cost €6.50; for frequent use, get a timed pass for unlimited travel within a set period (12/24/36/48/72 hour passes cost €16/18/23/28/33). Tickets, passes and maps are available at dockside Hello-Venezia ticket booths and www.hellovenezia.com.

Gondola Daytime rates run to €80 for 40 minutes (six passengers maximum) or €100 from 7pm to 8am, not including songs (negotiated separately) or tips.

Traghetto Locals use this daytime public gondola service (€0.50) to cross the Grand Canal between bridges.

Water taxi Sleek teak boats offer taxi service for €8.90 plus €1.80 per minute, plus €6 for hotel service and extra for night-time, luggage and large groups. Flat rates can be negotiated in advance.

For much more on **getting around**, see p253.

Sleeping

With many Venetians opening historic homes to visitors as B&Bs and rental getaways, you can become a local overnight here. Venice was once known for charmingly decrepit hotels where English poets quietly expired, but new designer-chic boutique hotels are spiffing up historic palaces and attracting a rock-star following. Expect to pay €120 to €220 midrange, plus hotel tax (hostels exempt). Some upscale hotels offer vouchers for overnight parking in Tronchetto; otherwise it's at least €24 per day. San Marco hotels are ideally located, but the trade-offs are light, space and noise.

Useful Websites

- **BB Planet** (www.bbplanet.it) Search Venice B&Bs by neighbourhood, price range and availability.
- **APT** (www.turismovenezia.it) Lists hundreds of licensed B&Bs and rental apartments in Venice proper.
- **Lonely Planet** (http://hotels.lonelyplanet.com) Expert author reviews, user feedback, booking engine.

For much more on **sleeping**, see p190.

Top Itineraries

Day One

San Marco (p50)

Begin your day in prison on the Secret Passageways tour of the **Palazzo Ducale**, then make a break for espresso in **Piazza San Marco** before the Byzantine blitz of golden mosaics inside **Basilica di San Marco**. Browse boutique-lined backstreets to **Museo Fortuny**, the palace fashion house whose slinky goddess gowns set standards for Bohemian glamour.

Lunch Enoteca al Volto (p65): handmade pasta in a hidden *calle*.

Dorsoduro (p77)

Pause atop wooden **Ponte dell'Accademia** for **Grand Canal** photo-ops, then discover visual splendours no camera can convey inside **Gallerie dell'Accademia** – now you see where Venetian painters get their reputations for vibrant colour and major drama. Wander to **Squero di San Trovaso** to watch gondolas being built, then bask in the afternoon sunlight and dazzling views of Palladio's **Il Redentore** along waterfront **Zattere**. Stop at tiny **Chiesa di San Sebastian**, packed with Veroneses, then troll artisan boutiques along Calle Lunga San Barnaba until it's '*spritz* o'clock' (cocktail hour) in **Campo Santa Margherita**.

Dinner Bacaro Da Fiore (p65): quick bites of seafood, superior Soave.

San Marco (p50)

The hottest ticket in town during opera season is at **La Fenice**, but classical music fans shouldn't miss Vivaldi played with contemporary verve by **Interpreti Veneziani.**

Day Two

Dorsoduro (p77)

Discover the modern art that caused uproars and defined the 20th century at the **Peggy Guggenheim Collection**, then confront contemporary art pushing 21st-century buttons inside **Punta della Dogana**, Venice's ancient customs house. Hop the *vaporetto* in front of Baldassare Longhena's domed **Chiesa di Santa Maria della Salute** up the **Grand Canal**.

Lunch Enjoy market-fresh feasts in miniature at All'Arco (p104).

San Polo & Santa Croce (p96)

Shop your way south to masterpieces facing off across Campo San Rocco: **I Frari**, featuring Titian's radiant altarpiece, and **Scuola Grande di San Rocco**, filled with stormy Tintoretto masterpieces. Antique shops and artisan studios line your route from Campo dei Frari to **Campo San Polo** and **Campo San Giacomo dell'Orio**, where the medieval church restores the senses with meditative calm. Test your orienteering skills on the winding back lanes of the former red-light district, heading across **Ponte delle Tette** (Tits Bridge) towards **Al Mercá** for happy hour.

Dinner Al Pesador (p104): Grand Canal seats, memorable market-inspired fare.

San Marco (p50)

Cross **Ponte di Rialto** to join overflow crowds grooving to DJ sets at **Osteria All'Alba**, or order your new favourite Veneto vintage at **I Rusteghi**.

Day Three

Castello (p125)

Wayward socialites were warehoused at **Chiesa di San Zaccaria**, but you're free to wander from these Byzantine marvels to Renaissance glories at frescoed **Palazzo Grimani**. Refuel with espresso and a jolt of modernism at Mario Botta–designed **QCoffee Bar**, then head to brick Gothic **Zanipolo** for blasts from the pasts: marble tombs of 25 dogi. The Renaissance is only two bridges away at **Chiesa di Santa Maria degli Miracoli**, a polychrome marble miracle made from Basilica di San Marco's leftovers.

Lunch Slow Food that goes down fast: try panini at Zenzero (p138).

Cannaregio (p114)

Turn away from shopping temptations along **Strada Nuova** to find sudden calm along **Fondamenta della Misericordia**. Pass statue sentries ringing **Campo dei Mori** to reach **Chiesa della Madonna dell'Orto**, the white-trimmed, red-brick Gothic church that was the object of Tintoretto's painterly attentions for decades. Tour the Ghetto's rooftop **synagogues** and enjoy quiet reflection in **Ikona Gallery** and **Old World Books**, until Venice's happiest hours beckon across the bridge at **Al Timon**.

Dinner Hearty meals to satisfy sailors await at Dalla Marisa (p121).

Cannaregio (p114)

Take a romantic **gondola** ride through Cannaregio's long canals, which seem purpose-built to maximise moonlight.

Day Four

Murano, Burano & the Northern Islands (p154)

Make your lagoon getaway on a *vaporetto* bound for rainbow-coloured **Burano** and green and gold **Torcello**. Follow the sheep-trail to Torcello's Byzantine cathedral, where a golden Madonna in the apse calmly stares down the blue devils opposite. Explore relics of this Byzantine capital and spot lagoon birds no longer hunted by Hemingway, then head to Burano to admire extreme home-design schemes and handmade lace.

Lunch Venissa (p160): Sunny Mazzorbo vineyards, inspired lagoon cuisine.

Murano, Burano & the Northern Islands (p154)

Witness the fiery passions of glass artisans in action at Murano's legendary *fornace* (furnaces), and see some of their finest moments at the **Museum of Glass**. After Murano showrooms close, hop the *vaporetto* all the way to **Giudecca** for one last, long view of San Marco glittering across glassy waters.

Dinner I Figli delle Stelle (p151): Hearty dishes and romantic canalside tables.

San Marco (p50)

Celebrate your triumphant tour of the lagoon with a *prosecco* toast and tango across Piazza San Marco at **Caffè Florian**; repeat as necessary.

If You Like...

Curiosities

Museo della Follia 'Museum of Madness' is as creepy as it sounds, featuring 'cures' happily no longer in use on this island. (p151)

Fondaco dei Turchi Bizarre scientific specimens brought home in jars by intrepid Venetian explorers, plus an entire dinosaur inside a Turkish fortress. (p103)

Mercantino dei Miracoli Postcards sent to Venetian sweethearts during WWII, talismans worn by sailors for safe passage, and Venetian offal cookbooks. (p44)

Atelier Alessandro Merlin Squid lurk in the bottom of hand-painted gelato bowls, and risqué coffee cups are definitely not safe for work. (p143)

Malefatte Organic lavender beauty products, fashion-forward man-bags and hand-silkscreened aprons, all expertly made by a non-profit Venetian prison cooperative. (p123)

Fashion

Museo Fortuny Glimpse inside the palatial, radical fashion house that freed women from corsets and innovated Bohemian chic. (p60)

Palazzo Mocenigo Find fashion inspiration in this museum of Venetian baroque style, from bustles to knee-britches. (p101)

Fiorella Gallery Rock subversive Venetian fashion, including lilac silk-velvet jackets hand-printed with red rats. (p74)

Gelateria display

Arnoldo & Battois Venetian designers sculpt silk dresses and finish handbags with findings from Venetian antique markets. (p75)

Spilli A fashion miracle: glamour made easy by young Venetian designers alongside Chiesa di Santa Maria dei Miracoli. (p123)

Boats

Gondola rides The most scenic routes in Venice are travelled by long, narrow, shallow boats, rowed by a single oar. (p254)

Squero di San Trovaso Witness the making of a gondola, shaped by hand and custom-sized to match the weight and height of the gondolier. (p84)

Museo Storico Navale Four floors of nautical wonders, from the *bucintoro* (ducal barge) to WWII battleships. (p136)

Gilberto Penzo Scale-model gondolas for your bathtub and build-your-own-boat kits from a master artisan. (p110)

Row Venice Learn to row across lagoon waters standing, like gondolieri do, from regatta champ Jane Caporal. (p26)

Hidden Gems

Chiesa di San Francesco della Vigna All-star Venetian art showcase and Palladio's first commission, down by Castello's boatyard docks. (p133)

Chiesa di Santa Maria dei Miracoli The little neighbourhood church with big Renaissance ideas and priceless marble, amid a maze of canals. (p118)

Cattedrale di Santa Maria Assunta Lambs bleat encouragement as you walk through this overgrown island towards golden glory in apse mosaics. (p156)

Ghetto synagogues Climb to rooftop synagogues on tours run by Museo Ebraico. (p117)

Malamocco Criss-crossed with canals and emblazoned with lions, this Lido hamlet is Venice in miniature. (p150)

Dessert

Alaska Gelateria Organic gelato in gourmet flavours invented on-site, including cardamom, white peach and artichoke. (p106)

Tearoom Caffè Orientale Tea cakes, crumbles and tarts fresh from the oven, with organic ingredients and fluffy, double-zero flour. (p106)

Grom Slow-food gelato devoured quickly in flavours like Sicilian strawberry, Amalfi lemon and Fair Trade coffee. (p85)

Pasticceria Tonolo Flakey apple strudel and mini-profiteroles bursting with hazelnut-chocolate mousse provide energy to take on Titian at I Frari. (p85)

Gelateria Suso Creamy gelato made in Venice, including mint-chocolate and signature 'doge' flavour: mascarpone laced with caramel and chocolate-covered almonds. (p72)

Backstreet Bacari (Bars)

Cantina do Spade Tasty snacks and house wines supplied by family winemakers make this centuries-old *bacaro* quite a find. (p108)

Osteria All'Alba Scrawled with thanks in multiple languages, this storefront behind the Rialto bridge serves DOC wines and DJ beats. (p73)

Un Mondo di Vino 'A world of wine' tucked into a cupboard-sized locale, with shelves replenished with *cicheti* until late. (p122)

Bacaro Risorto This corner *bacaro* the size of a newsstand overflows with *cicheti* and good spirits, whenever they feel like opening. (p140)

Osteria Alla Vedova Upholds hallowed Venetian happy hour traditions, including meaty €1 *polpette* (meatballs) and dainty *ombre* (glasses of wine). (p121)

For more top Venice spots, see

- Eating (p29)
- Drinking & Nightlife (p35)
- Entertainment (p38)
- Shopping (p43)

Local Hangouts

Lido Beaches When temperatures nudge upwards of 29°C, Venice races to the Lido-bound *vaporetto* to claim sandy beachfront. (p149)

Campo San Giacomo dell'Orio bars Kids tear through the *campo*, while parents watch through the bottom of glasses of natural-process *prosecco*. (p108)

Rialto Market Grandmothers drive hard bargains with joking grocers while photographers shoot heaps of glistening purple lagoon octopus. (p102)

Giudecca Artists sketch views from canalfront tables until it's time for bargain lunches at the boatyard or organic farmer's market picnics. (p145)

Lido di Jesolo Partiers with island fever take the bus to Lido di Jesolo clubs, and recover on Adriatic beaches the next day. (p162)

Month by Month

TOP EVENTS

Carnevale, February

Venice Bienniale, June–November

Venice International Film Festival, September

Vogalonga, May

Festa della Madonna della Salute, November

February

Costumes and wine fountains take the edge off chilly February nights, and revellers party like it's 1699 at masked balls until wigs itch and livers twitch – in its baroque heyday, Carnevale lasted three months.

Carnevale

Masqueraders party in the streets over two weeks in February before Lent. Tickets to La Fenice's masked balls run to €200, but there's a free-flowing wine fountain to commence Carnevale, public costume parties in every campo, and a Grand Canal flotilla marking the end. (www.carnevale.venezia.it)

April

The winning springtime combination of relaxed sightseeing, optimal walking weather and reasonable room rates lasts until Easter, when art history classes on holiday briefly flood the city.

Vinitaly

Good spirits abound at Italy's premier expo of wine and spirits, drawing 150,000 visitors to Verona's VeronaFiere pavilions. The three-day expo in early April starts in sober earnest, with expert-guided tastings of rare vintages and Slow Food and wine pairings – but by the final afternoon it's a proper bacchanal, with singing erupting midday over the dregs of more than a million bottles of wine. (www.vinitaly.com)

Su e Zo Per I Ponti

'Up and Down the Bridges' is a 13km non-competitive race through Venice, with 10,000 to 15,000 participants crossing 55 bridges to raise funds for charity – usually a clean-water initiative in developing nations – and enjoying free concerts at the finish line. (www.tgseurogroup.it/suezo/en/suezo_en.htm)

Festa di San Marco

Join the celebration of Venice's patron saint on 25 April, when Venetian men carry a *bocolo* (rosebud) in processions through Piazza San Marco, then bestow them on the women they love.

May

Summer is better known in Venice as regatta season, when Venetians limber up and row standing across the sun-dazzled lagoon for glory and *prosecco*.

Vogalonga

Not a race so much as a show of endurance, this 32km 'long row' starts with 1000 boats in front of the Ducal Palace, loops past Burano and Murano, and ends with cheers, *prosecco* and enormous blisters at Punta della Dogana. (www.turismovenezia.it)

June

Festivals kick off all month, from millennium-old mystical seafaring celebrations to freaky performance art marathons.

Festa della Sensa

If Venice loves the sea so much, why don't they get married? Consider it done. Vows have been professed annually since AD 1000 in the *Sposalito del Mar* (Wedding to the Sea), with celebrations including regattas, outdoor markets and mass on the Lido. (www.sensavenezia.it)

Festa di San Pietro di Castello

The Festival of St Peter of Castello takes place the last week of June at the steps of the church that was once the city's cathedral, with mass, games, puppetry, hearty rustic fare, and Abba tribute bands.

Venice Biennale (Biennale di Venezia)

In odd years the Art Biennale usually runs June to November, and in even years the Architecture Biennale kicks off in September – but every summer, the Biennale also features avant-garde dance, theatre, cinema, and music. (www.labiennale.org)

July

Fireworks over Giudecca and occasional summer lightning illuminate balmy summer nights on the lagoon, and performances by jazz greats end sunny days on a sultry note.

Festa del Redentore

Walk on water across the Giudecca Canal to Il Redentore via a bobbing, wobbly pontoon bridge the third Saturday and Sunday in July. Join the massive floating picnic along the Zattere, and don't miss the fireworks. (www.turismovenezia.it)

Venice Jazz Festival

International jazz legends from Wynton Marsalis to Cesaria Evora bring down the house at La Fenice, while crowd-favourite acts like Sting and Paolo Conte play Piazza San Marco with a full orchestra. Check the calendar for shows in Vicenza, Verona and Treviso through to August. (www.venetojazz.com)

September

Movie stars bask in Venice's golden autumnal light along film festival red carpets on the Lido, and musical interludes, island picnics and regattas make the most of the optimal weather on the lagoon.

Venice International Film Festival

The only thing hotter than Lido beaches in August is the red carpet at this star-studded event, which runs the last weekend in August through to the first week of September. (www.labiennale.org/en/cinema)

Regata Storica

Never mind who's winning, check out the gear: 16th-century costumes, eight-oared gondolas and ceremonial barks re-enact the Venice arrival of the Queen of Cyprus. A floating parade is followed by four races, where kids, women and gondolieri compete for boating bragging rights. (www.regatastoricavenezia.it)

Venezia Suona

Hear contemporary music from around the world where you least expect it, in Venice's medieval *campi* (squares), under bridges, on abandoned islands, even atop Tronchetto parking garages in free, free-form concerts performed over one glorious September weekend. (www.veneziasuona.it, in Italian)

Sagra del Pesce (Fish Festival)

Burano angles for attention with fish, polenta, white wine, traditional music and Venice's only mixed men's and women's rowing regatta – since this is the last serious match of the regatta season, rowers are out to settle grudges and claim definitive wins.

Riviera Fiorita

Party like it's 1627 along the Brenta River (p165) with a flotilla of antique boats, baroque costume balls at Villa Widman Rezzonico Foscari and Villa Pisani Nazionale, historically correct country fairs, period music and even gelato in baroque-era flavours; held the second Sunday in September.

October

When high tourism season ends, festival crowds disperse and rates come back down to earth, Venice unwinds with a glass of Sant'Erasmo wine and a brisk jog from the Brenta.

Festa del Mosto

A genuine country fair, on 'garden isle' Sant'Erasmo (first Sunday in October). The wine grape harvest is celebrated with a parade, farmers market, gourmet food stalls, live music and free-flowing *vino.*

Venice Marathon

Six thousand runners work up a sweat over 42km of spectacular scenery, dashing along the Brenta River past Palladian villas before crossing into Venice and heading to Piazza San Marco via a 160m floating bridge. Mind your step... (www.venicemarathon.com)

November

Venice takes a breather from its usual antics to give thanks for its miraculous survival against all odds, and carbo-load before kicking off another year of revelry, art and inspiration on 1 January.

Festa della Madonna della Salute

If you'd survived plague and Austrian invasion, you'd throw a party too. Every 21 November since the 17th century, Venetians have crossed a pontoon bridge across the Grand Canal to give thanks at Santa Maria della Salute and splurge on sweets.

Top: Carnevale in Piazza di San Marco

Bottom: *Wave UFO* by Mariko Mori, at the 2005 Venice Biennale

With Kids

Adults think Venice is for them; kids know better. This is where every fairy tale comes to life, where prisoners escape through the roof of a palace, Murano glass-blowers breathe life into pocket-sized sea dragons, and Pescaria fish balance on their tails as though spellbound. Top that, JK Rowling.

RYAN FOX / LONELY PLANET IMAGES ©

Feeding pigeons in a Venice piazza

Attractions

Venice is the ultimate for any kid who has ever believed in pirates and princesses: they really did sleep in Grand Canal palaces – possibly on peas – and launched swashbuckling adventures from these shores. Visit Museo Correr (p60) or Ca' Rezzonico (p82) to see where Venetians danced and flirted in secret at royal masked balls, and find out what they wore at Palazzo Mocenigo (p101). The explorers' ships are displayed at Museo Storico Navale (p136), and the samurai swords and armour they brought all the way from Asia are lined up ready for battle in the attic of Ca' Pesaro (p101). When kids staunchly refuse another church, savvy parents can play the trump card: Fondaco dei Turchi (p103), a fortress with a dinosaur, aquarium and secret garden.

Outdoor Activities

Beach Picnics

Lido beaches (p149) let the whole family relax in the sun, with the option of sun umbrellas and cabanas. Kids can pick out their own picnic ingredients at the Rialto Market (p102), and squeal over the squishy lagoon seafood.

Rowing & Sailing

Glide across the teal blue waters to desert islands on a customised sailing tour from Laguna Eco Adventures (p26), or learn to row standing up like gondolieri do with Row Venice (p26), with an optional stop on the cemetery island of San Michele (p159) for a picnic.

Biking

Explore the Lido by tandem bicycle (p149), and pedal all the way to Malamocco (p150) to discover a shrunken, kid-sized version of Venice.

Rainy-day Activities

Arts & Crafts

Kids inspired by watching Venetian artists and artisans at work can make their own Carnevale masks at Ca' Macana (p89), assemble their own Murano-glass necklaces

NEED TO KNOW

- **Change facilities** Available in public restrooms (p260)
- **Emergency care** Venice's main hospital (p258) offers emergency care and boat ambulance service.
- **Babysitting** Available at several hotels and B&Bs.
- **Strollers** Bring your own.
- **Nappies (diapers) & formula** Available at groceries citywide (p32).

at La Bottega di Giò (p113) or Campagnol & Salvadore (p163), or paint their own vivid Venetian masterpieces with supplies from Arcobaleno (p75). Those fascinated by gondolas can build their own with scale-model gondola kits from Gilberto Penzo (p110).

Secret Passageways Tour

Duck through hidden doorways to explore the secret attic prison hidden in the doge's pretty pink palace on the Itinerari Segreti tour of the Palazzo Ducale (p55).

Transport

Gondolas provide scenic ways to get around Venice once kids get worn out, and timed *vaporetto* tickets allow riders to hop on and off for bathroom breaks (p254). Adventurous kids might want to try the ultimate dare: riding a *traghetto*, an oversized gondola that transports riders across the Grand Canal, standing up. Strollers are helpful with toddlers, but bear in mind they have to be lifted over bridges.

Food

When spirits and feet begin to drag, there's pizza and pasta galore to pick them back up –though if your kids are anything like the Brangelina brood when they stay in Venice, they may demand nothing less than a double scoop of gelato. For tea parties and comfort food, Tearoom Caffè Orientale (p106) offers soups, sandwiches and house-baked cakes. Discerning young diners will want to sample *cicheti*, which are conveniently kid-sized and made to eat with your hands at Dai Zemei (p106) and Zenzero (p138). For a culinary challenge, try the freaky gelato flavours such as asparagus at Alaska Gelateria (p106) and chocolates in gourmet flavours like blueberry and olive oil at VizioVirtù (p110).

Toys & Gifts

As certain Venetian dogi and most parents know, a little bribery goes a long way. Wooden puzzles of the Rialto bridge inspire budding architects at Signor Bloom (p89), stuffed elephants and match-regulation Fair Trade footballs are kid-crowd-pleasers at Aqua Altra (p89), and teens freak out over glitter-gnome Fiorucci T-shirts at Elitre (p89). Treasure-hunting is best at outdoor markets, where antique toys and costumes surface from palace attics (p44). Giunti Al Punto (p124) stocks books for kids and young adults in multiple languages.

Kid Hangouts

Campo San Giacomo dell'Orio

Marathon games of tag in this *campo* (Map p292) probably started around the time its namesake medieval church was built, and kids can jump in anytime. Better still, the *campo* is ringed with bar tables where parents can keep an eye on kids through the bottom of a *prosecco* flute.

Giardini

Parents are wowed by the sweeping lagoon views and backdrop of Biennale pavilions, but kids know they've found paradise when they spot the swings, slides and sandlots of this island playground (p131).

Ghetto

Venice's past meets its future in this historic Jewish island (p116): once school lets out, the silent neighbourhood *campo* turns into a lively football pitch.

Campo San Polo

One of the biggest squares in Venice, this *campo* (Map p292) has plenty of room to run around, occasional puppet-shows and carnival rides in summer, and pizza to please the whole family at Antica Birreria della Corte (p107).

For Free

Despite its centuries-old reputation as a playground for Europe's elite, Venice's finest moments are freebies. Golden glimpses of heaven in Basilica di San Marco are gratis, Carnevale is best celebrated in the streets, and floating palaces are most extraordinary from outside, reflected in the Grand Canal.

Venice's Best Bargains

Glamorous Venice is known as a luxury destination, with five-star hotels, five-course meals and plush gondolas – but savvy visitors can live the *bea vita* (beautiful life) for less. B&Bs offer palatial settings and personal service for three figures, and Venice's best meals are gourmet *cicheti* (Venetian tapas) for €1 to €4 per dish, served at lunch and 6pm to 8pm daily. Splurge on a €80 gondola ride, or experience cheap thrills standing on the *traghetto* (public gondola) as you cross the Grand Canal (€0.50 per ride).

Discount Passes

Church and art aficionados can access some of Venice's finest masterpieces in 16 churches with a Chorus Pass (p256). It costs €10 (for a total saving of €35), and includes such spectacular sights as I Frari, Chiesa di Santa Maria dei Miracoli, Chiesa di San Sebastiano and Chiesa di Madonna dell'Orto.

For €1 more than a Palazzo Ducale ticket, museum lovers can explore five sights with San Marco Museum Plus (p256). The pass covers Palazzo Ducale, Museo Correr, Museo Archeologico Nazionale and Biblioteca Nazionale Marciana, plus one more of your choice. Get more history for your money: for €5 extra, buy the Civic Museum Pass, which is valid for six months and gives access to 11 civic museums (p256).

Historical Sites

Three of the most pivotal sites in Venetian history have free entry: Rialto Market (p102), where an empire sprang up around fishmongers; the Ghetto (p116), provider of funds and ideas to keep Venice afloat after its shipping empire declined; and Basilica di San Marco (p52), the apotheosis of Venice's millennium of brilliant self-invention.

Arts & Architecture

To defray substantial costs to the city, there's an entry fee to the main art and architecture Biennale shows and Venice film festival premieres – but many dance, music, cinema and ancillary arts programs are free of charge citywide, from summer through autumn (fall). Art galleries and Murano glass showrooms also offer free admission, and the entire city is an architecture showcase year-round. Discover hidden gems like Palazzo Contarini del Bovolo on your San Marco walking tour (p64).

Festivals & Events

Festivals fill Venetian *calli* with revelry all year, from Carnevale masquerades to raucous regattas (p20). Eternally grateful for being spared the plague, Venice gives thanks at Festa del Redentore and Festa della Madonna della Salute with fireworks, wobbly pontoon bridges and *prosecco.* Free movies and theatre illuminate nights in Summer Arena (p110); in September international musicians turn archways, bridges and public transport into concert venues for Venezia Suona (p21). In autumn, don't miss *sagre* (harvest festivals) with wine and live music on Sant'Erasmo and Burano (p21).

Tours

To get to know Venice from the inside out, first you have to see the lagoon city as Venetians have for a millennium – by water – then dive into the calli *(alleys) and ascend secret staircases for glimpses of Venetian life behind the scenes and above the fray.*

KIMBERLEY COOLE / LONELY PLANET IMAGES ©

Hidden backstreets of Venice

Tours on Water

Beyond brief jaunts on a gondola, *traghetto* (see the boxed text, p254) or *vaporetto* (city ferry), the following boating outings offer maritime adventures on traditional Venetian boats. Reserve ahead, bring sunscreen and check weather forecasts, since boat trips are subject to weather conditions.

Rowing

Learn to wield an oar like gondolieri do with Jane Caporal of **Row Venice** (☎345 241 52 66; www.rowvenice.com; 2hr lessons €40-50). Find your footing on the sparkling lagoon as Jane shows you how to propel her handcrafted Venetian *sandolo* (flat-bottomed boat) standing up, using a single oar. Glide past Venice's island cemetery, pause for a picnic (book ahead), and hop up on the *poppa* (stern) to learn to row while singing, gondolier-style.

Sailing

Laguna Eco Adventures (☎329 722 62 89; www.lagunaecoadventures.com; 2-8hr trips per person €40-150) lets you sail away into the lagoon blue in a Venetian *sampierota*, a narrow twin-sailed boat small enough to slip into canals but purpose-built to glide along open water. Boats accommodate five people maximum, so it's just you, the lagoon birds and the wind at your backs. Itineraries range from a circuit of outlying lagoon desert islands and Lido beaches to an easy, hour-long drift along Venice's canals at sunset.

Vento di Venezia (p159) offers sailing classes for the day or longer, plus stays at the hotel near the Isola di Certosa marina.

Boating

Terra e Acqua (☎347 420 50 04; www.veneziainbarca.it; day-long trips incl lunch €70-120) offers wild rides to the outer edges of the lagoon with skipper Cristina della Toffola, who shares a wealth of information about rare lagoon wildlife and juicy historical titbits (including a tale of nunneries closing due to scandal during Venice's notorious baroque party-era). Itineraries are customised, and can cover abandoned plague-quarantine islands, fishing and birdwatching hot spots, Burano, Torcello, and other lagoon architectural gems. Cristina makes a mean fish stew and *spritz*

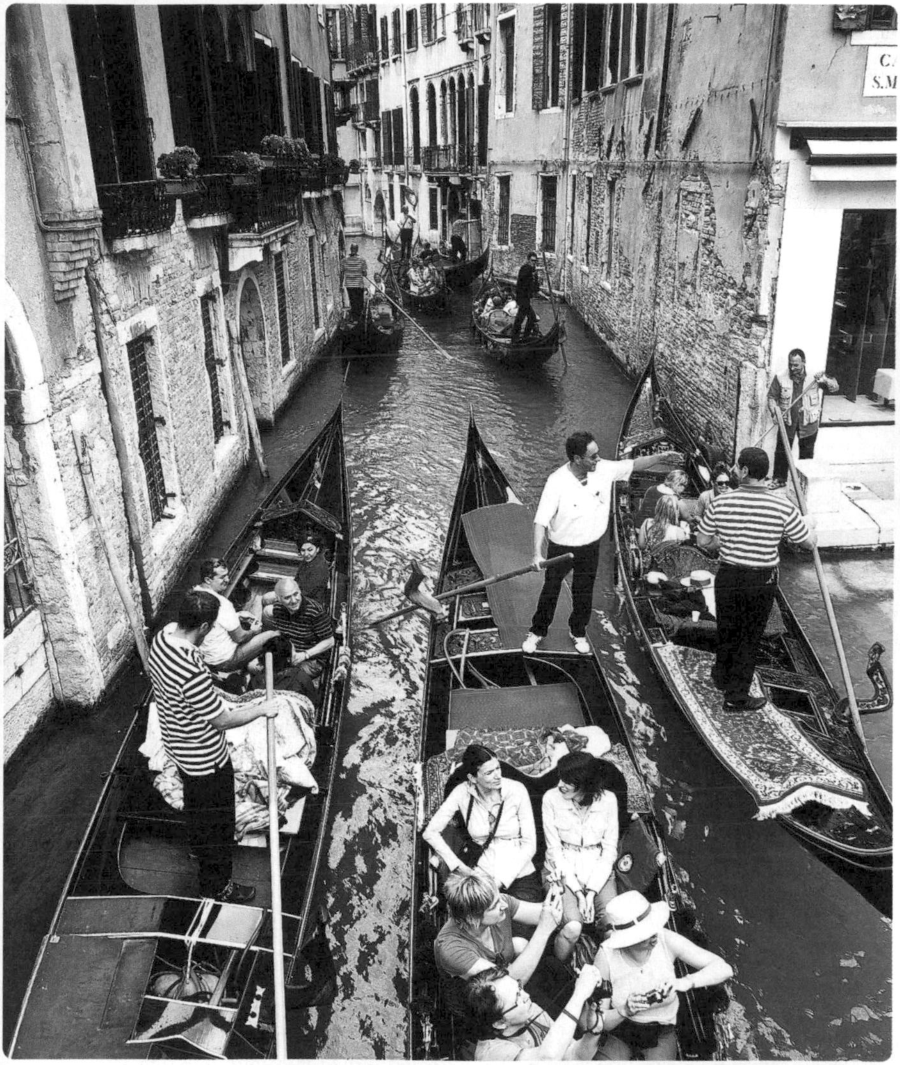

Top: Gondola rides

Bottom: Torre Dell'Orologio (p60)

KIMBERLEY COOLE / LONELY PLANET IMAGES ©

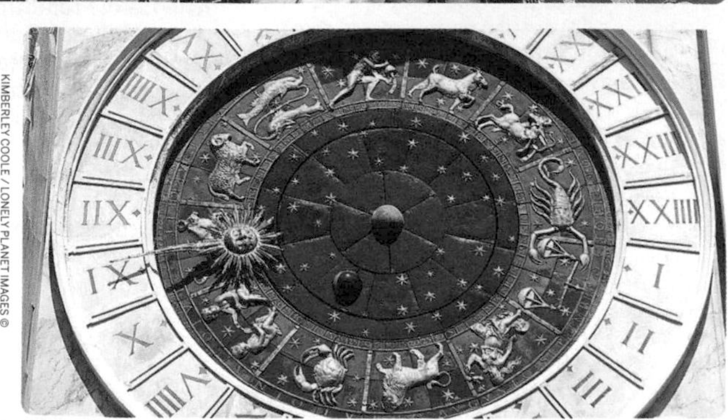

NEED TO KNOW

➡ **Options** Venice's tourism office APT (www.turismovenezia.it), provides suggested itineraries by interest area and lists free tours of major sights.

➡ **Accessibility** For a list of tour operators experienced in organising tours for travellers with disabilities, contact **Accessible Italy** (☎378 94 11 11; www.accessibleitaly.com); see p261.

➡ **Children** Historic sights and boats may not be not child-safe, and minimum age restrictions may apply; ask before reserving.

(*prosecco*-based drink), served on board at picturesque island mooring spots, and takes the utmost care to preserve the fragile lagoon ecosystem en route. Trips accommodate up to 10 people on a sunny, sturdy motorised *bragozzo* (Venetian barge), which makes trips sociable and easy-going for those not accustomed to boats. Reserve well ahead and bring your SPF30 sunscreen.

Eolo cruises (☎049 807 8032; Via Mantegna 11, Brugine) covers the lagoon on a double-masted, 1946 fishing *bragozzo* for three-day trips (per person from €2000, for six to 10 people) or on-board cooking tours. Guests sleep in selected villas and *palazzi* in Venice or around the lagoon, spend the day sailing and eat seafood lunches on board.

Rendez-Vous Fantasia (p200) lets you literally live on the lagoon by renting out houseboats; moorings are in Chioggia.

Tours on Land

Guided Tours of Major Sights

Many major sights offer guided tours – consult *Un Ospite di Venezia,* a free publication available in most hotels, for details of tours of Venetian churches and sights. Basilica di San Marco (p52) offers free mosaic tours run by the diocese; the Itinerari Segreti (Secret Passageways) tour of the Palazzo Ducale (p55) leads through hidden doorways to the attic prison inside the doge's pretty pink palace; and the only way to visit the Torre dell'Orologio (Clocktower; p60) is by pre-arranged tour.

Walking Tours

During Carnevale, don't miss storytelling walking tours written by leading Venetian historian **Alberto Toso Fei** (www.albertotosofei.it) and performed by a Venetian troupe.

At other times of year, there are several top walking tour organisers to choose from:

Venicescapes (☎041 520 63 61; www.venicescapes.org; 4-6hr tour incl book 2 adults US$150-290, additional adult US$50-60, under 18yr US$30) Intriguing walking tours run by a nonprofit historical society (proceeds support ongoing Venetian historical research) with themes such as 'A City of Nations', exploring multiethnic Venice through the ages; and 'A Most Serene Republic', revealing how Venice kept the peace through politics and espionage.

Walks Inside Venice (☎041 524 17 06; www.walksinsidevenice.com; per hr €75, for groups up to 6 people) Spirited tours, run by three local women, lead groups of up to six people on afternoon treks through the city's hidden backstreets to major monuments, off the tourist track through the Cannaregio district, or on grand tours of Venice with detours to Murano and the cemetery island of San Michele.

Azienda di Promozione Turistica (APT; ☎041 529 87 11; www.turismovenezia.it) APT tourist offices list guided tours ranging from an introduction to the greatest hits: inside La Fenice, a classic gondola circuit (per person €40), and a 'ghosts and legends' tour that unravels local mysteries (per person €20). If you don't find your interests covered, ask for an updated list of authorised guides who can take you on private walking tours of the city.

JULIET COOMBE / LONELY PLANET IMAGES ©

Cicheti (p30) on display in the window of a Rialto Bridge food stall

Eating

The visual blitz that is Venice tends to leave visitors bug-eyed, weak-kneed and grasping for the nearest panino (sandwich). But there's more to La Serenissima than simple carb-loading. For centuries Venice has gone far beyond the call of dietary duty, and lavished visitors with wildly inventive feasts. Today visitors enjoy impressive cicheti (Venetian tapas), decadent pastries and a lagoon's worth of fresh seafood.

Venetian Cuisine

'Local food!' is the latest foodie credo, but it's nothing new in Venice. Surrounded by garden islands and a seafood-rich lagoon, Venice offers local specialities that never make it to the mainland, because they're served fresh the same day in Venetian *bacari* (hole-in-the-wall bars) and *osterie* (taverns). A strong sea breeze wafts over the kitchens of the lagoon city, with the occasional meaty dish from the Veneto mainland and traditional local options of rice and polenta in addition to classic Italian pastas. But side dishes of Veneto vegetables often steal the show, and early risers will notice Venetians risking faceplants in canals to grab *radicchio trevisano* (bitter red chicory, a ruffled red leafy vegetable) and prized Bassano del Grappa asparagus from produce-laden barges.

Venice's cosmopolitan outlook has kept the city ahead of the locavore curve, and makes local cuisine anything but predictable. Don't be surprised if some Venetian dishes taste vaguely Turkish or Greek rather

NEED TO KNOW

Prices

In this book, a basic meal is defined as a main dish, glass of house wine, and *pane e coperto* (bread and cover charge). Price ranges for Venice are defined as follows:

€	under €20 a meal
€€	€20 to €40 a meal
€€€	over €40 a meal

Opening hours

Cafe-bars generally open from 8am to 8pm, although some stay open later and morph into drinking hangouts. Pubs and wine bars are mostly shut by 1am to 2am.

Reservations

Call ahead to book a table at restaurants and *osterie* whenever possible, especially at lunch in high season. You may get a table when you walk in off the street, but some restaurants buy ingredients according to how many bookings they've got – and when the food runs low, they stop seating. *Cicheti* are a handy alternative.

Pane e coperto

'Bread and cover' charges range from €1 to €6 for sit-down meals at most restaurants.

Service charges

Service may be included in *pane e coperto* (especially at basic *osterie*) or added onto the bill (at upscale bistros and for large parties). Read the fine print before you leave an additional tip.

than strictly Italian: with trade routes bringing imported tastes to Venice for over a millennium, Venetian cuisine is a highly refined fusion of flavours. Spice-route flavours from the Mediterranean and beyond can be savoured in signature Venetian recipes such as *sarde in saor,* traditionally made with sardines fried in a tangy onion marinade with pine nuts and sultanas. The occasional exceptional ingredient from another part of Italy sneaks in, such as Tuscan steaks, Campania *mozzarella di bufala* (fresh buffalo-milk mozzarella) and Sicilian blood oranges.

Cicheti

Even in unpretentious Venetian *osterie* and *bacari*, most dishes cost a couple of euros more than they might elsewhere in Italy – not a bad mark-up, considering all that fresh seafood and produce brought in by boat. But *cicheti*, or Venetian tapas, are some of the best foodie finds in Italy, served at lunch and from around 6pm to 8pm with sensational Veneto wines by the glass. *Cicheti* range from basic bar snacks (spicy meatballs, fresh tomato and basil bruschetta) to wildly inventive small plates: think white Bassano asparagus and plump lagoon shrimp wrapped with pancetta at All'Arco (p104); *crostini* (open-faced sandwiches) piled with soft local salami with marinated radicchio at Dai Zemei (p106); or fresh-baked whole-grain croissants with mortadella and pistachio salsa at Zenzero (p138).

Prices start at €1 for tasty meatballs and range from €3 to €6 for gourmet fantasias with fancy ingredients, typically devoured standing up or perched atop stools at the bar. Filling *cicheti* such as *crostini, panini* (sandwiches or filled bread rolls), and *tramezzini* (sandwiches on soft bread, often with mayo-based condiments) cost €1.50 to €4. Many *bacari* and *enoteche* (wine bars) also offer nightly *cicheti* spreads that could easily pass as dinner.

For *cicheti* with ultrafresh ingredients at manageable prices, seek out *osterie* and *bacari* in Venice's backstreets, especially in these *cicheti* hotspots:

Cannaregio (p119) Along Fondamenta degli Ormesini and off Strada Nuova.

San Polo & Santa Croce (p104) Around the Rialto Market and Campo San Giacomo dell'Orio.

Castello (p138) Via Garibaldi and Calle Lunga Santa Maria Formosa.

San Marco (p65) Around Campo San Bartolomeo, Campo Santo Stefano and Campo della Guerra.

The Menu

Cicheti are fresh alternatives to fast food worth planning your day around, but you'll also want to treat yourself to one leisurely sit-down meal while you're in Venice, whether it's in a back-alley *osteria* or canalside restaurant. Timid diners who stick to tourist menus are bound to be disappointed – but adventurous diners who order seasonal specialities are richly rewarded, and often spend less too.

PIATTI (COURSES)

No one expects you to soldier through three courses plus antipasti and dessert, but no one would blame you for trying either, given the many tempting *piatti* on the local menu. Consider your à la carte options:

Antipasti (appetisers) vary from lightly fried vegetables to lagoon-fresh *crudi* (Venetian sushi) such as sweet prawns, or a traditional platter of cured meats and cheeses.

Primi (first courses) usually include the classic Italian pasta or risotto; one Venetian speciality pasta you might try is *bigoli,* a thick wheat pasta. Many Venetian restaurants have adopted a hearty Verona speciality: gnocchi, small potato dumplings. Another traditional Venetian option is polenta, white or yellow cornmeal formed into a cake and grilled, or served semisoft and steaming hot. As the Venetian saying goes, '*Xe non xe pan, xe poenta*' (If there's no bread, there's still polenta), a charming way of expressing a Zen-like lack of anxiety or concern.

Secondi (second or main courses) are usually a seafood or meat dish. One common *secondo* is *fegato alla veneziana,* liver lightly pan-roasted in strips with browned onion and a splash of red wine – but if you're not an offal fan, you can find standard cuts of *manzo* (beef), *agnello* (lamb) and *vitello* (veal) on most menus. Committed carnivores might also try *carpaccio,* a dish of finely sliced raw beef served with a sauce of crushed tomato, cream, mustard and Worcestershire sauce dreamed up by Harry's Bar (p73) and named for the Venetian painter Vittore Carpaccio, famous for his liberal use of blood-red paint.

Contorni (vegetable dishes) are more substantial offerings of *verdure* (vegetables). For vegetarians, this may be the first place to look on a menu – and meat-eaters may want to check them out too, since *secondi* don't always come with a vegetable side dish. Go with whatever's fresh and seasonal.

Dolci (desserts) are often *fatti in casa* (house-made) in Venice, including tarts and cookies – but if not, *gelaterie* (ice-cream shops) offer tempting options for €1.50 to €2.50.

DAILY SPECIALS

Here's one foolproof way to distinguish a serious Venetian *osteria* from an imposter: lasagne, spaghetti Bolognese and pizza are not Venetian specialities, and when all three appear on a menu, avoid that tourist trap. Look instead for places where there's no menu at all, or one hastily scrawled on a chalkboard or laser-printed in Italian only, preferably with typos. This is a sign that your chef reinvents the menu daily, according to market offerings.

Although increasingly fish and seafood are imported, many Venetian restaurant owners pride themselves on using only fresh, local ingredients, even if that means getting up at the crack of dawn to get to the Pescaria (fish market; see p102). Lagoon tides and changing seasons on the nearby garden island of Sant'Erasmo (p158) bring a year-round bounty to Venetian tables at the Rialto Market (p102).

Eateries that make an exceptional effort in sustainable, seasonal local sourcing are acknowledged with ◪ in this book, and many top picks marked with TOP CHOICE also practise sustainable sourcing – see p34. Beware any menu dotted with asterisks indicating that several items are *surgelati* (frozen) – seafood flown in from afar is likely to be unsustainable, and indigestible besides.

DRINK MENU

No Venetian feast would be complete without at least one *ombra* (glass of wine) – and that includes lunch. Fishmongers at the Pescaria get a jumpstart on landlubbers, celebrating the day's haul at 9am by popping a cork on some *prosecco* (sparkling white wine), the Veneto's beloved bubbly. By noon, you already have some catching up to do: start working your way methodically through the extensive seafood menu of tender octopus salad, black squid-ink risotto, and *granseola* (spider crab), paired with appropriate *ombre.* Many Venetian dishes are designed with local wines specifically in mind to round out the flavours, so consult your server for a suitable selection; for popular local choices, see p35. Some *enoteche* and *osterie* have wine selections that run into the hundreds of labels; for best selections, see p36.

Vegetarians & Vegans

Even in a city known for seafood, vegetarians need not despair: with a little advance savvy, vegetarian visitors in Venice can enjoy an even wider range of food choices than they might at home. Island-grown produce is a point of pride for many Venetian restaurants, and *primi* such as polenta, pasta and risotto contorni make the most of such local specialities as asparagus, artichokes, raddichio and *bruscandoli* (wild hops). Venetian *contorni* include grilled local vegetables and salads, and *cicheti* feature marinated vegetables and Veneto cheeses.

Several eateries designated with 🥗 in this book serve a good range of meat-free dishes at all price points. Meat-free and cheese-free pizza is widely available, and gelaterie offer milk-free *sorbetto* (sorbet) and gelato with *latte di soia* (soy milk). Self-catering is always an option for vegans and others with restricted diets, but if you call ahead, specific dietary restrictions can usually be accommodated at restaurants and *osterie*.

Self-Catering

Picnicking isn't allowed in most *campi* (squares) – Venice tries to keep a lid on its clean-up duties, since all refuse needs to be taken out by barge – but you can assemble quite a feast to enjoy at your B&B, rental apartment or hotel. For lunch with sweeping lagoon views, pack a picnic and head to Lido beaches, Biennale gardens or the northern lagoon islands of Mazzorbo, Torcello, Le Vignole and Sant'Erasmo.

FARMERS' MARKETS

The Rialto Market (p102) offers superb local produce and lagoon seafood at the legendary Pescaria, Venice's 600-year-old fish market. For produce fresh from prison, head to Giudecca on Thursday mornings to the organic Farmers Market (p152), with fruit, vegetables and herbs grown by a cooperative in Giudecca's prison and proceeds funding job retraining programs. In fair weather, there's also a produce barge pulled up alongside Campo San Barnaba in Dorsoduro, near Ponte dei Pugni – but a half-kilo is the minimum purchase, so you may need to go elsewhere to get that single peach.

GROCERIES

The area around Rialto Market has gourmet delis and speciality shops, including an organic grocery. **Billa Supermarket** (Map p296; Strada Nuova 3660, Cannaregio; ⌚8.30am-8pm Mon-Sat, 9am-8pm Sun) meets most grocery needs, but the deli selection is better at **Coop** (Map p292; ☎041 296 06 21; Piazzale Roma, Santa Croce; ⌚9am-1pm & 4-7.30pm Mon-Sat; 🚉Piazzale Roma), an agricultural cooperative grocery with a branch at Campo San Giacomo dell'Orio. For a wider range of fresh-baked bread options, try Mauro El Forner de Canton (p108), and check out the pastry purveyors in the index.

Mealtimes

Restaurants and bars are generally closed one day each week, usually Sunday or Monday. If your stomach growls between official mealtimes, cafes and bars generally open from 7.30am to 8pm and serve snacks all day. In this book, opening times are mentioned only where they vary substantially from the norm, as stated here.

Prima colazione (breakfast) is eaten between 8am and 10am. Venetians rarely eat a sit-down breakfast, but instead bolt down a cappuccino with a *brioche* (sweet bread) or other type of pastry (generically known as *pastine*) at a coffee bar before heading to work.

Pranzo (lunch) is served from noon to 2.30pm. Few restaurants take orders for lunch after 2pm. Traditionally, lunch is the main meal of the day, and many shops and businesses close for two or three hours to accommodate it. Relax and enjoy a proper sit-down lunch, and you may be satisfied with *cicheti* for dinner. Bear in mind that restaurant lunch menus often cost the same as dinner in Venice, as most day-trippers make a mad dash on lunch places but clear out before dinner.

Cena (dinner) is served between 7pm and 10pm. Opening hours vary, but many places begin filling up by 7.30pm and few take orders after 10pm.

Dining Etiquette

With thousands of visitors trooping though Venice daily demanding to be fed, service can be slow, harried or indifferent. By showing an interest in what Venice brings to the table, you'll get more attentive service, better advice and a more memorable meal. You'll win over your server and the chef with these four gestures that prove your mettle as *una buona forchetta* ('a good fork', or good eater):

Ignore the menu. Solicit your server's advice about seasonal treats and house specials, pick two options that sound interesting, and ask your server to recommend one over the other. When that's done, snap the menu shut and say, *'Allora, facciamo cosi, per favore!'* (Well then, let's do that, please!) You have just made your server's day, and flattered the chef – promising omens for a memorable meal to come.

Drink well. Bottled water is entirely optional; *acqua del rubinetto* (tap water) is perfectly potable and highly recommended as an environment-saving measure. But fine meals call for wine, often available by the glass or half-bottle. Never mind that you don't recognise the label: the best small-production local wineries don't advertise or export (even to other parts of Italy), because their yield is snapped up by Venetian *osterie* and *enoteche*.

Try *primi* without condiments. Your server's relief and delight will be obvious. Venetian seafood risotto and pasta are rich and flavourful enough without being smothered in Parmesan or hot sauce.

Enjoy lagoon seafood. No one expects you to order an appetiser or *secondo*, but if you do, the tests of any Venetian chef are seasonal seafood antipasti and *frittura* (seafood fry). Try yours *senza limone* (without lemon) first: Venetians believe the delicate flavours of lagoon seafood are best complemented by salt and pepper. Instead, try washing down seafood with citrusy Veneto white wines that highlight instead of overwhelm subtle briny flavours.

Gourmet Hotspots

Bad advice has circulated for decades about how it's impossible to eat well and economically in Venice, which has misinformed day-trippers clinging defensively to congealed, reheated pizza slices in San Marco. Little do they realise that for the same price a bridge away, they could be dining on *crostini* topped with scampi and grilled baby artichoke, or tuna tartare with wild strawberries and balsamic reduction. Luckily for you, there's still room at the bar to score the best *cicheti* and reservations are almost always available at phenomenal eateries – especially at dinner, after the day-trippers depart.

To find the best Venetian food, dodge restaurants immediately around San Marco, near the train station and along main thoroughfares. If you haven't made reservations, try restaurants along these gourmet trails in hidden *campi* (squares) and backstreets:

Cannaregio (p119) Along Fondamenta Savorgnan, Fondamenta della Sensa, and Calle Larga Doge Priulli.

San Polo & Santa Croce (p104) Around the Rialto Market, Campo San Polo, Campo San Giacomo dell'Orio and Calle Larga dei Bari.

Castello (p138) Around Campo Bandiera e Moro, Zanipolo and Via Garibaldi.

San Marco (p65) Along Calle delle Botteghe, Calle Spezier and Frezzeria.

Dorsoduro (p85) Along Calle Lunga San Barnaba, Calle della Toletta and Calle Crosera.

Giudecca (p151) Along Fondamenta delle Zitelle.

Eating by Neighbourhood

- **San Marco** Backstreet *osterie*, Slow Food *cicheti* and panini.
- **Dorsoduro** Meat-based cuisine and light bites.
- **San Polo & Santa Croce** Market-inspired cuisine, creative *cicheti*, pizza and vegetarian cuisine.
- **Cannaregio** Traditional *cicheti*, authentic *osterie* and canalside dining.
- **Castello** Daring creative cuisine, pizza and bargain *cicheti*.
- **Giudecca, Lido & the Southern Islands** Traditional seafood and waterfront dining.
- **Murano, Burano & Northern Islands** Just-caught lagoon seafood and garden dining.

Lonely Planet's Top Choices

All'Arco (p104) Panini are decoys for day-trippers; stick around and let Venice's *cicheti* maestros ply you with market-fresh fantasias.

Venissa (p160) Lunch on the vineyard patio is an edible landscape painting, featuring lagoon specialities and culinary artistry.

Anice Stellato (p119) Venice redefines the neighbourhood bistro with lagoon seafood, canalside location and spice-route flair.

Trattoria Corte Sconta (p138) The hidden treasure of Castello: inventive, market-inspired dining in a secluded courtyard.

Al Pesador (p104) Delicate, Rialto-fresh flavours – finally, a Grand Canal restaurant with food as inspiring as the view.

Best by Budget

€

All'Arco (p104)

Pronto Pesce Pronto (p106)

Dai Zemei (p106)

Enoteca al Volto (p65)

Tearoom Caffè Orientale (p106)

€€

Anice Stellato (p119)

I Figli delle Stelle (p151)

Ristorante La Bitta (p85)

Antiche Carampane (p106)

Antica Adelaide (p120)

€€€

Venissa (p160)

Trattoria Corte Sconta (p138)

Al Pesador (p104)

Met (p138)

Al Covo (p138)

Best for Cicheti

All'Arco (p104)

Pronto Pesce Pronto (p106)

I Rusteghi (p72)

Zenzero (p138)

Dai Zemei (p106)

Best for Date Nights

Al Covo (p138)

Met (p138)

I Figli delle Stelle (p151)

Avogaria (p85)

Osteria San Marco (p65)

Best for Waterfront Dining

Al Pesador (p104)

Ai Canottieri (p121)

Taverna del Campiello Remer (p121)

La Palanca (p152)

Dalla Marisa (p121)

Best for Vegetarians

Le Spighe (p140)

Tearoom Caffè Orientale (p106)

Osteria La Zucca (p106)

La Cantina (p121)

Antica Adelaide (p120)

Best for Sustainable Food

Anice Stellato (p119)

Alaska Gelateria (p106)

Vecio Fritolin (p106)

Grom (p85)

Antica Ristorante agli Schioppi (p176)

Best for Garden Dining

Trattoria Corte Sconta (p138)

Trattoria da Ignazio (p107)

Al Nono Risorto (p107)

La Favorita (p153)

Al Profeta (p87)

Best for Classic Venetian

Dalla Marisa (p121)

Osteria al Garanghelo (p140)

Antiche Carampane (p106)

Al Pontil Dea Giudecca (p152)

Enoteca al Volto (p65)

Best for Inventive Venetian

Venissa (p160)

Trattoria Corte Sconta (p138)

Met (p138)

Cucina da Omar (see boxed text, p162)

Al Covo (p138)

Drinking & Nightlife

When the siren sounds for acqua alta (high tide), Venetians dutifully close up shop and head home to put up their flood barriers – then pull on their boots and head right back out again. Why let floods disrupt your evening's entertainment? It's not just a turn of phrase: come hell or high water, Venetians will find a way to have a good time.

Happy Hour(s)

The happiest hour (or two) in Venice begins around 6pm at boozing and *cicheti* (Venetian tapas) hot spots. If you're prompt, you might beat the crowds to the bar for *un ombra* (a 'shade', or small glass of wine) for as little as €1.50 and get *cicheti* while they're fresh. For *osterie* (taverns), *enoteche* (wine bars) and *bacari* (hole-in-the-wall bars) renowned for their food, see p29.

Giro d'Ombra

An authentic Venetian *giro d'ombra* (pub crawl) begins around the Pescaria by 9am, drinking *prosecco* with fishermen toasting a hard day's work that began at 3am. For layabouts, Venice offers a second-chance *giro d'ombra* with *cicheti* at *bacari* ringing the Rialto Market around noon. Afterwards, it's a long four-hour dry spell until the next *giro d'ombra* begins in hot spots around Campo Santa Margherita in Dorsoduro (p88), Campo Bella Vienna in San Polo (p108), Fondamenta degli Ormesini in Cannaregio (p121), and Campo Maria Formosa in Castello (p141). Some bars encourage drinkers to linger with occasional live music acts; for the best live-music venues, see p38.

What to Order

No rules seem to apply to drinking in Venice. No mixing spirits and wine? Venice's classic cocktails suggest otherwise, including spritz made with *prosecco*, soda water and bittersweet Aperol or bitter Campari. No girly drinks? Tell that to burly boat-builders enjoying frothy *prosecco*.

This makes knowing what to order where tricky. Price is not an indicator of quality – you can pay €2 for a respectable spritz, or live to regret that €15 Bellini tomorrow (ouch). If you're not pleased with your drink, leave it and move on to the next *bacaro*. Venice is too small and life too short to make do with ho-hum hooch. Don't be shy about asking fellow drinkers what they recommend; happy hour is highly sociable here.

LOCAL FAVOURITES

Prosecco The sparkling white that's the life of any Venetian party, from €1.50 nonvintage to €3.50 DOCG Conegliano Prosecco Superiore.

Spritz A stiff drink at an easy price (€1 to €2.50), this *prosecco* cocktail is a cross-generational hit with students and pensioners at bars across Venice – except *enoteche* (wine bars).

Soave A well-balanced white wine made with Veneto Garganega grapes, ideal with seafood in refreshing young versions (€2 to €5) or as a conversation piece in complex Classico versions (€2.50 to €6).

Amarone The Titian of wines: a profound, voluptuous red blended from Valpollicella Corvina grapes. Complex and costly (€6 to €18 per glass), but utterly captivating while it lasts, like a stormy love affair in a bottle.

Morgana beer A worthy Venetian craft beer from the owners of La Cantina (p121): unpasteurised, unfiltered and undeniably appealing on hot days.

Raboso del Piave Very James Bond: brash when young, brilliant with age. Save this one for speciality *enoteche*, or give it a whirl on your third glass.

NEED TO KNOW

Opening hours

Cafe-bars generally open from 8am to 8pm, although some stay open later and morph into drinking hangouts. Pubs and wine bars are mostly shut by 1am to 2am.

Events calendars

Check listings in free mags distributed citywide and online: **VeNews** (www.venezianews.it), **Venezia da Vivere** (www.veneziadavivere.com), and **2Venice** (www.2venice.it). For events in Lido di Jesolo and around the lagoon, see www.turismovenezia.it.

Noise regulations

Keep it down to a dull roar after 10pm: sound travels in Venice, and worse than a police bust for noise infractions is a scolding from a Venetian *nonna* (grandmother).

Tocai A dazzling, well-structured white worthy of Palladio, from neighbouring Friuli; a foodie favourite.

Refosco dal Peduncolo Rosso Intense and brooding, a Goth rocker that hits the right notes. This order is guaranteed to raise your sommelier's eyebrow, and probably your bill.

Cafes

To line your stomach with coffee and pastry before and after *giri d'ombra*, check out Venice's legendary cafe-bars, and skip cappuccino for a stronger, local-favourite espresso drink: *macchiatone* (espresso with a 'big stain' of hot milk). Historic baroque cafes around Piazza San Marco like Caffé Florian (p73) and Caffé Lavena (p73) serve coffee and hot chocolate with live orchestras, which might help your heart discover a different rhythm once you get the bill. But this is Venice, and decadence is always in order – might as well order *caffe correto*, espresso 'corrected' with liquor.

Enoteche

Request *qualcosa di particolare* (something interesting), and your sommelier will accept the challenge to reach behind the bar for one of Veneto's obscure varietals or innovative wine. Even ordinary varietals take on extraordinary characteristics in Veneto growing regions that range from marshy to mountainous, so a merlot or soave could be the most adventurous choice on the menu. Ask for an *ombra* for starters, or you might end up with a very interesting bill.

Speciality *enoteche* like I Rusteghi (p72), Enoteca Mascareta (p141) and Al Prosecco (p108) uphold Venice's time-honoured tradition of selling good stuff by the glass, so you can discover new favourites without committing to a bottle.

DOC VERSUS IGT

In Italy, the official DOC *(denominazione d'origine controllata)* and elite DOCG (DOC *garantita* – guaranteed) designations are usually assurances of top-notch vino, but Veneto bucks the system. Many small-production Veneto wineries can't be bothered with such external validation, because they already sell out to Venetian *osterie* and *enoteche*. Some top Veneto producers prefer the IGT designation, which guarantees grapes typical of the region, but leaves winemakers room to experiment with non-traditional blends and methods (such as natural-yeast fermentation). Once you get a taste for local wines, don't miss Verona's annual **Vinitaly** (www.vinitaly.com) in early spring (March/April), Italy's largest wine expo featuring 40,000 wines, including Veneto's finest IGTs and DOCGs.

Nightlife

In central Venice, every footstep reverberates along the *calle* (alleyway), and noise restrictions nix dance-club scenes. Things look up in summer, when beach clubs open on the Lido (p153), and at Lido di Jesolo (p162), about an hour's drive northeast of Venice along the Adriatic Coast. Padua also has a happening club scene (p172), including gay and lesbian venues.

Lonely Planet's Top Choices

I Rusteghi (p72) Gondoliers sing gratis after fourth-generation sommelier Giovanni d'Este's pairings of cult wines with boar salami.

Al Prosecco (p108) Organic grapes, wild-yeast fermentation, biodynamic methods: Italy's finest natural-process wines make naturally splendid toasts.

Al Mercà (p108) Top-notch wines, cheeses and *cicheti* enjoyed by the Grand Canal docks.

Cantinone Già Schiavi (p87) Tiny bottles of beer and outsized neighbourhood personalities keep this historic canalside joint hopping.

Al Timon (p121) Canalside tables, *crostini* (open-faced sandwiches), carafes of good house wine and occasional live music: idyllic.

Best for Beer

La Cantina (p121)

Agli Ormesini (p122)

Il Santo Bevitore (p121)

Cantinone Già Schiavi (p87)

Antica Birreria Della Corte (p107)

Best for Vino

Vinitaly (p36)

I Rusteghi (p72)

Al Prosecco (p108)

Enoteca Mascareta (p141)

Cantina di Millevini (p88)

Enoteca Al Volto (p65)

Best Signature Cocktails

Danieli at Bar Terazza Danieli (p142)

Spritz with olive at Ai Postali (p109)

Rialto at B-Bar (p73)

Bellini at Harry's Bar (p73)

Mojito at Muro Vino E Cucina (p109)

Best for Coffee & Tea

Caffè Florian (p73)

Caffè Lavena (p73)

Tearoom Orientale (p106)

Tea Room Beatrice (p87)

Teamo (p73)

Best Clubs

Terrazzamare (p162)

B.each (p153)

Flexoclub (p173)

Il Muretto (p162)

Marina Club (p162)

Best Wine-Tasting Destinations

Vinitaly (p36)

La Strada di Prosecco (p188)

Suavia (p189)

Enoteca Valpolicella (p189)

I Rusteghi (p72)

Best for Drinks with a View

Bar Terazza Danieli (p142)

Caffè Florian (p73)

Caffè Lavena (p73)

Harry's Dolci (p151)

Qcoffee Bar (p142)

Musicians performing at Caffè Florian (p73), overlooking Piazza San Marco

Entertainment

After the fall of Venice's shipping empire, the curtain rose on the city's music scene. A magnet for classical music fans for four centuries, Venice today supplies its own soundtrack of opera, baroque music and jazz. Given limited turf and loud echoes, sports events and rock concerts are comparatively limited – but Venice has earned a global reputation for regattas and cinema.

Opera

Venice is the home of modern opera and the legendary, incendiary Teatro La Fenice (p59), one of the world's top opera houses since its founding in 1792 and host to Giuseppe Verdi's premieres of *Rigoletto* and *La Traviata*. But the music doesn't stop when La Fenice takes its summer break: opera divas from around the world perform under the stars from June to August at Verona's Roman Arena (p179), Italy's top summer opera festival.

The tradition of high drama in high notes innovated by Monteverdi in Venice has attracted overflow crowds to Venetian premieres since the 17th century. But even before Venice constructed Europe's earliest public opera houses, Venetians enjoyed opera in private *palazzi* and (despite stern disapproval from Rome) in religious institutions. Today you can see opera as Venetians did centuries ago, inside a Grand Canal palace with Musica a Palazzo (p74), among heavenly frescoes at Scuola Grande di San Giovanni Evangelista (p102), and in period costume at Scuola Grande dei Carmini (p83). For ticket information, see p39.

Classical Music

Venice is the place to hear baroque music in its original and intended venues, with notes soaring to Tiepolo ceilings along the Grand Canal at Ca' Rezzonico (p82), creating a Tintoretto soundtrack at Scuola Grande di San Rocco (p98), filling the salon at Casa di Goldoni (p104) and reverberating through La Pietà (p135), the original Vivaldi venue. Between opera seasons, summer symphonies are performed by **La Fenice's Philharmonic Orchestra** (www.filarmonica-fenice.it) at the opera-house or affiliated Teatro Malibran. For Venice concert schedules, see p39.

Interpreti Veneziani (p74) plays Vivaldi and other baroque classics on original instruments with radical verve, in a style known in Italy as 'baroque-n-roll' or 'ba-rock'. Their primary venue when not touring internationally is San Vidal (p65), where a Carpaccio altarpiece makes a dramatic backdrop to strings played *con brio* – you might expect breakout star Davide Ammadio to smash his 18th-century cello at the end of the set. Tickets can be purchased onsite or at Museo della Musica (p63), an informative museum of baroque music and instruments with free admission provided by Interpreti Veneziani.

Music becomes a religious experience surrounded by Venetian art masterpieces in such organ-equipped Venetian churches as Chiesa dell'Arcangelo Raffaele (p85), and you might luck into a rare concert at Basilica di San Marco (p52). But the best Basilica soundtrack is provided by Caffè Lavena (p73) and Caffè Florian (p73), whose house orchestras inspire tangos and waltzes across Piazza San Marco at sunset.

Jazz

Never mind the costumed hawkers sheepishly sporting knee breeches and drumming up opera business in front of the Accademia – Venice's music scene is vital and varied, ranging from improvised jazz to upbeat ska. July's Venice Jazz Festival (p21) features international stars like Cesaria Evora and Omar Sosa, but tributes to Miles Davis, Chet Baker and Charles Mingus continue year-round at Venice Jazz Club (p88) and you might catch free-form jazz jams at Hosteria alla Poppa (p109) or Ai Postali (p109).

NEED TO KNOW

Advance Tickets

Shows regularly sell out in summer, so purchase tickets online at the venue website, www.veniceconnected.com or www.musicinvenice.com. Tickets may also be available at the venue box-office or from **HelloVenezia ticket outlets** (☎041 24 24; www.hellovenezia.it), located near key *vaporetto* stops and ACTV public-transport ticket points.

Business Hours

Event start times vary, with doors at evening concerts typically opening from 7pm to 8.30pm. Due to noise regulations in this small city with big echoes, live pop/rock venues are limited, and shows end by 11pm.

Music Calendar

For schedules of upcoming performances, Venetian discographies and online ticket sales, see www.musicinvenice.com. For upcoming openings, concerts, performances and other cultural events, check listings at www.veneziadavivere.com (mostly in Italian) and www.turismovenezia.it (in Italian, English and German).

Discounts

Last-minute, cut-price tickets are sometimes available at **Weekend a Venezia** (http://en.venezia.waf.it).

Cover

Entry is often free at bars, but cover runs from €10 to €20 for shows in established venues; pay at the door.

Free shows

Don't miss Venezia Suona and Venice Jazz Festival outdoor events, Lido di Jesolo beach concerts or outdoor happy-hour shows around Campo San Giacomo dell'Orio and Fondamenta degli Ormesini.

In summer, the Jazz Festival often culminates with a grand finale of La Fenice orchestra in Piazza San Marco performing with a special big-name act, ranging from rocker Sting to Italian melancholic troubadour Paolo Conte.

Rock & Pop

A handful of other bars sporadically host live music acts, usually rock, reggae, folk and *leggera* (pop). For all-ages alt-rock and punk, check events at Laboratorio Occupato Morion (p142). Bars with regular musical interludes include Paradiso Perduto (p123), Al Timon (p121), Bagolo (p109), Torino@Notte (p73), Il Santo Bevitore (p121) and Antica Osteria Ruga Rialto (p109). But don't expect to roll in late and still catch the show: according to local noise regulations, bars are supposed to end concerts at 11pm.

Free shows happen where you least expect them every September, when **Venezia Suona** (www.veneziasuona.it) invites international acts to perform in non-traditional, outdoor Venice venues: under bridges, atop a parking garage, on a vaporetto. Summer concerts are held on the beach in Lido di Jesolo (p162) – watch the local press in July and August, when international acts like Franz Ferdinand sometimes play for free. Another summer draw is **Marghera Estate Village** (www.villagestate.it, in Italian) in Mestre's Forte Marghera area, a program of nightly live music featuring eclectic international acts and Venetian favourites such as Ska-J and salsa band BatistoCoco.

Big-name acts sometimes play the Lido's PalaGalileo concert hall (Map p285) behind the Palazzo della Mostra del Cinema.

Cinema

International starpower and Italian fashion storm Lido red carpets during the Venice International Film Festival (p21), where films are shown in their original language. But the most cinematic crowd scenes are at free summer movies dubbed into Italian at Campo San Polo's Summer Arena (p110) and on Lido sands during the summer open-air movie series at B.each (p153). Year-round, catch revivals and rare cuts in the original language at the screening room of Casa del Cinema (p110), Venice's new video and film library, and at charming Cinema Giorgione Movie d'Essai (p123), which shows popular, dubbed films in a tiny hall that will remind Italian movie buffs of *Cinema Paradiso.*

Theatre & Dance

Dance performances are staged year-round in Venice, but especially in summer, during the Venice Biennale's International Festival of Contemporary Dance, usually held the first two weeks in June. For more modern movement, check the schedule at Teatro Fondamenta Nuove (p122); ballet performances are usually staged at Teatro Goldoni (p74), which also shows contemporary theatre and Shakespeare, usually in Italian.

Carnevale (p20) fills the streets of Venice with costume drama, but you don't have to wait for February to catch a show in Venice. For inspired staging, check out Il Lato Azzurro (p202), which hosts periodic workshops and a summer theatre festival at a ruined fort on the island of Sant'Erasmo. A former artillery warehouse has been creatively repurposed as Giudecca's cutting-edge Teatro Junghans (p153), where shows range from classic commedia dell'arte to staged readings of new plays.

Workshops Learn the art of mask-acting, costuming and pantomime at *commedia dell'arte* classes at Teatro Junghans.

Biennale venues International dance performances are often held inside the historic boatyards of the Arsenale and at Teatro Fondamenta Nuove.

Carnevale street theatre Don't miss roaming street theatre performances in Italian, French and English created by Venetian historian, storyteller and playwright **Alberto Toso Fei** (www.albertotosofei.it).

Sports & Activities

Boating is the sport of choice in Venice, with the Italian passion for football falling a distant second. The great Italian sport of **cycling** is actually banned in central Venice, though the Lido is a prime stretch of waterfront cycling turf (see Lido on Bike, p149) and the Veneto offers easy routes through patchwork flatlands and tougher challenges into the Dolomite foothills.

Running is gaining popularity in Venice, and though most locals stick to jogs through the Giardini, sure-footed runners attempt the mad dash from the Brenta riverbanks to San Marco via pontoon bridges during the Venice Marathon (p22).

ROWING

If this improbably floating city has one standing lesson to offer, it's that imagination makes anything possible – including rowing standing up *(voga alla veneta),* which is the closest non-Messiahs may get to walking on water. Regattas run from spring's ambitious 32km Vogalonga (p20) through to autumn's costumed Regata Storica (p21).

Lessons Learn to row from regatta champ Jane Caporal of Row Venice (p26), and you'll be hopping up on the *poppa* (rear oarlock footing) with the best of them.

Style Emilio Ceccato (p113) provides gondolier-standard striped boatneck tees, scarves and jackets; Pied á Terre (p111) makes original *furlane* (rubber-soled boat shoes) in fashion-forward shades.

Gondolas Get your seaworthy scale model for the bathtub at Gilberto Penzo (p110) or sign up on the waiting list at Squero Di San Trovaso (p84), where gondolas are still painstakingly hand-shaped and repaired.

Forcole Go *forcola* (oarlock) yourself: *forcola* artisans Saverio Pastor (p89) and Franco Furlanetto (p111) will custom-carve your wooden oarlock to suit your height and weight to propel your boat forward with minimum effort and maximum style – or at least make a compelling conversation piece.

SAILING

Sailing is a year-round passion, especially *vela al terzo*, in traditional, shallow-hulled lagoon vessels with triangular main sails. To get your feet wet in Venice's nautical scene, look into sailing tours (p26) of the Venice lagoon and boating trips up the Riviera Brenta (p165). You might try bringing your own boat to the lagoon, but be advised that navigation is tricky for newcomers to this treacherously shallow lagoon – even Napoleon was kept at bay by this daunting system of channels.

Sailing classes are available at Isola di Certosa (p159).

Navigational maps can be purchased at Mare di Carta (p112), which is an excellent source of information about lagoon boating routes and conditions.

Moorings may be available at Chioggia (p152) and Isola di Certosa (p159).

FOOTBALL

Football is a comparatively lesser passion here than in landlocked regions of Italy, although Venetian kids learn to aim quickly so balls kicked around the *campo* don't end up in the canal. Known as the *arancioneroverde* (orange, black and greens), **AC Venezia** (☎041 520 68 99; www.veneziacalcio.it, in Italian) was founded in 1907 and won major championships during WWII. Since then Venezia has shifted into Serie C (third division), where the team won a championship. Venezia plays at an island stadium, Stadio Penzo, on Isola di Sant'Elena, an island on the backside of Castello.

Tickets Match tickets are available at Stadio Penzo and from **HelloVenezia ticket outlets** (☎041 24 24; www.hellovenezia.it; tickets €15-20). Getting a ticket on the day is rarely a problem.

Transport to matches On match days, special ferry services run between Isola del Tronchetto's car parks and Sant'Elena, and all buses arriving in Venice stop at Tronchetto.

Footy on TV On big game nights, Venetians and visitors converge to watch the match at Inishark (p142) or Il Santo Bevitore (p121).

Casino

Fortunes have been won and entire empires lost for centuries in Venice's *ridotti* (gambling houses). Try your luck if you dare at Casinò di Venezia (p122), as long as you're at least 18 years old – they do check identification – and dressed to impress the bouncers (men are expected to wear jackets). Slot machines are less formal, open earlier, and lack the high-stakes drama of the roulette wheels and blackjack tables. Ask your hotel for a free casino entry coupon, which may also entitle you to a few euros' worth of free gaming.

VENICE BIENNALE

Europe's premier arts showcase since 1907 is something of a misnomer: the Venice Biennale is actually held every year, but the spotlight alternates between art (odd-numbered years, eg 2013, 2015, 2017) and architecture (even-numbered years, eg 2012, 2014, 2016). The summer art biennial is the biggest draw, with some 300,000 visitors viewing contemporary art showcases in 30 national pavilions in the Giardini, with additional exhibitions in venues across town. The architecture biennial is usually held in autumn (fall), with architects filling the vast boat-sheds of the Arsenale with avant-garde conceptual structures.

But the Biennale doesn't stop there. The city-backed organisation also organises an International Festival of Contemporary Dance and concert series every summer, and runs the Venice International Film Festival each September. For upcoming event listings, venues and tickets, check the Biennale website (www.labiennale.org).

Entertainment by Neighbourhood

➡ **San Marco** Opera, classical music, dance, theatre.

➡ **Dorsoduro** Jazz.

➡ **San Polo & Santa Croce** Cinema, outdoor theatre, live music nights.

➡ **Cannaregio** Dance, live music nights, cinema, casino.

➡ **Castello** Classical music, dance, live music nights.

➡ **Giudecca, Lido & the Southern Islands** Lido – cinema.

➡ **Murano, Burano & the Northern Islands** Sant'Erasmo – theatre.

Lonely Planet's Top Choices

Venice Biennale (p41) Europe's signature art and architecture biennials draw international crowds in alternate years, while musicians and dancers perform annually in Biennale summer showcases.

Teatro La Fenice (p59) Divas hit new highs in this historic jewel-box theatre for under 1000 lucky ticket-holders.

Venice International Film Festival (p21) Movie stars align along the Lido's red carpet, and thoughtful, stylish films earn top honours.

Verona's Roman Arena (p179) Larger-than-life tenors rock the Roman amphitheatre June to August, to choruses of *Bravo!* from 30,000 fans.

Interpreti Veneziani (p74) Venice's breakthrough classical talents play baroque with such bravado, you'll fear for their antique instruments.

Best Musical Events

Venice Jazz Festival (p21)

Venezia Suona (p21)

Carnevale (p20)

Venice Biennale (p41)

Best for Opera

Teatro La Fenice (p59)

Verona's Roman Arena (p179)

Musica a Palazzo (p74)

Scuola Grande di San Giovanni Evangelista (p102)

Scuola Grande dei Carmini (p83)

Best for Classical Music

Interpreti Veneziani (p74)

La Pietà (p135)

Scuola Grande di San Rocco (p98)

Ca' Rezzonico (p82)

Casa di Goldoni (p104)

Teatro La Fenice (p59)

Best Free Entertainment

Venezia Suona (p21)

Carnevale (p20)

Lido di Jesolo (see boxed text, p162)

Caffè Florian (p73)

Caffè Lavena (p73)

Best for Theatre & Dance

International Festival of Contemporary Dance (p41)

Teatro Goldoni (p74)

Teatro Junghans (p153)

Teatro Fondamenta Nuove (p122)

Il Lato Azzurro (p202)

Best for Cinema

Venice International Film Festival (p21)

Casa del Cinema (p110)

Summer Arena (p110)

Cinema Giorgione Movie d'Essai (p123)

B.each (p153)

Best Live Music Nights

Laboratorio Occupato Morion (p142)

Paradiso Perduto (p123)

Venice Jazz Club (p88)

Il Santo Bevitore (p121)

Bagolo (p109)

Shopping

Between world-famous museums and architecture, many visitors miss Venice's best-kept secret: the shopping. No illustrious shopping career is complete without trolling Venice for one-of-a-kind, artisan-made finds. All those kiosks hawking porcelain masks and souvenir tees are just there to throw less dedicated shoppers off the scent of major scores (though striped gondolier shirts are quite hip out of context).

Artisan Specialities

Your Venice souvenirs may be hard to describe back home without sounding like you're bragging. 'It's an original,' you'll say, 'and I met the artisan'. Venice has kept its artisan traditions alive and vital for centuries, especially mosaics, glass, paper and textiles.

STUDIO VISITS

For your travelling companions who aren't sold on shopping, here's a convincing argument: in Venice, it really is an educational experience. In backstreet artisans' studios, you can watch ancient techniques used to make strikingly modern *carta memorizzata* (marbled-paper) travel journals (from €12) and Murano glass waterfalls worn as necklaces (from €25). Studios cluster together, so to find unique pieces, just wander key artisan areas: San Polo around Calle dei Saoneri; Santa Croce around Calle Lunga and Calle del Tentor; San Marco, along Frezzeria; Dorsoduro around the Peggy Guggenheim Collection; and Murano.

Glass showrooms and shelves of fragile handicrafts may be labelled *'non toccare'* (don't touch) – instead of chancing breakage, just ask to see any piece. The person who shows it to you may be the artisan who made it, so don't be shy about saying *'Complimenti!'* (My compliments!) on impressive pieces. In a world of designer knockoffs and cookie-cutter culture, your support for handicrafts is a vote for Venice's enduring originality.

Venetian Style Signatures

Italian style earns its international reputation for impeccable proportions, eye-catching details, luxe textures and vibrant colours – but Venice goes one step further, with original fashion statements, artisan-made accessories and limited-edition sunglasses.

CLOTHING

Venice has the standard Italian designer brands you can find back home along Largo XXII Marzo and Calle dei Fabbri in San Marco, from Armani to Zegna – but for original fashion and better value, venture into Venice's backstreets. The odds of an office mate back home showing up to the holiday party in the same locally designed Spilli tunic, Venetia Studium goddess dress, hand-printed Fiorella Gallery smoking jacket or Arnoldo & Battois sculpted silk frock are infinitesimal. Pocket the difference in price between Venetian couture and mass-market logo merchandise, and you could get a return ticket to Venice.

ACCESSORIES

Don't call Venetian artisans designers: their highly skilled handcrafts can't be mass-produced, and stand out in a globalised fashion crowd. Paris' latest it bags seem uninspired compared to purses made of marbled paper at Cartè (p110) or in silkscreened velvet from Venetia Studium (p75), and Tiffany seems ho-hum once you've glimpsed the glass ring selection in Murano. When it comes to handcrafted boater hats from Antica Modisteria Giuliana Longo (p74) and custom-fit shoes with leather heels sculpted like gondola

NEED TO KNOW

Business Hours

Most shops open around 10am to 1pm and 3.30pm to 7pm Monday to Saturday. Some shops in tourist areas stay open 10am to 7pm daily, while shops off the main thoroughfares may remain closed on Monday morning. Many shops close for major Italian holidays, and for all or part of August. In this book, opening hours are provided only where they differ considerably from these general hours.

Shipping

Never mind arbitrary airline luggage limits: most home decor and Murano glass showrooms offer shipping services at reasonable costs, especially within Europe. On new merchandise, customs duties may apply in your home country – check before you buy.

Taxes

Visitors from outside the EU may be entitled to VAT sales tax refunds on major purchases; for details, see p259.

prows from Giovanna Zanella (p142), there really is no point of comparison.

EYEWEAR

Centuries before geek chic, the first eyeglasses known to Europe were worn in the Veneto c 1348, and Venetian opticians have been hand-grinding lenses and stylish frames ever since. Bring your prescription to Ottica Carraro (p74) or Ottica Vascellari (p112), or snap up a replica of Peggy Guggenheim's outrageous frames at the Peggy Guggenheim Collection gift shop (p81).

Bargains

Venetian treasures cost less than you'd think. From hand-blown *murrine* glass beads that make sensational pendants (€1 to €3) to custom chandeliers (€300-plus), Venice's handcrafted goods are quite reasonably priced for the highly specialised labour involved. Like the rest of Italy, Venice does have some January and July sales. Shops included in this book deliver good value for money, with the sweetest deals in the low-season months of November, March and July.

OUTDOOR MARKETS

From March through to October, treasures hidden in *palazzo* attics turn up at Venice's open-air markets. Upcoming dates are listed at www.turismovenezia.it (in Italian) for these not-to-be-missed markets:

Mercantino dei Miracoli (Campo Santa Maria Nova; ⏲9am-5pm, usually last weekends Mar & Apr, first weekends May, Sep, Oct & Dec; Fondamente Nuove) Recent finds include 1930s Murano glass buttons, marbled silk shawls and 19th-century cameos, at moderate prices.

Mercato delle pulci (flea market; Via Garibaldi; ⏲first Sun of month May-Jun, last Sun of month Sep-Oct; Giardini) Vintage Italian cookbooks, antique Murano perfume bottles and 1960s red ceramic pitchers have turned up at bargain prices on neighbours' jumble-sale tables.

Bochaleri in Giardini (www.bochaleri.it; Via Garibaldi, Castello; ⏲10am-6pm, weekends, May 1–mid-Jul; Giardini) The Association of Venetian Ceramists' annual showcase of Italian art pottery, from classic Renaissance portrait plates to freeform raku sculpture.

Mercantino dell'Antiquario (www.mercatinocamposanmaurizio.it; Campo San Maurizio; ⏲usually first weekend of Apr, Jun, Sep & Dec, see website; San Maurizio) Enamelled lockets, vintage Vespa ads and '70s sunglasses sell for prices approaching Sotheby's – but where else can you find a gondola prow, only slightly dinged?

Shopping Hotspots

Mall shopping can't compare to the thrill of treasure-hunting in Venice. Here's where to find Venetian specialities:

Contemporary art Between Biennales, Venice's contemporary art galleries make passers-by stop and stare around Campo San Maurizio in San Marco and along Fondamenta San Biagio on Giudecca.

Gourmet supplies Depending on your airplane's luggage limitations and home country's customs regulations, Venetian edibles and wines make tasty souvenirs from gourmet shops near the Rialto market .

Antiques Hidden gems surface in open-air markets and the backstreet shops of Cannaregio around the Ghetto and Dorsoduro along Calle delle Bottege.

Lonely Planet's Top Choices

ElleElle (p161) Murano art glass balancing modernity and tradition, with essential shapes and dramatic colours.

Cartè (p110) Marble endpaper breaks free of books and turns into handbags, statement necklaces and jewellery boxes.

Marina e Susanna Sent (p88) Minimalist Murano glass jewellery with vivid colours and architectural impact.

Sigfrido Cipollato (p143) Venetian pirate-king skull rings and enamelled Baroque diadems in gold and gems, exquisitely hand-crafted.

ArtigianCarta di Massimo Doretto (p74) Hand-bound musical composition books, leather travel journals, and stationery fit for a doge.

Best Venetian Home Decor

Fortuny Tessuti Artistici (p148)

Cartavenezia (p110)

Materialmente (p75)

Sabbie e Nebbie (p111)

Danghyra (p89)

Best Venetian Fashion

Spilli Lab & Shop (p123)

Giovanna Zanella (p142)

Fiorella Gallery (p74)

Lauretta Vistosi (p89)

Antica Modisteria Giuliana Longo (p74)

Best for Antiques & Vintage

Mercantino dei Miracoli (p44)

Galleria Rosella Junck (p62)

Old World Books (p123)

Antichità al Ghetto (p124)

Carpe Diem (p76)

Campiello Ca' Zen (p112)

Best for Art

Caterina Tognon (p62)

Galleria van der Koelen (p62)

Jarach Gallery (p62)

Galleria Traghetto (p62)

Ikona Gallery (p119)

le5venice (p62)

Best Non-touristy Venice Souvenirs

Scale-model gondola at Gilberto Penzo (p110)

Glass mosquitoes at I Vetri a Lume di Amadi (p110)

Furlane (gondolier shoes) at Pied à Terre (p111)

Calling cards with lion of San Marco from Gianni Basso (p123)

Forcola (carved gondola oarlock) by Saverio Pastor (p89)

Best Mementos for Musicians

CDs from Museo della Musica (p63)

Instruments from Mille e Una Nota (p112)

Vivaldi biographies from Libreria Studium (p75)

Diva-worthy opera wraps from Banco Lotto 10 (p144)

Concert gift card from www.musicinvenice.com

Best Gifts for Gourmets

Drogheria Mascari (p107)

Aliani (p107)

VizioVirtù (p110)

Atelier Alessandro Merlin (p143)

Madera (p88)

Explore Venice & the Veneto

VENICE'S TOP SIGHTS

Neighbourhoods at a Glance

1 Sestiere di San Marco (p50)

So many world-class attractions are packed into San Marco, some visitors never leave – and others are loath to visit, fearing crowds. But why deny yourself the pleasures of La Fenice, Basilica di San Marco, Palazzo Ducale and Museo Fortuny? Judge for yourself whether they earn their international reputations – but don't stop there. Far from a dusty museum-piece, San Marco's backstreets are packed with art galleries, artisan boutiques and well-stocked *enoteche* (wine bars).

2 Sestiere di Dorsoduro (p77)

Arty neighbourhoods in other cities are gritty, marginal districts, but Dorsoduro covers prime Grand Canal waterfront with art at Ca' Rezzonico, the Peggy Guggenheim Collection, Gallerie dell'Accademia and Punta della Dogana. Veronese covered a neighbourhood church

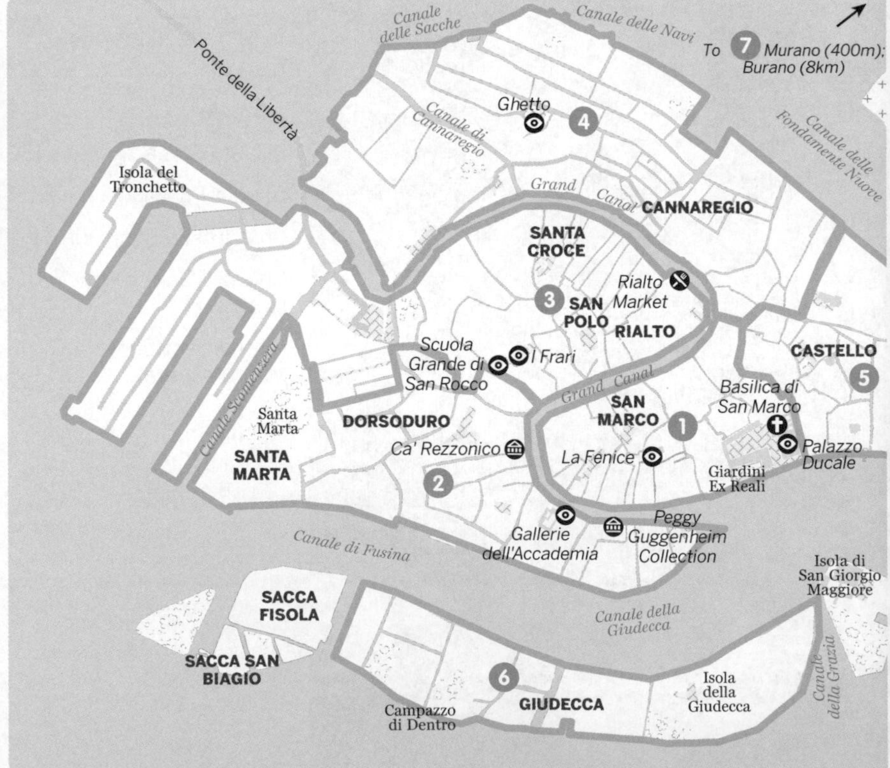

with masterpieces, Tiepolo made hostel ceilings heavenly, and Emilio Vedova transformed salt warehouses into rotating art installations – but the attention hasn't gone to Dorsoduro's head. The neighbourhood lazes days away on the Zattere, and convenes in Campo Santa Margherita for drinks.

3 Sestieri di San Polo & Santa Croce (p96)

Heavenly devotion and earthly delights are neighbours in San Polo and Santa Croce, featuring divine art alongside the ancient red-light district, now home to artisans' workshops and excellent *osterie* (taverns). Don't miss fraternal-twin masterpieces: Titian's glowing Madonna at I Frari and turbulent Tintorettos at Scuola Grande di San Rocco. Charmingly quirky museums occupy Grand Canal *palazzi*, while at the Rialto markets, island-grown produce resembles offerings to the gods.

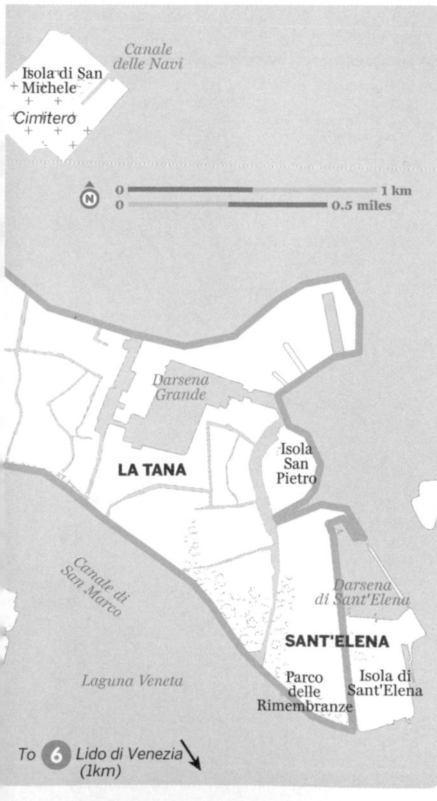

4 Sestiere di Cannaregio (p114)

Anyone could adore Venice on looks alone, but in Cannaregio you'll fall for its personality. A few streets over from bustling Strada Nuova, footsteps echo along moody Fondamenta della Misericordia without a T-shirt kiosk in sight. Between Gothic and Renaissance churches are Venice's top-value *osterie*, and the tiny island Ghetto boggles the mind, considering the outsized contributions of Venice's resilient Jewish community.

5 Sestiere di Castello (p125)

Sailors, saints and artists made Castello what it is today: home to seafood restaurants, ethereal icons and Biennale. Some 5000 shipbuilders once worked at Arsenale; relive those glory days at Museo Navale. Byzantine churches are gilt to the hilt, luxury hotels sprawl along the waterfront, and Vivaldi echoes from the orphanage he worked in. Despite the sublime, it remains down to earth in Giardini, *campo* cafes and *bacari* (bars).

6 Giudecca, Lido & the Southern Islands (p145)

Architecture binges have brought visitors here for centuries, and no wonder: have you seen the Palladios on Isola di San Giorgio Maggiore? Giudecca was an elite garden getaway before it became an industrial outpost; there's still a women's prison here alongside spas, art galleries and romantic restaurants. Lido is Venice's 12km island escape, with sandy beaches, an A-list film festival and Liberty villas. Resorts ring the Lido, alongside quarantine islands and the Museum of Madness.

7 Murano, Burano & the Northern Islands (p154)

Other cities have suburban sprawl; Venice has a teal-blue northern lagoon dotted with blown-glass sculptures and rare wildlife. Serious shoppers head to Murano for limited-edition art-glass. Escapists prefer lazy days boating on the lagoon, mooring for seafood feasts on the colourful fishing isle of Burano and glimpses of heaven in Torcello's golden mosaics.

Sestiere di San Marco

Neighbourhood Top Five

❶ Hear expressions of awe ripple through the crowd as you enter the **Basilica di San Marco** (p52) and look up to discover heavenly visions covering 8500 sq metres of glittering golden mosaics.

❷ Shout *brava!* for encore performances at **La Fenice** (p59), Venice's jewel-box opera-house.

❸ Discover dark secrets lurking in the attic behind the rosy facade of **Palazzo Ducale** (p55).

❹ Adopt a philosopher painted by Veronese, Titian or Tintoretto as your personal mentor at the Libreria Marciana in **Museo Correr** (p60).

❺ Tango across Piazza San Marco at sunset to the tune of the **Caffè Florian** (p73) orchestra.

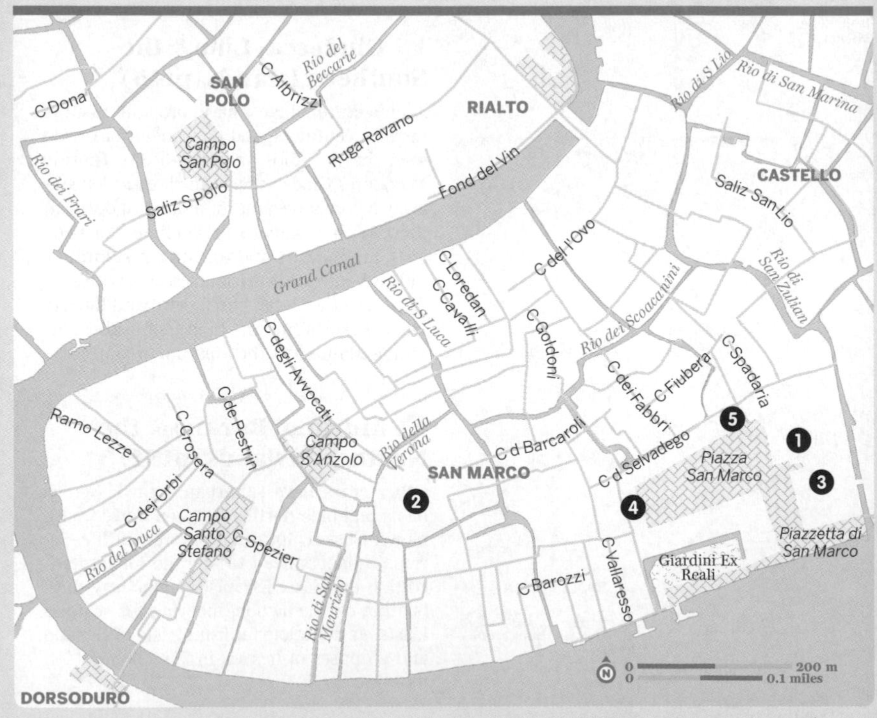

For more detail of this area, see map p286

Explore: San Marco

Take a walk through Venice's golden glories in the basilica and its dark secrets on the Palazzo Ducale Itinerari Segreti tour, then dive into backstreets to find artisan studios, contemporary art galleries and bargain *cicheti*. Detour for fashion and art shows at Museo Fortuny and sunset cocktails at Harry's bar, but don't miss the overture at La Fenice. Return to moonlit Piazza San Marco for a tango across the square, and watch the Moors strike midnight atop Torre dell'Orlogio, heralding another day in the life of San Marco's charmed existence.

Local Life

➡ **Cheap eats & fancy drinks** Skip sad congealed pizza slices around San Marco and trawl backstreets for bargain *cicheti* and top-notch Veneto wines at I Rusteghi (p72), Bacaro Da Fiore (p65) and Cavatappi (p72).

➡ **Musical stylings** Start on a high note at La Fenice (p59), go for baroque at Interpreti Veneziani (p74), tango at Caffè Florian (p73), tarantella at Caffè Lavena (p73) and hang on to your wine-glass through soaring arias at Musica A Palazzo (p74).

➡ **Galleries** Rising from the shadows of historic Santa Maria del Giglio and La Fenice are Venice's best contemporary art galleries (p62), where international and Italian artists supply steady inspiration between Biennales.

➡ **Artisan finds** Mass-market designers line thoroughfares from the Rialto and Accademia to Piazza San Marco – but along backstreets between, Venetian artisans still handcraft handbags, travel journals and glass jewellery (p74).

Getting There & Away

➡ **Vaporetto** Vaporetti 1 and N stop along the Grand Canal at several points in San Marco, including Rialto, Sant'Angelo, San Samuele, Santa Maria del Giglio and Vallaresso.

➡ **Walking** Follow yellow-signed shortcuts from the Rialto through shop-lined Marzarie to Piazza San Marco.

Lonely Planet's Top Tip

In San Marco, the price of a sit-down cappuccino seems more like rent. Take your coffee standing at a bar for just €1 to €2.50, spend a couple more euros for sunshine and people-watching at a campo table, or luxuriate in the baroque cafes of Piazza San Marco. There's usually a €6 music surcharge for outdoor seating in Piazza San Marco, so you may as well get your money's worth and tango.

Best Places to Eat

➡ Enoteca al Volto (p65)

➡ Osteria San Marco (p65)

➡ Bacaro Da Fiore (p65)

➡ I Rusteghi (p72)

➡ Osteria da Carla (p65)

For reviews, see p65 

Best Places to Drink

➡ I Rusteghi (p72)

➡ Caffè Florian (p73)

➡ Caffè Lavena (p73)

➡ Harry's Bar (p73)

➡ Osteria all'Alba (p73)

For reviews, see p72 

Best Interior Decor

➡ Basilica di San Marco (p52)

➡ Libreria Nazionale Marciana (p60)

➡ Palazzo Ducale (p55)

➡ Museo Fortuny (p60)

➡ Negozio Olivetti (p61)

KIMBERLEY COOLE / LONELY PLANET IMAGES ©

TOP SIGHTS
BASILICA DI SAN MARCO

Creating Venice's architectural wonder took nearly 800 years of labour and one saintly barrel of lard. Legend has it that in AD 828, Venetian merchants smuggled St Mark's corpse out of Egypt in a barrel of pork fat to avoid inspection by Muslim customs authorities. An impressive basilica was designed to house the relics. Church authorities in Rome took a dim view of Venice's tendency to glorify itself and God in the same breath, but Venice defiantly created the basilica in its own cosmopolitan image, with Byzantine onion-bulb domes, Greek cross layout and Egyptian marble walls. Occasionally higher purpose was clouded by construction dust: St Mark's bones were misplaced twice.

Exterior

The brick basilica is clad in patchworks of marbles and reliefs from Syria, Egypt and Palestine – priceless trophies from Crusades conquests and battles with Genova. On the southwest corner is the **Four Tetrarchs**, an Egyptian porphyry statue supposedly representing four emperors of ancient Rome looted from Constantinople. Rather than hide this stolen statue, as furtive art thieves might do, Venice made it a cornerstone of the official doge's chapel.

Facade

The front of the basilica ripples and crests like a wave, its five niched portals capped with shimmering mosaics and frothy stonework arches. In the left-most portal, lunette mosaics dating from 1270 show St Mark's stolen

DON'T MISS...

- 1270 lunette mosaics
- Dome of Genesis
- Dome of the Prophets
- Pala d'Oro
- Loggia dei Cavalli

PRACTICALITIES

- Map p286
- ☎041 241 38 17
- www.basilicasanmarco.it
- Piazza San Marco
- Basilica entry free
- Modest dress required
- Free, obligatory one-hour baggage deposit at Ateneo di San Basso (Map p286; ⏰9.30am-5.30pm)
- ⏰9.45am-5pm Mon-Sat, 2-4pm Sun & holidays

body arriving at the basilica – a story reprised in 1660 lunette mosaics on the second portal from the right. The far-right portal is a masterpiece of architectural thievery: over Greek columns and a Moorish arch is a lacy screen that seems lifted right from a Turkish harem. Grand entrances through the central portal pass between, under an ornate triple arch with Egyptian purple porphyry columns and 13th- to 14th-century reliefs of vines, virtues and astrological signs.

Dome Mosaics

Inside the basilica are 8500 sq metres of mosaics, many made with 24-carat gold to represent divine light. In niches flanking the main door as you enter the narthex (vestibule) glitters the stunning *Apostles with the Madonna*. At more than 950 years old, these are the oldest mosaics in the basilica. The atrium's medieval *Dome of Genesis* depicts the separation of sky and water with surprisingly abstract motifs, anticipating modern art by 650 years. *Last Judgment* mosaics cover the atrium vault and the *Apocalypse* looms large in vault mosaics over the gallery.

Mystical transfusions occur in the Dome of the Holy Spirit, where a dove's blood streams on to the heads of saints. In the central 13th-century Cupola of the Ascension, angels swirl overhead while dreamy-eyed St Mark rests on the pendentive. Scenes from St Mark's life unfold over the main altar, in vaults flanking the Dome of the Prophets (best seen from the Pala d'Oro).

Pala d'Oro

Tucked behind the main altar containing St Mark's sarcophagus is the **Pala d'Oro** (admission €2; ⌚9.45am-4pm Mon-Sat & 2-4pm Sun), studded with 2000 emeralds, amethysts, sapphires, rubies, pearls and other gemstones. Even more precious are biblical figures in vibrant cloisonné, begun in Constantinople in AD 976 and elaborated by Venetian goldsmiths in 1209. The enamelled saints have wild, unkempt beards and wide eyes fixed on Jesus, who glances sideways at a studious St Mark as Mary throws up her hands in wonder. Angels overlooking the scene appear to be clapping – an understandable reaction to this captivating scene.

Museum

San Marco remained the doge's chapel until 1807, and the ducal treasures upstairs in the **Museo** (adult €4; ⌚9.45am-4pm Mon-Sat, 2-4pm Sun) puts a king's ransom to shame. Gilt bronze horses taken by Venice from Constantinople were stolen in turn

PLANNING YOUR VISIT

The grandest entrances to the basilica are with a crowd, its polyglot expressions of wonder making a hive-like hum under honey-gold domes. Luckily, the queue moves quickly – waits are rarely more than 15 minutes, even when the queue extends past the door to Palazzo Ducale. Book online (www.venetoinside.com; €1 booking fee) to skip queues and head directly into the central portal. Arrive at odd times to avoid tour groups, which tend to arrive on the hour or half-hour. Free guided tours from the diocese explaining the theological messages in the mosaics also enjoy expedited entry through the central portal (open 11am Monday to Saturday April to October by prior reservation).

Attending evening vespers allows you to enter the basilica in the evening. Worshippers enter through a side door and are expected to sit quietly for the duration of services; visits beyond the side chapel are not allowed.

by Napoleon, but eventually returned to the basilica and installed in the 1st-floor gallery. Portals lead from the gallery on to the giddiness-inducing Loggia dei Cavalli, where reproductions of the horses gallop off the balcony over Piazza San Marco.

The Museum also offers close-up glimpses of recently restored mosaics and a look inside the doge's banquet hall, where dignitaries wined and dined right above the altar among lithe stucco figures of Music, Poetry and Peace. In 13th- to 14th-century mosaic fragments, the Prophet Abraham is all ears and raised eyebrows, as though scandalised by Venetian gossip. On an interior balcony, Salviati's restored 1542–52 mosaic of the Virgin's family tree shows Mary's ancestors perched on branches, alternately chatting and ignoring one another, as families often do.

Treasury

Holy bones and booty from the Crusades fill the **Tesoro** (Treasury; admission €3; ⌚9.45am-4pm Mon-Sat, 2-4pm Sun). Amid the jumble of jewelled chalices is a 10th-century rock-crystal ewer with a gazelle-shaped handle and winged feet made for Fatimid Caliph al-'Aziz-bi-llah. Velvet-padded boxes preserve doges' remains alongside saints' relics, including St Roch's femur, St Mark's thumb, the arm St George used to slay the dragon and even a lock of the Madonna's hair.

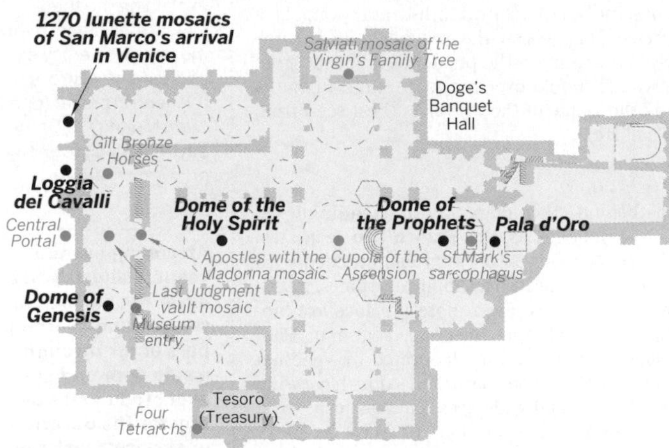

Ground Floor

TOP SIGHTS
PALAZZO DUCALE

CHRISTOPHER GROENHOUT / LONELY PLANET IMAGES ©

Don't be fooled by its genteel Gothic elegance: underneath that lacy, pink-chequered marble cladding, the doge's palace shows serious muscle and a steely will to survive. The seat of Venice's government for nearly seven centuries, this powerhouse stood the test of storms, wars, conspiracies and economic crashes. After fire gutted the building in 1577, the city considered Palladio's offer to build one of his signature neoclassical temples in its place. Instead, Antonio da Ponte won the commission to restore the magnificent Gothic facades in white Istrian stone and Veronese pink marble.

Exterior

Outside, the Palazzo mixes business with pleasure, capping a graceful colonnade with medieval capitals depicting key Venetian guilds. The loggia running along the *piazzetta* (little square) may seem like a fanciful architectural flourish but it served a solemn purpose: death sentences were read out between the ninth and 10th columns from the left. Facing the piazza, Zane and Bartolomeo Bon's 1443 **Porta della Carta** (Paper Door) was once an elegant point of entry for dignitaries, while also serving as the bulletin board for government decrees.

Courtyard

Entering through the colonnaded courtyard you'll spot Sansovino's brawny statues of Apollo and Neptune flanking Antonio Rizzo's **Scala dei Giganti** (Giants' Staircase). Recent restorations have preserved charming cherubim propping up the pillars, though slippery incised marble steps are

DON'T MISS

- Scala dei Giganti
- Sala del Scudo
- Scala d'Oro
- Sala delle Quattro Porte
- Anticollegio
- Sala Consiglio dei Dieci
- Piombi

PRACTICALITIES

- Map p286
- ☎041 271 59 11
- www.museicivici veneziani.it, in Italian
- Piazzetta San Marco 52
- adult/reduced incl Museo Correr €14/8 or Museum Pass
- 8.30am-7pm Apr-Oct, to 5.30pm Nov-Mar
- San Zaccaria

PALAZZO DUCALE'S TOP FIVE PROPAGANDA PAINTINGS

Veronese's *Juno Bestowing Her Gifts on Venice*, Tiepolo's *Venice Receiving Gifts of the Sea from Neptune*, Titian's *Doge Antonio Grimani Kneeling before Faith*, Tintoretto's *Minerva Dismissing Mars* and Veronese's 1578–82 *Virtues of the Republic* are not to be missed.

In Sala del Maggior Consiglio the wall frieze depicts the first 76 doges of Venice, but note the black space: Doge Marin Falier would have appeared there had he not lost his head for treason in 1355.

off-limits. On the east side of the courtyard arcade were the dreaded **Poggi** (Wells), where prisoners were kept below water level – but now a baggage deposit is installed in their place.

First Floor

Climb the Scala dei Censori (Stairs of the Censors) to the **Doge's Apartments**, where the doge lived under 24-hour guard with a short commute to work up a secret staircase capped with Titian's painting of St Christopher wading across troubled lagoon waters. Still, consider the real estate: a dozen salons with stone fireplaces, terrace garden and private entry to the basilica. **Sala del Scudo** (Shield Room) is covered with world maps that reveal the extents of Venetian power (and the limits of its cartographers) c 1483 and 1762. The upside-down New World map places Canada above Virginia and Florida near Asia, while the British Isles are essentially Scotland plus Newcastle.

Second Floor

Head up Sansovino's 24-carat gilt stuccowork **Scala d'Oro** (Golden Staircase) and emerge into rooms covered with gorgeous propaganda. In **Sala delle Quattro Porte** (Hall of the Four Doors), ambassadors awaited ducal audiences under a Palladio-designed ceiling frescoed by Tintoretto, showing Justice presenting sword and scales to Venice's Doge Girolamo Priuli. Other convincing shows of Venetian superiority include Titian's 1576 *Doge Antonio Grimani Kneeling before Faith* amid approving cherubs and Tiepolo's 1740s *Venice Receiving Gifts of the Sea from Neptune,* where Venice is a gorgeous blonde casually leaning on a lion.

Delegations waited in the **Anticollegio** (Council Antechamber), where Tintoretto drew parallels between Roman gods and Venetian government: *Mercury and the Three Graces* reward Venice's industriousness with beauty, and *Minerva Dismissing Mars* is a Venetian triumph of savvy over brute force. The recently restored ceiling is Veronese's 1577 *Venice Distributing Honours*, while on the walls is a vivid reminder of diplomatic behaviour to avoid: Veronese's *Rape of Europe*.

Few were granted an audience in the Palladio-designed **Collegio** (Council Room), where Veronese's *Virtues of the Republic* ceiling shows Venice as a bewitching blonde waving her sceptre like a wand. Father-son team Jacopo and Domenico Tintoretto attempt similar flattery, showing Venice keeping company with Apollo, Mars and Mercury in their *Triumph of Venice* ceiling for **Sala del Senato** (Senate Hall), but frolicking lagoon sea-monsters steal the scene.

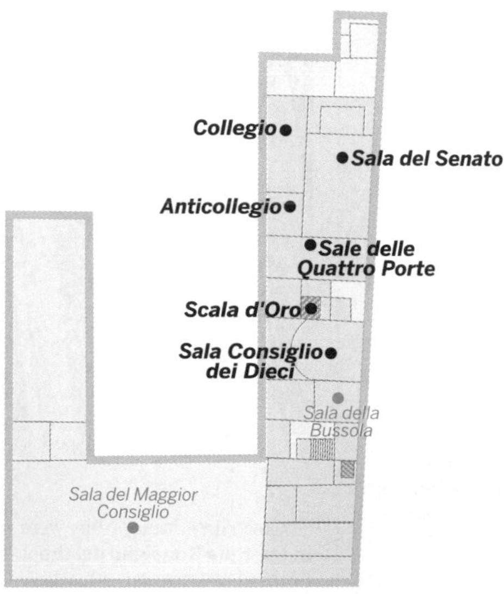

Second Floor

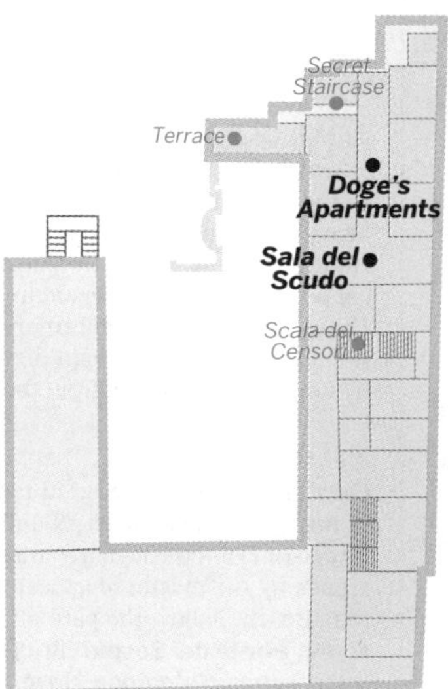

First Floor

SECRET PASSAGES TOUR

Discover Venice's state secrets in the Palazzo Ducale attic on a fascinating 75-minute guided tour: Itinerari Segreti (Secret Passages; ☎041 4273 0892; adult/reduced €18/12; tours in English 9.55am, 10.45am & 11.35am, Italian 9.30am & 11.10am, French 10.20am & noon). Follow your guide through a hidden passageway disguised as a filing cabinet in Sala del Consiglio dei Dieci (Chamber of the Council of 10), festooned with happy cherubim and Veronese's optimistic *Triumph of Virtue Over Vice*. Suddenly you're in the cramped, unadorned Council of 10 Secret Headquarters, adjoining a Trial Chamber lined with drawers of top-secret files. Follow the path of the accused into the windowless Interrogation Room. In 1756, Casanova was condemned to five years' confinement in the adjoining prison for corrupting nuns and a more serious charge of spreading Freemasonry – but he escaped through the roof.

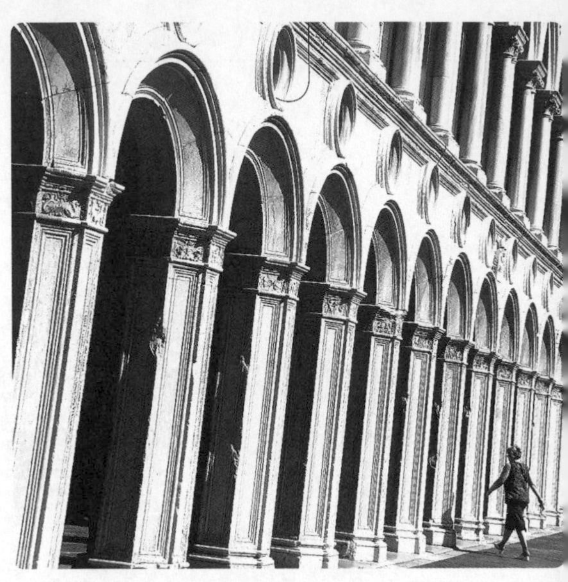

Government cover-ups were never so appealing as in the **Sala Consiglio dei Dieci** (Trial Chambers of the Council of 10; Room 20), where Venice's star chamber plotted under Veronese's *Juno Bestowing her Gifts on Venice*, a glowing goddess strewing gold ducats. Over the slot where anonymous treason accusations were slipped in **Sala della Bussola** (Compass Room; Room 21) is his *St Mark in Glory* ceiling.

The cavernous 1419 **Sala del Maggior Consiglio** (Grand Council Hall) features the doge's throne with a 22m-by-7m *Paradise* backdrop (by Tintoretto's son Domenico) that's more politically correct than pretty: heaven is crammed with 500 prominent Venetians, including several Tintoretto patrons. Veronese's political posturing is more elegant in his oval *Apotheosis of Venice* ceiling, where gods marvel at Venice's coronation by angels with foreign dignitaries and Venetian blondes rubbernecking from the balcony below.

Prisons

Only on the Itinerari Segreti tour can you access the Council of 10 headquarters and dreaded **Piombi** attic prison. Pass through a chamber featuring ominous scenes by the master of apocalyptic visions, Hieronymus Bosch. Follow the path of condemned prisoners across **Ponte dei Sospiri** (Bridge of Sighs) to Venice's 16th-century **Priggione Nove** (New Prisons). Dank cells are covered with graffitied protestations of innocence and paved with marble stolen by the doge in a state-sanctioned heist: the sacking of Constantinople.

TOP SIGHTS
TEATRO LA FENICE

Once La Serenissima's dominion over the high seas ended, Venice discovered the power of high Cs, hiring as San Marco choirmaster Claudio Monteverdi, the father of modern opera, and opening La Fenice (The Phoenix) opera house to much fanfare in 1792.

In the 19th century, Venice's great families were largely ruined and could not afford heating in their enormous *palazzi* (palaces or mansions), so La Fenice served as a members-only club where they would spend much of the day gambling, gossiping and providing running commentary during performances (especially in winter). When he first performed in La Fenice, German composer Richard Wagner miffed the notoriously chatty Venetians by insisting on total silence during performances.

Fires & Rebuilding

Rossini and Bellini staged operas at the house that was becoming the talk of Europe – until the building went up in flames in 1836. Venice without opera was unthinkable and, within a year, the opera house was rebuilt in grand form. Verdi premiered *Rigoletto* and *La Traviata* at La Fenice, and international greats Stravinsky, Prokofiev and Britten composed for the house. But La Fenice was again reduced to ashes in 1996 by arson; two electricians found guilty of the crime were apparently behind on their repair work. A painstaking €90 million replica of the 19th-century opera house reopened in late 2003, and though architectural reviews were mixed – some critics had lobbied for a more avant-garde design by Gae Aulenti – the reprise performance of *La Traviata* was a triumph.

DON'T MISS...

- Opera season
- Intermezzo (intermission) at the baroque bar
- Summer symphonies
- Carnevale balls
- Debating divas with *loggione* critics

PRACTICALITIES

- Map p286
- ☎box office 041 78 65 11
- www.teatrolafenice.it
- Campo San Fantin 1965
- Show tickets €40-120
- Self-guided audiotours adult/reduced €7/5

Opera Season

From January to July and September to October, you'll spot opera lovers in rustling silks and patched corduroy jackets casually loitering on La Fenice's steps with glasses of *prosecco* – until the curtains-up signal dings, starting the mad whoosh up the grand stairway so as not to miss the overture. Tours are possible with advance booking (☎041 24 24), but the best way to see La Fenice is in full swing with the *loggione,* opera buffs who pass judgment from on high in the top-tier cheap seats. With limited runs of bravura performances and a snug 900-seat venue, tickets sell out faster than you can say 'bravo!' Book ahead online for performances and tours.

Off-Season

Between operas, the theatre hosts symphonies and lavish events, ranging from gala Carnevale balls to star-studded private events like the 2009 wedding of François-Henri Pinault, son of billionaire art collector François Pinault, and actress Salma Hayek. Check also for chamber music concerts at La Fenice or operas staged at the charming, diminutive 17th-century **Teatro Malibran** (☎041 786611; Calle del Teatro 5870; Rialto).

SIGHTS

BASILICA DI SAN MARCO CHURCH

See p52.

PALAZZO DUCALE PALACE

See p55.

TEATRO LA FENICE THEATRE

See p59.

TORRE DELL'OROLOGIO LANDMARK

Map p286 (Clock Tower; ☎041 4273 0892; www.museiciviciveneziani.it; Piazza San Marco; adult/reduced €12/7 or Museum Pass; child 6yr & up only; ⊙visit by prebooked tour only, in English 10am & 11am Mon-Wed, 2pm & 3pm Thu-Sat, in Italian noon & 4pm daily, in French 2pm & 3pm Mon-Wed, 10am & 11am Thu-Sun; ⛴San Marco) Legend has it that the inventors of the gold-leafed timepiece tracking lunar phases and astrological shifts were blinded, so that no other city could boast a similar engineering marvel. The sinister plan backfired: the 1497 mechanism malfunctioned and the bells rang randomly because no one knew how to fix them.

A recent renovation has restored the works to full working order: moving barrels indicate the minutes and hour on the clock face, 132-stroke chimes keep time in tune and, on Epiphany and the Feast of the Ascension, wooden statues of Three Kings and the Angel emerge to wild cheers. Two bronze statues striking the hour on a bell atop the tower are known as 'Do Mori' (the Moors) due to their patina – these figures predate political correctness. Tours of Mauro Codussi's 1496–99 tower climb the steep, claustrophobia-triggering four-storey spiral staircase behind the clock to the terrace, for giddy, close-up views of the Moors in action.

MUSEO FORTUNY MUSEUM

Map p286 (☎041 4273 0892; www.museiciviciveneziani.it; Campo San Beneto 3758; adult/reduced €9/6 or Museum Pass; ⊙10am-6pm Wed-Mon; ⛴Sant'Angelo) Find design inspiration at the 15th-century Gothic home studio of Spanish-Venetian Art Nouveau designer Mariano Fortuny y Madrazo, whose shockingly uncorseted Delphi goddess frocks worn by Isadora Duncan set the standard for Bohemian chic. The 1st-floor salon walls are vast mood boards, swagged with Fortuny's art nouveau textiles and hung with his eclectic collection of Fortunato Depero

TOP SIGHTS
MUSEO CORRER

Napoleon filled his Piazza San Marco digs with the doges' riches, and took Venice's finest heirlooms back to France. Venice successfully reclaimed many ancient maps, statues, cameos and weapons, plus four centuries of artistic masterpieces in the **Pinacoteca**. But the real treasure couldn't be lifted: Jacopo Sansovino's spectacular **Libreria Nazionale Marciana**, covered with back-flipping sea creature miniatures and larger-than-life philosophers, by Veronese, Titian and Tintoretto. One of Europe's earliest public libraries, it included musical scores and operas, ancient Greek codices and Marco Polo's last will and testament.

Not to be missed are Paolo Veneziano's 14th-century sad-eyed saints (Room 25); Lo Schiavone's Madonna with a bouncing baby Jesus, wearing a coral good-luck charm and holding a bird (Room 31); Jacopo di Barbari's minutely detailed woodblock perspective of Venice (Room 32); an entire room of bright-eyed, peach-cheeked Bellini saints (Room 36); and a wonderful anonymous 1784 portrait of champion rower Maria Boscola, five-time regatta winner (Room 47). Temporary **Neoclassical Ballroom** shows on such themes as futurism and Italian unity are hit-and-miss, but Antonio Canova's 1777 statues of star-crossed lovers Orpheus and Eurydice are scene-stealers.

DON'T MISS...

- Libreria Nazionale Marciana
- Pinacoteca
- Canova's Orpheus and Eurydice
- Drinks in frescoed Caffé dell'Art

PRACTICALITIES

- Map p286
- ☎041 240 52 11
- www.museiciviciveneziani.it, in Italian
- Piazza San Marco 52
- adult/reduced incl Palazzo Ducale €14/8 or Museum Pass
- ⊙10am-7pm Apr-Oct, to 5pm Nov-Mar

posters, Persian chain mail helmets and paintings of scantily clad muses. Salons mood-lit with Fortuny's Moorish glass lanterns showcase original Fortuny dresses alongside more recent avant-garde fashion, such as Roberta di Camerino's trompe l'oeil velvet handbags and poly maxidresses.

Large-scale art installations in the **attic warehouse** are often overshadowed by the striking architecture but the **downstairs gallery** hosts fascinating rotating shows on Venetian themes, such as Paolo Venturi's moving photos of hand-built dioramas representing the Venice Ghetto c 1942. If these salons inspire decor schemes, visit Fortuny Tessuti Artistici (p148) in Giudecca, where wall coverings are still hand-printed according to Fortuny's top-secret methods.

PALAZZO GRASSI MUSEUM

Map p286 (☎044 535 70 99; www.palazzograssi.it; Campo San Samuele 3231; admission adult/reduced €15/10; ⏰10am-7pm Wed-Mon; Accademia) Just around the bend in the Grand Canal, unsuspecting gondola riders gasp with the shock of the new: installations by controversial contemporary artists like Richard Prince and Jeff Koons are parked right in front of Giorgio Masari's 1749 neoclassical palace. French billionaire François Pinault installed his provocative contemporary art collection at the Palazzo Grassi in 2005, providing Venice with sensation and scandal between Biennales.

Indoors, the palace's creatively repurposed interior architecture steals the show. In 1985–6 postmodern architect Gae Aulenti first peeled back twee rococo decor to highlight Masari's striking, muscular classicism. Minimalist architect Tadao Ando heightened the palace's stage-set drama in 2003–5, adding ethereal backlit scrims and strategic spotlighting to direct attention to modern art without detracting from ceiling frescoes and marble arcades.

Clever curation and shameless art-star namedropping are the hallmarks of rotating shows, often featuring Takashi Murakami's smiling Superflat daisies, Raymond Pettibon's poetically captioned cartoons ('I curse the happy for whom the unhappy is only a spectacle') and Barbara Kruger's provocative maxims ('We are astonishingly lifelike'). Don't miss the cafe overlooking the Grand Canal, with interiors redesigned by contemporary artists with each new show.

ART SMART

To see more of Pinault's collection of more than 2000 artworks, get a **combined ticket** (adult/reduced €20/15) that gives you three days to visit Palazzo Grassi and Punta della Dogana (p84), Venice's ancient customs houses renovated by Ando in 2009 to showcase larger art installations.

CHIESA DI SANTO STEFANO CHURCH

Map p286 (www.chorusvenezia.org; Campo Santo Stefano; admission €3 or Chorus Pass; ⏰10am-5pm Mon-Sat; Accademia) The free-standing **bell tower** behind it leans disconcertingly, but this soaring brick Gothic church has stood since 1325, even though a subterranean canal runs right under the inlaid wood choir stalls. Credit for ship-shape splendour goes to architect Bartolomeo Bon for the marble entry portal and to Venetian shipbuilders, who constructed the vast wood-ribbed carena di nave (ship's keel) ceiling that looks like an upturned Noah's Ark.

Enter the cloisters **museum** to see Canova's 1808 funerary stelae featuring gorgeous women dabbing their eyes with their cloaks, Tullio Lombardo's wide-eyed 1505 saint, and three brooding Tintoretto canvases: *Last Supper,* with a ghostly dog begging for bread; the gathering gloom of *Agony in the Garden;* and the abstract, mostly black *Washing of the Feet.*

NEGOZIO OLIVETTI NOTEWORTHY BUILDING

Map p286 (Olivetti Store; ☎041 522 83 87; www.fondoambiente.it; Piazza San Marco 101, Procuratie Vecchie; audiotours adult/reduced €5/3; ⏰10am-7pm Apr-Oct, to 5pm Nov-Mar; San Marco) Like a revolver pulled from a petticoat, starkly modern Negozio Olivetti was an outright provocation when it first appeared under the frilly arcades of Piazza San Marco in 1957. Venetian architect Carlo Scarpa won the coveted commission from high-tech pioneer Olivetti to transform a narrow, dim souvenir shop into a fitting showcase for its sleek, innovative typewriters and 'computing machines' (several 1948–54 models are still displayed).

Instead of fighting the elements, Scarpa slyly invited them indoors: he sliced away

GALLERY-HOP SAN MARCO

For all its splendours of bygone eras, San Marco is not just a museum piece. Slip into the backstreets behind Santa Maria del Giglio and you'll jump ahead of the art curve in galleries showcasing contemporary works ranging from glass sculpture to video installation. Entry is free and inspiration abundant at these six San Marco galleries:

➡ **Galleria van der Koelen** (Map p286; ☎041 520 74 15; www.galerie.vanderkoelen.de; Ramo Primo dei Calegheri 2566; ⏲10am-12.30pm & 3.30-6.30pm Mon-Sat; Santa Maria del Giglio) Hidden behind thundering Teatro La Fenice, this conceptual art gallery makes bold statements with Ai Weiwei's 'Fairytale', a line-up of Qing dynasty chairs waiting for the next imperious politicians to fill them, and Patrick Mimran's banners hung on Venetian museums, declaring 'Art is not where you think you're going to find it'.

➡ **Galleria Rossella Junck** (Map p286; ☎041 521 07 59; www.rossellajunck.it; Calle Larga XXII Marzo 2360; ⏲10am-12.30pm & 4-7.30pm Mon-Sat; Santa Maria del Giglio) Fragile beauty in unlikely forms, from Seguso's 1950 braying donkey in rose-tinted glass to Marie Aimée Grimaldi's contemporary Hamlet-in-Murano-crystal skull. Gallery displays cover 13th-century goblets through to modern art-glass.

➡ **Caterina Tognon Arte Contemporanea** (Map p286; ☎041 520 78 59; www.caterinatognon.com; Palazzo da Ponte, Calle delle Dose 2746; ⏲3-7pm Wed-Sat; Santa Maria del Giglio) Press the brass doorbell for 'stART' on this 17th-century palace to be buzzed up to the 2nd-storey gallery, where guest artists experiment with Venetian materials and ideas: Maurizio Donzelli tiled the floor with watery drawings, while Richard Marquis designed colourful glass camouflage for submarines to enter stealth mode off Murano.

➡ **Galleria Traghetto** (Map p286; ☎041 522 11 88; www.galleriatraghetto.it; Campo Santa Maria del Giglio 2543; ⏲3-7pm Mon-Sat; Santa Maria del Giglio) Gutsy shows of young Italian artists on the brink of international breakthroughs, including Serafino Maiorano's blurred digital photographs with bleeding reds evoking Carpaccio and Mirco Marchelli's tattered, patchworked Italian flag paintings.

➡ **Jarach Gallery** (Map p286; ☎041 522 19 38; www.jarachgallery.com; Campo San Fantin 1997; ⏲10am-1pm & 2.30-7.30pm Tue-Sat; Santa Maria del Giglio) Contemporary photography waits in the wings near La Fenice, with the quiet drama of shows such as Simone Bergantini's photos of abandoned dresses and spectral garbage bags casting film-noir shadows.

➡ **le5venice** (Map p286; ☎041 296 01 20; www.le5venice.com; Campo San Fantin 1891 & 1895; ⏲10am-7pm Mon-Sat; Santa Maria del Giglio) This new upstairs gallery showcases contemporary photography and painters such as Davide Battistin, whose Venetian nocturnes update Turner. Don't miss the ground floor's showcase of high-concept clothing designs, including coats printed with photorealistic rugs.

walls to let light flood in, included a huge planter for tall grasses and added a black Belgian marble slab fountain as a wink at *acqua alta*. The illuminated space enticed visitors to cross glittering Murano glass-tiled floors in appealing primary colours, scale a floating white marble stairway, pass satiny Venetian plaster walls and browse the teak-wood balcony. Semi-circular porthole windows resemble eyes open wide to the Piazza, but also possibilities on distant horizons.

PONTE DELL'ACCADEMIA — BRIDGE

Map p286 (btwn Campo di San Vidal & Campo della Carità; Accademia) The wooden Ponte dell'Accademia was built in 1933 as a temporary replacement for an 1854 iron bridge but, with its high arch curved like a cat's back, it remains a beloved landmark. Engineer Eugenio Miozzi moved on to bigger Fascist monuments such as the Lido Casino, but none has lasted like this elegant little footbridge – and recent structural improvements have preserved it for decades to come.

CHIESA DI SANTA MARIA DEL GIGLIO CHURCH

Map p286 (Santa Maria Zobenigo; www.chorusvenezia.org; Campo di Santa Maria del Giglio; admission €3 or Chorus Pass; ⏲10am-5pm Mon-Sat) Experience awe through the ages in this compact church with a 10th-century Byzantine layout, three intriguing masterpieces and a baroque facade featuring charmingly flawed maps of regions conquered by Venice c 1678. Standing tall among these possessions is a statue of Admiral Antonio Barbaro, who commissioned the reconstruction of the original 9th-century church by Giuseppe Sardi for the glory of the Virgin, Venice, and of course himself. This largely secular, self-glorifying architectural audacity enraged 19th-century architectural critic John Ruskin, who called it a 'manifestation of insolent atheism'.

Inside, Veronese's *Madonna with Child* hides behind the **altar**, Tintoretto's four evangelists flank the **organ**, and Northern Renaissance master Peter Paul Rubens makes a cameo appearance in the **Molin Chapel** with his painting of Mary with St John and charmingly chubby baby Jesus.

CAMPANILE LANDMARK

Map p286 (Bell Tower; Piazza San Marco; www.basilicasanmarco.it; admission €8; ⏲9am-9pm Jul-Sep, to 7pm Apr-Jun & Oct, 9.30am-3.45pm Nov-Mar) The basilica's 99m-tall tower has been rebuilt twice since its initial construction in AD 888, and Galileo Galilei found it handy for testing his telescope in 1609. Critics called Bartolomeo Bon's 16th-century tower re-design ungainly, but when this version suddenly collapsed in 1902, Venetians rebuilt the tower as it was, brick by brick.

Visitors head to the tower top for 360-degree lagoon views and close encounters with the Marangona, the booming bronze bell that could be heard in the Arsenale shipyards (bring earplugs on the hour). Due to ongoing stabilisation efforts and drainage works, the Sansovino-designed **marble loggia** at the base of the Campanile is currently partially enclosed behind a safety barrier.

FREE PALAZZO CONTARINI DEL BOVOLO PALAZZO

Map p286 (☎041 532 29 20; Calle Contarini del Bovolo 4299; entry to open courtyard free; ⏲10am-6pm) No need to wait for San Marco sunsets to inspire a snog: this romantic Renaissance 15th-century *palazzo* with an external spiral *bovolo* (snail-shell) stairwell is closed for restoration, but its shady courtyard offers stirring views and privacy.

FREE MUSEO DELLA MUSICA MUSEUM

Map p286 (☎041 241 18 40; Campo San Maurizio 2761; ⏲9.30am-7.30pm daily; ⛴Santa Maria del Giglio) Housed in the restored neoclassical Chiesa di San Maurizio, this collection of rare and curious 17th- to 19th-century instruments is accompanied by informative panels on the life and times of Venice's Antonio Vivaldi (see p235). To hear these instruments in action, check out the kiosk with early-music CDs and concert tickets for Interpreti Veneziani (p74), who fund this museum and play museum-piece instruments with modern verve around the corner at San Vidal (p65).

CHIESA DI SAN MOISÈ CHURCH

Map p286 (☎041 528 58 40; Campo di San Moisè; admission free; ⏲9.30am-12.30pm Mon-Sat; ⛴Vallaresso) Icing flourishes of carved-stone ornament across the 1660s facade make this church appear positively lickable, although 19th-century architecture critic John Ruskin found its wedding-cake appearance indigestible. From an engineering perspective, Ruskin had a point: several statues had to be removed in the 19th century to prevent the facade from collapsing under their combined weight.

The remaining statuary by Flemish sculptor Heinrich Meyring (aka Merengo in Italian) includes scant devotional works but a sycophantic number of tributes to church patrons. Among the scene-stealing works inside are Tintoretto's *The Washing of the Feet*, in the sanctuary to the left of the main altar, and Palma il Giovane's *The Supper*, on the right side of the church.

CHIESA DI SAN ZULIAN CHURCH

Map p286 (☎041 523 53 83; Campo San Zulian; ⏲9am-6.30pm Mon-Sat, 9am-7.30pm Sun; ⛴San Marco) Originally a modest church founded in 829, San Zulian got an Istrian stone makeover by Sansovino on a commission from the wealthy physician Tomasso Rangone, who made his fortune selling syphilis cures and a book revealing the secrets to living past 100 (he died at 84). The doctor is immortalised in bronze over the portal, holding sarsaparilla – apparently a key ingredient to his miracle cure for VD. Inside are works by Palma il Giovane and, on the right as you enter, Paolo Veronese's *The Dead Christ and Saints*.

START **PIAZZETTA DI SAN MARCO**
END **I RUSTEGHI**
DISTANCE **3KM**
DURATION **1½ HOURS**

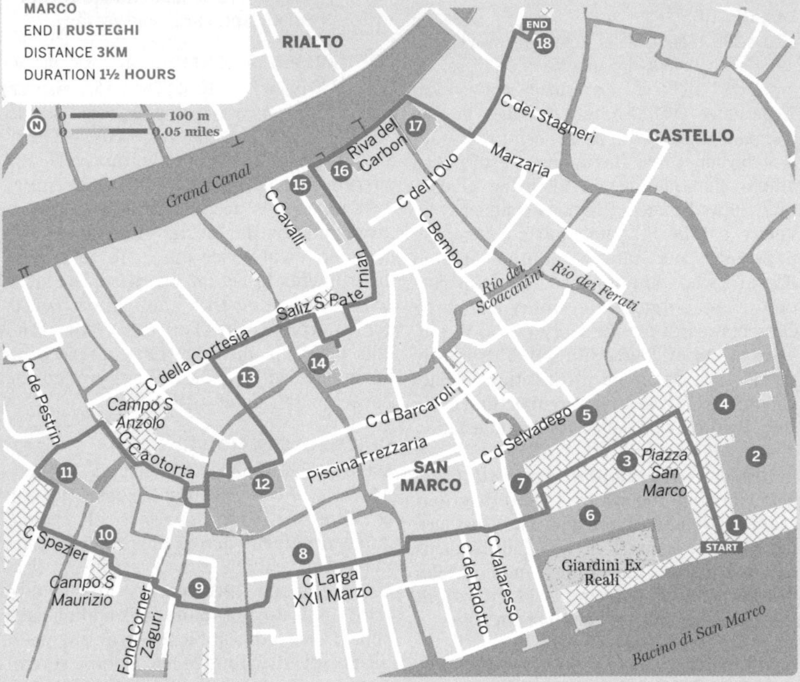

Neighbourhood Walk

San Marco Circuit

Venetians still hurry past the granite ❶ **Columns of San Marco**, site of public executions for centuries. Past ❷ **Palazzo Ducale** is ❸ **Piazza San Marco**, crowned by ❹ **Basilica di San Marco** and flanked by Mauro Codussi's 16th-century ❺ **Procuratie Vecchie** and Jacopo Sansovino–designed ❻ **Procuratie Nuove**. Today the Museo Correr occupies the upper storeys of the Procuratie Nuove and ❼ **Ala Napoleonica**, the palace Napoleon brazenly razed San Geminiano church to build.

Follow ❽ **Calle Larga XXII Marzo**, commemorating the anti-Austrian insurrection of 22 March 1848, towards baroque ❾ **Chiesa di Santa Maria del Giglio**, covered in peculiar maps – cartographers' best attempts to chart Venetian vassal states c 1678–81, including Crete, Croatia, Corfu and Padua. Further west, 15th-century ❿ **Santo Stefano bell tower** leans 2m from its intended perpendicular stance, as though it's had one *spritz* too many. Nearby, Bartolomeo Bon's marble Gothic portals grace brick ⓫ **Chiesa di Santo Stefano**.

Follow Calle Caotorta to ⓬ **Teatro La Fenice**, veering left onto ⓭ **Rio Terà dei Assassini**. Corpses were so frequently found here that, in 1128, Venice banned the full beards assassins wore as disguises. Snogging in *campi* is such an established Venetian pastime it's surprising dogi didn't find a way to tax it – but duck into ⓮ **Palazzo Contarini del Bovolo** courtyard for privacy.

Along Calle del Carbon, wander into city hall weekdays at ⓯ **Palazzo Loredan**. Outside, a plaque honours philosopher Eleonora Lucrezia Corner Piscopia, the first woman to earn a Padua University degree, in 1678. Along the quay is 14th-century Gothic ⓰ **Palazzo Dandolo**, home of blind doge and erstwhile Crusader Enrico Dandolo, who sacked Constantinople in 1203. Next door is Sansovino-designed ⓱ **Palazzo Dolfin-Manin** (1547), where the last doge, Ludovico Manin, died in seclusion in 1802 after handing over his doge's cap to Napoleon's guard with a sigh. End your grand tour at ⓲ **I Rusteghi**, with sighs over Amarone as red and powerful as a doge's cap.

PALAZZO FRANCHETTI PALAZZO

Map p286 (☎041 240 77 11; www.istitutoveneto.it; Campo Santo Stefano 2842; exhibits vary, cafe admission free; ⊙10am-7pm daily; Accademia) Three extended Venetian families originally lived at this 16th-century Grand Canal Palace and it seems they didn't always see eye to eye on decor. When archduke Frederick of Austria snapped up this Gothic palace in the 19th century, he attempted to unify competing styles with a spare, modern makeover. The Franchetti family lived here for decades after independence and commissioned architect Camillo Boito to reinstall a retro-Gothic look, plus a **formal garden** and grand **art nouveau staircase**.

The palace was home to a private bank from 1922 until 1999, when the Istituto Veneto di Scienze, Lettere ed Arti (Veneto Institute of Sciences, Letters and Arts) moved in and began hosting expositions and conferences (see website for listings). The latest addition is the 2009 **Palazzo Franchetti Caffè** in the enclosed garden cloisters, with patterned window screens harmonising the palace's Gothic, modern and art nouveau design schemes.

FREE **CHIESA DI SAN VIDAL** CHURCH

Map p286 (Campo di San Vidal 2862; admission free; ⊙9am-noon & 3.30-6pm Mon-Sat; Accademia) Originally built by Doge Vitale Falier in the 11th century in honour of his own namesake saint, Chiesa di San Vidal was upgraded by Antonio Gaspari to celebrate Doge Francesco Morosoni's triumph over Turkish foes in Morea, with a Palladian facade tacked on in 1706–14. The church has since been deconsecrated, and now serves as the chief venue and ticket point for Interpreti Veneziani (p74). Inside is *St Vitale on Horseback and Eight Saints,* an uncharacteristically gore-free work by Vittore Carpaccio, featuring traces of his signature traffic-light red and a miniaturist's attention to detail.

FONDACO DEI TEDESCHI NOTABLE BUILDING

Map p286 (Salizada del Fontego dei Tedeschi 5346; Rialto) You would never guess from its blank facade along the Grand Canal, but this *fondaco* (trading house) was the Wall Street of Venice's German community during its 13th- to 17th-century heyday. Creeping damp destroyed the original exterior frescoes by Giorgione and Titian; a few remaining fragments are preserved at Ca' d'Oro (p118). Traders here drove hard bargains: when Giorgione and Titian showed up to collect their payment of 150 ducats they were told their frescoes were worth only 130 ducats. An independent appraisal confirmed the original figure but the artists were advised to settle. Controversy continues to surround the fondaco, which is currently closed to the public. From 1937 to 2010, this building served as Venice's central post office, and negotiations are currently under way to convert the building into a cultural centre, shopping mall or some combination of the two.

EATING

TOP CHOICE **ENOTECA AL VOLTO** VENETIAN €

Map p286 (☎041 522 89 45; Calle Cavalli 4081; cicheti €2-4, mains €7-18; ⊙9.30am-3pm & 5.30-10pm Mon-Sat; Rialto) Join the bar crowd working its way through the vast selection of wine and *cicheti,* or come early for a table outdoors (in summer) or inside the snug backroom that looks like a ship's hold, for seaworthy bowls of pasta with *bottarga* (dried fish roe) or housemade ravioli. Cash only.

OSTERIA SAN MARCO MODERN ITALIAN €€€

Map p286 (☎041 528 52 42; www.osteriasanmarco.it; Frezzeria 1610; mains €20-30; ⊙12.30-11pm Mon-Sat; Vallaresso) Romance is in the air here – but top-notch wines lining the exposed brick walls surely help. Under strategic spotlights, dishes seem to arrive with a halo, especially heavenly lagoon clams with squid ink linguine. Wine selections by the glass are limited and meat dishes are modestly sized, but all is forgiven over *passito* (dessert) wine with artisan cheeses.

BACARO DA FIORE CICHETI, VENETIAN €

Map p286 (☎041 523 53 10; www.dafiore.it; Calle delle Botteghe 3461; meals €10-15; ⊙5.30-9pm Wed-Mon; Accademia) Attached to a posh trattoria, this *cicheti* counter attracts spillover Venetian crowds with classic dishes like *baccala mantecato* (creamed cod), polenta with *bruscandoli* (wild hops), and octopus-fennel salad to enjoy at the bar or on a stool in the *calle.* Even with gorgeous DOC Soave by the glass, meals cost a fraction of what you'd pay for table seating.

OSTERIA DA CARLA OSTERIA €

Map p286 (☎041 523 78 55; Frezzeria 1535; mains €8-13; ⊙10am-9pm Mon-Sat; Vallaresso) For

Continued on page 72

Grand Canal

The 3.5km route of *vaporetto* (passenger ferry) No 1, which passes some 50 *palazzi* (mansions), six churches and scene-stealing backdrops featured in four James Bond films, is public transport at its most glamorous.

The Grand Canal starts with controversy: **Ponte di Calatrava** 1 a luminous glass-and-steel bridge that cost triple the original €4 million estimate. Ahead are castle-like **Fondaco dei Turchi** 2, the historic Turkish trading-house; Renaissance **Palazzo Vendramin** 3, housing the city's casino; and double-arcaded **Ca' Pesaro** 4. Don't miss **Ca' d'Oro** 5, a 1430 filigree Gothic marvel.

Points of Venetian pride include the **Pescaria** 6, built in 1907 on the site where fishmongers have been slinging lagoon crab for 600 years, and neighbouring **Rialto Market** 7 stalls, overflowing with island-grown produce. Cost overruns for 1592 **Ponte di Rialto** 8 rival Calatrava's, but its marble splendour stands the test of time.

The next two canal bends could cause architectural whiplash, with Sanmicheli-designed Renaissance **Palazzo Grimani** 9 and Mauro Codussi's **Palazzo Corner-Spinelli** 10 followed by Giorgio Masari-designed **Palazzo Grassi** 11 and Baldassare Longhena's baroque jewel box, **Ca' Rezzonico** 12.

Wooden **Ponte dell'Accademia** 13, was built in 1930 as a temporary bridge, but the beloved landmark was recently reinforced. Stone lions flank **Peggy Guggenheim Collection** 14, where the American heiress collected ideas, lovers and art. You can't miss the dramatic dome of Longhena's **Chiesa di Santa Maria della Salute** 15, or **Punta della Dogana** 16, Venice's triangular customs warehouse reinvented as a contemporary art showcase. The Grand Canal's grand finale is pink Gothic **Palazzo Ducale** 17 and its adjoining **Ponte dei Sospiri** 18, currently draped in advertising.

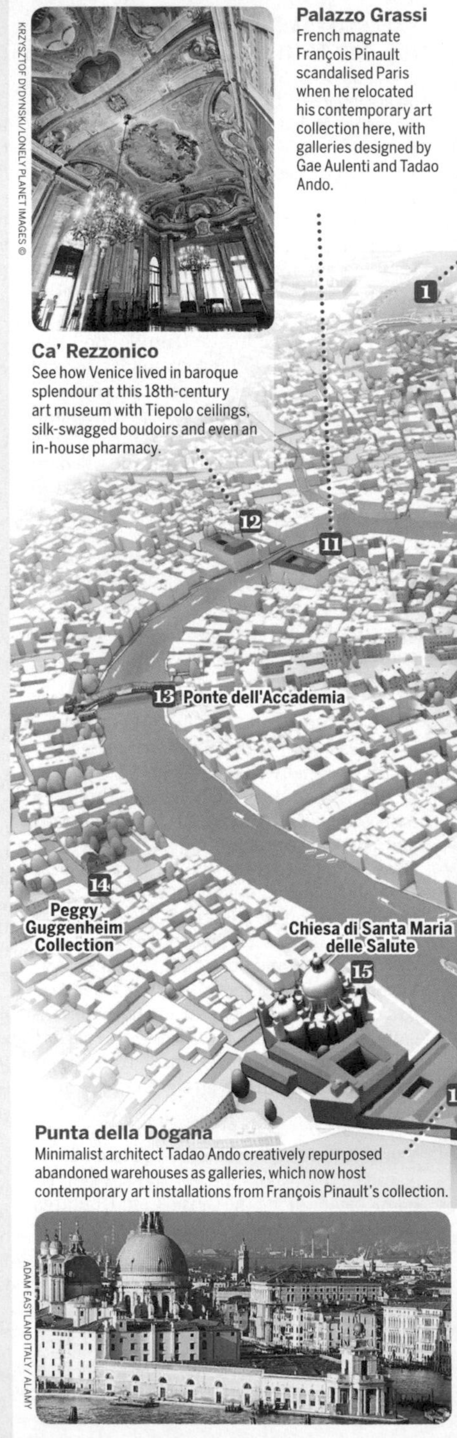

KRZYSZTOF DYDYNSKI/LONELY PLANET IMAGES ©

Palazzo Grassi
French magnate François Pinault scandalised Paris when he relocated his contemporary art collection here, with galleries designed by Gae Aulenti and Tadao Ando.

Ca' Rezzonico
See how Venice lived in baroque splendour at this 18th-century art museum with Tiepolo ceilings, silk-swagged boudoirs and even an in-house pharmacy.

Punta della Dogana
Minimalist architect Tadao Ando creatively repurposed abandoned warehouses as galleries, which now host contemporary art installations from François Pinault's collection.

ADAM EASTLAND ITALY / ALAMY

RUSSELL MOUNTFORD/LONELY PLANET IMAGES ©

Ponte di Calatrava

With its starkly streamlined fish-fin shape, the 2008 bridge is the first to be built over the Grand Canal in 75 years.

Fondaco dei Turchi

Recognisable by its polychrome, marble double colonnade, topped by 13th-century Byzantine capitals and flanked by watchtowers.

JEAN-PIERRE LESCOURRET/LONELY PLANET IMAGES ©

Ca' d'Oro

Behind the triple Gothic arcades are priceless masterpieces: Titians looted by Napoleon, a rare Mantegna and semi-precious stone mosaic floors.

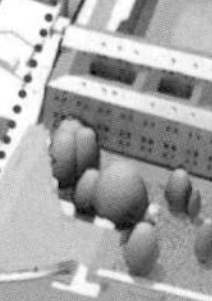

Ca' Pesaro

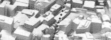

Originally designed by Baldassare Longhena, this palazzo was bequeathed to the city in 1898 to house the Galleria d'Arte Moderna and Museo d'Arte Orientale.

CUBOIMAGES SRL / ALAMY

Ponte di Rialto

Antonio da Ponte beat out Palladio for the commission of this bridge, but construction costs spiralled to 250,000 Venetian ducats – about €19 million today.

KRZYSZTOF DYDYNSKI/LONELY PLANET IMAGES ©

Venice: Building the Dream City

Impossible though it seems, Venetians built their home on 117 small islands connected by some 400 bridges over 150 canals. But if floating marble palaces boggle the mind, consider what's underneath them: an entire forest's worth of wood pylons, rammed through silty *barene* (shoals) into the clay lagoon floor. Some 100,000 petrified pylons support the brick and Istrian stone base of Baldassare Longhena's 1631 Chiesa di Santa Maria della Salute.

While pylons do the heavy lifting, Venice's upkeep is constant and painstaking. Punta della Dogana's salt-corroded foundations were recently repaired by injecting specially formulated cement into thousands of holes. Venice's canals must be regularly dredged, which involves pumping water out of canals, carefully removing pungent sludge and a ticklish technique Venetians call *scuci-cuci* (patching brickwork by hand).

When visitors marvel at their city, Venetians pass along the compliment to their extraordinary lagoon ecosystem. But deep channels dug to accommodate tankers and cruise ships allow more seawater into the lagoon, changing lagoon aquaculture and elevating *acque alte* (high tide). The controversial, multi-billion-euro mobile flood barrier known as Mose is intended to limit *acque alte,* but critics question its effectiveness, environmental impact and the diversion of funds critical for Venice's upkeep.

Solutions aren't easy, but simple gestures are. With 22 million visitors a year, minor adjustments in traveller behaviour will help keep Venice alive and dreaming.

HELP KEEP VENICE AFLOAT

- **Take the train to Venice** – instead of higher-impact cruise ships
- **Pick up litter** – to protect Venice's fragile ecosystem
- **Enjoy local products** – lagoon seafood, island-grown produce and Venetian handicrafts are Venice's pride, joy and livelihood
- **Go slowly on motorboats** – wakes expose and damage fragile foundations
- **Drink tap water** – to spare Venice the current burden of recycling 20 to 60 million water bottles annually

1. Isola di San Giorgio Maggiore (p147) **2.** Grand Canal (p66)

1

BRENT WINEBRENNER / LONELY PLANET IMAGES ©

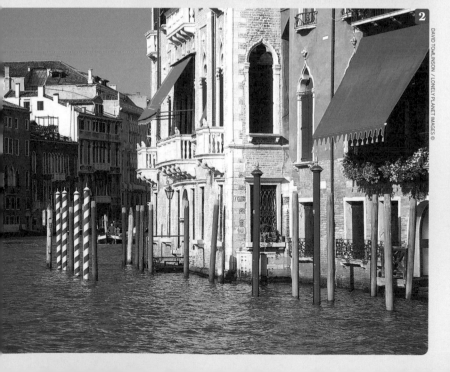

2

DAVID TOMLINSON / LONELY PLANET IMAGES ©

Secrets of the Calli

Yellow signs helpfully point the way to major sights, but the secret to any great Venetian adventure is: *ignore them*. That *calle* (backstreet) behind the thoroughfare leads to a wonderful world of artisan studios, backstreet *bacari* (bars) and hidden *campi* (squares).

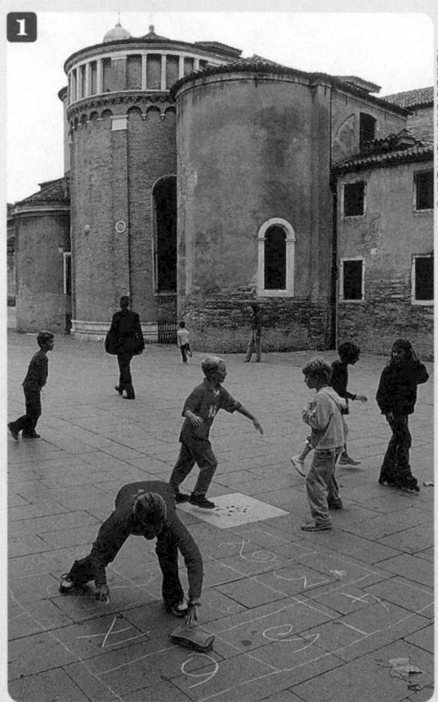

Chiesa della Madonna dell'Orto to the Ghetto

1 Cannaregio calm restores overloaded senses as you pass sculptures flanking Campo dei Mori, stroll sunny Fondamente della Miseriacordia and Ormesini, and reach bridges leading into the historic Ghetto.

Campo San Polo to San Giacomo dell'Orio

2 Take Calle Scalater past artisan studios to hidden Campiello Agostin for draught beer and dramatic glass jewellery; cross the bridge to join happy hour and tag games alongside medieval San Giacomo dell'Orio.

La Fenice to Bacino Orseolo

3 G alleries ring Campo San Fantin, where Frezzeria leads past studios where artisans craft books, masks and La Fenice opera costumes, before bumping into Bacino Orseolo, a picturesque gondola-parking lot.

Chiesa di San Sebastian to I Frari

4 Follow bargain *osterie* (taverns) along Calle Lunga San Barnaba to its bustling namesake campo, where Calle delle Botteghe leads past antiques, ceramics, shawls and chocolates to Titian's masterpiece.

San Zaccaria to Chiesa di Santa Maria dei Miracoli

5 Head north of San Marco past chatty Campo Santa Maria Formosa for *cicheti* (tapas) in Campo Santa Marina, or Venetian designers and antiques alongside the chapel.

Clockwise from top left

1. Campo San Giacomo dell'Orio (p24) **2.** Bacino Orseolo **3.** Campo Santa Maria Formosa

2

KRZYSZTOF DYDYNSKI / LONELY PLANET IMAGES ©

ROBERTO GEROMETTA / LONELY PLANET IMAGES ©

Continued from page 65

the price of hot chocolate in Piazza San Marco, diners in the know duck into this hidden courtyard to feast on handmade ravioli with poppyseed, pear and sheep's cheese. Expect a wait at lunch and happy hour, when gondolieri abandon ship for DOC Soave and *sopressa crostini* (soft salami on toast).

ANONIMO VENEZIANO CICHETI, VENETIAN €€

Map p286 (041 523 53 10; Calle del Fruttarol 1847; meals €15-25; noon-3pm & 5.30-9pm Mon-Wed & Fri & Sat, 5.30-9pm Sun; Santa Maria del Giglio) A casual charmer with classic fare at eminently reasonable prices – under €10 for pasta and €4 for a small carafe of house Tocai – and impeccable social graces. The dapper 80-something server may not allow you to leave until you've enjoyed a grappa-filled chocolate, and he nimbly helps you put on your coat afterwards.

CAVATAPPI OSTERIA €

Map p286 (041 296 02 52; Campo della Guerra 525/526; cicheti €2-4, mains €8-13; 10am-9pm Tue-Thu & Sun, 10am-11pm Fri & Sat; San Marco) A casual charmer offering *cicheti* and artisanal cheeses, DOC bubbly by the glass and that rarest of San Marco finds: a tasty sit-down meal under €20. Get the risotto of the day and sheep's cheese drizzled with Dolomite wildflower honey for dessert.

VINI DA ARTURO ITALIAN, STEAK €€€

Map p286 (041 528 69 74; Calle dei Assassini 3656; meals €50-70; 7-11pm Mon-Sat; Santa Maria del Giglio) Everyone in this corridor-sized restaurant comes for the same reason: the steak, studded with green peppercorn, soused in brandy and mustard or rare on the bone. Your host will happily trot out irrefutable proof that Nicole Kidman actually eats and that director Joel Silver managed to escape *The Matrix* for steak here.

DA MARIO VENETIAN €€

Map p286 (041 528 59 68; Fondamenta della Malvasia Vecchia 2614; meals €20-30; Sun-Mon; Santa Maria del Giglio) Squeeze in among the motley collection of fisherman's lamps, ceramic pitchers, watercolours, and the locals who made them, and make yourself at home with a generous plate of seafood pasta and wine by the litre. This classic *osteria* (wine bar) seems miles from tourist attractions and the 21st century, yet the Gallerie dell'Accademia and Palazzo Grassi are minutes away.

A DRINK WITH A VIEW

Eating options in San Marco boil down to a simple choice: good food or a view. Getting both is nearly impossible in San Marco, especially at reasonable prices – but you can always enjoy Piazza San Marco panoramas over coffee or *aperitivi*, then spelunk into San Marco's narrow alleyways for delightful meals at authentic *osterie*. For scenic canalside dining at more down-to-earth prices, try Cannaregio or Giudecca.

CAFFÈ MANDOLA PANINI €

Map p286 (041 523 76 24; Calle della Mandola 3630; panini €3-7; 9am-7pm Mon-Sat; Vallaresso) Carbo-load before the opera or between museums with fresh focaccia loaded with tangy tuna and capers or lean *bresaola,* rocket and seasoned Grana Padano cheese. Stools provide sweet relief for tired feet if you plan your break around the lunch peak and happy hour rushes.

GELATERIA SUSO ICE CREAM €

Map p286 (Calle della Bissa 5453; gelato €2-3; 10am-10pm; Rialto) Indulge in Suso's ostentatiously rich 'Doge' gelato: fig sauce and walnuts swirled into marscapone cream. All Suso's gelati are locally made and extra-creamy, but a waffle cone with hazelnut and extra-dark chocolate passes as dinner.

DRINKING & NIGHTLIFE

TOP CHOICE **I RUSTEGHI** WINE BAR

Map p286 (041 523 22 05; Corte del Tentor 5513; mini panini €2-5; 10.30am-3pm & 6-9pm Mon-Sat; Rialto) Honouring centuries of Venetian *enoteca* tradition, fourth-generation sommelier Giovanni will open any wine bottle on his shelves just to pour you an *ombra* (half-glass of wine) – including near-mythic collector's wines like 1996 Quintarelli Amarone. Request *'qualcosa di particolare'* (something exceptional) and Giovanni will reward you with a sensual Ribolla Gialla or heady Refosco you won't find elsewhere. Pair yours with 30 types of *cicheti*, including rolls packed with boar salami and truffle.

CAFFÈ FLORIAN CAFE

Map p286 (☎041 520 56 41; www.caffeflorian.com; Piazza San Marco 56/59; drinks €8-12; ⏰10am-midnight Thu-Tue; 🚢San Marco) Florian adheres to rituals established c 1720: uniformed waiters serve hot chocolate on silver trays, lovers canoodle in plush banquettes indoors and the orchestra strikes up a tango as fading sunlight illuminates San Marco's portal mosaics. Ever forward-thinking, this cafe was among the first to admit women, served as a clubhouse for Italy's independence movement and still hosts contemporary art and design events.

CAFFÈ LAVENA CAFE

Map p286 (☎041 522 40 70; www.lavena.it; Piazza San Marco 133/4; drinks €1-12; ⏰9.30am-11pm; 🚢SanMarco) Opera composer Richard Wagner had the right idea: when Venice leaves you weak in the knees, get a pick-me-up at Lavena. The €1 espresso at this mirrored 18th-century bar is the sweetest deal in Piazza San Marco, but get a table for *caffe corretto* (coffee 'corrected' with liquor) and live music. Florian's orchestra provides friendly competition across the square, but Lavena's lightning-speed tarantella usually wins by crowd roars.

HARRY'S BAR BAR

Map p286 (☎041 528 57 77; Calle Vallaresso 1323; cocktails €10-18; ⏰noon-11pm; 🚢Vallaresso) Aspiring auteurs throng the bar frequented by Ernest Hemingway, Charlie Chaplin, Truman Capote, Orson Welles and others, enjoying a signature €15 Bellini (Giuseppe Cipriani's original 1948 recipe: fresh-pressed white peach juice and *prosecco*) with a side of reflected glory. Despite basic bistro decor and minuscule tables, this is one of Italy's most expensive restaurants – stick to the bar to save financing for your breakthrough film.

OSTERIA ALL'ALBA WINE BAR

Map p286 (☎340 124 56 34; Ramo del Fontego dei Tedeschi 5370; ⏰7-1am; 🚢Rialto) That roar behind the Rialto means the DJ's funk set is kicking in at All'Alba. Squeeze inside to order salami sandwiches (€1 to €2.50) and DOC Veneto wines (€5 to €6), and check out walls festooned with vintage LPs and effusive thanks scrawled in 12 languages.

CAFFÈ QUADRI CAFE-BAR

Map p286 (☎041 522 21 05; Piazza San Marco 120; tea service €16-20; ⏰9am-11.30pm Tue-Sun; 🚢San Marco) Powdered wigs seem appropriate attire in this bodaciously baroque salon, a cafe since 1683 and Hapsburg hot spot during the 19th-century Austrian occupation. Venetians still veer instinctively towards Lavena or Florian, missing out on decadent desserts such as baked ice cream and the €16 hot chocolate service with *panna* (whipped cream) and Venetian cookies. Reserve ahead during Carnevale, when the Quadri is packed with costumed revellers partying like it's 1699.

TORINO@NOTTE BAR

Map p286 (☎041 522 39 14; Campo San Luca 4592; ⏰7pm-1am Tue-Sat; 🚢Rialto) Freeform, eclectic and loud, Torino adds an element of the unexpected to post-dinner drinks in otherwise staid San Marco. By day it's a cafe, but nights bring €2 to €5 drinks with live jazz most Saturdays, spontaneous college-student singalongs or marathon DJ sessions of vintage reggae on vinyl.

TEAMO CAFE-BAR

Map p286 (☎347 366 50 16; Rio Terà della Mandola 3795; ⏰8am-10pm; 🚢Sant'Angelo) Sunny tearoom by day, sleek backlit alabaster bar by night and full-time fabulousness. Arrive by 6.30pm for first choice of *cicheti* at the bar and lookers in the leather banquettes – this bar swings both ways, so there's something for everyone.

B-BAR LOUNGE-BAR

Map p286 (☎041 240 68 19; Campo di San Moisè 1455; ⏰6.30pm-1am Wed-Sun; 🚢Vallaresso) Pose as glitterati for the night at the gold-mosaic B-Bar, where top-shelf cocktails are thoughtfully served with bar nibbles and a piano player plays softly so as not to upstage VIP guests like you. There's an entire menu of creative twists on the classic Venetian *spritz,* such as the bittersweet Rialto (*prosecco*, gin and a splash of grenadine).

CENTRALE LOUNGE-BAR

Map p286 (☎041 296 06 64; www.centrale-lounge.com; Piscina Frezzaeria 1659b; cocktails €9-12; ⏰7pm-2am Wed-Mon; 🚢Vallaresso) Under moody Murano-chandelier lighting, you might spot Javier Bardem, Spike Lee, Charlize Theron or sundry Italian moguls within these exposed-brick walls. Meals are pricey and optional bodyguard service seems a bit much, but Centrale draws late-night crowds for mojitos, midnight snacks, chill-out DJ sets and occasional live jazz.

ENTERTAINMENT

TOP CHOICE TEATRO LA FENICE — OPERA

See p59.

TOP CHOICE INTERPRETI VENEZIANI — CLASSICAL MUSIC

Map p286 (041 277 05 61; www.interpretiveneziani.com; Chiesa San Vidal 2862; adult/reduced €25/20; doors open 8.30pm; Accademia) Everything you knew of Vivaldi from elevators and mobile ring-tones is proved fantastically wrong by Interpreti Veneziani, which plays Vivaldi on 18th-century instruments as a soundtrack for living in this city of intrigue – you'll never listen to *The Four Seasons* again without hearing summer storms erupting over the lagoon, or snow-muffled footsteps hurrying over footbridges in winter's night intrigues.

MUSICA A PALAZZO — OPERA

Map p286 (340 971 72 72; www.musicapalazzo.com; Palazzo Barbarigo-Minotto, Fondamenta Barbarigo o Duodo 2504; tickets €50; doors open 8pm) Hang on to your wineglass and brace for impact: in palace salons, the soprano's high notes might make you fear for your glassware, and thundering baritones reverberate in the base of the spine. The drama unfolds during 1½ hours of selected arias from Verdi to Rossini, progressing from receiving-room overtures to a parlour overlooking the Grand Canal, a Tiepolo-ceilinged dining room and heartbreaking finales in the bedroom.

TEATRO GOLDONI — THEATRE

Map p286 (041 240 20 14; www.teatrostabileveneto.it, in Italian; Calle Teatro Goldoni 4650b; tickets €7-30; box office 10am-1pm & 3-7pm Mon-Wed, 10am-1pm Thu; Rialto) Named after the city's greatest playwright, the city's main theatre has an impressive dramatic range that runs from Goldoni's comedy to Shakespearean tragedy (mostly in Italian), plus ballets and concerts. The box office opens Friday and Saturday when there is a performance.

SHOPPING

TOP CHOICE ARTIGIANCARTA DI MASSIMO DORETTO — PAPER CRAFTS

Map p286 (041 522 56 06; Frezzeria 1797; 10am-7pm Mon-Sat; Vallaresso) Conquer writers' block in style with one-of-a-kind hand-marbled note-cards, linen-bound composer's notebooks, travel journals emblazoned with vintage Venice postcards and gilt leather albums fit for a royal wedding. The hand-tanned leather must be handled with care, but Massimo is delighted to pull down any pieces for you – he made them all.

ANTICA MODISTERIA GIULIANA LONGO — HATS

Map p286 (041 522 64 54; www.giulianalongo.com; Calle l'Ovo 4813; Rialto) Shoe closets are for amateurs: Giuliana's shop is the dream hat-cupboard of any true sartorialist. Styles range from hand-woven Montecristi panama hats – as modelled by client Sean Connery – to a fuchsia felt number that looks like a doge's cap for Peggy Guggenheim. Giuliana is here most days, polishing leather aviator hats or affixing a broad band to a *bareteri,* wide-brimmed gondolier's hats best worn with a rakish tilt (from €45).

OTTICA CARRARO — EYEGLASSES

Map p286 (041 520 42 58; www.otticacarraro.it; Calle della Mandola 3706; 9am-1pm & 3.30-7pm Mon-Sat; Sant'Angelo) Lost your sunglasses on the Lido? Never fear: Ottica Carraro can make you a custom pair within 24 hours. The store has its own signature 'Venice' line, which ranges from retro-1980s shades with caution-yellow rims to arty matte-rubber frames in bronze and grape.

FIORELLA GALLERY — FASHION

Map p286 (041 520 92 28; www.fiorellagallery.com; Campo Santo Stefano 2806; 9.30am-1.30pm & 3.30-7pm Tue-Sat, 3-7pm Mon; Accademia) Groupies are the only accessory needed to go with Fiorella's crushed-velvet smoking jackets in louche shades of lavender and blood red, printed by hand with Venetian wallpaper patterns and a Fiorella signature: wide-eyed rats. Prices start in the mid-three figures, but check out your reflection in the graffitied Ettore Sotsass mirror and pretend you're not impressed. Hours are approximate; as the sign says, 'we open sometime'.

LIBRERIA STUDIUM BOOKSTORE

Map p286 (041 522 23 82; Calle di Canonica 337; 9am-7.30pm Mon-Sat, 9.30am-1.30pm & 2-6pm Sun; San Zaccaria) Consult bibliophile staff for worthy vacation reads, page-turning Venetian history or top picks from shelves groaning under the weight of Italian cookbooks. Many titles are available in English and French, and there's a respectably vast Lonely Planet section (not that we're biased).

ARNOLDO & BATTOIS FASHION, ACCESSORIES

Map p286 (041 5285944; www.arnoldoebattois.com; Calle dei Fuseri 4271; 10am-1pm & 3.30-7pm Mon Thu & Sat; Sant'Angelo) Handbags become heirlooms in the hands of Venetian designers Massimiliano Battois and Silvano Arnoldo, who handcraft their bags from boldly coloured leather and heraldic hardware found at Venice's antique markets. Artfully draped ochre and graphite silk dresses complete the look for Biennale openings.

DANIELA GHEZZO SHOES

Map p286 (041 522 21 15; Calle dei Fuseri 4365; Rialto) A gold chain is pulled across the doorway, but not because Daniela is out: she's chatting with a customer about shoe preferences while taking foot measurements. In this historic atelier, maestra Ghezzo continues the tradition of custom-making every pair to measure, so you'll never see your oxblood ankle boots on another art collector, or your charcoal-grey wingtips on a rival titan of industry.

VENETIA STUDIUM ACCESSORIES, FASHION

Map p286 (041 523 69 53; www.venetiastudium.com; Palazzo Zuccato 2425; 10am-7pm Mon-Sat; Santa Maria del Giglio) Get that 'just got in from Monaco for my art opening' look beloved of bohemians who marry well. The high-drama Delphos tunic dresses make anyone look like a high-maintenance modern dancer or heiress (Isadora Duncan and Peggy Guggenheim were both fans) and the hand-stamped silk-velvet bags are more arty than ostentatious (prices from €30).

ARCOBALENO ART SUPPLIES

Map p286 (041 523 68 18; Calle delle Botteghe 3457; Accademia) After umpteen Venetian art masterpieces, anyone's fingers will start twitching for a paint brush. Arcobaleno provides all the raw materials needed to start your own Venetian art movement, with shelves fully stocked with jars of all the essential pigments: Titian red, Tiepolo sky-blue, Veronese rose, Bellini peach and Tintoretto teal.

MATERIALMENTE JEWELLERY, DECOR

Map p286 (041 528 68 81; www.materialmente.it; Mercerie San Salvador 4850; 10am-7pm Mon-Sat; Rialto) No Venetian palace is complete without opulent mirrors and lavish tapestries, and Maddelena Venier and her brother Alessandro Salvadori have cleverly combined these luxe effects in modern mirrors hand-silkscreened with baroque patterns. The prolific siblings also create whimsical lamps that look like birdcages and signet rings ideal for sealing love letters in wax.

CHARTA BOOKS, PAPER CRAFTS

Map p286 (041 522 98 01; www.chartaonline.com; 831 Calle del Fabbri; 10am-1pm & 4-7.30pm; Vallaresso) Pulp fiction becomes high art at Charta, where favourite books are custom-bound: Tim Burton's *Edward Scissorhands* has artfully sliced edges, Houdini's secrets are bound in leather with embossed handcuffs and *Twilight* has a rising moon on the cover and black and silver shivers up the spine. Limited editions start around €30; a custom-illustrated magnum opus runs from €70 to €300.

ESPERIENZE GLASS, JEWELLERY

Map p286 (041 521 29 45; www.esperienzevenezia.com; Calle degli Specchieri 473b; 10am-noon & 3-7pm; San Marco) When Italian minimalist design meets Murano glassblowing talent and falls in love, the result is spare yet spirited glass jewellery. The creative minds behind Esperienze are Graziano and Sara, a husband-wife team raised in Murano with a shared love of Kandinsky, Miró and other Guggenheim Collection modernists. Every piece is a collaborative effort: he breathes life into her designs, which include oversize teardrop pendants and cracked-ice earrings.

BEVILACQUA FABRICS

Map p286 (041 241 06 62; www.bevilacquatessuti.com; Campo di Santa Maria del Giglio 2520; 10am-7pm; Santa Maria del Giglio) TV dens become grand salons with Venetian swagger at Bevilacqua, producers of Venetian brocades, damasks, and silken tassels since 1800. Fabrics are loom-woven in a time-honoured fashion, and custom cushions and upholstery are available.

PAOLO OLBI PAPER CRAFTS

Map p286 (☎041 528 50 25; http://olbi.atspace.com; Calle della Mandola 3653; ⊙10am-7pm Mon-Sat; Sant'Angelo) Thoughts worth committing to paper deserve Paolo Olbi's keepsake books, albums and stationery. Stock here is handcrafted with heavyweight paper, bound with either hand-tanned or affordable reclaimed leather bindings, and often emblazoned with the winged lion of San Marco, one paw resting on an open book.

LE BOTTEGHE GIFTS, HOUSEWARES

Map p286 (☎041 522 75 45; Rialto 5164; ⊙10am-7pm Mon-Sat; Rialto) Italian design sensibilities meet Venetian trading smarts at this fair-trade boutique on the steps of the Rialto. Gondola rides call for foldable straw hats made by a Bangladeshi collective, while kids are placated by recycled cans fashioned into toy aeroplanes and organic chocolate.

CAMUFFO GLASS

Map p286 (Calle delle Acque 4992; ⊙10am-1pm & 3.30-7pm Mon-Sat; Rialto) Kids, entomologists and glass collectors seek out Signor Camuffo, who wields a miniature blowtorch to fuse metallic foils to molten glass to make shimmering wings for the city's finest selection of lampworked glass beetles and dragonflies. Between bugs, he'll chat about his work and sell you strands of Murano glass beads at excellent prices.

LA PIETRA FILOSOFALE MASKS

Map p286 (☎041 528 58 85; Frezzeria 1735; ⊙10am-12:30pm & 3-7pm Tue-Sat; Vallaresso) Opera stars up the road at La Fenice know La Pietra Filosofale as the go-to artisan for dramatic entrances and Carnevale costumes. Here leather is moulded by hand into fiendish scowls and deceptively innocent grins, while papier-mâché masks are sketched with expressive pen and ink patterns reminiscent of a Ca' Pesaro Klimt painting.

GLORIA ASTOLFO JEWELLERY

Map p286 (☎041 520 68 27; www.gloriastolfo.com; Frezzeria 1581; ⊙10am-7pm; Vallareso) Take your fashion cues from Venetian painting masterpieces at this Venetian bead artisan's showcase. Garlands of beaded tiger lilies make open-necked T-shirts instantly glamorous, and those baroque pearl earrings would gently tickle your shoulders if you started to nod off at La Fenice. Prices starting at €35 are surprisingly down-to-earth for jewellery this original, especially so close to Piazza San Marco.

CARPE DIEM VINTAGE, WOMEN'S CLOTHING

Map p286 (☎041 528 98 03; Campo di Santa Maria del Giglio 2517; ⊙11am-7pm; Santa Maria del Giglio) Palazzo walk-in closets have been raided for this vintage boutique, where rare recent finds included a Roberta di Camerino trompe l'oeil scarf, Gucci backpacks and Chanel jackets galore. Prices quickly enter triple digits, especially for collectors' pieces.

FULL SPOT ACCESSORIES

(☎041 520 60 90; Salizada San Giovanni Gristosomo 5692; ⊙10am-7:30pm; Rialto) Right in style and on the money, this Padua-based watch designer sells affordable, interchangeable watch faces and rubber bands in fashion colours. Go tone-on-tone with a lagoon-teal-blue face and band, or mix it up with an orange-and-grey combo – a hit at the Milan design fair.

Sestiere di Dorsoduro

Neighbourhood Top Five

❶ Find out what all the fuss is about Venetian painting at **Gallerie dell'Accademia** (p79), a former convent that is now positively blushing with masterpieces of glowing colours, censored subjects and a newly restored dramatic finale.

❷ Hang out with priceless modern sculpture on the Grand Canal dock of **Peggy Guggenheim Collection** (p81).

❸ Waltz through baroque palace boudoirs filled with social graces and sharp wits at **Ca' Rezzonico** (p82).

❹ Compare, contrast and debate fearless contemporary art and boldly repurposed architecture at **Punta della Dogana** (p84).

❺ Be floored by wall-to-wall, floor-to-ceiling Veronese masterpieces at **Chiesa di San Sebastian** (p82).

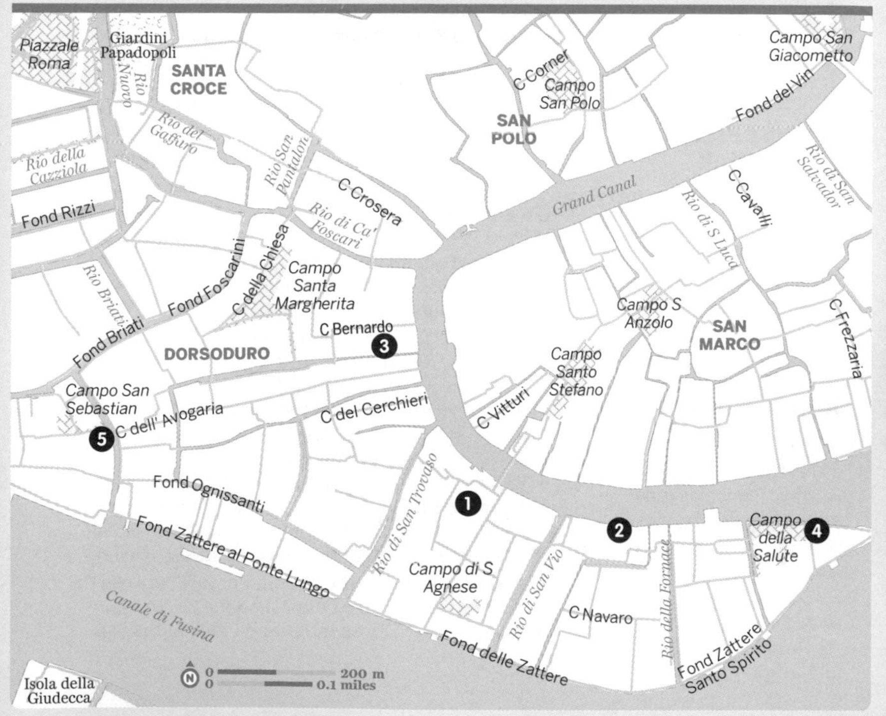

For more detail of this area, see map p290 ➡

Lonely Planet's Top Tip

Dorsoduro points into the lagoon like a bent gondola prow, and sites are spread out. Its museums are along the Grand Canal on the east side, while boisterous bars and upbeat eateries are clumped around Campo Santa Margherita and Campo San Barnaba to the northwest – a 20-minute walk from the Guggenheim or Punta della Dogana. To escape museums and revellers, head south along Zattere for quiet churches and sunshine.

Best Places to Eat

- Ristorante La Bitta (p85)
- Enoteca Ai Artisti (p85)
- Avogaria (p85)
- Grom (p85)
- Ristoteca Oniga (p85)

For reviews, see p85

Best Places to Drink

- Cantinone Giá Schiavi (p87)
- Il Caffè Rosso (p87)
- Imagina Caffé (p87)
- Osteria alla Bifora (p87)
- Tea Room Beatrice (p87)

For reviews, see p87

Best Venetian Views

- *Feast in the House of Levi*, Accademia (p80)
- Grand Canal alongside *Angel of the City*, Peggy Guggenheim Collection (p81)
- Ando's water-gate windows, Punta della Dogana (p84)
- Vedutisti Gallery, Ca' Rezzonico (p82)
- Zattere (p86)

Explore: Dorsoduro

Visual splendour and powerful drink are the eternal lures of artistically inclined Dorsoduro, so throw back an espresso and dive into the deep end of art history. Gallerie dell'Accademia is bound to leave you weak in the knees, so detour behind the museum for lunch among modern-art masters at Ristorante San Trovaso before resuming your Dorsoduro art blitz at Peggy Guggenheim Collection and controversial contemporary art installations at Punta della Dogana. Give your eyes a chance to refocus with a stroll along the Zattere, before they're boggled again by Veronese's floor-to-ceiling masterpieces at San Sebastian. Browse through boutiques along Calle Lunga San Barnaba and mingle with witty Venetian socialites of yore at Ca' Rezzonico before joining Venetian regulars for a *spritz* at Campo Santa Margherita. Dine near Campo San Barnaba, but don't be late for your hot concert date at one of Dorsoduro's historic venues – ideally Ca' Rezzonico's frescoed ballroom or Tiepolo-ceilinged Scuola Grande dei Carmini.

Local Life

- **Spritz o'clock** The best place to be when the clock strikes six *(spritz)* o'clock is Campo Santa Margherita (p88), Venice's nightlife hub.
- **Antique & avant-garde** Rummage through relics from Venice's past at Antiquariato Claudia Canestrelli (p88) or fast-forward to a Venetian-style future at Marina e Susanna Sent (p88), Lauretta Vistosi (p89) and Danghyra (p89).
- **Rush-hour detour** Dodge pedestrian traffic shuttling between Ponte dell'Accademia and Campo Santa Margherita in peak season and take the Zattere (p86) instead to bask in the late-afternoon sun.
- **Concert scene** Choose your music and your scene: chamber music in the grand ballroom at Ca' Rezzonico (p82), costume-drama arias in baroque Scuola Grande dei Carmini (p83), or swinging canalside tributes at Venice Jazz Club (p88).

Getting There & Away

- **Vaporetto** Grand Canal 1, 2 and N lines stop at Accademia; line 1 also calls at Ca' Rezzonico and Salute. Lines 51, 52, 61, 62 and the N night *vaporetto* (small passenger ferry) call at the Zattere and San Basilio.
- **Traghetto** To skip the 20-minute walk between Ca' Rezzonico and Palazzo Grassi, hop the Ca' Rezzonico *traghetto* (ferry) across the Grand Canal to the San Samuele stop.

TOP SIGHTS
GALLERIE DELL'ACCADEMIA

Hardly academic, these galleries contain more murderous intrigue, forbidden romance and shameless politicking than the most outrageous Venetian parties. The former Santa Maria della Carità convent complex maintained its serene composure for centuries, but ever since Napoleon installed his haul of Venetian art trophies in 1807, there's been nonstop visual drama inside these walls. To guide you through the ocular onslaught, the gallery layout is loosely organised by style and theme from the 14th to 18th centuries, though recent restorations have temporarily shuffled around masterpieces in eight of the galleries.

Architecture

The Accademia represents Venice's single most important art collection – and the work of several of its finest architects. Bartolomeo Bon completed the spare, Gothic-edged Santa Maria della Carità facade in 1448; in 1561, Palladio took a classical approach to the Convento dei Canonici Lateranensi, which was absorbed into the Accademia; and from 1949 to 1954, modernist Carlo Scarpa took a minimalist approach to restorations, taking care not to upset the delicate symmetries achieved between architects over the centuries.

Rooms 1–5

Early highlights include Paolo Veneziano's *Coronation of Mary* (Room 1), with Jesus bestowing the crown on his mother with a gentle pat on the head, an angelic orchestra performing above. For sheer, shimmering gore, check out Carpaccio's *Crucifixion and Glorification of the Ten Thousand Martyrs of Mount Ararat* (Room 2) – Harry's Bar was apt in naming its

DON'T MISS...

- Veronese's *Feast in the House of Levi*
- Titian's *Presentation of the Virgin*
- Tintoretto's *Creation of the Animals*
- Lotto's *Portrait of a Young Scholar*
- Bellini's *Madonna and Child*
- Veneziano's *Coronation of Mary*
- Titian/Palma il Giovane's *Pietá*

PRACTICALITIES

- Map p290
- ☎041 520 03 45
- www.gallerieaccademia.org
- Campo della Carità 1050
- adult/reduced €6.50/3.25
- 8.15am-2pm Mon, to 7.15pm Tue-Sun
- Accademia

OUTSMARTING ACCADEMIA QUEUES

To skip ahead of the Accademia ticket-booth queue in high season, book ahead online or by phone (booking fee €1). Otherwise, queues at the temporary booth alongside the museum tend to be shorter in the afternoon, after the school groups depart and the day-trippers begin their treks back to mainland hotels. Still, don't put off joining the queue too long, because the last entry is one hour before closing and proper visits take at least 90 minutes.

Leave any large items behind, or you'll have to drop them off at the baggage depot (€0.50 per piece). Also available at the baggage depot is an audio guide (€5) that is mostly descriptive and largely unnecessary – better to avoid the wait and just follow your bliss and the explanatory wall tags.

bloody, raw-beef dish after him. In Rooms 3 to 5, Andrea Mantegna's 1466 haughtily handsome *St George* and Giovanni Bellini's sweet-faced *Madonna and Child* haloed by neon-red cherubs show Venice's twin artistic tendencies: high drama and glowing colour.

Rooms 6–10

Here your visit advances rapidly through the Renaissance and such masterpieces as Tintoretto's *Creation of the Animals,* a fantastical bestiary suggesting God put forth his best efforts inventing Venetian seafood (no arguments here). A recent restoration brings new light to one of Titian's last efforts, which was possibly finished posthumously by Palma il Giovane: a 1576 *Pietà*, where form is secondary to emotion, with smears of paint Titian applied with his bare hands.

Artistic triumph over censorship dominates Room 10: Paolo Veronese's **Feast in the House of Levi**, originally called *Last Supper* until Inquisition leaders condemned him for showing dogs, drunkards, dwarves, Muslims and Reformation-minded Germans cavorting with Apostles. He refused to change a thing, besides the title, and Venice stood by this act of defiance against Rome. Follow the exchanges, gestures and eye contact among the characters, and you'll concede that not one Turkish trader, stumbling servant, gambler or bright-eyed lapdog could have been painted over without losing an essential piece of the Venetian puzzle.

Rooms 11–19

Here you're only halfway through Venice's contributions to art history – in these rooms though you will find a lighter baroque touch and down-to-earth subject matter. In Rooms 15 to 18 you'll see Canaletto's sweeping views of Venice and Giorgione's highly charged *The Storm,* a nursing mother, a passing soldier and a bolt of summer lightning. Adjoining portrait galleries can scarcely contain the larger-than-life Venetian characters: Giorgione's decidedly un-Botoxed *Old Woman*; Lorenzo Lotto's soul-searching *Portrait of a Young Scholar;* Rosalba Carriera's brutally honest self-portrait; Pietro Longhi's lovestruck violinist watching a debutante in *The Dance Lesson*; and Giambattista Piazzetta's saucy socialite in his *Fortune-Teller.*

Rooms 20–24

Gentile Bellini and Vittore Carpaccio pack Room 20 with multicultural merchant crowds embedded in Venetian versions of *Miracles of the True Cross.* The grand finale is the Sala dell'Albergo, fronted by Antonio **Vivarini**'s giant triptych and starring Titian's *Presentation of the Virgin* – a young Madonna dutifully trudging up an intimidating staircase as onlookers point to her example.

TOP SIGHTS
PEGGY GUGGENHEIM COLLECTION

After tragically losing her father on the *Titanic*, heiress Peggy Guggenheim befriended Dadaists, dodged Nazis and amassed avant-garde works by 200 modern artists at her palatial home on the Grand Canal. Peggy's Palazzo Venier dei Leoni became a modernist shrine, chronicling surrealism, Italian futurism and abstract expressionism, with a subtext of her romantic pursuits – the collection includes key works by Peggy's ex-husband Max Ernst as well as Jackson Pollock, among her many rumoured lovers.

Collection

Peggy collected according to her own convictions rather than for prestige or style, so her collection includes inspired folk art and lesser-known artists alongside Kandinsky, Picasso, Man Ray, Rothko, Mondrian, Joseph Cornell and Dalí. Major modernists also contributed custom interior decor, including the **Calder silver bedstead** hanging in the former bedroom. In the corners of the main galleries, you'll find photos of the rooms as they appeared when Peggy lived here, in fabulously eccentric style.

The Palazzo Venier dei Leoni was never finished, but that didn't stop Peggy Guggenheim from making art history with the available wall space and garden. More than a mere tastemaker, Peggy was a spirited advocate for contemporary Italian art, which had largely gone out of favour with the rise of Mussolini and the partisan politics of WWII. The Jewish American collector narrowly escaped Paris two days before the Nazis marched into the city, and arrived in Venice in 1948 to find the city's historically buoyant spirits broken by war. For this champion of Italian art who'd witnessed the dangers of censorship and party-line dictates, serious artwork deserved to be seen and judged on its merits.

Peggy sparked renewed interest in postwar Venetian and Italian art and resurrected the reputation of key Italian Futurists, whose dynamic style had been co-opted to make Fascism more visually palatable. Her support led to reappraisals of Umberto Boccioni, Giorgio Morandi, Giacomo Balla and Giorgio de Chirico, and aided Venice's own Emilio Vedova (see p83). Facing the Grand Canal on her palace's quay is deliberate provocation: Marino Marini's 1948 *Angel of the City*, a bronze male nude on horseback visibly excited by the possibilities on the horizon.

Garden & Pavilion

Wander outside, past bronzes by Moore, Giacometti and Brancusci, Yoko Ono's *Wish Tree* and a shiny black granite lump by Anish Kapoor in the **sculpture garden**, where the city of Venice granted Peggy honorary dispensation to be buried beneath the Giacometti sculptures and alongside her dearly departed lapdogs in 1979. Through the gardens is a pavilion housing a sunny cafe, bookshop, bathrooms, and temporary exhibits highlighting underappreciated modernist rebels. Around the corner from the museum on Fondamenta Venier dei Leoni is a larger **museum shop**, selling art books in several languages and replicas of Peggy's signature glasses – winged, like the lion of San Marco.

DON'T MISS...

- Rotating permanent collection
- Calder silver bedstead
- *Angel of the City*
- Sculpture garden
- Temporary pavilion shows

PRACTICALITIES

- Map p290
- ☎041 240 54 11
- www.guggenheim-venice.it
- Palazzo Venier dei Leoni 704
- adult/reduced €12/7
- ⌚10am-6pm Wed-Mon
- Accademia

SIGHTS

GALLERIE DELL'ACCADEMIA — MUSEUM

See p79.

PEGGY GUGGENHEIM COLLECTION — MUSEUM

See p81.

CHIESA DI SAN SEBASTIAN — CHURCH

Map p290 (www.chorusvenezia.org; Campo San Sebastiano 1687; admission €3, or with Chorus Pass; ⌚10am-5pm Mon-Sat; San Basilio) A hidden treasure of Venetian art in the heart of Dorsoduro, this otherwise humble neighbourhood church was embellished with floor-to-ceiling masterpieces by Paolo Veronese over three decades. Antonio Scarpignano's 1508–48 relatively austere classical facade creates a sense of false modesty from the outside, because inside, the interior decor goes wild.

Veronese's horses rear over the frames of the **coffered ceiling**; the **organ doors** are covered with vivid Veronese masterworks; and in Veronese's *Martyrdom of Saint Sebastian* near the altar, the bound saint defiantly stares down his tormentors amid a Venetian crowd of socialites, turbaned traders and Veronese's signature frisky spaniel. This last work may have held some personal significance for Veronese. According to popular local legend, Veronese found sanctuary at San Sebastian in 1555 after fleeing murder charges in Verona, and his works here deliver lavish thanks to the parish and an especially brilliant poke in the eye of his accusers.

Pay respects to Veronese, who chose to be buried here among his masterpieces, but don't miss Titian's *San Niccolo* and a couple minor works by Tintoretto and Palma Il Giovane in the **sacristy**. Ongoing restoration may limit access to some artworks, but even so, San Sebastiano offers glimpses of greatness.

CHIESA DI SANTA MARIA DELLA SALUTE — CHURCH

Map p290 (www.seminariovenezia.it, in Italian; Campo della Salute 1b; ⌚9am-noon & 3-5.30pm; Salute) A monumental sigh of relief, this dazzling church was built by survivors of Venice's plague as thanks for their salvation. The structure makes good on an official 1630 appeal by the Venetian Senate directly to the Madonna herself, promising her a church in exchange for her intervention on

TOP SIGHTS CA' REZZONICO

The original entry of Baldassare Longhena's dashingly handsome palace is along the Grand Canal, but the canal-side gate now in use opens onto a courtyard garden where you can picnic (rare in Venice). A sweeping marble staircase leads to baroque salons frosted with stucco and crowned with ceiling masterpieces by Giambattista Tiepolo. His **Throne Room ceiling** is a masterpiece of sensuous beauty and shameless flattery, showing gorgeous Merit ascending to the Temple of Glory clutching the Golden Book of Venetian nobles' names – including Tiepolo's patrons, the Rezzonico family.

Pietro Longhi Salon is covered with the artist's signature satires of society antics, observed by disapproving lapdogs. **Sala Rosalba Carriera** features Carriera's wry, unvarnished pastel portraits of socialites that aren't strictly pretty, but look like they'd be the life of any party. Giandomenico Tiepolo's swinging court jesters add cheeky humour to the reassembled **Zianigo Villa bedroom frescoes**, and don't miss Emma Ciardi's moody Venice canal views in the top-floor **Vedutisti galleries** (p232). Last entry is an hour before closing; check the schedule downstairs for chamber-music concerts in the **trompe l'oeil frescoed ballroom**.

DON'T MISS...

- Tiepolo's trompe l'oeil ceilings
- Pietro Longhi Salon
- Sala Rosalba Carriera

PRACTICALITIES

- Map p290
- ☎041 241 01 00
- www.museicivicivenezi ani.it
- Fondamenta Rezzonico 3136
- adult/reduced €8/5.50; Museum Pass
- ⌚10am-6pm Wed-Mon Apr-Oct, to 5pm Wed-Mon Nov-Mar
- Ca'Rezzonico

WORTH A DETOUR

CHIESA DI SAN NICOLÒ DEI MENDICOLI

Other churches in town are grander and glitzier, but none are more quintessentially Venetian. This striking brick Veneto-Gothic **church** (Map p290 (☎041 528 45 65; Campo San Nicolò 1907; ⏰10am-noon & 4-6pm Mon-Sat; 🚢San Basilio) dedicated to serving the poor hasn't changed much since the 12th century, when its cloisters functioned as a women's shelter and its **portico** sheltered *mendicoli* (beggars). The tiny, picturesque *campo* out front is Venice in miniature, surrounded on three sides by canals and featuring a pylon bearing the winged lion of St Mark – one of the few in Venice to escape target practice by Napoleon's troops.

Dim interiors are illuminated by an **18th-century golden arcade** and a profusion of clerestory paintings, including a Palma Il Giovane masterpiece: *Resurrection* shows onlookers taking cover in terror and amazement, as Jesus leaps from his tomb in a blaze of golden light. The right-hand **chapel** is a typically Venetian response to persistent orders from Rome to limit music in Venetian churches: Madonna in glory, thoroughly enjoying a concert by angels on flutes, lutes and violins. The parish's seafaring livelihood is honoured in Leonardo Corona's **16th-century ceiling** *San Niccolo Guiding Sailors Through a Storm*, which shows the saint as a beacon of light to guide sailors rowing furiously through a storm. You might recognise church interiors from the Julie Christie thriller *Don't Look Now* as the church Donald Sutherland was assigned to restore – no small task

behalf of Venice – never mind the labour involved. At least 100,000 pylons had to be driven deep into the *barene* (mud banks) to shore up the tip of Dorsoduro to support the weight of this baroque engineering marvel.

Baldassare Longhena's unusual domed octagon is an inspired design architectural scholars have compared to Greco-Roman temples and Jewish cabbala diagrams, and it remains the site of Venetians' annual pilgrimage to pray for health (Festa Della Madonna Della Salute; see p22). Extensive interior restorations may limit access to Tintoretto's surprisingly upbeat *The Wedding Feast of Cana* and 12 key works by Titian in the **sacristy** (admission €2) – including a vivid self-portrait in the guise of St Matthew and his earliest known work from 1510, *Saint Mark on the Throne*.

SCUOLA GRANDE DEI CARMINI — HISTORICAL BUILDING

Map p290 (☎041 528 94 20; www.scuolagrandecarmini.it; Campo Santa Margherita 2617; adult/reduced €5/4; ⏰11am-5pm; 🚢Ca' Rezzonico) Eighteenth-century backpackers must have thought they'd died and gone to heaven at the Scuola Grande dei Carmini, a shelter run by Carmelite nuns with interiors lavishly appointed by Giambattista Tiepolo and Baldassare Longhena. Longhena designed the gold-leafed stucco **stairway** to heaven, which is glimpsed upstairs in Tiepolo's **nine-panel ceiling** of a resplendent, rosy *Virgin in Glory*. The adjoining hostel room is a wonder of *boiserie* (carved woodwork). Sadly, cots are no longer available in this jewel-box building, but ask downstairs about occasional concerts by **Musica in Maschera** (Musical Masquerade; www.musicainmaschera.it), performed here in 1700s costume.

FREE MAGAZZINI DEL SALE — ART GALLERY

(www.fondazionevedova.org; Zattere 266; donation suggested; ⏰during shows 10.30am-6pm Wed-Mon; 🚢Zattere) A recent retrofit designed by Pritzker Prize–winning architect Renzo Piano transformed Venice's historic **salt warehouses** into city art galleries. Alongside a public art gallery and performance space is **Fondazione Vedova** (www.fondazionevedova.org), dedicated to pioneering Venetian abstract painter Emilio Vedova. At the Fondazione, shows are often literally moving and rotating: powered by renewable energy sources, **10 robotic arms** designed by Vedova and Piano move artworks in and out of storage slots.

Although the facade is a neoclassical job from the 1830s, the nine salt warehouses were built in the 14th century, establishing the all-important salt trade that made Venice's fortune. Before fridges and electricity, the only way to preserve foodstuffs was to cure or pack them in salt – and since preserved foods were essential for ocean voyages, salt became crucial to maritime

TOP SIGHTS
PUNTA DELLA DOGANA

Fortuna, the weathervane atop Punta della Dogana, swung Venice's way in 2005, when bureaucratic hassles in Paris convinced billionaire art collector François Pinault to showcase his artworks in long-abandoned customs warehouses at Punta della Dogana.

Art installations invade personal space and address personal fixations: Chen Zhen's pure crystal versions of his diseased internal organs; Edward Keinholz's full-scale brothel-parlour recreation; Abdel Abdessemed's drawings of Molotov cocktail throwers propped up on concert stands so as to orchestrate violence. Not all are intended for younger viewers, while others (Jeff Koons' dangling steel-balloon heart or Maurizio Cattelan's horse's hind end mounted on a wall) may speak to them exclusively.

The warehouses were built by Giuseppe Benoni in 1677 to ensure no ship entered the Grand Canal without paying duties. Opened in 2009 after a three-year reinvention by architect Tadao Ando, Venice's splashiest art space pays its dues to the city's seafaring history and pioneering modernist Carlo Scarpa. Windows in ancient watergates reveal cutaway views of canal ships; exposed-brick galleries are flooded with light through strategic polished-concrete channels and connected by floating staircases.

DON'T MISS...

- Fortuna
- Tadao Ando interiors
- Rotating art installations
- Quayside sculpture displays
- Bookshop

PRACTICALITIES

- Map p290
- ☎199 13 91 39
- www.palazzograssi.it
- adult/reduced €15/10, with Palazzo Grassi €20/15
- 10am-7pm Wed-Mon
- Salute

commerce. Today, warehouses not used for art are used by the Bucintoro rowing club for storage, and serve the city as environmental initiative labs.

CHIESA DEI GESUATI CHURCH
Map p290 (Church of Santa Maria del Rosario; www.chorusvenezia.org; Fondamenta delle Zattere 918; admission €3, or with Chorus Pass; 10am-5pm Mon-Sat; Zattere) No matter the weather outside, the outlook is decidedly sunny inside this high baroque church designed by Giorgio Massari. Luminous afternoon skies surrounding St Dominic in Tiepolo's 1737–39 **ceiling frescoes** are so convincing, you'll wonder whether you're wearing enough sunscreen. Striking a sombre note on the left side of the nave, Tintoretto's 1565 *Crucifixion* shows Mary fainting with grief – but in 1730–33 *Saints Peter and Thomas with Pope Pius V,* Sebastiano Ricci's chubby cherubs provide heavenly comic relief with celestial tumbling routines.

If you find the side door to the cloisters open, you might peek into the little-visited Chiesa di Santa Maria della Visitazione. Better known as **Chiesa di Santa Maria degli Artigianelli** for its role as the spiritual home to Venice's artisans, the otherwise modest church boasts a fine 15th-century chessboard ceiling embedded with scenes of the Visitation.

SQUERO DI SAN TROVASO HISTORICAL SITE
(Campo San Trovaso 1097; Zattere) When it's time for a tune-up, *gondolieri* head to the *squero* (small-scale shipyard). The wood cabin on the corner of the Rio di San Trovaso may look like a misplaced ski chalet, but it's actually part of one of the city's three working *squeri*. From the right bank, you can see refinished gondolas drying in the yard. If you find the door open during working hours, you can poke your head inside in exchange for a donation left in the can by the door – but no flash photography is allowed, as it might startle the gondola builders as they're completing a tricky bit of woodwork with sharp tools.

CA' DARIO PALAZZO
Map p290 (Ramo Ca' Dario 352; Salute) Grand Canal palaces rank among the world's most prime real estate, except for the perfectly gorgeous 1487 Ca' Dario. Its striking multicoloured marble facade casts a mesmerising

reflection in the Grand Canal, captured by no less than Claude Monet – but there's a catch. Starting with the daughter of its original owner, Giovanni Dario, an unusual number of its owners have lost fortunes, fallen ill and/or met tragic ends, which local gossips claim was enough to dissuade Woody Allen from buying the place in the 1990s. The former manager of The Who, Kit Lambert, once owned it, and one week after renting the place for a holiday in 2002, The Who's bass player, John Entwhistle, died of a heart attack. At this writing, Ca' Dario is for sale; any takers?

CHIESA DELL'ARCANGELO RAFFAELE CHURCH

Chiesa di San Basilio; Map p290 (041 522 85 48; Campo Anzolo Raffaele 1721; donation suggested; 9am-noon & 4-6pm Mon-Sat; San Basilio) The neighbours called, and they want their grime back: when a recent cleaning of Francesco Contino's 17th-century facade removed centuries of accumulated dirt on carved stone angels above the portals, it caused a local uproar. Had Venice lost its respect for the patina of age? But no similar argument was raised about the restoration of the baptistery, where Francesco Fontebasso's freshly restored baroque frescoes glow like dawn in shades of pink, gold and pale green. The cycle of paintings above the main altar has been attributed to the Guardi brothers, but no one is sure which one – the *vedutista* (landscape artist) Francesco or his lesser-known elder brother Gian Antonio (1699–1760). In the afternoons, the organist practises with fugues; ask the guardian about upcoming concerts.

EATING

RISTORANTE LA BITTA MEAT €€

Map p290 (041 523 05 31; Calle Lunga San Barnaba 2753a; meals €35-40; 7-10pm Mon-Sat; Ca' Rezzonico) The daily menu is presented on a miniature artist's easel, and the rustic fare served here looks like a still life and tastes like a dream: gnocchi is graced with pumpkin and herbs, and roast rabbit arrives on a bed of marinated rocket. This is one of few places in Venice to focus on meats instead of seafood – 'La Bitta' means 'the mooring post' – and only seats 35, so carnivores should book ahead. Wine isn't offered by the glass, but they'll cut you a deal on a half-bottle; cash only.

ENOTECA AI ARTISTI VENETIAN €€

Map p290 (041 523 89 44; www.enotecaartisti.com; Fondamenta della Toletta 1169a; mains €9-27; noon-4pm & 6.30-10pm Mon-Sat; Ca' Rezzonico) Heartwarming pastas, inspired cheeses and sliced steak with balsamic atop arugula are paired with exceptional wines by the glass by your oenophile hosts. Sidewalk tables for two make great people-watching, but book indoor tables for groups; space is limited, so book ahead.

AVOGARIA MODERN ITALIAN €€

Map p290 (041 296 04 91; Calle dell'Avogaria 1629; cicheti €1.5-4, mains €10-22; noon-3pm & 6-11pm Wed-Sun; San Basilio) Dates begin casually enough in this exposed-brick, wood-beamed restaurant, with happy-hour *cicheti* and *spritz* at the sleek glass bar – but a few bites of Venetian *crudi* (raw fish) laced with fresh herbs leads to seafood risotto for two, and by the time the tiramisu arrives, you'll be swooning.

 **GROM** GELATERIA €

Map p290 (041 099 17 51; www.grom.it; Campo San Barnaba, Dorsoduro 2461; gelato €2.50-4; noon-11pm; Ca' Rezzonico) Lick the landscape at Grom, featuring Slow Food ingredients from across Italy: lemon from Amalfi Coast, strawberries from Sicily, hazelnuts from Piedmont. Fair-trade chocolate and coffee sourcing helped win Turin-based Grom a coveted 'Master of Slow Food' designation, but with seasonal flavours like white peach with dark-chocolate chips, you may be tempted to give it another honorary title: lunch.

RISTOTECA ONIGA VENETIAN €€

Map p290 (041 522 44 10; www.oniga.it; Campo San Barnaba 2852; meals €17-30; noon-3pm & 7-10pm Wed-Mon; Ca' Rezzonico) Purists come for chef Annika's Venetian seafood platter with exemplary *sarde in saor* (sardines in tangy onion marinade), vegetarians are spoiled for choice with seasonal pastas (try broccoli rabe, pecorino and breadcrumbs), and everyone appreciates the selection of 150 wines and fixed-price menus starting at €17. Grab a sunny spot in the *campo*, or get cosy in a wood-panelled corner.

PASTICCERIA TONOLO PASTRIES & CAKES €

Map p290 (041 532 72 09; Calle dei Preti 3764; pastries €1-3; 8am-8pm Mon-Sat, 8am-1pm Sun; Ca' Rezzonico) Dire B&B breakfasts with packaged croissants are corrected

A HEALTHY STROLL: THE ZATTERE

On sunny days, the leisurely stretch of Dorsoduro's **Giudecca Canal** waterfront known as the Zattere becomes an idyllic seaside holiday resort, the perfect spot for a lazy stroll or sunbathing dockside – but a few centuries back, the Zattere was the absolute last resort for many Venetians. The imposing building at No 423 Zattere was once better known as **Ospedale degli Incurabili** (Hospital of the Incurables), built in the 16th century to address a problem spreading rapidly through Europe's nether regions. Euphemistically called the 'French sickness', syphilis quickly became a Venetian problem, passing from the ranks of its 12,000 registered prostitutes to the general populace.

With no known cure at the time, and blindness and insanity common side effects, Venetians urgently petitioned the state to create a hospice to assist the afflicted and the orphans they left behind. Venetian women were outspoken lobbyists for this forward-thinking effort, and funds were pledged early on by prostitutes and brothel madams with a particular interest in the problem. Venice was ahead of its time in dedicating public funds to this public health crisis, though at times even this large building was sometimes overcrowded. When penicillin provided a cure at last, the facility was happily rendered obsolete, and since 2003 the building has housed the **Accademia delle Belle Arti** (Fine Arts School), formerly located in the Gallerie dell'Accademia building.

Along the Zattere near the **Ponte degli Incurabili**, a plaque has been recently dedicated to Nobel Prize–winning Russian American poet **Joseph Brodsky**, a sometime local resident whose book *Watermark* captures Venice's ebbs and flows, its murky tragedies and crystalline graces. As the plaque says in Russian and Italian: 'He loved and sang this place'. Brodsky died in New York in 1996, but at his request, his body was buried in Venice's cemetery at Isola di San Michele.

at Tonolo, which serves flaky *apfelstrudel* (apple pastry) and oozing *pain au chocolat* (chocolate croissants). Chocolate-topped beignets are filled with hazelnut mousse as rich as a Venetian doge at tax time.

IMPRONTA CAFÉ — VENETIAN €

Map p290 (☎041 275 03 86; Calle Crosera 3815; meals €8-15; ⏲11am-1am Mon-Sat; San Tomá) Join Venice's value-minded jet set for *prosecco* and bargain polenta-salami combos, surrounded by witty architectural diagrams of cooking pots. Arrive by 6.30 to take advantage of Milan-style *aperitivi*, where access to an appetizer buffet is free with drink purchases.

PANE VINO E SAN DANIELE — ITALIAN €€

Map p290 (☎041 243 986; Calle Lunga San Barnaba 2861; meals €15-30; ⏲10am-2pm Tue-Sun; Ca' Rezzonico) Artists can't claim they're starving any more after a visit to this wood-beamed trattoria that's a favourite of art students and professors alike. Settle in to generous plates of gnocchi laced with truffle cheese, Veneto game such as roast rabbit and duck, lavish appetisers featuring the namesake San Daniele cured ham, and Friulian house wines made by the Fantinel family owners.

RISTORANTE SAN TROVASO — VENETIAN €€

Map p290 (☎041 5230835; www.tavernasantrovaso.it; Calle della Accademia 967; meals €15-30; ⏲noon-3.30pm & 7-11pm Fri-Wed; Accademia) After the Accademia leaves you delirious with visual overload, come to your senses with fried calamari, polenta, *sarde in saor* and a carafe of the house Soave. Just around the corner from the museum, this sensibly priced rustic restaurant hastens recovery with brisk service, sunny garden seating and an airy, wood-beamed dining room.

DO FARAI — SEAFOOD €€

Map p290 (☎041 277 03 69; Calle del Cappeller 3278; meals €25-35; ⏲11am-3pm & 7-10pm Mon-Sat; Ca' Rezzonico) Hidden away on a *calle* (street), this neighbourhood restaurant packs Venetian regulars into a wood-panelled room hung with football championship scarves and fragrant with aromatic seafood: pasta with clams, mussels and sweet prawns; herb-laced, grilled sea bass; and Venetian *tris di saor sarde, scampi e sogliole* (sardines, prawns and sole in the tangy Venetian *saor* marinade). Service is leisurely; bide your time with a superior Negroni cocktail.

AL PROFETA ITALIAN €€

Map p290 (041 5237466; Calle Lunga San Barnaba 2471; pizza €9-13; noon-3.30pm & 7-11pm Wed-Mon; Ca' Rezzonico) Switch up your Venetian seafood diet with respectable pizza, grilled meats, and duck *bigoli* (Venetian whole-wheat pasta) at this hideaway near Campo Santa Margherita. Garden seating is popular and service often overstretched; arrive early and not terribly famished.

PIZZA AL VOLO PIZZA BY SLICE €

Map p290 (041 522 54 30; Campo Santa Margherita 2944; pizza slices €2-4; noon-1am daily; Ca' Rezzonico) Peckish night owls run out of options fast in Venice once restaurants start to close at 10pm – but pizza slices here are cheap and tasty, with a thin, yet sturdy, crust that won't collapse on your bar-hopping outfit.

DRINKING & NIGHTLIFE

TOP CHOICE **CANTINONE GIÀ SCHIAVI** BAR

Map p290 (041 523 00 34; Fondamenta Nani 992; 8.30am-8.30pm Mon-Sat; Zattere) Good lungs and steady hands are instrumental to make your order heard and to transport *cicheti* (try creamy tuna with leeks), *ombre* and *pallottoline* (small bottles of beer) outside to the canal without spilling a drop on art historians and gondola builders. Chaos reigns until the neighbourhood *nonna* (grandmother) shows up and the crowd parts so that she can fetch her usual glass of Soave.

IL CAFFÈ ROSSO BAR

Map p290 (041 528 79 98; Campo Santa Margherita 2693; 7am-1am Mon-Sat; Ca' Rezzonico) Sunny piazza seating provides the perfect place to recover from last night's revelry and check out today's newspaper headlines, with espresso that opens eyes like a rip cord on Venetian blinds – until the cycle begins again at 6pm with *spritz* cocktails and standing-room-only student crowds. Locals affectionately call this no-name joint *caffè rosso* because of its red storefront, and it earns the nickname nightly with inexpensive *spritz* with a generous splash of bright-red Aperol.

IMAGINA CAFÉ BAR

Map p290 (041 241 06 25; www.imaginacafe.it; Rio Terà Canal 3126; 8am-2am Mon-Sat; Ca' Rezzonico) Emerging artists on the walls, comfortable booths and a vast display of Aperol behind the bar attract a regular creative, gay-friendly, chatty crowd that should probably start paying rent. Piazza tables are usually nabbed by locals and their little dogs, all basking in the sun and the admiration of passers-by.

OSTERIA ALLA BIFORA BAR

Map p290 (041 523 61 19; Campo Santa Margherita 2930; noon-3pm & 6pm-1am Wed-Mon; Ca' Rezzonico) Chandeliers and exposed-brick archways dating from the 12th century make this the most romantic butcher counter you've ever been to for happy hour. Other bars around this *campo* cater to *spritz*-pounding students, but this moodlit medieval hideaway caters to dreamers who flirt over glasses of big-hearted Veneto merlot. The Ferrari-red meat slicer behind the bar isn't as fast as it looks, so bide your time waiting for your *tagliere* (platter) of cured meats with a carafe of wine among new friends at the communal tables.

TEA ROOM BEATRICE TEA ROOM

Map p290 (041 724 10 42; Calle Lunga San Barnaba 2727A; 10am-6pm; Ca' Rezzonico) After a long day's sightseeing, Beatrice offers a welcome alternative to espresso bolted at a bar. Rainy days are good for iron pots of green tea and almond cake in the Japanese-themed tearoom, and sunny days are meant for iced drinks and salty pistachios on the patio.

AI PUGNI BAR

Map p290 (041 523 98 31; Ponte dei Pugni 2859; 6.30pm-midnight Mon-Sat; Ca' Rezzonico) Brawls on the bridge out the front once inevitably ended in the canal – hence the name 'ai Pugni' (the fighters) – but now Venetians settle differences with perfectly friendly drinks inside this arty new bolthole. Photography graces exposed-brick walls, Veneto and Friuli wines stock the bar, meatballs and salami appear at happy hour, and Thursdays sometimes bring live music.

CAMPO SANTA MARGHERITA

Even in the dead of winter and the heat of summer, you can count on action here, in Venice's nightlife hub. The oblong, unruly square boasts a bevy of beverage temptations – including Imagina Café, Osteria alla Bifora, Ai Do Draghi and Cantina di Millevini (see p87) – but it also hosts a regular weekday fish market, the odd flea market and periodic political protests. The nightly happy-hour scene unfolds like a live-action, 21st-century Veronese painting, with an animated, eclectic crowd of Italian architecture students, international hipsters, gay and straight Venetians, visiting Biennale curators, wise-cracking grandmothers and their little dogs.

AI DO DRAGHI BAR

Map p290 (041 528 97 31; Calle della Chiesa 3665; 7.30am-2am Fri-Wed; Ca' Rezzonico) *'Permesso!'* (Pardon!) is the chorus inside this historic *bacaro* (bar), where the standing-room-only crowd spills onto the sidewalk and tries not to spill drinks in the process. If you can squeeze inside, past the tiny wood-beamed bar, there's more seating out the back, or just let the crowd carry you to a table outside on the *campo*. In winter, the place shuts down at 10pm.

CANTINA DI MILLEVINI BAR

Map p290 (041 522 34 36; Campo Santa Margherita; www.millevini.com; 3pm-midnight Mon-Sat; Ca' Rezzonico) This respected Venetian wine merchant broadens Campo Santa Margherita happy-hour options considerably with bottle-lined brick walls, a small but select menu of Veneto vintages by the glass and the occasional tasting class (see website). Cocktails are creative, if alarming – 'Fire Orgasm' involves Baileys and flaming cognac – offset by a daily menu of soothing soups, salads and pastas for €6.50 to €8.

ENTERTAINMENT

VENICE JAZZ CLUB LIVE MUSIC

Map p290 (041 523 20 56; www.venicejazzclub.com; Ponte dei Pugni 3102; admission incl 1st drink €20; doors 7pm, set begins 9pm, closed Aug; Ca' Rezzonico) Jazz is alive and swinging in Dorsoduro, where the resident Venice Jazz Club Quartet swings to Miles Davis and Charles Mingus and grooves on Italian jazz standards. Drinks are steep, so starving artists booze beforehand and arrive by 8pm to pounce on free cold-cut platters.

SHOPPING

TOP CHOICE **MARINA E SUSANNA SENT** GLASS, JEWELLERY

Map p290 (041 520 8136; www.marinaesusannasent.com; Campo San Vio 669; 10am-1pm & 3-6.30pm Tue-Sat, 3-6.30pm Mon; Accademia) Warned that women couldn't handle working in molten glass, two sisters from Murano, trained as an architect and a jeweller, rose to the challenge – and created Murano's best-selling line of hand-blown glass statement jewellery. Museum shops around Venice feature their work, including ice-blue waterfall necklaces, traffic-stopping red-dot collars, and signature 'soap' necklaces: woven clear glass bubbles that make the wearer look both stylish and freshly scrubbed. There's also a branch at Ponte San Moisè in San Marco.

ANTIQUARIATO CLAUDIA CANESTRELLI ANTIQUES, JEWELLERY

Map p290 (041 522 70 72; Campiello Barbaro 364a; 11am-1pm & 3-5.30pm Mon & Wed-Sat, 11am-1pm Tue; Salute) Hand-coloured lithographs of 'prehistoric' lagoon fish and 19th-century miniatures of cats dressed as generals are charming souvenirs of Venice's past, but collector-artisan Claudia Canestrelli is bringing back bygone elegance with her repurposed antique earrings, including free-form baroque pearls dangling from tiny silver pigs.

MADERA HOME & GARDEN

Map p290 (041 522 41 81; www.shopmaderavenezia.it; Campo San Barnaba 2762; 10am-1pm & 4.30-7.30pm Tue-Sat; Ca' Rezzonico) Double-takes are a given at this modern design showcase, where porcelain birdhouses are covered with fish scales, wooden cutting boards are shaped like Venetian islands, and teapots in foam-rubber tea cosies seem ready to scuba-dive. These original design objects are by owner-designer Francesca Meratti and other Italian designers (with Scandinavian and Japanese influences) in a well-curated collection starting at €15.

LE FORCOLE DI SAVERIO PASTOR FORCOLE

Map p290 (041 522 56 99; www.forcole.com; Fondamenta Soranzo detta Fornace 341; 8.30am-12.30pm & 2.30-6pm Mon-Sat; Salute) Mick Jagger had his *forcola* made to measure here – and no, that's not as naughty as it sounds. A *forcola* is a forked tongue of wood where the gondola oar rests, hand-carved from acacia and hard oak; each one must be made to match a gondolier's exact height and weight so as not to upset the gondola's delicate balance. Sounds like a job for Saverio Pastor, who makes *forcole* that twist and lean in perfect balance – ideal for budding gondoliers, or as a customised sculpture.

DANGHYRA ARTISANAL

Map p290 (041 522 41 95; www.danghyra.com; Calle delle Botteghe 3220; 10am-1pm & 3-7pm Tue-Sun; San Tomá) Architect Carlo Scarpa's spare shapes meet exuberant Venetian colour in Danghyra's ultramodern ceramics, hand-thrown in Venice. Footed lilac bowls let spring tiptoe into any room, while gold crackle-glaze bowls make humble pasta dishes appear fit for a doge.

GUALTI JEWELLERY, ACCESSORIES

Map p290 (041 520 17 31; www.gualti.it; Rio Terà Canal 3111; 10am-1pm & 3-7.30pm Mon-Sat; Ca' Rezzonico) Either a shooting star just landed on your shoulder, or you've been to Gualti, where iridescent orange glass bursts from clear resin stems on a supernova brooch. Pleated-silk evening wraps are curled at the edges, like lagoon seaweed swaying with the current. One-off designs start at €60.

ARRAS FASHION, ACCESSORIES

Map p290 (041 522 64 60; Campiello del Squellini 3235; 10am-1pm & 3-7.30pm Mon-Sat; Ca' Rezzonico) The plush, handwoven silk and wool wraps piled high on Arras' shelves represent the combined efforts of this weaving cooperative, which offers vocational workshops for people with disabilities. Hand-woven wool jackets are draped for maximum effect by cooperative designers, taking the chill off sunset canal strolls in true local style.

AQUA ALTRA HOME & GARDEN

Map p290 (041 521 12 59; www.aquaaltra.it; Campo Santa Margherita 2898; 9.30am-12.30pm & 4-7.30pm Tue-Sat, 4-7.30pm Mon; Ca' Rezzonico) Global-minded but with Italian tastes firmly in mind, this volunteer-run fair-trade co-op sells single-origin chocolate from Sierra Leone growers' collectives, handbags made from Venetian vinyl museum banners and match-standard footballs made by a Pakistani cooperative.

LAURETTA VISTOSI

The Murano-born artisan made handcrafted shoes, stationery and dresses before she invented an entirely new craft: handstitched handbags, totes and journals, emblazoned with Murano-glass bullseye buttons. Contrasting-colour outstitching, vintage linen and handmade glass make each piece at this **store** (Map p290; 041 528 65 30; www.laurettavistosi.org; Calle Lunga San Barnaba 2866B; 10am-1pm & 3-7pm Tue-Sat) unique.

ELITRE FASHION

Map p290 (041 099 00 67; Calle Crosera 3949; 10am-7.30pm Mon-Sat; San Tomà) Extraterrestrial models stomp across the flatscreen TV, besotted garden gnomes radiate hearts on Fiorucci's Love Therapy T-shirts, and best friends square off over the last pair of purple polka-dotted Agatha Ruiz de la Prada Mary Janes only to re-bond over Hello Kitty housewares: it's just another day in the sale section at Elitre, Venice's trend store.

CA' MACANA MASKS, COSTUMES

Map p290 (041 277 61 42; www.camacana.com; Calle delle Botteghe 3172; 10am-6.30pm Sun-Fri, 10am-8pm Sat; Ca' Rezzonico) Glimpse the talents behind the Venetian Carnevale masks that so impressed Stanley Kubrick he placed a considerable order for his final film *Eyes Wide Shut*. Choose your own papier-mâché persona from the selection of long-nosed plague doctors' disguises or fine-featured courtesans' camouflage, or make your own at Ca' Macana's **mask-making workshops** (from €60; 11am Mon & 2.30pm Friday).

SIGNOR BLOOM TOYS, ARTISANAL

Map p290 (041 522 63 67; Campo San Barnaba 2840; 10am-6.30pm Mon-Sat; Ca' Rezzonico) Kids may have to drag the adults away from these 2D wooden puzzles of the Rialto bridge and grinning wooden duckies, because these clever handmade toys give grown-ups acute cases of nostalgia. Calder-esque mobiles made of carved red gondola prows would seem equally at home in an arty foyer or a nursery.

Venice in Art

Water may be the first thing you notice about Venice when you arrive, but as you get closer, you'll discover that this city is actually saturated with art.

Canals are just brief interruptions between artworks in this Unesco World Heritage Site, with more art treasures than any other city. Venice has always been a little in love with its own reflection – Basilica di San Marco's mosaic self-representations, the lagoon settings in Tintoretto's and Veronese's Biblical scenes, and city views by Romantic *vedustisti* (landscape artists). But even in abstract works by contemporary artisans, its mesmerising patterns, shimmering colours and rich patina leave their indelible watermarks.

Great Art In Situ

Until Napoleon grabbed every Venetian painting that he fancied, most remained in the churches and palaces for which they were painted. But lavishly painted ceilings weren't so easy to detach, and can still be seen in situ at Chiesa di San Sebastiano, Ca' Rezzonico, Palazzo Ducale and Scuola Grande dei Carmini. Tintoretto's masterworks for Scuola Grande di San Rocco and Chiesa della Madonna dell'Orto also escaped removal. Today, artwork returned after Napoleon's fall illuminates altars across Venice, and forms the basis of collections at Museo Correr, Accademia and Ca' d'Oro.

Mosaics

All that glitters is probably mosaic in Venice, where the art of making tiny glass *tesserae* (tiles) into wall-sized artworks dates from the lagoon's Byzantine heyday. Torcello is an astounding early example, with the beatific Madonna on a field of lagoon corn poppies in the apse facing off against blue devils tipping the scales of Final Judgment across the back wall. For closer examination of early mosaic techniques, thorough explanations accompany stunning mosaic fragments at Museo di Torcello and in the Museum of Glass in Murano.

The ancient Byzantine lagoon capital of Torcello was upstaged by the new doge's official chapel, the Basilica di San Marco, with golden mosaics rippling across 8000 sq metres. The Basilica di San Marco had no qualms about self-promotion: the Basilica is represented at least seven times in its own mosaics, including twice on the facade.

Today you don't have to be a guest of the doge in the Basilica's upstairs dining room to drink and snooze surrounded by golden mosaics. B-Bar offers a shimmering backdrop to make any happy hour golden, and Domus Orsoni B&B showcases the Orsoni mosaic company's work across tables, headboards, and dazzling bathrooms.

1. Ceiling fresco in Ca' Rezzonico (p82)
2. Mosaic detail on the facade of Basilica di San Marco (p52)

1

KRZYSZTOF DYDYNSKI / LONELY PLANET IMAGES ©

2

KRZYSZTOF DYDYNSKI / LONELY PLANET IMAGES ©

Frescoes

Things are perpetually looking up in Venice, thanks to the prolific maestro of ceiling frescoes, Giambattista Tiepolo. The sun seems to shine right through the roof of I Gesuati and Ca' Rezzonico in his staggering ceilings, where angels perch on balconies and late-afternoon light tint puffy clouds rose-gold. The heavenly frescoes that illuminate Venetian churches echo the striking early example of Giotto's 1303–05 frescoes for Padua's Cappella degli Scrovegni, with its glowing colours and dynamic interaction among a compelling cast of characters. Today guests can wake up to afternoon splendour at Palazzo Abadessa and Foresteria Valdese, in rooms frescoed for dignitaries and religious orders.

But Venetian artists saved some of their lightest, most fanciful frescoes for the private country villas of Venetian nobility. Giovanni Zelotti's sensuous frescoes of frolicking Roman goddesses for La Malcontenta converted this Palladian Brenta River villa into a delightful pleasure palace, even though it was intended as an exile for an unfaithful Venetian wife. Tiepolo and his son Domenico frescoed Villa Valmarana (Ai Nani), outside Vicenza, floor to ceiling with fantasias of their own invention, turning salons into a woodland wonderland, *commedia dell'arte* circus, and Chinoiserie curiosity cabinet. Without the Inquisition looking over his shoulder to spot any departure from church-sanctioned treatment of religious subjects, Veronese turned Palladio's already masterful Villa di Maser into a frescoed showstopper, cheekily painting a trompe-l'oeil painter's ladder propped up in one living room and himself and his favourite niece exchanging conspiratorial glances at the ends of adjoining salons.

Glass

For about 800 years now, one island on earth has been synonymous with glass: Murano. Venetians have actually been working in crystal and glass since the 10th century, but because of the inherent fire

1. Ceiling fresco by Paolo Veronese, Villa di Maser (p182)
2. Murano glass

HOLGER LEUE/ LONELY PLANET IMAGES ©

hazards of glass-blowing, the industry was moved to the island of Murano in the 13th century. Woe betide the glassblower with wanderlust: trade secrets were so jealously guarded that any glass-worker who left the city was considered guilty of treason and subject to assassination. For a short (not crash!) course in glass, don't miss Murano's Museo del Vetro (Museum of Glass), which strategically stays open a little later than the glass showrooms so that you can shop first, and ask questions later.

Today glass artisans quite openly ply their trade at workshops along Murano's Fondamenta dei Vetrai marked by 'Fornace' (Furnace) signs, secure in the knowledge that their wares set a standard that can't be replicated elsewhere. Centuries of tradition are upheld in Cesare Toffolo's winged goblets and Orovetro's Murano chandeliers, while striking modern glass designs by Nason Moretti at ElleElle, Marina e Susanna Sent, Campagnol & Salvadore and Ragazzi & Co keep the tradition moving forward.

In Venice proper, you'll find glass artisans working on a smaller scale, applying blowtorches and nerves of steel to molten, lampworked glass beads, especially in Santa Croce and San Marco. Captivating glass miniatures are a Venetian speciality – look for dragonflies at Camuffo, sea creatures at I Vetri a Lume di Amadi, and fish at Giuseppe Tinti. Bringing tradition and modernity together, Venice's Galleria Rosella Junck showcases miraculously intact antique glass alongside avant-garde art glass.

TOP FIVE FOR GLASS

- Museo del Vetro (p157)
- Galleria Rossella Junck (p62)
- ElleElle (p161)
- Marina e Susanna Sent (p88)
- I Vetri a Lume di Amadi (p110)

Paper

High tides are more than a fact of life in Venice: they're an inspiration. By submerging pulp, dragging paper through inky baths, and creating ripples across the surface, Venetian paper artisans have captured the city's every watery mood on paper. Embossing and marbling began in the 14th century as part of Venice's burgeoning publishing industry, but these bookbinding techniques and *ebru* (Turkish marbled paper) endpapers have taken on lives of their own in the hands of modern artisans. Artisan Rosanna Corrò of Cartè uses bookbinding techniques to create original marbled, book-bound handbags, screens and even furniture, while Cartavenezia turns hand-pulped paper into embossed friezes and free-form lamps. Gianni Basso uses 18th-century book symbols to make letter-pressed business cards with old-world flair, and you can watch a Heidelberg press in action most mornings at Veneziastampa, churning out menus and ex-libris (bookplates).

Books are still a prevailing passion in Venice, and marbled travel journals from Il Pavone di Paolo Pelosin may inspire one of your own. Librettists stock up on leather-bound musical composition books at ArtigianCarta di Massimo Doretto, and novelists dream of seeing their bestseller custom-bound and featured in the front window of Charta.

Textiles

Styles have changed since dandies rocked silk brocade knee britches and pink stockings at Palazzo Mocenigo, but Venice's obsession with artisan textiles continues. Anything that stands still long enough in this city is liable to end up curtained, swagged, tasselled and upholstered. Venetian lace was an 8th-century fashion must, and sunny days in Burano still bring ladies to their doorsteps to chat as they tat a bit of lace. Bevilacqua still weaves luxe tapestries in Venice, and donates scraps to nonprofit women prisoners' co-op Banco Lotto 10 to turn into La Fenice costumes and clever handbags.

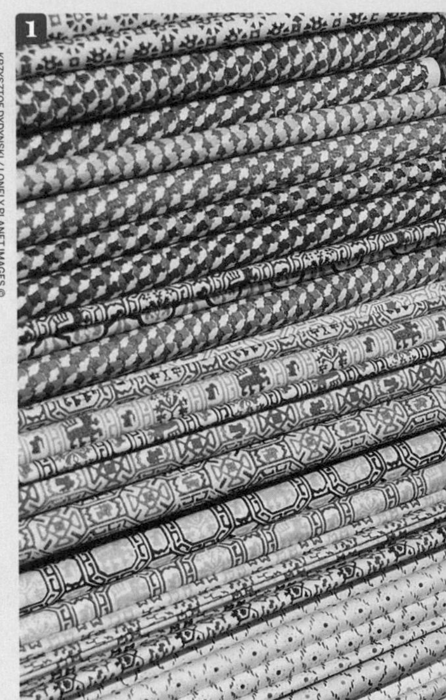

1

But the modern master of Venetian Bohemian textiles is Fortuny, whose showroom on Giudecca features hand-stamped wall coverings created in strict accordance with top-secret techniques innovated almost a century ago. But though the methods are secret, Fortuny's inspiration isn't: it's plastered all over the walls of the home studio, from Persian armour to portraits of rebellious socialites who tossed aside their corsets for Fortuny's signature Delphi gowns – now available for modern Boho goddesses at Venetia Studium. For modern art-fabric designs, don't miss the rotating design showcases at le5venice, or the lilac silk-velvet smoking jackets hand-printed with scarlet rats at Fiorella Gallery.

TOP FIVE FOR TEXTILES

- Museo Fortuny (p60)
- Palazzo Mocenigo (p101)
- Banco Lotto 10 (p144)
- Bevilacqua (p75)
- Fiorella Gallery (p74)

Clockwise from top left

1. Paper **2.** Venetian lace-making **3.** Textiles

2

ROBERTO GEROMETTA / LONELY PLANET IMAGES ©

3

ALBERTO CAMPANILE / PHOTOLIBRARY ©

Sestieri di San Polo & Santa Croce

Neighbourhood Top Five

❶ See lightning strike indoors at **Scuola Grande di San Rocco** (p98), where Tintoretto's streaky brushwork illuminates narratives with the gripping drama of a graphic novel.

❷ Watch Titian's red-hot Madonna light up the room in *Assunta* at **I Frari** (p100).

❸ Hear fishermen and island farmers sing the praises of lagoon ingredients at **Rialto Market** (p102).

❹ Watch Antonio da Ponte's marble wonder, **Ponte di Rialto** (p101), blush rose-gold at sunset.

❺ Graze your way through the *calli* on Venice's ultimate **gourmet crawl** (p101).

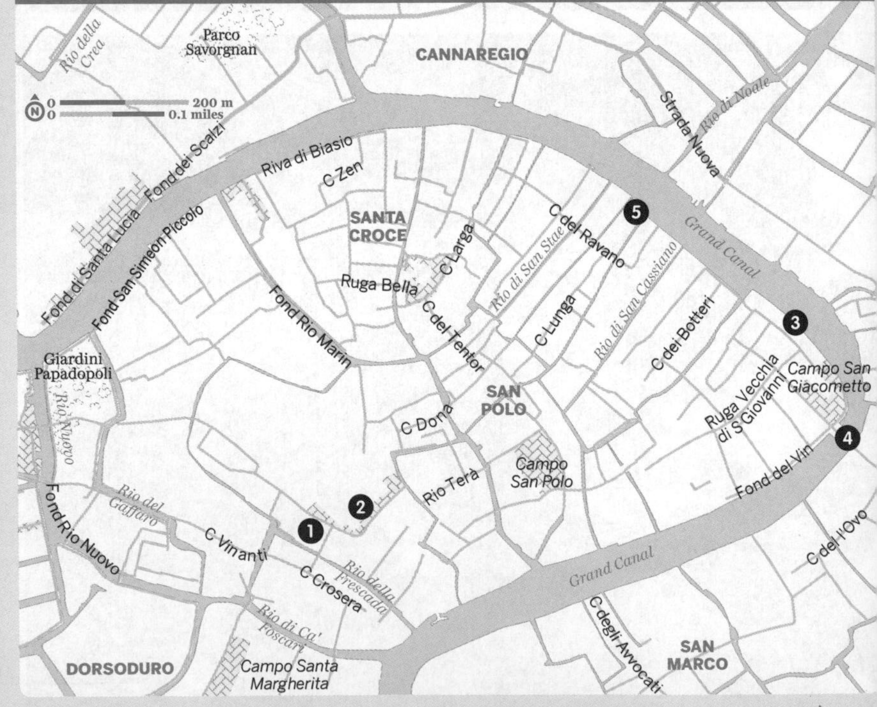

For more detail of this area, see map p292 and map p295

Explore: San Polo & Santa Croce

Start the morning among masterpieces at Scuola Grande di San Rocco, then bask in the glow of Titian's Madonna at I Frari. Shop backstreet boutiques all the way to the Rialto Market, where glistening purple octopi and feathery red *radicchio treviso* (chicory) present tantalising culinary photo-ops. Stop at All'Arco for *cicheti* (bar snacks), museum-hop from Ca' Pesaro to Palazzo Mocenigo, and take a breather in the Fondaco di Turchi garden or along the Grand Canal on sunny Riva di Biasio. Swing by Alaska for gelato en route to medieval San Giacomo dell'Orio, then wander the maze of Venice's former red-light district to Antiche Carampane for dinner. Classic movies at Casa del Cinema, opera at Scuola Grande di San Giovanni Evangelista or drinks at Al Muro provide suitably grand finales.

Local Life

➡ **Shopping obsessions** Museum collections are built around Venetian shopping habits at Ca' Pesaro (p101) and Palazzo Mocenigo (p101), and you can see how that might happen with museum-quality works at local artisans' studios (p110).

➡ **Hideouts** When Venetians shirk work, they bask in the sun at Campo San Giacomo dell'Orio, read novels along the canal at Tearoom Caffè Orientale (p106), play board games at Hosteria alla Poppa (p109), watch movie marathons at Casa del Cinema (p110), or daydream on the Grand Canal docks by Rialto Market (p102).

➡ **Cicheti central** Ringing the Rialto are authentic *bacari* (bars) offering inventive Venetian bites, best devoured standing with top-notch *ombre* (glasses of wine) at All'Arco (p104), Pronto Pesce Pronto (p106), Dai Zemei (p106), Al Mercà (p108), Al Pesador (p104) and Cantina Do Spade (p108).

➡ **Musical accompaniment** Look for upcoming opera in Scuola Grande di San Giovanni Evangelista (p110), live folk-rock acts around Campo San Giacomo dell'Orio (p109), Gregorian chants at Scuola Grande di San Rocco (p98) and summertime concerts in Summer Arena (p110) – or wait for jazz to spontaneously combust at Ai Postali (p109).

Getting There & Away

➡ **Vaporetto** Most *vaporetti* call at Piazzale Roma or Ferrovia at the northwest corner of Santa Croce. In San Polo, the Rialto stop is serviced by lines 1, 4 and N. Line 1 also calls at Riva de Biasio, San Stae (the N stops here too), San Silvestro and San Tomà (the N stops here as well). The Rialto-Mercato stop (line 1) is in use during the day only.

Lonely Planet's Top Tip

Many of the best restaurants, artisan studios and *bacari* (bars) are in the backstreets of San Polo and Santa Croce – if you can find them. This is the easiest place to get lost in, so allow extra time if you have dinner reservations. If totally lost, follow yellow Rialto or Ferrovia signs or red-and white Scuola Grande di San Rocco signs, or head to central Campo San Polo.

Best Places to Eat

➡ All'Arco (p104)
➡ Al Pesador (p104)
➡ Alaska Gelateria (p106)
➡ Pronto Pesce Pronto (p106)
➡ Antiche Carampane (p106)

For reviews, see p104 ➡

Best Places to Drink

➡ Al Prosecco (p108)
➡ Al Mercá (p108)
➡ Cantina Do Spade (p108)
➡ Caffè Dei Frari (p109)
➡ Muro Vino E Cucina (p109)

For reviews, see p108 ➡

Best Artisan Finds

➡ Marbled-paper handbags at Cartè (p110)

➡ Pocket-sized, seaworthy gondolas at Gilberto Penzo (p110)

➡ Glass groceries at I Vetri a Lume di Amadi (p110)

➡ Embossed San Marco lion sketchbooks at Cartavenezia (p110)

➡ Furlane shoes at Pied à Terre (p111)

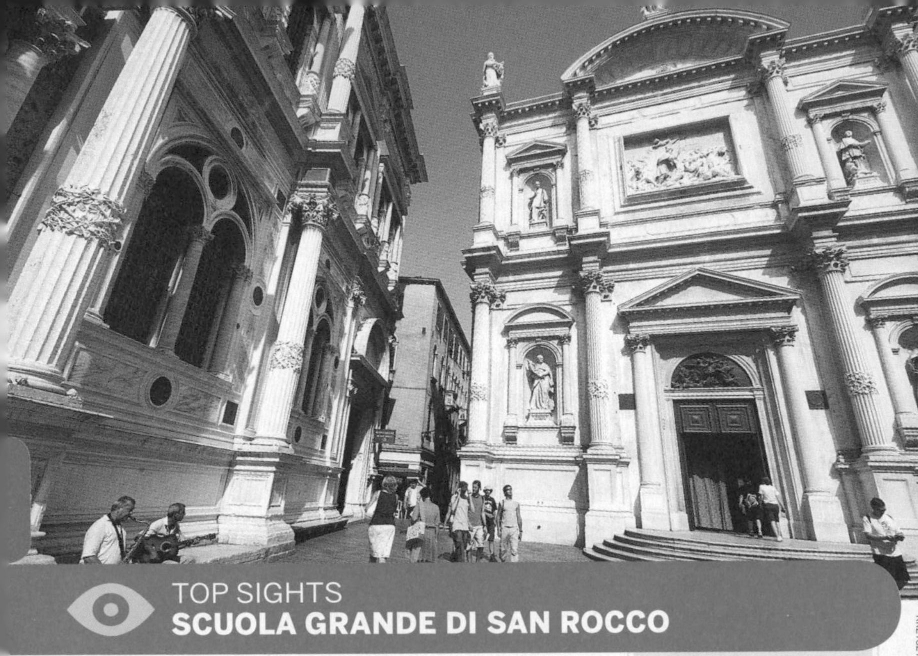

TOP SIGHTS
SCUOLA GRANDE DI SAN ROCCO

KRZYSZTOF DYDYNSKI / LONELY PLANET IMAGES ©

You'll swear the paint is still fresh on the 50 action-packed Tintorettos painted between 1575 and 1587 for the Scuola Grande di San Rocco. Every Venetian artist who'd survived the dark days of the Black Plague wanted the commission to paint this building, dedicated to the patron saint of the plague-stricken, so Tintoretto cheated a little: instead of producing sketches like his rival Paolo Veronese, Tintoretto painted a magnificent *tondo* (ceiling panel) and dedicated it to the saint, knowing such a gift couldn't be refused or matched by other artists.

Architecture

Take a moment to appreciate the architecture before you go in because Tintoretto's art-installation masterpiece is a near-impossible act to follow. Scarpagnino's uplifting, proto-baroque facade puts a brave face on the confraternity dedicated to San Rocco (aka St Roch).

Pity the architects of this carefully composed classical building: their work has been steadily ignored for centuries, even before it was completed. Bartolomeo Bon began the Scuola Grande di San Rocco in 1517, and at least three other architects were called in to finish the work by 1588. The facade is an impressive display of architectural handiwork: inlaid, veined marble frames the windows and doors, figures lean out from atop the capitals to greet visitors, and flowering garlands around pillars provided welcome signs of life after the plague. But once Tintoretto's painting cycle began to streak across the Scuola's walls in 1575 like indoor fireworks, it hardly mattered what the outside looked like any more.

DON'T MISS...

- *Ascension*
- Scarpagnino staircase
- *Elijah Fed by the Angels*
- New Testament wall scenes
- Francesco Pianta's sculpture of Tintoretto
- *St Roch in Glory* ceiling

PRACTICALITIES

- Map p292
- ☎041 523 48 64
- www.scuolagrandesanrocco.it
- Campo San Rocco, San Polo 3052
- admission adult/reduced €7/5
- 9.30am-5.30pm
- San Tomá

Assembly Hall

Downstairs, the assembly hall contains a handful of works on easels by Venetian A-list artists including Titian, Giorgione and Tiepolo. But Tintoretto steals the scene with the story of the Virgin Mary, starting on the left wall with *Annunciation* and ending with *Ascension* opposite; it's a dark and cataclysmic work, compared with Titian's glowing version at I Frari. **Gregorian chant concerts** are occasionally performed here (ask at the counter), and you can practically hear their echoes in Tintoretto's haunting paintings.

Sala Grande Superiore

Take the grand **Scarpagnino staircase** to the Sala Grande Superiore, where you may be seized with a powerful instinct to duck, given all the action in the **Old Testament ceiling scenes** – you can almost hear the *swoop!* overhead as an angel dives down to feed ailing Elijah. Grab a mirror to avoid the otherwise inevitable neck strain as you follow dramatic, superheroic gestures through these ceiling panels. Mercy from above is a recurring theme, with Daniel's salvation by angels, the miraculous fall of manna in the desert, and Elisha distributing bread to the hungry.

Tintoretto's **New Testament wall scenes** read like a modern graphic novel, with eerie lightning-bolt illumination striking his protagonists against the looming backdrop of the Black Death. Scenes from Christ's life aren't in chronological order: birth and baptism are followed by resurrection. The drama builds as background characters disappear into increasingly dark canvases, until an X-shaped black void looms at the centre of *Agony in the Garden* – a painting marked like a house doomed by plague contamination, with only a glimmer of light on a still-distant horizon.

When Tintoretto painted these scenes, Venice's outlook was grim indeed: the plague had just taken the great Venetian colourist Titian in 1576, and the cause and cure for the bubonic plague would not be discovered for centuries. By focusing his talents on dynamic lines instead of Titianesque colour, Tintoretto creates a shockingly modern, moving parable for epidemics through the ages. A portrait of the artist with his paintbrushes is captured in Francesco Pianta's recently restored 17th-century carved-wood sculpture, just below Tintoretto's New Testament masterpieces.

Sala Albergo

The New Testament cycle ends with the *Crucifixion* in the Sala Albergo, where things suddenly begin to look up – literally. On the ceiling, Tintoretto applies a lighter touch to *St Roch in Glory*, surrounded by representations of the four seasons and saving graces of Felicity, Generosity, Faith and Hope.

AN INTERFAITH EFFORT AGAINST THE PLAGUE

While the Black Death ravaged the rest of Europe, Venice mounted an interfaith effort against the plague. The city dedicated a church and *scuola* (religious confraternity) to San Rocco where Venetians could pray for deliverance from the disease, while also consulting resident Jewish and Muslim doctors about prevention measures. Venice established the world's first quarantine, with inspections and 40-day waiting periods for incoming ships at Lazaretto. Venice's forward-thinking, inclusive approach created artistic masterpieces that provide comfort to the afflicted and bereaved to this day, and set a public-health standard that has saved countless lives down the centuries.

In 1315, 20-year-old St Roch (aka San Rocco) began wandering southern France and northern Italy helping plague victims. Despite frequent exposure to contagion, he miraculously survived to continue his humanitarian work until his death at age 32. His body was transferred to Venice as a plague-prevention talisman in 1485.

TOP SIGHTS
I FRARI

As you've no doubt heard, there's a Titian – make that the Titian – altarpiece at Chiesa di Santa Maria Gloriosa dei Frari, but it's the 14th-century cathedral that is the towering achievement. The soaring Italian-brick Gothic church features marquetry choir stalls, a rare Bellini, and a creepy Longhena funeral monument. The cool, filtered light of the interior takes a moment's adjustment, but Canova's ethereal white marble tomb seems permanently moonlit at the end of the nave, and Titian's *Assunta* seems to shed its own sunlight in the apse.

Architecture

Built for the Franciscans in the 14th and 15th centuries of modest brick rather than stone, the Frari has none of the flying buttresses, pinnacles and the gargoyles typical of International Gothic – but its vaulted ceilings and broad, triple-nave, Latin-cross floor plan give this church a cathedral grandeur befitting its art masterpieces. The facade facing the canal has delicate scalloping under the roofline, contrasting red-and-white mouldings around windows and arches, and a repeating circle motif of *oculi* (porthole windows) around a high rosette window. The tall bell tower has managed to remain upright since 1386 – a rare feat, given the shifting *barene* (shoals) of Venice – and its bell-ringer still takes to the task with zeal when it's time for Mass.

DON'T MISS...

- Titian's *Assunta*
- Titian's Pesaro altarpiece
- Coro
- Bellini's *Madonna with Child*
- Doge Pesaro funeral monument
- Canova's pyramid mausoleum

PRACTICALITIES

- Map p292
- www.chorus venezia.org
- Campo dei Frari, San Polo 3004
- admission €3, or with Chorus Pass
- 9am-6pm Mon-Sat, 1-6pm Sun
- San Tomá

Assunta

Like moths to an eternal flame, visitors are inexorably drawn to the front of this cavernous, dimly lit Gothic church by a small altarpiece that seems to shed its own sunlight. This is Titian's 1518 *Assunta* (aka *Ascension*), capturing the split second the radiant Madonna reaches heavenward, finds her footing on a cloud, and escapes this mortal coil in a dramatic swirl of Titian-red robes. Both inside and outside the painting, onlookers gasp and point at the sight; Titian outdid himself here, upstaging his own **1526 Pesaro Altarpiece** near the entry. According to local lore, a glimpse of the Madonna's luminous wrist slipping from her cloak has led monks to recant their vows over the centuries.

Other Masterpieces

As though this weren't quite enough artistic achievement for one church or planet, there's minuscule puzzlework marquetry worthy of MC Escher in the **coro** (choir stalls), Bellini's achingly sweet *Madonna with Child* triptych in the **sacristy** and, by the side entry, Baldassare Longhena's eerie **Doge Pesaro funereal monument** hoisted by four burly, black-marble figures bursting from ragged white clothes like Invisible Hulks. Bringing up the rear are disconsolate mourners dabbing at their eyes with the hem of their cloaks on Canova's marble **pyramid mausoleum**, which he originally intended as a monument to Titian. The great painter was lost to the plague at 90 in 1576, but legend has it that in light of his contributions here, Venice's strict rules of quarantine were bent to allow Titian's burial near his masterpiece.

SIGHTS

SCUOLA GRANDE DI SAN ROCCO — HISTORICAL BUILDING

See p98.

I FRARI (CHIESA DI SANTA MARIA GLORIOSA DEI FRARI) — CHURCH

See p100.

PONTE DI RIALTO — BRIDGE

Map p292 (Rialto-Mercato) An amazing feat of engineering in its day, Antonio da Ponte's 1592 marble bridge was for centuries the only land link across the Grand Canal. The construction cost 250,000 gold ducats, a staggering sum that puts cost overruns for the new Calatrava bridge into perspective. Now that the Rialto is clogged with kiosks and foot-traffic jams, locals go out of their way to avoid it, or zip up the less scenic northern side of the bridge. The southern side faces San Marco, and when crowds of shutterbugs and tour groups clear out around sunset, it offers a romantic long view of gondolas pulling up to Grand Canal *palazzi* at striped moorings that look like floating barber poles.

CA' PESARO — MUSEUM

Map p292 (041 72 11 27; www.museiciviciveneziani.it; Fondamenta de Ca' Pesaro, Santa Croce 2070; adult/reduced €8/5, or with Museum Pass; 10am-6pm Tue-Sun Apr-Oct, to 5pm Nov-Mar; San Stae) Like a Carnevale costume built for two, the stately exterior of this Baldassare Longhena-designed 1710 palazzo hides two quirky museums: the Galleria d'Arte Moderna and Museo d'Arte Orientale. At **Galleria d'Arte Moderna** three storeys of Venetian modern-art history begin with flag-waving early Biennales, showcasing Venetian landscapes and Venetian socialites by Venetian painters (notably Giacomo Favretto and Guglielmo Ciardi). Savvy Biennale organisers soon diversified, showcasing Gustav Klimt's 1909 *Judith II (Salome)* and Marc Chagall's *Rabbi of Vitebsk* (1914–22). The 1st-floor 1961 De Lisi Bequest added Kandinskys and Morandis to the modernist mix of de Chiricos, Mirós and Moores, plus radical abstracts by postwar Venetian artists Santomaso and Vedova. Climb the creaky attic stairs of the **Museo d'Arte Orientale** past a phalanx of **samurai warriors**, girded for battle: they mark the start of an epic 1887–89 souvenir-shopping spree across Asia that Prince Enrico di Borbone preserved for posterity in vintage curio cabinets. The prince reached Japan when Edo art was discounted in favour of modern Meiji, and Edo-era netsukes, screens and a lacquerware palanquin are standouts in his collection of 30,000 *objets d'art*. The collection has been left much as it was organised in 1928, with displays periodically covered to preserve against light damage. Check the schedule for upcoming screenings of documentaries and vintage Japanese films, co-curated by the Japanese embassy.

CHIESA DI SAN GIACOMO DELL'ORIO — CHURCH

Map p292 (Campo San Giacomo dell'Orio, Santa Croce 1457; admission €3, or with Chorus Pass; 10am-5pm Mon-Sat; Riva de Biasio) La Serenissima seems as serene as ever inside the cool gloom of this Romanesque church, founded in the 9th and 10th centuries and built in its current form by 1225. The basic blueprint is a Latin cross, but it's hardly strict: chapels bubble along the edges, and pillars were added inside seemingly at random for decorative value. Under the striking 14th-century **carena di nave (ship's keel) ceiling** is decor dragged here from far-flung Venetian territories, including a **Lombard pulpit** perched atop a 6th-century **Byzantine green marble column**.

Lurking in the dark, cool interior are some notable 14th- to 18th-century artworks, including luminous **sacristy** paintings by Palma Il Giovane, rare Lorenzo Lotto *Madonna with Child and Saints,* and an exceptional **Veronese crucifix** (currently undergoing restoration). Don't miss Gaetano Zompini's macabre *Miracle of the Virgin,* which shows a rabble-rouser rudely interrupting the Virgin's funeral procession, only to have his hands miraculously fall off when he touches her coffin.

PALAZZO MOCENIGO — MUSEUM

Map p292 (041 72 17 98; www.museiciviciveneziani.it; Salizada di San Stae 1992; admission adult/reduced €5/3.30, or with Museum Pass; 10am-5pm Tue-Sun Apr-Oct, to 4pm Nov-Mar; San Stae) Costume dramas unfold in the Mocenigo family's swanky 18th-century **Grand Canal** palace, now a fascinating museum showcasing the fashions of Venice's power elite. Necklines plunge in the **Red Living Room**, lethal corsets come undone in the **Contessa's Bedroom** and men's paisley silk knee-breeches show some leg in the **Dining Room**. Yet even at the most risqué parties in the **Green Living Room** under Jacopo Guarana's 1787 **Allegory of Nuptial Bliss ceiling**, guests had to mind their tongues: the Mocenigos reported philosopher and sometime houseguest Giordano Bruno for heresy to the Inquisition, who subsequently tortured and burnt the betrayed philosopher at the stake in Rome.

IL GOBBO MONUMENT

Map p292 (Rialto-Mercato) Along the north end of the square fronted by the Fabbriche Nuove (New Buildings), you'll spot an iron railing around the 1541 statue of Il Gobbo (The Hunchback), who is propping up a step. This was a podium for official proclamations and punishments: those found guilty of misdemeanours might be forced to run a gauntlet of jeering citizens from Piazza San Marco to the Rialto, but the minute they touched Il Gobbo, their punishment was complete. Rubbing Il Gobbo was believed to confer luck, to the point that a railing was put up to save the hunchback from being worn out by his superstitious admirers.

SCUOLA GRANDE DI SAN GIOVANNI EVANGELISTA HISTORICAL BUILDING

Map p292 (041 718234; www.scuolasangiovanni.it; Campiello della Scuola 2454; admission €3; vary, check website; Ferrovia) Political power had its perks for this influential Venetian confraternity, including a polychrome marble 1st-floor meeting hall designed in 1729 by Giorgio Massari, a grand, Codussi-designed double staircase, and Pietro Lombardo's 1481 carved marble courtyard entry arch topped by the eagle of patron saint John the Baptist. Bellini and Titian turned out world-class works for the *scuola* (religious confraternity) that have since been moved to the **Gallerie dell'Accademia** (p79) – but Palma Il Giovane's works still illuminate the Sala d'Albergo, and Pietro Longhi's charming *Adoration of the Wise Men* is still here, with its bright-eyed, wriggling baby Jesus.

One of the six major Venetian *scuole*, this confraternity was founded in 1261 by an order of *battuti* (flagellants) and became a social club of the Council of Ten, Venice's dreaded secret service. With such illustrious and potentially deadly clients, Giandomenico Tiepolo was obliged to finish contracts left unfinished by his father Giambattista when

TOP SIGHTS RIALTO MARKET

Restaurants worldwide are catching on to a secret that the market has had for 700 years: food tastes better when it's fresh, seasonal and local. Before there was a bridge at the Rialto or palaces along the Grand Canal, there was a **Pescaria** (fish market) and a produce market. So loyal are locals to their market that recent talk of opening a larger, convenient mainland market was swiftly crushed.

More vital to Venetian cuisine than any top chef are Pescaria fishmongers, calling out today's catch: glistening mountains of *moscardini* (baby octopus), crabs ranging from tiny *moeche* (soft-shell crabs) to *granseole* (spider crabs), and inky *seppie* (squid) of all sizes. Sustainable fishing practices are not a new idea at the Pescaria; marble plaques show regulations set centuries ago for the minimum allowable sizes for lagoon fish. Note the line-caught lagoon seafood here, and you'll recognise tasty, sustainable options on dinner menus.

Compared with tame supermarket specimens, Veneto veggies look like they landed from another planet. Tiny purplish Sant'Erasmo *castraure* (baby artichokes) look like alien heads, white Bassano asparagus seems to have sprouted on the moon, and *radicchio trevisano* looks like a mutant Martian flower.

DON'T MISS...

- Lagoon seafood displays
- Produce barges by Grand Canal docks
- Veneto speciality produce
- Seasonal fruit

PRACTICALITIES

- Map p292
- 7am-2pm; Pescaria closed Mon
- Rialto-Mercato

THE OTHER RIALTO MARKET: PONTE DELLE TETTE

No one remembers the original name of **Ponte delle Tette** (Rialto-Mercato), known since the 15th century as 'Tits Bridge'. Back in those days, the shadowy porticos flanking this bridge were a designated red-light zone where neighbourhood prostitutes were encouraged to display their wares in windows, instead of taking their marketing campaigns to the streets in their signature platform shoes. The most ambitious working girls might be found studying: for educated conversation, *cortigiane* (courtesans) might charge 60 times the basic rates of the average prostitutes.

Church authorities and French dignitaries repeatedly professed dismay at Venice's lax attitudes towards prostitution, but Venice's idea of a crackdown was to prevent women prostitutes from luring clients by cross-dressing (aka false advertising) and to ban prostitutes from riding in two-oared boats – lucky that gondolas only require one oar. Fees were set by the state and posted in Rialto brothels (soap cost extra), the rates of high-end *cortigiane* were published in catalogues extolling their various merits, and the height of platform shoes was limited to a staggering 30cm.

he left for Spain. The order was suppressed by Napoleon, and today the *sculoa* hosts conferences and concerts (see p110), and opens occasionally to the public during the day.

If you get the chance to visit the *scuola*, ask at the front desk to look inside the chapel across the street. The deconsecrated **Chiesa di San Giovanni Evangelista** has a Tintoretto *Crucifixion*, and the adjoining private chapel founded by the Badoer family in 970 has a wonderful image by Pietro Vecchia of St John the Evangelist holding a pen, eagerly awaiting dictation from God.

CHIESA DI SAN POLO CHURCH

(Campo San Polo 2118; admission €3, or with Chorus Pass; 10am-5pm Mon-Sat; San Tomà) Travellers speed past this modest 9th-century Byzantine brick church between I Frari and the Rialto, with no idea of the major dramas unfolding behind these modest portals. Under the medieval wooden **carena di nave ceiling**, Tintoretto's *Last Supper* shows apostles alarmed and outraged by Jesus' announcement that one of them will betray him. Giandominico Tiepolo's disturbing *Stations of the Cross* **sacristy** cycle shows Jesus tormented by jeering onlookers, only to leap triumphantly from his tomb in a ceiling panel.

FONDACO DEI TURCHI HISTORICAL BUILDING

Map p292 (041 275 02 06; www.museicivici veneziani.it; Salizada del Fontego dei Turchi, Santa Croce 1730; adult/reduced €8/5.50, or with Museum Pass; 10am-6pm daily Jun-Oct, 9am-5pm Tue-Fri & 10am-6pm Sat & Sun Nov-May; San Stae) The dukes of Ferrara had the run of this 12th-century mansion until they were elbowed aside in 1621 to make room for Venice's most important trading partner: Turkey. Turkish merchants were a constant in Venice throughout the maritime powers' rocky romance, celebrated with favoured-nation trading status and inter-Adriatic weddings, and tested by periodic acts of piracy, invasion and looting. The Fondaco dei Turchi remained rented out to the Turks until 1858, after which the place underwent a disastrous modernisation. Original facade features were sacrificed to the architectural fancies of the time, including odd crenellations that made the gracious Gothic building look more like a prison.

Today the Fondaco houses a scientific library and the rather curious **Museo Civico di Storia Naturale** (Natural History Museum). Downstairs is a fish tank of Venetian coastal specimens bubbling for attention, while upstairs is a more exciting display of dinosaurs, including an *ouransaurus* from the Sahara, a 12m-long prehistoric crocodile skeleton, and a 120-million-year-old *psittacosaurus mongoliensis*, a 0.5m-long skeleton of a baby dinosaur found in the Gobi Desert. A new exhibit follows the footsteps of Venetian explorers, and looks at how the scientific specimens they collected were used to serve science, social agendas and macabre fascinations. The back garden is open during museum hours and is ideal for picnics.

CHIESA DI SAN ROCCO CHURCH

Map p292 (041 523 48 64; Campo San Rocco, San Polo 3053; admission free; 8am-12.30pm & 3-5.30pm Mon-Sat; San Tomà) After staggering out of the Scuola Grande di San

Rocco (p98), thunderstruck by Tintoretto, you might want to take a moment to regain the sensation in your ocular nerves inside this cheery pink church across the way. Here, a couple of the comparatively quiet Tintorettos are safely tucked away inside the church's Sala dell'Albergo, including *San Rocco Healing the Animals*. The original church was built by Bartolomeo Bon in 1489–1508, but once Tintoretto undertook his 1564–88 painting cycle for the Scuola, Bon's church was immediately downgraded to next-best status. The church was given a baroque facelift in 1765–71 to make its facade look more like the Scuola, with a grand portal flanked by statues by Giovanni Marchiori. Bon's rose window that once fronted the building was moved to the side of the church – it's been recently restored, along with Bon's original side door.

CASA DI GOLDONI — MUSEUM

Map p292 (☎041 275 93 25; www.museicivicivene ziani.it; Calle dei Nomboli, San Polo 2794; adult/ reduced €5/3, or with Museum Pass; ⏰10am-5pm Thu-Tue Apr-Oct, to 4pm Nov-Mar; ⛴San Tomà) Comedians, musicians and writers looking for inspiration seek out the birthplace of Carlo Goldoni (1707–93), Venice's greatest playwright and maestro of delicious social satire and *opera buffa* (comic opera). As the 1st-floor display explains (in Italian), Goldoni was a master of second and third acts: he was a doctor's apprentice before switching to law, a backup career that proved handy when some comedies didn't sell. But Goldoni had the last laugh, with salon sitcoms that made socialites laugh at themselves. The main draws in the museum are the 18th-century marionettes and puppet theatre, but don't miss the **chamber-music concerts** held here (see the website). Otherwise, the entrance is the most striking part of the 15th-century Gothic house, with its quiet courtyard, private well and Istrian stone stairway.

CHIESA DI SAN STAE — CHURCH

Map p292 (Campo San Stae, Santa Croce 1981; admission €3, or with Chorus Pass; ⏰10am-5pm Mon-Sat, 1-5pm Sun; ⛴San Stae) An aficionado of Venetian light, English painter William Turner loved painting the sun-washed Palladian exterior of this church, with its facade dotted by statues of angels and cardinal virtues. You can see what a painter obsessed with light effects might admire in this church: for all its gleaming white classical grandeur, it retains a languid seaside air, with early-morning lagoon mists that collect mystically around its base. The church was founded in 966 but finished in 1709, and though the interiors are surprisingly spare for a baroque edifice, there are a couple notable works: Giambattista Tiepolo's *The Martyrdom of St Bartholomew* and Sebastiano Ricci's *The Liberation of St Peter*.

CHIESA DI SAN GIOVANNI ELEMOSINARIO — CHURCH

Map p292 (Ruga Vecchia di San Giovanni, San Polo 477; admission €3, or with Chorus Pass; ⏰10am-5pm Mon-Sat, 1-5pm Sun; ⛴Rialto-Mercato) You could easily stride right past this Renaissance brick church, built by Scarpagnino (aka Antonio Abbondi) after a disastrous fire in 1514 destroyed much of the Rialto area. The church and its separate bell tower are camouflaged by surrounding houses and tucked behind kiosks selling T-shirts with 'Venezia' spelled out in rhinestones, so their sober, soaring presence comes as a surprise – but inside, a Titian of the namesake *St John the Almsgiver* (freshly restored and returned from the Accademia), a Mannerist altarpiece and recently restored dome frescoes by Pordenone are brilliant finds.

EATING

TOP CHOICE ALL'ARCO — VENETIAN €

Map p292 (☎041 520 56 66; Calle dell'Arco, San Polo 436; cicheti €1.50-4; ⏰noon-8.30pm Mon-Sat Apr-Jun & Sep, to 3.30pm Oct-Mar, closed Jul-Aug; ⛴Rialto-Mercato) Maestro Francesco and his talented son Matteo invent Venice's best *cicheti* daily with Rialto Market finds and, if you ask nicely and wait patiently, they'll invent a seasonal speciality for you. On Mondays when the Pescaria is closed, Francesco might wrap wild asparagus in rare roast beef with grainy mustard; when Saturday's seafood haul arrives, Matteo might create Sicilian tuna tartare with mint, Dolomite strawberries and aged balsamic. Even with copious *prosecco*, hardly any meal here tops €20 or falls short of five stars – might as well book your return ticket to Venice now.

TOP CHOICE AL PESADOR — MODERN ITALIAN €€€

Map p292 (☎041 523 94 92; www.alpesador.it; Campo San Giacometto, San Polo 125; mains €15-30; ⏰noon-3pm & 7-11pm Mon-Sat; ⛴Rialto-Mercato) Watch the world drift down the

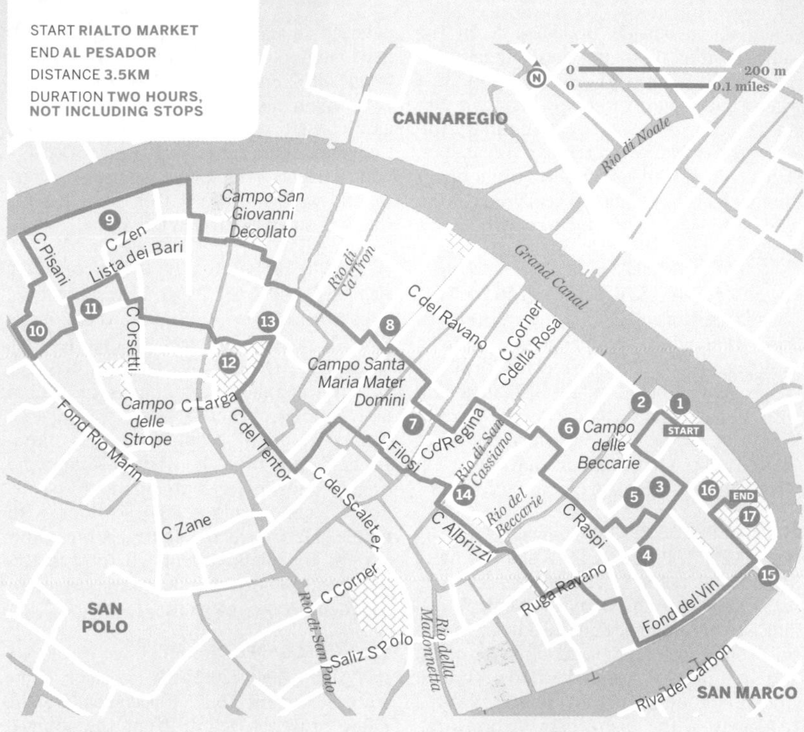

Neighbourhood Walk

Venice Gourmet Crawl

A trip through gourmet history starts where great Venetian meals have begun for centuries: **1 Rialto Market**. Hear the chants of grocers singing the praises of island-grown produce; be lured to the **2 Pescaria** by the glint of silver fishtails curved in their final flips atop hillocks of ice. Around the corner, glimpse the treasures that made Venice's fortune: trade-route spices, in pyramid mounds in historic **3 Drogheria Mascari** shop windows. Down the road, the tantalising displays of *sopressa* (soft salami), San Daniele hams, and Taleggio cheese-wheels at **4 Aliani** remind you that Veneto's culinary fame wasn't built on seafood and imported spices alone.

Duck into **5 All'Arco** for the city's best *cicheti* – ask for *una fantasia* (a fantasy), and father-son chefs Francesco and Matteo will invent a dish with ingredients you just saw at the market. Wander northwest past **6 Carté**, where you'll spot recipe albums hand-bound in lagoon-rippled marble paper, and over a couple of bridges until you smell the ink drying on letterpress menus (also sold blank for swanky dinner parties) at **7 Veneziastampa**. Walk further northwest past **8 Palazzo Mocenigo** until you hit a sunny stretch of Grand Canal along **9 Riva de Biasio**, allegedly named for 16th-century butcher Biagio (Biasio) Cargnio whose sausages contained a special ingredient: children. When found out, Biasio was drawn and quartered by order of the doge.

By now you'll be glad to hear there's a vegetarian restaurant nearby, **10 Tearoom Caffè Orientale**, where speciality teas are served with excellent in-house pastries. Leave room for **11 Alaska**'s organic roasted pistachio gelato, which may change your life, or at least tomorrow's travel plans. Over in **12 Campo San Giacomo dell'Orio**, a generous pour of natural-process *prosecco* awaits at **13 Al Prosecco** to help you glide over **14 Ponte delle Tette** toward **15 Ponte di Rialto**, all the way to **16 Il Gobbo**'s feet. As with any Venetian accomplishment – a university degree, a haul of lagoon crab, waking up in the morning – the end of your tour deserves a toast and gourmet *cicheti* at **17 Al Pesador**.

Grand Canal outside, or canoodle in the vaulted dining room, but once the food arrives, you'll sit up and pay attention. Just when you thought you knew Venetian cuisine, Pesador reinvents it with culinary finesse: *cicheti* feature a terrine of tiny lagoon clams topped with lemon *gélee,* while *primi* (mains) include red-footed scallops kicking wild herbs across squid-ink gnocchi.

TOP CHOICE ALASKA GELATERIA GELATERIA €

Map p292 (041 71 52 11; Calle Larga dei Bari 1159, Santa Croce; gelato €1-2; noon-8pm; Riva de Biasio) Outlandish organic gelato: enjoy a Slow Food scoop of house-roasted local pistachio, or two of the tangy Sicilian lemon with vaguely minty Sant'Erasmo *carciofi.* Kids who choose fresh strawberry granita (shaved ice) can top the confection with a leaf plucked from the basil plant on the counter.

PRONTO PESCE PRONTO SEAFOOD, CICHETI €

Map p292 (041 822 02 98; Rialto Pescheria, San Polo 319; cicheti €3-8; noon-2.45pm Tue-Sat; Rialto-Mercato) Alongside Venice's fish market, this designer deli specialises in artfully composed *crudi* (Venetian-style sushi) and well-dressed seafood salads. Grab a stool and a (unfortunately) plastic glass of DOC Soave with *folpetti* (baby octopus) salad and plump prawn *crudi,* or enjoy yours dockside along the Grand Canal.

ANTICHE CARAMPANE VENETIAN €€

Map p292 (0415240165; www.antichecarampane.com; Rio Terà delle Carampane 1911, San Polo; meals €30-45; noon-2.30pm & 7-11pm Tue-Sat; San Stae) Hidden in the once-shady lanes behind Ponte delle Tette, this culinary indulgence is a trick to find, and you may wonder who you have to, erm, know to get a reservation. The sign proudly announcing 'no tourist menu' signals a welcome change: say goodbye to soggy lasagne and hello to lagoon-fresh *crudi,* asparagus and *granseola* (lagoon crab) salad, *bottarga* pasta, and *filetto di San Pietro* (fish with artichokes or *radicchio trevisano*).

DAI ZEMEI VENETIAN €

Map p292 (041 520 85 46; www.osteriadaizemei.it; Ruga Vecchia San Giovanni, San Polo 1045; cicheti €2-5; 9am-8pm Wed-Mon; San Silvestro) The *zemei* (twins) who run this corner joint are a blur of motion by 10am, preparing for the onslaught of regulars and the odd well-informed foodie tourist by 11.45am for the first crack at these small meals with outsized imagination: octopus salad with marinated rocket, duck breast drizzled with truffle oil, or *crostini* (toast) loaded with velvety tuna mousse. Arrive early, grab a stool and consult twin gourmet masterminds Giovanni and Franco for ideal DOC/IGT wine pairings – think past the usual *prosecco,* and wash it down with a floral Ribolla Gialla or sophisticated Refosco.

VECIO FRITOLIN MODERN VENETIAN €€

Map p292 (041 522 28 81; www.veciofritolin.it; Calle della Regina 2262, Santa Croce; meals €30-50; noon-2.30pm & 7-10.30pm Tue-Sun; San Stae) Order the langoustine-and-zucchini spaghetti that packs in Italian Slow Foodies, or choose today's special with confidence – all produce here is hand-selected daily from the Rialto Market, and breads and desserts are made in-house. Roast lagoon seafood like scallops with truffle salt are worthy splurges, but savvy budget gourmets call ahead for the €10 *frittura* (seafood fry) takeaway, perfect for decadent picnics by Rialto docks.

TEAROOM CAFFÈ ORIENTALE VEGETARIAN €

Map p295 (041 520 17 89; Rio Marin, Santa Croce 888; meals €6-12; noon-9pm Fri-Wed; Riva de Biasio) Detour from the tourist-trail espresso bars and seafood restaurants to this art-filled canalside tearoom, which offers vegetarian delights ranging from asparagus-studded quiches to hearty bean soups. Baked goods are made in-house with extra-fluffy, high-protein Italian '00' flour – so after that whisper-light apple crumble, you'll be raring to tackle the museums.

SACRO E PROFANO ITALIAN €€

Map p292 (041 523 79 24; Ramo Terzo del Parangon 502, San Polo; meals €15-25; 11.30am-1pm & 6.30pm-1am Mon-Tue & Thu-Sat, 11.30am-2pm Sun; Rialto-Mercato) Musicians, artists and philosophising regulars make this hideaway under the Rialto exceptionally good for eavesdropping your way into conversation – but once that handmade gnocchi or spaghetti *alla búsara* (Venetian prawn sauce) arrives, all talk is reduced to oohs and aahs. The place is run by a Venetian ska-band leader, which explains the trumpets on the wall and the upbeat, arty scene.

OSTERIA LA ZUCCA MODERN ITALIAN €€

Map p292 (041 524 15 70; www.lazucca.it; Calle del Tentor, Santa Croce 1762; small plates €5-12; 12.30-2.30pm&7-10.30pmMon-Sat; SanStae)

Vegetable-centric, seasonal small plates bring spice-trade influences to local produce: zucchini with ginger zing, cinnamon-tinged pumpkin flan, and raspberry spice cake. Herbed roast lamb is respectable here too, but the island-grown produce is the breakout star. The snug wood-panelled interior gets toasty, so reserve canalside seats in summer.

ANTICA BIRRERIA DELLA CORTE PIZZERIA €

Map p292 (☎041 275 05 70; Campo San Polo 2168; pizzas €8-13; ⊙noon-11pm Mon-Fri; San Tomà) An outpost of wood-fired pizza and beer in a city of wine and fish seems like a deliberate provocation, but it's hard to protest with your mouth full. This former bullfight pen became a brewery in the 19th century to keep Venice's Austrian occupiers occupied, and even as a modern eatery it's still obsessed with beer and beef. Go with bresaola and rocket or buffalo mozzarella pizzas, washed down with German beer on tap or Italian artisan brews in bottles. With room for 150, there's hardly ever a wait, and piazza seating is prime for outdoor movie screenings in summer.

TRATTORIA DA IGNAZIO ITALIAN €€

Map p292 (☎041 523 48 52; Calle dei Saoneri 2749, San Polo; meals €25-30; ⊙noon-3pm & 7-11pm Mon-Sat; San Tomà) Dapper waiters serve simply prepared grilled lagoon fish and pasta made in-house ('of course') with a proud flourish, on tables bedecked with yellow linens and orchids. On sunny days and warm nights the neighbourhood converges beneath the garden grape arbour.

AL NONO RISORTO ITALIAN, PIZZERIA €€

Map p292 (☎041 524 11 69; Sottoportego della Siora Bettina 2338, Santa Croce; pizzas €7-9, meals €20-30; ⊙noon-3pm & 6-10pm Fri-Tue, 6-10pm Thu; San Stae) Manifesto or menu? At Al Nono Risorto, pizzas are listed alongside urgent action alerts: 'No abandoning animals!', 'More rights for gays and domestic partners!' Prices are left of centre, radical-chic servers graciously indulge petty bourgeois pizza orders, and on sunny days, all of Venice converges on the garden for squid with polenta, the bargain house *prosecco,* and cross-partisan bonding.

ANTICO PANIFICIO PIZZERIA €

Map p292 (☎041 277 09 67; Campiello del Sol 929, San Polo; pizzas €8-10; ⊙noon-3pm & 7-11pm Wed-Mon; San Silvestro) Most Venetian pizzerias pander to tourists, but this wood-fired pizza joint is packed with a neighbourhood crowd – be prepared to lunge at open tables when you get the nod and order decisively. Basic options like pizza *margherita* (with basil, mozzarella and tomato) or sausage insult the chef's intelligence – go with anchovies, squash blossoms or whatever seasonal topping your neighbours are enjoying.

OSTERIA MOCENIGO VENETIAN €€

Map p292 (☎041 523 17 03; Salizzada San Stae 1919, Santa Croce; meals €15-25; ⊙noon-2.30pm & 7-10pm Tue-Sun; San Stae) Times and dining habits have changed since dogi strained waistcoat buttons across the street at the Palazzo Mocenigo: here you can make light meals of *cicheti* at the bar, including an upstanding *sarde in saor,* or sit down to a casually elegant meal of grilled local asparagus and scallops, with homemade pastas including ravioli stuffed with radicchio and whitefish. Dishes ranging from €7 to €12 are plentiful enough for lunch and you can wash them down with Veneto wine by the glass.

VENICE'S GOURMET CENTRAL: THE RIALTO DISTRICT

Rialto Market (Map p292) offers superb local produce next to the legendary **Pescaria** (Map p292), Venice's 600-year-old fish market. Nearby, backstreets are lined with bakeries, *bacari* (bars; see p108) and two notable gourmet shops: **Aliani** (Map p292; ☎041 522 49 13; Ruga Vecchia di San Giovanni, San Polo 654; Rialto-Mercato), with cheeses, cured meats and gourmet specialities from balsamic vinegar (aged 40 years) to *bottarga* (dried fish-roe paste); and **Drogheria Mascari** (Map p292; ☎041 522 97 62; Ruga degli Spezieri 381; ⊙8am-1pm & 4-7.30pm Mon-Tue & Thu-Sat, 8am-1pm Wed; Rialto-Mercato), an emporium lined with copper-topped jars, spices and truffles galore, plus an entire backroom of speciality Italian wines. For organic edibles and sustainably produced wines, visit **Rialto Biocenter** (Map p292; ☎041 523 95 15; www.rialtobiocenter.it; Calle della Regina, Santa Croce 2264; ⊙8.30am-1pm & 4.30-8pm Mon-Thu, 8.30am-8pm Fri & Sat; Rialto-Mercato).

SNACK BAR AI NOMBOLI PANINI €

Map p292 (041 523 09 95; Rio Terà dei Nomboli 271c, San Polo; panini €3-4; 8am-8pm Mon-Sat; San Tomà) A snappy Venetian comeback to McDonald's: scrumptious, right-sized sandwiches on fresh, crusty rolls, well packed with local cheeses, roast vegetables, savoury salami, prosciutto, roast beef and other cold cuts. Sprightly greens are more than garnishes in these sandwiches, and condiments range from spicy mustard to wild nettle sauce. Two of these make a filling lunch for €4 to €5, and three is a proper feast deserving of a glass of Brunello on a stool at the bar.

MAURO EL FORNER DE CANTON PASTRIES & CAKES €

Map p292 (041 522 28 90; Ruga Vecchia di San Giovanni 603, San Polo; pastries €1-4; 7am-7pm Mon-Sat; Rialto-Mercato) A boutique of bread by the Rialto, with the ubiquitous *bovoli* (snail-shaped rolls), crusty loaves for all your pressing *panino* needs, rich hazelnut-studded biscuits called *pan dei dogi* (doge's bread) and, for some fibre and a change of pace, wholegrain breads.

PASTICCERIA TREVISAN PASTRIES & CAKES €

Map p295 (041 71 85 23; Calle Sechera 636, Santa Croce; pastries €1-3; 7am-6.30pm Mon-Sat; Ferrovia) Mini-profiteroles bursting with dark-chocolate mousse and flaky croissants laced with apricot jam are perfect pick-me-ups after train rides or packaged B&B breakfasts, especially with a proper, scorching-hot Venetian *macchiatone* (an espresso liberally 'stained' with milk).

LA RIVETTA CICHETI €

Map p292 (041 71 84 98; Calle Sechera 637a, Santa Croce; cicheti €1-3; 9am-9.30pm Mon-Sat; Ferrovia) Cabernet Franc comes out of a hose and platters of hearty fare are passed around at this *bacaro* (old-style bar), a favourite of salty sailors and neighbourhood eccentrics. Go for mixed plates with thick slabs of salami, translucent sheets of pancetta and grilled vegies with crusty bread. Angle for a canalside spot, or duck inside to admire the decor of bicycle parts and dusty English gin bottles, drained before the war.

PASTICCERIA RIZZARDINI PASTRIES €

Map p292 (041 522 38 35; Campiello dei Meloni 1415, San Polo; pastries €1-3; 7.30am-8pm Wed-Mon; San Silvestro) 'From 1742' reads the modest storefront sign, and inside you'll find irresistible cream puffs and doughnuts that have helped this little bakery survive many an *acqua alta* – in a peculiarly Venetian boast, samples of waters bailed from the store floor over the years are preserved in bottles on the top shelf. Troll the biscuit section in search of wagging *lingue di suocere* (mother-in-law's tongues), suggestively sprinkled *pallone di Casanova* (Casanova's balls), and other *dolci tipici venexiani* (typical Venetian sweets) – but act fast if you want that last slice of tiramisu.

DRINKING & NIGHTLIFE

TOP CHOICE **AL PROSECCO** WINE BAR

Map p292 (041 524 02 22; Campo San Giacomo da l'Orio, Santa Croce 1503; www.alprosecco.com; 9am-9pm Mon-Sat; San Stae) The urge to toast sunsets in Venice's loveliest *campo* is only natural – and so is the wine at Al Prosecco. This forward-thinking bar specialises in *vini naturi* (natural process wines) – organic, biodynamic, wild-yeast-fermented – and memorable *ombre,* from the signature €3.5 unfiltered 'cloudy' *prosecco* to the silky, €5 Veneto Venegazzú that trails across the tongue and lingers in the imagination.

TOP CHOICE **AL MERCÀ** WINE BAR

Map p292 (393 992 47 81; Campo Bella Vienna, San Polo 213; 9am-3pm & 4-9pm Mon-Sat; Rialto-Mercato) Discerning drinkers throng this cupboard-sized bar crammed with *cicheti* and 60 different wines, including top-notch *prosecco* and DOC wines by the glass (€2 to €3.50). Arrive by 6.30pm for meatballs and mini-*panini* (€1 to €2) and easy bar access, or mingle with crowds stretching to Grand Canal docks – there's no seating, and it's elbow-room-only at this little gem of a bar.

CANTINA DO SPADE BAR

Map p292 (041 521 05 83; www.cantinadospade.it; Calle delle Do Spade, San Polo 860; 10am-3pm & 6-10pm Mon-Sat; Rialto-Mercato) Since 1488, this bar has kept Venice in good spirits, and the friendly young management extends warm welcomes to both *spritz*-sipping Venetian regulars and visiting connoisseurs, here for double-malt Dolomite beer and bargain Venetian DOC Cab Franc. Come early for market-fresh *fritture* (batter-fried seafood; €2 to €6) and stick around for local gossip (free).

CAFFÈ DEI FRARI CAFE

Map p292 (☎041 524 18 77; Fondamenta dei Frari 2564, San Polo; ⏰8am-9pm Mon-Sat; 🚢San Tomà) Take your espresso with a heaping of history at this century-old carved wooden bar, or recover from the sensory overload of I Frari with a sandwich, glass of wine and easy conversation at the dinky indoor cafe tables downstairs or on the Liberty-style wrought-iron balcony upstairs.

HOSTERIA ALLA POPPA CAFE

Map p292 (☎041 524 65 54; Calle de le Oche, Santa Croce; ⏰6pm-1am; 🚢Riva de Biasio) A living room where drinks are served, Hosteria alla Poppa comes complete with creaky sofas, scuffed tables and board games for marathon sessions mastering the Italian version of Risk. Service is brusque but drinks are cheap, and Wednesdays are live music nights (usually jazz).

AI POSTALI BAR

Map p292 (☎041 71 51 76; Fondamenta Rio Marin 821, Santa Croce; ⏰6pm-2am Mon-Sat; 🚢Ferrovia) Jazz provides a backbeat to buzzing conversation until the wee hours, and local musicians have been known to break into impromptu jam sessions around midnight. Long ago, off-duty mailmen had the run of the place – hence the name – but now the hipper half of Santa Croce vies for seats along the canal and an unconventional *spritz* served with an olive.

ANTICA OSTERIA RUGA RIALTO BAR

Map p292 (☎041 521 12 43; Ruga Rialto 692, San Polo; ⏰11am-3pm & 6.30pm-midnight; 🚢Rialto-Mercato) Although seafood salads and the classic *fritto misto e pattatine* (lightly fried lagoon seafood and potatoes) – Venice's answer to fish and chips – earn this *osteria* (pub-restaurant) a loyal following, drink is the common bond at this place by night's end. The back room doubles as a gallery for local emerging artists, and the occasional live-music set fills the narrow alleyway with revellers all the way to the Grand Canal.

BAGOLO BAR

Map p292 (☎041 71 75 84; Campo San Giacomo dell'Orio 584, Santa Croce; ⏰7am-midnight; 🚢Riva de Biasio) Creaky wood floors and mood lighting indoors, and candlelit tables outside on the *campo*, add romance from another era to leisurely happy hours on this picturesque square, with *cicheti*, cocktails and occasional live-music acts.

EASYBAR BAR

Map p292 (☎041 524 03 21; Campo Santa Maria Mater Domini 2119, Santa Croce; 🚢San Stae) Leave it to Venice to give the usual sports bar crossover appeal. The sleek bar makes this the watering hole of choice for Università di Foscari architecture students, while bargain *ombre* starting at €1 and football matches on TV reel in the masses.

MURO VINO E CUCINA BAR

Map p292 (☎041 241 23 39; Campo Bello Vienna 222, San Polo; ⏰9am-3pm & 5pm-1am Mon-Sat; 🚢Rialto-Mercato) No velvet rope here, though it's the kind of snazzy urban place you'd expect to find one, given the aluminium bar, sexy backlighting and see-and-be-seen picture windows. Prices are friendly too, with wines by the glass starting at €2, respectable cocktails from €5, and €1.50 to €3.50 *cicheti* at the bar. The upstairs restaurant is swanky, but low tables out in the *campo* are more happening than any VIP lounge.

TAVERNA DA BAFFO BAR

Map p292 (☎041 520 88 62; Campiello Sant'Agostin 2346, Santa Croce; ⏰5pm-2am; 🚢San Tomà) This bar, named for Casanova's licentious poet pal Giorgio Baffo, is actually a converted chapel, stripped down to its naked brick walls and then plastered with Baffo's explicit odes to womanly curves. The young, upbeat crowds are hardly scandalised – and when strong *spritz,* draught beer and well-priced wines are flowing, there may be some impromptu poetry from the crowd before the night is through. In summer, arrive early to stake your claim on outdoor tables and the bartender's attention.

CAFFÈ DEL DOGE CAFE

Map p292 (☎041 522 77 87; www.caffedeldoge.com; Calle dei Cinque 609, San Polo; ⏰8.30am-8pm Mon-Sat, 9am-1pm Sun; 🚢San Silvestro) Sniff your way to the Doge, where hyperactive coffee connoisseurs slurp their way through the menu of speciality imported coffees from Ethiopia to Guatemala, all roasted on the premises. The decor is more laboratory than classic Venetian cafe and the looped video ad seems like hype, but these beans have earned an international following.

ENTERTAINMENT

CASA DEL CINEMA CINEMA

(041 524 13 20; Salizada San Stae, Santa Croce 1990; admission adult/reduced €6/5; shows afternoon Mon-Sat; San Stae) Venice's public film archive shows art films in a new 50-seat, wood-beamed screening room inside Palazzo Mocenigo. Original-language classics are shown Mondays and first-run independent films on Friday nights and Saturday afternoons; check online for prerelease previews and revivals with introductions by directors, actors and scholars. Show up early for prime seating.

SUMMER ARENA CINEMA, THEATRE

Map p292 (Campo San Polo; Jul-Aug; San Silvestro) Where bullfights were once held by rowdy Austrians, the city now hosts open-air movies, concerts and theatre performances from July to September – but watch this space year-round though for kiddie carousels, political rallies and street musicians.

OPERA AT SCUOLA GRANDE DI SAN GIOVANNI EVANGELISTA OPERA HOUSE

Map p292 (041 426 65 59; www.scuolasangiovanni.it; Campiello della Scuola 2454; adult €30-35, reduced €20-25; concerts begin 8pm; Ferrovia) Perennial Italian opera favourites – Puccini's *Tosca*, Verdi's *La Traviata*, Rossini's *Il Barbiere di Seviglia* – are performed by local opera troupes in the highly operatic setting of the Scuola Grande di San Giovanni Evangelista. Sweep up the grand 15th-century staircase designed by Mauro Codussi to your concert venue: Giorgio Massari's 1729 Scuola meeting hall, lined with paintings by Giandomenico Tiepolo. Not bad for an evening's entertainment.

SHOPPING

TOP CHOICE CARTÈ CRAFTS, STATIONERY

Map p292 (041 024 87 76; www.cartevenezia.it; Calle di Cristi, San Polo 1731; 10am-6.30pm Mon- Sat; San Tomà) Lagoon ripples mysteriously appear on marbled-paper necklaces and hand-bound portfolios thanks to the steady hands and restless imagination of *carta marmorizzata* (marbled paper) maestra Rosanna Corrò. After years restoring ancient Venetian manuscripts and books, Rosanna began creating original, bookish beauties: aquatic marbled-paper cocktail rings, hypnotically swirled statement necklaces, op-art jewellery boxes and surreal book-bound handbags featuring woodgrain patterns.

TOP CHOICE GILBERTO PENZO ARTISANAL

Map p292 (041 71 93 72; www.veniceboats.com; Calle 2 dei Saoneri 2681, San Polo; 9am-12.30pm & 3-6pm Mon-Sat; San Tomà) Yes, you actually can take a gondola home in your pocket. Anyone fascinated by the models at the Museo Storico Navale (p136) will go wild here, amid handmade wooden models of all kinds of Venetian boats, including some that are seaworthy (or at least bathtub-worthy). Signor Penzo also creates kits so crafty types and kids can have a crack at it themselves.

I VETRI A LUME DI AMADI GLASS

Map p292 (041 523 80 89; Calle Saoneri 2747, San Polo; 9am-12.30pm & 3-6pm Mon-Sat; San Silvestro) Glass menageries don't get more fascinating than the one created before your eyes by Signor Amadi. Fierce little glass crabs approach pink-tipped sea anemones, and glass peas spill from a speckled peapod. You might be tempted to swat at eerily lifelike glass mosquitoes, and the outlines of galloping horses in blue glass would do Picasso proud.

VIZIOVIRTÙ CHOCOLATE

Map p292 (041 275 01 49; www.viziovirtu.com; Calle del Campaniel 2898a, Santa Croce; 10am-6.30pm; Ca' Rezzonico) Work your way through Venice's most decadent vices and tasty virtues with repeat visits to the Willy Wonka–esque chocolatier for extra-creamy house-made gelato and chocolates filled with ganache in a five-course meal of flavours: Barolo wine, pink pepper, ginger-curry, chestnut honey and mimosa flower. A second location on Campo San Tomá offers more cakes, mousses, pralines and upscale gift-wrapped treats.

CARTAVENEZIA ARTISANAL

Map p292 (041 524 12 83; www.cartavenezia.it; Calle Lunga 2125, Santa Croce; 11am-1pm & 3.30-7.30pm Tue-Sat, 3.30-7.30pm Mon; San Stae) Paper is anything but two-dimensional here: instead of being marbled, as has been the custom in Venice for 150 years, paper maestro Fernando di Masone embosses and sculpts handmade cotton paper into seamless raw-edged lampshades, hand-bound sketchbooks and paper versions of marble friezes that would seem equally at home in a Greek temple or modern loft.

DROGHERIA MASCARI FOOD, WINE

Map p292 (☎041 522 97 62; www.imascari.com; Ruga degli Spezieri 381, San Polo; ⊙8am-1pm & 4-7.30pm Mon-Tue & Thu-Sat, 8am-1pm Wed; Rialto-Mercato) Ziggurats of cayenne, leaning towers of star anise and chorus lines of spotlit olive oils attract crowds of awestruck foodies to Drogheria Mascara's windows. Indoors, customers clutch tiny jars of white truffles like holy relics, and staff help dazed first-timers navigate the selection of Sicilian capers and 50 kinds of aromatic honeys. For memorable small-production Italian wines at €10 to €30 – including Veneto cult winemakers like Quintarelli – don't miss the backroom *enoteca* (wine bar).

PIED À TERRE SHOES SHOES

Mapp292(☎0415285513;www.piedaterre-venice.com; Sottoportico degli Oresi 60; ⊙10am-1pm & 3-7pm Tue-Sat, 3-7pm Mon; Rialto-Mercato) Though 18th-century Rialto courtesans started a craze for 30cm-high heels, the fashion for slippers never left Venice. Pied à Terre's colourful baroque *furlane* (slippers) are handcrafted with recycled bicycle tyre treads, ideal for finding your footing on a gondola. Choose from velvet, brocade or raw silk in jewel tones like emerald and fuschia, with the option of contrasting piping. Bring your own fabric, and you can have shoes made to measure.

VENEZIASTAMPA ARTISANAL

Map p292 (☎041 71 54 55; www.veneziastampa.com; Campo Santa Maria Mater Domini 2173, Santa Croce; ⊙8.30am-12.30pm & 2.30-7.30pm Mon-Fri, 8.30am-12.30pm Sat; San Stae) Mornings are the best time to stop by to see the ancient blackened gears of the 1930s Heidelberg machine in action – but any time you stop by, you'll smell printer's ink drying and find fresh racks of etchings hot off the proverbial press. The stock here is a thrilling throwback to another time, when postcards were gorgeously lithographed, custom bookplates gently reminded book borrowers of their rightful owners and Casanovas invited dates upstairs to 'look at my etchings'. Pick up original hand-stamped stationery with your choice of symbols – a meteor shower, a leaking faucet, a dandy – or invitation cards, menus and posters by local artists.

SERENA VIANELLO ACCESSORIES

Map p292 (☎041 522 33 51; www.serenavianello.com; Campo Sant'Aponal 1226, San Polo; ⊙10am-1.30pm & 2.30-7pm Mon-Sat; San Silvestro) Opulent Como silks and minute finishing set these timeless Venetian designs apart from the faddish crowd. Clever ruffled wraps take the chill off La Fenice opening nights in diva-worthy silvery lilac, swooping, broad-brimmed Florentine straw hats that would suit royals riding gondolas, and lagoon-teal shoes evoke a walk through Venice.

FRANCO FURLANETTO ARTISANAL

Map p292 (☎045 209 544; Calle delle Nomboli 2768, San Polo; ⊙10am-6.30pm Mon-Sat; San Tomá) Masks and violins inspire maestro Franco's sleek, original designs for *forcole* (gondola oarlocks), which he hand-carves on-site from blocks of walnut, cherry and pear wood. There's a science to each piece, which must be perfectly weighted and angled to propel the boat forward, but also an obvious art: for its sculptural finesse, Franco's work has been shown in New York's Metropolitan Museum of Art.

SABBIE E NEBBIE HOME & GARDEN

Map p292 (☎041 71 90 73; www.sabbienebbie.com; Calle dei Nomboli 2768a, San Polo; ⊙10am-12.30pm & 4-7.30pm Mon-Sat; San Tomà) The latest East–West trade-route trends begin here, with Japanese-inspired Rina Menardi ceramics, woven opera wraps that are saffron on one side and paprika on the other, and handmade books from Bologna made with Japanese paper-marbling techniques.

LABERINTHO JEWELLERY

Map p292 (☎041 71 00 17; www.laberintho.it; Calle del Scaleter 2236, San Polo; ⊙10am-12.30pm & 3-7pm Tue-Sat; San Stae) A token jewel in the window is a tantalising hint of the original custom jewellery this versatile goldsmiths' atelier can create for you, with designs that nod at Venice's seafaring, Byzantine past: a nautilus-inspired ring inset with opal and turquoise mosaic, a square gold bracelet inlaid with ebony and amber, a necklace of seascape agate lozenges that float on the collarbone like islands.

DIETRO L'ANGOLO DESIGN STORE

Map p292 (☎041 524 30 71; www.dietrolangolo2657.com; Calle Seconda dei Saoneri 2657, San Polo; San Tomá) A totally Venetian concept store: modern Italian design finds hidden on a backstreet behind I Frari, with affordable, original pieces by young local artisans. Clothespins shaped like pigeons lighten household chores with San Marco memories, and cocktail rings featuring rubber daisies with a Murano-glass centre will remind you it's time for a *spritz*.

IL PAVONE DI PAOLO PELOSIN ARTISANAL

Map p292 (☎041 522 42 96; Campiello dei Meoni 1478, San Polo; San Silvestro) Consider Paolo's hand-bound marbled-paper journals and photo albums a challenge: now it's up to you to come up with Venice memories worthy of such inspired workmanship. Recipe books come in scrumptious violet and gold art-deco patterns, lagoon-swirled blue sketchbooks inspire sudden seascapes, and paper-wrapped pen sets seem to catch fire with flickers of orange and red.

IL BAULE BLU TOYS, VINTAGE

Map p292 (☎041 71 94 48; www.ilbaeleblu.com; Campo San Tomà 2916a, San Polo; 10.30am-12.30pm & 4-7.30pm Mon-Sat; San Tomà;) A curiosity cabinet of elusive treasures, which on recent inspection included antique Steiff teddy bears, a pelican-shaped lamp, vintage Murano *murrine* (glass beads) and an asymmetrical, acid-green Marni jacket. If travel has proved tough on your kid's favourite toy, first aid and kind words will be administered at the in-house teddy hospital.

MARE DI CARTA BOOKSTORE, MAPS

Map p295 (☎041 71 63 04; www.maredicarta.com; Fondamenta dei Tolentini 222, Santa Croce; 9am-1pm & 2.30-7pm Tue-Sat; Ferrovia) Sailors, pirates and armchair seafarers should navigate their way to this canalside storefront, which stocks every maritime map and DIY boating aid needed for lagoon exploration, boat upkeep and spotting local sea life. If you're considering rowing lessons or a sailboat excursion – and who doesn't after a few days on the lagoon? – stop here to check out the schedule of boating classes and trips.

OTTICA VASCELLARI EYEGLASSES

Map p292 (☎041 522 93 88; www.otticavascellari.it; Ruga Rialto 1030, San Polo; Rialto-Mercato) Second-generation opticians and first-class eyewear stylists, the Vascellari family intuit eyewear needs with a glance at your prescription and a long look to assess your face shape and personal style. Angular features demand Vascellari's signature bold architectural eyewear line with two-tone laminates, delicate features are set off with sleek satin-finish specs, and fabulous gold-rimmed sunglasses will have the crowds parting for you at the Venice film festival.

GMEINER SHOES

Map p292 (☎338 896 21 89; www.gabrielegmeiner.com; Campiello del Sol 951, San Polo; Rialto-Mercato) London, Paris, Tokyo: Gabriele Gmeiner honed her shoemaking craft in sartorial centres around the globe, and jet-setters now seek out her hidden Venice workshop for ultrasleek Oxfords with hidden 'bent' seams and brogues minutely detailed with hand-stitching, all made to measure for men and women. If Gabriele's not stitching on-site, she's probably at the women's prison on Giudecca, where she leads a job-training program in shoe design.

MARCO FRANZATO VETRATE ARTISTICHE GLASS, JEWELLERY

Map p292 (☎041 24 07 70; www.marcofranzato.it; Calle Lunga 2155a, Santa Croce; 10am-6pm Mon-Sat, noon-5pm Sun; San Stae) Slumped, fused and foiled again: glass goes wild in this experimental co-op gallery of emerging glass designers. Mod glass clocks are the work of studio ringleader Marco Franzato, who also stocks a well-priced selection of necklaces of matte glass discs that look like UFOs orbiting around the neck, and jars of handmade Murano beads embedded with rosebuds or stars that start at €0.40 each.

CAMPIELLO CA' ZEN ANTIQUES

Map p292 (☎041 71 48 71; www.campiellocazen.com; Campiello Zen 2581; 9am-1pm & 3-7pm Mon- Sat; San Tomà) Antique Murano glass lamps are the last thing you'd want to cram in your luggage – or so you thought before you saw the 1940s Salviati silver chandelier and the rare Scarpa table lamp. That hand-blown golden goblet seems practical in comparison, but here's a dangerous thought: they ship.

MILLE E UNA NOTA MUSICAL INSTRUMENTS

Map p292 (☎041 523 18 22; Calle di Mezzo 1235, San Polo; 9.30am-1pm & 3.30-7.30pm Mon-Sat; San Tomà) The same thought occurs to almost everyone after hearing a concert in Venice: is it too late to take up an instrument? The easiest would be the harmonica, and Mille e Una Nota has an impressive range of vintage and modern ones from the Italian Alps. If you're feeling very ambitious, you can pick up some Albinoni sheet music and a lute here too.

LA PEDRERA JEWELLERY

Map p292 (041 244 01 44; www.lapedrera.it; Campo Sant'Agostino 2279a, San Polo; 10am-1pm & 2-6.30pm Mon-Sat & 10am-1pm Sun; San Stae) Made you look: these Murano glass jewels in bold colours and essential shapes have the attention-getting powers of traffic lights, and will make you stop in your tracks between Campo San Polo and Campo San Giacomo dell'Orio. Arches of chartreuse beads form a Grand Canal balcony around the collarbone, and a 1920s flapper-inspired drop necklace made with antique scarlet beads demands a Venetian jazz concert.

LA MARGHERITA ARTISANAL

Map p292 (393 210 02 73; lamargheritavenezia.com; Campo San Cassian 2345, Santa Croce; 10am-7pm Mon-Fri, 10am-2pm Sat; Rialto-Mercato) The charm of Venice is captured in a squiggle of Gothic archways by Margherita Rossetto, a cartoonist who also applies her graphic talents to ceramics at this studio. Hand-drawn cards feature Venetian signoras leaning over ironwork balconies, kitchen tiles feature cats sunning on Gothic windowsills, and grinning fish greet diners with a knowing wink on oval fish platters.

IL GUFO ARTIGIANO CRAFTS

Map p292 (041 523 40 30; Ruga degli Speziali 299, San Polo; 10am-3.30pm Mon-Sat; Rialto-Mercato) Hot copper and extremely careful handling is the secret to the embossed leather designs gracing journals, handbags and wallets in this artisan's atelier. Ancient ironwork patterns in Venetian windows and balconies inspire the swirling designs, with vibrantly coloured leather adding an unexpected modern twist: orange satchels, saffron-yellow photo albums and verdant day planners.

LA BOTTEGA DI GIÒ JEWELLERY

Map p292 (041 71 46 64; www.labottegadigio.it; Fondamenta dei Frari 2559a, San Polo; 10am-1pm & 3-7pm; San Tomà) Murano glass jewellery you see in the shops not quite your style? Make your own with lampworked Murano glass beads beginning at €2 and choose your own coloured wire, silk thread or leather cord from this DIY jewellery shop. If you're not crafty, they'll finish a necklace or earrings professionally for you.

EMILIO CECCATO FASHION

Map p292 (041 520 89 89; Orafecio 16, San Polo; 9am-12.30pm & 3-6.30 Mon-Sat; San Silvestro) Gondoliers pull up at the Rialto bridge to do their one-stop shopping at this historic Venetian uniform shop for boatneck shirts, matching red-and-white striped scarves, navy rowing jackets and straw boaters, all at strictly fair prices. Chefs stop by for regulation whites and industrial-strength aprons, and custom orders are available. You may find cheaper knock-offs at souvenir stands, but this is the real deal, and built to last.

GIUSEPPE TINTI GLASS

Map p292 (041 524 12 57; www.tintimuranoglass.com; Campo San Cassian 2343, Santa Croce; 9am-1pm & 3-7pm Mon-Sat; Rialto-Mercato) Watch Giuseppe turn molten glass into a colourful, cartoony fish with a blowtorch and very steady hands. The results are all around you in this tiny, packed corner shop: highly portable, affordable souvenirs, including violet glass earrings with gold-foil swirls (€8 to €12), stackable glass-band rings (€3 for €6) and Tinti's signature glass fish magnets (€4 to €7).

FANNY FASHION

Map p292 (041 522 82 66; Calle dei Saoneri 2723, San Polo; 10am-7.30pm; San Tomà) Quit snickering about the name – when that Venice chill hits your extremities, you'll be seriously glad you found this trove of artisan-crafted leather gloves. No need to sacrifice style for warmth here: check out the cashmere-lined purple pair with yellow piping, or those polka-dotted aqua numbers. At these prices, you might spring for a sleek chocolate bowling-ball bag to haul around your glove purchases.

Sestiere di Cannaregio

Neighbourhood Top Five

❶ Explore the tiny island that offered refuge from the Inquisition, bailed out the Venetian empire and sparked a Renaissance in thought: the **Ghetto** (p116), where synagogues, art galleries, bookshops and the Museo Ebraico honour the traditions of Venice's historic Jewish community.

❷ Discover the little neighbourhood corner chapel that marked a turning point in art history: **Chiesa di Santa Maria dei Miracoli** (p118).

❸ Pay respects to the patron saint of travellers and the genius of Tintoretto at **Chiesa della Madonna dell'Orto** (p120).

❹ Find Grand Canal photo-ops, stolen masterpieces and priceless pavement at **Ca' d'Oro** (p118).

❺ Detour from well-travelled Rialto routes to find Venice's best-priced *cicheti* and *ombre* at Cannaregio **happy hours** (p121).

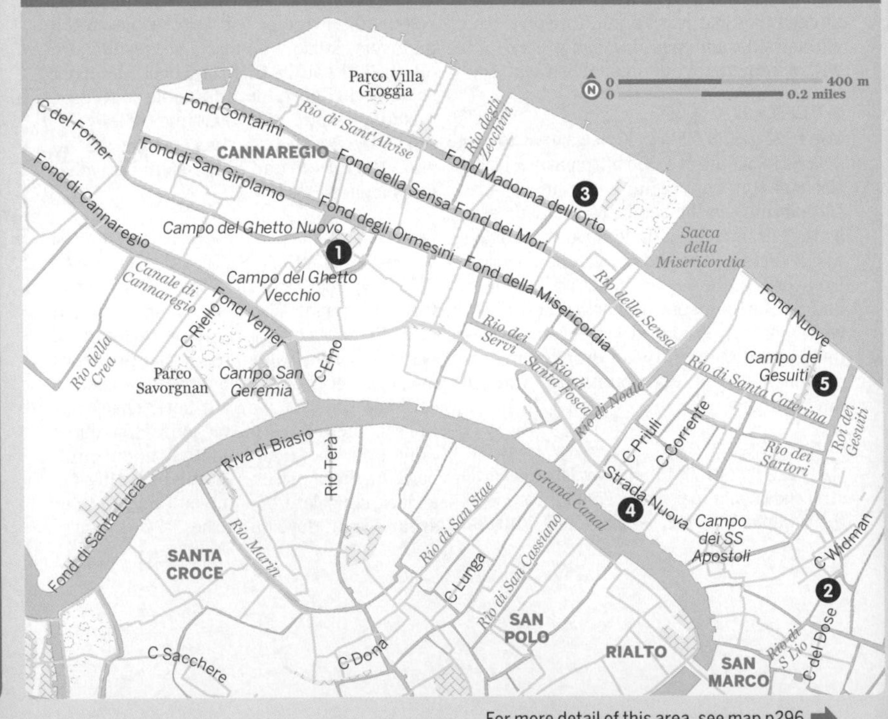

For more detail of this area, see map p296

Explore: Cannaregio

Ignore the Ferrovia signs trying to rush you through Cannaregio, and detour behind the Rialto to Chiesa di Santa Maria dei Miracoli. Wander up to Fondamente Nouve, and turn to glimpse baroque splendour at I Gesuiti and follow aptly named Fondamenta Zen and misnomer Fondamenta Misericordia towards Campo dei Mori and Madonna dell'Orto. Break for a stellar lunch at Anice Stellato, followed by a fascinating tour of historic Ghetto synagogues. Browse through poetry, antiques and Ikona Gallery in the Ghetto until it's time for a legendary Cannaregio *cicheti* crawl: Al Timon, Osteria Ai Osti, Alla Vedova and Mondo di Vino.

Local Life

➡ **Canalside dining** Romance comes naturally to candlelit tables reflected in the canal at Dalla Marisa (p121), Ai Canottieri (p121), Anice Stellato (p119) and Taverna del Campiello Remer (p121).

➡ **Shopping secrets** Campo Santa Maria Nova hosts a monthly outdoor antiques market from spring to autumn (p44), but you'll also find antiques, artisans and fashion-forward Spilli (p123) in this Cannaregio corner.

➡ **Hidden happy hours** Commuters rushing along Strada Nuova are missing some of Venice's best happy-hour venues just steps off the thoroughfare at La Cantina (p121), Alla Vedova (p121) and Osteria Ai Osti (p122).

➡ **Nightlife** Cannaregio's timeless calm is broken at night by modern music acts at Il Santo Bevitore (p121), Al Timon (p121), Paradiso Perduto (p123) and Teatro Fondamenta Nuove (p122).

Getting Around

➡ **Vaporetto** After the busy Ferrovia stop, there are two more Grand Canal stops in Cannaregio: San Marcuola (lines 1 and 82 and N) and Ca' d'Oro (1 and N). Lines 41, 42, 51 and 52 head from Ferrovia into the Canale di Cannaregio and onwards to Fondamente Nuove. Ferries head from Fondamente Nuove to the northern islands, including San Michele, Murano, Burano, Le Vignole and Sant'Erasmo.

Lonely Planet's Top Tip

Napoleon created the wide pedestrian boulevard that links the train station to the Rialto, and it's a lot like a highway, with rush-hour pedestrian traffic and chain stores. But one of Venice's most scenic walks runs parallel to it, along the sunny *fondamente* (canal banks) running north of the Ghetto and along the lagoon on the Fondamente Nouve. Follow the *fondamente* to find your bliss, plus Venice's top-value happy hours and tasty canalside dining.

Best Places to Eat

➡ Anice Stellato (p119)

➡ Dalla Marisa (p121)

➡ Osteria Boccadoro (p119)

➡ Antica Adelaide (p120)

➡ Osteria l'Orto dei Mori (p120)

For reviews, see p119 ➡

Best Places to Drink

➡ Al Timon (p121)

➡ Il Santo Bevitore (p121)

➡ Algiubagió (p122)

➡ Agli Ormesini (p122)

➡ Osteria Ai Osti (p122)

For reviews, see p121 ➡

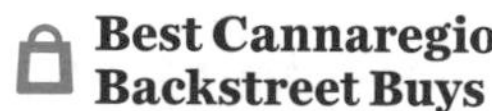

Best Cannaregio Backstreet Buys

➡ Tough-guy man-bags by prison co-op Malefatte (p123)

➡ Biennale tunic dresses designed at Spilli (p123)

➡ Hand-stamped Venetian-motif calling cards at Gianni Basso (p123)

➡ Modern poetry on timeless Venetian themes at Old World Books (p123)

➡ Ghetto grand-dame cameos at Antichità al Ghetto (p124)

For reviews, see p123 

KRZYSZTOF DYDYNSKI / LONELY PLANET IMAGES ©

TOP SIGHTS
THE GHETTO

In medieval times, this Cannaregio outpost housed a *getto* (foundry) on an island to contain the risk of fire – but its role as the designated Jewish quarter from the 16th to 18th centuries gave the word a whole new meaning. In accordance with the Venetian Republic's 1516 decree, Jewish artisans and lenders stocked and funded Venice's commercial enterprises by day, while at night and on Christian holidays, most were restricted to the gated island of the Ghetto Nuovo.

Campo del Ghetto Nuovo

Unlike most European cities of the era, pragmatic Venice granted Jewish communities the right to practise certain professions key to the city's livelihood, including medicine, trade, banking, fashion and publishing. But after workdays, Jewish Venetians returned to the island of Campo del Ghetto Nuovo (Map p296). When the Inquisition forced Jewish communities out of Spain, many fled to Venice. Around Campo del Ghetto Nuovo, upper storeys were added to house new arrivals, synagogues and publishing houses.

According to official orders c 1516, the island's bridges were closed at midnight. Such laws were abolished under Napoleon in 1797, when some 1626 Ghetto residents gained standing as Venetian citizens. However, Mussolini's 1938 Racial Laws were throwbacks to the 16th century, and in 1943 most Jewish Venetians were deported to concentration camps. As a **memorial** on the northeast end of the campo notes, only 37 returned. Today few of Venice's 400-person Jewish community actually live in the Ghetto, but their children come to Campo del Ghetto Nuovo to

DON'T MISS...

- Campo del Ghetto Nuovo
- Schola Italiana cupola
- 1704 decree
- 1943 memorial
- Museo Ebraico synagogue tour

PRACTICALITIES

- Map p296
- ☎041 71 53 59
- www.museoebraico.it
- Museo Ebraico: Campo del Ghetto Nuovo 2902b
- museum adult/reduced €3/2
- synagogue tours incl museum €8.50/7
- Museo Ebraico 10am-7pm Sun-Fri except Jewish holidays Jun-Sep, to 6pm Oct-May
- Guglie

play, surrounded by the Ghetto's living legacy of bookshops, art galleries and religious institutions.

At the Ghetto's heart, **Museo Ebraico** (Jewish Museum; see boxed text left) explores the history of Venice's Jewish community through everyday artefacts, and showcases its pivotal contributions. Inquire at the museum about guided tours to the Antico Cimitero Israelitico (Old Jewish Cemetery; p150) on the Lido.

Synagogues

As you enter Campo del Ghetto Nuovo, look up: atop private apartments is the wooden cupola of the 1575 **Schola Italiana** (Italian Synagogue). The Italians were the poorest in the Ghetto, and their synagogue is simple, with beautifully carved woodwork.

Recognisable from the square by its five long windows, the **Schola Tedesca** (German Synagogue) has been the spiritual home of Venice's Ashkenazi community since 1528. By 16th-century Venetian law, only the German Jewish community could lend money, and the success of this trade shows in the handsome decor. The baroque pulpit and carved benches downstairs are topped by a gilded, elliptical women's gallery, modelled after a Venetian opera balcony.

Above the Schola Tedesca in the corner of the campo, you'll spot the wooden cupola of **Schola Canton** (the Corner or French Synagogue), built c 1531 with gilded rococo interiors added in the 18th century. Though European synagogues typically avoid figurative imagery, this little synagogue makes an exception to the rule with eight charming landscapes taken from Biblical parables.

Refugees from Portugal and Spain raised two synagogues over the bridge in **Campo del Ghetto Vecchio**, considered among the most beautiful in northern Italy, with interiors renovated in the 17th century that may be the work of Baldassare Longhena. The **Schola Levantina** (Levantine Synagogue) has a magnificent 17th-century woodworked pulpit, while the main hall of the **Schola Spagnola** (Spanish Synagogue) is reached by a sweeping staircase. This Sephardic synagogue founded by refugees from Spain in 1583 shows how Venetian the community became within a generation or two, with the addition of classical high-arched windows, repeating geometric details, and exuberant marble and carved-wood baroque interiors.

Hour-long English-language tours of the synagogues leave from Museo Ebraico four times daily starting at 10.30am, and lead inside three of the Ghetto's synagogues: Schola Tedescha, Schola Canton, and either Schola Italiana or still-active Schola Spagnola. The Schola Levantina is still used for Saturday prayers in winter (it has heating), while the Schola Spagnola is used in summer.

RENAISSANCE IN THE GHETTO

Despite a 10-year censorship order issued by the church in Rome in 1553, Jewish Venetian publishers contributed hundreds of titles popularising new Renaissance ideas on religion, humanist philosophy and medicine. In the 17th century, the Schola Italiana's learned rabbi Leon da Modena was so widely respected as a thinker and scientist that Christians began attending his services, and Modena accommodated them by delivering his sermons in Italian. Ghetto literary salons organised by Modena, bestselling philosopher Sara Copia Sullam and other notable intellectuals brought leading thinkers of all faiths to the Ghetto.

On the wall at No 1131 Calle del Ghetto Vecchio, an official 1704 decree of the Republic remains carved in stone. This announcement forbids Jews converted to Christianity entry into the Ghetto or into Jewish homes on pain of punishment that might include 'the rope [hanging], prison, galleys, flogging...and other greater punishments, depending on the judgment of their excellencies (the Executors Against Blasphemy)'.

SIGHTS

THE GHETTO — HISTORICAL SITE

See p116.

CA' D'ORO — MUSEUM

Map p296 (Golden House; ☎041 520 03 45; www.cadoro.org; Calle di Ca' d'Oro 3932; adult/reduced €6/3; ⏲8.15am-2pm Mon, to 7.15pm Tue-Sun; ⛴Ca' d'Oro) Along the Grand Canal, you can't miss the stunning 15th-century Ca' d'Oro, its lacy Gothic facade resplendent even without the original gold-leaf details that gave the palace its name (Golden House). The lacy **Gothic arcade** framing the double loggia balcony is Venice's most irresistible photo-op, and the intricate semiprecious stone mosaics paving the **water door entry** make a grander entrance than any red carpet.

Ca' d'Oro was donated to the city by Baron Franchetti with an impressive art collection, now displayed in the upstairs **Galleria Franchetti**, alongside a jackpot of artwork plundered from Veneto churches during Napoleon's Italy conquest. Napoleon had excellent taste in souvenirs, including bronzes, tapestries, paintings and sculpture ripped (sometimes literally) from Veneto churches; they were warehoused at Milan's Brera Museum as Napoleonic war trophies until they were reclaimed by Venice for display here. Collection highlights include Andrea Mantegna's teeth-bearing, arrow-riddled *Saint Sebastian*; Pietro Lombardo's tender *Madonna and Child* in glistening Carrara marble; Titian fresco fragments rescued after Venice's 1967 flood; and Tullio Lombardo's *Last Supper* centrepiece for Santa Maria dei Miracoli (p118), a stunning carved-marble homage to Leonardo Da Vinci.

I GESUITI — CHURCH

Map p296 (☎041 528 65 79; Salizada dei Specchieri 4880; ⏲10am-noon & 4-6pm daily; ⛴Fondamente Nuove) Giddily over the top even by rococo standards, this gaudy, glitzy 18th-century Jesuit church is difficult to take in all at once, with a staggering spaceship of a **pulpit** and undulating marble walls. The church is lavishly decorated with white-and-gold stucco, white-and-green marble floors, and marble flourishes filling in any blank space. Gravity is provided by Titian's uncharacteristically dark, gloomy *Martyrdom of St Lawrence*, on the left as you enter

TOP SIGHTS
CHIESA DI SANTA MARIA DEI MIRACOLI

When Nicolò di Pietro's Madonna icon started miraculously weeping in its outdoor shrine around 1480, crowd control became impossible in this cramped corner of Cannaregio. By pooling resources and scavenging multicoloured marble from San Marco slag heaps, the neighbours built this chapel (1481–89) to house the painting and its ecstatic admirers. But there was another miracle in store for the neighbourhood: Pietro and Tullio Lombardo's design, which dropped grandiose Gothic in favour of a human-scale, classical approach that would come to be known as Renaissance architecture.

The patchworked marble exteriors are a marvel of creative repurposing: you might recognise **polychrome marbles** plundered from Egypt to Syria from the sides of Basilica di San Marco. Note the careful placement of each coloured marble panel, creating a rhythmic rippling across the building's exterior.

Look closely at the **chancel staircase** – there are angels carved right into the railings by Tullio Lombardo. In a prime example of Renaissance humanism, Pier Maria Pennacchi filled each of the 50 wooden **coffered ceiling panels** with a bright-eyed portrait of a saint or prophet dressed as a Venetian, like a class photo in a school yearbook.

DON'T MISS...

- Pietro Lombardo's Renaissance design
- Repurposed polychrome marble cladding
- Nicolò di Pietro's Madonna
- Tullio Lombardo's chancel staircase

PRACTICALITIES

- Map p296
- Campo dei Miracoli 6074
- admission €3; Chorus Pass
- ⏲10am-5pm Mon-Sat
- ⛴Fondamente Nuove

the church. Also playing against type here is Tintoretto's *Assumption of the Virgin,* in the northern transept. This image is the antithesis of his dark images in the Scuola Grande di San Rocco (p98), showing the Virgin on her merry way to heaven, with the light step of Tiepolo and a rosy glow that nods at Titian.

CAMPO DEI MORI PIAZZA

Map p296 (Madonna dell'Orto) A gent in an outsized turban hangs out at the corner of the Calle dei Mori, just as he's done since the Middle Ages. This is one of four such figures on building facades ringing the Campo dei Mori (Square of the Moors) – probably a misnomer, since these statues are believed to represent the Greek Mastelli family (the one on the corner is known as Sior Rioba), 12th-century merchants from Morea. The Mastelli brothers became notorious for their shady dealings and eager participation in Doge Dandolo's sack of Constantinople. According to Venetian legend, Mary Magdalene herself turned them into stone for their hard-hearted business dealings.

PONTE DI CALATRAVA BRIDGE

Map p296 (Piazzale Roma, Ferrovia) Modern Spanish architect Santiago Calatrava's 2008 bridge over the Grand Canal between Santa Croce and Cannaregio has been called many things: a fish tail, a glass-and-steel fantasy, unnecessary, overdue, pleasingly streamlined and displeasingly wheelchair inaccessible. Its detractors point out that its €15 million costs are triple the original 2001 estimate, and engineers are still working to correct a 4cm tolerance to ensure its stability. A wheelchair lift is currently being installed, but at an estimated 16-minute round-trip plus wait times, the *vaporetto* may remain the faster way for disabled travellers to cross the canal.

Even among its supporters, there is disagreement. Some claim the bridge is best seen at night from afar, when it looks like a meteoric streak of light across the Grand Canal; others prefer it by day, when you can appreciate the red ribbed-steel underbelly. Judge for yourself whether the time and money has paid off, and join the ongoing debates on the bridge's relative merits at happy hours across Venice.

IKONA GALLERY ART GALLERY

Map p296 (041 528 93 87; www.ikonavenezia.com; Campo del Ghetto Nuovo 2909; admission free; during shows 11am-7pm Sun-Fri; Guglie) Art provides the missing link between the Ghetto's history and its contemporary context at Ikona, a showcase for think pieces and themed installations. Recent shows have considered photography as memory, Michele Bubacco's looming, spectral black and white wall paintings, and Luigi Viola's powerful *Kaddish* series, commemorating the Ghetto's vanished generation.

SPEZERIA ANTICA SANTA FOSCA HISTORICAL SITE

Map p296 (041 720 600; Campo Santa Fosca 2234a; 9am-12.30pm & 3-7.30pm Mon-Fri, 9am-12.45pm Sat; Ca' d'Oro) Medical advances are historically key to the life and livelihood of Venice, where laws guaranteed the free movement of Muslim and Jewish doctors and forward-thinking public-health policies included such historic developments as quarantine. This perfectly preserved storefront pharmacy illustrates how medical advice was dispensed three centuries ago, with curatives in ceramic jars lined up on hand-carved shelves, and etchings of wise doctors hanging beneath gilded wood-beam ceilings. An adjoining modern pharmacy and homeopathy centre offers the latest health aids, from baby formula and orthopaedic insoles to trendy, tin-boxed 'fashion condoms'.

EATING

TOP CHOICE **ANICE STELLATO** VENETIAN €€

Map p296 (041 72 07 44; Fondamenta della Sensa 3272; meals €25-40; 9.30am-3.30pm & 6.30-11.30pm Wed-Sun; Madonna dell'Orto) If finding this obscure corner of Cannaregio seems like an adventure, wait until dinner arrives: herb-encrusted lamb chops, ravioli made in-house, and lightly fried *moeche* (soft-shelled crab) crunched whole. Tin lamps and recycled-paper placemats on communal tables keep the focus on local food and local company – all memorable. Book ahead.

OSTERIA BOCCADORO VENETIAN €€€

Map p296 (041 521 10 21; www.boccadorovenezia.it; Campiello Widmann 5405a; noon-3pm & 7-10pm Tue-Sun; Fondamente Nuove) Birds sweetly singing above your table in this bucolic *campo* are probably angling for your leftovers, but they don't stand a chance.

Chef-owner Luciano's creative *crudi* (raw seafood) are two-bite delights – tuna with blood orange, sweet prawn atop a sliver of tart green apple – and the cloudlike gnocchi topped with spider crab are gone entirely too soon. Pair your seafood dishes with mineral-rich Traminer white, and save room for luxuriant mousse made with six kinds of chocolate.

OSTERIA L'ORTO DEI MORI MODERN ITALIAN €€
Map p296 (☎041 524 36 77; Campo dei Mori 3386; meals €20-40; ⏲12.30-3.30pm & 7.30pm-midnight Wed-Mon; ⛴Madonna dell'Orto) Not since Tintoretto lived next door has this sleepy neighbourhood stayed up so late, thanks to this smart new *osteria*. Sicilian chef Lorenzo makes fresh pasta daily, including squid atop spinach *tagliolini* and bow-tie pasta with sausage and *radichio di Treviso*. Upbeat staff and fish-shaped lamps add a playful air to evenings here, and you'll be handed *prosecco* to endure the wait for tables (book ahead).

ANTICA ADELAIDE VENETIAN €€
Map p296 (☎041 523 26 29; Calle Priuli 3728; meals €25-35; ⏲noon-3pm & 7-11pm; ⛴Ca' d'Oro; 🖉) In a Venetian home that's been serving food to neighbourhood crowds since the 18th century, dishes range from classic to modern, with impeccable lagoon-clam linguine and inventive *orechiette* (little ear) pasta with almonds and gorgonzola. With a well-priced selection of small-production wines (especially whites) and artisanal beer; call ahead and make a summer night of it.

BENTIGODI VENETIAN €€
Map p296 (☎041 822 37 14; Calle Sele 822 37 14; meals €18-35; ⏲11.30am-2pm & 6.30-10pm Sun-Wed, to midnight Fri & Sat; ⛴San Marcuola) Follow the sound of animated conversation to this Ghetto *osteria*, where excitement over heaping dishes of *seppie in nero* (squid in its own ink) and *fegato Veneziano* (Venetian calf's liver with slow-cooked onions) raise conviviality levels to the wooden rafters around lunchtime, when fixed-price meals run from €18. Dishes are scrupulously prepared according to historically researched recipes with Veneto ingredients, top-notch local cheeses and an abundance of top Veneto and Friuli wines.

PASTICCERIA DAL MAS PASTRIES €
Map p296 (☎041 71 51 01; Rio Terà Lista di Spagna 150a; pastries €0.90-1.50; ⏲7am-6pm daily; ⛴Ferrovia; 🖉) Early departures and commuter cravings call for flaky pastries near the train station, devoured warm with a *macchiatone* (espresso stained with milk): apple turnovers, *krapfen* (doughnuts) and the classic *curasan* (croissant).

CHIESA DELLA MADONNA DELL'ORTO

Dedicated to the patron saint of *gondolieri*, merchants and travellers – basically, all of Venice – this sublime 1365 Italian Gothic **cathedral** (Map p296; Campo della Madonna dell'Orto 3520; admission €3 or Chorus Pass; ⏲10am-5pm Mon-Sat; ⛴Madonna dell'Orto) somehow remains one of Venice's best-kept secrets. A red-brick marvel edged in white Istrian stone and statuary, Chiesa della Madonna dell'Orto and its adjoining monastery were originally intended to honour St Christopher. But when the Madonna statue parked in the monastery's kitchen *orto* (garden) began to work miracles, the statue won pride of place at the altar, and the design was upgraded to cathedral quality with a doorway designed by Bartolomeo Bon. Still, the monastery had difficulty keeping monks in this remote corner of Cannaregio, and the church was eventually downgraded to a parish church and allowed to deteriorate in the 18th and 19th centuries.

Yet even after the Madonna dell'Orto's initial tide of admirers had ebbed, it held the eternal devotion of one key parishioner: Tintoretto. Madonna dell'Orto is just over the footbridge from the Venetian Renaissance master's home studio, and he lavished the church with attention for decades. Tintoretto and his family were buried in the corner chapel, and he saved some of his best work for the apse: *Presentation of the Virgin in the Temple*, with throngs of star-struck angels and mortals vying for a glimpse of Mary; and his 1546 *Last Judgment*, where lost souls attempt to hold back a teal tidal wave while an angel rescues one last person from the ultimate *acqua alta*. Tintoretto is better known for nocturnal drama, but these works show he could handle colour with the best Venetian painters.

AI CANOTTIERI VENETIAN €€

Map p296 (☎041 715 408; Fondamenta del Macello 690; meals €20-35; Crea) Architecture students pack this out-of-the-way *osteria* for the €15 pasta lunch special, and starry-eyed Slow Foodies arrive at night for candlelit, canalside seafood feasts of exemplary polenta with *schie* (lagoon shrimp) and strictly line-caught Sicilian tuna. Book ahead for canalside seating during regattas, which row furiously past this turning point.

OSTERIA DA ALBERTO SEAFOOD €€

Map p296 (☎041 523 81 53; Calle Larga Gallina 5401; meals €15-25; noon-3pm & 6-11pm Mon-Sat; Fondamente Nuove) All the makings of a true Venetian *osteria* – hidden location, casks of wine, chandeliers that look like medieval torture devices – plus fair prices on spaghetti *alla busara* (with shrimp sauce), seasonal *cicheti*, crispy Venetian seafood fry, and silky panna cotta with strawberries. Call ahead, because the kitchen closes early when the joint's not jumping.

LA CANTINA VENETIAN €€

Map p296 (☎041 522 82 58; Campo San Felice 3689; cicheti €3-6, mains €15-30; 11am-11pm Mon-Sat; Ca' d'Oro;) Talk about slow food: grab a stool and local Morgana beer while you await seasonal bruschette made to order and hearty bean soups. Seafood platters require larger appetites and deeper pockets – the market price varies, so ask today's rate – but mullet with roast potatoes, *scampi crudi* (sweet prawn Venetian-style sushi) and corn-breaded fried anchovies are worthy investments.

OSTERIA ALLA VEDOVA VENETIAN, CICHETI €€

Map p296 (☎041 528 53 24; Calle del Pistor 3912; cicheti €1-3.50, meals €15-40; 11.30am-2pm & 6.30-10.30pm Mon-Wed & Fri-Sat, 6.30-10.30pm Sun; Ca' d'Oro) Culinary convictions run deep here at one of Venice's oldest *osterie,* which is why you won't find *spritz* or coffee on the menu or pay more than €1 for a bar snack of Venetian meatballs. Enjoy superior seasonal *cicheti* and *ombre* with the local crowd at the bar, or call ahead for brusque, pricey table service and strictly authentic Venetian pastas.

TAVERNA DEL CAMPIELLO REMER TRADITIONAL ITALIAN, CICHETI €€

Map p296 (☎349 336 51 68; Campiello del Remer 5701; cicheti €5-7, meals €20-40; 9.30am-2.30pm & 5.30pm-1am Wed-Mon; Rialto) Off the tourist routes and close to any Venetian bargain-hunter's heart, this vaulted cavern opens onto a secluded square along the Grand Canal. Buffet-style lunches come fully loaded with *affettati* (especially Trevisana sausages and cured meats) and pasta for about €20 – but the best deal is in the afternoons before 7.30pm, when a *cicheti* buffet and drink runs from €5 to €7. At dinner, abundant *primi* are served family-style with about a pound of pasta for two, and specials are recited rather than written down. As the sign says: *menú turistico non ghe xe* (there's no tourist menu).

WORTH A DETOUR

DALLA MARISA

At **Dalla Marisa** (Map p296; ☎041 720 211; Fondamenta San Giobbe 652b; set menu €30-35; 11am-3pm & 7-11pm Tue & Thu-Sat; Crea), you're treated like a friend of the family. You'll be seated where there's room and get no menu – you'll have whatever Marisa's cooking, and like it – but you will be informed that the abundant menu is meat- or fish-based when you book, and house wine is included in the fixed price. Venetian regulars confess Marisa's *fegato alla veneziana* (Venetian calf's liver) is better than their grandmothers', while fish nights (usually Tuesdays) bring hauls of lagoon seafood grilled, fried and perched atop pasta and arugula.

DRINKING & NIGHTLIFE

TOP CHOICE **AL TIMON** WINE BAR

Map p296 (☎041 524 60 66; Fondamenta degli Ormesini; 11am-1am Thu-Tue & 6pm-1am Wed; Guglie) Pull up your director's chair along the canal and watch the motley parade of drinkers and dreamers arrive for *crostini* (open-face sandwiches) and quality organic and DOC wines by the *ombra* or carafe. Folk singers sometimes play sets, which turn to singalongs as the evening unfolds.

IL SANTO BEVITORE BAR

Map p296 (☎041 71 75 60; Calle Zancani 2393a; 8am-midnight Mon-Sat; Ca' d'Oro) San Marco may have its glittering cathedral,

WORTH A DETOUR

ALGIUBAGIÓ

Pretty much any other bar in town can claim a more central location than **Algiubagió** (Map p296; ☎041 523 60 84; Fondamente Nuove 5039; ⏰7.30am-midnight Wed-Mon; ⛴Fondamente Nuove), which is really only convenient to Murano shoppers and Burano photographers – but for modern romance, none quite compare. The long indoor bar is a most promising start to date nights, with some 300 wine options and moody spotlighting under the exposed-beam ceiling. Casual drinks may lead to cosy, candlelit tables for two and ambitious (if pricey) meals of goose and truffle ravioli.

but here at the shrine of the 'Holy Drinker', enticing offerings include blonde beers and Trappist ales, canalside seating, the footy match on TV, afternoon internet access and the occasional live band at night (Irish groups and all-girl rock bands are perennial favourites).

AGLI ORMESINI PUB

Map p296 (Da Aldo; ☎041 71 58 34; Fondamenta degli Ormesini, Cannaregio 2710; ⏰8pm-1am Mon-Sat; ⛴Madonna dell'Orto) While the rest of Venice is awash in wine, Ormesini offers 120 brews, including local Birra Venezia. The cheery, beery scene often spills into the street – but keep it down, or the neighbours get testy.

OSTERIA AI OSTI BAR

Map p296 (☎041 520 79 93; Corte di Pali Testori 3849; ⏰9.30am-8pm Mon-Sat; ⛴Ca' d'Oro) Behind the old well and between a kebab joint and an Irish pub is this authentic *ombra* outpost, where Venetians stop in throughout the day for friendly glasses of wine at friendly prices. It also offers a good selection of *sopressa* (Venetian soft salami) and *cicheti* that easily pass as lunch or an early dinner.

UN MONDO DI VINO BAR

Map p296 (☎041 521 10 93; Salizada San Canciano 5984a; ⏰11am-3pm & 6.30-11pm Tue-Sun; ⛴Rialto) Get there early for first crack at the fresh and largely unfried bar noshes – marinated artichokes and mussels if you're lucky – and a few square inches of ledge to help you balance your overflowing plate and glass of wine. There are 45 wines offered by the glass here, with prices ranging from €1.50 to €5, so take a chance on whatever the bartender recommends.

CAFFÈ COSTA RICA CAFE, BAR

Map p296 (☎041 71 63 71; Rio Terà San Leonardo 1337; ⛴San Marcuola) Sudden detours en route to the train station are caused by enticing aromas wafting out of this little shopfront lined with burlap coffee bags. Since 1930, the Marchi family has been importing beans from Costa Rica and other speciality coffee locales, roasting them fresh daily on the premises, and grinding them on the spot to suit coffee connoisseurs.

ENTERTAINMENT

CASINÒ DI VENEZIA CASINO

Map p296 (☎041 529 71 11; www.casinovenezia.it; Palazzo Vendramin-Calergi, Cannaregio 2040; admission €5, or with €10 gaming token purchase free; ⏰11am-2.30am Sun-Thu, 11am-3am Fri & Sat) No opera can match the dramas that have occurred at Venice's palatial gambling house since the 16th century: Richard Wagner survived the 20-year effort of composing his stormy *Ring* cycle only to expire here in 1883. Wagner's suite has been turned into a **museum** (☎041 276 04 07; ⏰Tue & Sat noon by reservation at least one day in advance), with Wagner memorabilia that includes a request from Wagner's wife to deliver champagne to their favourite gondolier and, in a rather macabre touch, a copy of the sofa on which he had his fatal heart attack.

But the real draws here are on the casino floor, especially roulette wheels and marathon blackjack sessions. Hotel guests can usually get a coupon for free casino entry from their concierge. Slots open at 11am; to take on the gaming tables here, arrive after 3.30pm wearing your best jacket and poker face.

TEATRO FONDAMENTA NUOVE THEATRE, DANCE

Map p296 (☎041 522 44 98; www.teatrofondamentanuove.it; Fondamente Nuove 5013; ticket prices vary; ⛴Fondamente Nuove) Expect the unexpected in Cannaregio's experimental corner: dances inspired by water and arithmetic, freeform jazz and improvised electronica, British performance art in Italian, and a steady stream of acclaimed artists from Brazil to Finland playing to a full house of 200.

PARADISO PERDUTO LIVE MUSIC

Map p296 (☎041 72 05 81; Fondamenta della Misericordia 2540; ⏱7pm-1am Thu-Mon; ⛴Madonna dell'Orto) 'Paradise Lost' is a find for anyone craving a cold beer canalside on a hot summer's night, with occasional live-music acts. Over the past 25 years, troubadour Vinicio Capossela, Italian jazz great Massimo Urbani and Keith Richards have played the small stage at the Paradiso. On Sundays, jam sessions hosted by two independent local labels alternate with local art openings.

CINEMA GIORGIONE MOVIE D'ESSAI CINEMA

Map p296 (☎041 522 62 98; Rio Terà di Franceschi 4612; adult/student €7.50/5.50; ⛴Fondamente Nuove) Screenings of Oscar winners and recently restored classics share top billing at this modern cinema in the heart of Venice. There are two screens (one tiny) and as many as three screenings a day (roughly 5pm, 7.30pm and 10pm).

SHOPPING

TOP CHOICE **MALEFATTE** GIFTS, ACCESSORIES

Map p296 (☎041 521 02 72; www.rioteradeipensieri.org, in Italian; Calle Zancani 2433; ⏱10am-7pm Mon-Sat; ⛴San Marcuola) 'Misdeeds' is the name of this nonprofit initiative by and for incarcerated workers, but their hand-silkscreened fashion, organic body-care products and pop-art bowling bags made from recycled vinyl museum banners are not at all badly made – they're actually quite brilliant. Aprons with the recipe for *spritz*, T-shirts showing the measurements of *acqua alta* and art journals made from Venice art-show ads are souvenirs with a difference: all proceeds support training and transitions from jail on Giudecca to new lives and productive careers in Venice.

TOP CHOICE **OLD WORLD BOOKS** BOOKS

Map p296 (☎041 275 94 56; Punto del Ghetto Vecchio; ⏱10am-1pm & 4-7pm Mon-Fri; ⛴Guglie) Rare books, local histories and speciality titles for Venice obsessives (such as *Chimney Pots of Venice, Abandoned Islands of the Lagoon*) draw book-lovers of every stripe, but the poets are probably here for free *prosecco*, celebrating the publication of the house's latest chapbook. Poems celebrating Venetian preoccupations – water, lust, secrecy, ribald humour – are available here in limited-edition printings, along with original artworks by Ghetto artists.

GIANNI BASSO PRINTER

Map p296 (☎041 523 46 81; Calle del Fumo 5306; ⏱9am-1pm & 2-6pm Mon-Sat; ⛴Fondamente Nuove) All the advertising Signor Basso needs for his letterpressing services are the calling cards crowding his small front window with familiar names and fitting symbols. Restaurant critic Gale Greene's title is framed by a knife and fork; conductor Michael Tilson Thomas' title rises from a grand piano; and Hugh Grant's moniker appears next to a surprisingly tame lion. Bring cash if you want to commission your own business cards, menus or invitations, and trust Gianno Basso to deliver via post if need be – posted hours are approximate.

LE MASCHERE DI ALE ACCESSORIES

Map p296 (☎041 241 25 92; www.lemascherediale.com; Calle Dolfin 5648a; ⏱10am-7pm Mon-Sat; ⛴Rialto) Everything in Venice looks better upholstered, as you can plainly see from these clever marbled-silk bracelets, stamped velvet masquerade masks, tapestry *furlane* (slippers) and brocade handbags. Each one-of-a-kind piece is handmade in Venice, and with prices from €12 to €79, a handy bargain.

WORTH A DETOUR

SPILLI LAB & SHOP

Glamour comes easily at **Spilli Lab & Shop** (Map p296; ☎340 276 72 96; www.spilli-venezia.com; Ponte dei Miracoli 6019; ⏱9.30am-12.30pm & 3.30-7.30pm Tue-Sun, 3.30-7.30pm Mon; ⛴Fondamente Nuove), a Venetian design showcase with gold-embroidered cotton tunic dresses, straw fedoras and raw-edged canvas handbags. Alessia Sopelsa has an eye for luxe textures and original details – yet everything here is surprisingly affordable, with double-digit fashion statements that command attention in five-digit Biennale crowds.

VLADI SHOES
SHOES

Map p296 (☎041 244 00 84; www.vladishoes.it; Rio Terá della Maddalena 2340; ⏲10.30am-7.30pm Wed-Mon; Ca' d'Oro) Step out in stylish, well-heeled and surprisingly practical shoes, made right here in Venice. Algae-green oxfords, navy suede peep-toes and scarlet strappy sandals turn Cannaregio *fondamente* into your own personal runways at happy hour, without leaving your arches aching for a *vaporetto*.

ANTICHITÀ AL GHETTO
ANTIQUES

Map p296 (☎041 524 45 92; Calle del Ghetto Vecchio 1133/4; ⏲9.30am-noon & 2.30-6pm Wed-Sat, 2.30-6pm Tue, 10am-1pm Sun; Guglie) Instead of souvenir T-shirts, this antique shop authors mementos of Venetian history: ancient maps of the canals, etchings of Venetian dandies daintily alighting from gondolas, and 18th-century cameos worn by the most fashionable ladies in the Ghetto.

GIUNTI AL PUNTO
BOOKS

Map p296 (☎041 524 37 28; Rio Terà Maddalena; ⏲9am-8pm Mon-Wed, to midnight Fri & Sat, 10am-10pm Thu & Sun; Guglie) Late hours, decent paperbacks in several languages, useful cookbooks and maps of Venice make this a handy outlet for further information and vacation reading.

DOLCEAMARO
FOOD, WINE

Map p296 (☎041 523 87 08; Campo San Canciano 6051; ⏲10am-1pm & 4-7.30pm Mon-Sat, 11.30am-1.30pm & 4.40-7.30pm Sun; Rialto) For the well-travelled foodie who's been there, eaten that, here's something original: a miniature platter of Italian cheeses and cured meats, made out of artisan chocolate. Dolceamaro also stocks wines, speciality Veneto grappa (spirits), and other gourmet temptations, including aged balsamic vinegars and whole truffles.

Sestiere di Castello

Neighbourhood Top Five

❶ Get an insider's view during special events at the **Arsenale** (p127), the Venetian Republic's vast honeycomb of a shipyard and once the world's best-kept industrial secret.

❷ Gawk at the sheer scale of **Zanipolo** (p129), a 14th-century church packed with master works of painting and sculpture.

❸ Take an early-morning stroll along **Riva degli Schiavoni** (p134), Castello's breathtaking waterfront promenade.

❹ Take a break from brick and marble amid the leafy byways of Napoleon's **Giardini Pubblici** (p131).

❺ Hear Vivaldi's music in acoustically tuned, frothily rococo **La Pietà** (p135), built in his honour.

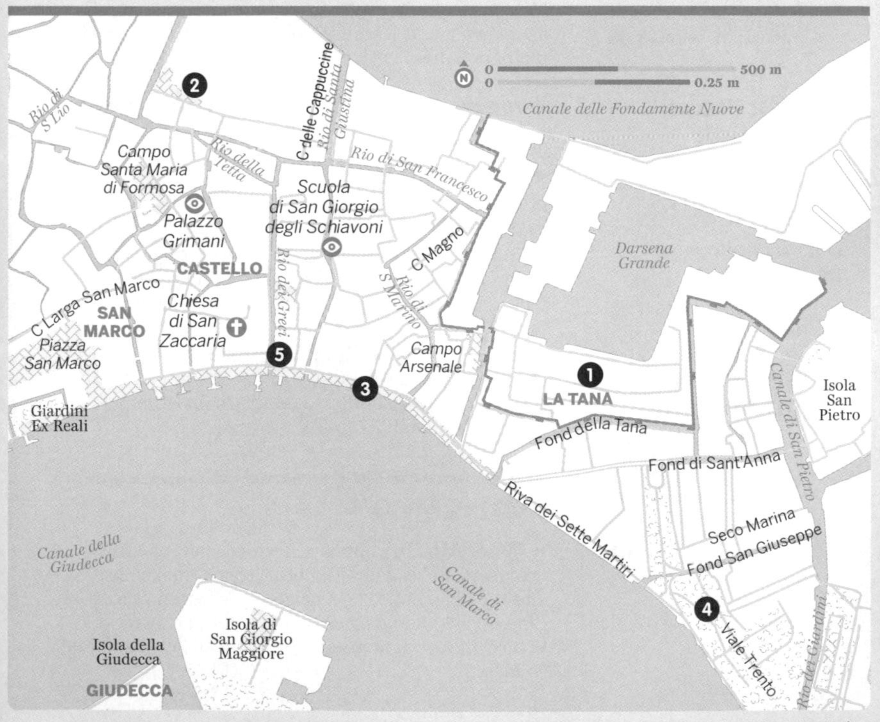

For more detail of this area, see Map p298

Lonely Planet's Top Tip

Venice is always best early in the morning or after the crowds thin in the evening. This is especially true of the Riva degli Schiavoni, which is crowded from 9am to 9pm with day-trippers as cruises disgorge their maddening crowds. But if you can get yourself out of bed at sunrise, the seafront promenade makes for a magnificent and remarkably solitary morning constitutional – it's also a great chance to get people-free photos.

Best Places to Eat

- Trattoria Corte Sconta (p138)
- Met (p138)
- al Covo (p138)

For reviews, see p138

Best Places to Drink

- Enoteca Mascareta (p141)
- Bar Terazza Danieli (p142)
- L'olandese Volante (p142)

For reviews, see p141

Best Places to Shop

- Giovanna Zanella (p142)
- Sigfrido Cipolato (p143)
- Atelier Alessandro Merlin (p143)

For reviews, see p142

Explore: Castello

Stretching from San Marco to the eastern edges of Venice, Castello is the city's most sprawling *sestiere* and exploring its entirety in one day will test walking shoes. Start with its most illustrious sites – the masterfully cavernous Zanipolo church, the golden glow of Carpaccio's paintings in the Scuola di San Giorgio degli Schiavoni and the light-filled galleries of Palazzo Grimani. All are within a stone's throw of San Marco and Rialto. Moving east, you'll reach the engine of the city's maritime might: the sprawling shipyards known simply as Arsenale. While the Arsenale is only open for special events, the nearby Museo Storico Navale helps fill in the city's watery history. East of the Arsenale lies a working-class stronghold where the phalanx of tourists thins dramatically. You're most likely to hear the Venetian dialect here, and it's good for a rough-and-ready *aperitivo* or hearty lunch. Continuing on, the leafy Giardini Pubblici is ground zero for Biennale events. Consider continuing on to the city's remotest reaches: Venice's cathedral on the island San Pietro del Castello and leafy, residential Isola di Sant'Elena – a kitsch, early-20th-century version of Venice itself. At sunset, head back along the Riva degli Schiavoni (perfect for a crowd-free early-morning jog), or climb aboard a *vaporetto* at one of the stops along the Riva. Or, consider staying on for dinner at the high-flying Met or rustically elegant Corte Sconta. Alternately, an *aperitivo* might lead naturally into a night of revelry – the bars lining Via Garibaldi will happily oblige.

Local Life

- **Drinking** Salt-of-the-earth Venetians mix promiscuously with their Bohemian neighbours in the bars along Via Garibaldi (p141).
- **Quick Eats** Locals drop in all day for *cicheti* at Bacaro Risorto (p140); *gondolieri* prefer their daily *spritz* (*prosecco* cocktail) at Pasticceria Da Bonifacio (p140).
- **Hangouts** *Nonne* (grandmothers) gather for afternoon gossip while their young charges kick balls across Campo di Bandiera e Mori, Campo Zanipolo and the Giardini Pubblici (p131).

Getting There & Away

- **Vaporetto** Line 1 makes all stops along the Riva Schiavoni, linking it with both Grand Canal stops and the Lido. Line 2 also heads up the Grand Canal. Lines 41, 42, 51 and 52 circle the outer perimeter of Venice, including stops along Riva degli Schiavoni and Giudecca.

TOP SIGHTS
ARSENALE

Founded in 1104, the Arsenale quickly grew into Europe's greatest medieval shipyard, employing up to 16,000 people and capable of turning out a new galley in a single day. In fact, historians have called it a unique pre-industrial example of mass production, since it was based on centralised, standardised methods and based on interchangeable parts. Spread out over 45 hectares (100 acres), the Arsenale occupied nearly 15% of the city. It is still, even today, completely surrounded by some 3.2km (2 miles) of walls high enough to ward off prying eyes. Such secrecy is understandable, since the naval and merchant ships produced here enabled Venice to dominate the eastern Mediterranean for centuries.

DON'T MISS...

- Porta Magna
- Corderia
- Artigliere

PRACTICALITIES

- Map p298
- ☎041 521 87 11
- www.labiennale.org
- Campo Arsenale 2407
- admission varies
- ⏲vary
- Arsenale

At its peak, the Arsenale must have made an enormous impression, with its boiling black pitch, metalworking and timber cutting. Indeed, Dante used it as a model scene for hell in his *Divina Commedia* (Divine Comedy; Canto XXI, lines 7 to 21). In the 1590s, Galileo served as a special consultant to the Arsenale, helping the Venetians rationalise production and build ships that could be equipped with increasingly powerful munitions. The treatise he later wrote, drawing on his experience, is considered a seminal text of materials science.

At the core of the complex is the **Arsenale Vecchio** (Old Arsenal), which included storage for the *bucintoro,* the doge's ceremonial galley. In 1303–04 came the first expansion, known as **La Tana**. Occupying almost the whole length of the southern side of the Arsenale and performing essential rope-making work – sometimes by children – it was refashioned in 1579 by Antonio da Ponte (of Rialto bridge fame). The **Arsenale Nuovo** (New Arsenal) was added in 1325, followed in 1473 by the **Arsenale Nuovissimo** (Very New Arsenal). In the 16th century, production of *galeazze* (large war vessels with a deep draught) required further workshops and construction sheds, along with

BUCINTORO

Seven centuries before *Pimp My Ride*, there was the Bucintoro. The most lavish creation of the Arsenale, it was the doge's official galley. There were four versions of the Bucintoro, the first of which was built in 1311. However, the most extravagant was the fourth and last. Completed in 1727, the multistorey floating *palazzo* was clad entirely in gold leaf and had seating for 90 – the main salon alone boasted 48 windows. And it required 168 oarsmen to manoeuvre. You can see a scale model in the Museo Storico Navale (p136), plus a few original details salvaged when Napoleonic troops burned it in 1798.

The Fondazione Bucintoro is now leading an effort to build a life-sized recreation of the 1727 Bucintoro for an estimated €20 million. Originally planned to be ready in 2010, it's now expected to be completed in 2015.

the creations of a deeper Canale delle Galeazze to provide access.

Perhaps the most revolutionary aspect of the Arsenale was that it used canals as moving assembly lines. The growing ship would move through the canals from one stage of construction to the next – a system that was not reproduced at such a scale until Henry Ford's 'revolutionary' car factory in the 20th century. As a result of this innovation, as many as 100 galleys could be in production at a single time.

Now, large parts of the Arsenale have been retooled for peaceful purposes. Large, long-neglected swaths have been taken over and partly restored for use as exhibition space during the Architecture Biennale and other special events.

Note that the Arsenale is not open for the public except for special events like the Art and Architecture Biennales; for more insight into the city's maritime past, head to the Museo Storico Navale (p136).

Porta Magna

Capped by the lion of St Mark that somehow eluded destruction by Napoleon's troops, the Arsenale's land gateway is considered by many to be the earliest example of Renaissance architecture in Venice; it was probably executed in 1460. A plaque was installed commemorating the 1571 victory at Lepanto, and the fenced-in terrace was added in 1692. Below the statues is a row of carved lions; the biggest one, regally seated, was taken as booty by Francesco Morosini from the Greek port of Piraeus, which must have taken some doing. On the right flank of the lion, you'll notice some Viking runes, said to be a kind of 11th-century war trophy inscription left behind by Norwegian mercenaries. They boast of their role in helping Byzantium quell a Greek rebellion – the mercenary equivalent of leaving behind a résumé.

Biennale Exhibition Spaces

Architecture and Art Biennale exhibitions are mounted in the construction sheds of the Arsenale; the Herculaean effort involving boats, hand-carrying materials, and tight organisation harkens back to earlier times. Unfortunately, the Arsenale is only accessible to the public during these events. Biennale shows do often offer peeks inside, including the former **Corderia** (where ships' cables were made), the **Artiglierie** (guns) and various wharves. More creative repurposing lies ahead: ongoing work to transform the entire Arsenale will create modern ship-maintenance areas, shops, restaurants, exhibition spaces, a study centre and more.

TOP SIGHTS ZANIPOLO

When the Dominicans began building Zanipolo (also known as Chiesa dei SS Giovanni e Paolo) in 1333 to rival the Franciscans' Chiesa di Santa Maria Gloriosa dei Frari (p100), the church stirred passions and partisanship more common to Serie A football than architecture. Both structures feature red-brick facades with high-contrast detailing in white stone. But since Zanipolo's facade remains unfinished, the Frari won a decisive early decision over Zanipolo with its soaring grace – and its Titlan's *Assunta* altarpiece. Over the centuries, Zanipolo has at least tied the score thanks to its sheer scale and variety of masterpieces.

In Venetian dialect, Zanipolo is an elision of 'Giovanni e Paolo'. The name refers not to the two apostles but two martyrs of the early Christian Rome. Don't miss the brilliantly coloured stained glass in the south transept. Created on Murano, it richly illuminates designs by Bartolomeo Vivarini and Girolamo Mocetto.

Bellini's Triptych

Through his innovative use of slow-drying oil paints, Giovanni Bellini introduced a vivid sensuousness to Venetian painting that became its hallmark. Located above the second altar of the right aisle, his *SS Vincent Ferrer, Christopher and Sebastian* is a stunning case in point: the three saints depicted in three life-sized panels manage to outglow their elaborately gilded frame.

Tombs of the Dogi

For centuries, Zanipolo was the official site for the doges' funeral, 25 of whom decided to stay on after the ceremonies ended. The basilica's bare brick walls are punctuated by the doges' lavish marble tombs. To the left as you enter the basilica, Pietro Lombardo's tomb for Pietro Mocenigo (1406–76), modelled on a Roman triumphal arch, is particularly impressive. Lombardo and his clan are also responsible for the tombs of Pasquale Malipiero, Nicolo Marcello and Alvise Diedo.

Architecture

Built in classic Italian Gothic style, the brick basilica was designed to hold virtually the entire population of 14th-century Castello. Its soaring nave, held aloft by gently pointed arches, is also reinforced by a clever series of cross-beams – necessary because of Venice's water-logged soil. Typical of Italian Gothic and different from French Gothic, its exteriors and interiors have a barnlike simplicity. This plainness makes the church's paintings and sculpture seem to shine all the more brightly.

Reni, Lorenzetti & Veronese

Guido Reni's *San Giuseppe* is a rare expression of holy bonding, with Joseph exchanging adoring looks with baby Jesus. The dome on the southwest end of the nave boasts Giambattista Lorenzetti's *Jesus the Navigator* – Jesus scans the skies like an anxious Venetian sea captain. In the **Cappella del Rosario**, Paolo Veronese's *Assunta* ceiling depicts the rosy Virgin ascending a staggering staircase to be crowned by cherubs, while angels flip with joy.

DON'T MISS...

- Giovanni Bellini's *SS Vincent Ferrer, Christopher and Sebastian*
- Pietro Lombardo's tomb for Pietro Mocenigo
- Stained glass in the south transept
- Guido Reni's *San Giuseppe*
- Giambattista Lorenzetti's *Jesus the Navigator*

PRACTICALITIES

- Map p298
- ☎041 523 59 13
- Campo Zanipolo
- admission €2.50
- ⏰9am-6pm Mon-Sat, noon-6pm Sun
- Ospedale

TOP SIGHTS
PALAZZO GRIMANI

The approach through dark, narrow alleyways makes this light-filled Renaissance *palazzo* all the more startling. The Grimani family built the *palazzo* in the 16th century to house its extraordinary Graeco-Roman collection, much of which can be glimpsed today in the Museo Correr (p60). Unusual for Venice, the *palazzo* is blessed with a huge courtyard – a nod to Roman architecture and a brilliant way to shed a flattering light on the family's archaeological curiosities.

These days, the *palazzo* hosts high-calibre temporary exhibitions, though the *palazzo*'s bedazzling interiors are reason enough to visit. So is the serene and often empty cafe off the main courtyard. The cafe's whitewashed, Zen-like interior is furnished entirely in recycled materials, including bean-bag chairs fashioned from old coffee sacks. Officially you need a museum ticket to enjoy your organic espresso, but usually no one asks.

There is debate about who designed the building. Credit generally goes to Michele Sanmicheli, born in Verona and educated in Rome at the height of the Renaissance. However, some believe that Jacopo Sansovino also played a role. In addition, some theorise that the grand staircase is the work of Palladio. What is certain is that Giovanni Grimani (1501–93) himself played a large role in a design that consciously recalls the glories of ancient Rome. The result is a unique amalgam of Florentine, Roman and Venetian architecture.

DON'T MISS...

- Ganymede hanging in La Tribuna
- Corn stalks in Sala ai Fogliami
- The courtyard cafe

PRACTICALITIES

- Map p298
- ☎041 520 03 45
- www.palazzogrimani.org
- Ramo Grimani 4858
- adult/reduced €9/7
- 9am-7pm
- Ospedale, Rialto

La Tribuna

While its niches are now empty, the marble atrium known as La Tribuna once held more than a hundred classical statues; it now feels like a bright, melancholy hymn to a lost past. A soaring ceiling, capped with a trompe l'œil coffered vault, is dramatically lit by a four-sided lantern at the top. Amid this strange space floats a statue of Ganymede. Made of precious marble and suspended from the room's ceiling, Zeus's beloved is believed to have originally come from Constantinople.

Sala ai Fogliami

Painted by Mantovano, the 'Foliage Room' is perhaps the most memorable of the *palazzo*'s frescoes. Ceiling and walls are awash in remarkably convincing plant and bird life that almost has you convinced you're looking past the plaster into the great outdoors. Mantovano even included New World species that had only recently been discovered by Europeans, including two that would come to be staples of Venetian life: tobacco and corn.

Other Roman-Style Frescoes

Besides Mantovano, Grimani hired a dream team of fresco painters specialised in fanciful grotesques and vibrant, Pompeii-style mythological scenes. Francesco Salviati applied the glowing, Raphael-style colours he'd used for Florence's Palazzo Vecchio and Rome's Palazzo Farnese, working alongside Francesco Menzocchi, responsible for Vatican frescoes. Roman painter Giovanni da Udine, considered among the brightest pupils of Raphael and Giorgione, devoted three rooms to the stories of Ovid. Another in this impressive list, Federico Zuccari, painted the ceiling of the main entrance hall with designs culled from the Grimanis' own collection of Roman motifs.

TOP SIGHTS
GIARDINI PUBBLICI

During the Art Biennale, it may be hard to see the forest for the tree-art installations, but these public gardens represent the broadest swath of green space in Venice. The Giardini were founded around 1807, when Napoleon decided that Venice needed a little breathing space. Never mind that an entire residential district, including four churches, had to be demolished: the emperor needed his shrubbery. In addition, many acres of swampland were converted into terra firma, making this one of the most recent parts of Venice proper to be reclaimed from the lagoon. Today, the Giardini Pubblici offers a winning a combination of formal gardens, winding pathways and, in summer, the welcome shade of palm, plane and acacia trees.

In addition, a large swath of the gardens has been given over to the **Art Biennale** (p41), with its 30 hodgepodge pavilions, each allocated to an individual nation. While not all are equally beautiful, they tell a fascinating story of 20th-century architecture. Note that the Biennale grounds are only open during Biennale events and other special events held on site.

DON'T MISS...

- Venezuelan Pavilion
- Austrian Pavilion
- Garibaldi Monument
- Serra dei Giardini

PRACTICALITIES

- Map p298
- www.labiennale.org
- Giardini, Biennale

Biennale Pavilions

During the Art Biennale's June to September run in odd years, curators and connoisseurs swarm national showcases ranging from Geza Rintel Maroti's 1909 Secessionist-era **Hungarian Pavilion**, glittering with mosaics, to Philip Cox's 1988 boxy yellow **Australian Pavilion**, frequently mistaken for a construction trailer.

Designed by Josef Hoffmann, the whitewashed 1934 **Austrian Pavilion** is another Secessionist masterpiece, while the overblown 1938 **German Pavilion** was designed, ominously, to project a 'new spirit of Art.' Nazi blazons have long since been removed.

Venetian architect Carlo Scarpa contributed in one way or another from 1948 to 1972, trying to make the best of Duilio Torres' Fascist 1932 Italian Pavilion (now the **Palazzo delle Esposizioni**) and building the entrance courtyard. Scarpa is also responsible for the daring 1956 raw-concrete-and-glass **Venezuelan Pavilion** and the winsome, bug-shaped **Biglietteria** (Ticket Office). The 1958 **Canadian Pavilion** looks like a kind of retro ski lodge, except for the tree growing right through it. The neoclassical **United States Pavilion**, constructed in 1930, looks like Palladio by way of Thomas Jefferson. Another nod to Palladio with its elegant front and back porticos, the 1909 **British Pavilion** actually began its life as a cafe before being converted into a gallery. More recently, the light-filled, postmodern 1996 **Korean Pavilion** has taken over an electrical plant in ingenious ways.

Garibaldi Monument

As you enter the gardens from Via Garibaldi, you can't miss the moss-covered mini-mountain capped off rather anomalously by a classical, 19th-century statue of a Giuseppi Garibaldi (1807–82) with a ferociously large lion at his feet. Hero of Italian unification, the bronze Garibaldi was completed by sculptor Augusto Benvenuti in 1885.

Serra Dei Giardini

The gardens' late-19th-century **greenhouse** (www.serradeigiardini.org; Viale Giuseppe Garibaldi 1254; admission free; 9am-12.30pm & 2-6.30pm Mon-Sat, 10am-6.30pm Sat & Sun) has been refurbished as a cultural centre, plant shop, kid-friendly play space and organic cafe. Special events range from book readings to yoga classes.

TOP SIGHTS
CHIESA DI SAN ZACCARIA

When 15th-century Venetian girls showed more interest in sailors than saints, they were sent for a stint at the convent adjoining Chiesa di San Zaccaria. Venice's spoiled daughters passed their time in prayer here, with breaks for concerts and the occasionally scandalous masked balls. The wealth showered on this church by their grateful (or at least hopeful) parents is evident. Vast, lavish 17th-century canvases crowd its walls. And the church itself is like a brief history of Venetian architecture, from its watery, 9th-century Romanesque crypt to its Gothic nave on to its elegant, early-Renaissance facade. Inside, it harbours a remarkable stash of paintings, including works by Bellini, Tintoretto, Salviati, Tiepolo and even Flemish master Anthony Van Dyck.

Founded in the 9th century, the church claims to possess the remains of San Zaccaria, father of John the Baptist, as well as the remains of eight early doges. For six centuries, doges visited San Zaccaria with great pomp each Easter, a tradition that began in the 12th century when the church's Benedictine monks donated land for the enlargement of Piazza San Marco. The church also possesses a feature typical of northern European Gothic churches but unique in Venice: a rounded ambulatory with tall, stained-glass windows behind the altar.

DON'T MISS...

- Bellini's altarpiece
- Mauro Cadussi's facade
- Cappella di San Tarasion
- 9th-century crypt

PRACTICALITIES

- Map p298
- ☎041 522 12 57
- Campo San Zaccaria 4693
- admission free; Cappella di San Atanasio & crypt €1
- ⏲10am-noon & 4-6pm Mon-Sat, 4-6pm Sun
- San Zaccaria

Bellini's Altarpiece

Bellini's *Virgin Enthroned with Jesus, an Angel Musician and Saints* glows like it's plugged into an outlet. The 1505 masterpiece marks a new phase in Bellini's development, illustrating his new mastery with oil paints. Not only are the colours more vivid than earlier works, but he also uses them to create a diffused sense of air and light that would become a hallmark of Venetian painting.

Mauro Cadussi's Facade

Gothic and Renaissance fans alike can admire the church's remarkable facade. Antonio Gambello began in the Gothic manner on the lower sections, but Mauro Cadussi took over the project in the late 15th century, creating a crescendo of harmoniously rounded embellishments in white Istrian stone. It is one of the great works in the city's transition into the Renaissance.

Cappella di San Atanasio

To your right as you enter, the late Renaissance **Cappella di San Atanasio** (admission €1) holds Tintoretto's depiction of the birth of St John the Baptist, while Tiepolo depicts the Holy Family fleeing to Egypt in a typically Venetian boat. Both hang above magnificently crafted choir stalls. Behind this chapel you'll find the Gothic **Cappella di San Tarasion** (also called Cappella d'Oro or Golden Chapel), with frescoes by Andrea del Castagno and Francesco da Faenza from the 1440s. Keep an eye out for Antonio Vivarini's 1443 painting of St Sabina keeping her cool as angels buzz around her head like lagoon mosquitoes. Finally, wander downstairs to the waterlogged 10th-century Romanesque crypt, the last remnant of an earlier church on the site.

SIGHTS

CHIESA DI SAN FRANCESCO DELLA VIGNA CHURCH

Map p298 (☎041 520 61 02; Campo San Francesco della Vigna 2786; ⏰9.30am-12.30pm & 3-6pm Mon-Sat, 3-6pm Sun) Designed and built by Jacopo Sansovino with a facade by Palladio – his first church commission – this enchanting Franciscan church is one of Venice's most underappreciated attractions. The Madonna positively glows in Bellini's 1507 *Madonna and Saints* in the **Capella Santa**, just off the flower-carpeted cloister **courtyard**, while swimming angels and strutting birds steal the scene in the delightful *Virgin Enthroned,* by Antonio da Negroponte c 1460–70.

Palladio and the Madonna are tough acts to follow, but father-son sculptors Pietro and Tullio Lombardo make their own mark with their 15th-century marble reliefs that recount the lives of Christ and an assortment of saints. Housed in the **Cappella Giustiniani**, just left of the altar, they are storytelling triumphs. Breezes seem to ripple through carved-marble trees, and lifelike lions seem prepared to pounce right off the wall. And keep your eye on the expressive reactions of minor figures in these biblical narratives. They provide a running commentary on the action, right down to the startled mule.

Out the back, the bell tower looks like the long-lost twin of the Campanile di San Marco and, facing north, a couple of steps leading to a portico of classical columns make the *campo* (square) look like a proper ancient Roman agora. This makes a sociable setting for Venice's best annual block party, the **Festa di Francesco della Vigna**, with wine and rustic fare served up in the stately shadow of Palladio; usually held the third week in June.

PALAZZO QUERINI STAMPALIA MUSEUM

Map p298 (☎041 271 14 11; www.querinistampalia.it, in Italian; Campiello Querini Stampalia 5252) The outer shell of this *palazzo* dates from the first half of the 16th century, but the inside could not be more surprising: a 1963 bridge, 1940s entrance and garden, and a 1959 1st-floor library all designed by Scarpa, with noteworthy 1990s embellishments by Mario Botta.

TOP SIGHTS
SCUOLA DI SAN GIORGIO DEGLI SCHIAVONI

In the 15th century, Venice annexed Dalmatia – an area roughly corresponding to the former Yugoslavia – and large numbers of Dalmatians, known as *Schiavoni*, immigrated to Venice. In a testament to Venetian pluralism, they were granted their own *scuola* (religious confraternity) in 1451. Around 1500, they began building their headquarters, making the brilliant decision to hire Vittore Carpaccio to complete an extraordinary cycle of paintings of Dalmatia's patron saints George, Tryphone and Jerome. Carpaccio's luminous works dominate the ground-floor hall, while upstairs hides a fine stash of works by Palma il Giovane.

Though Carpaccio never left Venice, his scenes with Dalmatian backdrops are so minutely detailed that some Slavic visitors claim to recognise the locations as their home region. Carpaccio's imagined worlds, with their rich honeyed glow, are so convincing that the dragon slayed by St George looks like something that might be hauled in with the day's catch at the Pescaria. Scattered around the dragon are the bloody remnants of his victims – sundry limbs, bones and the half-eaten corpse of a young woman.

DON'T MISS...

- Carpaccio's *St George and the Dragon*
- Carpaccio's *St Gerome and the Lion*
- Carpaccio's *St Augustine in His Study*

PRACTICALITIES

- Map p298
- ☎041 522 88 28
- Calle dei Furlani 3259a
- adult/reduced €4/2
- ⏰2.45-6pm Mon, 9.15am-1pm & 2.45-6pm Tue-Sat, 9.15am-1pm Sun
- 🚢San Zaccaria

VENICE'S SECRET WEAPON: ARSENALOTTI

In an early version of the assembly line, ships built in the Arsenale progressed through sequenced design phases, each staffed by *arsenalotti* (Arsenale workers) specialised in a particular aspect of construction, ranging from hull assembly and pitch application through to sail rigging. Women specialised in sails; children started apprenticeships at age 10, and did their part twisting hemp into rope.

But this wasn't a low-paid, low-status job. The *arsenalotti* were well remunerated, with cradle-to-grave fringe benefits. This helped keep them remarkably faithful to the Republic, and throughout Venetian history, *arsenalotti* repeatedly proved both their loyalty and their brawn during periods of war and rebellion. Using their proven shipbuilding techniques, they also constructed the vast *carena di nave* (ship's keel) ceilings you see in Venetian churches and in the Palazzo Ducale's Sala del Maggior Consiglio (see p55).

Job requirements for *arsenalotti* included manual dexterity, strength and silence. Even in raucous Castello *bacari* (old-style bars), *arsenalotti* remained carefully vague about the specifics of their workday, in an 'I could tell you, but then I'd have to kill you' kind of way. Shipbuilding processes were top secret, and industrial espionage was considered an act of high treason, punishable by exile or death. For centuries the crenellated walls of the Arsenale hid the feverish activity inside from view. Even outside the walls, the *arsenalotti* tended to stick to their own kind. They intermarried, and even had their own market gardens to reduce contact with the rest of the city.

If other maritime powers had learned to make warships as fast and as fleet as Venice, the tiny lagoon republic might have lost its outsized advantage and been obliterated by its foes. In 1379, when Venetian commander Carlo Zeno's fleet was otherwise engaged, maritime rival Genoa surrounded Venice and tried to starve it into submission. But Genoa hadn't counted on the *arsenalotti*, who worked furiously to produce a fleet able to sustain a counterattack until Zeno arrived on the horizon. In 1570, when requested to produce as many ships as possible for an emergency fleet, the *arsenalotti* put out an astounding 100 galleys in just two months – despite a fire that had decimated the Arsenale the previous year.

However, things soon went downhill. A bout of plague wiped out a third of the city's population, including *arsenalotti*, and Venice's maritime rivals Austria and the Ottoman Empire discovered their own secret weapon: free-trade agreements that excluded Venice. By 1797 naval production had all but ceased, and La Serenissima surrendered to Napoleon without a fight.

Enter through the Botta-designed bookshop to get a free pass to the cafe and its garden. Design-savvy drinkers take their *spritz* with a twist of high modernism in the Carlo Scarpa–designed courtyard garden or the Mario Botta–designed Qcoffee Bar (p142).

Alternately, buy a ticket and head upstairs to the 2nd-floor **Museo della Fondazione Querini Stampalia** (adult/reduced €10/8; ⏲10am-7pm Tue-Sun). The museum occupies a series of sumptuous, well-preserved 18th-century salons that look largely as they did when the Querinis redecorated in the 1860s. You'll also find some 400 paintings, mostly minor works and portraits of illustrious family members. The clear standout is Giovanni Bellini's arresting *Presentation of Jesus at the Temple*, where the hapless child looks like a toddler mummy, standing up in tightly wrapped swaddling clothes. In a small annexe off a large hall before the Bellini is *Scenes of Public Life in Venice*, a series of some 39 folksy paintings by Gabriele Bella (1730–99).

RIVA DEGLI SCHIAVONI PROMENADE

Map p298 (San Zaccaria) Stretching west from the Palazzo Ducale in San Marco all the way to the city's eastern edges, this paved boardwalk is one of the world's great promenades.

Schiavoni (literally, 'Slavs') refers to fishermen from Dalmatia (a region roughly equivalent to the former Yugoslavia) who arrived in Venice in medieval times and found this a handy spot for casting their nets. For centuries, vessels would dock and disembark here, right into the heart of Venice – if they could find a parking space between galleons and gondolas. A Rosetta Stone's worth of languages were spoken here, as traders, dignitaries, sailors and servants arrived from ports around the Mediterranean and beyond. Paolo Veronese's *Feast in the House of Levi,* in the Gallerie dell'Accademia (p79), gives you some idea of how the crowd might have looked and dressed, with Turkish, German, North African and Greek merchants wheeling and dealing along the banks. The great poet Petrarch was among those who found lodgings and inspiration at No 4175, east of Rio della Pietà.

Today the scene is as busy as ever, with some adjustments. The gondolas are still here, but *vaporetti* have mostly replaced galleons – though you might spot the Italian navy's tall ship *Amerigo Vespucci* occasionally docked down by the Arsenale. Tourists hail from even further afield than the merchants of yesteryear, and their main challenge is negotiating the tourist menus in San Marco (hint: skip them all and order à la carte). Some of the grand old mansions now function as pricey hotels, so you too can bunk here.

MUSEO DELLE ICONE CHURCH

Map p298 (Museum of Icons; ☎041 522 65 81; www.istitutoellenico.org; Campiello dei Greci 3412; adult/student €4/2; ⏰10am-5pm; San Zaccaria) Glowing colours and all-seeing eyes fill this treasure box of some 80 Greek icons made in 14th- to 17th-century Italy. Keep your own eye out for the expressive *San Giovanni Climaco,* which shows the saintly author of a Greek spiritual guide distracted from his work by visions of souls diving into hell. The museum goes by a confusing variety of names: it's also known as the 'Museo dei Dipinti Sacri Bizantini' (Museum of Holy Byzantine Paintings), and technically it's housed in the Istituto Ellenico (Hellenic Institute).

CHIESA DI SAN GIORGIO DEI GRECI CHURCH

Map p298 (☎041 522 65 81; Campiello dei Greci 3412; admission free; ⏰9am-12.30pm & 2.30-4.30pm Wed-Sat & Mon, 9am-1pm Sun; San Zaccaria) Greek Orthodox refugees who fled to Venice from Turkey with the rise of the Ottoman Empire built a church here in 1536, with the aid of a special dispensation from Venice to collect taxes on incoming Greek ships. Nicknamed 'St George of the Greeks,' the little church has an impressive iconostasis, plus a range of Byzantine icons and fine incense still in use at services. The separate, slender **bell tower** was completed in 1603 though it began to lean right from the start; these days, it seems poised to dive into the canal on which the church sits.

LA PIETÀ CHURCH

Map p298 (☎041 522 21 71; Riva degli Schiavoni; admission €3; ⏰10am-5pm Thu-Sun & for concerts; San Zaccaria) Originally called Chiesa di Santa Maria della Visitazione but fondly nicknamed La Pietà, this light-filled and harmonious church designed by Giorgio Massari is best known for its association with the composer Vivaldi, who was concertmaster here in the early 18th century. Though the current church was built after Vivaldi's death, its acoustic-friendly oval shape honours his memory, and it is still regularly used as a concert hall (p142). Be sure to look up: on the ceiling, Giambattista Tiepolo's gravity-defying *Coronation of the Virgin* seems to open up the church to the vast heavens themselves.

SCUOLA GRANDE DI SAN MARCO NOTABLE BUILDING

Map p298 Instead of a simple Saturday father-son handyman project, sculptor Pietro Lombardo and his sons had something more ambitious in mind: a high Renaissance polychrome marble facade for the most important confraternity in Venice; Codussi was brought in to put the finishing touches on this Renaissance gem. Magnificent lions of St Mark prowl above the portals, while sculpted trompe l'œil perspectives beguile the eye.

The *scuola* now serves as the main entrance to the Ospedale Civile, the city's public hospital. You are welcome to peek inside at the ancient hall with its beamed ceiling held up by two ranks of five columns. However, sightseeing among the sick is considered poor form.

OSPEDALETTO CHURCH

Map p298 (☎041 271 90 12; Barbaria delle Tole 6691; ⏰guided visits only; Ospedale) So much for Rome's attempt to limit Venice's love affair with music: a musical theme runs right this chapel and adjacent music room. Designed by Baldassare Longhena in the 1660s, they are part of an historic hospice and orphanage. The chapel is uplifting by design, with a trumpeting angel who flits overhead, and a mirror image of the mighty organ painted on the ceiling to draw the eye upward. Jacopo Guarana painted the elegant frescoes that cover the **Sala da Musica**, where orphan girls performed in celebrated concerts.

At the time of writing, the church was being restored and was only open to groups by appointment, at a cost of €60.

MUSEO STORICO NAVALE MUSEUM

Map p298 (☎041 244 13 99; Riva San Biagio 2148; adult/reduced €1.55/0.77; ⏲8.45am-1.30pm Mon-Fri, to 1pm Sat; ⛴Arsenale) Maritime madness spans four storeys and 42 rooms at this museum of Venice's seafaring history, featuring scale models of the Venetian-built vessels as well as Peggy Guggenheim's not-so-minimalist gondola. On the ground floor, you'll find sprawling galleries of fearsome weaponry – cannons, blunderbusses, swords and sabres – with hardly any noticeable bloodstains. These big guns were rarely needed in Venice itself, since the shallows of the lagoon provided the city's best protection against invaders. Also on the ground floor you'll find 17th-century dioramas of forts and ports. They illustrate the incredible span of Venetian power across the Adriatic and Mediterranean.

Among the many large-scale models of sailing vessels on the 1st floor, you'll find a not-so-miniature version of the *bucintoro,* the doge's impossibly sumptuous ceremonial barge – Napoleon's French troops destroyed the real thing in 1798. The 2nd floor covers Italian naval history and memorabilia, from unification to the present day, and on the 3rd floor is a room devoted to gondolas, including Peggy Guggenheim's swanky version. A small room set above the 3rd floor is dedicated to – wait for it – Swedish naval history.

The ticket also gets you entrance to the **Padiglione delle Navi** (Ships Pavilion; Fondamenta della Madonna), though at writing it was only open for special exhibitions. Of the many boats on display here, the most eye-catching is the *Scalé Reale,* an early-19th-century ceremonial vessel used to ferry King Vittorio Emanuele to Piazza San Marco in 1866 when Venice joined the nascent Kingdom of Italy. The ship last set sail in 1959, when it brought the body of the Venetian Pope Pius X to rest at the Basilica di San Marco.

CATTEDRALE DI SAN PIETRO DI CASTELLO CHURCH

Map p298 (☎041 275 04 62; Campo San Pietro 2787; admission €3, or with Chorus Pass; ⏲10am-5pm Mon-Sat; ⛴San Pietro) Unlikely though it may seem, this sleepy church on the far-flung island of San Pietro served as Venice's cathedral from 1451 to 1807. Despite its glamour and central location, the Basilica di San Marco was 'merely' the doge's chapel. The island of San Pietro (originally known as Olivolo) was among the first to be inhabited in Venice, and the original church here was the seat of a bishopric as early as 775. The present church is an almost-but-not-quite Palladio design. Palladio had been awarded the contract in the 1550s, but the death of the patriarch (Venice's version of a bishop) led to a project hiatus that lasted beyond the genius's own demise. Palladio's successors largely respected his initial ideas, taking their cue from Giudecca's Chiesa del SS Redentore (p148) to complete the monumental facade by the end of the 16th century. Note the fine work on the expansive 54m **dome**, which rivals Michelangelo's at the Vatican in width (though not height). Inside, Baldassare Longhena is responsible for the **baroque main altar**.

Between the second and third altars on the right side of the church, you'll spot a chair with an intricately carved stone back referred to as **St Peter's Throne**. According to one of Venice's many architectural urban legends, the impressive chair was used by the Apostle Peter in Antioch, and the Holy Grail was later hidden in it. This story has all the makings of an *Indiana Jones* sequel, but there's very little truth to it: the seat back is in fact made from a scavenged Muslim tombstone that postdates the Apostle's death by many centuries.

Also on the premises, you'll spot San Pietro's blinding white **bell tower** of Istrian stone by Codussi (finished in 1490) leaning at an odd angle. Next door is the crumbling former **patriarchate**, retired from its use as military barracks and now partly occupied by private apartments.

CHIESA DI SAN GIOVANNI IN BRAGORA CHURCH

Map p298 (☎041 296 06 30; Campo di Bandiera e Mori 3790; admission free; ⏲9-11am & 3.30-5.30pm Mon-Sat, 9.30-noon Sun; ⛴Arsenale) This serene, 15th-century brick church harmonises Gothic and Renaissance styles with remarkable ease, setting the tone for a young Antonio Vivaldi who was baptised here. Look for Bartolomeo Vivarini's 1478 *Enthroned Madonna with St Andrew and John the Baptist,* which shows the Madonna bouncing a delighted baby Jesus on her knee. Bartolomeo's nephew Alvise depicts Jesus in later years in his splendidly restored 1494 *Saviour Blessing,* with a cloud-like beard and eyes that seem to follow you around the room.

CHIESA DI SAN MARTINO CHURCH

Map p298 (☎041 523 04 87; Campo San Martino 2298; admission free; ⊙9am-noon & 4.30-7.30pm daily; Arsenale) Stick your hand into the lion's mouth by the door, and say something nice about your neighbours: maybe that will help atone for all the dangerous rumours spread through the years via this *bocca di leone* (the mouth of the lion of San Marco). Venetians were encouraged to slip anonymous denunciations of their neighbours through these slots, reporting unholy acts ranging from cursing (forgivable) to Freemasonry (punishable by death). Denunciations were investigated by Venice's dreaded security service, led the Council of Ten.

The theme of persecution continues indoors with Palma Il Giovane's canvases of Jesus being flogged and then marched towards Calvary. The pair is hung almost out of sight in the choir stalls but can be glimpsed in front of the altar. Ironically, the church's namesake St Martin of Tours (AD 316–97) was actually the first Christian saint to die a natural death rather than as a martyr. Martin was a Hungarian priest who experienced a conversion experience after serving the Roman army in Gaul (France).

CHIESA DI SANTA MARIA FORMOSA CHURCH

Map p298 (Campo Santa Maria Formosa 5267; admission €3, or with Chorus Pass; ⊙10am-5pm Mon-Sat, 1-5pm Sun; San Zaccaria) Rebuilt in 1492 by Mauro Codussi on the site of a 7th-century church, this house of worship bears a curious name (Shapely St Mary) that has spawned two local legends. One claims the church got its nickname because its address was confused with that of a local courtesan in a 16th-century guidebook. Alternately, you can choose to believe that the name comes via San Magno, Bishop of Oderzo, who had a vision of a particularly beautiful and *formosa* Virgin Mary on this spot. To match its rival legends, the cross-shaped church also has, oddly enough, two separate facades, one facing the canal and one facing the adjacent *campo* (square). With its generous baroque curves and serene symmetries, the latter makes good on the church's shapely name.

Inspired by the Florentine churches of Brunelleschi, the interior was designed by Mauro Codussi in the 1490s. It was damaged by an Austrian bomb in 1916, but fortunately, the altarpiece by Palma il Vecchio was unharmed. It depicts St Barbara, a bevy of saints, and the body of Christ in his mother's arms. Just inside and to the right from the canal entrance, look for a 16th-century Byzantine icon of *St Mary of Lepanto.* Nearby you'll also find an 8th-century Egyptian Coptic garment, said to be the veil of St Marina – a rare relic of the saint's namesake church demolished in the nearby Campo Santa Marina.

STATUE OF BARTOLOMEO COLLEONI MONUMENT

Map p298 (Campo SS Giovanni e Paolo; Ospedale) You'll know you've crossed from Cannaregio into Castello when you spot Bartolomeo Colleoni galloping out to meet you. The bronze equestrian statue is one of only two such public monuments in Venice – and an extraordinary example of early-Renaissance sculpture. It commemorates one of Venice's most loyal mercenary commanders. From 1448, Colleoni commanded armies for the Republic, though in true mercenary form he switched sides a couple of times when he felt he'd been stiffed on pay or promotions. On his death in 1474, he bequeathed 216,000 gold and silver ducats to Venice, on one condition: that the city erect a commemorative statue to him in Piazza San Marco. Since not even a doge had ever won such pride of place in Venice, the Senate found a rather dubious workaround, placing the monument in front of the Scuola Grande di San Marco instead. At least Colleoni can rest easy knowing that the Republic didn't scrimp on the statue, sculpted with imposing grandeur by Florentine master Andrea del Verrocchio (1435–88).

MUSEO DIOCESANO DI VENEZIA MUSEUM

Map p298 (☎041 522 91 66; www.museodiocesanovenezia.it; Chiostro di Sant'Apollonia 4312; adult/reduced €4/2, cloister only €1; ⊙10am-4.30pm Thu-Tue; San Zaccaria) Housed in a former Benedictine monastery dedicated to Sant'Apollonia, this museum has a fairly predictable collection of religious art and the occasional standout temporary show – but the exquisite Romanesque cloister is a rare example of the genre in Venice. The adjoining building was a church until 1906, and now houses exhibition spaces.

CHIESA DI SAN LIO CHURCH

Map p298 (Campo San Lio; admission free; ⌚3-6pm Mon-Sat; Rialto) Giandomenico Tiepolo sure did know how to light up a room. If you find this church open, duck into the atmospheric gloom of its baroque interior and as your eyes adjust to the light, look up at Tiepolo's magnificent ceiling fresco, *The Glory of the Cross and St Leon IX*. On your left by the main door is Titian's *Apostle James the Great,* but this church is better known for yet another Venetian artist: the great *vedutista* (landscapist) Canaletto, who was baptised and buried in this, his parish church.

SOTOPORTEGO DEI PRETI LANDMARK

Map p298 (off Campo di Bandiera e Mori; Arsenale) Under the arch of this *sotoportego* (covered passageway), there's hidden a reddish, heart-shaped stone about the size of a hand. Legend has it that couples that touch it together will remain in love forever. Not ready to commit just yet? This is also a nice private spot for a smooch.

EATING

Castello offers extremely varied dining choices, from casual *cicheti* (bar snacks) at raucous neighbourhood bars to wildly inventive feasts in the city's most upmarket eateries.

TRATTORIA CORTE SCONTA MODERN VENETIAN €€€

Map p298 (☎041 522 70 24; Calle del Pestrin 3886; meals €45-65; ⌚12.30-2.30pm & 7-9.30pm Tue-Sat, closed Jan & Aug) Biennale types seek out this vine-covered *corte sconta* (hidden courtyard) for imaginative house-made pasta and ultrafresh, visually striking seafood. Crustaceans are arranged on a platter like dabs of paint on an artist's palette, black squid-ink pasta is artfully topped with bright-orange squash and tender *cappesante* (scallops), and roast eel loops like the Brenta River in a drizzle of balsamic reduction.

AL COVO VENETIAN €€€

Map p298 (☎041 522 38 12; www.ristoranteal covo.com; Campiello della Pescaria 3968; meals €55-75; ⌚lunch & dinner Fri-Sun, lunch Mon-Tue; Arsenale) Featuring all the markings of a classic Venetian trattoria – low-beamed ceilings, exposed brick wall, regulars installed in the corner – but with twists on the typical dishes. Caprese salad gets the Covo treatment with basil and *mozzarella di bufala* served with a heavenly cherry tomato gelée. Squid-ink pasta is served with clams and squash blossoms. And Adriatic tuna swims in no fewer than five sauces – at once. Prices are understandable given the top-quality, lagoon-fresh ingredients, and are offset by reasonably priced, limited-production wine.

MET MODERN ITALIAN €€€

Map p298 (☎041 520 50 44; www.hotelmetropole .com; Hotel Metropole, Riva degli Schiavoni, Castello 4149; meals from €100; ⌚dinner Tue-Sun; San Zaccaria) Michelin stars don't mean much in Venice. In fact, the last French critic Venetians took seriously was Napoleon himself, and he had an army backing him up. Still, locals who would not normally patronise a hotel restaurant concede that Met chef Corrado Fasolato certainly earns his starry reputation. Moonlit lagoon panoramas and mesmerising blown-glass constellations recede once the food starts to arrive. Confident and playful takes on local game and seafood dishes might include savoury pheasant cannelloni or decadent eel-stuffed pasta that makes foie gras seem trifling. One main arrives with red wine and horseradish transformed into sorbet and gelato. Bring a hot date, a sense of adventure and a fat wallet.

ZENZERO CAFE, BAR €

Map p298 (☎041 241 28 28; http://barzenzero. it; Campo Santa Marina 5902; sandwiches €2-4; ⌚7am-8pm Mon-Fri, 7am-3pm Sat; Rialto) One of the best quick eats in Venice, Zenzero pairs the eye-opening powers of espresso with great little sandwiches and freshly baked pastries that tend to disappear in a flash. Return for top-shelf *aperitivi* (predinner drinks) in the *campo.* It's closed for two weeks at Christmas and two weeks in August.

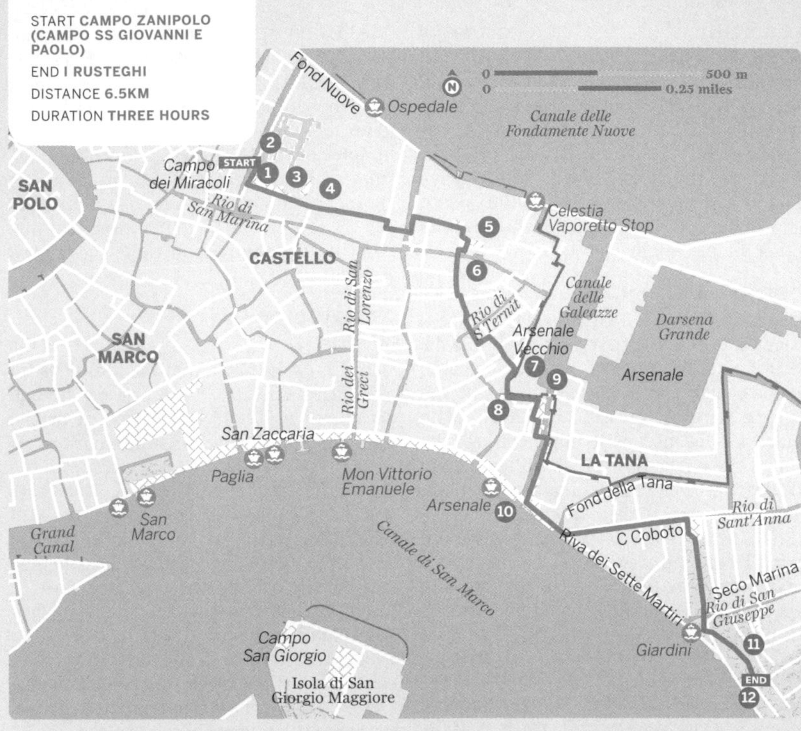

Neighbourhood Walk

Castello's Byways

This walk takes you through the back alleys, where tourist hoards thin out dramatically. Start in Campo Zanipolo, where you can't miss the 1 **Bartolomeo Colleoni statue**. A 15th-century mercenary commander, Colleoni left a generous sum on the condition that Venice erect a statue in his honour in Piazza San Marco. Venice took the money but changed the terms slightly – it erected the statue in front of the 2 **Scuola Grande di San Marco**, with its remarkable, early-Renaissance trompe-l'oeil facade. Next door rise the imposing Gothic heights of the treasure-packed 3 **Zanipolo.** Don't miss Bellini's technicolour altarpiece inside.

A block west, pass the 4 **Ospedaletto**, an orphanage chapel designed by Palladio and Longhena. Burly statues loom from the facade like heavenly bouncers. Strolling east along narrow residential alleys, Palladio's massive, classical facade of 5 **Chiesa di San Francesco della Vigna** comes as a sudden but pleasant shock.

Turn south and back to the future – just over the next canal lies 6 **Laboratorio Occupato Morion**, an avant-garde cultural centre and art lab. Further south past Campo delle Gatte, cross a canal and enter a tight nest of alleys, once housing works of the 7 **Arsenale**, whose walls rear up ahead. Turn right at the walls, following them to 8 **Chiesa di San Martino**. To the right of its doorway, look for the *bocca di leoni* (mouth of the lion), where Venetians could slip anonymous denunciations of their neighbours.

Keep following the Arsenale's walls until you reach the 9 **Arsenale's Porta Magna** (Main Entrance), considered the city's earliest example of Renaissance architecture. From here, head south to 10 **Riva degli Schiavoni** and gawk at the views across the Bacino before turning down the Venetian boulevard Via Giuseppe Garibaldi, built to remind Napoleon of Paris.

After hours of cobblestones, your feet will naturally gravitate towards the greenery of the 11 **Giardini Pubblici** off Via Garibaldi. Follow the paths through the park towards the hodgepodge of pavilions that make up the grounds of the 12 **Biennale**.

LE SPIGHE
VEGETARIAN €

Map p298 (041 523 81 73; Via Garibaldi 1341; meals €10-15; 9.30am-2pm & 5.30-7.30pm Mon-Sat) All vegetarian, all organic and vegan-friendly, this little spot offers quick but delicious eats based on seasonal produce, from crunchy fennel salads to delicious potato-and-squash pies. And the vegan chocolate cake tastes divine, whatever its other virtues might be.

OSTERIA AL GARANGHELO
VENETIAN €€

Map p298 (041 520 49 67; www.garanghelo.com; Via Garibaldi, Castello 1621; meals €35-45; lunch & dinner Wed-Mon; Giardini Pubblici) It looks like a ramshackle version of the typical Venetian tourist joint, but this little place has been consistently honoured by Italy's Slow Foodies for its adherence to traditional Venetian culinary practices. You won't regret the *margherite ripiene all'astice com sugo di pesce* (ravioli stuffed with lobster in fish sauce) or the tangy *spaghetti alla búsera* with shrimp and zucchini. Sweet tooths shouldn't miss the tiramisu.

TAVERNA SAN LIO
MODERN VENETIAN €€€

Map p298 (041 277 06 69; www.tavernasanlio.com; Salizada San Lio 5547; meals €40-50; noon-11pm Tue-Sat; Rialto) Modern without losing Venice's essential quirkiness, the seafood dishes here are delicately handled: think scallops infused with thyme or a tuna steak in a delicate clam and lobster sauce. The duck breast with plums and leeks is also tempting. Low wood tables encourage diners to lean towards one another conspiratorially, amoeba-shaped lamps set the mood for free-form conversation, and huge windows let you in on the catwalk action outdoors. Note that the kitchen is open nonstop from noon till 11pm.

PIZZERIA ALLA STREGA
PIZZERIA €

Map p298 (041 528 64 97; Barbaria delle Tole 6418; pizzas €7-12; lunch & dinner; Ospedale) Dozens of creative pizza toppings are the real secret at Alla Strega ('the Way of the Witch'), including the Calabrian pepper-laced Inferno pizza. A collection of witch dolls keep a beady eye on proceedings in the pizzeria's otherwise bright, airy rooms. To escape their gaze, head out back to the winning terrace. A new €11 lunch menu includes a pasta or risotto, plus a serving of grilled meat or fish and vegies – a real bargain for Venice.

TRATTORIA ALLA RAMPA
VENETIAN €

Map p298 (041 528 53 65; Via Garibaldi 1135; meals €12-20; noon-2pm Mon-Fri; Giardini) Hidden behind a little working-class bar hides a low-slung dining room that serves up some of Venice's heartiest lunch specials, from roasted meat and fish to generous stews, accompanied by vegies and bread to sop the sauces – all for €13. Tourists are discovering this gem, so go while the going's good.

OSTERIA DI SANTA MARINA
MODERN VENETIAN €€€

Map p298 (041 528 52 39; Campo Santa Marina 5911; meals €60-80; lunch & dinner Tue-Sat, dinner Mon; Rialto) Don't be fooled by the casual piazza seating and simple dark-wood interiors: this restaurant is saving up all the drama for your plate. Given the à la carte prices, you might as well go for the €55 fixed-price menu or the all-out adventure of the €75 tasting menu, where each course brings two bites of reinvented local fare – a prawn in a nest of shaved red pepper, black squid-ink ravioli stuffed with *branzino* (sea bass), artichoke and soft-shell crab with squash *saor* (Venice's tangy marinade). Dessert is a must, especially the house-made gelati and hot chocolate pie.

BACARO RISORTO
CICHETI €

Map p298 (Campo San Provolo 4700; cicheti €1.50-4; 9am-9pm Mon-Sat; San Zaccaria) Just a footbridge from Piazza San Marco, this shoebox of a corner bar offers quality wines and abundant *cicheti,* including *crostini* heaped with *baccalà mantecato,* grilled vegies, soft cheeses and melon tightly swaddled in prosciutto. Note that opening times are 'flexible.'

PASTICCERIA DA BONIFACIO
PASTRIES & CAKES €

Map p298 (041 522 75 07; Calle degli Albanesi 4237; pastries €1.50-4; 7am-8pm Fri-Wed; San Zaccaria) Down a narrow alley just around the corner from the Palazzo Ducale, this little bakery attracts hard-bitten gondoliers as well as hunger-dazed tourists with its selection of *pizzette* (mini-pizzas), petits fours, and traditional Venetian biscuits including *zaletti* (cornmeal biscuits with sultanas). As afternoon wanes, the bakery turns into a makeshift bar as locals pop in for the signature Americano cocktail (sweet vermouth, bitters and soda).

THE VENETIAN 'BURBS

At the easternmost reaches of Venice, Sant'Elena is the city's most far-flung island and also its most anomalous, lacking both the ancient sites and sloping charms that make up the rest of the city. Few tourists ever make it all the way to its leafy *piazze*. Those who do are rewarded with an odd surprise, since the island is in fact an intriguing, if strangely sanitised, copy of Venice itself.

Sant'Elena began as a refuge for Augustine and then Benedictine monks, who provided shelter for pilgrims to the Holy Land. The island takes its name from the mother of Roman emperor Constantine, whose body was stolen and brought here when Venice sacked Constantinople in 1211. Eventually Napoleon turned the sleepy monastery to military purposes in 1807; after his defeat, the defunct cloisters were rented out to the occasional holidaymaker. Then in the 1880s, the city greatly expanded the island, reclaiming swampland in order to build a new manufacturing zone. However, like much of the city's efforts at industrialisation, it proved inefficient by the 1920s and was abandoned.

The island took on its current aspect during the 1920s, when it was developed as the city's newest residential area. Deliberately eschewing the Modernist trends of its time, the middle-class apartments are faithful copies of the city's aristocratic palaces. However, they lack the quirks and elegant decay that define the rest of Venice. In fact, the whole neighbourhood feels a little like a Disney version of the city of which, ironically, it is an integral part.

Today Sant'Elena has become a favourite of joggers for its shady byways and distinct lack of crowds. But it is also worth a stroll just for its anachronistic charms – and as a lesson, by way of contrasts, in what makes Venice inimitable.

CIP CIAP PIZZERIA €

Map p298 (☎041 523 6621; Calle del Mondo Novo 5799/a; ⊙9.30am-9pm Wed-Mon; Rialto) The cooks at this to-go pizza joint take their job seriously enough to dress in traditional chef's whites, and their thick-crust pizzas (€12 per kilo) are a cut above the competition, thanks to fresh, high-quality ingredients. If you can snag one of the half-dozen stools, you'll even get a canal view thrown in with your cheap, quick meal.

CONCA D'ORO PIZZERIA €€

Map p298 (☎041 522 9293; www.concadorovenice.com; Campo SS Fillipo e Giacomo 4338; meals €20-30; ⊙lunch & dinner daily; San Zaccaria) Pizza is not a local speciality, in case you hadn't guessed from the cardboard pies you'll find at most pizzerias around San Marco – but this place is the exception. This local joint brought pizza to Venice in 1960 and has been slinging generous thin-crust pies (€7 to €10) with creative toppings ever since, though the nonpizza items are better avoided. Service is not especially quick on busy days, so relax and enjoy the sun in the piazza. Note: the restaurant sometimes closes on Tuesdays in low season.

DRINKING & NIGHTLIFE

Around sunset, the inhabitants of Castello converges along the waterfront and the Giardini for the *passeggiata* (evening stroll), then disperses into the *campi* for *aperitivi*. Cafes in Campo Santa Maria di Formosa, Campo di Bandiera e Mori and Campo Zanipolo become prime drinking spots by night – though for cocktails with views of islands and glowing Palladio monuments across the lagoon, you could splash out at designer hotel bars along the Riva degli Schiavoni. Or you can join locals at the rather interchangeable bars that line Via Garibaldi, where salty locals mix with both travellers and Biennale types.

ENOTECA MASCARETA WINE BAR

Map p298 (☎041 523 07 44; Calle Lunga Santa Maria Formosa 5138; meals €30-45; ⊙7pm-2am Fri-Tue; Ospedale) Oenophiles love this cosily traditional *enoteca* for its stellar wines by the glass – including big Amarones and cloudily organic *prosecco*. If you're hungry, the excellent *taier misto* (platters of cured meats and cheeses) could pass for a light meal for two – all for €15.

VENEZIA CAFFÉ CAFE

Map p298 (041 296 01 83; Calle del Cafetier 6661A; 8am-7pm Mon-Sat, 8am-5pm Sun; Ospedale) Proud owner Stefano has revived the coffee company founded by his great-great-grandfather. His trim little shop just off Campo Zanipolo stars a wood-burning roaster Stefano uses to toast up carefully selected arabica beans, which you can sip standing or smuggle home in airtight packages.

QCOFFEE BAR CAFE

Map p298 (041 099 13 07; Fondazione Querini Stampalia 5252; 10.30am-10pm Tue-Sun; San Zaccaria) One drink grants you access to the works of two modernist master architects through the Querini Stampalia bookshop. Rainy days are right for hot chocolate in Mario Botta's neoclassical cafe, with white walls framed with black polished-concrete floors and a harmonious repeating-rectangle theme. Outside, Carlo Scarpa's clever, Levant-inspired concrete irrigation channels bring Venice's canals indoors, adding industrial cool to your *spritz* in the sunny garden. The *cicheti* are especially scrumptious.

BAR TERAZZA DANIELI BAR

Map p298 (041 522 64 80; www.starwoodhotels.com; Riva degli Schiavoni 4196; 3-6.30pm, Apr-Oct; San Zaccaria) Gondolas glide in to dock along the quay, while across the lagoon, the white marble edifice of Palladio's San Giorgio Maggiore turns from gold to pink in the waters of the canal: the late afternoon scene from the Hotel Danieli's top-floor balcony bar definitely calls for a toast. Arrive after lunch and linger the afternoon away over a *spritz* (€10) or cocktail (€18 to €22) – preferably the sunset-tinted signature Danieli cocktail of gin, apricot and orange juices, and a splash of grenadine.

L'OLANDESE VOLANTE BAR

Map p298 (041 528 93 49; Campo San Lio 5658; 8am-1am; Rialto) Go home happily hoarse after another chaotic night at the Flying Dutchman, where study-abroad students mingle easily with local eccentrics over cheap beer. Outdoor seating is highly prized, though you might be sharing it by last call.

INISHARK BAR

Map p298 (041 523 53 00; www.inisharkpub.com; Calle del Mondo Novo 5787; 6-11.30pm Tue-Sun; Rialto) This hearty Venetian version of an Irish pub comes complete with Guinness, Kilkenny Cream and Bulmer's cider, plus Sky Sport TV for those who can't long forgo football and rugby. Usually closes two weeks in May or June.

PARADISO CAFE

Map p298 (041 241 39 72; Giardini della Biennale 1260; 9am-7pm, later during Biennale; Biennale) This cheery yellow mini-*palazzo* is fuelled by a steady stream of coffee and cocktails that cost less than you'd expect given the designer chairs, waterfront terrace and lack of competition – this is the only cafe within reach of anyone in stilettos at the Biennale. Watch curators woo shy artists as starchitects hold court under sun umbrellas – even between Biennales.

☆ ENTERTAINMENT

CONCERTS AT LA PIETÀ LIVE MUSIC

Map p298 (041 522 21 71; www.pietavenezia.org, in Italian; Riva degli Schiavoni; San Zaccaria) With fine acoustics, soaring Tiepolo ceilings and a long association with Vivaldi (p135), this church makes an ideal venue for live baroque music.

LABORATORIO OCCUPATO MORION CULTURAL CENTRE

Map p298 (041 520 84 37; Calle di Morion 2951; Celestia) When not busy staging environmental protests or avant-garde performance art, this counterculture social centre throws one hell of a dance party, with performances by bands from around the Veneto. Events are announced via wheat-paste posters thrown up around town.

SHOPPING

Castello is more of a residential area than a tourist zone, so the artisans you'll find in these quiet alleyways are less beholden to the mainstream tourist trade, and freer to experiment.

GIOVANNA ZANELLA SHOES

Map p298 (041 523 55 00; Calle Carminati 5641; 9.30am-1pm & 3-7pm Mon-Sat; Rialto) Woven, sculpted and crested like lagoon birds, Zanella's shoes practically demand that red carpets unfurl before you. The Venetian

LOCAL KNOWLEDGE

ART BIENNALE: A LOCAL'S GUIDE

For the last decade, designer and art director **Pamela Berry** (www.pamelaberry.com, www.veniceetc.com) has made Venice her home – and helped create tailor-made itineraries for the city and its surrounding countryside. An Art Biennale (p21) veteran, she's learned to navigate the crowds and wring the most from the sprawling phenomenon.

If you only have a weekend The first day, I would visit the pavilions in the Giardini Pubblici (p131) and then head over to the Arsenale (p127). The second day, I'd choose from the list of other exhibitions and just start wandering throughout the city.

Beating the crowds The first week of Art Biennale is the busiest, though in some ways the most interesting – the crowd is educated, sophisticated and international. After June it really quiets down, and you can easily visit without elbowing others. However, the rest of the city grows hot and crowded. September and October are wonderful, after summer crowds and heat subside.

For the glamour of it all The opening of the Biennale is very glamorous – the city fills with cocktails, events and parties until late hours. Yachts and celebrities are eager to out-do, out-party and out-glam one another. For the best people-watching, head to Harry's Bar (p73) or B-Bar (p73) at the Bauer's L'Hotel.

Refuelling Favourite places within a stone's throw of the Giardini include Corte Sconta (p138) and al Covo (p138). For fresh, organic and vegetarian takeaway, head to organic Le Spighe (p140). And for inexpensive, *casalinga* (homemade) meals, try Trattoria Alla Rampa (p140). If you have your heart set on a particular place, be sure to reserve well ahead during the weeks of Biennale.

Treasure-hunting There are collateral exhibitions and temporary pavilions scattered throughout the city during the Biennale (printed material with indications and maps is available at the entrances). Some are interesting, some not, but even if you don't end up liking the art, the locations are often worth visiting. It's like going on a treasure hunt to find some of them. There are exhibitions in palaces and churches, galleries and monasteries, abandoned buildings and far-flung islands.

Favourite far-flung venue The Scuola della Misericordia in Cannaregio is worth the hike. It was built in the mid-1500s, and its high ceilings and massive columns are attributed to the architect Jacopo Sansovino. Many Venetians still remember it as a basketball court and gym in the '70s. It's especially worth seeking out since it's only open to the public during Biennale.

designer makes shoes custom, so the answer is always: yes, you can get those peep-toe numbers in yellow and grey, size 12, extra narrow. Closed last two weeks of August.

ATELIER ALESSANDRO MERLIN ARTISANAL

Map p298 (041 522 58 95; Calle del Pestrin 3876; 3-7pm Fri, 10am-noon & 3-7pm Sat-Tue; Arsenale) Enjoy your breakfast in the nude, on a horse or atop a jellyfish – Alessandro Merlin paints them all on striking black and white cappuccino cups and saucers. His expressive characters are modern, but the sgraffito technique he uses on some of his work dates back to Roman times: designs are scratched white lines against a black background.

SIGFRIDO CIPOLATO JEWELLERY

Map p298 (041 522 84 37; San Lio Caselleria 5336; San Zaccaria) Booty worthy of pirate royalty is displayed in this fishbowl-sized window display: a constellation of diamonds in star settings on a ring, a tiny enamelled green snake sinking its fangs into a pearl, and diamond drop earrings that end in enamelled gold skulls. Though they look like heirlooms, these small wonders were worked on the premises by master jeweller Sigfridio – and you'll pay as little as half what you would at the high-end jewellery showrooms near San Marco that carry Cipolato's work.

KALIMALA CUOIERIA ARTISANAL

Map p298 (☎041 528 35 96; www.kalimala.it; Salizada San Lio 5387; ⏰9.30am-7.30pm Mon-Sat; ⛴Rialto) Sleekly supple belts with brushed-steel buckles, modern satchels, man-bags and knee-high red boots: Kalimala makes leather goods with comfort and modern style in mind. Given the natural tanning and top-flight leather, the prices are remarkably reasonable, with handmade shoes starting at around €100.

BANCO LOTTO 10 FASHION

Map p298 (☎041 522 14 39; Salizada Sant'Antonin 3478a; ⏰3.30-7.30pm Mon; 10am-1pm, 3.30-7pm Tue-Sat; ⛴San Zaccaria) Prison orange is out and plum silk velvet is in at this nonprofit boutique, whose hand-sewn fashions are the fruit of a retraining program at the women's prison on Giudecca. Designed and made by women inmates, the smartly tailored jackets, dresses and handbags often incorporate opulent silks, velvets and tapestry donated by Fortuny (p148) and Bevilacqua (p75). Even La Fenice has dressed its divas in Banco Lotto ensembles. Volunteers run the boutique and purchases fund the women prisoners' continuing career training and reintegration into society after their release.

ARTE VETRO MURANO ARTISANAL

Map p298 (☎041 523 75 14; www.artevetromurano.com; Calle delle Rasse 4613; ⏰10am-5.30 daily; ⛴San Zaccaria) Shatter glass conventions with new styles by this family of Murano glass designers. Davide Penso makes a necklace of flat puddles of orange glass that have a molten-lava look about them, and his brother Artematte's concatenation of silver and glass shimmers uncannily. Now Davide's daughter Elisa has joined in the act, mixing glass with her own felt work. Note the store sometimes closes Wednesdays when Venice is slow.

PROFILI ARTISANAL

Map p298 (☎333 674 48 52; Via Garibaldi 1596; ⏰10am-1pm & 3.30-8pm Mon-Sat; ⛴Arsenale) Francesco Vittorelli crafts a beautiful range of picture frames (made-to-measure on request) that vary from 18th-century baroque to 20th-century modernist. Besides his dextrous ways with wood and gold leaf, he is happy to share his enthusiasm for an ancient craft.

PAPIER MÂCHÉ LABORATORIO ARTISANAL

Map p298 (☎041 522 99 95; Calle Lunga Maria Formosa 5175; ⏰9am-7.30pm Mon-Sat, 10am-7pm Sun; ⛴Ospedale) Go incognito in style with the highly original masquerade masks revealing influences as diverse as Canaletto and Modigliani. Masks are moulded and painted from scratch on the premises, as are a smaller selection of ceramics.

PAOLO BRANDOLISIO ARTISANAL

Map p298 (☎041 522 41 55; www.paolobrandolisio.altervista.org; ⏰vary; ⛴Zaccaria) Inside an unassuming shed on a Castello back street, master woodcarver Paolo Brandolisio handcrafts his remarkable *forcole* – the sinuous rowlock that supports the gondolier's oar. If you order one for your gondola back home, you'll need to provide your vitals, as *forcole* are crafted to individual rowers' height and weight. Or you can settle for a miniature replica on sale in the workroom.

Giudecca, Lido & the Southern Islands

ISOLA DI SAN GIORGIO MAGGIORE | GIUDECCA | LIDO DI VENEZIA | ISOLA DI SAN LAZZARO DEGLI ARMENI | ISOLA DO SAN SERVOLO

Neighbourhood Top Five

❶ Immerse yourself in the bright serenity of two Palladio masterworks – **Chiesa di San Giorgio Maggiore** (p147) and **Chiesa del SS Redentore** (p148).

❷ Ascend San Giorgio Maggiore's soaring **campanile** (p147) to gain purchase on the labyrinth that is Venice.

❸ Rent a bike on the **Lido** (p149) and pedal your way along both the seafront promenade and the island's pastoral byways.

❹ Rub elbows with locals at Giudecca's **farmer's market** (p152) featuring organic produce grown inside Giudecca's women's prison.

❺ Suck on lagoon-sourced molluscs at one of the **unassuming eateries** (p151) along Giudecca's canalside promenade.

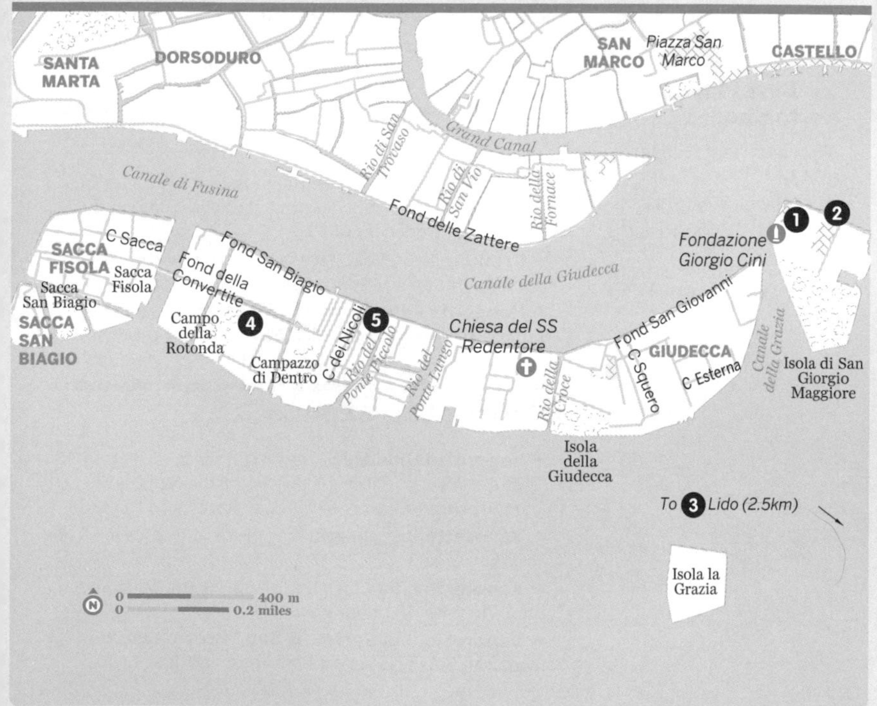

For more detail of this area, see map p301 and map p285

Lonely Planet's Top Tip

Instead of braving the lines at San Marco's campanile, seek out San Giorgio Maggiore's campanile (p147), which offers comparable views for a fraction of the wait time.

Best Places to Eat

- I Figli delle Stelle (p151)
- La Palanca (p152)
- La Favorita (p153)

For reviews, see p151

Best Places to Drink

- Skyline Rooftop Bar (p153)
- B.each (p153)
- Harry's Dolci (p151)

For reviews, see p153

Best Places to Shop

- Galleria Santa Eufemia (p149)
- Giudecca 795 (p149)
- Fortuny Tessuti Artistici (p148)

For reviews, see p148

Explore: Giudecca, Lido & the Southern Islands

Other cities have suburban sprawl; Venice has primordial monasteries floating upon a teal-blue lagoon. A welcome break from the human congestion of Venice proper, the islands do require negotiating Venice's *vaporetti*, but the views back to San Marco alone are worth the hassles. Note that some island restaurants and bars close down from November to March, especially on the Lido.

Across from Piazza San Marco lie the restrained Palladian splendours of San Giorgio Maggiore. A few more minutes by *vaporetto* lands you on Giudecca, the unofficial seventh *sestiere*. An aristocratic retreat, then industrial centre, Giudecca is now in its third act as factories become artists' lofts. Visit both islands in half a day – weekends are best, when you can also visit the Fondazione Giorgio Cini.

Beyond Giudecca lies the Lido, a svelte barrier protecting Venice from the hazards of the Adriatic. In fine weather, the Lido is worth the trip, whether it's to lie lizardlike on the sand or pedal around the island's back roads. Come for a few hours or the whole day. You can also make it your cheaper, roomier base for excursions into Venice.

Closer by, San Lazzaro degli Armeni, a refuge for 18th-century monks escaping Ottoman persecution, remains an important repository of Armenian culture. A working monastery, it can only be visited by organised tour. On the way, consider stopping at Isola di San Servolo, an insane asylum until 1978 and now a leafy university campus and home to the Museum della Follia (Madness Museum).

Local Life

- **Eating** Slick artists join rough-and-ready locals for generously served lunches at La Palanca (p152) and Al Pontil Dea Giudecca (p152).
- **Drinking** Even Venetians head to the rooftop Skyline Rooftop Bar (p153) for vast views and a vacation vibe.
- **Hangouts** Rub elbows with Venetian artists at the galleries (p149) along Giudecca's waterfront promenade.

Getting There & Away

- **Vaporetto Giudecca** *Vaporetti* lines 2, 41, 42 and N (night) make Giudecca an easy hop from San Marco or Dorsoduro, and handy to Piazzale Roma and the Lido.
- **Vaporetto San Giorgio Maggiore** Line 2 leaves from San Zaccaria.
- **Vaporetto Lido** Lines 1, 2, 51, 52, 61 and 62 connect the Lido with all major stops in Venice.
- **Vaporetto San Servolo & San Lazzaro** Line 20 from San Zaccaria serves both these islands.

TOP SIGHTS
CHIESA DI SAN GIORGIO MAGGIORE

Sunglasses are a must as you approach the Chiesa di San Giorgio: the white Istrian marble of Palladio's masterful facade is practically blinding when seen head-on. Though it's just a quick *vaporetto* ride away, most visitors only see San Giorgio across the water from San Marco. It's a great view – Palladio chose the white stone to stand out clearly across the blue lagoon waters, and cleverly set it at an angle that creates an intriguing drama while also ensuring that it catches the sun all afternoon.

The island of San Giorgio Maggiore has belonged to Benedictine monks since the 10th century, though current constructions date from the 16th century. When Palladio arrived in Venice in the 1560s, the monks asked him to remodel their dining hall. They liked his work so much, they asked him rebuild their church as well.

DON'T MISS...

- Tintoretto's *Fall of Manna* and *Last Supper*
- Views from the bell tower

PRACTICALITIES

- Map p301
- Isola di San Giorgio Maggiore
- adult/reduced €3/2
- 9.30am-12.30pm & 2.30-6.30pm Mon-Sat, to 4.30pm Oct-Apr
- San Giorgio Maggiore

Palladio's Facade

Palladio was the first architect to gracefully solve the problem of trying to graft a classical-style triangular pediment onto the facade of a Christian church, with its high central nave and much lower side aisles. Palladio's innovation: have your cake and eat it too. He uses one pediment to crown the central nave, and a lower, much wider pediment that spans both side aisles. The two interlock with a rhythmic harmony. In another fine piece of showmanship, Palladio gave the facade depth with three-quarter columns, deeply incised capitals and cornices, and shadowy sculptural niches. The dramatic play of light and shade makes it hard to look away.

Church Interior

Palladio's interior is an uncanny combination of brightness and serenity. Sunlight enters almost mysteriously through high thermal windows and is then softened and diffused by the white stucco surfaces, playing gently across the geometrical harmonies of the church's individual parts. Floors inlaid with black, white and red stone draw the eye toward the altar, beyond which lies a particularly large choir. With its rigorous application of classical motifs, it's reminiscent of a Roman theatre.

Campanile

Avoid the lines at the Campanile in Piazza San Marco and instead head to the back of this church and take the lift (€3) to the top of the 60m-high **bell tower** for stirring panoramas of Venice and its lagoon.

Tintorettos

Two enormous late works by Tintoretto flank the church's altar. On one side hangs his *Fall of Manna*, in which soft light is diffused as generously as the bread that falls from heaven. On the other side of the altar, *Last Supper* depicts Christ and his apostles at a table set at a rakish angle and depicted in a scene that looks suspiciously like a 16th-century Venetian tavern. Nearby hangs what is considered Tintoretto's last work, the moving *Deposition of Christ*.

PRISONERS, PARTIERS & PAINTERS: A SHORT HISTORY OF GIUDECCA

Giudecca's disputed history begins with its name. In southern Italy, 'Giudecca' was a common term for a city's Jewish neighbourhood. But there is little evidence that Venetian Jews made this island their home. More likely, the name comes from the Venetian term *zudega*, meaning *giudicato*, or 'the judged' – referring to the rebel families banished here during the 9th century.

However, Giudecca's most illustrious exile was not Venetian but Florentine. Michelangelo fled here from Florence in 1529, though by the time he had arrived, the aristocratic Dandolos, Mocenigos and Vendramins had transformed the island from a prison into a neighbourhood of garden villas with sweeping lagoon views – the perfect escape from the close confines of central Venice. When Venice established definitive control over the Veneto, the nobles headed inland to build villas along the Riviera Brenta and beyond. However, Giudecca continued its devil-may-care ways, and by the 18th century its pleasure gardens had become scandal-ridden for their bacchanalian revelries – this despite the presence of a half-dozen monasteries.

Napoleon put an end to both the partying and the praying, first by extinguishing the Venetian Republic in 1797 and then shutting down the monasteries in 1807. And so over the next century, Giudecca underwent yet another transformation – this time from pleasure garden to workhorse. Gardens made way for factories, tenements and military barracks. The convent of SS Cosma e Damiano was converted into a factory, its bell tower becoming a smokestack.

However, even this experiment was not meant to last. The opening of a much more efficient port in nearby Marghera spelled an early end to industrial production in Venice itself, and soon Giudecca became something of a backwater. In recent years, the large abandoned spaces and relatively cheap rents attracted a new set of exiles – artists who could no longer afford rents in central Venice. Today, SS Cosma e Damiano, first a church and then a factory, has live-work loft spaces, while a munitions depot is now the cutting-edge Teatro Junghans (see p153).

SIGHTS

Giudecca

FORTUNY TESSUTI ARTISTICI LANDMARK

Map p301 (041 522 40 78; www.fortuny.com; Fondamenta San Biagio 805; 9am-noon & 2-5pm Mon-Fri; Palanca) Marcel Proust waxed rhapsodic over Fortuny's silken cottons printed with boho-chic art nouveau patterns. Find out why at Fortuny's version of a factory outlet. Visitors can browse 260 textile designs in the showroom, but fabrication methods have been jealously guarded in the garden studio for a century. To see more of Fortuny's original designs and his home studio, head to Museo Fortuny (p60).

CHIESA DEL SS REDENTORE CHURCH

Map p301 (Campo del SS Redentore 194; admission €3, or with Chorus Pass; 10am-5pm Mon-Sat) Even from afar, you can't miss Palladio's 1577 Il Redentore, a triumph of white marble along the Grand Canal. Built to celebrate the city's deliverance from the Black Death, this magnificent edifice was completed under Antonio da Ponte (of Rialto bridge fame) in 1592. Inside the church there are scattered works by Tintoretto, Veronese and Vivarini, but the most striking work is often overlooked. Inside, over the portal, Paolo Piazza's strikingly modern 1619 *Gratitude of Venice for Liberation from the Plague* shows the city held aloft by angels in sobering shades of grey.

Survival is never taken for granted in this tidal town, and to give thanks during the **Festa del Redentore** (Feast of the Redeemer; p21), Venetians have been making the wobbly pilgrimage across the canal on a shaky pontoon bridge from the Zattere since 1578.

CHIESA DI SANT'EUFEMIA CHURCH

Map p301 (041 532 29 20; Fondamenta Sant'Eufemia 680; by appointment for groups of 20 or more; Palanca) Four women saints were crowded under the roof of the original AD 890 church here, but Sts Dorothy, Tecla and Erasma weren't as big a draw as Byzantine Christian martyr Euphemia. She was thrown to hungry lions, but after biting off her hand, the lions refused to eat her holy virgin flesh. The simple Veneto-Byzantine structure you see today dates from the 14th century, with some capitals and columns inside preserved from the 11th century. The pleasing Doric portico attributed to Michele Sanmicheli was added c 1596. If you can't get up a group of 20 other people, try attending Mass on Sundays at 11am.

GIUDECCA 795 GALLERY

Map p301 (☎340 8798327; www.giudecca795.com; Fondamenta San Biagio 795; ⏱3-8pm; ⛴Palanca) Founded to promote local artists of all kinds, this quirky and welcoming gallery displays (and sells) a wide range of works by both established and young artists, most of whom have a strong connection with Venice itself. There is also a shop attached with quirky, Venice-related keepsakes.

GALLERIA SANTA EUFEMIA GALLERY

Map p301 (☎041 296 02 40; www.eufemiagallery.com; Fondamenta Santa Eufemia 597; ⏱10am-12.30pm & 3-6.30pm Mon-Sat; ⛴Palanca) Specialising in paintings and drawings of Venice itself, this sophisticated little gallery is about five notches above the usual tourist paint-by-numbers fare. If you can't afford the paintings, small original drawings and engravings (from €40) make an original, and relatively affordable, memento of your trip.

Lido Di Venezia

LIDO BEACHES BEACH

(Lido di Venezia; deposit/chair/umbrella & chair/hut around €5/6/11/17; ⏱most beaches 9.30am-7pm May Sep; ⛴Lido) Beach chairs and bronzed lifeguards may seem a world apart from muggy, ripe Venice in summer, but they're only a 15-minute ferry ride away. Most Lido beaches charge for chair, umbrella and hut rental, but the tanning crowd thins out and rates drop a couple of euros after 2pm. To avoid obligatory fees and throngs of local weekenders, rent a bike and head south to Alberoni and other more pristine beaches.

LIDO ON BIKE CYCLING

Map p285 (☎041 526 80 19; www.lidoonbike.it in Italian; Gran Viale 21b; bikes per 90min/day €5/9; ⏱9am-7pm daily, weather permitting, mid-Mar–Sep;

TOP SIGHTS
FONDAZIONE GIORGIO CINI

A defunct naval academy has been cleverly converted into a shipshape gallery for the Fondazione Giorgio Cini. Founded in the 1950s by industrialist Vittorio Cini – a survivor of Dachau – the foundation houses a remarkable collection of original manuscripts and also hosts temporary exhibitions and other cultural events. The organisation also helps organise tours of the remarkable Benedictine monastery attached to Palladio's San Giorgio Maggiore.

The monastery encompasses a 17th-century library as well as a **monumental staircase** by Baldassare Longhena. The **Chiostro dei Cipressi** is the oldest extant part of the complex, completed in 1526 in an early-Renaissance style. A stroll through the monastery's gardens leads to the outdoor **Teatro Verde**, built in the 1950s and sometimes used for summer performances.

Palladio also designed the monastery's impressive **refectory**, where Veronese's masterpiece *Nozze di Cana* (Wedding at Cana) took pride of place – at least until Napoleon sent it home to the Louvre. In its place hangs Tintoretto's *Wedding of the Virgin*. Palladio also designed the **Chiostro del Palladio**, whose arches line up with military precision.

DON'T MISS...

- Chiostro del Palladio
- Palladio's Refectory
- Longhena's staircase
- Tintoretto's *Wedding of the Virgin*

PRACTICALITIES

- Map p301
- ☎041 220 12 15
- www.cini.it
- adult/reduced €12/10
- Isola di San Giorgio Maggiore
- ⏱guided visits in English & French from 11am Sat & Sun
- ⛴San Giorgio Maggiore

LIDO & THE TEMPTATION OF THOMAS MANN

In 1857, pleasure-friendly Venice invented a newfangled temptation to lure Europe's leisured classes – beachgoing. In a few years, Lido became the world's most exclusive seaside resort, and is still defined by the 'Stile Liberty' (art nouveau) villas from its heyday from 1890 until WWI.

When Thomas Mann paid a visit in 1911, he stayed at the Grand Hotel des Bains (currently closed while it is being turned into private residences) where, famously, he caught a glimpse of a beautiful 13-year-old Polish boy. According to his wife, the boy was 'tremendously attractive' and perhaps succumbing to Venetian permissiveness, Mann allowed himself to grow 'fascinated' by the boy. 'My husband was always watching him and his companions on the beach,' wrote his wife Katia in her 1976 memoir *Unwritten Memories*.

A year later, Mann had transformed this 'fascination' into the great novella: *Death in Venice*. 'My husband transferred to Aschenbach [the novel's main character] the pleasure he actually took in this charming boy, stylising it into extreme passion,' writes Katia in her memoir. Mann's powerful story has itself been transformed into an opera by Benjamin Britten and a critically acclaimed movie by Luchino Visconti – parts of which were filmed on location at the Grand Hotel des Bains itself.

Lido) To tour at your own pace, rent a set of wheels from this friendly bike place near the Lido *vaporetto* stop, with reasonable prices that includes a free map with recommended routes. You must have official identification showing you're at least 18 to rent. And remember to mind the traffic.

MALAMOCCO TOWN

off Map p285 (Lido) Pass over Ponte di Borge to explore the canals and *calli* (lanes) of a less overwhelming lagoon town, with just a few *campi* (fields), churches, *osterie* (wine bar), and a Gothic *palazzo* (mansion) to explore. A miniature version of Venice right down to the lions of St Mark on medieval facades, Malamocco was actually the lagoon capital from 742 to 811 before Venice took over.

ANTICO CIMITERO ISRAELITICO CEMETERY

Map p285 (041 71 53 59; admission through Museo Ebraico, adult/student €8.50/7; Lido) This quiet, overgrown garden was Venice's main Jewish community cemetery from 1386 until the 18th century. The bulk of the tombstones were discovered by construction workers in the late 19th century, and it was decided to set them up in some sort of orderly fashion. They range in design from Venetian Gothic to distinctly Ottoman, and one-hour tours organised by the Museo Ebraico (p117) provide insights into the life and times of the people buried here. There are no fixed times for tours; advanced reservations are required.

PALAZZO DELLA MOSTRA DEL CINEMA NOTABLE BUILDING

Map p285 (Lido) A seaside Fascist monument, this rigid airport-terminal structure seems as ill-suited to the playboy Lido as a woolly bathing suit. And C+S Associates' 2003 'Wave' entrance just begs for a skateboard. But once the red carpets are rolled out and the stars arrive for the Venice International Film Festival (see p21), it all makes sense.

Isola di San Lazzaro degli Armeni

Once the site of a Benedictine hospice for pilgrims and then a leper colony, this island was given to Armenian monks fleeing Ottoman persecution in 1717. The entire island is still a working monastery. To visit San Lazzaro, you must take the 3.10pm *vaporetto* 20 from San Zaccaria.

MONASTERY OF SAN LAZZARO DEGLI ARMENI CHURCH

Map p301 (041 526 01 04; adult/student & child €6/4.50; tours 3.25-5pm Sun) This monastery became an important centre of learning as well as a repository of Armenian culture. And because it was the only monastery in Venice spared pillaging by Napoleon's troops, it remains so today. Access to the island is by tour only. You generally start in the **church**, which sparkles with mosaics. After passing through the 18th-century **refectory**, you'll head upstairs to the **library**, which is divided into several rooms with curio cabinets of antiquities from Ancient Egypt, Sumeria and India, plus a precious collection of books. One room is reserved specifically for Armenian art and artefacts.

An Egyptian mummy and a 15th-century Indian throne are the rather quirky main features of the room dedicated to the memory of **Lord Byron**, who stayed on the island in search of inner peace. True to his eccentric nature, he could often be seen swimming from the island to the Grand Canal – Byron was never one to let a body of water come between him and a hot date.

Lastly, you reach a modern circular gallery that contains precious **manuscripts**, many of them Armenian, including one dating to the 6th century.

Isola di San Servolo

From the 7th to the 17th centuries, Benedictine monks made this island their home. From the 18th century, San Servolo served as hospital for plague victims and then an insane asylum until 1978. Venice International University is now headquartered on the island, offering accredited university coursework through reciprocal arrangements with several European, US and Japanese universities. Program strengths are art history, musicology and history.

While the museum requires advance booking, the grassy island itself is public and makes for a pleasantly leafy stroll not so far from the madding crowds.

For San Servolo, take *vaporetto* 20 from San Zaccaria.

MUSEO DELLA FOLLIA MUSEUM

(Museum of Madness; ☎041 524 01 19; www.fondazionesanservolo.it; admission €3; ⊙phone bookings 9.30am-5.30pm Mon-Thu, to 3.30pm Fri) Part of San Servolo's former insane asylum has been turned into a museum. Two intriguing rooms are full of paraphernalia and explanations of the days when a stint at San Servolo rarely guaranteed a cure. In the first room, find a series of before and after photos of 19th-century inmates, many of whose chief malady was extreme poverty, with hallucinations and nonspecific symptoms resulting from bad nutrition and vitamin deficiency. In the main room, you'll see instruments used for electroshock therapy, while in an annexe there are other 'therapeutic' instruments, including chains and straitjackets.

Of particular interest is the ancient pharmacy, where for centuries many of Venice's medicines were concocted – including various 'cures' for syphilis, a common cause of mental-health problems in Venice, even after the discovery of penicillin. Since most penicillin in Italy was set aside for the military well into the 20th century, it remained a sought-after street drug. The guided tour of the island, which must be booked in advance, also takes in the park and modest church.

EATING

Giudecca

TOP CHOICE I FIGLI DELLE STELLE ITALIAN €€

Map p301 (☎041 523 00 04; www.ifiglidellestelle.it; Zitelle 70; meals €30-40; ⊙12.30-2.30pm & 7-10pm Tue-Sun; closed mid-Nov–mid-Mar; Zitelle) Beware of declarations of love at one of Venice's most romantic restaurants: are you sure that's not Pugliese chef Luigi's velvety, heartwarming pasta and soup talking? A creamy fava-bean mash with biting chicory and fresh tomatoes coats the tongue in a naughty way, and the lagoon-fresh mixed grill for two with langoustine, sole and fresh sardines is quite a catch. Given the cuisine and waterfront views of San Marco, this place also makes for a surprisingly reasonably priced date.

HARRY'S DOLCI MODERN VENETIAN €€€

Map p301 (☎041 522 48 44; www.cipriani.com; Fondamenta San Biagio 773, Giudecca; meals €80-120; ⊙10.30am-11pm Wed-Mon Apr-Oct; Palanca) The sun-washed Tiffany-blue sun canopy along the waterfront marks out this home away from home for the designer-sunglasses set. The service is low-key and the decor retro (think bistro chairs and subway tile), though the prices have more than kept up with inflation. Still, for the €15 price of *dolci* (sweets), you could linger through the better part of an afternoon inside this bosom of the good life.

MISTRÀ VENETIAN €€

Map p301 (☎041 522 07 43; Calle Michelangelo 53c, Giudecca; meals €20-35; ⊙lunch & dinner Tue-Sun; Zitelle) Head here for authentically Venetian seafood, including generous plates

WORTH A DETOUR

PELLESTRINA & CHIOGGIA

Stretching south of Lido and repeating its long sinuous shape, Pellestrina reminds you what the lagoon might have been like if Venice had never been dreamed of. Almost perfectly flat and impinged on by only a trickle of cars, Pellestrina makes ideal biking country for enthusiasts of all levels. Your best bet is to wait for a sunny day and then rent a bike (p149) near the Lido *vaporetto* stop. Head south until you reach the ferry that crosses the narrow channel dividing Lido from Pellestrina.

The 11km-long barrier island is dotted with little villages, mostly populated by farmers and fishermen (population about 2900). On the lagoon side, look for the shantylike fishermen's shacks built over beds of mussels. Enjoy these and other lagoon specialities at **Ristorante Da Celeste** (041 96 70 43; Via Vianelli 625; closed Nov-Mar). Towards the southern end of the island, you'll find a bird-watching sanctuary in the region of Ca' Roman.

Much of Pellestrina's seafront is lined by a remarkable feat of 18th-century engineering known as the **Murazzi**. Although not immediately impressive to modern eyes, these massive sea walls represent Herculean handiwork from a preindustrial age. Designed to keep high seas from crashing into the lagoon, they remain an effective breakwater even today. On calm days, long stretches of grey-sand beaches separate the Murazzi from the sea; in rough weather, the waves crash against the stones.

If you've started out early, consider catching the ferry at the southern tip of Pellestrina to explore Chioggia, the lagoon's other island city. Like Venice, Chioggia is laced with canals and medieval churches done up in baroque clothing, including a **cathedral** (www.cattedralechioggia.it; Rione Duomo 77) rebuilt in the 17th century by Baldassarre Longhena. Remember to look both ways before crossing the street because Chioggia also has cars.

of briny clam pasta and genuine Genovese pesto. The chef, who hails from Liguria, also recommends *zuppa di pesce* (soup thick with seafood) and ravioli stuffed with shrimp. Terrace seating in warm weather completes the picture. You won't regret the calories in the homemade desserts.

LA PALANCA — VENETIAN €€

Map p301 (041 528 77 19; Fondamenta al Ponte Piccolo 448, Giudecca; meals €20-30; 8am-8.30pm Mon-Sat) Lunchtime competition for canalside tables is stiff, but the views of the Zattere make *tagliolini ai calamaretti* (narrow ribbon pasta with tiny calamari) and tuna steak with sesame and balsamic vinegar taste even better. At €7 to €9 for full plates of pasta, you'll be forking over half what diners pay along the waterfront in San Marco, while enjoying what are arguably even better views. Dinner is not served, but you can get *cicheti* at the bar right up to closing time.

AL PONTIL DEA GIUDECCA — VENETIAN €

Map p301 (041 528 69 85; Calle Redentore 197a, Giudecca; meals €15; 8am-8pm Mon-Sat; Redentore) Asking for a menu here is like asking for one at your grandma's house. You'll have one of the three daily specials and like it – really – and by the time lunch is over you'll feel like you should offer to help tidy up. For €12, you can expect a generous plate of pasta, a savoury meat or fish dish, a *contorno* (a vegie side dish), and a view of Venice – if you get the one window seat. Note that the bar is open for *cicheti* all day, but solid meals are only available at lunchtime Monday to Friday.

ESU — ITALIAN €

Map p301 (Corte Grande, Giudecca; meals €12; noon-2.30 Mon-Fri & 7-9pm Mon-Thu; Santa Eufemia) Once a communist collective and now a cafeteria catering to university students, this place looks like a former boatshed because, well, that's what it is. Meals are better than your average dorm fair, and include pasta, a main, a vegie or salad and both water and wine – all for €12.

THURSDAY ORGANIC MARKET — SELF-CATERING €

Map p301 (Fondamenta delle Convertite, Giudecca; Thursday morning; Palanca) Every Thursday morning, locals jostle for the best of the organic produce available at this unusual twist on a farmer's market. In this case, the farmers happen also to be prisoners of the adjacent women's correctional facility. Proceeds help pay for job retraining and postrelease reintegration.

Lido Di Venezia

LA FAVORITA SEAFOOD €€

Map p285 (041 526 1626; Via Francesco Duodo 33, Lido; meals €35-50; lunch Wed-Sun, dinner Tue-Sun, closed Jan–mid-Feb; Lido) Spider-crab *gnochetti* (mini-gnocchi), fish risotto and *crudi* have all helped La Favorita earn its name. Book ahead for the wisteria-filled garden and well ahead during the film festival, when songbirds are practically out-sung by the ringtones of movie moguls.

BUDDHA INDIAN €

Map p285 (041 77 06 18; Gran Viale 28/b, Lido; meals €15-30; 10am-midnight Tue-Sun, to 2am Jun-Aug; Lido) A short walk from the beach, this simple but stylishly mod eatery offers up an intriguing fusion of Italian and Indian cuisines, from curry-inflected *cicheti* (available all day) to mains combining Veneto produce and fish infused with Indian spices and condiments.

DA TIZIANO PIZZA, CICHETI €

Map p285 (041 526 72 91; Via Sandro Gallo 96, Lido; pizzas €6-8.50; lunch & dinner Tue-Sun; Lido) Keeping it low-key on the Lido, this local hangout serves decent pizza at fair prices, plus respectable *cicheti* to a regular happy-hour crowd. If movie stars drop by, that can't be helped – this is the handiest pizzeria to the Palazzo della Mostra del Cinema.

PIZZERIA ALLA BOTTE PIZZA €

Map p285 (041 526 06 81; Gran Viale 57/a, Lido; pizzas €6-10; 11.30am-3.30pm & 6-10.30pm, closed Nov, Dec & Jan; Lido) Boasting one of the only wood-burning ovens in Venice, this touristy-looking place actually offers up good pizza with a thickish crust that has just the right proportion of chewiness. While there are other dishes available, it's best to stick to pizza.

MAGICHE VOGLIE GELATO €

Map p285 (041 526 13 85; Gran Viale 47/g, Lido; Lido) The best gelato in Lido is made on premises at this family-owned place right between the *vaporetto* stop and the beach.

DRINKING & NIGHTLIFE

Currently, the Lido's famous Grand Hotel des Bains is undergoing renovations, but when it reopens, the scene-makers are sure to flock once again to the hotel's illustrious Colony Bar.

SKYLINE ROOFTOP BAR BAR

Map p301 (041 272 33 11; www.molinostuckyhilton.com; Fondamenta San Biagio 810, Giudecca; noon-3.30pm & 5pm-1am; Palanca) From white-sneaker cruise passengers to the €1000 sunglasses set, the rooftop bar at the Hilton Molino Stucky wows everyone with its vast panorama over Venice and the lagoon, with drink prices to match. From May to September, the bar offers a lunch buffet from noon to 3pm. Note that the bar closes on Mondays from November to February.

B.EACH NIGHTCLUB

Map p285 (Lungomare D'Annunzio 20, Lido; 8.30am-midnight, May–mid-Sep; Lido) After a taxing day on a Lido lounge chair, there's nothing better than unwinding on a four-poster beach bed. At this bold beach venue, days flow into nights with a parade of diversions: a free library of books and magazines, designated beach sport and chill-out zones, live-music sets, cocktail bars, open-air cinema and weekend DJ sets that will keep you dancing until you face-plant on the sand.

ENTERTAINMENT

TEATRO JUNGHANS THEATRE

Map p301 (041 241 19 74; www.teatrojunghans.it, in Italian; Piazza Junghans 494, Giudecca; prices vary; Redentore) Cutting-edge theatre takes on a literal meaning at this three-sided stage, nicknamed Teatro Formaggino (Little Cheese Theatre) because it looks like a wedge of cheese. The experimental theatre seats 150, but you're not expected to just sit there: Teatro Junghans offers workshops on costume design, mask-acting, and commedia dell'arte (archetypal improvisational comedy). If you'd rather leave that sort of thing to professionals, check the online calendar for performances when the company is in residence.

Murano, Burano & the Northern Islands

MURANO | BURANO | TORCELLO | LE VIGNOLE & SANT' ERASMO | ISOLA DI CERTOSA | ISOLA DI SAN MICHELE

Neighbourhood Top Five

❶ Watch and learn as tiny glass squares form vivid cautionary tales at **Cattedrale di Santa Maria Assunta** (p156), where devilish imps steal souls and the attention away from a glittering, golden heaven, filled with heavenly creatures and lagoon poppies.

❷ Witness artistry in action at the glass-blowing showrooms in **Murano** (p161) and reward their originality with your purchases.

❸ Bask in sun and culinary glory with a feast on the vineyard patio at **Venissa** (p160).

❹ Watch colourful houses wiggle with delight at their reflections in the canals of **Burano** (p157).

❺ Explore remote islands by sailboat, barge or houseboat, or row like a regatta champ (p26).

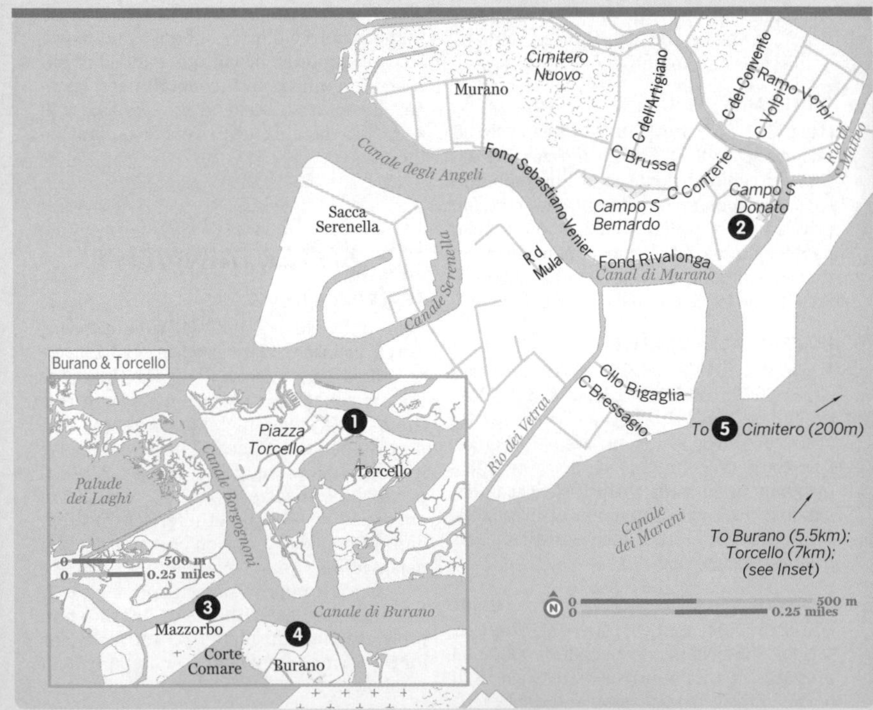

For more detail of this area, see Map p302

Explore: Murano, Burano & the Northern Islands

Reaching the northern corner of the lagoon takes awhile, but once you've made the trip, you'll wish it took longer. On the way to the glass-blowing furnaces of Murano and stunning mosaics of Santa Assunta on Torcello, you'll pass the haunting island cemetery of Isola di San Michele, lagoon ibis thoughtfully perched on narrow *barene* (shoals) off San Francesco del Deserto, and colourful fishermen's houses on Burano. Boating trips to wild Le Vignole and sailing lessons on Isola di Certosa are handy excuses to linger on the lagoon – and with freshly caught seafood, island-grown vegetables and even local vineyards, there might never be a convincing enough reason to leave.

Local Life

➡ **Picnics** Lunch is a highlight of sunny northern lagoon days, even without reservations at Venissa (p160). Pack a picnic to enjoy on Mazzorbo (p157), the meadow behind Cattedrale di Santa Maria Assunta (p156) on Torcello, or among the picturesque ruins of Forte Sant'Andrea on Le Vignole (p159).

➡ **Regatta revelry** The biggest event on the northern lagoon calendar is the 32km Vogalonga long row (p20) from Venice to Murano and Burano and back each May. Find a patch of grass on Mazzorbo, invite the rowers to pull over by waving a bottle of *prosecco* and let the party unfold.

➡ **Islands after hours** Stores and restaurants close up shop quickly once day-trippers clear out around 5.30pm, but stick around to enjoy happy hour with the local crowd at Caffè-Bar Palmisano (p161) or Gelateria Al Ponte (p160).

➡ **Overnight retreats** Quit worrying about ferry schedules and enjoy a relaxed stay at affordable rates at Locanda Cipriani (p202), Murano Palace (p202), or Venissa (p202).

Getting There & Away

➡ **Vaporetto** To reach Murano, the most regular services are the DM line from Ferrovia and the 41 and 42 lines from Fondamente Nouve. To reach Burano and Mazzorbo, take the LN line from Fondamente Nuove or from the Murano-Faro stop. From Burano, the T line is a short hop to Torcello. Line 13 heads from Fondamente Nuove to Murano and onward to Le Vignole and Sant'Erasmo.

Lonely Planet's Top Tip

Plan your trip carefully around your priorities – or it can be tricky to squeeze in Murano glass, Burano photography, Mazzorbo lunches and Torcello nature and history between the *vaporetto* hours (9am to 5.30pm). Hit the outer islands first, and work your way back to Murano – it's faster and easier to reach from Venice if you need to return for more glass. Also, you don't want to carry glass purchases around the nature trails.

Best Places to Eat

➡ Venissa (p160)

➡ Locanda Cipriani (p161)

➡ Cucina da Omar (p162)

➡ Alla Maddelena (p161)

➡ Busa alla Torre (p160)

For reviews, see p160 

Best Places to Drink

➡ Terrazzamare (p162)

➡ Il Muretto (p162)

➡ Marina Club (p162)

➡ Caffè-Bar Palmisano (p161)

➡ Locanda Cipriani (p161)

For reviews, see p160 

Best Lagoon Photo-Ops

➡ Brightly painted houses reflected in Burano canals (p157)

➡ Poses in Attila the Hun's throne in Torcello (p158)

➡ Flowers on poets' graves at Isola di San Michele (p159)

➡ Cormorants holding their wings out to dry on sunny Mazzorbo (p157)

➡ Rock-star shots at ruined Forte Sant'Andrea on Le Vignole (p159)

TOP SIGHTS
CATTEDRALE DI SANTA MARIA ASSUNTA

Life choices are presented in no uncertain terms in Santa Maria Assunta's vivid mosaic cautionary tale: look ahead to a golden afterlife amid hovering saints and a beatific Madonna in the apse, or turn your back on her to face the wrath of a blue devil gloating over lost souls. This scene has all the drama of a major motion picture, only it is told in over a million tiny, individually hand-cut glass tesserae – and it first premiered at least a millennium ago.

Architecture
Restrained brick exteriors betray no hint of the colourful scenes unfolding inside the Byzantine cathedral of Santa Maria Assunta, first built c AD 639. The structure you see today dates from the first expansion of the church c 824 and rebuilding in 1008, making it the oldest Venetian monument still in its original Byzantine-Romanesque condition. The soaring bell tower offers commanding bird's-eye lagoon vistas, but is currently undergoing restoration.

Madonna & Last Judgment Mosaics
You can't miss the Madonna, rising like the sun above a field of lagoon corn poppies in the 12th-century golden eastern apse mosaic. To ensure medieval pilgrims left the cathedral set on redemption, the back wall vividly depicts the dire consequences of dodging biblical commandments. The Last Judgment mosaic shows the Adriatic as a sea nymph ushering souls lost at sea towards St Peter, who's jangling the keys to Paradise like God's own bouncer. A sneaky devil tips the scales of justice that angels are using to weigh souls, while the Antichrist's minions drag sinners into a hell already crammed with greedy bejewelled merchants, bloated gluttons chewing on their own hands, and envious cadavers with snakes coming out of their eye-sockets.

At the centre, in a mystical almond (representing the seed of salvation), is Jesus, offering reassuring words to troubled souls: 'I am God and Man; I am not far from the guilty, but close to the repentant.' Oversized angels flanking the scene are the result of a 19th-century restoration; one of the original is shown tidying up after the apocalypse, wrapping up the starry sky.

Chapel Mosaics
The right-hand chapel is capped with another 12th-century mosaic with traces of an earlier 9th-century design, showing saints Augustine, Ambrose, Martin and Gregory amid splendid, symbolic plants: lilies (representing purity), grapes and wheat (representing the wine and host of the holy sacrament), and corn-poppy buds (evoking Torcello's island setting). The mosaic inscription in Latin is mystical poetry: 'God is three people at once, but one in essence/He covers the earth with grass, lays down the sea and illuminates the sky.'

Key Works
Polychrome marble floors are another medieval masterpiece, with swirling designs and interlocking wheels forming an intricate, almost mechanical geometry. Saints line up like holy soldiers atop the gilded iconostasis, their gravity foiled by a Byzantine screen teeming with peacocks, rabbits and lion cubs and other tumbling, fanciful beasts. Commanding the scene at the front is a bishop's throne atop 10 steps representing the Ten Commandments.

DON'T MISS...
- Last Judgment mosaic
- Madonna apse mosaic
- Chapel saints mosaic
- Polychrome marble floors
- Iconostasis
- Bishop's throne

PRACTICALITIES
- Map p303
- Piazza Torcello
- admission & cathedral audio-guide €6, incl museum €8
- 10.30am-6pm Mar-Oct, 10am-5pm Nov-Feb; last entry 30min before closing
- Torcello

SUNDAY ISLAND-HOPPING

➡ **Lido** (p149) Take a 15-minute *vaporetto* ride to beaches, bicycling and tours of the Antico Cimitero Israelitico.

➡ **Murano** (p157) Many shops are closed, but major attractions are open: Museo del Vetro, Murano Collezioni and Chiesa dei SS Maria e Donato.

➡ **Burano** (p157) Find photo-ops galore amid the artist's palette of brightly coloured houses, enjoy inspired lagoon cuisine at Venissa and loll the day away in Mazzorbo.

➡ **Torcello** (p158) Discover glittering, hidden treasures in the wilds of Torcello at Cattedrale di Santa Maria Assunta and Museo di Torcello, and get cosy in Hemingway's room at Locanda Cipriani.

➡ **Le Vignole** (p159) Drift the day away on a boat trip with **Terra e Acqua** (p14), enjoy lunch moored along the canal and a hike to Venice's deserted island fortress.

SIGHTS

Murano

Venetians have been working in crystal and glass since the 10th century, but due to the fire hazards of glass-blowing, the industry was moved to the island of Murano in the 13th century. Woe betide the glass-blower with wanderlust: trade secrets were so jealously guarded that any glass worker who left the city was guilty of treason and subject to assassination. Today, glass artisans ply their trade at workshops along Murano's **Fondamenta dei Vetrai** marked by *'Fornace'* (Furnace) signs, secure in the knowledge that their wares set a standard that can't be replicated elsewhere.

Glass-blowers are no longer obliged to live near the *fornaci* (furnaces), and after many head home at night to Venice or Mestre, Murano seems deserted. To Murano, the most regular services are the 41 and 42.

MUSEO DEL VETRO — MUSEUM

Map p302 (Museum of Glass; ☎041 73 95 86; www.museicivicivenezian i.it; Fondamenta Giustinian 8; adult/reduced €8/5.50, or with Museum Pass free; ⏰10am-6pm Thu-Tue Apr-Oct, to 5pm Nov-Mar; ⛴Museo-Murano) Since 1861, Murano's glass-making prowess has earned pride of place in this palace. Downstairs there are priceless and surprisingly intact 1500-year-old examples of iridescent Roman glass, but upstairs, Murano truly shows off in the frescoed **Salone Maggiore** (Grand Salon), with displays ranging from gold-flecked 17th-century winged aventurine goblets to a botanically convincing 1930s glass cactus. An adjoining salon geeks out with the technical details of glass-making processes innovated on Murano, helpfully illustrated with examples of Murano specialities ranging from mosaic miniatures to *murrine* (flower-patterned beads), including blue-and-white Venetian trade beads. The museum building itself is a 15th-century mansion that served as the seat of the Torcello bishopric from 1659 until its dissolution in the early 19th century, when it briefly became Murano's town hall.

CHIESA DEI SS MARIA E DONATO — CHURCH

Map p302 (☎041 73 90 56; Campo San Donato; ⏰9am-noon & 3.30-7pm Mon-Sat, 3.30-7pm Sun) Fire-breathing is the unifying theme of Murano's medieval church, with its 12th-century gilded glass **Madonna apse mosaic** made in Murano's red-hot *fornace* (furnaces) and the legendary bones of a dragon hanging behind the **altar**. According to local lore, these are bones of a beast slayed by San Donato, whose mortal remains were also brought all the way from Cephalonia as relics. The other masterpiece here is underfoot: a Byzantine-style, 12th-century mosaic pavement. Save the church visit until after the museum and stores close around 5pm to 6pm.

Burano & Mazzorbo

Once Venice's lofty Gothic architecture leaves you feeling slightly loopy from all those flights of fancy, Burano brings you down to earth and back to your senses with a reviving shock of colour. The 50-minute Laguna Nord (LN) ferry ride from the Fondamente Nuove is packed with photographers bounding into

Burano's backstreets, snapping away at pea-green stockings hung to dry between hot-pink, royal-blue and caution-orange houses.

Burano is also famed for its lemon-scented S-shaped *buranelli* biscuits and handmade lace. At the time of writing, the **Museo del Merletto** (Lace Museum; www.museiciviciveneziani.it) remains closed for expansion, and much of the lace stock for sale in Burano boutiques was imported – be sure to ask for a guarantee of authenticity. Near the Museo, one tree stands in a quiet, sombre *campo,* recently renamed to commemorate a tragedy with ripple effects all the way to Burano: Corte Settembre 11, 2001.

Neighbouring Mazzorbo is a prime spot for a stroll past pleasant gardens, a playground, seemingly sacrilegious pit stops in a public toilet in the apse of a former chapel, and leisurely, worth-the-ferry-ride lunches (see p160). For both Burano and Mazzorbo, take the LN from Fondamente Nuove via Murano.

FREE CHIESA DI SAN MARTINO CHURCH

Map p303 (041 73 00 96; Piazza Galuppi; 8am-noon & 3-7pm Mon-Sat; Burano) This 16th-century church is worth a peek for the Giambattista Tiepolo's 1725 *Crocifissione,* showing Mary gone grey with grief, and Giovanni di Niccolo Mansueti's fanciful *Flight from Egypt* (c 1492), which looks suspiciously like Torcello, plus sundry griffons, lions and what appears to be a llama. The Russian icon near the altar is the Madonna di Kazan, a masterpiece of enamelwork with astonishingly bright, lifelike eyes.

Torcello

On the pastoral island of Torcello, a three-minute T line ferry-hop from Burano, sheep outnumber the 14 or so human residents. This bucolic backwater was once a Byzantine metropolis of 20,000, but rivalry with Venice and a succession of malaria epidemics systematically reduced its splendour and population. Of its original nine churches and two abbeys, all that remain are mosaic-filled Cattedrale di Santa Maria Assunta (p156) and simple but striking 11th-century brick **Chiesa di Santa Fosca** (10am-4.30pm daily), which houses the bones of an early Roman martyr transported here from Libya by a Venetian sailor named Vitale.

On leisurely walks around the island, you'll spot a few relics, including a worn stone throne Attila the Hun is said to have occupied when he passed through the area in the 5th century, along with a variety of lagoon birds – it's been 80 years since Ernest Hemingway's hunting parties gave them cause to fear.

From Burano, the T *vaporetto* runs every half hour to Torcello until evening. Follow the path along the canal, Fondamenta Borgognoni, which leads you on a 10-minute walk from the ferry stop to the heart of the island.

MUSEO DI TORCELLO MUSEUM

Map p303 (Piazza Torcello; admission incl cathedral €8; 10.30am-5pm Tue-Sun Apr-Oct; Torcello) Across the square from the cathedral in the 13th-century **Palazzo del Consiglio** is this museum dedicated to Torcello's bygone splendours. Downstairs are early Byzantine mosaics painstakingly assembled from half-centimetre tesserae; upstairs is a daunting display of heavy medieval culinary irons, used by nuns to stamp holy host wafers.

A captivating collection of ancient curiosities is upstairs in the 11th- to 12th-century **Palazzo dell'Archivio**, opposite the Palazzo del Consiglio. Roman items unearthed at the now-vanished Altino include charming, enigmatic bronze miniatures: a poppy, a chicken's claw, and a dolphin. Elegantly incised Egyptian bronze mirrors date from the 3rd to 4th century BC, while that creepy fibule shaped like a leech is from the 7th to 8th century BC. Venetian obsession with little dogs is witnessed in 3rd- to 5th-century bronzes, but the show-stopper is a lively first-century Greek marble bust of a baby, lips parted as though to utter his first word.

Le Vignole & Sant'Erasmo

Welcome to the Venetian countryside! Together the two islands of **Vignole Vecchie** and **Vignole Nuove** almost equal Venice in size, but any comparison ends there. Like nearby **Sant'Erasmo**, the rural lagoon landscapes of **Le Vignole** are covered in fields, groves and vineyards rather than endless monuments, and people are few and far between. *Vaporetto* 13 runs to Le Vignole and Sant'Erasmo from Fondamente Nuove via Murano (Faro stop).

Le Vignole

Le Vignole long produced most of the doge's wine, and its 50 inhabitants still live mainly from agriculture. The southeastern end is a disused military zone, but a couple of *osterie* on the inhabited southwestern tip of the island occasionally open on sunny weekends and in summer to accommodate intrepid lagoon explorers. A promontory off southeastern Le Vignole ends in the Isola di Sant'Andrea, which has the best-preserved fort on the lagoon: 16th-century **Forte Sant'Andrea**.

Built by Michele Sanmicheli and commonly known as the Castello da Mar (Sea Castle), the fort features low-level cannons pointing out to sea. The last time these guns were fired was in 1797; they managed to dissuade one of Napoleon's warships. There was once a chain from the fort across to the (now gone) Forte di San Nicolò on the Lido, rendering entry into the heart of the lagoon by enemy warships virtually impossible. The guns and chain were rarely needed, since the lagoon was notoriously difficult to navigate without insider knowledge. The Venetian Municipality is reclaiming the disused military zone on Isola di Sant'Andrea as a park, and you'll find a well-kept path and informational signage amid the barracks and fort; visits are possible on lagoon boat trips (see p26).

Sant' Erasmo

Sant' Erasmo is known as the *orto di Venezia* (Venice's garden), and if you're visiting in mid-May, don't miss the island's **Sagra di Violetti** (Festival of Sant'Erasmo purple artichokes; www.carciofosanterasmo.it, in Italian). About 750 people live on the island, many around the Chiesa ferry stop. According to the Roman chronicler Martial, Sant'Erasmo was once dotted with the country villas of wealthy citizens of the now-disappeared mainland centre of Altinum (Altino). The island bore the direct brunt of waves rolling in from the Adriatic until the 1800s, when construction of dykes at the Porto del Lido lagoon entrance led to a build-up of sediment that created Punta Sabbioni, buffering Sant'Erasmo from sea tides.

It's a half-hour walk from the Chiesa stop to the more southern Capannone stop, and another 15 minutes east to a beach near the round, partly ruined **Torre Massimiliana**, a 19th-century Austrian fort sometimes used for art exhibitions. **Il Lato Azzurro** (p202) is a favourite summertime retreat for artists, offering on-site cultural events and inexpensive lodging near the lagoon, located a 25-minute ferry ride from the Biennale.

Isola La Certosa

Once home to Carthusian monks (hence the island's name), La Certosa served as a military zone from about the time Napoleon waltzed into Venice until after WWII. Today, this long-abandoned island is being revived as a marina; the rest of the island is being revamped as parkland, with free public entry to groves of poplar and ash trees. *Vaporetti* 41 and 42 connect Certosa with Castello stops at San Pietro and Sant'Elena, but schedules are subject to the season (see p253).

VENTO DI VENEZIA MARINA

(☎041 520 85 88; www.ventodivenezia.it) The initiative behind Certosa's yacht marina is now launching a full-fledged sustainable tourism project on the island, with public nature trails, revived vineyards and a restored 15th-century charterhouse for educational programs that sits alongside a hotel with 18 spacious rooms and a restaurant-bar, plus boat-charter services and sailing classes.

Isola Di San Michele

Shuttling between Murano from the Fondamente Nuove, *vaporetti* 41 and 42 stop at Venice's **city cemetery**.

CIMITERO HISTORICAL SITE

(admission free; 7.30am-6pm daily Apr-Sep, 7.30am-4pm Oct-Mar; Cimitero) Until Napoleon established a city cemetery on Isola di San Michele, Venetians had been buried in parish plots across town – not the most salubrious solution, as Napoleon's inspectors realised. Today, goths, incorrigible romantics and music-lovers pause here to pay respects to Ezra Pound, Joseph Brodsky, Sergei Diaghilev and Igor Stravinsky. Architecture buffs stop by to see the Renaissance **Chiesa di San Michele in Isola**, begun by Codussi in 1469, and the ongoing **cemetery extension** scheduled for completion in 2013 by David Chipperfield Architects, including the recently completed **Courtyard of the Four**

VENISSA

A single roasted scallop daintily dips its red foot in a black espresso reduction: starting with her highly amusing *amuse bouche*, chef Paola Budel treats local ingredients with the evident delight of a Italian chef returned home from restaurants abroad. The culinary stars (including the Michelin variety) are aligning over **Mazzorbo**, the lush garden island over the bridge from Burano where anything grows – you can practically eat the island landscape here in Budel's bowl of breadcrumb gnocchi swimming in a fragrant, herbal broth of wild fennel and asparagus shoots, young mint and basil. A dish of 63 minuscule whole octopi fished by hand in Chioggia and served on a *barene* (shoal) of garlicky fava-bean puree gives you some inkling what it's like to be a ravenous Venetian sea monster, satisfied at last. Call ahead, budget at least €60 per person, and wear sunblock to take advantage of the sunny outdoor patio overlooking Venissa's **vineyard** (☎041 527 22 81; www.venissa.it; Fondamenta di Santa Caterina 3, Mazzorbo; ⏰noon-3pm & 7-9.30pm Tue-Sun).

Evangelists – a rather gloomy bunker, with a concrete colonnade and basalt-clad walls engraved with the Gospels.

Isola di San Francesco del Deserto

On this island wilderness, in the heart of the lagoon, the only souls around are the Franciscans who have been caretakers of the island for centuries. Evidence of an early Roman presence has been found here, and legend has it that Francis of Assisi sought shelter on the island after a long, arduous journey to Palestine in 1220. It's said that gentle saint planted his walking stick in the ground here, and in its place grew a tree. The Franciscans took this as a sign, and chose this spot for an island retreat – but with malaria rampant and harsh living conditions, the surviving monks were forced to desert the island (hence the name) in 1420. The tenacious order returned, and has remained on the island since the 19th century.

Today, visits to the island are possible by prior arrangement with the **monastery** (☎041 528 68 63; admission free, donations appreciated; ⏰9-11am & 3-5pm Tue-Sun). Phone ahead, since tours are subject to the availability of a Franciscan brother to usher you through grounds that retain some of its 13th-century elements, including the first cloister. Visitors are kindly requested to speak in hushed tones, as this remains a sacred space of prayer and contemplation among the whispering cypress trees.

Getting there is another matter. You may be able to arrange a visit as part of a day trip boating on the lagoon (p26); otherwise, you'll need to hire a private boat or water taxi from Burano. If you decide to go the taxi route, ask around at the *vaporetto* stop on Burano, and expect to pay about €80 to €100 for up to four passengers for the return trip, including a 40- to 60-minute wait time. Spiritual retreats of up to one week are possible; contact the monastery.

EATING

Murano

BUSA ALLA TORRE SEAFOOD €€

Map p302 (☎041 73 96 62; Campo Santo Stefano 3, Murano; meals €35-50; ⏰11.30-3.30pm; 🚢Faro)
Glassy-eyed shoppers are drawn to Murano's classic eatery for its sunny disposition and €13 set menu. Arrive early for piazza seating with tempting views of glass showrooms, and settle in for a parade of tangy *sarde in saor* (marinated sardines), crispy fried *moeche* (tiny lagoon crab), plump prawn pasta and respectable house Soave.

GELATERIA AL PONTE GELATERIA, SANDWICH SHOP €

Map p302 (☎041 73 62 78; Riva Longa 1c, Murano; snacks €2-5; ⏰9am-5pm Mon-Sat; 🚢Museo)
Toasted prosciutto-and-cheese *panini* and gelato give shoppers a second wind, without cutting into Murano glass-buying budgets – sandwiches run at €3 to €5 and ice creams €2. Service can be slow at tables out front and in the back room, so if you're in a rush, order at the bar.

Burano & Mazzorbo

ALLA MADDALENA SEAFOOD €€

Map p303 (041 730 151; Fondamenta di Santa Caterina 7c, Mazzorbo; meals €30; 8am-8pm Fri-Wed; Mazzorbo) Just a footbridge away from Burano's frantic, photo-snapping crowds are lazy seafood lunches on the island of Mazzorbo. Relax by the canal or in the garden out the back with fresh fish dishes and, during autumn hunting season, the signature pasta with wild duck ragú.

TRATTORIA AL RASPO DE UA VENETIAN €€

Map p303 (041 730 095; www.alraspodeua.it; Via Galuppi 560, Burano; meals €20-30; lunch; Burano) Lunches alongside the piazza let you take in the lace-shopping frenzy from a safe distance, while enjoying a plate of delicate prawn pasta made in the sparklingly clean kitchen. Linger over *vin santo* and *essi buranelli* – postprandial spirits served with the classic S-shaped Burano biscuit. For a quicker, cheaper lunch, grab a steel bistro table at its new pizzeria just up Via Galuppi for some of the better pizza in the lagoon.

CAFFÈ-BAR PALMISANO CAFE €

Map p303 (Via San Martino 351, Burano; snacks €2-5; 7am-8pm; Burano) Refuel with espresso and a sandwich between Burano and Torcello at this cafe on the sunny side of the street, and return later to celebrate photo-safari triumphs over *spritz* or DOC wine with regular crowds of fishermen and university students before catching the boat back to Venice.

Torcello

LOCANDA CIPRIANI ITALIAN €€€

Map p303 (041 73 01 50; www.locandacipriani.com; 30142 Torcello; meals €30-45; by reservation, closed Tue & Jan; Torcello) A restorative, rustic retreat smartly run by the Cipriani family since 1934, the Locanda is Harry's Bar gone wild. Go with seasonal specialities like squid-ink gnocchi with calamari and Sant'Erasmo artichokes, or plan a lazy afternoon around the €45 Torcello menu fit for a famished Hemingway, with *bigoli* (fat whole wheat spaghetti) with rabbit, lamb with wild herbs, and dessert. Lunches and dinners are served by the fireplace or in the garden under the rose pergola, admiring the back side of Cattedrale di Santa Maria Assunta – at least until the flaming cognac *crepe suzette* is served tableside. Bargain alert: the Bellini is made to Harry's Bar standards and served in the rose garden, and here it's only €7.

RISTORANTE AL TRONO DI ATTILA VENETIAN €€

Map p303 (041 73 00 94; www.altronodiattila.it; Fondamenta Borgognoni 7a, Torcello; meals €20-30; noon-3.30pm Apr-Oct, closed Sun-Mon Nov-Mar; Torcello) Good cheer and honest prices make this spot the pick of the three canalside restaurants lining the path from the *vaporetto* stop to Cattedrale di Santa Maria Assunta. Unwind under the pergola with *risotto di pesce* (fish risotto, €20 for two people), house wine, and Torcello's bucolic soundtrack of shorebirds and bleating sheep. Like the neighbouring restaurants, this place generally opens for lunch only, unless you book ahead for a group dinner.

SHOPPING

Venice's outlying islands have their artisanal specialities: Murano is world renowned for glass art (look for 'Vero Artistico Murano' guarantee that glass is handmade in Murano) and Burano has been famed for handmade lace since the 17th century. Watch red-hot home decor emerge from the fiery glass-blowing *fornaci* (furnaces) of Murano, hidden behind the glitzy showrooms along **Fondamenta Vetrai** and **Ramo di Mula**. Showroom staff let you handle pieces if you ask first, but wield parcels and handbags with care – what you break, you buy. On sunny Burano days, you might glimpse local ladies tatting lace on brightly painted front stoops. The island's main drag, **Via Galuppi**, is, ahem, laced with lace shops – look for a seal guaranteeing *'fatto a Burano'* (made in Burano), since much of the less-expensive stock is imported.

Murano

TOP CHOICE **ELLEELLE** GLASS

Map p302 (041 527 48 66; www.elleellemurano.com; Fondamenta Manin 52, Murano; 10am-6pm Mon-Sat; Colonna) Burlesque dancers inspire curvy, red-hot wineglasses, crystal icebergs become champagne flutes and lagoon waters seem to swirl inside freeform, two-tone green and blue flower vases.

WORTH A DETOUR

JESOLO & THE ADRIATIC COAST

The arc of waterfront northeast of Venice is the Adriatic coast, lined with beach resorts. On summer weekends and sunny days, the beaches crowded with recliners and umbrellas may not be everyone's ideal Mediterranean beach getaway. But at night, an Ibiza mood sets in at local beach nightclubs, and DJs work a groove until the crowd abandons hard-won loungers to dance barefoot in the sand. Most resorts and clubs are clustered around Jesolo (population 23,620), a beach town at the northern end of a long Adriatic peninsula.

For Adriatic Coast information, try the **Palazzo del Turismo** (☎041 37 06 01; www.turismojesoloeraclea.it) in Piazza Brescia, Jesolo, or the **APT office** (☎042 18 10 85) in Caorle. Getting to Jesolo takes about an hour by car, and can be reached by public transport: take ATVO bus 10a from Piazzale Roma, which takes about 70 minutes to Jesolo, and costs €3.80 (€6.70 return). The problem is getting back – keep in mind that the last bus usually leaves at 11.20pm in summer, and taxis cost upwards of €80. If you can make it to Punta Sabbioni at the tip of the peninsula, you might be able to catch the LN late-night *vaporetto* back to Venice.

Caorle

For a more laid-back beach experience, head 30km east of Jesolo to sleepy Caorle (population 11,800); a Roman port in the first century BC, today it remains a fishing town. Independent-minded Caorle resisted Venetian annexation until the 15th century, and retains a distinct medieval character with the cylindrical bell tower of its 11th-century cathedral. But like neighbouring Burano (p157), Caorle has modern-art sensibilities, with houses painted in bold contrasting colour schemes that would make pastel-prone Venetian decorators blanch. Caorle's beaches are also busy in summer, but the whole place has a mellow seaside vibe that sets it apart from jumping Jesolo resorts. The town centre is easy to walk around, with a few hotels and plenty of restaurants offering simple, fresh fish dinners.

Lido di Jesolo

This strand of sand a couple of kilometres away from Jesolo is far and away Venetians' preferred beach, with fine, clean sand, warm, calm waters and beach nightclubs. The most memorable entertainment options are often spontaneous or quasi-organised – so while perfecting a tan by day in July and August, keep an eye out for flyers offering free admission to clubs (a €5 to €20 value) and announcements of free beach concerts by international acts like Franz Ferdinand.

Bring a stylish change of clothes to pass bouncer scrutiny around midnight, and in case of dinner reservations at **Cucina da Omar** (☎042 19 36 85; www.ristorantedaomar.it; Via Dante Alighieri 21, Lido di Jesolo; ⏲noon-2pm & 7.30-10pm Thu-Tue). At this stark, serious little bistro, lagoon seafood and French finesse are blended in a Venetian-style bouillabaisse to make the French Riviera gnash its teeth in envy and delight.

A beach scene ripped from an Italian decor magazine, **Terrazzamare** (☎042 13700 12; www.terrazzamare.com, in Italian; Vicolo Faro 1, Lido di Jesolo; admission €15; ⏲6pm-4am Tue-Sat Apr-Jun, nightly Jul-Sep) is populated by bronzed regulars in enormous sunglasses lounging on lipstick-red club chairs and sun-deprived Biennale-goers making out behind art installations. With open cabanas on a raised platform, dance scenes on the sand and occasional DJ duels, the Terazza earns its 'theatre-bar' fame.

An army of DJs spins mostly house music at one of the hippest summer dance locales, **Il Muretto** (☎393 410 11 20; www.ilmuretto.net, in Italian; Via Roma Destra 120d, Lido di Jesolo; admission from €20; ⏲11pm-4am Wed & Fri-Sun Apr-Sep), set inland from Jesolo and the beach; you'll need a car or taxi to get here. While clubbers at Muretto watch dawn arrive through the retractable roof, hook-ups head down the road to **Marina Club** (☎042 13706 45; www.marinaclubjesolo.com, in Italian; Via Roma Destra 120b, Lido di Jesolo; admission free; ⏲8pm-4am Apr-Sep), where breezy gazebos, candles and weekend DJs set the mood for summertime patio parties and private convos in cosy lounges.

Nason Moretti have been making modernist magic happen in glass since the 1950s, and the third-generation glass designers are in rare form in this showroom. Prices start at €30 for signed, hand-blown drinking glasses.

CAMPAGNOL & SALVADORE GLASS

Map p302 (☎041 73 67 72; Fondamenta San Giovanni dei Battuti 8; ⏲10.30am-6pm Mon-Sat; Colonna) A light touch is key to the delicate art of Murano mouth-blown glass, but the Japanese-Murano couple behind Campagnol & Salvadore make creations that are light-hearted, too: their aqua and sunshine-yellow bead necklaces look like strands of tiny beach balls, and the hypnotically swirled orange and burgundy earrings appear to have been pulled from a magician's hat. Psychedelic, Tim Burton–esque colour schemes make these baubles circus-fabulous and runway-ready, and aspiring designers are encouraged to create their own looks from individual blown-glass beads (€3 to €15 per bead).

BARBARA PROVERBIO GLASS

Map p302 (☎041 527 47 17; www.barbaraproverbio.com; Calle delle Agostiniane 4, Murano; ⏲by appointment Mon-Sat; Venier) Call ahead to witness a master glass artisan in the hot seat, crafting molten glass into spiky, volcanic black collars, bracelets with a single talismanic bead as bright and spellbinding as an eye of newt, and honeycomb pendants carefully cold-worked for that chiselled effect. Her style is organic minimalist, mixing textured glass with natural materials like wool, leather and feathers into statement jewellery.

RAGAZZI & CO GLASS

Map p302 (☎041 73 68 18; www.ragazzimurano.it; Ramo da Mula 16, Murano; ⏲9.30am-5.30pm Mon-Sat; Museo) Bullseyes cluster by the hundreds into mesmerising matte-glass dessert plates, mod choker necklaces and surprisingly durable steel-topped key chains. Ragazzi's design signature is an abstraction of traditional Murano *millefiori* (thousand-flower) pattern, and though it's been much imitated, these originals have unmistakable pop-art appeal. Prices start around €28.

TOFFOLO GALLERY GLASS

Map p302 (☎041 73 64 60; www.toffolo.com; Fondamenta Vetrai 37, Murano; ⏲10am-6pm Mon-Sat; Colonna) Classic gold-leafed winged goblets and mind-boggling miniatures are the trademarks of this Murano glass-blower, but you'll also find some dramatic departures: chiselled cobalt-blue vases, glossy black candlesticks that look like Dubai minarets, and highly hypnotic pendants.

OROVETRO MURANO GLASS

Map p302 (☎041 73 66 78; www.orovetro.it; Fondamenta Vetrai 45, Murano; ⏲10am-6.30pm Mon-Sat; Colonna) Not all Murano glass chandeliers require baroque ballrooms. These dramatic modern designs in black, red, and acid-green glass could turn studio bedrooms into boutique hotel suites and dens into swanky lounge-bars. Prices begin under €1000 for limited-edition lighting; architect-designed chandeliers with more waving arms than Kali hit five digits.

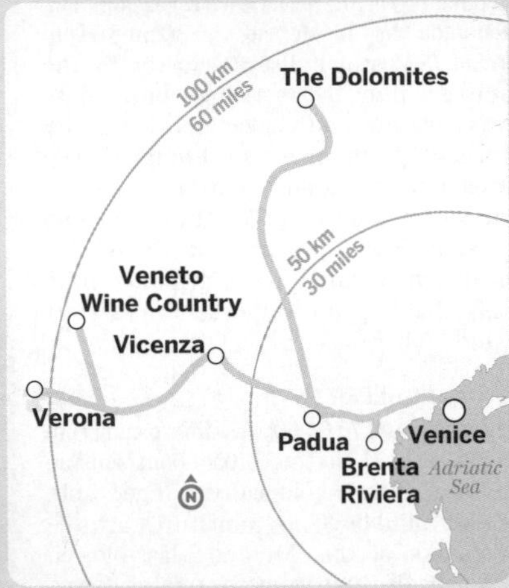

Day Trips from Venice

Riviera Brenta

Explore

For centuries, summer officially started on 13 June as a flotilla of fashionable Venetians headed for their villas along the banks of the Brenta. Today, private ownership and privacy hedges leave much to the imagination, but four historic villas are open as museums, including Palladio's exquisite La Malcontenta and the ramblingly grand Villa Pisani. They can be seen in one day, especially on an organised tour. If on your own, note that sites are scattered, so cars are a better option than trains – this very flat country also begs for biking. If you decide to linger, seek shelter in a villa-turned-B&B – or keep heading inland and spend the night in nearby Padua.

The Best...

- **Sight** Villa Foscari (p165)
- **Place to Eat** Da Conte (p167)
- **Place to Drink** Da Conte (p167)

Top Tip

The Riviera Brenta is best seen from the decks of flat-bottomed riverboats (p166) – the same way Venetians did, at least until Napoleon's troops shut down the centuries-long party in 1797.

Getting There & Away

Boat Organised boat tours leave from both Venice and Padua (p166).

Train Local trains between Venice and Padua stops at Dolo (€2.40, 30 minutes, one to two per hour) en route to Padua.

Bus ACTV's Venezia–Padova Extraurbane bus 53 leaves from Venice's Piazzale Roma (p251) about every half hour, stopping at key Brenta villages en route to Padua.

Car Take SS11 from Mestre-Venezia towards Padova (Padua), and take the Autostrada A4 towards Dolo/Padova.

Need to Know

- **Area Code** ☎041
- **Location** 15km to 30km west of Venice
- **Tourist Office** (☎041 560 06 90; Villa Widmann Foscari, Via Nazionale 420, Mira Porte; ⏲10.30am-1pm Sat, 1.30-4.30pm)

SIGHTS

VILLA FOSCARI HISTORIC BUILDING

(☎041 520 39 66; www.lamalcontenta.com; Via dei Turisti 9, Malcontenta; adult/student €10/8; ⏲9am-noon Tue & Sat, closed Nov-Apr) The most romantic Brenta villa, the Palladio-designed 1555–60 Villa Foscari got its nickname La Malcontenta from a grand dame of the Foscari clan who was reputedly exiled here for cheating on her husband – though these bright, highly sociable salons hardly constitute a punishment. The villa was abandoned for years, but Giovanni Zelotti's frescoes have recently been restored to daydream-inducing splendour, from Fame in the study to the Bacchanalian bedroom with Bacchus and Cupid among trompe l'oeil grapevines over the bed. Palladio's glorious facade faces the river, with soaring Ionic columns capped by a classical tympanum that draw the eye and spirits upward.

VILLA WIDMANN REZZONICO FOSCARI HISTORIC BUILDING

(☎041 560 06 90; www.riviera-brenta.it; Via Nazionale 420, Mira; adult/student €5.50/4.50; ⏲10am-5pm Tue-Sun Mar-Oct, 10am-5pm Sat & Sun Nov-Feb) To appreciate both gardening and Venetian-style social engineering, stop just west of Oriago at Villa Widmann Rezzonico Foscari. Originally owned by Persian-Venetian nobility, the 18th-century villa captures the Brenta's last days of rococo decadence, with Murano sea-monster chandeliers and a frescoed grand ballroom with upper viewing gallery. Head to the gallery to reach the upstairs ladies' gambling parlour where, according to local lore, villas were once gambled away in high-stakes games. Ignore the incongruously modernised bathrooms and puzzling modern crafts displays in the bedrooms and head instead into the garden, where an albino peacock loudly bemoans bygone glories amid moss-covered nymphs and cherubs. The gatehouse ticket counter doubles as an **APTV Info Point** (☎041 560 06 90) offering brochures on the Brenta.

VILLA BARCHESSA VALMARANA HISTORIC BUILDING

(☎041 426 63 87; www.villavalmarana.net; admission €6; ⏲10am-6pm Tue-Sun Mar-Oct, by appointment rest of the year) Across the Brenta from Villa Widmann Foscari and behind the hedgerows is the Villa Barchessa Valmarana, which was built a century later and now serves mainly as a conference centre – though it must be hard to concentrate on business in that double-height dining room lined with fanciful frescoes.

VILLA PISANI NAZIONALE HISTORIC BUILDING

(049 50 22 70; www.villapisani.beniculturali.it; Via Doge Pisani 7, Stra; adult/reduced €10/7.50, grounds only €7.50/5; 9am-5pm Tue-Sun, to 8pm Apr-Sep) To keep hard-partying Venetian nobles in line, Doge Alvise Pisani provided a Versailles-like reminder of who was in charge. The 1774 Villa Pisani Nazionale is surrounded by huge gardens, a labyrinthine hedge-maze and pools to reflect the doge's glory. And if the walls of these 114 rooms could talk, they'd name-drop shamelessly. Here you'll find the gaming rooms where Venice's powerful Pisani family racked up debts that forced them to sell the family mansion to Napoleon; the grand bathroom with a tiny wooden throne used by Napoleon during his 1807 reign as king of Italy; a sagging bed where Vittorio Emanuele II apparently tossed and turned as the head of newly independent Italy; and, in historical irony, the grand reception hall where Mussolini and Hitler met for the first time in 1934 under Tiepolo's ceiling masterpiece depicting the *Geniuses of Peace*. Occasionally there are also some outstanding temporary exhibitions in upstairs salons and the gardens, from old masters to contemporary artists.

VILLA FOSCARINI ROSSI HISTORIC BUILDING

(049 980 03 35; www.villafoscarini.it; Via Doge Pisani 1/2, Stra; admission €7; 9am-1pm & 2.30-6pm Mon-Fri, 2.30-6pm Sat & Sun Apr-Oct; 9am-1pm Mon-Fri Nov-Mar) Well-heeled Venetians wouldn't have dreamt of decamping to the Brenta without their favourite cobblers, sparking a local tradition of high-end shoemaking. Today, 950 companies in the Brenta region produce 20 million pairs of shoes annually. The lasting contribution of Brenta cobblers is commemorated with a **Shoemakers' Museum** at the 18th-century Villa Foscarini Rossi, a multiroom dream wardrobe that includes 18th-century slippers, kicks created for trendsetters Marlene Dietrich and Katharine Hepburn, and heels handcrafted in the Brenta for Yves Saint Laurent, Pucci and the like. The building itself also has an impressive pedigree: among the many architects involved was Vincenzo Scamozzi (one of the city's leading 16th-century architects), working from designs by Palladio, although the present building is largely the result of a later neoclassical reworking.

SLEEPING IN RIVIERA BRENTA

➡ **Villa Tron Mioni** (041 41 01 77; www.villatron.it; Via Ca' Tron 23, Dolo; d from €92-130;) Surrounded by gardens, this 19th-century villa provides aristocratic flourishes at middle-class prices. Rooms in the main villa are done up in simple good taste, and a few new apartments are handsomely decorated in rustic chic style. However, the ramblingly romantic gardens are the real draw. Works best if you have your own car.

RIVER BOAT TOURS BOAT TOURS

Seeing the Brenta by boat lets you witness an engineering marvel: the hydraulic locks system developed in the 15th century to divert the river to the sea, ingeniously preventing river silt from dumping into the lagoon and turning Venice into a mudflat. Most boats move only at a walking pace, and when water levels are low, views of the surrounding countryside are not as panoramic. But since most villas face the river, you'll be seeing them as Palladio and his contemporaries intended: at a leisurely pace befitting Venetian nobility.

Burchiello (049 820 69 10; www.ilburchiello.it; half-day cruise adult/reduced €51/40, full day from €71/56) is a modern luxury barge offering full-day cruises that stop at Malcontenta, Widmann and Pisani villas; half-day tours cover two villas. Full-day cruises leave from Venice's Stazione Marittima (Tuesday, Thursday and Saturday) or Padua (Wednesday, Friday and Sunday), with bus transfers to train stations.

I Batelli del Brenta (049 876 02 33; www.battellidelbrenta.it; half-day tours adult/reduced from €47/39, full day from €85/40; by reservation Tue-Sun Mar-Nov) offers a range of half-day and full-day excursions, with departures from both Venice and Padua.

RENTAL BIKE VENICE BIKE RENTAL

(346 847 114; www.rentalbikevenice.blogspot.com; Via Gramsci 85, Mira; bicycle per day city & mountain/foldable from €10/14; 8am-8pm) The scenic Brenta Riviera plains make an easy, enjoyable bicycle ride, and you can speed past those tour boats along 150km of cycling routes. Rental Bike Venice is a friendly bike-rental spot accessible by bus from Venice,

Mestre or Padua (see website for directions) offering city bikes with baskets, mountain bikes and handy foldable bikes to take on buses, plus guided tours, free parking, roadside assistance and advice in English on itineraries, local restaurants and shops.

EATING

DA CONTE CONTEMPORARY VENETIAN **€€**

(☎049 50 23 70; Via Caltana 133, Mira; meals €35-45; ⏰lunch & dinner Tue-Sat) This unlikely bastion of sophistication is lodged practically underneath an overpass. Da Conte has one of the best wine lists in the region, plus creative takes on classic lagoon cuisine, from roasted quail to ginger-infused langoustines.

Padua (Padova)

Explore

Though under an hour from Venice, Padua (Padova; population 212,500) seems a world away. In fact, it's more reminiscent of Milan, with its arcaded sidewalks, oddly shaped medieval piazzas, hip student population and Fascist-era facades. As a medieval city-state and home to Italy's second-oldest university, Padua challenged both Venice and Verona for regional hegemony. A series of vivid fresco cycles recalls this medieval golden age – including Giotto's remarkable Capella degli Scrovegni. With cheap, convenient train connections and a dense historic heart within walking distance of the station, you can easily see all the main sights in a day. A brand-new tramline from the train station makes this easier than ever. Stay into the evening to watch the *piazze* come alive as the highly social Padovans gather for their evening *aperitivo*.

The Best...

- **Sight** Capella degli Scrovegni (p167)
- **Place to Eat** Godenda (p172)
- **Place to Drink** Enoteca Santa Lucia (p172)

MAKING THE MOST OF YOUR EURO

A **PadovaCard** (per 48/72hr €16/21) gives one adult plus one child under 14 free use of city public transport and access to almost all of Padua's major attractions, including the Cappella degli Scrovegni (plus €1 booking fee; reservation essential). PadovaCards are available at Padua tourist offices and monuments covered by the pass.

Top Tip

Reservations are required to see Giotto's extraordinary Capella degli Scrovegni – sometimes as much as a few weeks ahead for summer weekends and during holidays.

Getting There & Away

Car The A4 (Turin–Milan–Venice–Trieste) passes to the north of town, while the A13 to Bologna starts south of town.

Bus SITA buses (☎049 820 68 34; www.sitabus.it, in Italian) from Venice's Piazzale Roma (€3.70, 45 to 60 minutes, hourly) arrive at Piazzale Boschetti, 500m south of the train station. Check online for buses to Colli Euganei towns (see p170).

Train Trains are the easiest way to reach Padua from Venice (€3 to €15, 25 to 50 minutes, three or four per hour).

Need to Know

- **Area Code** ☎049
- **Location** 37km west of Venice
- **Tourist Office** (www.turismopadova.it) Train Station (☎049 875 20 77; ⏰9am-7pm Mon-Sat, 9am-12.30pm Sun); Galleria Pedrocchi (☎049 876 79 27; ⏰9am-1.30pm & 3-7pm Mon-Sat)

SIGHTS

CAPELLA DEGLI SCROVEGNI CHURCH

(☎049 201 00 20; www.cappelladegliscrovegni.it; Giardini dell'Arena; admission with PadovaCard free, adult/reduced 13/8; ⏰9am-7pm, by reservation only, call centre 9am-7pm Mon-Fri & 9am-6pm Sat) Almost 200 years before Michelangelo's Sistine Chapel and da Vinci's *Last Supper* came Padua's Renaissance breakthrough:

Padua

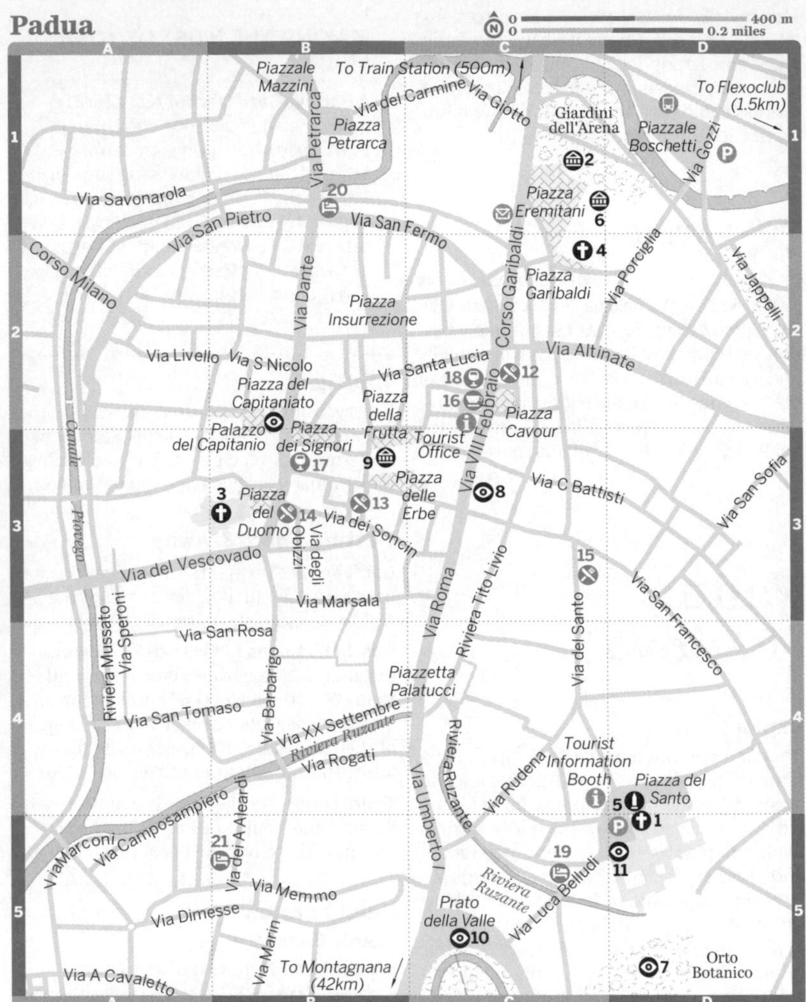

Giotto's moving, modern 1303–05 frescoes in the Capella degli Scrovegni. Medieval churchgoers were accustomed to blank stares from flat saints perched high on gold Gothic thrones, but Giotto introduces Biblical figures as characters in recognisable settings, caught up in extraordinary circumstances. Onlookers gossip as middle-aged Anne tenderly kisses Joachim, and then late in life gives birth to miracle-baby Mary; exhausted new dad Joseph falls asleep sitting up in the manger, as sheep and angels take the night watch over baby Jesus; and Jesus stares down Judas as the traitor puckers up for the kiss that seals Jesus' fate.

Dante, da Vinci, Boccacio and Vasari all honour Giotto as the artist who officially ended the Dark Ages in a blaze of glowing colour. Giotto's startlingly humanist approach not only changed how people saw saints, it changed how they saw themselves; not as lowly vassals but as vessels for the divine, however flawed. This humanising approach was especially well suited for the chapel Enrico Scrovegni commissioned in memory of his father, who as a moneylender was denied a Christian burial. In the new multimedia gallery, a mandatory 10-minute video provides a helpful introduction before you enter the church itself.

Padua

Sights

1 Basilica di Sant'Antonio....D5
2 Cappella degli Scrovegni....C1
3 Cathedral & Baptistry....B3
4 Chiesa degli Eremitani....C2
5 Gattamelata Statue....D4
6 Musei Civici agli Eremitani....C1
Museo del Risorgimento e dell'Età Contemporanea....(see 16)
Oratorio di San Giorgio....(see 11)
7 Orto Botanico....D5
8 Palazzo del Bò....C3
9 Palazzo della Ragione....B3
10 Prato della Valle....C5
11 Scoletta del Santo....D5

Eating

12 Caffè Cavour....C2
13 Godenda....B3
14 Osteria Dal Capo....B3
15 Piadineria Italiana....C3

Drinking & Nightlife

16 Caffè Pedrocchi....C2
17 Caffetteria Manin....B3
18 Enoteca Santa Lucia....C2

Sleeping

19 Belludi37....C5
20 Hotel Sant'Antonio....B1
21 Ostello Città di Padova....B5

The chapel is a five-minute walk from the train station, but daily visits are by reservation only and booking is required online or by phone. Pick up tickets at the box office of the adjacent Musei Civici agli Eremitani. Plan to book well ahead, especially for weekends and any time from April to October. Chapel visits last 15 minutes, plus another 15 minutes for the orientation video, though the 'double turn' night session ticket (adult/reduced/child under seven years €12/6/1; open 7pm to 9.20pm) allows a 30-minute stay in the church.

MUSEI CIVICI AGLI EREMITANI MUSEUM
(☎049 820 45 51; Piazza Eremitani 8; museum adult/reduced €10/8, with PadovaCard or Capella degli Scrovegni ticket free; ⏰9am-7pm Tue-Sun) The ground floor of this monastery houses artefacts dating from Padua's Roman and pre-Roman past. Upstairs, a rambling but interesting collection boasts a few notable 14th to 18th-century works by Bellini, Giorgione, Tintoretto and Veronese. The show-stopper is a crucifix by Giotto, showing a heartbroken Mary wringing her hands as Jesus' blood drips through the rocky earth, right into the empty eye sockets of a human skull.

CHIESA DEGLI EREMITANI CHURCH
☎049 875 64 10; Piazza Eremitani; ⏰7.30am-12.30pm & 3.30-7pm Mon-Fri, 9am-12.30pm & 4-8pm Sat & Sun) When a 1944 bombing raid demolished the extraordinary 1448–57 frescoes by Andrea Mantegna in the Capella Overtari in the Chiesa degli Eremitani, the loss to art history was incalculable. After half a century of painstaking reconstruction, the shattered, humidity-damaged stories of Saints James and Christopher have been puzzled together, revealing action-packed compositions and extreme perspectives that make Mantegna's saints look like superheroes.

PALAZZO DEL BÒ HISTORIC BUILDING
(☎049 827 30 47; Via VIII Febbraio; adult/reduced €5/3.50; ⏰tours 9.15am, 10.15am & 11.15pm Tue, Thu & Sat, 3.15pm, 4.15pm & 5.15pm Mon, Wed & Fri) This Renaissance *palazzo* is the seat of Padua's history-making **university**. Founded by renegade scholars from Bologna seeking greater intellectual freedom, the university has employed some of Italy's greatest and most controversial thinkers, including Copernicus, Galileo, Casanova and the world's first woman doctor of philosophy, Eleonora Lucrezia Cornaro Piscopia (her statue graces the stairs). Guided tours cover Galileo's lecture hall and the world's first Anatomy Theatre, a six-tiered hall built for scientific autopsy in 1594 before biohazards were understood – dissected corpses were dumped into an underground stream.

Note that there are generally only two tours per day from November to March.

PALAZZO DELLA RAGIONE HISTORIC BUILDING
(☎049 820 50 06; Piazza delle Erbe; adult/reduced €4/2; ⏰9am-7pm Tue-Sun, to 6pm Nov-Jan) Ancient Padua can be glimpsed in elegant twin squares framed separated by the triple-decker Gothic Palazzo della Ragione, the city's tribunal dating from 1218. Inside, frescoes by Giotto acolytes Giusto de' Menabuoi and Nicolò Mireto depict the astrological theories of Padovan professor Pietro d'Abano, with images representing the months, seasons, saints, animals and noteworthy Paduans (not necessarily in that order). D'Abano's work, which drew

WORTH A DETOUR

COLLI EUGANEI (EUGANEAN HILLS)

Southwest of Padua, the Colli Euganei (Euganean Hills) feel a world away from the urban sophistication of Venice and the surrounding plains. To explore the walled hilltop towns, misty vineyards and bubbling hot springs, the Padua tourist office offers area maps, accommodation, hiking and transport information online (www.turismoterme euganee.it). Trains serve all towns except Arquá Petraca.

Just south of Padua lie the natural-hot-spring resorts of **Abano Terme** and **Montegrotto Terme**. The towns are uninspired, but the waters do cure aches and pains.

In the medieval village of **Arquà Petrarca**, look for the elegant little **house** (0429 71 82 94; Via Valleselle 4; adult/reduced €4/2; 9am-12.30pm & 3-7pm Tue-Sun Mar-Oct, 9am-12.30pm & 2.30-5.30pm Tue-Sun Nov-Feb) where great Italian poet Petrarch spent his final years in the 1370s.

At the southern reaches of the Euganei, you'll find three walled medieval towns: **Monselice**, with its remarkable **medieval castle** (www.castellodimonselice.it; 1hr guided tours 9am, 10am, 11am, 3pm, 4pm Tue-Sun Apr-Nov); **Este**, whose **archaeological museum** (Via Guido Negri 9c; adult/reduced €3/1.50; 8.30am-7.30pm) has an important collection of artefacts from the pre-Roman Veneti tribes; and **Montagnana**, with its magnificent 2km defensive perimeter. Just outside Montagnana's east gate, look for Palladio's small but important Villa Pisani, still a private residence.

on Arab sources, brought him into conflict with the Church, and he was convicted posthumously of heresy. Unfortunately, the frescoes had to be restored after a fire in 1420 and storm damage in 1756. Though much of the original work was lost, reproductions are of a high quality.

CATHEDRAL CHURCH

(049 66 28 14; Piazza del Duomo; 7.30am-noon & 4-7.30pm Mon-Sat, 8am-1pm & 4-8.45pm Sun & holidays) South of the *palazzo* is the city's cathedral, built from a much-altered design of Michelangelo's. Its whitewashed symmetry is a far cry from its rival in Piazza San Marco. The adjoining 13th-century **Baptistry** (adult/reduced €2.80/1.80, with PadovaCard free; 10am-6pm) is a Romanesque gem that's completely frescoed with luminous Biblical scenes by Giusto de' Menabuoi, a follower of Giotto. His cupola depicts hundreds of male and female saints posed as though for a school graduation photo, exchanging glances and stealing looks at the Madonna. The inside of the dome shows Christ Pantocrator holding an open book inscribed with the words *Ego sum alpha et omega* (I am the beginning and the end), and the rear apse wall illustrates his meaning with frescoes that illuminate Biblical stories of creation, redemption and the apocalypse.

BASILICA DI SANT'ANTONIO CHURCH

(049 822 56 52; www.basilicadelsanto.org; Piazza del Santo; 6.30am-7.45pm, to 6.45pm Nov-Mar) The soul of the city is this basilica, a key pilgrimage site and burial place of the town's patron saint, St Anthony of Padua (1193–1231). Construction of the church, nicknamed Il Santo, began in 1232, and over the years took on an unmistakable polyglot style: atop a Latin cross base is the brick Italian Gothic structure, topped by a series of domes and towers that seem to take their cue from the east.

Once inside, you'll notice people clustering along the right transept, where the saint's tomb is covered with requests and thanks for the saint's intercession in curing illness and recovering lost objects. His resting place is a remarkable, light-filled Renaissance confection attributed to the Padua-born Lombardo brothers and probably completed around 1510.

Behind the high altar at the rear of the church radiates a series of nine chapels, mostly decorated in the 20th century. The central chapel is the baroque Cappella del Tesoro (Treasury Chapel), where the relics of St Anthony were transferred in 1745. True to centuries-old tradition, parts of the saint are on show for the edification of the faithful: his chin and grey-green tongue are showcased in two separate, exquisitely worked gold monstrances. For the faithful, the tongue became a particular object of veneration, perhaps because in his lifetime the saint had been a convincing orator as well as a mediator in times of civil strife.

Under the church's vaulted Gothic ceilings, you will find notable works: the lifelike 1360s crucifix by Veronese master Altichiero da Zevio in the frescoed Chapel of St James; the wonderful 1528 sacristy fresco of Saint Anthony preaching to spellbound fish by a follower of Girolamo Tessari; and 1444–50 high altar reliefs by Florentine Renaissance master Donatello (ask guards for access). Through the east door of the basilica you reach the attached monastery with its five cloisters. The oldest (13th century) is the **Chiostro della Magnolia**, so-called because of the magnificent tree in its centre. Nearby, the **Museo Antoniano** (☎049 822 56 56; Piazza del Santo; admission free; ⏲9am-1pm & 2-6pm) holds a kitschy but interesting collection of art and religious objects, many by amateurs, donated by grateful pilgrims over the centuries.

Outside, in the **Piazza del Santo**, is Donatello's 1453 equestrian statue commemorating the 15th-century Venetian mercenary leader known as **Gattamelata** (Honeyed Cat). It's considered the first great Italian Renaissance bronze.

ORATORIO DI SAN GIORGIO CHURCH

(☎049 875 52 35; admission incl Scoletta del Santo €4; ⏲9am-12.30pm & 2.30-5pm, to 7pm Apr-Oct) Just across the square from the basilica hide two of Padua's most overlooked treasures. Downstairs, the walls of Oratorio di San Giorgio are completely covered with frescoes recounting the lives of St George, St Lucy and St Catherine of Alexandria – all told in jewel-like colour by Altichiero da Zevio and Jacopo Avanzi in 1378. The church was briefly used as a prison by Napoleon, who apparently missed the message of St George's liberation from the torture wheel by avenging angels. Your ticket allows entry next door to the upstairs **Scoletta del Santo**, which houses a few dramatic Titian paintings including a 1511 portrait of St Anthony calmly reattaching his own foot as an onlooker gasps. There is also a riveting parable, painted by Titian's brother Francesco Vecellio, in which a doctor discovers a miser's heart is missing, just as a neighbour pulls the bloody heart from a treasure chest.

ORTO BOTANICO GARDEN

(☎049 827 21 19; www.ortobotanico.unipd.it; via dell'Orto Botanico; adult/reduced €4/1; ⏲9am-1pm & 3-7pm Apr-Oct, 9am-1pm Mon-Sat Nov-Mar) South of Piazza del Santo, a Unesco World Heritage Site is growing. Padua's Orto Botanico was planted in 1545 by Padua University's medical faculty to study the medicinal properties of rare plants, and served as a clandestine Resistance meeting headquarters in WWII. The oldest tree in here is nicknamed 'Goethe's palm'; it was planted in 1585 and mentioned by the great German writer in his *Voyage in Italy*.

SLEEPING IN PADUA

The **tourist office** (www.turismopadova.it) publishes accommodation brochures and lists dozens of B&Bs and hotels online. The **Koko Nor Association** (www.bbkokonor.it; d €60-80) offers Tibetan-themed apartments, terrace rooms and artists' garrets owned by welcoming, worldly Italian families; ask about informal Italian conversation classes. Additional B&B listings outside Padua are listed on an affiliated website: www.bedandbreakfastpadova.it (in Italian).

➡ **Belludi37** (☎049 66 56 33; www.belludi37.it; Via Luca Belludi 37; s €80, d €120-150; ❄@☎) A sleek boutique hotel with soul: expect generous beds, modern yet serene rooms, and helpful staff quick with budget-friendly shopping advice, free drinks, biking itineraries and speciality-food-sampling walking tours.

➡ **Hotel Sant'Antonio** (☎049 875 13 93; www.hotelsantantonio.it; Via San Fermo 118; s €63-69, d €82-94; ❄) A calm, canalside hotel near the historic city gate, this place offers unfussy, airy rooms, most with new bathrooms and a few with canal views. There are also some cheaper singles with a shared bathroom (€39 to €42).

➡ **Ostello Città di Padova** (☎049 875 22 19; www.ostellopadova.it; Via dei A Aleardi 30; dm €19; ⏲7-9.30am & 3.30-11.30pm) This central hostel has decent dorm rooms with four to six beds on a quiet side street. Sheets and wi-fi are free, but there is no open kitchen. Note there is an 11.30pm curfew, except when there are special events, and you must check out by 9.30am. Take bus 3, 8 or 12 or the city's new tram from the train station.

PRATO DELLA VALLE PARK

At the southern edge of the historical centre this odd, elliptical garden was long used for public markets. Today it serves as a favourite spot for locals to soak in the summer sun. Surrounding the grassy park is a slim canal lined by 78 statues of sundry great and good of Paduan history, plus 10 empty pedestals. Ten Venetian dogi once occupied them, but Napoleon had them removed after he took Venice in 1797.

EATING

TOP CHOICE GODENDA MODERN ITALIAN €€

(☎049 877 41 92; www.godenda.it; Via Squarcione 4/6; meals €30-50; ⏰10am-3pm, 7pm-1am Mon-Sat, closed Aug) Though hidden under an ancient portico, this local foodies' favourite is airy and modern. The seasonal menu offers creative takes on old Venetian classics such as a sublime monkfish with fava beans and house-made pasta sprinkled with jerked horsemeat. Fortunately, the biggest hits – tartare of tuna and beef, as well as its signature tiramisu – are available year round.

ENOTECA ANGELO RASI MODERN ITALIAN €€

(☎049 871 97 97; Riviera Paleocapa 7; meals €30; ⏰dinner Tue-Sun) Come for a glass of wine and *cicheti* on a sunny day and inevitably you'll pull up a chair by the canal and stay for dinner under the lime trees. Rustic fare is reinvented with a touch of whimsy: creamed cod comes with savoury squid-ink polenta doughnuts, ricotta gnocchi is topped with a decadent zucchini mousse sauce, and cheeses are presented in the form of a clock.

OSTERIA DAL CAPO OSTERIA €€

(☎049 66 31 05; Via degli Obizzi 2; meals €25-35; ⏰lunch & dinner Tue-Sat) Rub elbows with locals – literally – at tiny tables precariously piled with traditional Venetian seafood and a few inspired novelties, such as *caviale di melanzane con bufala* (eggplant caviar with buffalo mozzarella atop crispy wafer bread). Reservations and a sociable nature advised.

CAFFÈ CAVOUR PASTRIES & CAKES €

(☎049 875 12 24; www.caffecavour.com; Piazza Cavour 10; pastries €1.50-4; ⏰7.30am-8pm Wed-Sun, to midnight May-Sep) Pistachio macaroons, wild-berry tarts and other two-bite indulgences sweeten the expressions of traffic cops bolting espresso at the curved granite bar.

PIADINERIA ITALIANA SNACKS €

(☎340 294 64 80; Via del Santo 7; meals €5-10; ⏰10am-5pm Mon-Sat) Students from the nearby university head here for a fast, cheap and delicious variation on pizza known as the *piadina*, a classic quick eat from the region around Ravenna.

DRINKING & NIGHTLIFE

Sundown isn't official until you've had your *spritz* (*prosecco*-based drink) in Piazza delle Erbe or Piazza dei Signori. Also note that Padua is the region's unofficial capital of gay and lesbian life.

TOP CHOICE ENOTECA SANTA LUCIA WINE BAR

(☎049 875 94 83; Piazza Cavour 15; ⏰7pm-midnight Mon-Sat) Taking its cue from Milan, Santa Lucia offers upscale wines by the glass (€5 to €10) with a free buffet of local specialities and cheeses from 7pm to 10pm nightly. Occupy your battle station at the glassed-in bar for buffet forays with Padua's budget fashionistas, or head inside the ancient stone-walled tavern with the aficionados.

CAFFÈ PEDROCCHI CAFE

(☎049 878 12 31; www.caffepedrocchi.it, in Italian; Via VIII Febbraio 15; ⏰9am-10pm Sun-Wed, to 1am Thu-Sat) Since 1831, this neoclassical landmark has been a favourite of Stendhal and other pillars of Padua's cafe society, thanks mostly to its heart-poundingly powerful coffee and *caffè correto* (coffee cocktails). The grand 1st floor is decorated in post-Napoleonic styles ranging from ancient Egyptian to Imperial. During the day you can visit the upstairs **Museo del Risorgimento e dell'Età Contemporanea** (☎049 878 12 31; Galleria Pedrocchi 11; adult/child €4/2.50; ⏰9.30am-12.30pm & 3.30-6pm Tue-Sun), recounting local and national history from the fall of Venice in 1797 until the republican constitution of 1848 in original documents, images and mementos.

CAFFETTERIA MANIN CAFE

(☎049 876 16 09; Via Manin 56; ⏰7am-7pm Mon-Fri, to 12.30pm Sat) Top-flight coffee is still roasted on the premises at this old-fashioned cafe, where locals pop in all day for a frothy jolt at the bar only – no tables. For an extra euro, you can have your espresso made with Jamaica Blue Mountain beans.

FLEXOCLUB NIGHTCLUB

(☎049 807 47 07; www.flexoclub.it, in Italian; Via Turazza 19; ⏲from 10pm Wed-Sun) This sprawling gay venue located about 2km east of the train station features a bar-disco, with occasional live music and drag shows, plus an adjacent sauna.

Vicenza

Explore

When Palladio escaped an oppressive employer in his native Padua in the 1520s, few could have guessed the humble stonecutter would transform not only Vicenza (population 113,500) but also the history of European architecture. Today, Vicenza's historic centre is thick with Palladio's work, and his iconic La Rotonda, as well as the delightful Villa Valmarana 'ai Nani', lie a 20-minute walk to the south. Frequent train connections and a dense city centre make it an easy city to tackle as a day trip. Despite its outsized heritage, this charming town remains quietly unpretentious – a fine place to join locals lingering over rustic lunches of local *salumi* (cured meats), game and handmade pasta. Centrally located and with good-value accommodation, Vicenza also makes an ideal base for the rest of the Veneto.

The Best...

➡ **Sight** La Rotonda (p173)

➡ **Place to Eat** Antico Ristorante agli Schioppi (p176)

➡ **Place to Drink** Antica Casa della Malvasia (p179)

Top Tip

Palladio's Teatro Olimpico was built for live performances, and that is still the best way to absorb the complex harmonies of this extraordinary space (p174).

Getting There & Away

Train Trains are the easiest way to reach Vicenza from Venice (€4.40 to €14, 45 to 90 minutes, three or four per hour).

Car Vicenza lies just off the A4 connecting Milan with Venice, while the SR11 connects Vicenza with Verona and Padua. Large car parks are located near Piazza Castello and the train station.

Need to Know

➡ **Area Code** ☎0444

➡ **Location** 62km west of Venice

➡ **Tourist Office** (☎0444 32 08 54; www.vicenzae.org; Piazza Matteotti 12; ⏲9am-1pm & 2-6pm) Especially knowledgeable and helpful.

SIGHTS

LA ROTONDA HISTORICAL BUILDING

(☎049 879 13 80; www.villalarotonda.it; Via della Rotonda 45; admission villa/gardens €10/5; ⏲gardens 10am-noon & 3-6pm Tue-Sun, villa open Wed & Sat only, closed mid-Nov–mid-Mar) No matter how you look at it, this villa is a show-stopper: the namesake dome caps a square base, with identical colonnaded facades on all four sides. This is one of Palladio's most admired creations, inspiring variations across Europe and the USA, including Thomas Jefferson's Monticello (La Rotonda's late owner, Mario di Valmarana, was a retired University of Virginia architecture professor; he died in 2010). Inside, the circular central hall is frescoed from the walls to the soaring cupola with trompe l'oeil frescoes. Catch bus 8 or 13 (€1.20) from in front of Vicenza's train station, or just walk (about 25 minutes by foot).

VILLA VALMARANA 'AI NANI' HISTORICAL BUILDING

(☎0444 32 18 03; www.villavalmarana.com; Stradella dei Nani 8; admission €8; ⏲10am-noon & 3-6pm Tue-Sun Apr-Oct, 10am-noon & 2.30-5pm Sat & Sun Nov-Mar) From La Rotonda, a path leads about 500m to the elegantly neoclassical Villa Valmarana 'ai Nani', whose interior shelters sublime 1757 frescoes by Giambattista Tiepolo and his son Giandomenico. Giambattista painted the Palazzina wing with his signature mythological epics, while his son painted the Foresteria with rural, carnival and Chinese themes. Nicknamed 'ai Nani' (gnomes) for the 17 garden-gnome statues around the garden walls, this estate with its carefully maintained grounds is a superb spot for the occasional summer concert; check dates online.

Vicenza

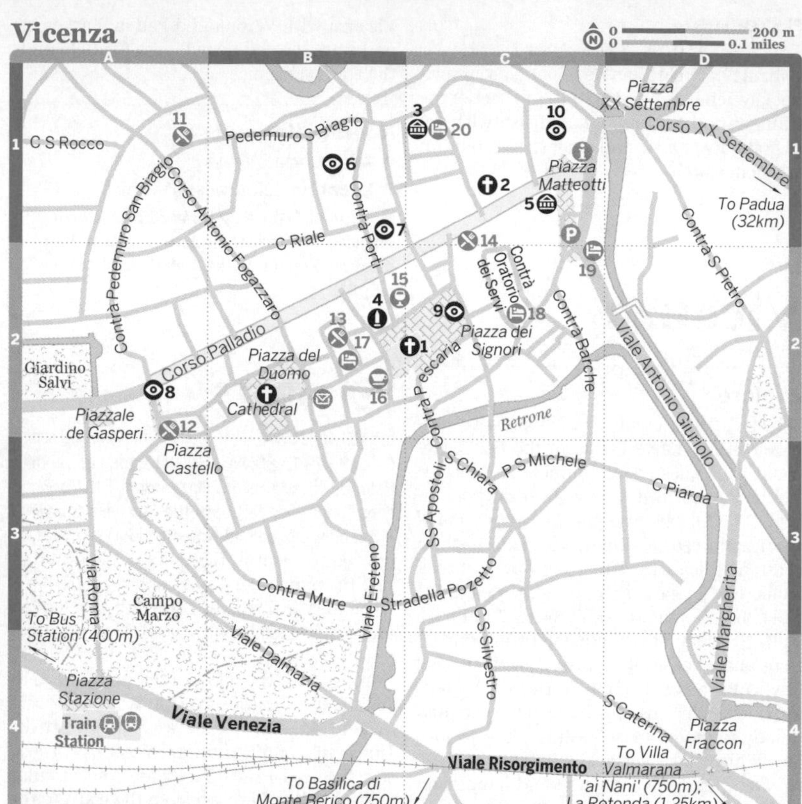

TEATRO OLIMPICO THEATRE

(☎0444 22 28 00; www.olimpico.vicenza.it; Palazzo Matteotti 11; combined ticket with Museo Civico adult/reduced €8/6; ⏲9am-5pm Tue-Sun) Behind a charming walled garden lies a Renaissance marvel: the Teatro Olimpico, which Palladio began in 1580 with inspiration from Roman amphitheatres. Vincenzo Scamozzi finished the elliptical theatre after Palladio's death, adding a stage set modelled on the ancient Greek city of Thebes, with streets built in steep perspective to give the illusion of a city sprawling towards a distant horizon. The theatre was inaugurated in 1585 with a performance of *Oedipus Rex* but soon fell into disuse. Eventually the ceiling caved in, and the theatre remained abandoned for centuries until it was finally restored in 1934. Today, Italian performers vie to make an entrance on this gem of a stage; check online for opera, classical and jazz performances.

MUSEO CIVICO MUSEUM

(☎0444 22 28 11; www.museicivicivicenza.it; Palazzo Chiericati, Piazza Matteotti 37/39; combined ticket with Teatro Olimpico adult/reduced €8/6; ⏲9am-5pm Tue-Sun) This little museum is housed in one of Palladio's finest buildings, designed in 1550 with a colonnaded ground floor and double-height loggia flanked by vast sun porches. The lavishly frescoed ground floor includes the ultimate baroque party room: the Sala dal Firmamento (Salon of the Skies), with Domenico Brusasorci's ceiling fresco of Diana the moon goddess in her chariot, galloping across the sky to meet a bare-arsed Helios, god of the Sun. The upstairs galleries present works by Vicenza masters in the context of a handful of major works by Venetian masters such as Veronese, Tiepolo and Tintoretto. Also look out for Hans Memling's minutely detailed Crucifix, action-packed works by Jacopo Bassano, Elisabetta Marchioni's bodacious still lifes, and Giambattista Piazzetta's swirling, high-drama 1729 masterpiece, *The Ecstasy of St Francis.*

GALLERIE DI PALAZZO LEONI MONTANARI MUSEUM

(☎800 57 88 75; www.palazzomontanari.com; Contrà di Santa Corona 25; adult/reduced €5/4; ⊙10am-6pm Tue-Sun) From the outside it looks like a bank, but a treasure beyond accountants' imagining awaits inside the Gallerie di Palazzo Leoni Montanari. Ascend past the nymphs along the extravagant stuccoed staircase to grand salons filled with Canaletto's misty lagoon landscapes and Pietro Longhi 18th-century satires such as *Tutors of Venier's House,* in which a sassy child with hand on hip wears out exasperated tutors, who've collapsed in their chairs.

Head upstairs to see Banca Intesa's superb collection of some 400 Russian icons, gorgeously spotlit in darkened galleries in which recordings of soft Gregorian chants set the scene. Each room elicits audible gasps: bright-eyed saints haloed in silver peer from 16th-century doors; 19th-century menologies show 99 miniature saints with detailed heads no larger than pencil erasers; and a phalanx of bejewelled, miraculous Madonna icons makes you understand why bags must be left in ground-floor lockers. Such a collection is rare anywhere, particularly outside Russia.

PIAZZA DEI SIGNORI & AROUND HISTORICAL BUILDINGS

The heart of historic Vicenza is Piazza dei Signori, where Palladio lightens the mood of government buildings with his trademark play of light and shadow. Dazzling white Piovene stone arches frame shady double arcades in the **Basilica Palladiana**. Temporary exhibitions are held in its upstairs hall, but at the time of writing the whole complex was closed for renovations. Across the piazza, white stone and stucco grace the exposed red brick colonnade of the 1571-designed **Loggia del Capitaniato**.

PALAZZO THIENE HISTORICAL BUILDING

(Contrà San Gaetano Thiene; ⊙8.20am-1.20pm & 2.35pm-4.05pm) The bank building at No 12 Contrà Porti is in fact Palladio's renowned Palazzo Thiene, begun under his supervision around 1556. Notice the rustic stone arches capped by gabled windows, and how elegant Corinthian pilasters draw the eye skyward. During bank hours you can wander into the courtyard, but otherwise the building is not open to the public.

Further along the street at No 21, you can't miss Palladio's blinding white, unfinished 1549–53 **Palazzo Isoppo da Porto**, rippling with eight inset Ionic columns on the 1st floor and crowned with sculpture and pilasters along the attic. At the time of writing, this building was also not open to the public.

CHIESA DI SANTA CORONA CHURCH

(☎0444 22 28 11; Contrá Santa Corona at Corso Palladio) Two blocks east of Contrà Porti is another splendid side street: Contrà di Santa Corona, named after Chiesa di Santa Corona. Built by the Dominicans in 1261 to house a relic from Christ's crown of thorns, this Romanesque brick church also houses three light-filled masterpieces: Palladio's 1576 Valmarana Chapel in the crypt; Paolo Veronese's *Adoration of the Magi,* much praised by Goethe; and Giovanni Bellini's radiant *Baptism of Christ,* where the holy event is witnessed by a trio of Veneto beauties and a curious red bird. At the time of writing, the church was closed for restoration, with no definite reopening date.

PALLADIO

When it comes to coffee-table art, no one beats Andrea Palladio. As you flip past photos of his villas, your own problematic living room begins to dissolve, and you find yourself strolling through more harmonious country. Nature is governed by pleasing symmetries. Roman rigour is soothed by rustic charms. He managed to synthesise the classical past without doggedly copying it, creating buildings that were at once inviting, useful and incomparably elegant. From Scotland to St Petersburg, his work – cleverly disseminated by his own 'Quattro Libri', a how-to guide for other architects – shaped the way Europe thought about architecture.

And yet when Palladio turned 30 in 1538, he was little more than a glorified stonecutter in the provincial backwater of Vicenza. His big break came when a local nobleman recognised his potential. Believing it was too late to turn him into a truly learned man, Count Giangiorgio Trissino decided at least to make him into a pleasing and useful one – a fellow who could shore up a sagging garden wall and perhaps jazz it up with a set of antique columns.

To that end, Trissino sent Palladio to Rome to sketch both crumbling antiquities and new works like Michelangelo's dome for St Peter's. Something mysterious happened on those trips, because when the stonecutter returned to Vicenza, he was designing not just whole buildings but forging a completely new way of thinking about architecture – one that married his humble beginnings with the dazzling new knowledge he had lately required. Like Pallas Athena, from whom he took his name, Palladio's ideas seemed to spring full-born from his head.

For Palladio, the search for perfection was never at odds with ruthless practicality – such are the minds of great architects. In his villas, he squeezed stables beneath the most elegant drawing rooms. Lacking funds to line San Giorgio Maggiore with marble, he came up with a superior solution: humble, monochrome stucco walls that diffuse light and fill the church with a revelation of ethereal softness. Constraint became perfection.

A Palladian villa never masters its landscape like, say, Versailles, but neither does it appear to grow naturally out of the earth, like a Kyoto palace. Palladio makes his mark, but tactfully, as if he has merely gathered the natural forces of the land and translated them into an ideal – and distinctly human – response. His Rotonda, for example, crowns a rise in the terrain, and famously looks out on it from four, virtually identical facades. No building like it had ever been built before. Yet when you see it *in situ*, the structure seems to be the rational – even the inevitable – outcome of the site itself.

BASILICA DI MONTE BERICO CHURCH

(☎0444 55 94 11; Viale X Giugno 87; ⏰6am-12.30pm & 2.30-7pm Mon-Sat, 6am-7pm Sun & holidays) Also south of the city, the hilltop Basilica di Monte Berico offers panoramic views of the Palladian city below. The basilica was built in the 18th century to replace a Gothic structure where the Virgin Mary herself is said to have made two appearances in 1426. An impressive 18th-century colonnade runs uphill to the church, roughly parallel to Viale X Giugno.

PIAZZA CASTELLO PIAZZA

The first square you come to along Corso Palladio is Piazza Castello, featuring several grand edifices including the oddly truncated, unfinished **Palazzo Breganze** on the south side, designed by Palladio and built by Vincenzo Scamozzi. Its couple of outsize columns look strange in isolation, but show the makings of an imposing classical structure.

EATING

TOP CHOICE **ANTICO RISTORANTE AGLI SCHIOPPI** OSTERIA €€

(☎0444 54 37 01; www.ristoranteaglischioppi.com; Contrà Piazza del Castello 26; meals €30-40; ⏰dinner Mon, lunch & dinner Tue-Sat) Tucked under an arcade just off Piazza del Castello lies one of the city's simplest and best restaurants. The owners are devotees of locally sourced products, from wild forest greens to baby river trout, but without any pretensions about it; it's just what they know best.

The menu changes with the season, but think quails stuffed with dandelion greens in spring and gamey pasta with musky wild mushrooms in the fall.

DAI NODARI TRATTORIA €€

(☎0444 54 40 85; Contrà do Rode 20; meals €20-30; ⏱noon-3.30pm & 7-11pm) Rustic fare gets hip in the heart of historic Vicenza, attracting young and old alike with hearty yet reasonably priced dishes like duck in beer sauce or a thick soup of orzo, beans and radicchio. Finish with a sweet Sachertorte or a hunk of grappa-washed Bastardo di Grappa cheese.

GASTRONOMIA IL CEPPO TRADITIONAL ITALIAN €

(☎0444 54 44 14; www.gastronomiailceppo.com, in Italian; Corso Palladio 196; prepared dishes per 100g €3-5; ⏱8am-1pm & 3.30-7.45pm Mon, Tue & Thu-Sat, 8am-1pm Wed) San Daniele hams dangle over the vast glass counter, which is filled with ready-made specialities like fresh seafood salads, house-made pastas and speciality cheeses. Never mind that there's no seating available at this temple to local gastronomy: ask counter staff to pair your food selections with a local wine from their shelves for a dream picnic across the street in the Teatro Olimpico.

ANTICO GUELFO MODERN ITALIAN €€

(☎0444 54 78 97; www.anticoguelfo.it; Contrà Pedemuro San Biagio 90; meals €30-40; ⏱dinner Mon-Sat) This culinary hideaway is a hit with slow foodies for its inventive daily market menu, making the most of local specialities in such dishes as Amarone risotto or buckwheat crepes with Bastardo di Grappa cheese. The chef is a specialist in gluten-free cooking, and is usually willing to adapt dishes to any food sensitivity.

RISTORANTE IL CASTELLO TRADITIONAL ITALIAN €€

(☎0444 37 90 32; www.ristoranteilcastellosovizzo.it, in Italian; Via Castello 2, Montemezzo di Sovizzo; meals €35-45; ⏱dinner Tue-Fri, lunch & dinner Sat & Sun) You won't regret the 20-minute drive to this extraordinary hilltop restaurant, which occupies a 15th-century villa of thick stone walls and nobly proportioned rooms. The menu, too, is equally noble and rustic, including perfectly grilled meats and home-made pastas confected with seasonal vegetables and local cheeses.

SLEEPING IN VICENZA

Dozens of hotels in greater Vicenza are listed on the tourism board website (www.vicenzae.org), and a dozen or so B&Bs can be found at www.vitourism.it (in Italian).

➡ **Relais Ca' Muse** (☎0444 37 64 43; www.camuse.it; Via Valle 62, Sovizzo; d from €140; P ❄ @ 🛜 ≋) Impossible to categorise, this gallery-hotel-social experiment in an old stone farmhouse is well worth the 15-minute drive from Vicenza for its serene rooms, remarkable and racy collection of contemporary art, well-tended grounds, and breakfasts of the freshest, best local ingredients.

➡ **Relais Santa Corona** (☎0444 32 46 78; www.relaissantacorona.it; Contrà Santa Corona 19; s/d €100/150; P ❄ @ 🛜) This boutique bargain offers stylish stays in an 18th-century palace ideally located on a street dotted with landmarks. Guestrooms are soothing and soundproofed, with excellent mattresses, minimal-chic decor and free wi-fi.

➡ **Hotel Palladio** (☎0444 32 53 47; www.hotel-palladio.it; Contrà Oratorio dei Servi 25; s/d €110/170; P ❄ @ 🛜) The top choice in central Vicenza, this four-star hotel boasts well-appointed rooms done up in whitewashed minimalism, while preserving key details of the Renaissance *palazzo* it occupies.

➡ **Albergo Due Mori** (☎0444 32 18 86; www.hotelduemori.com; Contrà do Rode 26; d/tr €85/100, s/d with shared bathroom €40/60; @ 🛜) Right off Piazza dei Signori on a boutique-lined cobblestone street, this historic 1854 hotel has a modicum of period charm – especially for the price – with *stile liberty* (Liberty style) bedsteads and antique armoires. There are fans instead of air-con and no TV, but in a nod to modernity there's disabled access and wi-fi. Breakfast extra.

➡ **Ostello Olimpico** (☎0444 54 02 22; www.ostellovicenza.com; Via Antonio Giuriolo 9; dm €20, s/d €28/48; ⏱reception 7.30-9.30am & 3.30-11.30pm; 🛜) A convenient HI youth hostel set in a fine building by the Teatro Olimpico. There is no curfew and wi-fi is free.

WORTH A DETOUR

IN PALLADIO'S FOOTSTEPS SOUTH OF VICENZA

Palladio's most famous works are scattered across the Veneto countryside, and because many remain private homes, visiting hours tend to be short, seasonal, sporadic and/or by reservations only. That makes it nearly impossible to see all his major works in a day or two. Still, those with a car (or a bike and strong legs) can see a healthy dose of his innovative works – plus extraordinary villas by those who followed closely in his footsteps – by taking a 110km loop south of Vicenza.

Starting just west of Vicenza in **Montecchio Maggiore**, seek out the exquisite **Villa Cordellina Lombardi** (0444 69 60 85; Via Lovara 36; adult/reduced €2.10/1; 9am-1pm Tue & Fri, 9am-1pm & 3-6pm Wed-Thu & Sat & Sun Apr-Oct, by appointment only Nov-Mar), built in the 1740s by Giorgio Massari. Despite its easy Palladian graces, this villa has seen its share of hard work: it was used during both World Wars for military purposes, and served as a farm for breeding silkworms. Now, thanks to careful restoration of the interiors, Giambattista's Tiepolo's fresco *Intelligence Triumphing over Ignorance* glows freshly once again. Impressive Intelligence blows into the room to the trumpets of Fame, as mighty Ignorance is struck by a putto's arrow and tumbles from the ceiling.

From Montecchio Maggiore, head south to the village of Sarego, where you can see the incomplete and somewhat dilapidated Palladian complex of **Villa Trissino** (not open to the public). A couple of kilometres south of Sarego through rolling vineyard country, **Lonigo** is surrounded by horses, cattle and Scamozzi's 1576 domed, hilltop **Rocca Pisana** (0444 83 16 25; admission €5; by prior appointment 3-5.30pm Tue Mar-Nov), which pays careful homage to Palladio's La Rotonda. About 4km further south, the village of **Bagnolo** is home to the proud Palladian **Villa Pisani Ferri Bonetti** (0444 83 11 04; admission €7; 10am-noon & 2-6pm Apr-Nov, visits by prior appointment only), a 16th-century facade standing tall above rolling lawns and a stream.

From Bagnolo, a series of winding country lanes leads southeast to **Pojana Maggiore** and another of Palladio's designs just south out of town on the road to Legnago: the frescoed 1550 **Villa Pojana** (0444 89 85 54; admission €4; 10am-12.30pm & 2-4pm Sat & Sun Nov-Mar, 10am-12.30pm & 2-4pm daily Apr-Oct), which was inspired by ancient Roman baths. Three kilometres east in **Noventa Vicentina** is the 17th-century **Villa Barbarigo** (0444 78 85 11; www.comune.noventa-vicentina.vi.it; admission free; 10am-1pm Tue, Wed & Fri, 10am-1pm & 3-5pm Mon & Thu), which these days makes a mighty impressive town hall for a country village; beyond the deep porch and two massive tiers of columns, frescoes on the walls of the grand salons have been lovingly restored. Just east, lies **Finale** (just south of Agugliaro) and Palladio's **Villa Saraceno** (0444 89 13 71, Landmark Trust in UK 01628-825925; www.landmarktrust.org.uk; Via Finale 8, Finale di Agugliaro; to the public 2-4pm Wed Apr-Oct; P), a beautifully restored villa that is also available for temporary rental.

Heading back toward Vicenza, stop at the pretty village of **Costozza**, whose star attraction is the complex known as the **Ville da Schio** (gardens admission €5; 9.30am-7.30pm Tue-Sun), in which frescoed mansions are set against a hillside of magnificent baroque gardens dotted with sculpture. Get your entry tickets to see the gardens from the neighbouring Botte del Covolo wine bar. In the shadow of the **Colli Berici** hills (some great walking), the village is worth a stroll and wine stop in a handful of *enoteche* (wine bars). Finally, head to **Vancimuglio,** home of the privately owned **Villa Chiericati da Porto Rigo**. It is not open, but you can see its weather-worn but winsome facade from the road.

From here, it's a straight shot back to Vicenza. If you haven't already done so, end on a grand note with a stop at Palladio's La Rotonda (p173) – perhaps his single most influential building.

DRINKING

ANTICA CASA DELLA MALVASIA WINE BAR

(☎0444 54 37 04; Contrà delle Morette 5; ⏰11am-12.30pm Mon-Thu & Sat, 5.30pm-2am Fri) This purveyor of wines has been in business since 1200, when Malvasia wine was imported from Greece by Venetian merchants. Its menu covers 80 wines, including prime Italian Malvasia, plus 100 types of grappa from just up the road in Bassano del Grappa. Its **wine bar** (⏰11am-12.30pm Mon-Thu & Sat, 5.30pm-2am Fri) next door offers quick bites and good local wines by the glass.

SORARÙ CAFE

(☎0444 32 09 15; Piazzetta Palladio; ⏰7.30am-12.30pm & 3.30-7.30pm Thu-Tue) Drink in the history at this marble-topped bar, serving bracing espresso and pastries made on the premises. There are also tempting jars of sweets stashed on the elaborately gilded shelves. A few outdoor tables offer views of one of Italian's finest piazzas.

Verona

Explore

A key crossroads since Roman times, Verona (population 264,500) has a 1st century AD arena that still serves as one of the world's great opera venues. Book tickets (and accommodation) well ahead during summer. Verona's historic centre also bristles with masterful Romanesque churches and the highly defended medieval digs of the wrathful Scaligeri clan. Today, Verona's entering its third act as a small but prosperous industrial centre – and mainstay of Italy's hard right. While it's larger than Padua and Vicenza and farther away from Venice, it's still possible to see most of its key sights in a day, though it'll take an earlier start and more careful planning. Consider spending the night if you want to delve deeper – or explore Verona's remarkable wine country (p187).

The Best...

- **Sight** Roman Arena (p179)
- **Place to Eat** Pintxos Bistrot (p183)
- **Place to Drink** Antica Bottega del Vino (p184)

Top Tip

VeronaCard (2/5 days €15/20), available at tourist sights as well as tobacconists, is great value, providing access to virtually all major monuments and churches, plus unlimited use of local buses.

Getting There & Away

Train There are at least three trains hourly to Venice (€6.35 to €20, 1¼ to 2½ hours). The station is about a 20-minute walk south of the historic centre. From just in front of the station, there are also frequent local bus connections to the centre.

Car Verona is at the intersection of the A4 (Turin–Trieste) and A22 motorways.

Need to Know

- **Area code** ☎045
- **Location** 120km west of Venice
- **Tourist office** (☎045 806 86 80; www.tourism.verona.it; Via degli Alpini 9; ⏰10am-1pm & 2-6pm Mon-Tue, 9am-6pm Wed-Sat, 10am-4pm Sun, shorter hours Jan & Feb)

SIGHTS

ROMAN ARENA ARCHAEOLOGICAL SITE

(☎045 800 03 60; www.arena.it; Piazza Brà, ticket office Ente Lirico Arena di Verona, Via Dietro Anfiteatro 6b; opera tickets €20-150, tours adult/student/child €6/4.50/1; ⏰8.30am-7.30pm Tue-Sun, 1.30-7.30pm Mon, last admission 6.30pm) This Roman-era arena, built of pink-tinged marble in the 1st century AD, survived a 12th-century earthquake to become Verona's legendary open-air opera house, with seating for 30,000 people. You can visit the arena year-round, though it's at its best during the June-to-August opera season, which features around 50 performances by some of the world's top names – Placido Domingo made his debut here. In winter months, concerts are held at the adjacent 18th-century **Ente Lirico Arena**.

BASILICA DI SAN ZENO MAGGIORE CHURCH

(www.chieseverona.it; Piazza San Zeno; with Verona Card free, combined Verona church ticket/single church entry €6/2.50; ⏰8.30am-6pm Tue-Sat, 12.30-6pm Sun Mar-Oct; 10am-1pm & 1.30-5pm Tue-Sat, 12.30-5pm Sun Nov-Feb) A masterpiece of

Verona

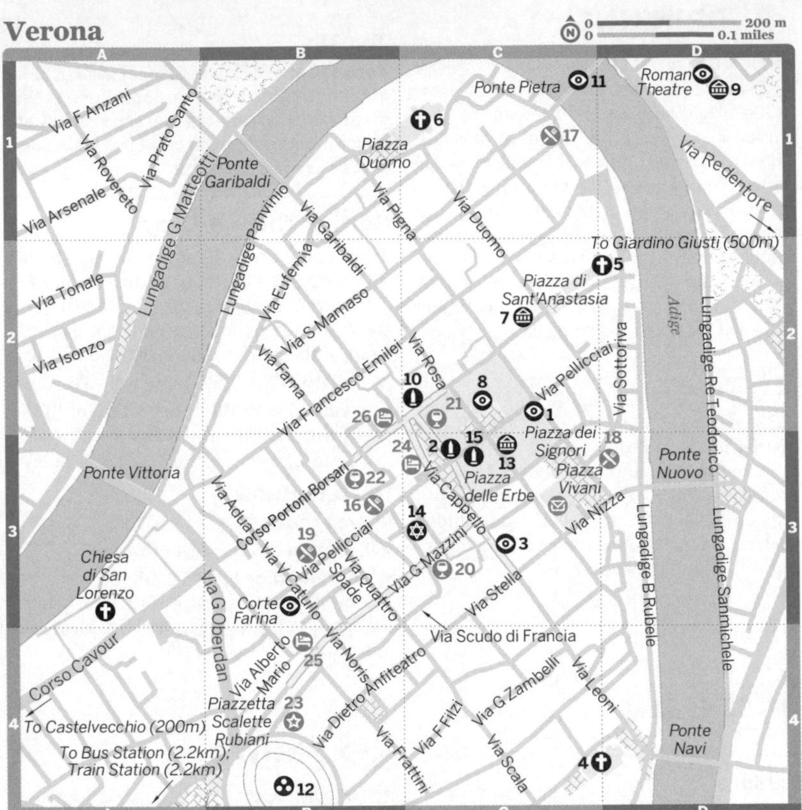

Romanesque architecture, the striped brick and stone Basilica di San Zeno Maggiore was built in honour of the city's patron saint from the 12th to 14th centuries. Enter through the graceful, flower-filled cloister into the nave – a vast space lined with 12th- to 15th-century frescoes, including Mary Magdalene modestly covered in her curtain of golden hair and St George casually slaying a dragon atop a startled horse. Under the rose window depicting the Wheel of Fortune, you'll find meticulously detailed 12th-century bronze doors, including a scene of an exorcism with a demon being yanked from a woman's mouth (under restoration at the time of writing). Painstaking restoration has already revived Mantegna's 1457–59 *Majesty of the Virgin* polyptych altarpiece, painted with such astonishing perspective and convincing textures that you actually believe there are garlands of fresh fruit hanging behind the Madonna's throne. Below the main altar is a fascinatingly eerie crypt, with faces carved into medieval capitals and St Zeno's corpse glowing in a transparent sarcophagus.

CASTELVECCHIO MUSEUM

(☎045 806 26 11; Corso Castelvecchio 2; with Verona Card free, adult/reduced €6/4.50; ⏲8.30am-7.30pm Tue-Sun & 1.30-7.30pm Mon) Bristling with battlements along the back of the River Adige, Castelvecchio was built in the 1350s by the tyrannical Cangrande II. The fortress was so severely damaged by Napoleon's troops and then WWII bombings that many feared it was beyond repair. But instead of erasing the Castelvecchio's chequered past with restorations, Carlo Scarpa reinvented the building 1960s-style, building bridges over exposed foundations, filling gaping holes with glass panels, and balancing a statue of Cangrande I above the courtyard on a concrete gangplank. Scarpa's revived Castelvecchio makes a fitting home for Verona's largest museum, with a diverse collection of frescoes, jewellery, medieval arte-

Verona

Sights

1	Arche Scaligere	C2
2	Arco della Costa	C3
3	Casa di Giulietta	C3
4	Chiesa di San Fermo	C4
5	Chiesa di Sant'Anastasia	D2
6	Duomo	C1
7	Galleria D'Arte Moderna	C2
	Jewish Ghetto	(see 14)
8	Loggia del Consiglio	C2
9	Museo Archeologico	D1
10	Palazzo Maffei	C2
11	Ponte Pietro	C1
12	Roman Arena	B4
13	Scavi Scaligeri	C3
14	Synagogue	C3
15	Torre dei Lamberti	C3

Eating

16	Café Noir	B3
17	Gelateria Ponte Pietra	C1
18	Pintxos Bistrot	D3
19	Pizzeria Du de Cope	B3

Drinking & Nightlife

20	Antica Bottega del Vino	C3
21	Caffè Filippini	C2
22	Osteria del Bugiardo	B3

Entertainment

	Ente Lirico Arena di Verona	(see 23)
23	Roman Arena Ticket Office	B4

Sleeping

24	Albergo Aurora	C3
25	Anfiteatro B&B	B4
26	Hotel Gabbia d'Oro	B2

facts and paintings by Pisanello, Giovanni Bellini, Tiepolo, Carpaccio and Veronese. The museum also hosts interesting temporary exhibitions ranging from Old Master retrospectives to modernist arts and crafts.

DUOMO CHURCH

(www.chieseverona.it; Piazza del Duomo; with Verona Card free, combined Verona church ticket/single church entry €6/2.50; 10am-5.30pm Mon-Sat, 1.30-5.30pm Sun Mar-Oct, 10am-1pm & 1.30-5pm Tue-Sat, 1.30-5pm Sun Nov-Feb) Verona's 12th-century cathedral is a striking, striped Romanesque building, with polychrome reliefs and the bug-eyed statues of Charlemagne's paladins Roland and Oliver, crafted by medieval master Nicolò, on the west porch. Nothing about this sober facade hints at the extravagant interior, frescoed over during the 16th to 17th centuries with angels aloft amid trompe l'oeil architecture. At the left end of the nave is the Cartolari-Nichesola Chapel, designed by Renaissance master Jacopo Sansovino and featuring a vibrant Titian *Assumption,* in which astonished crowds gape at an airborne Madonna.

CHIESA DI SANT'ANASTASIA CHURCH

(Piazza di Sant'Anastasia; www.chieseverona.it; combined church ticket/single entry €6/2.50; 10am-1pm & 1.30-5pm Tue-Sat, 1-5pm Sun) Dating from the 13th to 15th centuries, the Gothic Chiesa di Sant'Anastasia is Verona's largest church and a showcase for local art. The multitude of frescoes is overwhelming, but don't overlook Pisanello's storybook-quality fresco *St George Setting out to Free the Princess from the Dragon* in the Pisanelli Chapel (undergoing restoration at the time of writing), or the 1495 holy water font featuring a hunchback carved by Paolo Veronese's father, Gabriele Caliari.

PIAZZA DELLE ERBE & PIAZZA DEI SIGNORI HISTORICAL SITE

Originally a Roman forum, Piazza delle Erbe is ringed with buzzing cafes and some of Verona's most sumptuous buildings, including the elegantly baroque **Palazzo Maffei** (now a corporate headquarters) at its northern end.

Separating Piazza delle Erbe from Piazza dei Signori is the monumental gate known as **Arco della Costa**, hung with a whale's rib that, according to legend, will fall on the first just person to walk beneath it. So far, it remains intact, despite visits by popes and kings. On the northern side of Piazza dei Signori stands Verona's early-Renaissance **Loggia del Consiglio**, the 15th-century city council (not open to visitors). Through the archway at the far end of the piazza are the open-air **Arche Scaligere** – elaborate Gothic tombs of the Scaligeri family where murderers are interred next to the relatives they killed.

Dividing the two piazzas, the striped **Torre dei Lamberti** (045 927 30 27; adult/reduced €6/4.50; 8.30am-7.30pm, to 8.30pm Jun-Sep) rises a neck-craning 85m. Begun in the 12th century and finished in 1463 – too late to notice invading Venetians – this watchtower still offers panoramic views of the city and nearby mountains, which are snowcapped in winter. A lift whisks you up two-thirds of the way; for the last few

WORTH A DETOUR

BASSANO DEL GRAPPA, ASOLO & PALLADIO'S VILLA DI MASER

A road trip north of Vicenza takes you through one of Italy's most sophisticated stretches of countryside, including the most splendid villa in the Veneto – and one of the most important in all Europe. With a car and an early start, you can visit all the key sites in a day – including a leisurely lunch.

Head first to **Bassano del Grappa**, which sits with charming simplicity on the banks of the River Brenta where it winds its way free from Alpine foothills. Located 35km northeast of Vicenza, the town is famous above all for its namesake spirit, grappa – a fiery distillation of leftovers from winemaking: skins, pulp, seeds and stems. At the **Poli Museo della Grappa** (☎0424 52 44 26; www.poligrappa.com; Via Gamba 6; admission free; ⏰9am-7.30pm), you can drink in four centuries of the history of Bassano's signature spirits (including a free tasting).

About 17km east of Bassano rises **Asolo**, known as the 'town of 100 vistas' for its panoramic hillside location – and a long favourite of literary types. Robert Browning spent time in Asolo, but the ultimate local celebrity is Caterina Corner, the 15th-century queen of Cyprus who was given the town, its **castle** (now used as a theatre, only open for performances) and surrounding county in exchange for her abdication. She promptly became the queen of the local literary set, holding salons that featured writer Pietro Bembo. It is believed that it was Bembo who coined the verb *asolare*, which can be loosely translated as 'to do nothing but take pleasure in the passing of time'. In Asolo's **Museo Civico** (☎0423 95 23 13; Via Regina Cornaro 74; adult/reduced €4/3; ⏰10am-noon & 3-7pm Sat & Sun), you can explore the town's prehistoric and Roman past and wander through a small collection of local paintings ranging from the Renaissance to Impressionism, plus a pair of portraits by Tintoretto. The museum also includes rooms devoted to Eleonora Duse (1858–1924) – a major actress romantically and politically linked with nationalist poet Gabriele d'Annunzio – and British traveller and writer Freya Stark (1893–1993), who retreated to Asolo between Middle Eastern forays.

Another 5km east lies **Villa di Maser** (☎423 92 30 04; www.villadimaser.it; adult/reduced €6/5; ⏰10am-6pm Tue-Sat & 11am-6pm Sun Apr-Jun, Sep & Oct, 10.30am-6pm Tue, Thu, Sat & 11am-6pm Sun Mar, Jul & Aug, 11am-5pm Sat & Sun Nov & Dec, 11am-5pm Sat & Sun Jan & Feb), where Palladio and Paolo Veronese conspired to create the Veneto countryside's finest monument to *la bella vita*. Palladio set the arcaded yellow villa into a verdant hillside with a fanciful grotto out the back. Inside, Paolo Veronese nearly upstages his collaborator with wildly imaginative trompe l'oeil architecture of his own. Vines climb the walls of the Stanza di Baccho; an alert watchdog keeps one eye on the painted door of the Stanza di Canuccio (Little Dog Room); and in a corner of the frescoed grand salon, the painter has apparently forgotten his spattered shoes and broom. At the wine-tasting room by the villa's parking lot, you can raise a toast to Palladio and Veronese with Maser estate-grown DOC (*denominazione d'origine controllata*; quality-controlled) *prosecco*. And just east of the villa's gates, you can admire Palladio's **Tempietto**. The domed, centrally-planned church is a graceful, miniature version of the Pantheon in Rome. Note that the church is rarely open.

storeys you will have to rely on your own thigh power.

GIARDINO GIUSTI GARDEN

(☎045 803 40 29; Via Giardino Giusti 2; admission €6; ⏰9am-8pm Apr-Sep, 9am-sunset Oct-Mar) Across the river from the historic centre, these lushly sculpted gardens, considered a masterpiece of Renaissance landscaping, are well worth seeking out. Named after the noble family that has looked after them since opening them to the public in 1591, the gardens have lost none of their charm over the centuries. The vegetation is an Italianate mix of the sculpted and natural, graced by soaring cypresses, one of which the German poet Goethe immortalised in his travel writings. According to local legend, lovers who manage to find each other in the little labyrinth on the right side of the garden are destined to stay together. On the back end of the garden, a short but steep climb rewards with sweeping views over the city.

MUSEO ARCHEOLOGICO ARCHAEOLOGICAL SITE

(☎045 800 03 60; Regaste Redentore 2; adult/student/child €4.50/3/1; ⏲8.30am-7.30pm Tue-Sun, 1.45-7.30pm Mon) Just north of the historic centre you'll find a **Roman theatre**. Built in the 1st century BC, it is cunningly carved into the hillside at a strategic spot overlooking a bend in the river. Take the lift at the back of the theatre to the former convent above, which houses an interesting collection of Greek and Roman pieces.

PONTE PIETRA ARCHAEOLOGICAL SITE

At the northern edge of the city centre, this bridge is a quiet but remarkable testament to the Italians' love of their artistic heritage. Two of the bridge's arches date from the Roman Republican era in the 1st century BC, while the other three were replaced in the 13th century. The ancient bridge remained largely intact until 1945, when retreating German troops blew it up. But locals fished the fragments out of the river, and painstakingly rebuilt the bridge stone by stone in the 1950s.

GALLERIA D'ARTE MODERNA MUSEUM

(☎045 800 19 03; www.palazzoforti.it; Palazzo Forti, off Corso Sant'Anastasia near Via Duomo; adult/student €6/5; ⏲10.30am-7pm Tue-Sun) In a rambling Renaissance and baroque palace, this interesting collection ranges from Italy's late 19th-century Impressionists to recent avant-garde works. It also holds occasionally interesting international shows.

SCAVI SCALIGERI MUSEUM

(☎045 800 74 90; Cortile del Tribunale; with Verona Card free, adult/reduced €6/4.50; ⏲vary) Find well-curated contemporary photography displayed amid the Roman ruins that archaeologists uncovered right underneath Verona's medieval and Renaissance city centre in the 1980s.

CASA DI GIULIETTA HISTORICAL BUILDING

(Juliet's House; ☎045 803 43 03; Via Cappello 23; with Verona Card free, adult/reduced €6/4.50; ⏲8.30am-7.30pm Tue-Sun, 1.30-7.30pm Mon) Never mind that Romeo and Juliet were fictional characters with no resemblance to Veronese nobility, or that there's hardly room for two on the narrow stone balcony. Romantics flock to this 14th-century house anyway, first adding their lovelorn pleas to the graffiti on the courtyard causeway and then rubbing the right breast of the bronze statue of Juliet for luck.

JEWISH GHETTO SYNAGOGUE

Off Piazza delle Erbe to the southwest is Verona's historic Jewish Ghetto. Tall buildings frame the narrow side street **Via Rita Rosani**, named for the Resistance heroine who commanded a band of partisans in Verona until 1944, when she was caught and summarily executed at age 24. On the southeast side of Via Rosani is Verona's newly restored **synagogue**, where you might find the doors open to Jewish visitors and others who express a sincere interest.

CHIESA DI SAN FERMO CHURCH

(Stradone San Fermo; www.chieseverona.it; combined church ticket/single entry €6/2.5; ⏲10am-1pm & 1.30-5pm Tue Sat, 1-5pm Sun) At the river end of Via Leoni, Chiesa di San Fermo is actually two churches in one: Franciscan monks raised the 13th-century Gothic church right over an original 11th-century Romanesque structure. Inside the main Gothic church, you'll notice a magnificent timber *carena di nave,* a ceiling reminiscent of an upturned boat's hull. In the right transept are 14th-century frescoes, including some fragments depicting episodes in the life of St Francis. Stairs from the cloister lead underground to the spare but atmospheric Romanesque church below.

EATING

PINTXOS BISTROT MODERN ITALIAN €€€

(☎045 59 42 87; www.ristorantealcristo.it, in Italian; Piazzetta Pescheria 6; meals €40-60; ⏲lunch & dinner Tue-Sun) Taking its inspiration from Catalan-style tapas, this airy bistro offers an excitingly eclectic menu that mixes Italian pastas, Catalan cheeses and hams, and small plate dishes perfumed with exotic ingredients like lemon grass and tamarind – even sushi and sashimi. A local foodie favourite, it gets packed during the summer opera season – book ahead. There is no sign for the restaurant. Instead, look for Ristorante al Cristo, which shares the same entrance.

GELATERIA PONTE PIETRA GELATERIA €

(☎340 471 72 94; Via Ponte Pietra 23; ⏲2.30-7.30pm, to 10pm Jun-Aug, closed Nov-Feb) Impeccable gelato is made on the premises, with flavours like *bacio bianco* (white chocolate and hazelnut), candied orange with cinnamon, and *mille fiori* (cream with honey and bits of pollen gathered from local hillsides).

SLEEPING IN VERONA

Cooperativa Albergatori Veronesi (☎045 800 98 44; www.veronapass.com) offers a no-fee booking service for two-star hotels. For home-style stays outside the city centre, check **Verona Bed & Breakfast** (www.bedandbreakfastverona.com). Try to book well ahead if you plan to be here during the summer opera season.

➡ **Anfiteatro B&B** (☎347 248 84 62; www.anfiteatro-bedandbreakfast.com; Via Alberto Mario 5; s €60-90, d €80-130, tr €100-150) Opera divas and fashionistas rest up steps from the action in this 19th-century townhouse, one block from the Roman Arena and just off boutique-lined Via Mazzini. Spacious guestrooms have high wood-beamed ceilings, antique armoires for stashing purchases, and divans for swooning after shows.

➡ **Hotel Gabbia d'Oro** (☎045 59 02 93; www.hotelgabbiadoro.it; Corso Porta Borsari 4a; d from €220; P ❄ @ 📶) One of the city's top addresses and also one of its most romantic, the Gabbia d'Oro features luxe rooms inside an 18th-century *palazzo* that manage to be both elegant and cosy. The rooftop terrace and central location are icing on the wedding cake.

➡ **Villa Francescati** (☎045 59 03 60; www.ostelloverona.it; Salita Fontana del Ferro 15; dm €18-20; ⏲7am-midnight) This HI youth hostel is housed in a 16th-century villa on a garden estate a 20-minute walk from central Verona. Dinners cost €9 (reservations required); there are no cooking facilities. Rooms are off-limits 9am to 5pm, but you can use the common rooms. Catch bus 73 (weekdays) or bus 90 (Sunday and holidays) from the train station.

➡ **Albergo Aurora** (☎045 59 47 17; www.hotelaurora.biz; Piazza XIV Novembre 2; s €90-135, d €100-160; ❄) Right off bustling Piazza Erbe yet cosy and blissfully quiet, this hotel has spacious, unfussy doubles, some with city views. There are cheaper single rooms with shared bathroom (€58 to €80). Head to the sunny terrace for drinks overlooking the Piazza.

PIZZERIA DU DE COPE — PIZZERIA €

(☎045 59 55 62; www.pizzeriadudecope.it; Galleria Pellicciai 10; pizzas 6-12; ⏲noon-2pm & 7-11pm) This fashion-forward pizzeria manages to blend refinement with relaxed ease in its airy and vividly coloured dining space. You can peek over the counter and watch your pizza bubbling in the wood-fired oven, or ease up on the carbs with one of the high-quality salads.

CAFÉ NOIR — CAFE €

(☎045 803 05 00; Via Pellicciai 12; meals €10-15; ⏲7.30am-7.30pm Mon-Sat) In addition to excellent coffee, teas and wickedly thick hot chocolate, this trim little cafe also serves up economical two-course lunches for under €12. No dinner.

DRINKING

ANTICA BOTTEGA DEL VINO — TRADITIONAL ITALIAN €€€

(☎045 800 45 35; www.bottegavini.it; Via Scudo di Francia 3; meals €50-60; ⏲lunch & dinner Wed-Mon) Wine is the primary consideration at this historic *enoteca* with beautiful wood panelling and backlit bottles of Valpolicella vintages. The sommelier will gladly recommend a worthy vintage for your lobster *crudo* salad, Amarone risotto or suckling pig – some of the best wines here are bottled specifically for the Bottega. Note they sometimes close in November and February, so call ahead.

OSTERIA DEL BUGIARDO — WINE BAR

(☎045 59 18 69; Corso Portoni Borsari 17a; ⏲11am-11pm, to midnight Fri & Sat) On busy Corso Portoni Borsari, traffic converges at Bugiardo for glasses of upstanding Valpolicella bottled specifically for the *osteria*. Polenta and *sopressa* make worthy bar snacks for the powerhouse Amarone.

CAFFÈ FILIPPINI — BAR

(☎045 800 45 49; Piazza delle Erbe 26; ⏲4pm-2am Thu-Tue, daily Jun-Aug) On the town's most bustling square, the hippest joint in town has been here since 1901, perfecting the house speciality Filippini, a killer cocktail of vermouth, gin, lemon and ice.

The Dolomites

Explore

The spiked peaks and emerald-green valleys of the Dolomites are so beautiful, and their ecosystem so unique, they've won Unesco protection. Though a world away, on clear days these peaks are visible from Venice itself. Perched on bluffs above the River Piave, historic Belluno (population 35,600) makes a scenic, strategic base to explore the region. For breathtaking hikes, head to the nearby Parco Nazionale delle Dolomiti Bellunesi. In winter, Cortina d'Ampezzo is the place to be, with fashion-conscious snow bunnies crowding its excellent slopes. By car, you can get a flavour of the region in a day from Venice, but you need at least a night or two if you want to get off-road and explore its natural wonders – more if you rely on regional trains and buses.

The Best...

➡ **Sight** Parco Nazionale delle Dolomiti Bellunesi (p186)

➡ **Place to Eat** Al Borgo (p187)

➡ **Place to Drink** Al Borgo (p187)

Top Tip

Don't miss Belluno's remarkable cheeses, including Schiz (semisoft cow's-milk cheese, usually fried in butter) and the flaky, butter-yellow Malga Bellunense.

Getting There & Away

Bus Cortina Express (☎0437 86 73 50; www.cortinaexpress.it) has daily direct service to Cortina d'Ampezzo from the Mestre train station (2¼ hours) and the Venice airport (two hours). The regional

Car To reach Belluno, take the A27 from Venice (Mestre), which avoids traffic around Treviso. To reach Cortina, look for the SS51 just east of Belluno.

Dolomiti Bus (☎0437 21 71 11; www.dolomitibus.it) offers regular service between Belluno, Cortina d'Ampezzo and smaller mountain towns.

Train Trains from Venice (€6, two to 2½ hours, five to 10 daily) serve Belluno via Treviso and/or Conegliano. Changing trains can sometimes add another hour to travel times. There is no train service to Cortina d'Ampezzo.

Need to Know

➡ **Area Code** Belluno ☎0437; Cortina d'Ampezzo ☎0436

➡ **Location** Belluno is 106km north of Venice; Cortina d'Ampezzo is 161km north of Venice

➡ **Tourist Office** Belluno (☎0437 94 00 83; www.infodolomiti.it; Piazza Duomo 2; ⏲9am-12.30pm & 3.30-6.30pm Mon-Sat, 9am-12.30pm Sun); Cortina d'Ampezzo (☎0436 32 31; www.infodolimiti.it; Piazetta San Francesco 8; ⏲9am-12.30pm & 3.30-6.30pm Mon-Sat).

THE DOLOMITES: A SCIENTIFIC SEA CHANGE

In explaining the Dolomites' World Heritage status, Unesco cites their sheer beauty, which 'derives from a variety of spectacular vertical forms such as pinnacles, spires and towers, with contrasting horizontal surfaces including ledges, crags and plateaux'. Unesco also singles out the 'great diversity of colours...provided by the contrasts between the bare pale-coloured rock surfaces and the forests and meadows below'.

But the Dolomites aren't just good-looking – they have inspired great thinkers too. From the 18th-century, they played a key role in the development of modern geology. The mountains are named for 18th-century geologist Déodat de Dolomieu, who was the first to identify dolomite – the carbonate mineral that is largely responsible for the mountains' distinctive colours and shapes. More importantly, geologists discovered that portions of the mountains were made up of fossilised atolls. In the struggle to explain how these tropical sponges and coral found their way to the tops of the Italian Alps, geologists were forced to come up with revolutionary new ideas about the earth's development.

SIGHTS & ACTIVITIES

Belluno

PARCO NAZIONALE DELLE DOLOMITI BELLUNESI NATURE RESERVE

(www.dolomitipark.it) Northwest of Belluno, the Parco Nazionale delle Dolomiti Bellunesi is a magnificent national park offering trails for hikers at every level, wildflowers in spring and summer and restorative gulps of crisp mountain air year-round. Between late June and early September, hikers walking six **Alte Vie delle Dolomiti** (high-altitude Dolomites walking trails) pass Belluno en route to mountain refuges. Route 1 starts in Belluno and, in about 13 days, covers 150km of breathtaking mountain scenery to Lago di Braies in Val Pusteria to the north. For more information about other hikes of all lengths and levels of difficulty, including themed itineraries and maps, check out www.parks.it/parco.nazionale.dol.bellunesi/Eiti.php.

PIAZZA DEI MARTIRI PIAZZA

Belluno's main pedestrian square is the Piazza dei Martiri (Martyrs' Sq), named after the four partisans hanged here in WWII. On sunny days and warm nights, its cafes overflow with young and old alike.

PIAZZA DEL DUOMO PIAZZA

At the heart of the old town, Piazza del Duomo is framed by the early-16th-century Renaissance **Cattedrale di San Martino**, the 16th-century **Palazzo Rosso** and the **Palazzo dei Vescovi** with a striking 12th-century tower.

SLEEPING IN THE DOLOMITES

To explore hotel, B&B, camping and *agriturismo* (rustic lodging, usually with half board) options in the Dolomites, check www.infodolomiti.it and www.dolomitipark.it.

➡ **Azienda Agrituristica Sant'Anna** (☎0437 274 91; www.aziendasantanna.it; Via Pedecastello 27, Belluno; d per night €50-80, per week €330-460) This idyllic stone farmhouse 4km outside Belluno in the Castion neighbourhood proffers mod cons without losing rustic charms: think iron bedsteads, timber floors and beamed ceilings, all with shared or private kitchens. Enthusiastic, English-speaking hosts happily orient visitors, from hiking to eating, and also offer hands-on classes in agricultural practices on the adjacent farm. No breakfast.

➡ **Baita Fraina** (☎0436 36 34; www.baitafraina.it; Via Fraina 1, Cortina d'Ampezzo; d Jan-Nov €60-100, Dec €100-140; ⏲closed May & Nov; P) Reserve ahead in high season at this beloved, Swiss-style inn with simple but spotless rooms of knotty pine. The fine restaurant has a menu inspired by local ingredients, from mountain herbs to wild game.

➡ **Ostello Imperina** (☎0437 624 51; www.parks.it/ost/imperina; Località Le Miniere; dm €20, half/full board €37/50; ⏲7.20am-10pm Apr-Oct) The area's only youth hostel lies inside the Parco Nazionale delle Dolomiti Bellunesi, 35km northwest of Belluno at Rivamonte Agordino. Book ahead in summer. To get there, take the Agordo bus (50 minutes) from Belluno.

➡ **Hotel Montana** (☎0436 86 21 26; www.cortina-hotel.com; Corso Italia 94; Cortina d'Ampezzo; s €52-65, d €88-97; @) Right in the heart of Cortina, this friendly, vintage 1920s Alpine hotel offers simple but well-maintained rooms. In winter, there's a seven-night minimum (€310 to €580 per person), but call for last-minute cancellations. Reception areas double as gallery space for local artists.

➡ **Albergo Cappello e Cadore** (☎0437 94 02 46; www.albergocappello.com; Via Ricci 8, Belluno; s €45-75, d €90-103; P) At this rose-coloured, 19th-century inn just off Piazza dei Martiri, guestrooms are small and monastery-modest, with plain pine bedsteads. A few top-floor rooms have views. Reserve ahead, as this is the only affordable option in town.

Cortina d'Ampezzo

CORTINA D'AMPEZZO SKI COOPERATIVE SKIING

Two cable cars whisk skiers and walkers from Cortina's town centre to a central departure point for chair lifts, cable cars and trails. Lifts usually run from 9am to 5pm daily from mid-December to at least 1 April. Artificial snow makes up for what nature lacks. Runs range from bunny to the legendary Staunies black mogul run: starting at 3000m, Staunies isn't for the faint of heart or weak of knee. Passes are sold at the **ski pass office** (☎0436 86 21 71; Via G Marconi 15; 1-/2-/3-day/week pass €46/91/132/247; ⏱vary).

OLYMPIC ICE STADIUM ICE SKATING

(☎0436 88 18 11; Via dello Stadio 1; adult/child incl skate rental €10/9; ⏱vary) During white-outs, take a spin around this rink built for the 1956 Winter Olympics.

GUIDE ALPINE CORTINA D'AMPEZZO HIKING, ROCK-CLIMBING

(☎0436 86 85 05; www.guidecortina.com; Corso Italia 69a) In milder weather, guides from this reputable outfit run rock-climbing courses (three-day climbing course including gear rental €260), mountain-climbing excursions and guided nature hikes (prices vary). In winter they also offer ad hoc courses in off-trail skiing, snowshoeing and more.

EATING

TOP CHOICE **AL BORGO** TRADITIONAL ITALIAN €€

(☎0437 92 67 55; www.alborgo.to; Via Anconetta 8, Belluno; meals around €30-40; ⏱lunch Mon, lunch & dinner Wed-Sun) If you have wheels or strong legs, seek out this delightful restaurant in an 18th-century villa in the hills about 3km south of Belluno. Considered Belluno's best, the kitchen produces everything from homemade salamis and roast lamb to artisanal gelato. Wines are also skilfully chosen.

LA TAVERNA TRADITIONAL ITALIAN €€

(☎0437 251 92; Via Cipro 7, Belluno; meals €25-30; ⏱lunch & dinner Mon-Sat) This place just off Piazza dei Martiri features top-notch seasonal bruschetta with *prosecco* at the bar. In the adjoining restaurant, carbo-load for your hike with fresh *porcini tagliolini* (mushrooms with ribbon pasta), or go gourmet with Taverna's seasonal house specialities: wintertime eel with snails or springtime rabbit with zucchini flowers.

IL MELONCINO TRADITIONAL ITALIAN €€

(☎0436 44 32; www.ilmeloncino.it; Locale Rumerlo 1, Cortina d'Ampezzo; meals around €45; ⏱lunch & dinner Wed-Mon) With a rustically elegant dining room inside and spectacular terrace seating when weather permits, Il Meloncino is one of the few finer restaurants that stays open almost year-round (though it does close for part of May and June). The roasted boar and venison-stuffed ravioli in a hazelnut sauce are as jaw-dropping as the Alpine views.

Veneto Wine Country

Explore

No matter how you like your wine – red, white or sparkling – Veneto's wine country can slake your thirst. Northwest of Verona, Valpolicella is celebrated for Amarone – an intense red made from partially dried grapes. Between Vicenza and Verona, Soave delivers its crisp, namesake whites amid storybook medieval walls. In the foothills of the Dolomites, Conegliano yields dry, crisp *prosecco* in *spumante* (bubbly), *frizzante* (sparkling) and still varieties. And for harder stuff, head to Bassano del Grappa (p182). You'll need wheels to visit far-flung vineyards, though the towns of Soave and Conegliano are within striking distance of train stations. Most growing areas are also bike-friendly. Since vineyards are spread across the Veneto, each individual region requires a full day for relaxed appreciation, including a long, vinous lunch.

The Best...

- **Sight** Castello di Soave (p188)
- **Place to Eat** Locanda Lo Scudo (p189)
- **Place to Drink** Enoteca Valpolicella (p189)

WORTH A DETOUR

FELTRE

From the ramparts of this walled hill town, you can look south to the green pastures of the Alpine foothills and north to the craggy, snow-topped drama of the Alps themselves. A city since at least Roman times, Feltre was largely levelled in 1509 as Venice was battling the League of Cambrai. It was quickly rebuilt in a remarkably unified architectural style – namely a rustic version of Renaissance classicism. Piazza Maggiore, the town's main square, is especially winning with its harmonious arrangement of public and private buildings.

Just inside the northern entrance to the old city, you'll find the **tourist office** (Piazza Trento e Trieste; ⏲9am-12.30pm & 3.30-6.30pm Mon-Sat). Up the street, **Hostaria Novecento** (☎0439 830 43; Via Messaterra 24; meals €25-35; ⏲lunch & dinner Thu-Tue) offers a cosy dining room and, weather permitting, a charming terrace on the adjacent piazza. The menu features fresh pasta with seasonal vegetables, *pastins* (flattened meatballs typical of the region) and very good wine by the glass. It is open nonstop from noon to 10pm for wine and *panini* breaks.

Top Tip

Before heading into wine country, educate your palate at an *enoteche* (wine bars) like Verona's Antica Bottega del Vino (p184), Vicenza's Antica Casa della Malvasia (p179) or Venice's Enoteca Mascareta (p141).

Getting There & Away

Train To get to Soave from Venice, take the train to San Bonifacio (90 minutes, €5.40, hourly), then catch the local ATV bus 30 (€1.50, 10 minutes, about two hourly). For Conegliano, head from Venice to the Mestre station, where there are two to three trains per hour to Conegliano (one hour, €4). Trains do not serve Valpolicella.

Car Your own wheels are your best option for visiting individual wineries. Valpolicella lies just past Verona's northwest suburbs, just off E45. Soave lies just of the A4, which connects Verona and Mestre. For Conegliano, head north from Mestre along the A27.

Need to Know

- **Area Code** ☎041
- **Location** Valpolicella (140km west of Venice); Soave (85km west of Venice); Conegliano (62km north of Venice)
- **Tourist Office** Valpolicella tourist office (☎045 770 19 20; www.valpolicellaweb.it; Via Ingelheim 7; ⏲9am-1pm Mon-Fri, 9am-noon Sat); Conegliano tourist office (☎0438 212 30; Via XX Settembre 61; ⏲9am-12.30pm Tue-Wed, to 12.30pm & 3-6pm Thu-Sun).

SIGHTS & ACTIVITIES

Conegliano

LA STRADA DI PROSECCO WINE ROUTE

(www.coneglianovaldobbiadene.it) Running through a landscape of rolling vineyards, this driving route takes you from Conegliano to Valdobbiadene via some of the region's best wineries. The website provides an itinerary, background information on *prosecco*, and details about stops along the way.

Soave

CASTELLO DI SOAVE HISTORICAL BUILDING

(☎045 768 00 36; www.castellodisoave.it; admission €6; ⏲9am-noon & 3-6pm Tue-Sun Apr–mid-Oct, to 5pm mid-Oct–Mar) Built on a medieval base by Verona's fratricidal Scaligeri family, the Castello complex encompasses an early-Renaissance villa, grassy courtyards, the remnants of a Romanesque church and the Mastio (the defensive tower apparently used as a dungeon): during restoration, a mound of human bones was unearthed here. Be sure to make your way to the upper ramparts for fine views of the town and surrounding countryside.

AZIENDA AGRICOLA COFFELE WINERY

(☎045 768 00 07; www.coffele.it; Via Roma 5; ⏲9am-12.30pm & 2-7pm Mon-Sat & by appointment) Across from the old-town church, this family-run winery offers tastings of lemon-zesty DOC Soave Classico and nutty, faintly sweet bubbly DOCG (guaranteed-quality) Recioto di Soave. The family also rents out rooms among vineyards a few kilometres from town.

SUAVIA WINERY

(☎045 767 50 89; www.suavia.it; Via Centro 14, Fitta; ⌚9am-1pm & 2.30-6pm Mon-Fri & 9am-1pm Sat, & by appointment) Soave is not known as a complex white, but this trailblazing winery, located 8km outside Soave via SP39, is changing the equation. Don't miss DOC Monte Carbonare Soave Classico, with its mineral, ocean-breeze finish.

Valpolicella

MONTECARIANO CELLARS WINERY

(☎045 683 83 35; www.montecariano.it; Via Valena 3, San Pietro in Cariano; ⌚by appointment Mon-Sat) Sample award-winning Amarone at this winery in the town of San Pietro in Cariano, just off central Piazza San Giuseppe.

AZIENDA AGRICOLA CORTE ALEARDI WINERY

(☎045 770 13 79; www.cortealeardi.com; Via Giare 15, Sant'Ambrogio di Valpolicella; ⌚by appointment) A few kilometres west of San Pietro di San Cariano, this winery is renowned for Amarone, and if you call ahead, you can taste excellent DOC Amarone and lighter DOC Valpolicella reds.

PIEVE DI SAN GIORGIO CHURCH

(San Giorgio; ⌚7am-6pm) In this tiny hilltop village of San Giorgio a few kilometres northwest of San Pietro in Cariano, you'll find this fresco-filled, cloistered 8th-century Romanesque church. Not old enough for you? In the little garden to its left, you can also see a few fragments of an ancient Roman temple.

EATING

TOP CHOICE **ENOTECA VALPOLICELLA** ITALIAN €€€

(☎045 683 91 46; Via Osan 47, Fumane; meals €25-35; ⌚lunch & dinner Tue-Sat, lunch Sun) Foodies flock to the town of Fumane, just a few kilometres north of San Pietro in Cariano, where an ancient farmhouse has been converted in a rustically elegant restaurant. The chef keeps flavours pure – puree of asparagus, risotto with wild herbs, game with polenta – so as not to compete with 700 Italian wines on the menu.

TOP CHOICE **LOCANDA LO SCUDO** MODERN ITALIAN €€

(☎045 768 07 66; www.loscudo.vr.it; Via Covergnino 9, Soave; meals €35-45; ⌚lunch & dinner Tue-Sat) Just outside the medieval walls of Soave, Lo Scudo is half country inn and half high-powered gastronomy. Arrive early and order fast – or miss out on daily fish specials or risotto made with Verona's zesty Monte Veronese cheese. Above the restaurant, the owners rent out four bright, lovely rooms (singles/doubles €75/110) that continue the theme of countrified sophistication. Both restaurant and inn are closed in August.

LA TARTARE DELL'HOTEL CRISTALLO ITALIAN €€€

(☎0438 354 45; www.hotelcristallo.tv.it; Corso Mazzini 45, Conegliano; meals around €50; ⌚lunch & dinner Tue-Sun) This Conegliano classic is beloved by locals for the rustic elegance of its decor as well as the menu, which fuses ingredients from both the rich Veneto plains and the rugged slopes of the nearby Alps. Think albino asparagus puree and wild game cooked over an open flame.

CAFFÉ CREMERIA MATTIELLI GELATERIA €

(☎331 299 53 72; www.cremeriamattielli.com; Via Roma 16, Soave; ⌚7.30am-12.30pm & 2.30-7.30pm Thu-Tue, to 11pm Jun-Aug) Expect top-notch *gelati*, including ambitious daily specials like celery and goat cheese, at this old-fashioned cafe on the main street of Soave's historic centre.

Sleeping

Want to wake up in a palazzo *to the sound of lagoon waters lapping at the* fondamente *(canal banks)? It's an unforgettable experience – and probably more affordable than you think. High-end hotels are no longer your only option. Many Venetians are opening historic homes as* locande *(guesthouses), B&Bs,* affittacamere *(rooms for rent) and holiday rental apartments.*

More Options than Ever

Venice still offers plenty of luxe hotels along the Grand Canal and Riva degli Schiavone, and there's also a growing inventory of boutique sleeps. But the real news is the concerted effort to make overnight stays affordable. In the last decade, the number of Venetian properties dedicated to tourist lodgings has nearly quintupled. At the same time, the internet has made it much easier for locals to rent out their homes (or extra rooms).

For budget travellers, Venice offers a range of hostels (called *foresterie*). Some bunks at Giudecca's hostel even have canal views. The palatial Palazzo Zenobio and frescoed Foresteria Valdese also offer private rooms at unbeatable prices. During summer, university housing also opens to tourists.

Location, Location, Location

Of course, it is always preferable to stay as close to key sights as possible – for example near San Marco or anywhere within striking distance of the Grand Canal. However, a much-improved *vaporetto* system makes it less crucial to stay near the action. Outlying areas – including the lagoon's other islands like Giudecca and Lido – are often cheaper, quieter and more authentically Venetian.

Season Matters

In low season – November, early December, and January to March (except around New Year's, Carnevale and Easter) – you can expect discounts of 40% or more off peak rates. July and August also bring bargains, though usually not quite as steep. Even in high season, midweek rates tend to be lower than weekends. By contrast, expect to pay a hefty premium during Carnevale, New Year's and Easter.

Rates cited here should be considered a guide, since hotels often make constant adjustments according to season, day of week and holidays of varying importance.

Amenities

In general, rooms tend to be small in Venice – and sometimes dark or awkwardly shaped as per the quirks of ancient *palazzi*. Unless otherwise stated in our reviews, guestrooms come with private bathroom, often with a shower rather than a bathtub. Business centres are rarely well equipped, even in swanky hotels, since the assumption is you're here for pleasure. Only a few large hotels have a pool – mostly on the Lido. While increasingly available, wi-fi doesn't always penetrate thick stone walls and may only be available in common areas.

Buyer Beware

Not all hotels in Venice are grand: some are cramped, frayed and draughty, with lackadaisical service. Budget and midrange places around the train station tend to be especially drear – sometimes despite glowing internet 'reviews'. Note also that many hotels boast of 'Venetian-style' rooms. Sometimes this implies real antiques and Murano chandeliers, but it means a kitsch version of baroque in rooms whose former charms have been remodelled out of existence.

Lonely Planet's Top Choices

Novecento (p193) Trade-route chic at its best, with eclectic, comfortable digs catering to world travellers.

Palazzo Soderini (p199) A tranquil, all-white retreat with garden and lily pond.

Oltre Il Giardino (p197) A garden getaway where tradition meets modernity in distinctive designer rooms.

Ca' dei Dogi (p199) Cheerful digs at reasonable prices steps from San Marco.

Hotel Danieli (p200) A classic as eccentric and sumptuous as Venice itself.

Locanda Cipriani (p202) Ernest Hemingway's lagoon literary retreat, with original furnishings, rose-garden views and roast duck by the fireplace.

Best by Budget

€

Foresteria Valdese (p200)

Locanda Sant'Anna (p200)

Ostello Venezia (p201)

Hotel Galleria (p195)

Giò & Giò (p193)

€€

Pensione Accademia Villa Maravege (p194)

Oltre Il Giardino (p197)

Palazzo Soderini (p199)

Ca' Dei Dogi (p199)

Ca' Angeli (p197)

La Calcina (p195)

€€€

Hotel Danieli (p200)

Bauer Palladio Hotel & Spa (p201)

Palazzo Abadessa (p198)

Hotel Palazzo Barbarigo (p197)

Charming House DD.724 (p194)

Ca' Pisani (p195)

Best Design/ Boutique

Palazzo Soderini (p199)

Domus Orsoni (p198)

Hotel Palazzo Barbarigo (p197)

Residenza Cannaregio (p199)

AD Place Venice (p193)

Ca' Pozzo (p198)

Most Romantic

Bauer Palladio Hotel & Spa (p201)

Palazzo Abadessa (p198)

Hotel Flora (p193)

Hotel Al Duca (p197)

Bloom/7 Cielo (p194)

Locanda San Barnaba (p196)

Best Heritage

Hotel Danieli (p200)

Gritti Palace (p193)

Antica Locanda Montin (p196)

Pensione Guerrato (p197)

Hotel Abbazia (p199)

Palazzo Zenobio (p196)

Best Views

Hotel Danieli (p200)

Ostello Venezia (p201)

Gritti Palace (p193)

Hotel Galleria (p195)

Locanda Leon Bianco (p198)

La Calcina (p195)

NEED TO KNOW

Price Ranges

Price ranges are for standard double rooms with private bathroom.

€	less than €120
€€	€120–220
€€€	over €220

Reservations

- Book ahead at weekends and anytime during high season.
- The best, and best-value, hotels are always in high demand; book well ahead.
- Check individual hotel websites for increasingly common internet specials.
- Best to confirm arrival at least 72 hours in advance – some hotels may assume you've changed your plans.

Getting to Your Hotel

- Pack light to better negotiate twisting alleys, footbridges and narrow staircases.
- Try to arrive during daylight to avoid getting lost in night-time Venice.
- Get directions from your hotel, plus a detailed map.
- Though expensive, water-taxis can be worth the price for night arrivals or if you're heavily laden.

Breakfast

Except in higher-end places, breakfast tends to be utilitarian. *Affittacamere* generally don't offer breakfast because of strict dining codes. However, you're never far from a great local cafe.

Where to Stay

Neighbourhood	For	Against
San Marco	Historic and design hotels in central location, optimal for sightseeing and shopping.	Rooms often small with little natural light; streets crowded and noisy in the morning; fewer good-value restaurant options.
Dorsoduro	Lively art and student scenes, with design hotels near museums and seaside getaways along Zattere.	Lively student scene can mean noise echoing from Campo Santa Margherita until 2am, especially on weekends.
San Polo & Santa Croce	Good-value B&Bs with prime local dining, Rialto markets, drinking and shopping, convenient to train and bus.	Easy to get lost in maze of streets, and it may be a long walk to a *vaporetto* stop.
Cannaregio	Quiet and largely residential, but with happy-hour canal-bank scenes and restaurants frequented by locals.	Long walk or *vaporetto* ride to San Marco sightseeing; pedestrian traffic between train station and Rialto.
Castello	Calmer and fewer tourists as you move away from San Marco; good budget options.	The outskirts are quite far away from key sights.
Giudecca, Lido & the Southern Islands	Better value-for-money; quieter and fewer tourists.	Far from the action; must rely on *vaporetti*.
Murano, Burano & the Northern Islands	Far from Venice crowds, excellent island-fresh cuisine.	Far from Venice; sporadic *vaporetti* after 5.30pm.

Sestiere di San Marco

TOP CHOICE NOVECENTO BOUTIQUE HOTEL €€
Map p286 (041 241 37 65; www.novecento.biz; Calle del Dose 2683/84; d incl breakfast €130-260;) World travellers put down roots in nine bohemian-chic rooms with Turkish kilim pillows, Fortuny draperies and 19th-century scallop-shell carved bedsteads. Linger over breakfast in the garden under an Indian sun parasol, meet the artists at hotel-organised art exhibitions, go for a massage at sister property Hotel Flora, or mingle around the honesty bar.

GRITTI PALACE HOTEL €€€
Map p286 (041 794 611; www.hotelgrittipalacevenice.com; Campo di Santa Maria del Giglio 2467; d €285-2800; Santa Maria del Giglio) You might not ever get around to sightseeing if you stay at the Gritti, the landmark 1525 doge's palace. Modern hotels are bigger, but the Gritti remains the grandest hotel along the Grand Canal with 90 individually decorated guestrooms. Updated deluxe rooms show elegant restraint, except for beds the size of ducal barges, Murano chandeliers and antique writing desks – but Venetian-style rooms are glorious anachronisms with fainting couches, beds in silk-swagged niches, and hand-painted vanities. Luxury specialist Starwood manages operations efficiently, and chef Daniele Turco creates inspired Venetian spice-route cuisine for fabulous dockside meals.

HOTEL FLORA HOTEL €€
Map p286 (041 520 58 44; www.hotelflora.it; Calle Bergamaschi 2283a; d €150-290; Santa Maria del Giglio) Down a lane from glitzy Calle Larga XXII Marzo, this ivy-covered garden retreat quietly outclasses brash top-end neighbours with its plush rooms, delightful tearoom and gym offering shiatsu massage. Guestrooms feature antique carved beds piled with soft mattresses and fluffy duvets; ask for opulent gilded No 3 or No 32, which opens onto the garden.

HOTEL NOEMI B&B €€
Map p286 (041 523 81 44; www.hotelnoemi.com; Calle dei Fabbri 909; d incl breakfast €80-230; San Marco) Gilded baroque beds, damask-clad walls and beamed ceilings give this place undeniable Venetian charm – but Noemi doesn't just get by on looks. Besides its superb location 50m behind Piazza San Marco, Noemi offers exceptional convenience, including garage space up the Grand Canal and 24-hour reception for late arrivals and early departures.

GIÒ & GIÒ B&B €
Map p286 (347 366 50 16; www.giogiovenice.com; Calle delle Ostreghe 2439; d €90-150; Santa Maria del Giglio;) Restrained baroque sounds like an oxymoron, but here you have it: polished wood floors, pearl-grey walls, bronze silk curtains, burl-wood dressers and spotlit art. It's ideally located near Piazza San Marco along a side canal; angle for rooms overlooking the gondola stop, and wake to choruses of *Volare, oh-oh-oooooh*!

AD PLACE VENICE DESIGN HOTEL €€
Map p286 (041 241 23 24; www.adplacevenice.com; Fondamenta della Fenice 2557a; d incl breakfast €125-290; Santa Maria del Giglio) Taking its cue from Teatro La Fenice across the canal, AD Place goes for romantic high drama, from the lobby's patchwork curtains and candlelit lanterns to patent-leather bedsteads and gilded mirrors upstairs. Let savvy staff arrange gondola pick-ups and custom art tours, and don't skip sumptuous buffet breakfasts on the cushion-strewn terrace.

PALAZZO SELVADEGO HOTEL €€
Map p286 (041 520 02 11; www.hotelmonaco.it; Calle Selvadego 1238; d incl breakfast €170-280; @Vallaresso) Sister property to the Hotel Monaco, Palazzo Selvadego offers stylish, wood-beamed rooms with travertine bathrooms in a quieter location behind Piazza San Marco – all at a better price. Ask for rooms on upper floors, which have more natural light; some offer glimpses of the Grand Canal down the *calle*. Breakfast, check-in and check-out are at the Hotel Monaco, which gives you an excuse to see the premises of Venice's favourite Ridotto (gaming hall) c 1648. When Selvadego is full, you might be upgraded to the Hotel Monaco.

LOCANDA ART DECO B&B €€
Map p286 (041 277 05 58; www.locandaartdeco.com; Calle delle Botteghe 2966; d incl breakfast €80-170; Accademia) Rakishly handsome, cream-coloured guestrooms with parquet floors and comfy beds in custom wrought-iron bedsteads. The top-floor loft is a bargain if you don't mind the steps or the low wood-beamed ceiling. Helpful B&B staff arrange in-room massages and boat rides with Venice's pioneering woman gondolier.

BLOOM/7 CIELO B&B €€

Map p286 (☎340 149 8872; www.bloom-venice.com, www.settimocielo-venice.com; Campiello Santo Stefano 3470; d incl breakfast €170-250; ❄ Accademia) Fraternal-twin B&Bs occupy two upper floors of a historic home overlooking Santo Stefano right across the *calle*. Bloom features splashy baroque decor schemes in crimson, cobalt and lemon silk damask with gilded beds and cathedral-window views. 7 Cielo (aka Seventh Heaven) is artfully romantic, with sleek tubs in shimmering Murano glass-tiled bathrooms and designer beds setting a honeymoon mood. Take breakfast on the sunny top-floor terrace.

LOCANDA CASA PETRARCA B&B €

Map p286 (☎041 520 04 30; www.casapetrarca.com; Calle delle Schiavine 4386; d incl breakfast €105-155, with shared bathroom €80-125; ❄ Rialto) A budget option with heart and character, this family-run place offers six unfussy, sparkling rooms in an ancient apartment building in the heart of San Marco, with breakfast serenades from passing gondolas. Count on a 10-minute walk from the *vaporetto*: from Campo San Luca, follow Calle dei Fuseri, take the second left, and turn right into Calle delle Schiavine.

LOCANDA ORSEOLO B&B €€

Map p286 (☎041 520 48 27; www.locandaorseolo.com; Corte Zorzi 1083; d incl breakfast €150-240; ❄@ Vallaresso) No one will know you're hiding out right behind Piazza San Marco but the *gondolieri,* who ply the waters out front where two canals meet. Consistently warm greetings and comfortable wood-trimmed rooms – some with Carnevale murals – make this the ideal launch-pad for San Marco sightseeing and forays to nearby Rialto restaurants and boutiques.

HOTEL AI DO MORI HOTEL €

Map p286 (☎041 520 48 17; www.hotelaidomori.com; Calle Larga San Marco 658; d €50-110; ❄ San Marco) Cosy artist garrets just off Piazza San Marco; book ahead to score an upper-floor room with wood-beamed ceilings, parquet floors and views over the basilica. Ask for No 11, with a private terrace – but pack light, because there is no lift here.

LOCANDA BARBARIGO B&B €€

Map p286 (☎041 241 36 39; www.locandabarbarigo.com; Fondamenta Barbarigo 2503a; d incl breakfast €125-170; ❄ Santa Maria del Giglio) Your *palazzo* hideaway awaits beneath the arcade of historic Palazzo Barbarigo, just off the Grand Canal. These cosy rooms have outsized baroque swagger, with damask walls, gilded mirrors, bow-legged vanities and fanciful chandeliers, plus small TVs and humming air-conditioning. Angle for the snug corner room in a lemon-lime colour scheme with views over a side canal, or the little yellow garret room with a wrought-iron bed and exposed timber beams. Reception closes around 2pm, so ask questions over breakfast.

LOCANDA ANTICO FIORE B&B €

Map p286 (☎041 522 79 41; www.anticofiore.com; Corte Lucatello 3486; d €100-160; ❄@ Sant'Angelo) Local colour is the draw in this cosy B&B in a quiet courtyard, from the arty mother-daughter owners to the eight Venetian-style guestrooms spread out over the top two floors. Ask for the top-floor green canal-view room or the sweet yellow room tucked under eaves; larger downstairs rooms are noisier, as they're just off the breakfast room.

Sestiere di Dorsoduro

TOP CHOICE PENSIONE ACCADEMIA VILLA MARAVEGE INN €€

Map p290 (☎041 521 01 88; www.pensioneaccademia.it; Fondamenta Bollani 1058; d €135-320; ❄ Accademia) Once you step through the gate of this 17th-century garden villa just off the Grand Canal, you'll forget you're just a block from the Accademia. Buffet breakfasts are served on the lawn in summer, sunsets are toasted with a complimentary drink at the bar, and garden swings for two promise romance under the stars. All rooms are comfortably furnished with parquet floors, pale walls and modern bathrooms – but a few are a cut above with four-poster beds, wood-beamed ceilings, even glimpses of the canal. Ask for Thelma, a superior double with its own patch of greenery, named after a regular who loved reading in the garden. Handicap-accessible rooms and wheelchairs available on request.

CHARMING HOUSE DD.724 B&B €€€

Map p290 (☎041 277 02 62; www.thecharminghouse.com; Ramo de Mula 724; d incl breakfast d €200-400; ❄@ Accademia) Hole up in your own art-filled, modernist-chic Venetian bolthole, with lavish breakfast buffets in the library and movies to watch in the multime-

LONGER-TERM RENTALS

For longer stays and groups of three or more, renting an apartment is an economical option that gives you the freedom to cook your own meals. Generally, flats are let by the week or month.

ApartmentsApart (www.apartmentsapart.com) Offers flats for rent by the day, starting at about €70.

Guest in Italy (www.guestinitaly.com) Has apartments and B&Bs ranging from €100 to €350 a night, though you may have to fill out a booking form to see the prices on many places.

Interhome (www.interhome.co.uk) Has a selection of mostly small flats (about 50 sq metres) that sleep three to four (a little cramped) for around UK£700 to UK£1400 a week.

Venetian Apartments (www.venice-rentals.com) Arranges accommodation in flats, often of a luxurious nature. Two- to four-person apartments start at around €895 per week.

There are several other sites featuring rentals in Venice proper:

BB Planet (www.bbplanet.it)

Bianco Holidays (www.apartmentinitaly.com)

RentalinItaly (www.rentalinitaly.com)

Venice Apartment Rental (www.veniceapartment.com)

If you plan to stay for a month or more, you'll want to seek out longer-term rental, which you might find through **Craigslist Venice** (http://venice.it.craigslist.it) or word of mouth. If you don't mind sharing with students, check out the **Università Ca' Foscari noticeboards** (Map p290; Calle Larga Foscari, San Polo), where you might find rooms in a shared apartment for about €300 to €600 a month (usually the low-end places are in mainland Mestre). To rent a studio for yourself, expect to pay €800 to €1200 per month.

dia room. Guestrooms are designer-sleek yet cosy; splash out for the superior double with a bathtub and balcony overlooking Peggy Guggenheim's garden. Babysitting, massages and guided tours are available on request.

LA CALCINA — INN €€

Map p290 (041 520 64 66; www.lacalcina.com; Fondamenta Zattere ai Gesuati 780; d incl breakfast €110-310; Zattere) An inspiring seaside getaway, with breakfasts on the roof terrace, elegant canalside restaurant and 29 airy, parquet-floored guestrooms, several facing the Giudecca Canal and Palladio's Redentore church. Book ahead for rooms with ensuite bathrooms and/or views, especially No 2, where John Ruskin stayed while he wrote his classic (and inexplicably Palladio-bashing) 1876 *The Stones of Venice*.

HOTEL GALLERIA — INN €

Map p290 (041 523 24 89; www.hotelgalleria.it; Campo della Carità 878a; d incl breakfast €100-200; Accademia) Smack on the Grand Canal at the Ponte dell'Accademia is this classic hotel in a converted 17th-century mansion. Nos 7 and 9 are small doubles overlooking the Grand Canal, No 8 has Liberty furnishings with Grand Canal views and No 10 sleeps five, with an original frescoed ceiling and Grand-Canal-facing windows. Most rooms share updated bathrooms, and two rooms accommodate larger families.

CA' PISANI — BOUTIQUE HOTEL €€€

Map p290 (041 240 14 11; www.capisanihotel.it; Rio Terà Antonio Foscarini 979/a; d €162-333; Accademia) An ideal spot right behind the Accademia to hide from paparazzi, yet still get the star treatment. Custom-decorated in a retro-glam style, this hotel features Jacuzzi tubs, art-deco walnut marquetry sleigh beds, and all the latest technology hidden behind clever cabinetry so as not to kill the mood. Rooms in the eaves (31 is one of the best) feature sloping timber ceilings, and are handy to the steam bath and terrace with outdoor shower that rather naughtily

…oks the Salute Church. Enjoy outdoor breakfasts and ask about wine-tasting at the on-site wine bar.

LOCANDA SAN BARNABA B&B €€

Map p290 (041 241 12 33; www.locanda-sanbarnaba.com; Calle del Traghetto 2785-6; d incl breakfast €120-180; Ca' Rezzonico) The stage is set for intrigue at this 16th-century *palazzo,* where the 1st-floor salon features unusual monochromatic 19th-century frescoes, and corner cupboards cleverly conceal a hidden staircase. Ask for the romantic 'Poeta Fanatico' room under the eaves or 'Campiello', which offers suggestive views of a neighbouring bell tower *(campiello)* through a skylight. Superior rooms feature 18th-century frescoed ceilings, and one has two balconies over the canal. Downstairs in the garden are sun umbrellas, patio seating and a bar.

CASA REZZONICO B&B €€

Map p290 (041 277 06 53; www.casarezzonico.it; Fondamenta Gherardini 2813; d €160; Ca' Rezzonico) 'La Serenissima' lives up to its name at this tranquil B&B, with handsome antique bedsteads, Fortuny lamps and parquet floors in whitewashed rooms. Opt for a room peeking over the quiet canal, and unwind over breakfast or drinks in the courtyard garden – or head just up the canal bank to Campo Santa Margherita for the liveliest happy hours in town.

LA CHICCA B&B €

Map p290 (041 552 55 35; www.lachicca-venezia.com; Calle Franchi 644; d incl breakfast €50-200;) Neatly wedged among Dorsoduro's trifecta of museums – Accademia, Peggy Guggenheim, Punta della Dogana – yet all you'll hear at night in this new family-run B&B is the lapping of the canal at the end of the *calle.* Venetian damask-clad guestrooms are spacious and blessedly uncluttered after a museum binge; book ahead to nab one with a tub.

ANTICA LOCANDA MONTIN B&B €

Map p290 (041 522 71 51; www.locandamontin.com; Fondamenta di Borgo 1147; d €100-160, with shared bathroom €75-120; Ca'Rezzonico) Artists can finally stop suffering for their art at Locanda Montin, where sleepless nights are highly unlikely in tranquil rooms facing the pergola-shaded garden. After feasting in the downstairs restaurant where Brad Pitt, David Bowie and Yoko Ono have dined, head up the back stairway and pass through the art-filled salon to eclectic guestrooms where Ezra Pound, Modigliani and Gabriele D'Annunzio have stayed. Works by D'Annunzio grace the walls of No 12, and even Modigliani couldn't pull a long face in rooms 5 and 8, where balconies overlooking the canal keep the inspiration coming.

LOCANDA CA' DEL BROCCHI B&B €

Map p290 (041 522 69 89; www.cadelbrocchi.it; Rio Tera San Vio 470; d incl breakfast €72-105; P Accademia) A colourful character smack in the centre of Dorsoduro's museum district, Ca' del Brocchi has small yet over-the-top baroque-styled rooms, all tasselled, gilt-edged and upholstery-padded with matching scrollwork wallpaper – and some have Jacuzzi tubs. Family-friendly, with babysitting and cradles available.

CA' DELLA CORTE B&B €€

Map p290 (041 715 877; www.cadellacorte.com; Corte Surian 3560; d incl breakfast €100-180; Piazzale Roma) Live like a Venetian in this 16th-century family home 10 minutes from Piazzale Roma and Campo Santa Margherita, with guestrooms overlooking the courtyard, a frescoed grand music salon, breakfasts in the room and a top-floor terrace overlooking terracotta rooftops and neighbouring Gothic palaces.

HOTEL TIVOLI INN €

Map p290 (041 524 24 60; www.hoteltivoli.it; Crosera San Pantalon 3838; d incl breakfast €55-150, with shared bathroom €40-100; San Tomá) Watch day-trippers rush to trains and San Marco as you kick back with drinks in Campo Santa Margherita or browse backstreet boutiques – your comfortable, simply furnished 1930s-style inn is nearby, and it's a bargain. Close to restaurants, museums, *vaporetto,* train and bus stations, yet not touristy.

PALAZZO ZENOBIO HOSTEL €

Map p290 (041 522 87 70; www.collegioarmeno.com; Fondamenta del Soccorso; s €30-65, d €56-100; Ca' Rezzonico) A gilded 1690 palace that formerly housed a school for Venice's Armenian community recently opened its doors to hostel guests. Accommodation is monastic and chilly, lower-priced rooms have shared bathrooms, and there's a 1.30am curfew – but the location is superb, the overgrown formal garden is among Venice's largest and loveliest, and guests are invited to on-site concerts and art events.

Sestieri di San Polo & Santa Croce

TOP CHOICE OLTRE IL GIARDINO B&B €€

Map p292 (041 275 00 15; www.oltreilgiardino-venezia.com; Fondamenta Contarini 2542, San Polo; d €150-350; San Tomá) Live the designer dream in guestrooms brimming with historic charm and modern comforts: marquetry composer's desks and flat-screen TVs, candelabra and Bulgari bath products, 19th-century poker chairs and babysitting services. Light fills all six high-ceilinged bedrooms, and though Turquoise is sprawling and Green occupies a private corner of the walled garden, Grey has a sexy wrought-iron bedframe under a cathedral ceiling.

TOP CHOICE HOTEL PALAZZO BARBARIGO BOUTIQUE HOTEL €€€

Map p292 (041 740 172; www.palazzobarbarigo.com; Grand Canal, San Polo 2765; d incl breakfast €240-380; San Tomá) Not your grandmother's Grand Canal getaway, the Palazzo Barbarigo is Venice's splashiest new design hotel. The traditional watergate entryway has been turned into a watering hole, with a deco-inspired bar and disco-inspired accent lighting. But the 18 guestrooms get modern low-key luxury just right, with sumptuous velvets and contemporary, curvaceous furniture graced with the occasional silken tassel or feather fringe. Whether you opt for junior suites overlooking the Grand Canal (get triple-windowed Room 10) or standard rooms overlooking Rio San Polo, expect compact, sleek bathrooms and positively royal breakfasts.

CA' ANGELI B&B €€

Map p292 (041 523 24 80; www.caangeli.it; Calle del Traghetto de la Madonnetta 1434, San Polo; d €80-250; San Silvestro) Brothers Giorgio and Matteo inherited this Grand Canal mansion and converted it into an antique showplace, with original Murano glass chandeliers, namesake angels from the 16th century and a restored Louis XIV sofa in the canalside reading room. Breakfasts are made with organic products and served on antique plates in the dining room, overlooking the Grand Canal.

STUDENT STAYS

From July to mid-September, **ESU** (041 524 67 42; www.esuvenezia.it), the city's student administration agency, opens its residences to students and academics visiting town. Singles, doubles and triples are available. Prices run around €30 to €40 per person per night.

PENSIONE GUERRATO PENSIONE €

Map p292 (041 528 59 27; www.pensioneguerrato.it; Ruga due Mori 240a, San Polo; d incl breakfast €95-140; Rialto) In a 1227 landmark that once served as a hostel for knights heading off on the Third Crusade, updated guestrooms haven't lost their sense of history – ask for one with frescoes or glimpses of the Grand Canal. The prime Rialto Market location and reliable dining recommendations make Pensione Guerrato the Holy Grail for visiting foodies, and the newly restored apartment is equipped with a kitchen.

AL PONTE MOCENIGO HOTEL €€

Map p292 (041 524 4797; www.alpontemocenigo.com; Fondamenta Rimpetto Mocenigo 2063, Santa Croce; d €85-170; San Stae) A doge of a deal right off the Grand Canal, steps from the San Stae *vaporetto* stop and a 10-minute walk through crooked *calli* to the Rialto. Swanky boudoir guestrooms with chandeliers hung from high wood-beamed ceilings are often spacious enough for gymnastic routines, even with four-poster beds, gilt-edged armoires and salon seating. Ask for rooms overlooking Rio San Stae or the private courtyard.

HOTEL AL DUCA HOTEL €€

Map p292 (041 812 3069; www.alducadivenezia.com; Fontego dei Turchi 1739, Santa Croce; d €120-220; San Stae) Plush red rooms with black Murano chandeliers are Venetian bordello chic, honouring the courtesans that once ruled these backstreets – but for a soothing place to actually get some sleep, go with all-bronze or pearl-grey rooms. A 24-hour reception is at your service, and babysitting is available.

DOMINA HOME CA' ZUSTO BOUTIQUE HOTEL €€

Map p292 (051 639 18 01; www.dominavacanze.it; Campo Rielo 1358, Santa Croce; d incl breakfast €118-225; Riva di Biasio) Like a Venetian in masquerade, the stately exteriors of this Gothic palace disguise a colourful wild streak. With a wink at the nearby Fondaco dei Turchi, the historic Turkish trading house, guestrooms are named after Turkish women and decked out in harem stripes and silk brocade, with plush beds fit for pashas and amenities including cushy slippers and Jacuzzi tubs.

LOCANDA ARCO ANTICO BOUTIQUE HOTEL €€
Map p292 (041 241 12 27; www.arcoanticovenice.com; Corte Petriana 1451, San Polo; d €60-190; San Silvestro) Under the Gothic archway and through the courtyard, this 16th-century *palazzo* offers charming hideaways footsteps from the Grand Canal at a fraction of San Marco hotel rates. Guestrooms feature handsome dark woods, cream and yellow brocades, leaded windows, marquetry dressers and exposed wood beams – but best of all is the sunny upper room overlooking the courtyard.

AL CAMPANIEL B&B €
Map p292 (041 275 07 49; www.alcampaniel.com; Calle del Campaniel 2889, San Polo; d incl breakfast €55-105; San Tomá) A find off quiet Campo San Tomá: steps from the *vaporetto* stop and I Frari, handy to action-packed Campo Santa Margherita and overlooking a chocolate shop. Rooms are surprisingly spacious and inviting, in tasteful shades of cream and crimson; standard doubles have ensuite toilets but shared showers.

CA' SAN POLO B&B €
Map p292 (041 244 03 31; www.casanpolo.it; Calle dei Saoneri 2696, San Polo; d incl breakfast €60-115; San Tomá) Welcome to the neighbourhood: in this hidden location on a quiet *calle*, you're within shouting distance of I Frari, but you'll enjoy neighbourly greetings and get to know your local gondoliers. Climb steep stairs to cosy wood-beamed bedrooms with cheerful red-and-gold-striped brocade bedspreads and matching curtains, with small but clean ensuite bathrooms.

HOSTEL DOMUS CIVICA HOSTEL €
Map p295 (041 522 71 39; www.domuscivica.com, in Italian; Campiello Ciovare Frari 3082, San Polo; s/d €30/60; Jun-Sep only, 12.30am curfew; Piazzale Roma) A women's dorm during the school year welcomes visitors as a hostel in summer, with shared facilities that include a living room with TV and free internet access. Simple, clean dorm rooms in a graceful 1918 building are equipped with single beds, desks and sinks, and there are five bathrooms per floor. Light sleepers should bring earplugs – the hallways reverberate, as do the church bells across the street.

Sestiere di Cannaregio

TOP CHOICE PALAZZO ABADESSA BOUTIQUE HOTEL €€€
Map p296 (041 241 37 84; www.abadessa.com; Calle Priuli 4011; d €125-345; Rialto) Evenings seem enchanted in this opulent 1540 Venetian *palazzo,* with staff fluffing pillows, plying guests with *prosecco,* arranging water taxis to the opera and plotting romantic wedding proposals. Sumptuous guestrooms feature plush beds, silk-damask walls and 18th-century vanities; go for baroque and request a larger room with ceiling frescoes, Murano chandeliers and canal or garden views.

TOP CHOICE DOMUS ORSONI B&B €€
Map p296 (041 275 95 38; www.domusorsoni.it; Corte Vedei 1045; s incl breakfast €80-150, d €100-250; San Marcuola) Surprise: along a tranquil back lane near the Ghetto are five of Venice's most stylish guestrooms. In summer, breakfast is served in the garden by Orsoni mosaic works, located here since 1885 – hence the mosaic fantasias glittering across guestroom walls, headboards and bathrooms.

CA' POZZO INN €€
Map p296 (041 524 05 04; www.capozzovenice.com; Sotoportego Ca' Pozzo 1279; d €80-170; Guglie) Biennale-bound travellers find a home away from home-design catalogues in this minimalist-chic hotel near the Ghetto. Several guestrooms have balconies, two accommodate disabled guests, and spacious No 208 could house a Damien Hirst entourage.

ALLA VITE DORATA B&B €€
Map p296 (041 241 30 18; www.allavitedorata.com; Rio Terà Barba Frutariol 4690b; d incl breakfast €90-150; Ca' d'Oro) *Venexianárse* (become Venetian) at this family home recently converted to a B&B in a pleasant, untouristed neighbourhood. Romantics upgrade to rooms with brocade-curtained beds overlooking a canal, but all rooms are airy and charming, with high wood-beamed ceilings, wrought-iron furnishings, and colourful drapery.

LOCANDA LEON BIANCO B&B €€
Map p296 (041 523 35 72; www.leonbianco.it; Corte Leon Bianco 5629; d incl breakfast €80-250; Ca' d'Oro) Turner used to paint at this

canalside hotel, and you can see what he saw in the place: sloping *terrazzo alla Veneziana* (Venetian chipped marble) floors, heavy wooden doors and hulking antique furniture that hasn't changed much since Turner's day. Three slightly larger 'deluxe' rooms overlook the Grand Canal, including No 4, a corner room with wraparound postcard views – but bring your earplugs for canalside rooms, because the Rialto Market opposite starts at 4am.

RESIDENZA CANNAREGIO B&B €€

Map p296 (041 524 43 32; www.hotelresidenzacannaregio.com; Dei Reformati 3210a; d incl breakfast €79-345; St Alvise) A former monastery gone mod, this B&B offers a rosy outlook on a remote corner of the lagoon and cleverly repurposed interiors for maximum cool factor – it's like sleeping inside Tadao Ando's Punta della Dogana. The original brickwork and exposed-beam ceilings have been carefully preserved, with the strategic additions of industrial steel railings and low-slung leather chairs. Rooms are spacious and comfortable, with sleeping lofts and backlit bedsteads, and the far-flung canalside location is close to the historic Ghetto, Madonna dell'Orto, romantic restaurants and local-favourite happy hours.

HOTEL ABBAZIA B&B €€

Map p296 (041 717 333; www.abbaziahotel.com; Calle Priuli dei Cavaletti 68; d incl breakfast €80-210; Ferrovia) Common spaces have uncommon appeal at this converted Carmelite retreat. The dining hall has been converted into a heavenly lobby-bar, and the love seats in the garden are so serene, you'd never guess you were just around the corner from the train station (great for late arrivals). Rooms are comfortable and quiet, featuring striped-brocade, Venetian-gone-corporate decor.

RESIDENZA CA' RICCIO B&B €

Map p296 (041 528 23 34; www.cariccio.com; Campo dei Miracoli 5394/a; d incl breakfast €85-150; @ Fondamente Nuove) Down the street from Casanova's house in a convenient yet hidden location near the Rialto is the Riccio family's lovingly restored 14th-century residence. Seven rooms on the two top floors look out onto a courtyard, and feature simple wrought-iron beds, wood-beamed ceilings, terracotta tiled floors, and whitewashed walls.

HOTEL VILLA ROSA INN €

Map p296 (041 716 569; www.villarosahotel.com; Calle delle Misericordia 389; d incl breakfast €70-140; Ferrovia) Blooming window-boxes and cheery staff make arrivals feel at home around the corner from the train station. Guestrooms are compact but high-ceilinged, with damask wallpaper, tapestry bedspreads and modern bathrooms. Best-value rooms have balconies overlooking the small garden; garden rooms are cheap but dark.

Sestiere Di Castello

For luxury with lagoon views, grand hotels along the Riva degli Schiavoni have reeled in visitors for two centuries. But bargain-hunters, take note: some Castello lodgings are closer to Piazza San Marco than ones with a San Marco address, often at a substantially lower price. For even better rates, walk another 15 minutes from the Piazza towards the Arsenale, where rates plummet up to 50% from central city rates.

TOP CHOICE PALAZZO SODERINI B&B €€

Map p298 (041 296 08 23; www.palazzosoderini.it; Campo di Bandiera e Mori 3611; d incl breakfast €150-200; Arsenale) Whether you're coming from cutting-edge art at the Biennale or baroque masterpieces at the Ducal Palace, this tranquil all-white retreat with a lily pond in the garden is a welcome reprieve from the visual onslaught of Venice. Minimalist decor emphasises spare shapes and clean lines, with metal-edged furniture and bare walls, and an unexpected blue lobby sofa for the element of surprise. The three rooms have all the mod cons: TVs, wi-fi, minibars, air-con and heating. Book well ahead.

CA' DEI DOGI BOUTIQUE HOTEL €€

Map p298 (041 241 37 51; www.cadeidogi.it; Corte Santa Scolastica 4242; d incl breakfast from €100-140; @ San Zaccaria) Even the nearby Bridge of Sighs can't dampen the high spirits of the sunny yellow Ca' Dei Dogi, with guestroom windows sneaking peeks into the convent cloisters next door. Streamlined, modern rooms look like ships' cabins, with tilted wood-beamed ceilings, dressers that look like steamer trunks, and compact mosaic-covered bathrooms – ask for the one with the terrace and Jacuzzi

(€140 to €300). Friendly staff can arrange concerts, free trips to Murano and sunset gondola rides. Book well ahead.

HOTEL DANIELI LUXURY HOTEL €€€

Map p298 (041 522 64 80; www.starwoodhotels.com/luxury; Riva degli Schiavoni 4196; d from €850; San Zaccaria) As eccentric, luxurious and exuberant as Venice itself, the Danieli has attracted artistic bohemians, minor royalty and their millionaire lovers for over a century. The hotel sprawls along the lagoon next to the Palazzo Ducale in three landmark buildings: the 14th-century *casa vecchia* (old house), built for Doge Enrico Dandolo, with frescoed, antique-filled rooms; the 18th-century *casa nuova* (new house), with cosier Venetian-style rooms and gilt to the hilt; and the Danielino, a stark Fascist edifice with a multimillion-euro 2008 modern-luxe interior redesign by Jacques Garcia, preserving original bathtubs and chandeliers but adding hand-rubbed Venetian-plaster walls, crimson silk curtains and blissful beds with dramatic damask headboards. In summer weather, breakfast is served on the rooftop terrace with its extraordinary views of San Marco and the lagoon.

HOUSEBOAT RENTALS

It seems too good to be true, but in fact you really can rent a houseboat by the week or half-week and turn the entire lagoon into your own hotel – all without any special operating licence – thanks to **Rendez-Vous Fantasia** (041 551 04 00; www.charterboat.it; Via Roma 1445, Chioggia; 9am-12.30pm & 3-6pm Mon-Tue & Thu-Sat, 9am-12.30pm Wed & Sun). Rates vary with season and boat size, but begin at €819 per week for two to three people in low season (October to April) and range up to €3000 per week for six to eight people in high season (July and August).

You don't just have to stick to the lagoon. The company provides itineraries like the Brenta Riviera, along the River Po, and even as far afield as Trieste. Note you have to pick up the boat at the company's marina in Chioggia. The company's website provides complete information, including how to get to the Chioggia marina.

FORESTERIA VALDESE HOSTEL €

Map p298 (0415286797; www.foresteriavenezia.it; Palazzo Cavagnis 5170; dm per person €25-30, d from €82; Ospedale) Holy hostel: this rambling palace retreat owned by the Waldensian church has 1st-floor guestrooms with 18th-century frescoes by Bevilacqua, and one floor up guestrooms have canal views. Dorm beds are available only for families or groups; book well ahead. Rates include breakfast.

LOCANDA SANT'ANNA PENSIONE €

Map p298 (041 528 64 66; www.locandasantanna.com; Corte del Bianco 269; d incl breakfast €100-120, with shared bathroom €70-85; @ Giardini) Escape the madding crowd on a quiet *campiello* (small square) on the sleepy side of Castello, where tourists are scarce, boats drift past and seagulls circle aimlessly all day. Antique vanities, marquetry bedsteads and parquet floors add character to spacious whitewashed rooms, some with views of canals and Isola San Pietro. A little terrace is ideal for sunny days, and the reading room makes a welcome retreat when lagoon mists roll in. Prices drop as much as 50% in low season.

LOCANDA LA CORTE B&B €€

Map p298 (041 241 13 00; www.locandalacorte.it; Calle Bressana 6317; d incl breakfast €90-180; @ Ospedale) It's the common areas in this 16th-century palace that are the real draw here, including the aristocratic reception area and the atmospheric courtyard where breakfast is served in warm weather. Rooms vary in size, but all are comfortably fitted out with good beds and bathrooms. Check the website for sometimes steep discounts.

LA RESIDENZA PENSIONE €€

Map p298 (041 528 53 15; www.venicelaresidenza.com; Campo di Bandiera e Mori 3608; s €50-100, d €80-200; Arsenale) Sleep like the dead in the comfort of this grand 15th-century mansion, presiding over a *campo* that was once the site of public executions. Generous-sized rooms of varying degrees of brightness are furnished in a reproduction of classic Venetian style, with cream lacquered wardrobes and beds with boldly striped bedspreads. The real luxury is the classic Venetian *salone* (great room) garlanded with 18th-century stucco, where breakfast is served and cushy chairs make for rainy-day cosiness.

HOTEL RIVA PENSIONE €

Map p298 (041 522 70 34; www.hotelriva.it; Ponte dell'Angelo 5310; s €80-90, d €90-120, with shared bathroom s €60-70, d €80-100; San Zaccaria) At the juncture of two canals, this is a prime location to drift off in an upholstered baroque bed to the whistling of passing gondoliers, awakening under high wood-beamed ceilings to the tolling bells of nearby San Marco. True to Venetian priorities, all rooms have Murano glass chandeliers and only some are air-conditioned – but the prices are hard to beat.

ALLOGGI BARBARIA PENSIONE €

Map p298 (041 522 27 50; www.alloggibarbaria.it; Calle delle Cappuccine 6573; s €40-120, d €60-150; Ospedale) Located in an authentic Venetian neighbourhood near the Fondamente Nuove, this *pensione* isn't easy to find – but that's part of its charm, and so are the intrepid fellow travellers you'll meet over breakfast on a shared balcony. All six rooms are simple but tidy, bright and airy, with tiled floors and rates that rarely hit the quoted maximums. Rates include breakfast.

HOTEL AL PIAVE HOTEL €€

Map p298 (041 528 51 74; www.hotelalpiave.com; Ruga Giuffa 4838; d €140-165; San Zaccaria) Steps from Campo Santa Maria Formosa, this neat-as-a-pin midrange option offers comfortably equipped rooms with beautifully polished *terrazzo* (marble chips set in mortar) floors, and 'traditional' Venetian designs, though everything looks brand new. Smallish digs and no views, but good value if comfort and location are your priority. Rates include breakfast.

ALBERGO DONI PENSIONE €

Map p298 (041 522 42 67; www.albergodoni.it; Calle del Vin 4656; d €60-125, with shared bathroom €50-100; San Zaccaria) In a miniscule 15th-century *palazzo*, this quirky, friendly, family-run inn offers a four-star location at budget prices. While more picturesque outside than in thanks to a rather dated 'modernisation', it still delivers clean, efficiently managed digs steps from Piazza San Marco. Rates include breakfast.

Giudecca, Lido & the Southern Islands

Take a breather from the palatial grandeur of Venice at seaside *stile liberty* villas on the Lido or bargain lodging on Giudecca. If you want to stay on the Lido during the Venice International Film Festival in September, plan to make reservations months in advance and to pay premium rates.

OSTELLO VENEZIA HOSTEL €

Map p301 (041 523 82 11; www.ostellovenezia.it; Fondamenta delle Zitelli 86, Giudecca; dm incl breakfast €22-27; Zitelle) Calming canal views make hostel bunks seem miles away from the stampeding crowds and inflated prices of San Marco. Sheets, blanket, and a pillow are provided in the bunk price, but you'll need to arrive promptly at the 3.30pm opening time to claim that perfect bunk by the window; reserve ahead for one of two viewless private rooms. Check-in is from 3.30pm to 10pm; check-out is at 9.30am. No curfew. A new bar-restaurant was being installed at the time of writing.

BAUER PALLADIO HOTEL & SPA LUXURY HOTEL €€€

Map p301 (041 520 70 22; www.palladiohotelspa.com; Fondamenta della Croce 33, Giudecca; d from €780; closed mid-Nov–mid-Mar; Zitelle) Splash out in a serene, Palladio-designed former cloister with San Marco views, private solar-powered boat service and a superb spa. These premises once housed nuns and orphans, but now offer heavenly comfort in 37 rosy, serenely demure guestrooms, many with garden terraces or Giudecca Canal views. Head downstairs for local organic breakfast buffets and ecofriendly spa treatments like the milk, honey and rose bath (€90) with complimentary sauna, Jacuzzi and marble steam-room access. Check online for discounts.

HOTEL VILLA CIPRO HOTEL €€

Map p285 (041 73 15 38; www.hotelvillacipro.com; Via Zara 2, Lido; d €50-140, d €80-170; P Lido) A world away from the narrow streets of Venice but only a few blocks from the *vaporetto* stop, this pine-shaded villa offers spacious rooms with high ceilings adorned with Murano chandeliers and tall windows, some with balconies overlooking the gardens. Breakfast is served in the courtyard when weather permits, and cocktails at the vintage bar or in the gardens; the beach is two blocks away.

HOTEL PANORAMA HOTEL €€

Map p285 (☎041 276 04 86; www.hpanorama.com; Piazzale Santa Marie Elisabetta 1/B, Lido; d €60-140, with lagoon views €80-160; Lido) Steps from the Lido *vaporetto* stop, this cheerful, lemon-yellow hotel offers airy rooms with huge windows, many of which look out onto the lagoon. Double-paned windows keep out noise from the busy waterfront, while Murano-glass light fixtures, recently refurbished rooms and a terrace complete the pleasant picture. Makes for a great off-season deal.

HOTEL VILLA STELLA HOTEL €€

Map p285 (☎041 526 07 45; www.villastella.com; Via Sandro Gallo 111, Lido; d €60-160; Lido) Three generations of women have made visitors feel comfortable in this 19th-century villa. Rooms are old-fashioned looking but provide the modern comforts. Extra touches include leafy grounds, a generous breakfast with homemade cakes and jams, and afternoon tea.

CASA GENOVEFFA B&B €€

Map p301 (☎347 250 78 09; www.casagenoveffa.com; Calle del Forno 472, Giudecca; d around €120; Palanca) Down a narrow alley hides this simple but welcoming bed-and-breakfast, with snug but recently remodelled rooms with tile floors, kitchenettes and a bit of atmosphere thanks to wood-beamed ceilings and four-poster beds.

Murano, Burano & the Northern Islands

TOP CHOICE LOCANDA CIPRIANI B&B €€

Map p303 (☎041 73 01 50; www.locandacipriani.com; Piazza Santa Fosca 29, Torcello; per person €100-180, half board €150-230; closed Tue & month of Jan; Torcello) Not much has changed since this rustic wineshop was transformed into a country inn in 1934 by Harry's Bar founder Giuseppe Cipriani. You won't see Ernest Hemingway hauling in his hunting trophies or working on his manuscripts any more, but you can still enjoy hearty pastas and *anatra* (wild duck) by the *fogher* (fireplace) or under the rose pergola in the garden. The six spacious rooms are more like suites, with stocked libraries and easy chairs in lieu of TVs for a true literary retreat – and you're bound to find inspiration for your next novel in Hemingway's favourite room, Santa Fosca, with its balcony overlooking the garden and original creaky oak floors.

TOP CHOICE MURANO PALACE B&B €

Map p302 (☎041 73 96 55; www.muranopalace.com; Fondamenta Ventrai 77, Murano; d incl breakfast €90-130; Colonna) Come here for designer fabulousness at an outlet price. Jewel-toned colour schemes and (naturally) Murano glass chandeliers illuminate high-ceilinged, parquet-floored rooms, and there are free drinks and snacks in the minibar. Expect canal views and unparalleled art-glass shopping, but eerie calm once the shops close around 6pm. Ask the front desk about fishing excursions and Venetian rowing lessons.

IL LATO AZZURRO INN €

(☎041 523 06 42; www.latoazzurro.it; Via Forti 13, Sant'Erasmo; dm €25-30, s €50-55, d €70-80; Sant'Erasmo Capannone) Sleep among the artichokes on Venice's garden isle of Sant'Erasmo in a red-roofed country villa, 25 minutes by boat from central Venice. Spacious guestrooms with parquet floors and wrought-iron beds open onto a wrap-around veranda. Meals are largely home-grown, organic and fair trade, bicycles are available, and the lagoon laps at the end of the lane – bite-prone guests should bring mosquito repellent. The guesthouse supports a nonprofit cultural organisation, and guests are invited to participate in nature excursions, archaeological digs, theatre performances and cultural exchange programs.

VENISSA INN €€

(☎041 527 22 81; www.venissa.it; Fondamenta Santa Caterina 3, Mazzorbo; d €130-220; Mazzorbo) Gourmet getaways are made in the shade of the vineyards at Venissa, which offers some of the lagoon's finest, freshest dining as well as six large, strikingly contemporary rooms under the manor-house rafters. For less dedicated diners, the twin islands of Mazzorbo-Burano may seem like a long haul from Venice for dinner and an overnight, but it takes about 15 minutes to arrive by private boat launch from the mainland near the airport, where free private car parking is available. Breakfast is extra, either prix fixe or à la carte.

Understand Venice & the Veneto

Venice Today

Look around: all those splendid palaces, paintings and churches were created by a handful of Venetians. In the city's thousand-year history, only about three million Venetians can claim grandparents from Venice. Despite its decadent reputation, it's not just a city of the idle rich. Most Venetians work in services, tourism and the arts, and live in flats – 1000 Venetian palaces are now hotels and B&Bs. Resting on past glories would be easy, and topping them seems impossible, but as usual, Venetians are opting for the impossible.

Best on Film

Pane e Tulipani (Bread & Tulips) (2000) An AWOL housewife starts life anew in Venice.

Casanova (1976) Donald Sutherland's sly take on Venice's seducer tops winsome Heath Ledger's.

Don't Look Now (1973) A couple's demons follow them to Venice in Nicolas Roeg's taut thriller.

Casino Royale (2006) James Bond hits the Grand Canal (don't worry, that palace survived).

Best in Print

Watermark (1992) Nobel Laureate Joseph Brodsky's 17-year fascination with Venice spills onto every page.

Invisible Cities (1972) Italo Calvino imagines Marco Polo recounting his travels to Kublai Khan – yet every city he describes is Venice.

The Passion (1987) In Jeanette Winterson's fable, Napoleon's cook pursues a Venetian con artist.

Shakespeare in Venice (2007) Venetian historian Alberto Toso Fei unravels local legends intertwined with Shakespearean dramas.

Changing Demographics

With 60,000 official residents outnumbered by visitors on any given day, Venetians sometimes seem like a rarity in their own city. The population has halved in size since 1848, and a quarter of the city's population is retired. But there are 2000 children still playing tag in Venice's *campi* (squares) and local universities attract 23,000 students, keeping the city young and full of ideas. If you don't always encounter locals on the main thoroughfares, that's because Venetians prefer the city's 3000 backstreets. Join them, and you'll discover a whole other city backstage, keeping Venice's mainstage production running, and dreaming up its next act.

Living by its Wits

Since the fall of its shipping empire, Venice has primarily lived by its wits. The city's extraordinary support for opera, orphan orchestras and satirical theatre kept Monteverdi, Vivaldi and Goldoni gainfully employed, and helped establish Venice as Europe's entertainment capital. Even in the dark days of the plague, Venetian artists Titian and Tintoretto filled the city with light and colour. Venice's Biennale and film festival kept inspiration coming to the city, and the Peggy Guggenheim Collection helped raise the city's spirits and expand its outlook after WWII.

Today Venice's traditions are upheld by civic institutions such as La Fenice, Goldoni Theatre, the Biennale and a dozen museums. Yet for local talent that has kept these institutions so vibrant, staying in Venice isn't easy. Housing is among Europe's most costly; many Venetian musicians now drag instruments back and forth to mainland Mestre. With Italy's ongoing recession straining resources for arts programming, public and private arts gigs are tough to find. Mose barriers are intended to prevent flooding in Venice (see p247), but with billions of euros directed towards its establishment by 2014, it has drained funds that might have supported other programs essential to city life – including the arts.

This is where you enter the picture. Venice's admirers have been the heroes of its story many times, not only funding vital restorations after the devastating flood of 1966, but also filling its concert halls, buying its books, attending its parties and art openings. So when Venetians thank you for coming to local arts events, they mean it.

Good & Bad Publicity

Even as Venice thinks ahead to its next act, its spectacular past remains both a blessing and burden. For decades, a 'Special Law' for Venice allowed the city to keep a portion of its tax revenues to defray city upkeep. This revenue has been gradually eroded as Italy redirects funds to service its growing debt, which has reached 120% of GDP. International nonprofit organisations have generously donated funds to help keep Venice afloat – but often their grants are earmarked for the preservation of Venice's heritage rather than projects essential to Venice's future, such as public works maintenance or support for its living legacy of artisans and musicians.

To cover €20 million in delayed maintenance projects that are now urgent, Venice has had to come up with fundraising workarounds. A hotel tax was introduced in 2011 to help provide local funds for local programs – a modest rise of up to €4.50 per person for luxury hotels – and public transport prices have been raised.

But the most controversial measure has been relaxing some historic preservation rules to allow advertising in public places, including glaringly anachronistic banners lining the Bridge of Sighs and Piazza San Marco. Fashion magnate Renzo Rosso of Diesel, the Italian jeans brand, pledged funds in 2011 to reinforce Ponte di Rialto, after chunks of stone mysteriously dropped from the bridge. The announcement was greeted with relief, tempered with wariness: what fresh publicity horrors might await the city from the creators of the controversial 'Be Stupid' campaign?

While public outcry may help prevent further advertising, existing ads can be eliminated by directing positive attention to the city's many attractions. When the city's restaurants, artisans, concerts and museums merit rave reviews, visitors who pass the good word online are effectively helping Venice raise maintenance funds through hotel, restaurant and retail taxes. Vinyl banners might then be put to better use by Malefatte (p123), the prison cooperative that upcycles them into slick messenger bags.

if Venice were 100 people

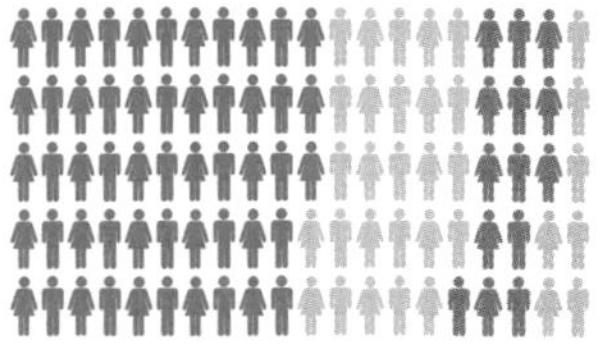

53 are adults
26 pensioners
14 children
7 university students

ethnicity

(% of population)

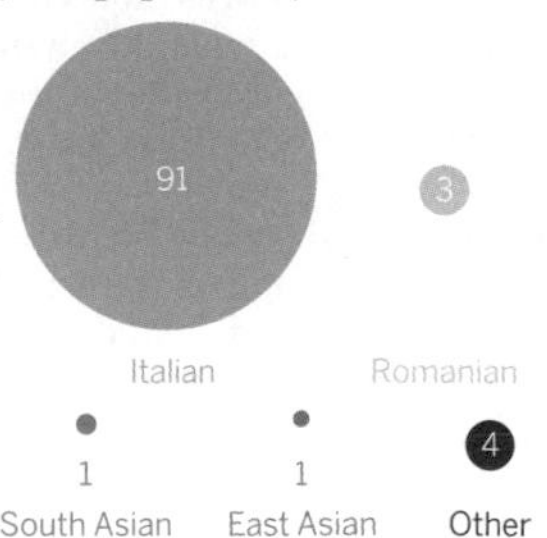

population per sq km

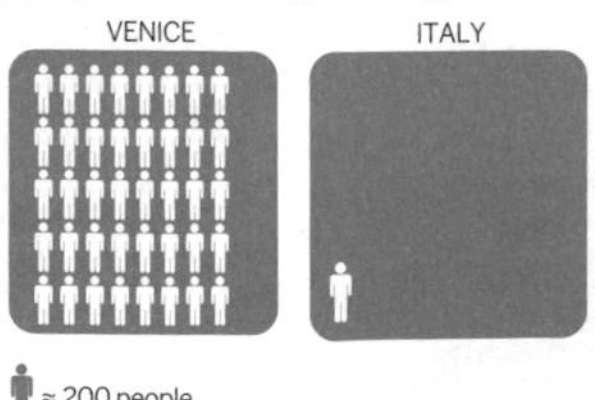

History

Not content with conquering the known world with its naval fleets, Venice dispatched explorers like Marco Polo to destinations right off the map to expand its trade horizons. When its maritime empire passed its high-water mark, Venice refused to concede defeat on the world stage. Instead the city itself became a stage, attracting global audiences with its vivid painting, baroque music, modern opera, independent thinkers, and parties without parallel. In its audacious thousand-year history, Venice has not only risen above sea level, but repeatedly risen to the occasion.

FROM SWAMP TO EMPIRE

A malarial swamp seems like a strange place to found an empire, unless you consider the circumstances: from the 5th to the 8th century AD, Huns, Goths and sundry other barbarians repeatedly sacked Roman Veneto towns along the Adriatic, and made murky wetlands off the coast seem comparatively hospitable. Celtic Veneti had lived in the area relatively peacefully since 1500 BC, had been Roman citizens since 49 BC, and were not in the habit of war. When Alaric led a Visigoth invasion through the province of Venetia in AD 402, many Veneti fled to marshy islands in the lagoon that stretches along the province's Adriatic coast. Some Veneti tentatively returned to the mainland when the Visigoths left, but after Attila, king of the Huns, attacked in 452, many refugees took up permanent residence on the islands.

The nascent island communities elected tribunes and in 466 met in Grado, south of Aquileia, forming a loose federation. When Emperor Justinian claimed Italy's northeast coast for the Holy Roman Empire in 540, Venetia (roughly today's Veneto region) and the island's elected representatives to local Byzantine government in Ravenna, which reported to central authority in Constantinople (now called Istanbul). But when warring French Lombards swept across the Po plains eastward in 568, Veneti refugees headed for the islands in unprecedented numbers, and the marsh began to look like a city. Thousands settled on the commercial centre of Torcello (p158); others headed to the now submerged island of Malamocco,

Top Five for Byzantine Splendour

- *Gallerie dell'Accademia (Dorsoduro)*
- *Basilica di San Marco (San Marco)*
- *Torcello (Torcello)*
- *Chiesa di San Zaccaria (Castello)*
- *Chiesa di San Giacomo dell'Orio (Santa Croce)*

TIMELINE

c 1500 BC

Celtic Veneti tribes, possibly from Anatolia (in present-day Turkey), arrive in northeast Italy to inhabit the region now known as the Veneto.

AD 726

Orso Ipato becomes the first elected Venetian doge. The Byzantines consider Ipato's election an act of rebellion, and if not behind it, are not devastated by Ipato's assassination in 737.

810

The seat of the Venetian empire is moved from the hamlet of Malamocco on the Lido to the bustling market centre of Rivo Alto, known today as the Rialto.

bucolic Chioggia, and the fishing and local trading centre of Rivoalto (colloquially known as Rialto).

Crafty Venetian settlers soon rose above their swampy circumstances, residing on land lifted above tides with wooden pylons driven into some 30m (100ft) of soft silt. When the Byzantine grip slipped, Venice seized the moment: in 726 the people of Venice elected Orso Ipato as their *dux* (Latin for leader), or doge (duke) in Venetian dialect, the first of 118 elected Venetian dogi that would lead the city for more than a thousand years. Like some of his successors, Orso tried to turn his appointment into a hereditary monarchy. He was assassinated for overstepping his bounds; some later dogi with aspirations to absolute power were merely blinded. At first, no one held the doge's hot seat for long: Orso's successor, Teodato, managed to transfer the ducal seat to Malamocco in 742 before being deposed. Gradually the office of the doge was understood as an elected office, kept in check by two councillors and the Arengo (a popular assembly).

Crafty Venetian settlers soon rose above their swampy circumstances, residing on land lifted above tides

The Lombards had failed to conquer the lagoon, but the Franks were determined to succeed. When they invaded the lagoon, the Franks were surprised by resistance led by Agnello Partecipazio from Rivoalto, a shallow area of the lagoon unnavigable by large seafaring vessels except those familiar with the maze of deep-water channels criss-crossing the lagoon. Partecipazio was elected doge in 809, and the cluster of islets around Rivoalto became the focus of community development. Land was drained, canals cleared, and Partecipazio built a fortress on the eventual site of the Palazzo Ducale (p55). The duchy launched commercial and naval fleets that would become the envy of the Adriatic, with Venetian ships trading from Croatia to Egypt.

THE STOLEN SAINT

Venice had all the makings of an independent trading centre – ports, a defensible position against Charlemagne and the Huns, leadership to settle inevitable trade disputes – but no glorious shrine to mark Venice's place on the world map. So Venice did what any ambitious, God-fearing medieval city would do: it procured a patron saint. Under Byzantine rule, St Theodore (San Teodoro) had been the patron saint. But according to local legend, the evangelist St Mark (San Marco) had visited the lagoon islands and been told by an angel that his body would rest there – and some Venetian merchants decided to realise this prophecy.

828

According to legend, the corpse of St Mark the Evangelist is smuggled from Alexandria (Egypt) to Venice in a shipment of pork. St Mark is adopted as the patron saint of Venice.

957

Holy Roman Emperor Otto the Great formally recognises key trading rights for Venice, cutting the Eastern Byzantine Christian empire out of Venice's increasingly lucrative mercantile deals.

1094

Basilica di San Marco is consecrated. The doge's spectacular Chiesa d'Oro (Church of Gold) stands for the glory of Venice, St Mark and a brain-trust of Mediterranean artisans.

BETHUNE CARMICHAEL / LONELY PLANET IMAGES ©

Basilica di San Marco (p52) door

PIRATE BRIDES

Today the only pirates you're likely to spot in Venice are the ones selling knock-off Prada handbags at the Ponte dell'Accademia, but for centuries pirate ships prowled the waters around the Lido. In AD 944, a bevy of wealthy Venetian brides sparkling with golden dowries were sailing off into the sunset to weddings on the Lido when their boat was intercepted by pirates. The women were whisked off to a nearby harbour at Caorle, but Venetians in hot pursuit discovered the lair, slaughtered the pirates and delivered the rattled brides to their weddings. The event was long commemorated with the annual Festa delle Marie (Feast of the Marys), in which Venice's 12 wealthiest families presented money for dowries to 12 poor but beautiful young women. Today the 'Marys' are remembered during Carnevale (p20) with a procession and beauty pageant crowning the most beautiful of the 12 Marys.

In AD 828, Venetian smugglers stole St Mark's body from its resting place in Alexandria, Egypt, apparently hiding the holy corpse in a load of pork to deter inspection by Muslim customs officials. Venice summoned the best artisans from Byzantium and beyond to enshrine these relics in an official ducal church that would impress visitors with the power and glory of Venice. The usual medieval construction setbacks of riots and fires thrice destroyed exterior mosaics and weakened the underlying structure, and St Mark's bones were misplaced twice. While Basilica di San Marco (p60) was under construction, the winged lion of St Mark was adopted as the emblem of the Venetian empire, symbolically setting Venice apart from Constantinople and Rome.

WAR & SPOILS

Once terra firma was established, Venice set about shoring up its business interests. When consummate diplomat Pietro Orseolo was elected doge in 991, he positioned Venice as a neutral party between the western Holy Roman Empire and eastern territories controlled by Constantinople, and won the medieval equivalent of most-favoured-nation status from both competing empires.

Even at the outset of the Crusades, Venice maintained its strategic neutrality, continuing to trade with Muslim leaders from Syria to Spain while its port served as the launching pad for crusaders bent on wresting the Holy Land from Muslim control. With rivals Genoa and Pisa vying to equip crusaders, Venice established the world's first assembly lines in the Arsenale (p127), capable of turning out a warship per day. Officially, La Serenissima ('The Most Serene'; the Venetian Re

1167

About 200,000 Venetians occupy their own quarter in Constantinople, subject to their own laws and making a nuisance of themselves without legal recourse for complaint.

1171

After attacking Genoese in Constantinople and pointing the finger at Venice, Byzantium orders the arrest of all Venetians. A noticeable chill sets in over the Adriatic.

1172

Venice establishes an elected Maggior Consiglio (Great Council). Though citizenry makes up 80% of the population, nobles are elected councillors.

1204

Doge Dandolo leads a Venetian fleet hired to take Frankish Crusaders on a detour to Constantinople, where Venetian-led armies massacre and pillage before returning laden with booty.

public) remained above the fray, joining crusading naval operations only sporadically – and almost always in return for trade concessions.

Constantinople knew who was supplying the crusaders' ships, and in the wake of the First Crusade in 1095, Venice's relations with Byzantium were strained. Byzantine emperor Manuele Comnenus played on Venetian–Genoese rivalries, staging an 1171 assault on Constantinople's Genoese colony and blaming it on the Venetians in Constantinople, who were promptly clapped into irons. Venice sent a fleet to the rescue, but the crew contracted plague from stowaway rats, and the ships limped home without having fired a shot.

Meanwhile, Venice was under threat by land from Holy Roman Emperor Frederick Barbarossa's plans to force Italy and the Pope to recognise his authority. Back in 1154, Barbarossa's strategy must have seemed like an easy win: divide and conquer competing Italian city-states frequently on the outs with the papacy. But after several strikes, Barbarossa found northern Italy a tough territory to control. When his army was struck by plague in 1167, Barbarossa was forced to withdraw to Pavia, only to discover that 15 Italian city-states, including Venice, had formed the Lombard League against him. Barbarossa met with spectacular defeat, and when things couldn't get any worse, he was excommunicated. Venice quickly recognised that it could only handle one holy war at a time, and through nimble diplomatic manoeuvres, convinced Pope Alexander III and the repentant emperor to make peace in Venice in 1177.

Once terra firma was established, Venice set about shoring up its business interests.

THE DODGY DOGE

But for fast talking, even the shrewdest Venetian merchant couldn't top Doge Enrico Dandolo. The doddering nonagenarian doge who'd lost his sight years before might have seemed like an easy mark to Franks seeking Venice's support in the Fourth Crusade. But Doge Dandolo drove a hard bargain: Venice would provide a fleet to carry 30,000 Crusaders, but not for less than 84,000 silver marks – approximately double the yearly income of the king of England at the time.

Only one-third of the proposed Frankish forces turned up in Venice the following year, and their leaders couldn't pay. But Venice had the ships ready, and figured it had kept its side of the bargain. To cover the balance due, Doge Dandolo suggested the Crusaders might help Venice out with a few tasks on the way to Palestine. This included invading Dalmatia and a detour to Constantinople in 1203 that would last a year, while Venetian and Frankish forces thoroughly pillaged the place.

1271

Traders Nicolò and Matteo Polo set sail for Xanadu, the court of Kublai Khan, with Nicolò's 20-year-old son, Marco. The Polos make a fortune in the jewellery business in Asia.

1297

Venice ends constitutional monarchy, allowing only those from noble families to participate in the Assembly – until it runs low on funds, and allows merchants to buy noble titles.

1309

For openly defying orders, Venice is excommunicated from the Church for the first (but not last) time. Through its wealth and negotiation skills, Venice convinces Rome to relent.

1310

With rebellion afoot, a temporary security force called Consiglio dei Dieci (Council of Ten) is convened to handle the emergency; it lasts almost five centuries, effectively running Venice for two.

Finally Doge Dandolo claimed that Constantinople had been suitably claimed for Christendom, and at age 96 declared himself 'Lord of a Quarter and a Half-Quarter of the Roman Empire' of Byzantium – a title that conveniently awarded Venice three-eighths of the spoils, including monumental gilt-bronze horses in Basilica di San Marco (p60). Venetian ships opted to head home loaded with booty instead of onward to Christian duty, leaving the Franks to straggle onwards to the Crusades. With its control of the Adriatic secured, Venice began sending ships directly to the Holy Land – only this time, they were in the tourism business, ferrying pilgrims to and from holy sites.

VENICE VERSUS GENOA

The puppet emperor Doge Dandolo put on the throne in Constantinople didn't last long: the Genoese soon conspired with the Byzantines to overthrow the pro-Venetian regime. Having taken Constantinople for all it was worth, Venice set its sights on distant shores. Through the overland trip of native son Marco Polo to China in 1271–91, Venetian trade routes extended all the way to China. Rival Genoa's routes to the New World were proving slower to yield returns, and the impatient empire cast an envious eye on Venice's spice and silk-trade routes.

While the plague struck Italy's mainland as many as 50 more times before 1500, the outbreaks often seemed to miraculously bypass Venice.

In 1372 Genoa and Venice finally came to blows over an incident in Cyprus, initiating eight years of maritime warfare that took a toll on Venice. To make matters worse, the plague decimated Venice in the 1370s. Genoa's allies Padua and Hungary took the opportunity to seize Venetian territories on the mainland, and in 1379 a Genoese fleet appeared off the Lido. Venetian commander Carlo Zeno's war fleet had been sent out to patrol the Mediterranean, leaving the city outflanked and outnumbered.

But the Genoese made a strategic mistake: instead of invading, Genoa attempted to starve out the city. With stores of grain saved for just such an occasion, Venice worked day and night to build new ships and defences around the islands. Mustering all of Venice's might, Venetian commander Vittore Pisani mounted a counter-attack on the Genoese fleet – but his forces were inadequate. All hope seemed lost for Venice, until ships flying the lion of St Mark banner appeared on the horizon: Carlo Zeno had returned. Venice ousted the Genoese, exerting control over the Adriatic and a backyard that stretched from Dalmatia (Croatia) to Bergamo (Northern Italy).

1348–49

A horrific bout of the Black Death hits Venice, killing some 60% of the population. Venetian doctors observe that the worst-hit areas are by Dorsoduro's docks, where rats arrive.

1386

A Jewish cemetery is established on the Lido, with land granted by the state. The cemetery remains in use until its abandonment with Mussolini's racial laws in 1938.

1403

The world's first quarantine is established when arriving ships, merchandise and sailors are required to spend a *quarantena* (40 days) on Isola di Lazzaretto Nuovo.

Ponte di Rialto (p101)

RATS & REDEMPTION

As a maritime empire, ships came and went through Venice's ports daily, carrying salt, silks, spices and an unintentional import: rats infested with fleas carrying bubonic plague. In 1348 the city was still recovering from an earthquake that had destroyed houses and drained the Grand Canal, when the plague struck the city. Soon, as many as 600 people were dying every day, and undertakers' barges raised the rueful cry: *'Corpi morti! Corpi morti!'* (Bring out your dead!) Within the year, more than a third of Venice's population had died.

No one was sure how the disease had spread, but Venice took the unprecedented step of appointing three public health officials to manage the crisis. Observing that outbreaks seemed to coincide with incoming shipments, Venice decided to take precautions in 1403, and intercept all incoming ships arriving from infected areas on Isola di Lazzaretto Nuovo. Before any ship was allowed to enter the city, it was required to undergo inspection, and its passengers had to wait for a *quarantena* (40-day period), to be sure no signs of plague emerged. This was the world's first organised quarantine station, setting a precedent that saved untold lives from plague and other infectious diseases since.

While the plague struck Italy's mainland as many as 50 more times before 1500, the outbreaks often seemed to miraculously bypass Venice. The city's faithful chalked up their salvation to divine intervention, and built two spectacular churches by way of thanks: the Chiesa del SS Redentore (p148) and Chiesa di Santa Maria della Salute (p82). The confraternity dedicated to San Rocco, the patron saint of the plague-stricken, commissioned one of the city's greatest art masterpieces: floor-to-ceiling Tintoretto paintings for the Scuola Grande di San Rocco (p98).

HISTORY OF VENICE

John Julius Norwich's *History of Venice* (1981) is a massive, engrossing epic account of the city's maritime empire, if a bit long on naval battles and short on recent history.

TRADERS & TRAITORS

Like its signature Basilica di San Marco, the Venetian empire was dazzlingly cosmopolitan. Venice turned arrivals from every nation and creed into trading partners with a common credo: as long as everyone was making money, cultural boundaries need not apply. Armenians, Turks, Greeks and Germans became neighbours along the Grand Canal, and Jewish refugees and other groups widely persecuted in Europe settled into established communities in Venice.

Commerce provided a common bond. At the height of Venice's maritime prowess, 300 shipbuilding companies in the Arsenale had 16,000 employees. By the mid-15th century, Venice's maritime ventures had left it swathed in golden mosaics, rustling silks and incense to cover mucky summer smells that were the downsides of a lagoon empire. In case of

1444

The second Rialto Bridge collapses under spectators watching a wedding flotilla. After 148 years and huge cost overruns, Antonio da Ponte provides a spectacular stone replacement.

1470

Cyprus is the latest of Venice's conquests, now stretching across the mainland to Bergamo, through the Aegean to Crete, and Middle East trading outposts in Jaffa, Beirut and Alexandria.

1492

Genoese Cristoforo Colombo's voyage kicks off the age of discovery and Venice's long slide into obsolescence, as the Portuguese and Spanish bypass its customs controls.

1494

Aldo Manuzio founds Aldine Press, introducing italics and cheap paperbacks. Venice's literary reputation soars; by 1500 one in six books published in Europe is printed in Venice.

trade disputes or feuds among neighbours, La Serenissima retained its calm through a complex political system of checks, balances and elections, with the doge as the executive presiding over council matters.

Yet inside the red velvet cloak of its ruling elite, Venice was hiding an iron hand. Venice's shadowy secret service, the Consiglio dei Dieci (Council of Ten), thwarted conspiracies by deploying Venetian James Bonds throughout Venice and major European capitals. Venice had no qualms about spying on its own citizens to ensure a balance of power, and trials, torture and executions were carried out in secret. Still, compared with its neighbours at the time, Venice remained a haven of tolerance.

Occasionally, the Council made examples of lawbreakers. Denunciations of wrongdoers were nailed to the door of Palazzo Ducale (p55) and published by Venice's presses – and when that failed to convey the message, the Council of Ten ordered the bludgeoning or decapitation of those found guilty of crimes against the doge. Severed heads were placed atop columns outside the Palazzo Ducale and sundry parts distributed for display in the *sestieri* (neighbourhoods) for exactly three nights and four days, until they started to smell.

KING HENRY III

Venetian party planners outdid themselves with the 1574 reception for King Henry III of France. The king's barge was greeted with glass-blowers performing on rafts, bevvies of Venetian beauties dressed in white, a 1200-course meal, and decorations provided by an all-star committee of Palladio, Veronese and Tintoretto.

FRIENDLY FOES

As it turns out, overripe heads were the least of Venice's dangers. Never mind that Venice sacked Constantinople, or that Constantinople sided with Genoa against Venice: warfare wasn't enough to deter the two maritime powers from doing brisk business with one another for centuries. When Constantinople fell to Ottoman rule in 1453, business carried on as usual. The rival powers understood one another very well; the Venetian language was widely spoken across the eastern Mediterranean.

There were some awkward moments in diplomatic relations, however. Both sides periodically took prisoners of war, and seldom released them. Prisoners were routinely forced into servitude and/or conversion. In 1428 Venice established a special prison in Dorsoduro to convert Muslim Turkish women prisoners to Christianity. Ottomans tended to hold Venetians for ransom, though it wasn't always an especially profitable gambit. Though Venice officially installed collection boxes in churches in 1586 to raise funds for POW ransom, they remained mostly empty.

Prisoners & Princesses

After Suleiman the Magnificent took over Cyprus in 1571, Venice felt its maritime power slipping, and became allied with the papal states, Spain and even arch-rival Genoa to keep the Ottoman sultan at bay. The same year a huge allied fleet (much of it provided by Venice) routed the

1498

Portuguese explorer Vasco da Gama sails around the Cape of Good Hope, and the boom in trans-Atlantic trade shuts out many Venetian merchants.

1508

The Holy Roman Empire, papal states, Spain and France form the League of Cambrai against Venice – but with Venice cutting side deals, ensuing war doesn't change the map much.

1516

A proclamation declares that Jewish residents of Venice are to live in a designated zone known as the Ghetto, with access to the area closed at midnight by guards.

1564

When Venetian noblewoman Bianca Cappello runs off with a Florentine clerk, she is sentenced to death for treason – but once she becomes the Grand Duchess of Tuscany, all is forgiven.

Turks off Lepanto, in Greece, and Sebastiano Venier and his Venetian fleet sailed home with 100 Turkish women as war trophies.

Legend has it that when Turkish troops took over the island of Paros, the POWs included Cecilia Venier-Baffo, who was apparently the illegitimate daughter of Venice's noble Venier family, a niece of the doge, and possibly the cousin of Sebastiano (of Lepanto fame). Cecilia became the favourite wife of Sultan Salim II in Constantinople, and when he died in 1574 she took control as Sultana Nurbani (Princess of Light). Regent of Sultan Murad III, she was a faithful pen pal of Queen Elizabeth I of Britain and Catherine de Medici of France. According to historian Alberto Toso Fei, the Sultana's policies were so favourable to Venetian interests that the Venetian senate set aside special funds to fulfil her wishes for Venetian specialities, from lapdogs to golden cushions. Genoa wasn't pleased by her favouritism, and in 1582 she was poisoned to death by what appears to have been Genoese assassins.

Top Five Hallmarks of Venetian Decadence

- *Carnevale*
- *Ca' Rezzonico (Dorsoduro)*
- *Ponte delle Tette (San Polo)*
- *Palazzo Mocenigo (Santa Croce)*
- *Palazzo Fortuny (San Marco)*

THE AGE OF DECADENCE

While Italy's city-states continued to plot against one another, they were increasingly eclipsed by marriages cementing alliances among France, Henry VIII's England and the Habsburg Empire. As it lost ground to these European nation-states and the seas to pirates and Ottomans, Venice took a different tack, and began conquering Europe by charm.

Artistic Sensations & Scandals

Venice's star attractions were its parties, music, women and art. Nunneries in Venice held soirées to rival those in its *ridotti* (casinos), and Carnevale lasted up to three months. Claudio Monteverdi was hired as choir director of San Marco in 1613, introducing multi-part harmonies and historical operas with crowd-pleasing tragicomic scenes. Monteverdi's modern opera caught on: by the end of the 17th century, Venice's opera season included as many as 30 different operas, including 10 brand-new operas composed for Venetian venues.

New orchestras required musicians, but Venice came up with a ready workforce: orphan girls. Circumstances had conspired to produce an unprecedented number of Venetian orphans: on the one hand were plague and snake-oil cures, and on the other were scandalous masquerade parties and flourishing prostitution. Funds poured in from anonymous donors to support *ospedaletti* (orphanages), and the great baroque composers Antonio Vivaldi and Domenico Cimarosa were hired to lead orphan orchestras. The Venetian state took on the care and musical training of the city's orphan girls, who earned their keep by performing at public functions

1571

Venice and the Holy League of Catholic states defeat Ottoman forces at the naval Battle of Lepanto, thanks in part to a technical advantage: cannons and guns versus archers.

1575

Plague claims many lives, including Titian's. Quarantine aids Venice's recovery; a new painting cycle by Tintoretto is dedicated to San Rocco, patron saint of the plague-stricken.

1609

Venice passes a law defining penalties for casino employees caught cheating: cutting the ears and nose, plus 10 to 20 years of incarceration.

1630

The plague kills a third of Venice's population within 16 months. With few leaders surviving, Venice allows wealthy Venetians to buy their way into the Golden Book of nobles.

VENICE'S 'HONEST COURTESANS'

High praise, high pay and even high honours: Venice's *cortigiane oneste* were no ordinary strumpets. An 'honest courtesan' earned the title not by offering a fair price, but by providing added value with style, education and wit that reflected well on her patrons. They were not always beautiful or young, but *cortigiane oneste* were well-educated, dazzling their admirers with poetry, music, philosophical insights and apt social critiques. In the 16th century, some Venetian families of limited means spared no expense on their daughters' educations: beyond an advantageous marriage or career, educated women who become *cortigiane oneste* could command prices 60 times the average *cortigiana di lume* ('courtesan of the lamp' – streetwalker).

Far from hiding their trade, a catalogue of 210 of Venice's *piu honorate cortigiane* (most honoured courtesans) was published in 1565, listing contact information and going rates, payable directly to the courtesan's servant, her mother or, occasionally, her husband. A *cortigiana onesta* might circulate in Venetian society as the known mistress of one or more admirers, who compensated her for her company rather than services rendered, and with an allowance rather than pay per hour – though on rare occasion, an exceptionally clever Petrarchan sonnet might win her favours. Syphilis was an occupational hazard, and special hospices were founded for infirm courtesans.

One better-paid courtesans was Veronica Franco (1546–91), the daughter of a *cortigiana onesta*. She married a wealthy doctor and had a child as a teenager, but by 20 left her stormy marriage to become a courtesan. By age 30, Franco's patrons included King Henry III of France, and she'd published an acclaimed volume of her poetry. When an outbreak of the plague forced Franco to flee the city in 1575, her home was looted, and she returned to the city two years later to provide for her six children and orphaned relatives only to face Inquisition accusations of witchcraft. Franco defended herself successfully, and went on to publish 50 of her letters (including two sonnets to Henry III) in 1580. With the proceeds, she established a charity for courtesans and their children.

and *ospedaletti* fund-raising galas. Visiting diplomats treated to orphan concerts were well advised to tip the orphan performers: you never know whose illegitimate daughter you might be insulting otherwise.

Socialites began gifting snuffboxes and portraits painted by Venetian artists as fashionable tokens of their esteem, and salon habitués across Europe became accustomed to mythological and biblical themes painted in luminous Venetian colours, with the unmistakable city on the water as a backdrop. On baroque church ceilings across Venice, frescoed angels play heavenly music on lutes and trumpets – instruments officially banned from churches by Rome. Venetian art became incredibly daring with Titian and Veronese, bringing voluptuous reds and sly social commentary to familiar religious subjects.

1669

The Venetian colony of Crete is lost to the Ottoman Turks, yet the two powers continue to trade with one another – despite repeated objections from Rome.

1678

Venetian scholar Eleonora Lucrezia Cornaro Piscopia is the first woman to receive a university degree in Europe, earning her doctor of Philosophy at the University of Padua.

1703–40

Antonio Vivaldi is musical director at La Pietà, composing hundreds of concertos for orchestras of orphan girls. He is fired in 1709 but swiftly recalled, to Venice's immense credit.

1718

Venice and Austria sign Treaty of Passarowitz with the Ottoman Empire, splitting prime coastal territory and leaving Venice with only nominal control and a smattering of Ionian islands.

Pulling Rank: The Pope & the Doge

Rome repeatedly censured Venice for depicting holy subjects in an earthy, Venetian light, and playing toe-tapping tunes in churches – but such censorship was largely ignored within Venice. According to late-16th-century gossip, Cardinal Camillo Borghese had a beef with the Venetian ambassador to Rome, Leonardo Donà, ever since the two exchanged heated words in the Roman halls of power. The cardinal hissed that, were he pope, he'd excommunicate the entire Venetian populace. 'And I would thumb my nose at the excommunication,' retorted Donà.

As fate would have it, by 1606 cardinal and ambassador were promoted to Pope Paul V and doge, respectively. Rome had never appreciated Venice's insistence on reserving a degree of control over Church matters, and when Venice claimed that zoning laws required its approval of church expansion plans within the city, Pope Paul V issued a papal bull excommunicating Venice. As promised, Doge Donà defied the bull, ordering all churches to remain open on Venetian territory. Any church that obeyed the bull would have its doors permanently closed, property seized and clergy exiled from Venice.

Venetian-born monk and philosopher Paolo Sarpi (see the boxed text, p219) convincingly argued Venice's case, claiming Venice's right to self-determination came directly from God, not through Rome. Before the excommunication could cause further loss of Church property in Venice, or other Catholic territories became convinced by Sarpi's argument, Pope Paul V rescinded his bull.

Finally, after Rome issued its umpteenth official reprimand of Venice, the Venetian state decided to do some paperwork of its own. Venice conducted an official 1767 audit of 11 million golden ducats in revenues rendered to Rome in the previous decade, and decided to cut its losses: 127 Veneto monasteries and convents were closed, cutting the local clerical population in half and redirecting millions of ducats to Venice's coffers.

One of Italy's most beloved graphic novels, *Corto Maltese in Fables of Venice* (originally published 1967) follows Hugo Pratt's cosmopolitan sea captain as he cracks the mysteries of the *calli* (alleyways).

RED LIGHTS, WHITE WIDOWS & GREY AREAS

While Roman clerics furiously scribbled their disapproval, Venetian trends stealthily took over drawing rooms across the continent, and Grand Canal *palazzi* (palaces) and Veneto villas lining the Riviera Brenta (p165) became playgrounds for Europe's upper crust.

Venetian women's lavish finery, staggering platform shoes up to 50cm high and masculine quiff hairdos scandalised visiting European nobility, until Venice felt obliged to enact sumptuary laws preventing women from adopting manly hairstyles and blinding displays of jewels

1797

The segregation of Jewish Venetians comes to an end and the gates of the Ghetto are opened, just as Napoleon arrives in the city.

1807

Napoleon suppresses religious orders to quell dissent, but it continues until Independence, when some churches are reconsecrated. Many aren't, serving as archives or tourist attractions.

1814

Austria takes Venice as a war trophy and imposes order with thousands of troops, a house-numbering system and heavy taxes that push Venice to the brink of starvation.

1836

Fire guts Venice's legendary public opera house, but a new version soon rises from the ashes. When La Fenice (The Phoenix) burns again in 1996, an exacting replica is rebuilt.

on dipping décolletages. Venetian noblewomen complained to the doge and the Pope, and the restrictions were soon dropped.

With maritime trade revenues dipping and the value of the Venetian ducat slipping in the 16th century, Venice's fleshpots brought in far too much valuable foreign currency to be outlawed. Instead, Venice opted for regulation and taxation. Rather than baring all in the rough-and-ready streets around the Rialto, prostitutes could only display their wares from the waist up in windows, or sit bare-legged on windowsills. Venice decreed that to distinguish themselves from noblewomen who increasingly dressed like them, ladies of the night should ride in gondolas with red lights. By the end of the 16th century, the town was flush with some 12,000 registered prostitutes, creating a literal red-light district. Today red beacons mostly signal construction, but you can enjoy decadent dinners at Antiche Carampane (Old Streetwalkers; p106) near Ponte delle Tette (Tits Bridge; see the boxed text, p103).

Director Luchino Visconti takes on Nobel Prize–winner Thomas Mann's story of a Mahler-esque composer, an infatuation and a deadly outbreak in *Death in Venice* (1971).

Beyond red lights ringing the Rialto, 16th- to 18th-century visitors encountered broad grey areas in Venetian social mores. Far from being shunned by polite society, Venice's 'honest courtesans' became widely admired as poets, musicians and tastemakers (see the boxed text, p214). As free-spirited, financially independent Venetian women took lovers and accepted lavish gifts from admirers in the 16th to 18th centuries, there became a certain fluidity surrounding the definition of a *cortigiana* (courtesan). With their husbands at sea for months or years, Venice's 'white widows' took young, handsome *cicisbei* (manservants) to tend their needs. Not coincidentally, Venetian ladies occasionally fell into religious fervours entailing a trimester-long seclusion.

During winter masquerades and Carnevale, Venice's nobility regularly escaped the tedium of salons and official duties under masks and cloaks, generating enough gossip to last until the summer social season in Riviera Brenta villas provided fresh scandal. Some Venetians dropped the mask of propriety altogether, openly cohabitating with lovers year-round and acknowledging illegitimate heirs in their wills. By the 18th century, less than 40% of Venetian nobles bothered with the formality of marriage, and the regularity of Venetian annulments scandalised even visiting French courtiers.

FROM COLONISATION TO REVOLUTION

When Napoleon arrived in 1797, Venice had been reduced by plague and circumstances from 175,000 to fewer than 100,000 people, and their reputation as fierce partiers did nothing to prevent the French and Austrians from handing the city back and forth as a war trophy. Venice declared its

1840

At La Serenissima's height, Venice's fabled Golden Book of nobles included more than 1200 families – but by 1840, all but 200 were destitute and subsisting on charity.

1846

The first train crosses to the mainland. The feat is bittersweet: churches were demolished for the station, trains brought occupying Austrian troops, and Venetians footed the bill.

1848

Daniele Manin leads an anti-Austrian rebellion and declares Venice a republic for 17 months. Austrians retake the city in 1849, and Venice remains under Austrian control for 17 years.

1866

Venice and Veneto join the new Kingdom of Italy. The unification of Italy is complete when Rome is made the capital of Italy in 1870.

PRINCE OF PLEASURE

Never was a hedonist born at a better time and in a more appropriate place. Eighteenth-century Venice had retired from the arduous business of running a maritime empire, and was well into its new career as the pleasure capital of Europe when Giacomo Casanova (1725–98) arrived on the scene. He was abandoned as a young boy, and became a gambler and rake on the make while studying law in Padua. He graduated by age 17 to take up a position with the Church in Venice, but adventuring soon became Casanova's primary career, with minor sidelines in penning love letters for cardinals, looking good in military uniform, and playing violin badly in an orchestra of drunkards. His charm won him warm welcomes into the homes of wealthy patrons – and the beds of their wives, lovers and daughters.

Venice was a licentious place, but some political limits still applied. Though Casanova's escapades may have been dangerous to marriages, his dalliances with Freemasonry and banned books were considered nothing less than a threat to the state. After an evening foursome with the French ambassador and a couple of nuns, Casanova was arrested on the nebulous charge of 'outrages against religion' and dragged to the Piombi, the Palazzo Ducale's dreaded attic prison. Sentenced to five years in a sweltering, flea-infested cell, Casanova complained bitterly, and carved an escape hatch through the wooden floor – but just when he was ready to make his getaway, a sympathetic warden had him moved to a more comfortable cell. Casanova soon devised plan B: he escaped through the roof of his new cell, entered the palace, and casually breezed past the guards in the morning.

Casanova fled Venice to make his fortune in Paris and serve briefly as a French spy. But his extracurricular habits caused him no end of trouble: he went broke in Germany, survived a duel in Poland, fathered and abandoned several children (possibly including a child by one of his daughters), and contracted venereal diseases in England (despite occasional use of a linen condom prototype). Late in life, he returned to Venice as a celebrity, and served the government as a spy – but he was exiled for publishing a satire of the nobility. He wound up as a librarian in an isolated castle in Bohemia, where boredom drove him to finally write his memoirs. In the end, he concludes, 'I can say I have lived.'

neutrality in the war between France and Austria, but that didn't stop Napoleon. Venetian warships managed to deter one French ship by the Lido, but when Napoleon made it clear he intended to destroy the city if it resisted, the Maggior Consiglio (Grand Council) decreed the end of the Republic. The doge reportedly doffed the signature cap of his office with a sigh, saying, 'I won't be needing this anymore'. Rioting citizens were incensed by such cowardice, but French forces soon ended the insurrection, and began systematically plundering the city.

1895

The first Biennale reasserts the city as global tastemaker. Other nations are eventually invited, though a provocative Picasso piece is removed from the Spanish pavilion in 1910.

San Marco campanile (p63)

1902

The San Marco campanile (bell tower) suddenly collapses. Miraculously, the only casualty is the caretaker's cat. A replica is built by 1912; restorations continue, just in case.

1918

Austro-Hungarian planes drop almost 300 bombs on Venice in WWI, but their aim is off, resulting in mercifully little loss of life or damage.

Though Napoleon only controlled Venice sporadically for a total of about 11 years, the impact of his reign is still visible. Napoleon grabbed any Venetian art masterpiece that wasn't nailed down, and displaced religious orders to make room for museums and trophy galleries in the Gallerie dell'Accademia and Museo Correr. Napoleon's city planners lifted remaining restrictions on the Jewish Ghetto, filled in canals and widened city streets to facilitate movement of troops and loot; his decorators established a style of gaudy gold cornices and whimsical grotesques. Napoleon lost control of Venice in 1814, and two years later one-quarter of Venice's population was destitute.

Top Five Landmarks of Multicultural Venice

- *Ghetto (Canna-reggio)*
- *Museo delle Icone (Castello)*
- *Scuola di San Giorgio degli Schiavoni (Castello)*
- *Fondaco dei Turchi (Santa Croce)*
- *Palazzo Zenobio (Dorsoduro)*

But Austria had grand plans for Venice, and expected impoverished Venetians to foot the bill. They were obliged to house Austrian soldiers, who spent off-duty hours carousing in *campi* (squares) with bullfights and beer gardens and their new happy-hour invention, the *spritz* (a *prosecco*-and-bitters cocktail). Finding their way back home afterwards was a challenge in Venetian *calli* (alleyways), so the Austrians implemented a street-numbering system. To bring in reinforcements and supplies, they dredged and deepened entrances to the lagoon for ease of shipping access and began a train bridge in 1841 – all with Venetian labour and special Venetian taxes. To make way for the new train station in 1846, *scuole* (religious confraternity) convents and a palace were demolished.

With no say in the Austrian puppet government running Venice, many Venetians voted with their feet: under the Austrians, the population fell from 138,000 to 99,000. When a young lawyer named Daniele Manin suggested reforms to Venice's puppet government in 1848, he was tossed in prison – sparking a popular uprising against the Austrians that would last 17 months (see the boxed text, p219). Austria responded by bombarding and blockading the city. In July, Austria began a 24-day artillery bombardment raining some 23,000 shells down on the city and its increasingly famished and cholera-stricken populace, until Manin finally managed to negotiate the surrender to Austria with a guarantee of no reprisals. Yet the indignity of Austria's suppression continued to fester, and when presented with the option in 1866, the people of Venice and the Veneto voted to join the new independent kingdom of Italy under King Vittorio Emanuele II.

LIFE DURING WARTIME

Glamorous Venice gradually took on a workaday aspect in the 19th century, with factories springing up on Giudecca and around Mestre and Padua, and textile industries setting up shop around Vicenza and

1932
The world's first film festival is initially considered a dubious ploy for attention, but Greta Garbo, Clark Gable, the international press and 25,000 movie-goers prove the formula a success.

1933
Mussolini opens the Ponte della Libertà (Freedom Bridge) from Mestre to Venice. The 3.85km-long, two-lane highway remains the only access to Venice by car.

1943
From the Ghetto, 256 Jewish Venetians are rounded up and deported to concentration camps. A memorial in the Campo del Ghetto commemorates those lost in the camps.

1948
Peggy Guggenheim arrives with major modernists, renewing interest in Italian art, reclaiming Futurism from the Fascists and championing Venetian abstract expressionism.

VENETIANS WHO CHANGED HISTORY

Doge Marin Falier (1285–1355)

Claim to fame The hot-headed doge was in power for eight months. After a Venetian courtier apparently made a joke at his expense, the doge plotted to overthrow Venice's noble council. Details leaked out and he was arrested and beheaded within the hour.

Legacy In the Palazzo Ducale's Sala del Maggior Consiglio, Doge Falier's portrait is blacked out, and his sarcophagus was emptied and used as a washbasin in Venice's public hospital. The thwarted coup justified consolidation of power by Venice's security service, the Consiglio dei Dieci (Council of Ten), which encouraged Venetians to spy on their neighbours.

Paolo Sarpi (1552–1623)

Claim to fame When the Pope excommunicated the republic of Venice in 1606 for ignoring Rome's rulings, Servite monk Paolo Sarpi defended Venice's 'God-given' right to govern its people. Under Sarpi's direction, Venice ordered churches to ignore the excommunication, and Venetian religious orders that failed to hold Mass were closed and had their property seized. The excommunication was lifted a year later.

Legacy Six months after Rome recanted, five assassins stabbed Sarpi in Campo Santa Fosca and fled to papal territories. Sarpi survived, writing legal and scientific tracts for 13 more years. Venice raised a monument in Sarpi's honour on the site of the attempted assassination in Cannaregio.

Daniele Manin (1804–1857)

Claim to fame After suggesting reforms to Austrian rulers, this young Venetian lawyer was arrested for treason. On 22 March 1848, fellow Venetians rescued him from jail to lead an insurrection. Manin was declared president of Venice, and for 17 months the republic survived Austrian bombardment, starvation and cholera. Manin negotiated favourable terms for surrender, with amnesty granted to all Venetians except himself.

Legacy Manin was exiled to France, where he agitated for independent Italy. Manin did not live to see his dream fulfilled, but in 1868, his remains were returned to Venice for a state funeral. Today, Via Lunga XXII Marzo (22 March St) commemorates the Venice uprising.

Treviso. As an increasingly strategic industrial area, Venice began to seem like a port worth reclaiming. But when Austro-Hungarian forces advanced on Venice, they were confronted by Italy's naval marines. Two days after Italy declared war on Austria in 1915, air raids on the

1955

Venice opens Italy's first museum of Jewish history, the Museo Ebraico, in the historic Ghetto. The museum opens the Ghetto's historic synagogues and Lido cemetery to visitors.

1966

Record floods cause widespread damage and unleash debate on measures to protect Venice.Its admirers around the world rally to save the city, and rescue its treasures from lagoon muck.

1996

La Fenice burns down for the second time; two electricians are found guilty of arson. A €90 million replica of the 19th-century opera house is completed in 2003.

2003

After decades of debate, Berlusconi launches the construction of Modulo Sperimentale Elettromeccanico (Mose) to prevent disastrous flooding from rising sea levels.

city began, and would continue intermittently throughout WWI until 1918. Venice was lucky: the bombardments caused little damage or loss of life.

When Mussolini rose to power after WWI, he was determined to turn the Veneto into a modern industrial powerhouse and a model Fascist society – despite Venice's famously laissez-faire reputation. Mussolini constructed a roadway from the mainland to Venice, literally bringing the freewheeling city into line with the rest of Italy. While Italy's largest Fascist rallies, with up to 300,000 participants, were held in the boulevards of Padua (p167), Italian Resistance leaders met in Padua's parks to plot uprisings throughout northern Italy. When Mussolini's grip on the region began to weaken, partisans joined Allied troops to wrest Veneto from Fascist control.

Venice emerged relatively unscathed by Allied bombing campaigns that targeted mainland industrial sites, and was liberated by New Zealand troops in 1945 – but the mass deportation of Venice's historic Jewish population in 1943 shook Venice to its very moorings. When the Veneto began to rebound after the war, many Venetians left for the mainland, Milan and other postwar economic centres. The legendary lagoon city seemed mired in the mud, unable to reconcile its recent history with its past grandeur, and unsure of its future.

In *Wings of the Dove* (1902), a dapper con man and sickly heiress meet in Venice, with predictable consequences – but Henry James' gorgeous storytelling makes for riveting reading.

ACQUE ALTE

On 4 November 1966, disaster struck. Record floods poured into 16,000 Venetian homes in terrifying waves, and residents were stranded in the wreckage of 1400 years of civilisation. Given Venice's historic, cosmopolitan charms, the response was instantaneous and international: assistance from admirers poured in, from Mexico to Australia, millionaires and pensioners alike, and Unesco coordinated some 27 private organisations to redress the ravages of the flood. Photographs of the era (available online at www.albumdivenezia.it) show Venetians drying ancient books one page at a time and gondolas gliding into bars for a *spritz,* served by bartenders in hip-high waders.

Venice's *acque alte* (high tides) bravado may be its saving grace. Today, with 60,000 official residents matched by a daily influx of visitors, Venetians could be overwhelmed in their own city. Yet despite dire predictions, Venice has not yet become a Carnavale-masked parody of itself or a lost Atlantis. The city remains relevant and realistic, continuing to produce new music, art and crafts even as it seeks sustainable solutions to rising water levels. Venice remains anchored not merely by ancient pylons, but by the people who put them there: the Venetians.

2006

With support from the city, François Pinault moves his world-class contemporary art collection to Giorgio Masari's 1749 Palazzo Grassi, redesigned by Tadao Ando.

KRZYSZTOF DYDYNSKI / LONELY PLANET IMAGES ©

Palazzo Grassi (p61)

2008

The first new bridge across the Grand Canal since before WWII, Ponte di Calatrava opens to pedestrians amid controversy over its modernity, cost and wheelchair accessibility.

2009

Tadao Ando reinvents abandoned Punta della Dogana customs houses as a gallery for French billionaire Pinault's collection of provocative contemporary-art installations.

Architecture

Lulls in Venetian happy-hour conversation are easily resolved with one innocent question: so what is Venetian architecture? Everyone has a pet period in Venice's chequered architectural history, and hardly anyone agrees which is Venice's defining moment. Ruskin waxed rhapsodic about Venetian Gothic and detested Palladio; Palladians rebuffed baroque; fans of regal rococo were scandalised by the Lido's louche Liberty (Italian art nouveau); and pretty much everyone was horrified by the inclinations of industry to strip Venice of any ornamentation. Now that the latest architectural trend is creative repurposing, it's all making a comeback.

ENGINEERING MARVELS

Over the centuries, Venetian architecture has evolved into such a dazzling composite of materials, styles and influences that you might overlook its singular defining feature: it floats. Thousands of wood pylons sunk into lagoon mud support stone foundations, built up with elegant brickwork and rustic ceiling beams, low *sotoportegi* (passageways) and lofty loggias, grand watergates and hidden *cortile* (courtyards). Instead of disguising or wallpapering over these essential Venetian structural elements, modern architects have begun highlighting them. With this approach, the Fondazione Giorgio Cini (p149) converted a naval academy into a gallery, Tadao Ando turned Punta della Dogana (p84) customs houses into a contemporary art showplace, and Renzo Piano transformed historic salt warehouses into a rotating gallery space for Fondazione Emilio Vedova (p83). With original load-bearing supports and brickwork exposed to public admiration, Venice's new-old architecture seems more fresh and vital than ever.

More than 1000 years of architectural history are covered on the short trip down the Grand Canal, lined with 200 palaces that range from Venetian Gothic with Moorish flourishes (the Ca' d'Oro) to radically repurposed postmodern neoclassical (Palazzo Grassi).

VENETO-BYZANTINE

If Venice seems to have unfair aesthetic advantages, it did have an early start: cosmopolitan flair has made Venetian architecture a standout since the 7th century. While Venice proper was still a motley, muddy outpost of refugee settlements, the nearby island of Torcello was a booming Byzantine trade hub of 20,000. At its spiritual centre was the Cattedrale di Santa Maria Assunta (p156), which from afar looks like a Byzantine-style basilica on loan from Ravenna. But look closely: those 7th- to 9th-century apses have Romanesque arches, and the iconostasis separating the central nave from the presbytery is straight out of an Eastern Orthodox church. Back in Torcello's heyday, traders from France, Greece or Turkey could have stepped off their boats and into this church, and all felt at home.

But to signal to visitors that they had arrived in a powerful trading centre, Santa Maria Assunta glitters with 12th- to 13th-century golden mosaics. Recent excavations reveal Torcello glassworks dating from the 7th century, and those furnaces would have been kept glowing through the night to produce the thousands of tiny glass tesserae (tiles) needed to create the mesmerising Madonna with child keeping company with saints over the altar – not to mention the rather alarmingly detailed Last Judgment mosaic, with hellfire licking at the dancing feet of the damned.

TOP FIVE CONTROVERSIAL BRIDGES

➡ **Ponte di Calatrava** (p119) Officially known as Ponte della Costituzione (Constitution Bridge), Spanish architect Santiago Calatrava's modern bridge between Piazzale Roma and Ferrovia was commissioned for €4 million in 1999, and for a decade was variously denounced as unnecessary, inappropriate and wheelchair inaccessible. Though the bridge has cost triple the original estimate, it has also received private backing by retailers with offices at the foot of the bridge, and some Venetians refer to it as 'Benetton Bridge'. Foot traffic is noticeably diverting over this minimalist arc of steel, glass and stone, and wheelchair access is being added – but with a projected 15-minute crossing limited to one wheelchair at a time, the *vaporetto* (waterbus) seems comparatively efficient.

➡ **Ponte di Rialto** (p101) The main bridge across the Grand Canal was disaster-prone for centuries: the original 1255 wooden structure burned during a 1310 revolt, and its replacement collapsed under spectators watching a 1444 wedding parade. The state couldn't gather funds for a 1551 stone bridge project pitched for by Palladio, Sansovino or Michelangelo, and the task fell to Antonio da Ponte in 1588. Cost overruns were enormous: as the stonework settled, the bridge cracked, and legend has it that only a deal with the Devil allowed da Ponte to finish by 1592. Architect Vincenzo Scamozzi sniffed that the structure was doomed, but da Ponte's bridge has remained a diabolically clever masterpiece of engineering – at least until chunks of bridge pylons abruptly dropped into the canal in 2011. Renzo Rosso of Diesel, the Italian jeans brand, pledged funds in 2011 to restore the bridge. Fearing that Diesel will seize the opportunity to advertise on the bridge, some Venetians are calling it a new deal with the Devil.

➡ **Ponte dei Pugni** (Bridge of the Fists) Turf battles were regularly fought on this pugnacious Dorsoduro bridge between residents of Venice's north end, the Nicolotti, and its south end, the Castellani. Deadly brawls evolved into full-contact boxing matches, with starting footholds marked in the corners of the bridge (which was restored in 2005). It was all fun and games even after someone's eye was put out; bouts ended with fighters bloodied, bruised and bobbing in the canal. King Henry III of France apparently enjoyed the spectacle, but escalation into deadly knife fights in 1705 ended the practice, and today Venetians compete for neighbourhood bragging rights with regattas instead.

➡ **Ponte delle Tette** (p103) 'Tits Bridge' got its name in the late 15th century, when neighbourhood prostitutes were encouraged to display their wares in the windows of buildings above the bridge instead of taking their marketing campaigns to the streets. According to local lore (and rather bizarre logic), this display was intended to curb a dramatic increase in sodomy. The bridge leads to Rio Terà delle Carampane, named after a noble family's house (Ca' Rampani) that became a notorious hangout for local streetwalkers (dubbed *carampane*).

➡ **Ponte dei Sospiri** (p58) Built by Antonio Contino in 1600 and given its 'Bridge of Sighs' nickname by Lord Byron, the bridge connects the upper storeys of the Palazzo Ducale and Prigioni Nuove (New Prisons). According to Byron's conceit, doomed prisoners would sigh at their last glimpse of lovely Venice through the bridge's windows – but as you'll notice on Palazzo Ducale tours, the lagoon is scarcely visible through the stonework-screened windows. Legend has it that couples kissing under the bridge will remain in love forever, but no doubt Venice's prisoners took a less romantic view of the construction.

Breakout Byzantine Style

When Venice made its definitive break with the Byzantine empire in the 9th century, it needed a landmark to set the city apart, and a platform to launch its golden age of maritime commerce. Basilica di San Marco (p52) captures Venice's grand designs in five vast gold mosaic domes, refracting stray sunbeams like an indoor fireworks display – even today, the sight elicits audible gasps from crowds of international admirers. The basilica began with a triple nave in the 9th century but, after a fire, two wings were added to form a Greek cross, in an idea borrowed from the Church of the Holy Apostles in Constantinople. The East-meets-West style was the ideal showcase for Venice's position as the new powerhouse in the Adriatic. The finest artisans from around the Mediterranean were brought in to raise the basilica's dazzle factor to mind-boggling, from 11th- to 13th-century marble relief masterpieces over the Romanesque entry arches to the intricate Islamic geometry of the 12th- to 13th-century inlaid semiprecious stone floors.

Since the basilica was the official chapel of the doge, every time Venice conquered new territory by commerce or force, the basilica displayed the doge's share of the loot – hence the walls of polychrome marble pilfered from Egypt, and 2nd-century Roman bronze horses looted from Constantinople's hippodrome in 1204. The basilica's ornament changed over the centuries with architectural tastes that swung from Gothic to Renaissance, but the message to visiting dignitaries remained the same: the glory above may be God's, but the power below rested with the doge.

POGGI

Next to bridges, Venice's most common architectural features are its *poggi*, (well-heads). Before Venice's aqueduct was constructed, more than 6000 wells collected and filtered rainwater for public use across Venice. Even today, overflow happy-hour crowds at neighbourhood *bacari* (bars) gossip around these ancient watering holes.

ROMANESQUE

Romanesque was all the rage across Western Europe in the 9th century, from the Lombard plains to Tuscany, southern France to northeast Spain, and later, Germany and England. While the materials ranged from basic brick to elaborate marble, the rounded archways, barrel-vaulted ceilings, triple nave and calming cloisters came to define medieval church architecture. This austere, classical style was a deliberate reference to the Roman empire and early martyrs that sacrificed all for the Church, reminding the faithful of their own duty through the Crusades. But in case the architecture failed to send the message, sculptural reliefs were added, heralding heroism on entry portals – and putting the fear of the devil into unbelievers, with angels and demons carved into stone capitals in creepy crypts.

As Venice became a maritime empire in the 13th century, many of the city's smaller Byzantine and early Romanesque buildings were swept away to make room for International Gothic grandeur. The finest examples of Romanesque in the Veneto – and possibly in Northern Italy – are Verona's vast 12th- to 14th-century Basilica di San Zeno Maggiore (p179) and Padua's frescoed jewel of a Romanesque Baptistry (p170). Within Venice, you can admire Romanesque simplicity in Chiesa di San Giacomo dell'Orio (p101).

VENETIAN GOTHIC

Soaring spires and flying buttresses rose above Paris in the 12th century, making the rest of Europe suddenly seem small and squat by comparison. Soon every European capital was trying to top Paris with Gothic marvels of their own, featuring deceptively delicate ribbed cross-vaulting that distributed the weight of stone walls and allowed openings for vast stained glass windows.

Europe's medieval superpowers used this grand international style to showcase their splendour and status – but Venice one-upped its neighbours not with height, but by inventing its own version of Gothic. Venice had been trading across the Mediterranean with partners from Lebanon to North Africa for centuries, and the constant exchange of

TOP FIVE DIVINE ARCHITECTURAL EXPERIENCES

- **Basilica di San Marco** (p52) Domes glimmer with golden mosaics.
- **Chiesa di San Giorgio Maggiore** (p147) Palladio's expansive, effortlessly uplifting interiors.
- **Scuola Grande dei Carmini** (p83) Longhena's stairway to heaven.
- **Chiesa di Santa Maria dei Miracoli** (p118) The little Renaissance miracle in polychrome marble.
- **Schola Spagnola** (Spanish Synagogue; p117) Lofty, elliptical women's gallery with operatic drama.

building materials, engineering innovations and aesthetic ideals led to a creative cross-pollination in Western and Middle Eastern architecture. Instead of framing windows with the ordinary ogive (pointed) arch common to France and Germany, Venice added an elegantly tapered, Moorish flourish to its arches, with a trilobate (three-lobed) shape that became a signature of Venetian Gothic.

Brick Gothic

While Tuscany used marble for Gothic cathedrals like France and Germany, Venice showcased a more austere, cerebral style with clever brickwork and a Latin cross plan at I Frari (p100), completed in 1443 after a century's work, and Zanipolo (p129), consecrated in 1430. The more fanciful brick Madonna dell'Orto (p120) was built on 10th-century foundations, but its facade was lightened up with lacy white porphyry ornament in 1460–64. This play of white stone edging against red brick may have Middle Eastern origins: the style is pronounced in Yemen, where Venice's Marco Polo established trade relations in the 13th century.

Secular Gothic

Gothic architecture was so complicated and expensive that it was usually reserved for cathedrals in wealthy parishes – but Venice decided that if it was good enough for God, then it was good enough for the doge. A rare and extravagant secular Gothic construction, the Palazzo Ducale (p55) was built in grand Venetian Gothic style beginning in 1340, with refinements and extensions continuing through the 15th century. The palace was just finished when a fire swept through the building in 1577, leaving Venice with a tricky choice: rebuild in the original *gotico fiorito* (flamboyant Gothic) style, or go with the trendy new Renaissance style proposed by Palladio and his peers. The choice was Gothic, but instead of using brick, the facade was a puzzle work of white Istrian stone and pink Veronese marble with a lofty, lacy white loggia facing the Grand Canal. In 1853, critic and unabashed Gothic architecture partisan John Ruskin called the Palazzo Ducale the 'central building of the world'.

While the doge's palace is a show-stopper, many Venetian nobles weren't living too shabbily themselves by the 14th century – even stripped of its original gilding, the Ca' d'Oro (p118) is a Grand Canal highlight. The typical Venetian noble family's *palazzo* (palace) had a watergate that gave access from boats to a courtyard or ground floor, with the grand reception hall on the *piano nobile* (noble floor), usually the 1st floor. The *piano nobile* was built to impress, with light streaming through double-height loggia windows and balustraded balconies. The 2nd floor might also feature an elegant arcade topped with Venetian Gothic marble arches and trefoils, with decorative crenellation crowning the roofline.

RENAISSANCE

For centuries Gothic cathedrals soared to the skies, pointing the eye and aspirations heavenward – but as the Renaissance ushered in an era of reason and humanism, architecture became more down to earth and rational. Venice wasn't immediately sold on this radical new Tuscan world-view, but the revival of classical ideals gradually took root through Padua University (p169) and Venetian publishing houses.

With the study of classical philosophy came a fresh appreciation for strict classical order, harmonious geometry and human-scale proportions. A prime early example in Venice is the 1489 Chiesa di Santa Maria dei Miracoli (p118), a small church and great achievement by sculptor-architect Pietro Lombardo (1435–1515) with his sons Tullio and Antonio. The exterior is a near-riot of wildly veined multicolour marbles apparently 'borrowed' from Basilica di San Marco's slag-heap, kept in check by a steady rhythm of Corinthian pilasters. The glimmering marble interiors set off a joyous profusion of finely worked sculpture, and the coffered ceiling is filled in with portraits of saints in contemporary Venetian dress. This is ecclesiastical architecture come down to earth, intimate and approachable.

Wagering which of Venice's brick *campanile* (bell-towers) will next fall victim to shifting *barene* (mud-banks) is a morbid Venetian pasttime – but don't bet on the leaning tower of S Giorgio dei Greci, which has slouched ever since 1592. San Marco's *campanile* stood ramrod-straight until its 1902 collapse.

CAMPANILE

Sansovino's Humanist Architecture

Born in Florence and well versed in classical architecture in Rome, Jacopo Sansovino (1486–1570) was a champion of the Renaissance as Venice's *proto* (official city architect) whose best works reveal not just a shift in aesthetics, but a sea change in thinking. While the Gothic ideal was a staggeringly tall spire topped by a cross, his Libreria Nazionale Marciana (p60) is an ideal Renaissance landmark: a low, flat-roofed monument to learning, topped by statues of great men. Great men are also the theme of Sansovino's Scala dei Giganti in the Palazzo Ducale (p55), a staircase reserved for Venetian dignitaries and an unmistakable metaphorical reminder that in order to ascend to the heights of power, one must stand on the shoulders of giants.

Instead of striving for the skies, Renaissance architecture reached for the horizon. Sansovino changed the skyline of Venice with his work on 15 buildings, including the serenely splendid Chiesa di San Francesco della Vigna (p133), completed with a colonnaded facade by Palladio and sculptural flourishes by Pietro and Tullio Lombardo. But thankfully, one of Sansovino's most ambitious projects never came to fruition: his plan to turn Piazza San Marco into a Roman forum.

Renaissance Palaces

As the Renaissance swept into Venice, the changes became noticeable along the Grand Canal: pointed Gothic arcades relaxed into rounded archways, repeated geometric forms and serene order replaced Gothic trefoils, and palaces became anchored by bevelled blocks of rough-hewn, rusticated marble. One Grand Canal trendsetter was Bergamo-born Mauro Codussi (c 1440–1504), who first made his mark in Venice with the gracious Chiesa di San Michele (p159), but whose pleasing classical vocabulary translated just as easily to secular monuments and pleasure palaces. Codussi built the 15th-century Torre dell'Orologio (p60) and several stand-out *palazzi*, including Palazzo Vendramin-Calergi, better known today as Casinó di Venezia (p122).

Michele Sanmicheli (1484–1559) was from Verona but, like Sansovino, he worked in Rome until the sack of that city in 1527 spurred him to flee to Venice. The Venetian Republic kept him busy engineering defence works for the city, including Forte Sant'Andrea (p159), also known as the Castello da Mar (Sea Castle). Even Sanmicheli's private commissions have an imposing imperial Roman grandeur; the Grand Canal's Palazzo Grimani (built 1557–59), along the Grand Canal near the Rialto in San Marco, incorporates a triumphal arch on the ground floor, and feels more suited to its current use as the city's appeal court than a 16th-century pleasure palace.

Palladio

As the baroque began to add flourishes and curlicues to basic Renaissance shapes, Padua-born Andrea Palladio (1508–80) carefully stripped them away, and in doing so laid the basis for modern architecture. His facades are an open-book study of classical architecture, with rigorously elemental geometry – a triangular pediment supported by round columns atop a rectangle of stairs – that lends an irresistible logic to the stunning exteriors of San Giorgio Maggiore (p147) and Redentore (p148).

Top Five Palladio Landmarks

- *Chiesa di San Giorgio Maggiore (Isola di San Giorgio Maggiore)*
- *La Malcontenta (Riviera Brenta)*
- *La Rotunda (Vicenza)*
- *Villa di Maser (north of Vicenza)*
- *Teatro Olimpico (Vicenza)*

Critic John Ruskin detested Renaissance architecture in general and Palladio in particular, and ranted about San Giorgio Maggiore in his three-volume book *The Stones of Venice* (1851–53): 'It is impossible to conceive a design more gross, more barbarous, more childish in conception, more servile in plagiarism, more insipid in result, more contemptible under every point of rational regard… The interior of the church is like a large assembly room, and would have been undeserving of a moment's attention, but that it contains some most precious pictures'. But don't take his word for it: Palladio's blinding white Istrian facades may seem stoic from afar, but up close they become personal, with billowing ceilings and an easy grace that anticipated baroque and high modernism.

BAROQUE & NEOCLASSICAL

In other parts of Europe, baroque architecture seemed lightweight: an assemblage of frills and thrills, with no underlying Renaissance reason or gravitas. But baroque's buoyant spirits made perfect sense along the Grand Canal, where white-stone party palaces bedecked with tiers of ornament looked like floating wedding cakes. Baldassare Longhena (1598–1682) stepped into the role as the city's official architect at a moment when the city was breathing a sigh of relief at surviving the Black Death, and Longhena provided the architectural antidote to Venice's dark days with the gleaming white dome of Chiesa di Santa Maria della Salute (p82).

Architectural historians chalk up this unusual octagonal dome to the influence of Roman shrines, cabbala diagrams, and Palladio's soaring classical lines, but Longhena unleashes pure imagination on Santa Maria della Salute's exterior decoration, with exultant statues posing on the facade and reclining over the main entrance. The building has provided fodder for landscape artists from Turner to Monet, leading baroque-baiting Ruskin to concede that 'an architect trained in the worst schools, and utterly devoid of all meaning or purpose in his work may yet have such natural gift of massing and grouping as will render all his structures effective when seen from a distance'. Longhena's fanciful facade of giant sculptures at the Ospedaletto (p135) Ruskin deemed 'monstrous'; baroque fans will think otherwise. Longhena's marvel was Ca' Rezzonico (p82), sunny salons built for the good life with spectacular Tiepolo ceilings.

Neoclassicism

Venice didn't lose track of Renaissance harmonies completely under all that ornament, and in the 18th century, bombastic neoclassicism came into vogue. Inspired by Palladio, Giorgio Massari (c 1686–1766) created the **Chiesa dei Gesuati** (p84) as high theatre, setting the stage for Tiepolo's trompe l'œil ceilings. He built the gracious Palazzo Grassi (p61) with salons around a balustraded central light well, and brought to completion Longhena's Ca' Rezzonico on the Grand Canal.

Napoleon burst into Venice like a bully in 1797, ready to rearrange its face. The emperor's first order of architectural business was demolishing Sansovino's Chiesa di Geminiano to construct a monument in his own glory by Giovanni Antonio Selva (1753–1819), the Ala Napoleonica (see Museo Correr, p60). Napoleon had an entire district with four churches bulldozed to make way for the Giardini Pubblici (aka Biennale) and Via Garibaldi in Castello. Though Napoleon ruled Venice for only 11 years, French boulevards appeared where there were once churches across the city. Among others, Sant'Angelo, San Basilio, Santa Croce, Santa Maria Nova, Santa Marina, San Mattio, San Paterniano, San Severo, San Stin, Santa Ternita and San Vito disappeared under Napoleon.

Venice's first bridge to the mainland was built by the Austrians at Venetian taxpayers' expense in 1841–46, enabling troop and supplies transport by railway. The bridge spans 1.7 miles of lagoon waters and is propped up by 222 arches. Explosives were originally planted under the piers to be detonated in case of emergency, but these are said to have been quietly removed in later restorations.

THE 20TH CENTURY

After Giudecca's baroque buildings were torn down for factories and the Ferrovia (train station) was built, the city took decades to recover from the shock. Venice reverted to 19th-century *venezianitá*, the tendency to tack on exaggerated Venetian elements from a range of periods – a Gothic trefoil arch here, a baroque cupola there. Rather than harmonising these disparate architectural elements, interiors were swagged in silk damask and moodlit with Murano chandeliers. The resulting hodge-podge seemed to signal the end of Venice's architectural glory days.

Lido Liberty

But after nearly a century dominated by French and Austrian influence, Venice was ready to let loose on the Lido with the easygoing elegance of *stile liberty* (Liberty style, or Italian art nouveau). Ironwork vegetation wound around balconies of seaside villas and wild fantasy took root at grand hotels, including Giovanni Sardi's 1898–1908 Byzantine-Moorish Excelsior and Guido Sullam's Hungaria Palace Hotel. Eclectic references to Japanese art, organic patterns from nature and past Venetian styles in *stile liberty* tiles, stained glass, ironwork and murals give Lido buildings cosmopolitan flair and bohemian decadence.

Fascist Monuments

In the 1930s the Fascists arrived to lay down the law on the Lido, applying a strict, functional neoclassicism even to entertainment venues such as the 1937–38 Palazzo Della Mostra Del Cinema (p150) and former Casinò (now used for congresses). Fascist architecture makes occasional awkward appearances in central Venice too, notably the Hotel Bauer and the extension to the Hotel Danieli (p200), which represent an architectural oxymoron: the strict Fascist luxury-deco hotel.

Scarpa's High Modernism

The Biennale introduced new international architecture to Venice, but high modernism remained mostly an imported style until it was championed by Venice's own Carlo Scarpa (1906–78). Instead of creating seamless modern surfaces, Scarpa frequently exposed underlying structural elements and added an unexpectedly poetic twist in architectural redesigns like Negozio Olivetti (p61): mosaic and water channels mimicking *acqua alta* across the floor, rough concrete applied to walls as lovingly as marble, balconies jutting out midair like diving boards into the infinite. Scarpa's concrete-slab Venezuela Pavilion (p131) was ahead of its time by a full half-century and remains a star attraction even between Art Biennales. High modernist architecture aficionados make pilgrimages outside Venice to see Scarpa's Brioni Tomb near Asolo, and Castelvecchio (p180) in Verona. Scarpa's smaller works can be spotted all over Venice: the cricket-shaped former ticket booth at the Biennale, the entry and gardens of Palazzo Querini Stampalia (p133) and spare restorations to the doorway of the Accademia (p79).

CONTEMPORARY VENICE: WORKS IN PROGRESS

Modernism was not without its critics, especially among Venice's preservationists. Among the projects that never left the drawing board are a 1953 design for student housing on the Grand Canal by Frank Lloyd Wright, Le Corbusier's 1964 plans for a hospital in Cannaregio, and Luis Kahn's 1968 Palazzo dei Congressi project for the Giardini Pubblici. Yet there's more modern architecture here than you might think: fully one-third of all buildings in Venice have been raised since 1919.

But then came the flood of 1966, and it seemed all of Venice's architectural patrimony would be lost. Architecture aficionados around the globe put aside their differences, and aided Venetians in bailing out *palazzi* and reinforcing foundations across the city.

Today the city is open to a broader range of styles, though some controversies remain. The decade-long Ponte di Calatrava furore (see the boxed text, p222) overlapped with raging debates over the reconstruction of the Teatro Fenice after a 1996 arson attack. Architecture critics lobbied for an avant-garde La Fenice redesign by Gae Aulenti, but instead the city opted for a €90 million replica of the 19th-century opera house, completed in 2003.

TOP FIVE MODERN ARCHITECTURE LANDMARKS

- **Biennale Pavilions** (p131) High modernist pavilion architecture often steals the show at Art Biennales.
- **Punta della Dogana** (p84) Customs houses are creatively repurposed as a contemporary art showcase by Tadao Ando.
- **Negozio Olivetti** (p61) Forward-thinking Carlo Scarpa transformed a dusty souvenir shop into a showcase for high technology c 1958.
- **Fondazione Giorgio Cini** (p149) Former naval academy rocks the boat as an avant-garde art gallery.
- **Palazzo Grassi** (p61) Tadao Ando's minimalism rescues Massari's palace from neoclassical ornament overload.

The Ando Effect

But more startling are the number of avant-garde projects achieved in Venice, given strict building codes and the challenges of construction with materials transported by boat, lifted by crane and hauled by handcart. With support from the city and financing from his own deep pockets, French billionaire art collector François Pinault hired Japanese minimalist architect Tadao Ando to repurpose two historic buildings into showcases for his contemporary art collection. Instead of undermining their originality, Ando's careful repurposing revealed the muscular strength of Giorgio Masari's 1749 neoclassical Palazzo Grassi (p61) and Punta della Dogana customs houses (p84), built c 1675, vacated in 2002, and relaunched as an art museum in 2009.

Giudecca's Creative Comeback

Meanwhile, MIT-trained Italian architect Cino Zucci kicked off the creative revival of Giudecca in 1995 with his conversion of 19th-century brick factories and waterfront warehouses into art spaces and studio lofts. A triangular bunker-warehouse for bombs during WWII has been transformed into Teatro Junghans (p153), inaugurated in 2005 as Venice's hotspot for experimental theatre. Ernest Wullekopf's 1896 Molino Stucky flour mill has been reincarnated as a megacomfort Hilton hotel, with a full-service spa and rooftop bar (p153).

Watch this Space

New projects are cropping up in unlikely places around the lagoon. On the cemetery island of San Michele, David Chipperfield Architects are building extensions to echo the firm's sombre, minimalist Courtyard of the Four Evangelists (see Cimitero, p159). Tronchetto is mostly an island of parking lots, but for the shiny new People Mover monorail system (p255). Historic Arsenale shipyards now host the Architecture Biennale, with a sleek new courtyard cafe and medieval assembly-line sheds now used as interlinked galleries. Within Venice proper, the glam-rock-deco interiors of upscale Ca' Pisani kicked off a design-hotel trend, followed by Alvin Grassi's luxe redesign for the Grand Canal's Palazzo Barbarigo (p197).

Venice is becoming a space to watch for contemporary architecture. On the Lido, plans for a brand-new conference and cinema complex to host the Venice International Film Festival are in the works, since the current cinema is too small and – let's be honest – looks like a fascist airport. Venice's other drab airport structure, Marco Polo Airport, is scheduled for a facelift and much-needed new marina as part of a planned Venice Gateway complex by architecture star Frank Gehry.

Venetians avoid walking between the San Marco quay pillars, where criminals were once executed. According to legend, anyone wandering between these pillars will meet an untimely demise – doomed Marin Falier was beheaded eight months after supposedly passing between them to accept the post of doge.

SAN MARCO QUAY PILLARS

The Arts

By the 13th century, Venice had already accomplished the impossible: building a maritime empire on a shallow lagoon, with palaces rising majestically from mud banks. But its dominance didn't last. Plague repeatedly decimated the city from 1348 to 1349, new trade routes to the New World c 1492 bypassed Venice and its tax collectors, and the Ottoman Empire dominated the Adriatic by the middle of the 15th century. Yet when Venice could no longer prevail by wealth or force, it triumphed with new forms of art, music, theatre and poetry.

VISUAL ARTS

The sheer number of masterpieces packed into Venice might make you wonder if there's something in the water here, but the reason may be more simple: historically, Venice tended not to starve its artists and architects. Multiyear commissions from wealthy private patrons, the city and the Church gave them some sense of security. Artists were granted extraordinary opportunities to create new artwork without interference, with the city frequently declining to enforce the Inquisition's censorship edicts. Instead of dying young, destitute and out of favour, painters such as Titian and Giovanni Bellini survived into their 80s to produce late, great works. The side-by-side innovations of emerging and mature artists created schools of painting so distinct, they set Venice apart from the rest of Italy and Europe.

ST MARK

Winged lions carved onto Venetian facades symbolise St Mark, Venice's patron saint, but some served sinister functions. In the 1500s, the *Consigli dei Dieci* (Council of Ten) established *bocca dei leoni* (lion's mouths), stone lions' heads with slots for inserting anonymous denunciations of neighbours for crimes raging from cursing to conspiracy.

Early Venetian Painting

Once you've seen the mosaics at the Basilica di San Marco and Santa Maria Assunta in Torcello, you'll recognise some key aspects of early Venetian painting: wide eyes and serene expressions on larger-than-life religious figures floating on gold backgrounds or hovering above Gothic thrones. Byzantine influence can be seen in the *Madonna and Child with Two Votaries* painted c 1325 by Paolo Veneziano (c 1300–62) in Gallerie dell'Accademia (p79): like stagehands parting theatre curtains, two angels pull back the edges of a starry red cloak to reveal a hulking Madonna, golden baby Jesus, and two tiny patrons.

By the early 15th century, Venetian painters were breaking with Byzantine convention. *Madonna with Child* (c 1455) by Jacopo Bellini (c 1396–1470) in the Accademia is an image any parent might relate to: bright-eyed baby Jesus reaches one sandaled foot over the edge of the balcony, while an apparently sleep-deprived Mary patiently pulls him away from the ledge. Padua's Andrea Mantegna (1431–1506) took Renaissance perspective to extremes, showing bystanders in his biblical scenes reacting to unfolding miracles and martyrdoms with shock, anxiety, awe, anger, even inappropriate laughter .

Tuscan painter Gentile da Fabriano was in Venice as he was beginning his transition to Renaissance realism, and apparently influenced the young Murano-born painter Antonio Vivarini (c 1415–80), whose *Passion* polyptych in Ca' d'Oro (p118) shows tremendous pathos. Antonio's brother, Bartolomeo Vivarini (c 1432–99), created a delightful altarpiece in I Frari (p100) showing a baby Jesus wriggling out of the arms of the Madonna, squarely seated on her marble Renaissance throne.

Venice's Red-Hot Renaissance

Jacopo Bellini's sons used a new medium that would revolutionise Venetian painting: oil paints. The 1500 *Miracle of the Cross at the Bridge of San Lorenzo* by Gentile Bellini (1429–1507) at the Accademia shows the religious figure not high on a throne or adrift in the heavens, but floating in the Grand Canal, with crowds of bystanders stopped in their tracks in astonishment. Giovanni Bellini (c 1430–1516) takes an entirely different approach to his Accademia *Annunciation*, using glowing reds and oranges to focus attention on the solitary figure of the kneeling Madonna in a marble-panelled room, with the angel arriving in a rush of rumpled drapery.

From Venice's guild of house painters emerged some of art history's greatest names, starting with Giovanni Bellini's apt pupils: Giorgione (1477–1510) and Titian (c 1488–1576). The two worked together on the frescoes that once covered the Fondaco dei Tedeschi (only a few fragments remain in the Ca' d'Oro), with teenage Titian following Giorgione's lead. Giorgione was a Renaissance man who wrote poetry and music, is credited with inventing the easel, and preferred to paint from inspiration without sketching out his subject first, as in his enigmatic, Leonardo da Vinci–influenced 1508 *La Tempesta* (The Storm) at Gallerie dell'Accademia (p79).

When Giorgione died at 33, probably of the plague, Titian finished some of his works – but young Titian soon set himself apart with brushstrokes that brought his subjects to life, while taking on a life of their own. At Chiesa di Santa Maria della Salute (p82), you'll notice Titian started out a measured, methodical painter in his 1510 *St Marco Enthroned*. After seeing Michelangelo's expressive *Last Judgment*, Titian let it rip: in his final 1576 *Pietà* he smeared paint onto canvas with his bare hands.

But even for a man of many masterpieces, Titian's 1518 *Assunta* (Ascension) at I Frari (p100) is an astonishing accomplishment that mysteriously lights up the room. Vittore Carpaccio (1460–1526) rivalled Titian's reds with his own sanguine hues – hence the dish of bloody beef cheekily named in his honour by Harry's Bar (p73) – but it was Titian's *Assunta* that cemented Venice's reputation for glowing, glorious colour.

Not Minding Their Manners: Venice's Mannerists

Although art history tends to insist on a division of labour between Venice and Florence – Venice had the colour, Florence the ideas – the Venetian School had plenty of ideas that repeatedly got it into trouble. Titian was a hard act to follow, but there's no denying the impact of Venice's Jacopo Robusti, aka Tintoretto (1518–94) and Paolo Caliari from Verona, known as Veronese (1528–88).

A crash course in Tintoretto begins at Chiesa della Madonna dell'Orto (p120), his parish church and the serene brick backdrop for his action-packed 1546 *Last Judgment*. True-blue Venetian that he is, Tintoretto shows the final purge as a teal tidal wave, which lost souls are

VENETIAN PAINTINGS THAT CHANGED PAINTING

- *Feast in the House of Levi* (Veronese, Gallerie dell'Accademia, p79)
- *Assunta* (Titian, I Frari, p100)
- *Crucifixion* (Tintoretto, Scuola Grande di San Rocco, p98)
- *La Tempesta* (Giorgione, Gallerie dell'Accademia, p79)
- *Madonna with Child Between Saints Caterina and Maddalena* (Giovanni Bellini, Gallerie dell'Accademia, p79)

vainly trying to hold back, like human Mose barriers. A dive-bombing angel swoops in to save one last person – a riveting image Tintoretto reprised in the upper floor of the Scuola Grande di San Rocco (p98). Tintoretto spent some 15 years creating works for San Rocco, and his biblical scenes read like a modern graphic novel. Tintoretto sometimes used special effects to get his point across, enhancing his colours with a widely available local material: finely crushed glass.

Veronese's colours have a luminosity entirely their own, earning him Palazzo Ducale (p55) commissions and room to run riot inside Chiesa di San Sebastiano (p82) – but his choice of subjects got him into trouble. When Veronese was commissioned to paint the *Last Supper* (in Gallerie dell'Accademia; p79) his masterpiece ended up looking suspiciously like a Venetian party, with apostles dressed like Venetians mingling freely with Turkish merchants, Jewish guests, serving wenches, begging lapdogs and (most shocking of all) Protestant Germans. When the Inquisition demanded he change the painting, Veronese refused to remove the offending Germans and altered scarcely a stroke of paint, simply changing the title to *Feast in the House of Levi*. In an early victory for freedom of expression, Venice stood by the decision.

The next generation of Mannerists included Palma il Giovane (1544–1628), who finished Titian's *Pietá* posthumously and fused Titian's early naturalism with Tintoretto's drama. Another Titian acolyte who adopted Tintoretto's dramatic lighting was Jacopo da Ponte, called Bassano (1517–92) because his family of painters hailed from Bassano del Grappa. Jacopo's work can be seen in Gallerie dell'Accademia (p79), Chiesa di San Giorgio Maggiore (p147) and Bassano del Grappa's Museo Civico (p174).

MORI

Worn, turbaned figures appear across Venice on the corners of Campo dei Mori, on bronze door-knockers and propping up I Frari funerary monuments. Misleadingly referred to as 'Mori' (Moors), some represent Venetians from Morea, others Turkish pirates, and others enslaved West Africans who once rowed merchant ships across the Mediterranean.

Going for Baroque

By the 18th century, Venice had endured plague and seen its ambitions for world domination dashed – but the city repeatedly made light of its dire situation in tragicomic art. Pietro Longhi (1701–85) dispensed with lofty subject matter and painted wickedly witty Venetian social satires, while Giambattista Tiepolo (1696–1770) turned religious themes into a premise for dizzying ceilings with rococo sunbursts. The Ca' Rezzonico (p82) became a showplace for both their talents, with an entire salon of Pietro Longhi's drawing-room scenarios and Giambattista Tiepolo's trompe l'œil ceiling masterpieces.

Instead of popes on thrones, portraitist Rosalba Carriera (1675–1757) captured her socialite sitters on snuffboxes, and painted in a medium she pioneered: pastels. Her portraits at Ca' Rezzonico walk a fine line between Tiepolo's flattery and Longhi's satire, revealing her sitter's every twinkle and wrinkle.

As the 18th-century party wound down, the Mannerists' brooding theatricality merged with Tiepolo's pastel beauty in works by Tiepolo's son, Giandomenico Tiepolo (1727–1804). His 1747–49 *Stations of the Cross* in Chiesa di San Polo (p103) takes a dim view of humanity in light colours, illuminating the jeering faces of Jesus' tormenters. Giandomenico used a lighter touch working alongside his father on the frescoes at Villa Valmarana 'ai Nani' (p173) outside Vicenza, covering the walls with Chinese motifs, rural scenes and carnival characters.

The Vedutisti

Many Venetian artists turned their attention from the heavens to the local landscape in the 18th century, notably Antonio Canal, aka Canaletto (1697–1768). He became the leading figure of the *vedutisti* (landscape artists) with minutely detailed *vedute* (views) of Venice that leave admiring viewers with vicarious hand cramps. You might be struck how closely Canalettos resemble actual photos – and in fact, Canaletto created his works with the aid of a forerunner to the photographic camera, the *camera oscura* (camera obscura). Light entered this instrument and reflected the image on to a sheet of glass, which Canaletto then traced. After he had the outlines down, he filled in exact details, from lagoon algae to hats on passers-by.

Vedute sold well to Venice visitors as a kind of rich man's postcards. Canaletto was backed by the English collector John Smith, who introduced the artist to such a vast English clientele that only a few of his paintings can be seen in Venice today, in Gallerie dell'Accademia (p79) and Ca' Rezzonico (p82).

Canaletto's nephew Bernardo Bellotto (1721–80) also adopted the *camera oscura* in his painting process, though his expressionistic landscapes use strong *chiaroscuro* (shadow and light contrasts). His paintings hang in Gallerie dell'Accademia alongside *San Marco Basin with San Giorgio and Giudecca* by Francesco Guardi (1712–93), whose Impressionistic approach shows Venice's glories reflected in the lagoon. Among the last great *vedutisti* was Venetian Impressionist Emma Ciardi (1879–1933), who captured Venetian mysteries unfolding amid shimmering mists. Her work is on view at the Ca' Rezzonico (p82) and Ca' Pesaro (p101).

Lucky Stiffs: Venetian Funerary Sculpture

Bookending Venice's accomplishments in painting are its masterpieces in sculpture. Venice kept its sculptors busy, with 200 churches needing altars, fire-prone Palazzo Ducale requiring near-constant rebuilding for 300 years, and especially tombs for nobles with political careers cut short by age, plague and intrigue. The tomb of Doge Marco Corner in Zanipolo (p129) by Pisa's Nino Pisano (c 1300–68) is a sprawling wall monument with a massive, snoozing doge that somewhat exaggerated his career: Corner was doge for under three years.

Venice's Pietro Lombardo (1435–1515) and his sons Tullio (1460–1532) and Antonio (1458–1516) kept busy sculpting heroic, classical monuments to short-lived dogi: Nicolo Marcello, doge for a year (1473–1474); Pietro Mocenigo (1474–1476), and Andrea Vendramin (1476–1478). This last gilded marble monument was probably completed under Tullio, who literally cut corners: he sculpted the figures in half relief, and chopped away part of Pisano's Corner tomb to make room for Vendramin. Tullio's strong suit was the ideal beauty of his faces, as you can see in his bust of a young male saint at Chiesa di Santo Stefano (p61).

VENICE VIEWS INDOORS

- *Procession in San Marco* (1496, Gentile Bellini; Gallerie dell'Accademia, p79)
- *Rio dei Mendicanti* (1723–24, Canaletto; Ca' Rezzonico, p82)
- *Piazza San Marco, Mass after the Victory* (1918, Emma Ciardi; Museo Correr, p60)
- *The San Marco Basin with San Giorgio and Giudecca* (1770–74, Francesco Guardi; Gallerie dell'Accademia, p79)
- *Rio dei Mendicanti with the Scuola di San Marco* (1738–40, Bernardo Bellotto; Gallerie dell'Accademia, p79)

Antonio Canova (1757–1822) is the most prominent sculptor to emerge from the Veneto, whose pyramid tomb intended for Titian at I Frari (p100) would become his own funerary masterpiece. Mourners hang their heads and clutch onto one another in their grief, scarcely aware that their diaphanous garments are slipping off; even the great winged lion of St Mark is curled up in grief. Don't let his glistening Orpheus and Eurydice in Museo Correr (p60) fool you: Canova's seamless perfection in glistening marble was achieved through rough drafts modelled in gypsum, displayed at his studio, the Gipsoteca Canoviana.

Top Five for Modernism

Peggy Guggenheim Collection (Dorsoduro)

Ca' Pesaro (Santa Croce)

Fondazione Giorgio Cini (Isola di San Giorgio Maggiore)

Museo Fortuny (San Marco)

Fondazione Querini Stampalia (Castello)

Not Strictly Academic: Venetian Modernism

The arrival of Napoleon in 1797 was a disaster for Venice and its art. During his Kingdom of Italy (1806–14), Napoleon and his forces knocked down churches and systematically plundered Venice and the region of artistic treasures. Some works have been restored to Venice, including bronze horses of Basilica di San Marco (p52) that probably belong in Istanbul, since Venice pilfered them from Constantinople. Yet even under 19th-century occupation, Venice remained a highlight of the Grand Tour, and painters who flocked to the city created memorable Venice cityscapes (see p235).

After joining the newly unified Italy in 1866, Venice's signature artistic contribution to the new nation was Francesco Hayez (1791–1882). The Venetian painter paid his dues with society portraits, but is best remembered for Romanticism and frank sexuality, beginning with *Rinaldo and Armida* (1814) in Gallerie dell'Accademia (p79).

Never shy about self-promotion, Venice held its first Biennale (see p21) in 1895 to reassert Venice's role as global tastemaker, and provide an essential corrective to the brutality of the Industrial Revolution. A garden pavilion showcased a self-promoting, studiously inoffensive take on Italian art – principally lovely ladies, pretty flowers, and lovely ladies wearing pretty flowers. Other nations were granted pavilions in 1907, but the Biennale retained strict control, and had a Picasso removed from the Spanish pavilion in 1910 so as not to shock the public with modernity.

A backlash to Venetian conservatism arose from the ranks of Venetian painters experimenting in modern styles. Shows of young artists backed by the Duchess Felicita Bevilaqua La Masa found a permanent home in 1902, when the Duchess gifted Ca' Pesaro (p101) to the city as a modern art museum. A leader of the Ca' Pesaro crowd was Gino Rossi (1884–1947), whose brilliant blues and potent symbolism bring to mind Gauguin, Matisse and the Fauvists, and whose later work shifted toward Cubism. Often called the Venetian Van Gogh, Rossi spent many years in psychiatric institutions, where he died. Sculptor Arturo Martini (1889–1947) contributed works to Ca' Pesaro ranging from the rough-edged terracotta *Prostitute* c 1913 to a radically streamlined 1919 gesso bust.

Future Perfect: From Futurism to Fluidity

In 1910, Filippo Tommaso Marinetti (1876–1944) threw packets of his manifesto from Torre dell'Orologio promoting a new vision for the arts: futurism. In the days of the doge, Marinetti would have been accused of heresy for his declaration that Venice (a 'magnificent sore of the past') should be wiped out and replaced with a new industrial city. The futurists embraced industry and technology with their machine-inspired, streamlined look – a style that Mussolini co-opted in the 1930s for his vision of a monolithic, modern Italy. Futurism was conflated with Mussolini's brutal imposition of artificial order until championed in Venice by a heroine of the avant-garde and refugee from the Nazis: American expat art collector Peggy Guggenheim, who recognised in futurism the fluidity and flux of modern life.

Artistic dissidents also opposed Mussolini's square-jawed, iron-willed aesthetics. Emilio Vedova (1919–2006) joined the *Corrente* movement of artists, who openly opposed Fascist trends in a magazine shut down by the Fascists in 1940. After WWII, Vedova veered towards abstraction, and his larger works can now be found literally rotating at Magazzini del Sale (p83). Giovanni Pontini (1915–70) was a worker who painted as a hobby until 1947, when he discovered Kokoshka, van Gogh and Roualt, who inspired his empathic paintings of fishermen at Peggy Guggenheim Collection (p82).

Venetian Giuseppe Santomaso (1907–1990) painted his way out of rigid Fascism with lyrical, unbounded abstract landscapes in deep teals and brilliant blues. Rigidity and liquidity became the twin fascinations of another avant-garde Italian artist, Unesco-acclaimed, Bologna-born and Venice-trained video artist Fabrizio Plessi (b 1940), from his 1970s *Arte Povera* (Poor Art) experiments in humble materials to multimedia installations featuring Venice's essential medium: water. The fluidity that characterises Venice and its art continues into the 21st century, with new art galleries in San Marco and Giudecca showing a range of landscapes, abstraction, video and installation art.

Top Five for Contemporary Art

- *Venice Biennale*
- *Punta della Dogana (Dorsoduro)*
- *Palazzo Grassi (San Marco)*
- *Caterina Tognon Arte Contemporanea (San Marco)*
- *La Galleria van der Koelen (San Marco)*

MUSIC

Over the centuries, Venetian musicians developed a reputation for playing music as though their lives depended on it, which at times wasn't far from the truth. In its trade-empire heyday, La Serenissima had official

TOP FIVE ARTISTS IN RESIDENCE

- **Albrecht Dürer** (1471–1528) left his native Nuremberg for Venice in 1494, hoping to see Venetian experiments in perspective and colour that were the talk of Europe. Giovanni Bellini took him under his wing, and once Dürer returned to Germany in 1495, he began his evolution from Gothic painter into Renaissance artist. When Dürer returned to Venice in 1505, he was feted as a visionary.
- **William Turner** (1775–1851) was drawn to Venice three times (in 1819, 1833 and 1840), fascinated by the former merchant empire that, like his native England, had once commanded the sea. Turner's hazy portraits of the city are studies in light at different times of day; as he explained to art critic John Ruskin, 'atmosphere is my style'. Ruskin applauded the effort, but in London many critics loathed Turner's work.
- **James Whistler** (1834–1903) arrived in Venice in 1879, bankrupt and exhausted after a failed libel case brought against John Ruskin. The American painter rediscovered his verve and brush in prolific paintings of the lagoon city, returning to London in 1880 with a formidable portfolio that reestablished his reputation.
- **John Singer Sargent** (1856–1925) was a lifelong American admirer of Venice, visiting at a young age and becoming a part-time resident from 1880 to 1913. Sargent's intimate knowledge of the city shows in his paintings, which capture new angles on familiar panoramas and illuminate neglected monuments.
- **Claude Monet** (1840–1926) turned up in Venice in 1908, and immediately found Impressionist inspiration in architecture that seemed to dissolve into lagoon mists and shimmering waters.

musicians, including the distinguished directorship of Flemish Adrian Willaert (1490–1562) for 35 years at Capella Ducale. But when the city fell on hard times in the 17th to 18th century, it discovered its musical calling.

With shrinking trade revenues, the state took the quixotic step of underwriting musical education for orphan girls, and the investment yielded unfathomable returns. Among the maestri hired to conduct orphan orchestras was Antonio Vivaldi (1678–1741), whose 30-year tenure yielded hundreds of concertos and popularised Venetian baroque music across Europe. Visitors spread word of extraordinary performances by orphan girls, and the city became a magnet for novelty-seeking moneyed socialites. Modern visitors to Venice can still see music and opera performed in the same venues as in Vivaldi's day – *palazzi* (palaces), churches and *ospedaletti* (orphanages) – sometimes on 18th-century instruments.

Opera

Today's televised talent searches can't compare to Venice's ability to discover talents like Claudio Monteverdi (1567–1643), who was named the musical director of the Basilica di San Marco and went on to launch modern opera. Today, opera reverberates inside La Fenice (p59) and across town in churches, concert halls and *palazzi* – but until 1637 you would have been able to hear opera only by invitation. Opera and most chamber music were the preserve of the nobility, performed in private salons.

Then Venice threw open the doors of the first public opera houses. Between 1637 and 1700, some 358 operas were staged in 16 theatres to meet the musical demands of a population of 140,000. Monteverdi wrote two stand-out operas, *Il Ritorno di Ulisse al suo Paese* (The Return of Ulysses) and *L'Incoronazione di Poppea* (The Coronation of Poppea), with an astonishing range of plot and subplot, strong characterisation and power-

GIANANTONIO DE VINCENZO: MUSICIAN

Surround Sound

To enjoy concerts, first you have to find them – but our idea with Venezia Suona (p21) is to have wonderful concerts find people wherever they are. We've invited international musicians to play inside boats, at deserted island army barracks, even on top of the Tronchetto parking garage. That's the ugliest place in Venice, but for one afternoon, it was glorious.

Beyond Baroque

Vivaldi is like masquerade masks in Venice: it's everywhere, you can't miss it. When you encounter different music, stop and listen: this is how culture evolves, by paying attention to unexpected sensations. Otherwise, we're stuck with whatever's on TV.

Dinner and a Show

Restaurants close early, but you can find *cicheti* before and after concerts. I'll grab *panini* and natural-process *prosecco* at Al Mercà (p108) before shows, or hit the *cicheti* bar at Al Pesador (p104) afterwards.

Venetian Jazz

The creak of a gondola oar in the oarlock, followed by the rush of swirling water: those are the quiet, rhythmic sounds you can actually hear in Venice, because there is no aggressive traffic noise. Saturdays at Rialto Market (p102) you'll hear an improvised call-and-response between vendors and shoppers – it's Venice's own jazz.

Gianantonio De Vincenzo, musician, composer & director of Venezia Suona

HISTORIC PERFORMANCE VENUES

➡ **Teatro La Fenice** (p59) Opera in a blaze of glory.

➡ **Interpreti Veneziani** (p74) Baroque among masterpieces in Chiesa di San Vidal.

➡ **Musica a Palazzo** (p74) Arias in a rococo bedroom in Palazzo Barbarigo-Minotto.

➡ **Pietà** (p142) The Venetian baroque composer Vivaldi's work played at the orphanage where he was musical director.

➡ **Scuola di San Giovanni Evangelista** (p110) Arias in Venice's frescoed halls of power.

ful music. Critical response couldn't have been better: he was buried with honours in I Frari (p100).

A singer at the Basilica di San Marco under Monteverdi, Pier Francesco Cavalli (1602–76) became the outstanding 17th-century Italian opera composer, with 42 operas. With his frequent collaborator Carlo Goldoni (p241) and Baldassare Galuppi (1706–84), he added musical hooks to *opera buffa* (comic opera) favourites like *Il Filosofo di Campagna* (The Country Philosopher).

Classical

Are you ready to baroque-and-roll? Venetian classical musicians are leading a revival of 'early music' from medieval through to Renaissance and baroque periods, with historically accurate arrangements played *con brio* (with verve) on period instruments. Venetian baroque was the rebel music of its day, openly defying edicts from Rome deciding which instruments could accompany sermons and what kinds of rhythms and melodies were suitable for moral uplift. Venetians kept right on playing stringed instruments in churches, singing along to bawdy *opera buffa* and writing compositions that were both soulful and sensual.

Modern misconceptions about baroque being a nice soundtrack to accompany wedding ceremonies are smashed by baroque 'early music' ensembles. Among Vivaldi's repertoire of some 500 concertos is his ever-popular *Four Seasons*, instantly recognisable from hotel lobbies and ringtones – but you haven't heard summer-lightning strike and spring threaten to flood the room until you've heard it played *con brio* by Interpreti Veneziani (p74).

Look also for programs featuring Venetian baroque composer Tomaso Albinoni (1671–1750), especially the exquisite *Sinfonie e Concerti a 5*. For a more avant-garde take on classical music, look for works by Bruno Maderna (1920–73) or Luigi Nono (1924–90). Also, consider the venue: any classical performance in the intimate Casa di Goldoni (p104) or the Tiepolo-bedecked Ca' Rezzonico (p82) will transport you to the 18th century in one movement, and catapult you into the 21st with the next.

Leggera & Jazz

Most of the music you'll hear booming out of water-taxis and *bacari* (bars) is *musica leggera* ('light' or pop music). This term covers Italian rock, jazz, folk and hip-hop talents, plus perniciously catchy dance tunes and pop ballads. The San Remo Music Festival (televised on RAI 1) annually honours Italy's best songs and mercifully weeds out the worst early on, unlike the wildly popular Italian version of *X Factor*.

Besides Italian and international radio-ready fare and the odd reality-show winner, Venice has an indie music scene performing jazz, reggae and ska. Venice Jazz Club (p88) offers improvised sessions and tribute nights, and you may luck into a performance by Venetian jazz saxophonist Pietro Tonolo or Venetian trumpeter-musicologist Massimo Donà. With a natural affinity for island music, Venice grooves to 'reggae-n-roll' band Ciuke e I Aquarasa, and skanks to local ska band SkaJ – look for these bands and reggae DJs at Torino@Notte (p73).

LITERATURE

In a surprising 15th-century plot twist, shipping magnate Venice became a publishing empire. Johannes Gutenberg cranked out his first Bible with a movable-type press in 1455, and Venice became an early adopter of this cutting-edge technology. Venetian printing presses were in operation by the 1470s, with lawyers settling copyright claims soon thereafter. Venetian publishers printed not just religious texts, but histories, poetry, textbooks, plays, musical scores and manifestos.

Early Renaissance author Pietro Bembo (1470–1547) was a librarian, historian, diplomat and poet who defined the concept of platonic love and solidified Italian grammar in his *Rime* (Rhymes). Bembo collaborated with Aldo Manuzio on an invention that revolutionised reading and democratised learning: the Aldine Press, which introduced italics and paperbacks, including Dante's *La Divina Commedia* (The Divine Comedy). By 1500, nearly one in six books published in Europe was printed in Venice.

THE INFERNO

In trying to describe the Inferno to contemporary readers circa 1307, Dante compared it to Venice's Arsenale, with its stinking vats of tar, sparks flying from hammers and infernal clamour of 16,000 labourers working nonstop on its legendary ship-assembly lines.

Poetry

Duels, politics and romance seemed impossible in Venice without poetry. Shakespeare has competition for technical prowess from Veneto's Petrarch (aka Francesco Petrarca; 1304–74), who added wow to Italian woo with his eponymous sonnets. Writing in Italian and Latin, Petrarch applied a strict structure of rhythm (14 lines, with two quatrains to describe a desire and a sestet to attain it) and rhyme (no more than five rhymes per sonnet) to romance the idealised Laura. He might have tried chocolates instead: Laura never returned the sentiment.

Posthumously, Petrarch became idolised by Rilke, Byron, Mozart and Venice's *cortigiane oneste* (well-educated 'honest courtesans'). Tullia d'Aragona (1510–56) wrote sharp-witted Petrarchan sonnets that wooed men senseless: noblemen divulged state secrets, kings risked their thrones to beg her hand in marriage, and much ink was spilled in panegyric praise of her hooked nose.

Written with wit and recited with passion, poetry might get you a free date with a high-end courtesan, killed or elected in Venice. Leonardo Giustinian (1388–1446) was a member of the Consiglio dei Dieci (Council of Ten) who spent time off from spying on his neighbours writing poetry in elegant Venetian-inflected Italian, including *Canzonette* (Songs) and *Strambotti* (Ditties). Giorgio Baffo (1694–1768) was a friend of Casanova's whose risqué odes to the posterior might have affected his political career elsewhere – but in Venice, he became a state senator. To experience his bawdy poetry, head to Taverna da Baffo (p109), where his rhyme plasters the walls and may be chanted by night's end.

One of Italy's greatest poets, Ugo Foscolo (1778–1827) studied in Padua and arrived in Venice as a teenager amid political upheavals. Young Foscolo threw in his literary lot with Napoleon in a 1797 ode to the general, hoping he would revive the Venetian Republic, and even joined the French army. But Napoleon considered Foscolo a dangerous mind, and Foscolo ended his days in exile in London.

VENICE'S BESTSELLING WOMEN WRITERS

At a time when women were scarcely in print elsewhere in Europe, Venetian women became prolific and bestselling published authors in subjects ranging from mathematics to politics. Over 100 Venetian women authors from the 15th to 18th centuries remain in circulation today. Among the luminaries of their era:

➡ **Writer Sara Copia Sullam** (1592–1641) A leading Jewish intellectual of Venice's Accademia degli Incogniti literary salon, Sullam was admired for her poetry and spirited correspondence with a monk from Modena. A critic accused her of denying the immortality of the soul, a heresy punishable by death under the Inquisition. Sullam responded with a treatise on immortality written in two days; her manifesto became a bestseller. Sullam's writings remain in publication as key works of early modern Italian literature.

➡ **Philosopher Isotta Nogarola** (c 1418–66) The Verona-born teen prodigy corresponded with Renaissance philosophers and was widely published in Rome and Venice. An anonymous critic published attacks against her in 1439, claiming 'an eloquent woman is never chaste' and accusing her of incest. But she continued her correspondence with leading humanists and, with Venetian diplomat Ludovico Foscarini, published an influential early feminist tract: a 1453 dialogue asserting that since Eve and Adam were jointly responsible for expulsion from Paradise, women and men must be equals.

➡ **Musician and poet Gaspara Stampa** (1523–54) A true Renaissance intellectual, Gaspara Stampa was a renowned lute player, literary-salon organiser, and author of published Petrarchan sonnets openly dedicated to her many lovers. Historians debate her livelihood before she became a successful author; some claim she was a courtesan.

➡ **Dr Eleonora Lucrezia Cornaro Piscopia** (1646–84) Another prodigy, she became the first female university doctoral graduate in Europe in 1678 at the University of Padua, where a statue of her now stands. Her prolific contributions to the intellectual life of Venice are commemorated with a plaque inside Venice's city hall (p64).

Memoirs

Life on the lagoon has always been stranger than fiction, and Venetian memoirists were early bestsellers. Venice-born Marco Polo (1254–1324) captured his adventures across central Asia and China in c 1299 memoirs entitled *Il Milione,* as told to Rustichello da Pisa. The book achieved bestseller status even before the invention of the printing press, each volume copied by hand. Some details were apparently embellished along the way, but his tales of Kublai Khan's court remain riveting. In a more recent traveller's account, *Venezia, la Città Ritrovata* (Venice Rediscovered; 1998), Paolo Barbaro (b 1922) captures his reverse culture shock upon returning to the lagoon city.

Memoirs with sex and scandal sold well in Venice. 'Honest courtesan' Veronica Franco (1546–91; see p214) kissed and told in her bestselling memoir, but for sheer braggadocio it's hard to top the memoirs of Casanova (1725–98; see p217). Francesco Gritti (1740–1811) parodied the decadent Venetian aristocracy in vicious, delicious *Poesie in Dialetto Veneziano* (Poetry in the Venetian Dialect) and satirised the Venetian fashion for memoirs with his exaggerated *My Story: The Memoirs of Signor Tommasino Written by Him, a Narcotic Work by Dr Pifpuf.*

Modern Fiction

Venetian authors have remained at the forefront of modern Italian fiction. The enduring quality of Camillo Boito's 1883 short story *Senso* (Sense), a twisted tale of love and betrayal in Austrian-occupied Venice, made it a prime subject for director Luchino Visconti in 1954. Mysterious Venice proved the ideal setting for Venice's resident expat American mystery novelist Donna Leon, whose inspector Guido Brunetti uncovers the shadowy subcultures of Venice, from island fishing communities (*A Sea of Troubles*) to environmental protesters (*Through a Glass Darkly*). But the pride of Venice's literary scene is Tiziano Scarpa (b 1963), who earned the 2009 Strega Prize, Italy's top literary honour, for *Stabat Mater,* the story of an orphaned Venetian girl learning to play violin under Antonio Vivaldi.

Eighteenth-century Venetian grande dame Isabella Teotochi Albrizzi was practically wedded to her literary salon: when her husband received a post abroad, she got her marriage annulled to remain in Venice, and continue her discussions of poetry with the patronage of a new husband, her *cicisbeo* (manservant-lover) in devoted attendance.

FILM

Back in the 1980s, a Venice film archive found that the city had appeared in one form or another in 380,000 films – feature films, shorts, documentaries, you name it. But Venice's photogenic looks have proved a mixed blessing. This city is too distinctive to fade into the background, so the city tends to upstage even the most photogenic co-stars (ahem, 2010's *The Tourist*).

Since Casanova's escapades and a couple of Shakespearean dramas unfolded in Venice, the lagoon city was a natural choice of location for movie versions of these tales. In the Casanova category, two excellent accounts are Alexandre Volkoff's 1927 *Casanova* and Federico Fellini's 1977 *Casanova,* starring Donald Sutherland. Oliver Parker directed a 1995 version of *Othello,* but the definitive version remains Orson Welles' 1952 *Othello,* shot partly in Venice, but mostly on location in Morocco. Later adaptations of silver-screen classics haven't lived up to the original, including Michael Radford's 1994 *The Merchant of Venice* starring Al Pacino as Shylock, and Swedish director Lasse Hallström's 2005 *Casanova,* with a nonsensical plot but a charmingly rakish Heath Ledger in the title role.

After WWII, Hollywood came to Venice in search of romance, and the city delivered as the backdrop for Katherine Hepburn's midlife Italian love affair in David Lean's 1955 *Summertime*. Of all his films, Lean claimed this was his favourite, above *Lawrence of Arabia* and *Doctor Zhivago*. Gorgeous Venice set pieces compensated for some dubious singing in Woody Allen's musical romantic comedy *Everyone Says I Love You* (1996). But the most winsome Venetian romance is Silvio Soldini's *Pane e Tulipani* (Bread and Tulips; 1999), a tale of an Italian housewife who restarts her life as a woman of mystery in Venice, trying to dodge the detective-novel-reading plumber hot on her trail.

More often than not, romance seems to go horribly wrong in films set in Venice. It turns to obsession in *Morte a Venezia* (Death in Venice), Luchino Visconti's 1971 adaptation of the Thomas Mann novel, and again in *The Comfort of Strangers* (1990), featuring Natasha Richardson and Rupert Everett inexplicably following Christopher Walken into shadowy Venetian alleyways. A better adaptation of a lesser novel, *The Wings of the Dove* (1997) was based on the Henry James novel and mostly shot in the UK, though you can scarcely notice behind Helena Bonham-Carter's hair.

Venice has done its best to shock moviegoers over the years, as with Nicolas Roeg's riveting *Don't Look Now* (1973) starring Donald Sutherland, Julie Christie, and Venice at its most ominous and depraved. *Dangerous Beauty* (1998) is raunchier but sillier, a missed opportunity to show 16th-century Venice through the eyes of a courtesan. Venice-born Tinto Brass has directed some pseudo skin-flicks against a Venetian backdrop that make you wish the actors would quit blocking your view, including *Monamour!* (2005).

Always ready for action, Venice made appearances in *Indiana Jones and the Last Crusade* (1989) and the James Bond/Daniel Craig vehicle *Casino Royale* (2006), whose Grand Canal finale was shot in Venice with some help from CGI – no Gothic architecture was harmed in the making of that blockbuster. To see the latest big film to make a splash in Venice, don't miss the Venice International Film Festival (p21).

THEATRE & PERFORMING ARTS

Venice is a theatre, and whenever you arrive, you're just in time for a show. Sit on any *campo* (square), and the commedia dell'arte (archetypal comedy) and *opera buffa* commence, with stock characters improvising variations on familiar themes: graduating university students lurching towards another round of toasts, kids crying over gelato fallen into canals, neighbours hanging out laundry gossiping indiscreetly across the *calle*. Once you've seen Venice, you'll have a whole new appreciation for its theatrical innovations.

Commedia dell'Arte

During Carnevale, commedia dell'arte conventions take over, and all of Venice acts out with masks, extravagant costumes and exaggerated gestures. It may seem fantastical today, but for centuries, this was Italy's dominant form of theatre. Scholars attribute some of Molière's running gags and Shakespeare's romantic plots to the influence of commedia dell'arte – although Shakespeare would have been shocked to note that in Italy, women's parts were typically played by women. But after a couple of solid centuries of commedia dell'arte, 18th-century Venice began to tire of bawdy, slapstick shtick. Sophisticated improvisations had been reduced to farce, robbing the theatre of its subversive zing.

Comedy & Opera Buffa

Enter Carlo Goldoni (1707–93), by turns a doctor's apprentice, a lawyer, and librettist who attempted to write serious tragic opera. But of his 160 plays and 80 or so libretti, he remains best loved for *opera buffa*, unmasked social satires that remain ripe and delicious: battles of the sexes, self-important socialites getting their comeuppance, and the impossibility of pleasing one's boss.

Goldoni was light-hearted, but by no means a lightweight; his comic genius and deft wordplay would permanently change Italian theatre. His *Pamela* (1750) was the first play to dispense with masks altogether, and his characters didn't fall into good or evil archetypes: everyone was flawed, often hilariously so. Some of his most winsome roles were reserved for women and *castrati* (male soprano countertenors), from his early 1735 adaptation of Apostolo Zeno's *Griselda* (based on Boccaccio's *Decameron,* with a score by Vivaldi) to his celebrated 1763 *Le Donne Vendicate* (Revenge of the Women). Princess Cecilia Mahony Giustiniani commissioned this latter work, in which two women show a preening chauvinist the error of his ways with lethally witty retorts and co-ed swordplay.

But one Venetian dramatist was not amused. Carlo Gozzi (1720–1806) believed that Goldoni's comedies of middle-class manners were prosaic, and staged a searing 1761 parody of Goldoni – driving Goldoni to France in disgust, never to return to Venice. Gozzi went on to minor success with his fairy-tale scenarios, one of which would inspire the Puccini opera *Turandot.* But Gozzi's fantasias had little staying power, and eventually he turned to...comedy.

Venice's first movie role dates from the earliest days of cinema, as the subject of the 1897 short film *A Panoramic View of Venice*. But since Venice was complicated and expensive for location shooting, silver-screen classics set in Venice, such as the Astaire-Rogers vehicle *Top Hat,* were shot in Hollywood backlots.

SILVER SCREEN

While the Venice Art Biennale and International Film Festival are now major draws for international celebrities, the spring and autumn theatre programs of workshops and performances launched by the Venice Biennale remain experimental, drawing on a 400-year Venetian tradition of risk-taking theatre.

Meanwhile, Goldoni fell on hard times in France, after a pension granted to him by King Louis XVI was revoked by the Revolution. He died impoverished, but not entirely forgotten: at his French colleagues' insistence, the French state granted his pension to his widow. While Gozzi's works are rarely staged, Goldoni regularly gets top billing at the city's main theatre, Teatro Goldoni (p74), along with Shakespeare.

Contemporary Performing Arts

The modern performing-arts scene is not all Goldoni and Shakespeare reruns. Avant-garde troupes and experimental theatres such as Teatro Junghans (p153) bring new plays, performance art and choreography to Venetian stages. Elements of commedia dell'arte ballet periodically enjoy revivals on the contemporary dance scene, and contemporary dance is highlighted during the Biennale International Festival of Contemporary Dance in June. Dance is also championed by Fondazione Giorgio Cini (p149), which periodically hosts performances and workshops.

Life as a Venetian

With the world's most artistic masterpieces per square kilometre, you'd think the city would take it easy, maybe rest on its laurels. But Venice refuses to retire from the inspiration business. In narrow *calli* (alleyways), you'll glimpse artisans hammering out shoes crested like lagoon birds, cooks whipping up four-star dishes on single-burner hotplates, and musicians lugging 18th-century cellos to riveting baroque concerts played with punk-rock bravado. Your timing couldn't be better: the people who made walking on water look easy are already well into their next act.

As you can see, all those 19th-century Romantics got it wrong. Venice is not destined for genteel decay. Billionaire benefactors and cutting-edge biennales are filling up those ancient *palazzi* (palaces) with restored masterpieces and eyebrow-raising contemporary art and architecture, and back-alley galleries and artisan showrooms are springing up in their shadows.

FELLOW TRAVELLERS

Just don't go expecting to have the city to yourself. Even in the foot-stomping chill of January, Venice has its admirers. The upside is that you'll keep fascinating company here. More accessible than ever and surprisingly affordable given its singularity, Venice remains a self-selecting city: it takes a certain imagination to forgo the convenience of cars and highways for slow boats and crooked *calli*. Your fellow travellers probably share your passions for art, music, history, architecture, food and drink, since Venice really isn't big on business conventions, nightclubs or extreme sports (unless you include glass-shopping in Murano). Except for couples canoodling on gondolas and secluded corners of the *campo*, this is a highly sociable city, so don't be shy about sharing a table or striking up conversation.

Even in high season, Venice never hits maximum capacity. At its population peak circa 1563, Venice accommodated 170,000 residents. Today, on its busiest summer days, the city accommodates around 120,000 residents and visitors combined – comparatively uncrowded, by historical standards.

MINGLING AFTER-HOURS

Venetians don't always have time to join the conversation during their workdays, but stick around and you'll see a different city. Venice is best when caught between acts, after the day-trippers rush off to beat afternoon traffic, and before cruise ships dump dazed newcomers off in Piazza San Marco with three hours to see all of Venice before lunch. Those visitors may never get to see Venice in its precious downtime, when mosaic artisans converge at the bar for *tesserae* shoptalk and jokes over a *spritz* (*prosecco*-based drink).

The most sensitive happy-hour subject is still Mose (Modulo Sperimentale Elettromeccanico), the controversial flood barrier system currently under construction. But the combined effects of industrial pollution and global warming are also taken very seriously in this fragile lagoon ecosystem, and any effort you make to help mitigate the impact of travel – stay longer, eat and drink local specialities, support local artisans, tidy up after yourself – makes you a most welcome guest. Share your appreciation with Venetians, and they'll return the sentiment. 'There's only one Venice', explains one host as he pours another glass of fizzy Veneto *prosecco* well past the mark for *un ombra* (half glass). 'We might as well enjoy it.'

NOALTRÌ V VOALTRÌ (US VERSUS THEM)

The usual outside-insider dynamic doesn't quite wash in cosmopolitan Venice, whose excellent taste in imports ranges from Byzantine mosaics to the Venice Film Festival. Bringing a world-class art collection with you is one way to fit in, as Peggy Guggenheim and François Pinault (founder of Palazzo Grassi and Punta Dogana) discovered. But you don't have to be a mogul to *Venexianárse*, or 'become Venetian'. Of the 20 million visitors to Venice each year, only some three million stay overnight, and staying in a locally run B&B (p190) is a chance to experience Venice among Venetians. You can eat like a Venetian (p29), attempt a few words of Venet (p262), or learn a Venetian craft (p246). But the surest way to win over Venetians is to express curiosity about them and their city – so few rushed day-trippers stop to make polite conversation that the attempt is received with surprise and appreciation. As you'll find out, those other 17 million visitors are missing out on excellent company.

A DAY IN THE LIFE

At some point in your trip to Venice, you might notice a rental sign on a palace door that starts you daydreaming. If you were to wake up tomorrow as a Venetian, how might your day be different? By cross-referencing demographic statistics with interviews with Venetians, an answer can be approximated. But there's only one scientific way to find out: check out your rental options (p195) and cancel that return flight.

Morning

You might wake up feeling wiser, or at least older: the average age is four years older than in most Italian cities, at 46. Don't count on the usual urban street noise to wake you from your slumber, because there aren't technically any streets here. Instead of honks and squealing breaks, you may hear gondoliers warming up their vocal chords before work and toenails of small Venetian dogs clickety-clicking across marble footbridges. If you're in a rush to get to work, you may have to take the long way around – if you go your usual route, you'll be duty-bound to stop and say hello to so many neighbours and colleagues that you'll arrive even later.

No matter which way you take, you are likely to get stopped by a tourist asking for directions. You politely oblige, but you privately wish visitors would consult a map or follow yellow signs posted around town pointing towards San Marco, Accademia and Ferrovia. If each day-tripper asked one local for directions to San Marco, every Venetian would hear the question repeated some 350 times a year. Besides, you'd appreciate someone showing some personal interest in your thoughts instead, and asking a more interesting question – your current favourite Veneto wine, say, or your opinion about who should win the Golden Lion at this year's Venice Film Festival.

Since this is Venice, statistically you probably work in a service-related field, or you might be one of Venice's 2000 union-certified master artisans – but since this city is a costly place to live, you may have a couple of different jobs to pay the rent. On a coffee break, you once again debate with neighbours about the merits of moving to mainland Mestre for the lower cost of living and broader choices of amenities, including schools and hospitals. But you dread the commute, and can't quite convince yourself that mainland conveniences of cars and malls compensate for the sense of wonder Venice provides. Like most Venetians, you hit the mainland for sales around the holidays, and hurry back via train and *vaporetto*, hauling shopping bags across bridges and along canals, eager to reach your modest apartment in your glorious city.

Afternoon

Even if work is busy, you can't put off your break for a quick lunch at a backstreet *bacaro* (bar) for too long – otherwise, you'll be jostling for elbow room at the counter with sculptors, harpsichordists, sushi chefs and dreamers passing as accountants. Judging by the crowd, a newcomer to town might think the Art Biennale must be happening – but no, it's just an average Wednesday in Venice. But at your neighbourhood *bacaro*, the server who you've known since school days immediately recognises you're in a rush, and prepares an extra-heaped plate of *risotto di seppie* (squid risotto) on the double while *forestieri* (mainlanders) wait. Being Venetian may seem like an uphill struggle some days, but it does have its perks.

Towards the end of the workday, you coordinate with friends to meet for a drink; there's no particular hurry to get home. Like most Italians, you may have lived with family members until well into your adulthood – but unlike other Italians, more than half of Venetians live alone. There are statistically more women then men in Venice, which makes for a somewhat skewed dating scene. But with as many visitors every day to Venice as there are Venetians, there are fresh possibilities perpetually on the horizon. Though you avoid the crowds in major thoroughfares by taking winding backstreets there, you might chat, joke and flirt with visitors who linger over happy hour, kicking off promptly at 6pm.

Evening

So what if the siren just blasted out the signal for acqua alta? Neither rain nor high tides can dampen high spirits at Venice's happy hour, when even the most orthodox fashionistas gamely pull on *stivali di gomma* (rubber boots) over their stylish artisan-made shoes, and slosh out to the bar to get first dibs on *cicheti* (traditional bar snacks). At happy hour, you'll have the usual: *prosecco, crostini* (open-faced sandwiches) and a side of controversy. Did you hear about wheelchair-access issues on the Ponte di Calatrava, possible publicity on the Ponte di Rialto, the disappearance of funds for building a new Palazzo del Cinema, and art installations causing uproars at the latest Biennale and Punta della Dogana shows? Get your opinions and wisecracks ready, because diplomatic deferral is not an option, and joking always is a given here in the home of Goldoni and *opera di buffa* (comic opera).

Speaking of opera, it's not too late to decide to attend that friend's invitation to a recital or debut. If you accepted every invitation you received to the theatre performance, book reading, jazz concert or art opening of a relative, neighbour or friend-of-a-friend, your social calendar would be

VENETIAN ROAD RULES

Even though there are no cars in Venice, some pedestrian traffic rules apply:

- **Walk single file and keep right** along narrow streets to let people pass in either direction, and make way for anyone who says *permesso* (excuse me) – usually a local rushing to or from work or school.
- **Pull over to the side** if you want to check out a shop window or snap a photo, but don't linger for long: this is the pedestrian equivalent of double-parking your car.
- **Keep moving on smaller bridges**, where stalled shutterbugs can cause traffic jams. But feel free to snap away on the Rialto and Accademia bridges – everyone loves photographing these Grand Canal views, including locals.
- **Offer to lend a hand** if you see someone struggling with a stroller or heavy bag on a bridge, and you'll earn a grateful *Grazie!*

VENEXIANÁRSE (BECOME VENETIAN)

Learn the local lingo, whip up a Venetian signature dish, row like *gondolieri* or go incognito in a self-made mask with the following courses.

➡ **Get to know Venice inside out** Enjoy English-language, Venetian cultural immersion experiences from cuisine to glass-blowing organised through the **Venetian Club** (www.thevenetianclub.co.uk), a community group of Venetians by birth and inclination working together to promote and advance Venice's cultural heritage.

➡ **Masquerade like you mean it** Devise your own mask for Carnevale – or for back at the office when the boss is looking for you – at Ca' Macana (p89). Create your own costume and learn commedia dell'arte acting at Teatro Junghans (p153).

➡ **Drink like a local – not a fish** Sip your way to aficionado status wine-tasting classes at Ca' Pisani bar, self-guided tastings at I Rusteghi, and events at Vinitaly (p36).

➡ **Take to the water** Learn to row standing like *gondolieri* do with Row Venice (p26), or sail away into the blue lagoon with sailing classes at Isola di Certosa (p159).

as packed as Carnevale year-round. But some events you just can't skip – if Venice's history is any indication, you never know which show could be the one people will be talking about for decades or even centuries to come. Besides, that way you won't have to take the long way around to work tomorrow, to avoid inevitable delays from apologies and belated congratulations in the *calle*. Tomorrow you're on call to assist in Venice's encore performance, for a whole new audience of visitors – but tonight there's time for one last toast, to *la bea vita* (the beautiful life).

The Fragile Lagoon

White ibis perch on rock outcroppings, piles of lagoon crab are hauled in at the Pescaria (p102), and the waters shift from teal blue to oxidised silver: life on the lagoon is extraordinary, and extraordinarily fragile. Gazing across these waters to the distant Adriatic horizon, the lagoon appears to be an extension of the sea. But with its delicate balance of salty and fresh water, *barene* (mud banks) and grassy marshes, the lagoon supports a unique aquaculture.

RIVERS & TIDES

The lagoon is a great shallow dish, where ocean tides meet freshwater streams from alpine rivers. The salty-sweet lagoon is protected by a slender 50km arc of islands, halting the Adriatic's advances. Between Punta Sabbioni and Chioggia, three *bocche di porto* (port entrances) allow the Adriatic entry into the lagoon. When sirocco winds push ocean waves toward the Venetian gulf, or *seiche* (long waves) gently unroll along the Adriatic coast, *acque alte* ensue (see the boxed text, p248). These seasonal tides help wash the lagoon clean of extra silt and maintain the salty-sweet balance of its waters.

Of all the laws posted at Venetian *vaporetto* stops – including admonitions against strutting about town bare-breasted – the one most strictly observed by Venetians is against graffiti. Since solvents to remove graffiti damage Venice's brick foundations, Venetians appreciate visitors who take photos or paint pictures instead of marking city walls.

RISING WATERS

You may have heard that Venice is sinking, but that's not entirely accurate. The city is partially built on wooden foundations sunk deep into lagoon silt, and it's held up miraculously well for centuries. Well-drilling by coastal industries resulted in subsidence, but drilling has been halted since the 1960s.

At the same time, the dredging of deeper channels to accommodate supertankers and cruise ships allows more water to rush in from the sea during *acque alte*, posing danger to the city. Back in 1900, Piazza San Marco flooded about 10 times a year; now it's closer to 60. Engineers estimate that with technological advances, Venice may be able to withstand a 26cm to 60cm rise in water levels in the 21st century – great news, except that an intergovernmental panel on climate change recently forecasted increases as high as 88cm. In 2011, Unesco expressed concern about the impact of climate change in the Unesco-protected Venice lagoon.

You probably won't be sloshing through seawater while you're in Venice – extremely high tides happen only about once every three to five years – but rising tides threaten Venice all the same. The lagoon's salt content is increasing, endangering sealife and corroding stone foundations. Since 2003, the city has been raising the banks of the lowest spots in the city to 120cm above normal tide level, starting with San Marco.

MOSE

The hot topic of the last 30 years in Venice is a mobile flood barrier project known as Mose (Modulo Sperimentale Elettromeccanico – Experimental Electromechanical Module). With a planned completion date of 2014, these inflatable barriers 30m high and 20m wide are intended to seal the three entrances to Venice's lagoon whenever the sea approaches dangerous levels. Ever since the great flood of 1966, many Unesco-affiliated agencies have

THE TIDE IS HIGH

Sirens on a winter's afternoon don't send Venetians into a panic – though they might sport rubber boots at happy hour. The alarm from 16 sirens throughout the city is a warning that within three to four hours, *acqua alta* (high tide) is expected to reach the city. The sirens aren't heard that often: water levels only reach 110cm above normal lagoon levels four to five times a year, usually between November and April. When alarms sound, it's not an emergency situation, but a temporary tide that may only affect low-lying areas of the city.

- **One even tone** (up to 110cm above normal): barely warrants a pause in happy-hour conversation.
- **Two rising tones** (up to 120cm): you might need *stivali di gomma* (rubber boots).
- **Three rising tones** (around 130cm): check Venice's website (www.comune.venezia.it) to see where *passarelle* (elevated wooden walkways) are in use.
- **Four rising tones** (140cm and up) inspire shopkeepers to close up early, sliding low flood barriers across their doorsteps.

been urgently concerned about this jewel box of a city containing the world's great art treasures, and Mose proponents say the city must be saved at any cost.

But what are the costs, exactly? Current estimates top €5 billion for what is described even by its supporters as only a partial solution, since flooding is also caused by excessive rain, run-off and swollen inland rivers. As many Venetians point out, the city is their home, not just a treasure chest, and any stopgap measure must be considered for its public impact. Would flood barriers fill the lagoon with stagnant water, creating public health risks and driving away tourists? Could Mose change local aquaculture, and end fishing on the lagoon? Will it delay solutions to underlying problems? Debates continue as Mose's completion date nears, despite nine court appeals to halt its construction.

LAGOON CONSERVATION

High waters aren't the only concern. Venice's foundations are taking a pounding as never before, with new stresses from wakes of speeding motorboats and industrial pollutants. When pollution and silt fill in shallow areas, algae takes over, threatening building foundations and choking out other marine life. Since 1930 an estimated 20% of birdlife has disappeared, 80% of lagoon flora is gone, and lagoon water transparency has dropped 60%. The birds on their rocks, the plentiful crabs, the gleaming teal waters: all the distinctive features of Venice's remarkable setting are at risk.

But Venetians have made remarkable progress in preserving lagoon life. Industrial waste from Porto Marghera has been curbed over the years, and water is cleaner today than in the 1980s. The Venice city council has convinced most cruise lines to use fuel that emits less sulphur when entering port, reducing degradation of stone foundations. Plans are underway to convert inland industrial complexes into hi-tech parks, sustainable fisheries and wetland preserves.

Simple gestures also help. The conservation measures you already take at home – eating sustainably sourced, local food, conserving water, using products free of industrial chemicals – will also make a difference to the lagoon. To change Venice travel patterns for the greener, consider supporting Venetian businesses marked with 🍃 in this book, as well as environmentally savvy top picks indicated by TOP CHOICE.

Survival Guide

Transport

GETTING TO VENICE

Most people arrive in Venice by train, though for better or worse an increasing number are arriving by plane and cruise ship. There is a long-distance bus service to the city itself and it is also possible to drive to Venice, though you have to park at the end of the city and then walk or take a *vaporetto* (small passenger ferry).

Flights from London or Madrid to Venice take about 2½ hours; from New York nine hours; from Paris two hours; and from most other destinations in Europe between one and two hours.

Trains from Paris to Venice take about 13 hours; from London 17 hours; from Berlin 16 hours; from Frankfurt 11 hours; from Milan three hours; and from Rome four hours.

Flights, tours and rail tickets can be booked online at lonelyplanet.com/bookings.

Train

Prompt, affordable, scenic and environmentally savvy, trains are the preferred transport option to and from Venice (www.trenitalia.it). Trains run frequently to Venice's Stazione Santa Lucia (appearing on signs as Ferrovia within Venice). There is direct, intercity service to most major Italian cities, as well as major points in France, Germany, Austria, Switzerland, Slovenia and Croatia.

Local trains that link Venice to the Veneto are frequent, reliable, and remarkably inexpensive, including Padova (€3, 30 to 50 minutes, three to four per hour), Verona (€6.35, 1¾ hours, three to four per hour), and points in between. Faster intercity trains also serve these Veneto destinations, but the time saved may not be worth the 200% surcharge.

Train Stations

VENICE

When getting train tickets, be sure to specify **Venezia Santa Lucia** (VSL; Map p296), as opposed to Venezia Mestre, for the station in central Venice. The station has a rail-travel **information office** (⏲7am-9pm) opposite the APT office and a **deposito bagagli** (left luggage office; ☎041 78 55 31; per piece 1st 5hr €4, next 7hr €0.60, thereafter per hr €0.20; ⏲6am-midnight) opposite platform 1.

MESTRE

On the mainland (which is a 10-minute train ride from Santa Lucia), the **Venezia Mestre** station offers rail information, a hotel-booking office and a **deposito bagagli** (☎041 78 44 46; per piece 1st 5hr €4, next 7hr €0.60, thereafter per hr €0.20; ⏲7am-11pm). While many trains head all the way to Santa Lucia, some itineraries may require a change here.

To/From Venezia Santa Lucia

Vaporetti (p253) connect Santa Lucia train station with all parts of Venice. There is also a handy water taxi stand just out front if you are heavily laden. Useful routes include the following:

Line 1 Plies the Grand Canal to San Marco and Lido every 10 minutes.

Line 2 Follows the same route as Line 1, with fewer stops, returning via Giudecca.

Lines 41, 42 Circles the outside of Venice's perimeter in both directions.

Lines 51, 52 Follows the same route as 41 and 42 but has fewer stops and adds in Lido.

Line N All-night local service for Giudecca, the Grand Canal, San Marco and Lido (11.30pm to 4am, about every 40 minutes).

Tickets

Train tickets can be purchased at self-serve ticketing machines in the station, online at www.trenitalia.it, in the UK at **Rail Europe** (☎08448 484 064; www.raileurope.co.uk), or through travel agents.

Validate your ticket in the orange machines on station platforms before boarding your train. Failure to do so can result in embarrassment and a hefty on-the-spot fine when

CLIMATE CHANGE & TRAVEL

Every form of transport that relies on carbon-based fuel generates CO_2, the main cause of human-induced climate change. Modern travel is dependent on aeroplanes, which might use less fuel per kilometre per person than most cars but travel much greater distances. The altitude at which aircraft emit gases (including CO_2) and particles also contributes to their climate change impact. Many websites offer 'carbon calculators' that allow people to estimate the carbon emissions generated by their journey and, for those who wish to do so, to offset the impact of the greenhouse gases emitted with contributions to portfolios of climate-friendly initiatives throughout the world. Lonely Planet offsets the carbon footprint of all staff and author travel.

the inspector checks tickets on the train.

Air

Most flights to Venice fly in to **Marco Polo airport** (VCE; ☎041 260 92 60; www.veniceairport.it), 12km outside Venice, east of Mestre. Ryanair and some other budget airlines also use **Treviso airport** (TSF; ☎0422 31 51 11; www.trevisoairport.it), about 5km southwest of Treviso and a 30km, one-hour drive from Venice. Note that at the time of writing, Treviso's airport was closed for renovations, but was scheduled to reopen in December 2011.

Low-cost airlines are a benefit to travellers, but a burden on the environment and Venice's air quality; to travel with a cleaner conscience, consider a carbon-offset program.

To/From the Airport

VENICE AIRPORT

There is a range of options to get from the airport to the heart of Venice, including buses, water taxis and reliable passenger ferry links.

Azienda Trasporti Veneto Orientale (ATVO; ☎041 520 55 30; www.atvo.it) runs buses to the airport from Piazzale Roma (€5, 30 minutes, every 30 minutes from 8am to midnight).

Azienda del Consorzio Trasporti Veneziano (ACTV; ☎041 24 24; www.actv.it) runs bus 5 between Marco Polo airport and Piazzale Roma (€1.50, about one hour, four per hour).

A taxi ride to Venice's Piazzale Roma costs around €30 to €40, but Alilaguna boats are likely to get you much closer to your final destination at least as fast and at less than half the cost.

Alilaguna (☎041 240 17 01; www.alilaguna.com) operates four water taxi lines that link the airport with various parts of Venice at a cost of €13. Lines include the following:

Linea Blu (Blue Line) Stops at Lido, San Marco, Stazione Marittima and points in between.

Linea Rossa (Red Line) Stops at Murano and Lido.

Linea Arancia (Orange Line) Stops at Stazione Santa Lucia, Rialto and San Marco via the Grand Canal.

Linea Gialla (Yellow Line) Stops at Murano and Fondamento Nuovo.

TREVISO AIRPORT

While all ground transportation to Treviso airport was suspended at the time of writing, it is expected that **Barzi Bus Service** (☎0422 68 60 83; www.barziservice.com) will resume its direct service to Piazzale Roma in Venice (€7, about one hour, one to two per hour from 8am to 9pm). Taxis along the same route cost upwards of €70.

Bus

Urban, regional and long-distance buses all arrive in Venice's Piazzale Roma. Service includes:

Eurolines (☎041 538 21 18; www.eurolines.com) Operates a wide range of international routes from Piazzale Roma.

ACTV (☎041 24 24; www.actv.it) Buses leave from the bus station on Piazzale Roma for Mestre and surrounding areas.

ATVO (☎041 520 55 30) Operates buses from Piazzale Roma to destinations all over the eastern Veneto, including airport connections.

To/From Piazzale Roma

Vaporetti (p253) connect Piazzale Roma with all parts of Venice. There is also a water taxi stand if you come heavily laden. Useful *vaporetti* routes include the following:

Line 1 Plies the Grand Canal to San Marco and Lido every 10 minutes.

Line 2 Follows the same route as Line 1, with fewer stops, returning via Giudecca.

Lines 41, 42 Circles the outside of Venice's perimeter in both directions.

Lines 51, 52 Follows the same route as 41 and 42 but has fewer stops and adds in Lido.

Line 1 Plies the Grand Canal to San Marco and Lido every 10 minutes.

Line N All-night local service for Giudecca, the Grand Canal, San Marco and Lido (11.30pm to 4am, about every 40 minutes).

Car & Motorcycle

To get to Venice by car or motorcycle, take the often congested Trieste-Turin A4, which passes through Mestre. From Mestre, take the 'Venezia' exit. Once over Ponte della Libertà from Mestre, cars must be left at the car park at Piazzale Roma or Tronchetto. Expect to pay €24 or more for every 24 hours; parking stations in Mestre are cheaper. Car ferry 17 also transports vehicles from Tronchetto to the Lido.

If you are determined to drive, here's fair warning: visitors who drive across the bridge into Venice pay a hefty price in parking fees, and traffic back-ups at weekends and holidays can be infernal. Take the train instead.

Getting from Tronchetto to Piazzale Roma

If you park on Tronchetto, the new monorail known as the People Mover (p255) will whisk you from Tronchetto to Piazzale Roma.

To/From Piazzale Roma

Vaporetti (p253) connect Piazzale Roma with all parts of Venice. There is also a handy water taxi stand if you are heavily laden. Useful *vaporetti* routes from Piazzale Roma include the following:

Line 1 Plies the Grand Canal to San Marco and Lido every 10 minutes.

Line 2 Follows the same route as Line 1, with fewer stops, returning via Giudecca.

Lines 41, 42 Circles the outside of Venice's perimeter in both directions.

Lines 51, 52 Follows the same route as 41 and 42 but with fewer stops and adds in Lido.

Line N All-night local service for Giudecca, the Grand Canal, San Marco and Lido (11.30pm to 4am about every 40 minutes).

Driving Distances to Venice

Berlin 1135km

Budapest 564km

Florence 260km

Frankfurt 940km

Geneva 579km

London 1515km

Madrid 1820km

Milan 279km

Paris 1112km

Prague 798km

Rome 529km

Vienna 610km

Parking

If you're determined to drive across the Ponte della Libertà from the mainland, you'll find car parks in Piazzale Roma or on Isola del Tronchetto. Prices in Venice start at over €24 per day. At peak times, lots become completely full. However, you can book a parking place ahead of time at www.veniceconnected.com.

To avoid these hassles (and to make the most of the cheaper car parks) consider parking in Mestre, and take the bus or train into Venice instead. Remember to take anything that looks even remotely valuable out of your car, since thieves prowl local car parks.

For a range of parking options in Venice and Mestre, including prices and directions, head to www.asmvenezia.it. Some options include the following:

Garage Brega (☎041 92 64 78; Piazzale Favretti 1, Mestre; covered/outdoor per day €12/6) Only 350m from the Mestre train station.

Garage Europa Mestre (☎041 95 92 02; www.garageeuropamestre.com; Corso del Popolo 55, Mestre; 1st day €14, each additional day €12) ACTV bus 4 to/from Venice stops right outside the garage, or it's a 10-minute walk to the Mestre train station.

ASM Autoremissa Comunale (☎041 272 72 11; www.asmvenezia.it; Piazzale Roma; compact car in low/peak period per day €24/78, car over 185cm €27/31; ⏲24hr) Discounts available with online reservations; free six-hour parking for people with disabilities.

Garage San Marco (☎041 523 22 13; www.garagesanmarco.it; Piazzale Roma 467F; per 12hr/24hr €24/30; ⏲24hr) Guests of certain hotels get discounts; has 900 spaces.

Parking Sant'Andrea (☎041 272 73 04; Piazzale Roma; per 2hr or part thereof €4.50; ⏲24hr) 100 spots; best for short-term parking.

Tronchetto (☎041 520 75 55; www.veniceparking.it; Isola del Tronchetto; per 24hr €21; ⏲24hr)

Boat

Venice has regular ferry connections with Greece, Croatia and Slovenia. However, remember that long-haul ferries and cruise ships have an outsize environmental impact on tiny Venice and its fragile lagoon aquaculture. Consider the lower-impact train instead – Venice will be grateful.

Minoan Lines (www.minoan.gr) and **Anek** (www.anekitalia.com) run regular ferries between Venice and Greece.

Venezia Lines (www.venezialines.com) Runs high-speed boats to and

WAITING FOR YOUR SHIP TO COME IN

Vaporetto stops can be confusing, so check the signs at the landing dock to make sure you're at the right stop for the *vaporetto* line and direction you want. At major stops like Ferrovia, Piazzale Roma, San Marco and Zattere, there are often two separate docks for the same *vaporetto* line, heading in opposite directions. Check dock signage carefully or you could end up on the right *vaporetto*, heading the wrong way.

The cluster of stops near Piazza San Marco are especially tricky. If your boat doesn't stop right in front of Piazza San Marco, don't panic: it will probably stop at San Zaccaria, just past the Palazzo Ducale. Be sure to get off at San Zaccaria, though, as your next scheduled stop may be far-flung Arsenale.

from Croatia and Slovenia in summer.

To/From Stazione Marittima

Cruise ships usually provide free shuttles that connect the Stazione Maritima with Piazzale Roma. From Piazzale Roma, *vaporetti* (p253) head to all parts of Venice. Useful *vaporetti* routes include the following:

Line 1 Plies the Grand Canal to San Marco and Lido every 10 minutes.

Line 2 Follows the same route as Line 1, with fewer stops, returning via Giudecca.

Lines 41, 42 Circles the outside of Venice's perimeter in both directions.

Lines 51, 52 Follows the same route as 41 and 43 but has fewer stops and adds in Lido.

Line 1 Plies the Grand Canal to San Marco and Lido every 10 minutes.

Line N All-night local service for Giudecca, the Grand Canal, San Marco and Lido (11.30pm to 4am, about every 40 minutes).

GETTING AROUND VENICE

Vaporetto

The city's main mode of public transport is *vaporetto*. **ACTV** (☎041 24 24; www.actv.it) runs public transport in the Comune di Venezia (the municipality), covering mainland buses and all the waterborne public transport around Venice. The good news is that *vaporetti* service is much improved in recent years and quite punctual, though it comes at a rather hefty cost. One-way tickets cost €6.50, though discount passes are available (see p253).

Some lines make only limited stops, especially from 8am to 10am and 6pm to 8pm, so check boat signage. Most larger stops have digital displays that will indicate more limited service; if in doubt, ask the person charged with letting people on and off the boat.

Interisland ferry services to Murano, Torcello and other lagoon islands are usually provided on larger *motonave* (big interisland *vaporetto*), so those prone to motion sickness shouldn't worry too much about getting tossed about in a small boat.

Tickets

Tickets for *vaporetti* can be purchased from the **HelloVenezia** (☎041 24 24; www.hellovenezia.com) ticket booths at most landing stations, and free timetables and route maps are available at many of these ticket booths.

Instead of spending €6.50 for a one-way ticket, consider a VENICEcard – a timed pass for unlimited travel within a set period beginning when you first validate your ticket in the yellow machine located at ferry stations. Passes for 12/24/36/48/72 hours are €16/18/23/28/33. A one-week pass costs €50. Swipe your card every time you board, even if you have already validated it upon your initial ride. If you're caught without a valid ticket, you'll be required to pay a €60 fine (at the time of writing there was talk of increasing this fine significantly).

People aged 14 to 29 can get a three-day ticket for €18 with the Rolling VENICEcard (see p257).

Routes

From Piazzale Roma or the train station, *vaporetto* 1 zigzags up the Grand Canal to San Marco and onward to the Lido. If you're not in a rush, it's a great introduction to Venice. *Vaporetto* 17 carries vehicles from Tronchetto, near Piazzale Roma, to the Lido.

Frequency varies greatly according to line and time of day. *Vaporetto* 1 runs every 10 minutes throughout most of the day, while lines such as the 41 and 42 only run every 20 minutes. Services to Burano and Torcello are less frequent. Night services can be as much as one hour apart. Some lines stop running by around 9pm, so check timetables.

Keep in mind that routes, route numbers and schedules can change, and not all routes go both ways. Here are the key *vaporetto* lines and major stops, subject to seasonal changes:

No 1 Runs Piazzale Roma–Ferrovia–Grand Canal (all stops)–Lido and back (runs 5am to 11.30pm, every 10 minutes from 7am to 10pm).

No 2 Circular line: runs San Zaccaria–Redentore–Zattere–Trochetto–Ferrovia–Rialto–Accademia–San Marco.

No 5 Runs San Zaccaria–Murano and back.

No 8 Runs Giudecca–Zattere–Redentore–Giardini–Lido.

No 13 Runs Fondamente Nuove–Murano–Vignole–Sant'Erasmo–Treporti and back.

No 17 Car ferry: runs Tronchetto–Lido and back.

No 18 Runs Murano–Sant'Erasmo–Lido and back (summer only).

No 20 Runs San Zaccaria–San Servolo–San Lazzaro degli Armeni and back.

No 41 Circular line: runs Murano–Fondamente Nuove–Ferrovia–Piazzale Roma–Redentore–San Zaccaria–Fondamente Nuove–San Michele–Murano (6am to 10pm, every 20 minutes).

No 42 Circular line in reverse direction to No 41 (6.30am to 8.30pm, every 20 minutes)

No 51 Circular line: runs Lido–Fondamente Nuove–Riva de Biasio–Ferrovia–Piazzale Roma–Zattere–San Zaccaria–Giardini–Lido.

No 52 Circular line in reverse direction to No 51.

No 61 Circular line, limited stops, weekdays-only: runs Piazzale Roma–Santa Marta–San Basilio–Zattere-Giardini–Sant'Elena–Lido.

No 62 Circular line, limited stops, weekdays-only in reverse direction to No 61.

N All-stops night circuit, including Giudecca, Grand Canal, San Marco, Piazzale Roma, and the train station (11.30pm to 4am, every 40 minutes).

N (NMU) A second night service from Fondamente Nuove to Murano (all stops).

N (NLN) A third night run offering sporadic service between Fondamente Nuove and Burano, Mazzorbo, Torcello and Treporti.

DM (Diretto Murano) Runs Tronchetto–Piazzale Roma–Ferrovia–Murano and back.

T Runs Torcello–Burano and back (7am to 8.30pm, every 30 minutes).

Etiquette

Vaporetti can get crowded, and visitors anxious about missing their stops tend to cluster near exits. If you're standing near an exit, it is common practice to get off and let passengers behind you disembark before you get back on. Passengers with disabilities are first to embark or disembark, and offers of assistance are welcome. On smaller boats, leave luggage in designated areas or risk local ire.

Gondola

A gondola ride offers a view of Venice that is anything but pedestrian, with glimpses through water gates into palazzi courtyards. Official daytime rates are €80 for 40 minutes or €100 from 7pm to 8am, not including songs (negotiated separately) or tips. Additional time is charged in 20-minute increments (day/night €40/50). You may negotiate a price break in overcast weather or around midday, when other travellers get hot and hungry. Agree on a price, time limit and singing in advance to avoid unexpected surcharges.

Gondolas cluster at *stazi* (stops) along the Grand Canal, at the Ferrovia stop at the **Venezia Santa Lucia station** (☎041 71 85 43), the **Rialto** (☎041 522 49 04) and near major monuments (such as I Frari, Ponte Sospiri and Accademia), but you can also book a **pick-up** (☎041 528 50 75) at a canal near you.

Water Taxi

Licensed **water taxis** (☎041 522 23 03, 041 240 67 11) are a costly way to get around Venice, though they may prove handy when you're late for the opera or have lots of luggage or shopping in tow. Prices can be metered or negotiated in advance. Official rates start at €8.90 plus €1.80 per minute, €6 extra if they're called to your hotel. There are additional fees for night trips (10pm to 7am), luggage and for each extra passenger above the first four. Even if you're in a hurry, don't encourage your taxi driver to speed through Venice – this kicks up *moto-*

CHEAP THRILLS ON THE GRAND CANAL: TRAGHETTI

A *traghetto* is the gondola service locals use to cross the Grand Canal between its widely spaced bridges. *Traghetti* rides cost just €0.50 and typically operate from 9am to 6pm, although some routes finish by noon. For major *traghetto* crossings, consult the main map section (p283), though note that service can be spotty at times at all crossings, so be sure to have a back-up plan.

schiaffi (motorboat wakes) that expose Venice's ancient foundations to degradation and rot (p247).

Make sure your water taxi has the yellow strip with the licence number displayed. If approached by a craft without this sign, don't take it. Illegal water taxis have been known to whisk unsuspecting tourists off to places they don't necessarily want to go (a cousin's glass shop in Murano, for example) and charge staggering sums for the privilege. Illegal water taxi drivers have been a special problem on the Isola del Tronchetto, approaching freshly parked tourists and offering 'the only way' to get to central Venice.

Bicycle

Not that it's feasible with all those footbridges, but cycling is banned in central Venice. On the larger islands of Lido and Pellestrina, cycling is a pleasant way to get around and to reach distant beaches. Bicycle hire places are clustered around the Lido *vaporetto* stop (Map p285), including **Lido on Bike** (☎041 526 80 19; www.lidoonbike.it; Gran Viale 21b; bikes per 90min/day €5/9; ⏰9am-7pm Apr-Sep).

Boat Hire

Aspiring sea captains with nerves of steel can take on Venetian water traffic in a rented boat from **Brussa** (☎041 71 57 87; www.brussaisboat.it, in Italian; Fondamenta Labia 331, Cannaregio; ⏰7.30am-5.30pm Mon-Fri, 7.30am-12.30pm Sat). You can hire a 7m boat (including fuel) that can carry up to six people for an hour (€22) or a day (€140), or make arrangements for longer periods. You don't need a licence, but you will be taken on a test run to see if you can manoeuvre and park; be sure to ask them to point out the four boat petrol stations around Venice on a map. If you'd rather enjoy cocktails on board and leave the sailing to the experts, look into lagoon tours (see p26).

Alternatively you can also rent your own houseboat (see p200).

Car Hire

Obviously you can't drive in Venice proper, but Lido and Pellestrina allow cars, and they can be the most efficient way of seeing far-flung sites across the Veneto. The car-rental companies listed here all have offices both on Piazzale Roma and at Marco Polo airport. Several companies operate in or near Mestre train station as well.

Avis (☎041 523 73 77)

Europcar (☎041 523 86 16)

Hertz (☎041 528 40 91)

Monorail

Designed by the architect Francesco Cocco, Venice's **People Mover monorail** (APM; www.apmvenezia.com; per ride €1; ⏰7am-11pm Mon-Sat, 8am-9pm Sun) now connects the car parks on Tronchetto with the Stazione Maritima and Piazzale Roma.

Directory A–Z

Business Hours

The hours listed here are a general guide; individual establishments can vary, sometimes widely. Also note that hours at shops, bars and restaurants can be somewhat flexible in Venice as they are in the rest of Italy.

Shops 10am to 1pm and 3.30pm to 7pm (or 4pm to 7.30pm) Monday to Saturday

Supermarkets 9am to 7.30pm Monday to Saturday

Banks 8.30am to 1.30pm and 3.30pm to 5.30pm Monday to Friday, though hours vary; some open Saturday mornings

Restaurants Noon to 2.30pm and 7pm to 10pm

Customs Regulations

Import Limits

Duty-free sales within the EU no longer exist, but goods are sold free of value-added tax (VAT) in European airports. Visitors coming in to Italy from non-EU countries can import duty-free: 1L of spirits (or 4L of wine), 200 cigarettes and any other goods up to a total of €430 for air and sea travellers (€300 for all other travellers). Anything over this limit must be declared on arrival and the appropriate duty paid.

VAT Refunds

Non-EU citizens can get refunds on any VAT paid on purchases above €154.50 – an option that is often available at the time of purchase (see p259).

Discount Cards & Passes

An **International Student Identity Card** (ISIC; www.isic.org) can get you discounted admission prices at some sights (such as the Scuola Grande di San Rocco) and help with cheap flights out of Italy, but ISIC benefits are limited in Venice.

Chorus Pass

The association of Venice churches offers a **Chorus Pass** (☎041 275 04 62; www.chorusvenezia.org; adult/students under 30yr/family €10/7/20; ⏱visits 10am-5pm Mon-Sat) for single entry to 16 historic Venice churches anytime within one year, including I Frari, Chiesa di Santa Maria dei Miracoli, Chiesa di San Sebastiano, and Chiesa di Madonna dell'Orto. Otherwise, admission to these individual churches costs €3. Passes are for sale at church ticket booths; proceeds from the pass support restoration and maintenance of churches throughout Venice.

Civic Museum Passes

Available from the APT tourist office, the **Civic Museum Pass** (www.museiciviciveneziani.it; adult/child €18/12) is valid for six months and covers single entry to 11 civic museums, including Palazzo Ducale, Ca' Rezzonico, Ca' Pesaro, Palazzo Mocenigo, Museo Correr, and Museo del Vetro (Glass Museum) on Murano. Short-term visitors may prefer the **San Marco Museum Plus pass** (adult/child €14/8), which covers four museums around Piazza San Marco (Palazzo Ducale, Museo Correr and the attached Museo Archeologico Nazionale and Biblioteca Nazionale Marciana), plus one more of the visitor's choice. The pass also entitles bearers to discounts on admission to the Palazzo Ducale Itinerari Segreti (Secret Tour), Museo Fortuny and Torre d'Orlogio (Clock Tower).

Other Combined Museum Tickets

For art aficionados planning to visit the Gallerie dell'Accademia and the Franchetti art collections at Ca' d'Oro, consider the **combined ticket** (adult/child €12/6.50). The combined ticket is good for three months, but may not be available during special exhibitions.

A combined ticket to the Palazzo Grassi and Punta della Dogana costs €20, for a saving of €10 on adult admission.

Rolling VENICEcard

Visitors aged 14 to 29 years should pick up the €4 Rolling VENICEcard (from tourist offices and most ACTV public-transport ticket points), entitling purchase of a 72-hour public transit pass (€18) and discounts on museums, monuments and cultural events access, food, accommodation and entertainment.

Electricity

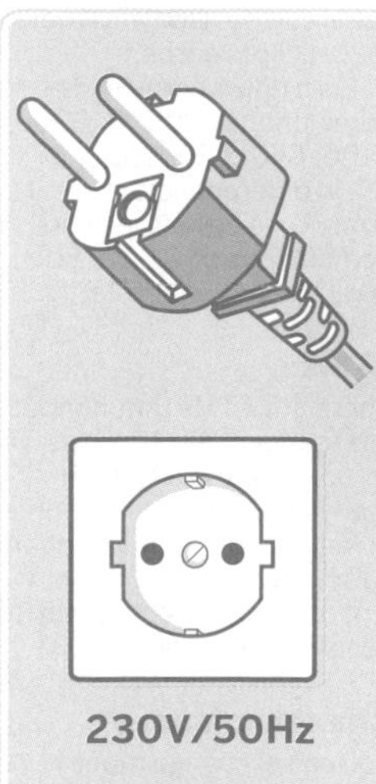

230V/50Hz

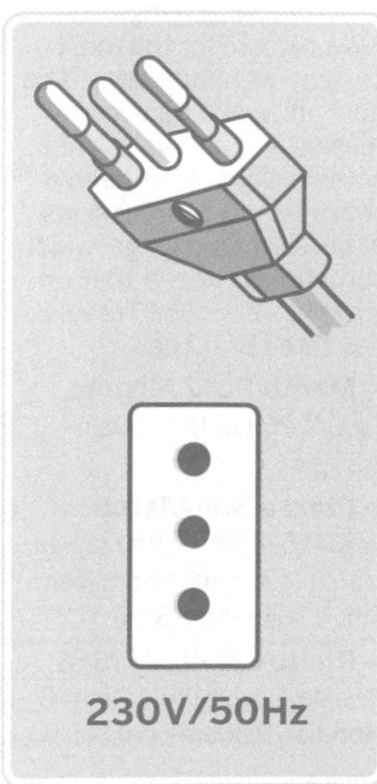

230V/50Hz

Embassies & Consulates

Most countries' embassies in Italy are located in Rome, though a limited number of countries maintain consulates in Venice:

Austria (☎041 524 05 56; Fondamenta Condulmer 251, Santa Croce)

France (☎041 522 70 79; Ramo del Pestrin 6140, Castello)

Switzerland (☎041 522 59 96; Campo di Sant'Agnese 810, Dorsoduro)

The Netherlands (☎041 528 34 16; Ramo Giustinian 2888, San Marco)

UK (☎041 505 59 90; Piazzale Donatori di Sangue 2, Mestre)

The nearest **US consulate** (☎02 29 03 51; Via Principe Amedeo 2/10) and **Australian consulate** (☎02 77 67 41; Via Borgogna 2) are in Milan. The **Canadian consulate** (☎049 876 48 33; Riviera Ruzzante 25) is in Padua.

Emergency

Ambulance (☎118)

Police station (☎112/113) Castello (Fondamenta di San Lorenzo 5053); Piazza San Marco (Piazza San Marco 67).

Gay & Lesbian Travellers

Homosexuality is legal in Italy and generally well tolerated in Venice and the Veneto, though extreme-right hate groups are on the rise in the Veneto. At the same time, federal officials, including Prime Minister Berlusconi, have made openly disparaging remarks about homosexuality. **ArciGay** (www.arcigay.it), the national gay, lesbian, bisexual and transgender organisation, has information on the GLBT scene in Italy. The useful website www.gay.it (in Italian) lists gay and lesbian events across the country, but options in Venice are slim. Head to Padua for a wider range of gay-friendly nightlife and the nearest GLBT organisation, **ArciGay Tralaltro** (☎049 876 24 58; www.tralaltro.it, in Italian; Corso Garibaldi 41).

Internet Access

If you plan to carry your notebook or palmtop computer, consider bringing a grounded power strip – it will allow you to plug in more appliances and protect your computer from the power fluctuations that can occur in Venice's older buildings.

Internet Cafes

There are internet cafes throughout Venice, though their numbers are slowly dwindling in the age of wi-fi and hand-held computing. Connections are generally fast, but prices are high: expect to pay €6 to €9 per hour. Note that at the time of writing, you still need to bring your passport on your first visit to an internet cafe, though this law was expected to be repealed.

Wi-fi

Wi-fi access is widely available in midrange and top-end accommodation, and increasingly even in budget sleeps – plus some public cafes and restaurants, though less than in other parts of Europe. Another option is to buy a PCMCIA card pack with one of the Italian mobile phone operators, which gives wireless access through the mobile telephone network. These are usually prepaid services that you can top up as you go. There is also a city-wide wi-fi service (see the boxed text, p258).

CITY-WIDE WI-FI ACCESS

In 2009, Venice launched an ambitious UK£9 million **city-wide wi-fi access plan** (www.veniceconnected.com; per day €8, 72hr €20, week €30) with the noble goal of providing access at 20 to 100 megabits per second – free to residents and €8 per day for visitors. In reality, the quality of connection varies dramatically depending on time of day and location: the signals have trouble penetrating thick old stone walls. Note that you can get a discount of about 30% if you sign up online in advance, but it is probably best to find out first if it will actually work where you need it to.

To purchase a connection once in Venice, select one of the //venice>connected network connections in among the available wi-fi networks and then open a browser window, which should take you straight to the welcome page where you can purchase a plan that works immediately.

Medical Services

All foreigners have the same right as Italians to free emergency medical treatment in a public hospital in Venice. However, other medical care is not necessarily covered.

EU, Switzerland, Norway and Iceland Citizens are entitled to the full range of health-care services in public hospitals free of charge upon presentation of a European Health Insurance Card (EHIC).

Australia Thanks to a reciprocal arrangement with Italy, Australian citizens are entitled to free public health care – carry your Medicare card.

New Zealand, the USA and Canada Citizens of these and other countries have to pay for anything other than emergency treatment. Most travel-insurance policies include medical coverage.

Emergency Clinics

The following medical services may be of use to travellers. Opening hours vary, though most are open 8am to 12.30pm Monday to Friday, and some open for a couple of hours on weekday afternoons and Saturday morning.

Guardia Medica (☎041 529 40 60) This service of night-time call-out doctors in Venice operates from 8pm to 8am on weekdays and from 10am the day before a holiday (including Sunday) until 8am the day after.

Ospedale Civile (☎041 529 41 11; Campo SS Giovanni e Paolo 6777) Venice's main hospital; for emergency care and dental treatment, ask for the *pronto soccorso* (casualty section).

Ospedale dell' Angelo (☎041 965 71 11; Via Paccagnella 11, Mestre) Vast modern hospital on the mainland.

Pharmacies

Most pharmacies in Venice are open from 9am to 12.30pm and 3.30pm to 7.30pm, and are closed on Saturday afternoon and Sunday. Information on rotating late-night pharmacies is posted in pharmacy windows and listed in the free magazine *Un Ospite di Venezia* as well as on their website (www.unospitedivenezia.it) under 'Night Chemists'.

Money

As in 12 other EU nations (Austria, Belgium, Finland, France, Germany, Greece, Ireland, Luxembourg, the Netherlands, Portugal, Slovenia and Spain), the currency in Italy is the euro. Each participating state decorates the reverse side of the coins with its own designs, but all euro coins can be used anywhere that accepts euros.

Euro notes come in denominations of €500, €200, €100, €50, €20, €10 and €5, in different colours and sizes. Euro coins are in denominations of €2, €1, 50c, 20c, 10c, 5c, 2c and 1c.

ATMs

There are ATMs that honour international ATM cards throughout the city, with many near San Marco, Ponte di Rialto and the train station. ATMs are the most convenient and cost-effective way to access cash in Venice.

Changing Money

You can exchange money in banks, at post offices or in bureaux de change. See www.ex.com for the most current exchange rates. The post office and banks are reliable, but always ask about commissions. Also, keep a sharp eye on commissions at bureaux de change, which sometimes exceed 10% on travellers cheques.Travelex has three branches:

➡ **Marco Polo Airport** (☎041 269 81 07; ⌚6am-8.30pm)

➡ **Piazza San Marco** (☎041 528 73 58; Piazza San Marco 142; ⌚9am-6pm Mon-Sat, 9.30am-5pm Sun)

➡ **Rialto** (☎041 528 73 58; Riva del Ferro 5126; ⌚9am-6pm Mon-Sat, 9.30am-5pm Sun)

Credit Cards

Major cards such as Visa, MasterCard, Maestro and Cirrus are accepted throughout Italy. Some banks may allow you to obtain cash advances over the counter with MasterCard or Visa, but be aware that this is a lengthy process. Check charges with your bank beforehand to avoid any nasty surprises later. American Express and Diners Club are also accepted, though not as widely.

Note also that most banks now build in a fee of around 2.75% into every foreign transaction. In addition, ATM withdrawals attract a fee, which can range from a flat fee to 1.5% of the withdrawal, or both.

Amex (☎800 87 43 33)

Diners Club (☎800 86 40 64)

MasterCard (☎800 87 08 66)

Visa (☎800 81 90 14)

Tipping

A 10% tip is customary at restaurants where a service charge is not included, and you can leave small change at cafes and bars. Tipping water-taxi drivers is not common practice; hotel porters are tipped €1 per bag.

Post

There are a couple of post offices in every Venetian *sestiere*, with addresses and hours online at www.poste.it (in Italian). Convenient offices:

Rialto (Calle San Salvador 5106, San Marco; ⌚8.30am-6.30pm Mon-Fri, until 1pm Sat)

Lista di Spagna (Lista di Spagna 233, Cannaregio; ⌚8.30am-2pm Mon-Fri, until 1pm Sat).

Public Holidays

For Venetians as for most Italians, the main holiday periods are summer (July and especially August), the Christmas–New Year period and Easter. Restaurants, shops and most other activity also grind to a halt around Ferragosto (Feast of the Assumption; 15 August). For information on the city's many festivals and other events, see p20. These are the national public holidays:

Capodanno/Anno Nuovo (New Year's Day) 1 January

Epifania/Befana (Epiphany) 6 January

Lunedí dell'Angelo (Good Friday) March/April

Pasquetta/Lunedì dell'Angelo (Easter Monday) March/April

Giorno della Liberazione (Liberation Day) 25 April

Festa del Lavoro (Labour Day) 1 May

Festa della Repubblica (Republic Day) 2 June

Ferragosto (Feast of the Assumption) 15 August

Ognissanti (All Saints' Day) 1 November

Immaculata Concezione (Feast of the Immaculate Conception) 8 December

Natale (Christmas Day) 25 December

Festa di Santo Stefano (Boxing Day) 26 December

Taxes

VAT (value-added tax) of around 20%, known as Imposta di Valore Aggiunto (IVA), is slapped onto just about everything in Italy. If you are a non-EU resident and spend more than €155 in a single transaction on selected purchases, you can claim a refund when you leave – or sometimes at the time of purchase. The refund only applies to purchases from affiliated retail outlets that display a 'tax-free for tourists' (or similar) sign.

Telephone

If you're calling an international number from an Italian phone, you must dial ☎00 to get an international line, then the relevant country and city codes, followed by the telephone number.

Directory inquiries (international) ☎476

Directory inquiries (national) ☎12

Costs

Using your own mobile (cell) phone in Venice could involve expensive roaming charges – check your plan details. Calling from a private landline is cheaper than a payphone, but beware hotel surcharges on phone calls. For international calls, you are sure to get a better deal via Skype or at one of the call centres that often operate in internet cafes (p257).

Local call A *comunicazione urbana* from a public phone costs around €0.10 per minute.

Long distance within Italy For a *comunicazione interurbana* you pay €0.10 when the call is answered and about €0.10 each minute thereafter.

Europe and North America A three-minute call from a payphone will cost about €2.

Australia Expect to pay about €4 for three minutes from a payphone.

Mobile Phones

GSM and tri-band mobile phones can be used in Italy with the purchase of a local SIM card at Vodafone and Telecom Italia Mobile outlets across the city. However, be sure to check with your provider before you leave home, as some phones may be code blocked. Prepaid plans are fairly reasonable, and most offer the option to have internet access for an additional fee.

US mobile phones generally work on a frequency of 1900MHz, so your US handset will have to be tri-band to be usable in Italy.

Unless you plan to live in Italy, it probably won't be worth your while to buy into a mobile phone contract. You'll need your passport to open any kind of mobile phone account, prepaid or otherwise.

Phone Codes

When calling Venice land lines, even from within the city, you must dial the ☎041 city code. To call from outside Italy, first dial the Italian country code ☎39.

Local mobile numbers have no initial ☎0. Italian mobile phone numbers begin with a three-digit prefix such as ☎330, ☎335, ☎347 or ☎368. Free-phone or toll-free numbers are known as *numeri verdi* (green numbers) and start with ☎800.

Public Phones

Many orange Telecom payphones only accept *carte/schede telefoniche* (phonecards, available in most newsstands and tobacconists), though there are payphones that accept coins around the Santa Lucia train station, Piazzale Roma, Campo Santa Margherita and Piazza San Marco. There's also a bank of telephones near the post office on Calle Galeazza.

Phonecards

You can buy phonecards (€2.50 or €5) at post offices, tobacconists and newsstands, and from vending machines in Telecom offices. Snap off the perforated corner before using it. Phonecards have an expiry date – usually 31 December or 30 June, depending on when you purchase it.

Stick to Telecom phonecards rather than the overpriced 'international calling cards' available in vending machines in Marco Polo Airport, which can charge as much as €1 per minute for local calls.

Time

Italy (and hence Venice) is one hour ahead of GMT/UTC during winter and two hours ahead during the daylight-saving period, which runs from the last Sunday in March to the last Sunday in October. Besides the UK, Ireland and Portugal, most other Western European countries are on the same time as Italy year-round; New York (Eastern Time) is six hours behind Italy. To compare Venice with other time zones, see www.worldtimezone.com. Note that times are often listed using a 24-hour clock (ie 2pm is written as 14 hours).

Toilets

Most bars and cafes reserve the restroom for paying customers only, so sudden urges at awkward moments call for a drink-buying detour – but be sure the place actually has a toilet before plunking down your cash. Look before you sit: even in women's bathrooms, some toilets don't have seats, and sometimes there is no toilet at all – just a hole with footrests. Public toilets (€1) are scattered around Venice near tourist attractions (look for the 'WC Toilette' signs), and are usually open from 7am to 7pm (sometimes closing earlier in winter).

Tourist Information

The useful monthly booklet *Un Ospite di Venezia* (A Guest in Venice; www.unospitedivenezia.it), published by a group of Venetian hoteliers, is distributed in many hotels and can also be viewed online. In tourist offices, ask for *La Rivista di Venezia,* a bimonthly free magazine with articles in Italian and English, with a handy *Shows & Events* listings insert. Another useful listings freebie in Italian and English is *Venezia da Vivere* (www.veneziadavivere.com), which you can check out online. You may find it in printed form in bars and shops. The Veneto section of *Corriera della Sera* (www.corriere.it, in Italian) is also useful for current and upcoming events.

Tourist Offices

Azienda di Promozione Turistica (APT; ☎041 529 87 11; www.turismovenezia.it) has several branches that can provide information on sights, suggested itineraries, day trips from Venice, transport, special events, shows and temporary exhibitions. Official APT outlets providing tourist information include the following – all open daily:

Marco Polo airport (Arrivals Hall; ⌚9am-8pm)

Piazzale Roma (Map p295; Santa Croce; ⌚9.30am-3.30pm)

Piazza San Marco (Map p286; ☎041 529 87 11; Piazza San Marco 71f, San Marco; ⌚9am-3.30pm Mon-Sat) Main tourist office.

Stazione di Santa Lucia (Map p296; Cannaregio; ⌚8am-6.30pm)

Travellers with Disabilities

With all the footbridges, stairs, and scant guard railings along canals, Venice might not seem like the easiest place to visit for travellers with disabilities. But the city has been making a more conscientious effort lately to provide access to key monuments, especially after the considerable embarrassment of paying millions for the Calatrava Bridge without considering its wheelchair accessibility. The city of Venice is also developing a project for the sight-impaired, including tactile maps that literally give a feel for the city and its extraordinary layout. Information (in Italian only) is available at www2.comune.venezia.it/letturagevolata/.

A **disabled assistance office** (⌚7am-9pm) is located in front of platform 4 at Venice's Santa Lucia station.

Maps

One useful tool for disabled travellers navigating Venice is a map available from APT offices with city areas that can be negotiated without running into one of Venice's many bridges shaded in yellow.

Public Transport

Vaporetto have access for wheelchairs, offering an easy way to get around town. Passengers in wheelchairs travel for free on the *vaporetto*; a companion pays just €1.20.

Virtually all local buses connecting Venice with mainland destinations are also wheelchair accessible.

Organisations

Accessible Italy (☎378 94 11 11; www.accessibleitaly.com) Specialises in holiday services for the disabled, with proceeds helping pay for accessibility improvements sorely needed throughout Italy.

Cittá per Tutti (☎041 274 81 44, 041 965 5440; www.comune.venezia.it/informahandicap, in Italian; Ca' Farsetti 4136, San Marco) This city program is devoted to improving disabled access in Venice and can provide the latest information about access issues around the city.

Holiday Care (☎0845 124 9971; www.holidaycare.org.uk; 7th fl, Sunley House, 4 Bedford Park, Croydon, Surrey CR0 2AP, UK) Provides listings of hotels with disabled access, suggestions on where to hire equipment, and tour operators experienced in managing Italy's accessibility issues.

Visas

Citizens of EU countries, Iceland, Norway and Switzerland do not need a visa to visit Italy. Nationals of some other countries, including Australia, Brazil, Canada, Israel, Japan, New Zealand and the USA, do not require visas for tourist visits of up to 90 days. For more information and a list of countries whose citizens require a visa, check the website of the **Italian foreign ministry** (www.esteri.it).

The standard tourist visa issued by Italian consulates is the Schengen visa, valid for up to 90 days. This visa is valid for travel in Italy and in several other European countries with which Italy has a reciprocal visa agreement (see www.eurovisa.info for the full list). These visas are not renewable inside Italy.

Permits

EU citizens do not need permits to live, work or start a business in Italy, but are advised to register with a *questura* (police station), if they take up residence. Non-EU citizens coming to Venice for work or long-term study require study and work visas, which you must apply for in your country of residence.

Women Travellers

Of the major travel destinations in Italy, Venice is among the safest for women, given the low rate of violent crime of any kind in Venice proper. Chief annoyances would be getting chatted up by other travellers in Piazza San Marco or on the more popular Lido beaches, usually easily quashed with a '*Non mi interessa*' (I'm not interested) or that universally crushing response, the exasperated eye roll.

Centro Anti-Violenza (Anti-Violence Centre; ☎041 269 06 30; Villa Franchin, Viale G Garibaldi 155a, Mestre; ⌚9am-6pm Mon-Fri) is a violence prevention organisation that includes a women's centre offering legal advice, counselling and support to women who have been assaulted, regardless of nationality. All services are free. Take bus 2 from Piazzale Roma.

Language

Standard Italian is spoken throughout Italy, but regional dialects are an important part of identity in many parts of the country, and this also goes for Venice where you'll no doubt hear some Venexian spoken or pick up on the local lilt standard Italian is often spoken with. This said, you'll have no trouble being understood – and your efforts will be much appreciated – if you stick to standard Italian, which we've also used in this chapter.

Italian pronunciation is straightforward as most sounds are also found in English. If you read our coloured pronunciation guides as if they were English (with the stressed syllables in italics), you'll be understood. Note that ai is pronounced as in 'aisle', ay as in 'say', ow as in 'how', dz as the 'ds' in 'lids', and that r is a strong, rolled sound. Keep in mind that Italian consonants can have a stronger, emphatic pronunciation – if the consonant is written as a double letter, it should be pronounced a little stronger, eg *sonno* son·no (sleep) and *sono* so·no (I am).

BASICS

Italian has two words for 'you' – use the polite form *Lei* lay if you're talking to strangers, officials or people older than you. With people familiar to you or younger than you, you can use the informal form *tu* too.

In Italian, all nouns and adjectives are either masculine or feminine, and so are the articles *il/la* eel/la (the) and *un/una* oon/oo·na (a) that go with the nouns.

WANT MORE?

For in-depth language information and handy phrases, check out Lonely Planet's *Italian phrasebook*. You'll find it at **shop.lonelyplanet.com**, or you can buy Lonely Planet's iPhone phrasebooks at the Apple App Store.

In this chapter the polite/informal and masculine/feminine options are included where necessary, separated with a slash and indicated with 'pol/inf' and 'm/f'.

Hello.	*Buongiorno.*	bwon·*jor*·no
Goodbye.	*Arrivederci.*	a·ree·ve·*der*·chee
Yes./No.	*Sì./No.*	see/no
Excuse me.	*Mi scusi.* (pol) *Scusami.* (inf)	mee *skoo*·zee *skoo*·za·mee
Sorry.	Mi dispiace.	mee dees·*pya*·che
Please.	*Per favore.*	per fa·vo·re
Thank you.	*Grazie.*	*gra*·tsye
You're welcome.	*Prego.*	*pre*·go

How are you?
Come sta/stai? (pol/inf) — *ko*·me sta/stai

Fine. And you?
Bene. E Lei/tu? (pol/inf) — *be*·ne e lay/too

What's your name?
Come si chiama? pol — *ko*·me see *kya*·ma
Come ti chiami? inf — *ko*·me tee *kya*·mee

My name is ...
Mi chiamo ... — mee *kya*·mo ...

Do you speak English?
Parla/Parli inglese? (pol/inf) — *par*·la/*par*·lee een·*gle*·ze

I don't understand.
Non capisco. — non ka·*pee*·sko

ACCOMMODATION

I'd like to book a room, please.
Vorrei prenotare una camera, per favore. — vo·*ray* pre·no·*ta*·re *oo*·na *ka*·me·ra per fa·*vo*·re

Is breakfast included?
La colazione è compresa? — la ko·la·*tsyo*·ne e kom·*pre*·sa

How much is it per ...?	*Quanto costa per ...?*	*kwan*·to *kos*·ta per ...
night	*una notte*	*oo*·na *no*·te
person	*persona*	per·*so*·na

air-con	*aria condizionata*	a·rya kon·dee·tsyo·*na*·ta
bathroom	*bagno*	*ba*·nyo
campsite	*campeggio*	kam·*pe*·jo
double room	*camera doppia con letto matrimoniale*	*ka*·me·ra *do*·pya kon *le*·to ma·tree·mo·*nya*·le
guesthouse	*pensione*	pen·*syo*·ne
hotel	*albergo*	al·*ber*·go
single room	*camera singola*	*ka*·me·ra *seen*·go·la
youth hostel	*ostello della gioventù*	os·*te*·lo de·la jo·ven·*too*
window	*finestra*	fee·*nes*·tra

DIRECTIONS

Where's ...?
Dov'è ...? do·ve ...

What's the address?
Qual'è l'indirizzo? kwa·*le* leen·dee·*ree*·tso

Could you please write it down?
Può scriverlo, per favore? pwo *skree*·ver·lo per fa·*vo*·re

Can you show me (on the map)?
Può mostrarmi (sulla pianta)? pwo mos·*trar*·mee (soo·la *pyan*·ta)

at the corner	*all'angolo*	a·*lan*·go·lo
behind	*dietro*	*dye*·tro
far	*lontano*	lon·*ta*·no
in front of	*davanti a*	da·*van*·tee a
left	*a sinistra*	a see·*nee*·stra
near	*vicino*	vee·*chee*·no
next to	*accanto a*	a·*kan*·to a
opposite	*di fronte a*	dee *fron*·te a
right	*a destra*	a *de*·stra
straight ahead	*sempre diritto*	*sem*·pre dee·*ree*·to

EATING & DRINKING

I'd like to reserve a table.
Vorrei prenotare un tavolo. vo·*ray* pre·no·*ta*·re oon *ta*·vo·lo

What would you recommend?
Cosa mi consiglia? *ko*·za mee kon·*see*·lya

What's in that dish?
Quali ingredienti ci sono in questo piatto? *kwa*·li een·gre·*dyen*·tee chee *so*·no een *kwe*·sto *pya*·to

What's the local speciality?
Qual'è la specialità di questa regione? kwa·*le* la spe·cha·lee·*ta* dee *kwe*·sta re·*jo*·ne

That was delicious!
Era squisito! e·ra skwee·*zee*·to

KEY PATTERNS

To get by in Italian, mix and match these simple patterns with words of your choice:

When's (the next flight)?
A che ora è (il prossimo volo)? a ke o·ra e (eel *pro*·see·mo *vo*·lo)

Where's (the station)?
Dov'è (la stazione)? *do*·ve (la sta·*tsyo*·ne)

I'm looking for (a hotel).
Sto cercando (un albergo). sto cher·*kan*·do (oon al·*ber*·go)

Do you have (a map)?
Ha (una pianta)? a (*oo*·na *pyan*·ta)

Is there (a toilet)?
C'è (un gabinetto)? che (oon ga·bee·*ne*·to)

I'd like (a coffee).
Vorrei (un caffè). vo·*ray* (oon ka·*fe*)

I'd like to (hire a car).
Vorrei (noleggiare una macchina). vo·*ray* (no·le·*ja*·re oo·na *ma*·kee·na)

Can I (enter)?
Posso (entrare)? *po*·so (en·*tra*·re)

Could you please (help me)?
Può (aiutarmi), per favore? pwo (a·yoo·*tar*·mee) per fa·*vo*·re

Do I have to (book a seat)?
Devo (prenotare un posto)? *de*·vo (pre·no·*ta*·re oon *po*·sto)

Cheers!
Salute! sa·*loo*·te

Please bring the bill.
Mi porta il conto, per favore? mee *por*·ta eel *kon*·to per fa·*vo*·re

I don't eat ...	*Non mangio ...*	non *man*·jo ...
eggs	*uova*	*wo*·va
fish	*pesce*	*pe*·she
nuts	*noci*	*no*·chee
(red) meat	*carne (rossa)*	*kar*·ne (*ro*·sa)

Key Words

bar	*locale*	lo·*ka*·le
bottle	*bottiglia*	bo·*tee*·lya
breakfast	*prima colazione*	*pree*·ma ko·la·*tsyo*·ne
cafe	*bar*	bar
cold	*freddo*	*fre*·do
dinner	*cena*	*che*·na

drink list	*lista delle bevande*	*lee*·sta *de*·le be·*van*·de
fork	*forchetta*	for·*ke*·ta
glass	*bicchiere*	bee·*kye*·re
grocery store	*alimentari*	a·lee·men·*ta*·ree
hot	*caldo*	*kal*·do
knife	*coltello*	kol·*te*·lo
lunch	*pranzo*	*pran*·dzo
market	*mercato*	mer·*ka*·to
menu	*menù*	me·*noo*
plate	*piatto*	*pya*·to
restaurant	*ristorante*	ree·sto·*ran*·te
spicy	*piccante*	pee·*kan*·te
spoon	*cucchiaio*	koo·*kya*·yo
vegetarian (food)	*vegetariano*	ve·je·ta·*rya*·no
with	*con*	kon
without	*senza*	*sen*·tsa

Meat & Fish

beef	*manzo*	*man*·dzo
chicken	*pollo*	*po*·lo
duck	*anatra*	*a*·na·tra
fish	*pesce*	*pe*·she
herring	*aringa*	a·*reen*·ga
lamb	*agnello*	a·*nye*·lo
lobster	*aragosta*	a·ra·*gos*·ta
meat	*carne*	*kar*·ne
mussels	*cozze*	*ko*·tse
oysters	*ostriche*	*o*·stree·ke
pork	*maiale*	ma·*ya*·le
prawn	*gambero*	*gam*·be·ro
salmon	*salmone*	sal·*mo*·ne
scallops	*capasante*	ka·pa·*san*·te
seafood	*frutti di mare*	*froo*·tee dee *ma*·re
shrimp	*gambero*	*gam*·be·ro
squid	*calamari*	ka·la·*ma*·ree
trout	*trota*	*tro*·ta
tuna	*tonno*	*to*·no
turkey	*tacchino*	ta·*kee*·no
veal	*vitello*	vee·*te*·lo

Fruit & Vegetables

apple	*mela*	*me*·la
beans	*fagioli*	fa·*jo*·lee
cabbage	*cavolo*	*ka*·vo·lo
capsicum	*peperone*	pe·pe·*ro*·ne
carrot	*carota*	ka·*ro*·ta
cauliflower	*cavolfiore*	ka·vol·*fyo*·re
cucumber	*cetriolo*	che·tree·*o*·lo
fruit	*frutta*	*froo*·ta
grapes	*uva*	*oo*·va
lemon	*limone*	lee·*mo*·ne
lentils	*lenticchie*	len·*tee*·kye
mushroom	*funghi*	*foon*·gee
nuts	*noci*	*no*·chee
onions	*cipolle*	chee·*po*·le
orange	*arancia*	a·*ran*·cha
peach	*pesca*	*pe*·ska
peas	*piselli*	pee·*ze*·lee
pineapple	*ananas*	*a*·na·nas
plum	*prugna*	*proo*·nya
potatoes	*patate*	pa·*ta*·te
spinach	*spinaci*	spee·*na*·chee
tomatoes	*pomodori*	po·mo·*do*·ree
vegetables	*verdura*	ver·*doo*·ra

Other

bread	*pane*	*pa*·ne
butter	*burro*	*boo*·ro
cheese	*formaggio*	for·*ma*·jo
eggs	*uova*	*wo*·va
honey	*miele*	*mye*·le
ice	*ghiaccio*	*gya*·cho
jam	*marmellata*	mar·me·*la*·ta
noodles	*pasta*	*pas*·ta
oil	*olio*	*o*·lyo
pepper	*pepe*	*pe*·pe
rice	*riso*	*ree*·zo
salt	*sale*	*sa*·le
soup	*minestra*	mee·*nes*·tra
soy sauce	*salsa di soia*	*sal*·sa dee *so*·ya
sugar	*zucchero*	*tsoo*·ke·ro
vinegar	*aceto*	a·*che*·to

Drinks

beer	*birra*	*bee*·ra
coffee	*caffè*	ka·*fe*
(orange) juice	*succo (d'arancia)*	*soo*·ko (da·*ran*·cha)
milk	*latte*	*la*·te
red wine	*vino rosso*	*vee*·no *ro*·so

soft drink	*bibita*	*bee*·bee·ta
tea	*tè*	te
(mineral) water	*acqua (minerale)*	*a*·kwa (mee·ne·*ra*·le)
white wine	*vino bianco*	*vee*·no *byan*·ko

EMERGENCIES

Help!
Aiuto! — a·*yoo*·to

Leave me alone!
Lasciami in pace! — *la*·sha·mee een *pa*·che

I'm lost.
Mi sono perso/a. (m/f) — mee *so*·no *per*·so/a

Call the police!
Chiami la polizia! — *kya*·mee la po·lee·*tsee*·a

Call a doctor!
Chiami un medico! — *kya*·mee oon *me*·dee·ko

Where are the toilets?
Dove sono i gabinetti? — *do*·ve *so*·no ee ga·bee·*ne*·tee

I'm sick.
Mi sento male. — mee *sen*·to *ma*·le

SHOPPING & SERVICES

I'd like to buy ...
Vorrei comprare ... — vo·*ray* kom·*pra*·re ...

I'm just looking.
Sto solo guardando. — sto *so*·lo gwar·*dan*·do

NUMBERS

1	*uno*	*oo*·no
2	*due*	*doo*·e
3	*tre*	tre
4	*quattro*	*kwa*·tro
5	*cinque*	*cheen*·kwe
6	*sei*	say
7	*sette*	*se*·te
8	*otto*	*o*·to
9	*nove*	*no*·ve
10	*dieci*	*dye*·chee
20	*venti*	*ven*·tee
30	*trenta*	*tren*·ta
40	*quaranta*	kwa·*ran*·ta
50	*cinquanta*	cheen·*kwan*·ta
60	*sessanta*	se·*san*·ta
70	*settanta*	se·*tan*·ta
80	*ottanta*	o·*tan*·ta
90	*novanta*	no·*van*·ta
100	*cento*	*chen*·to
1000	*mille*	*mee*·le

Signs

Entrata/Ingresso	Entrance
Uscita	Exit
Aperto	Open
Chiuso	Closed
Informazioni	Information
Proibito/Vietato	Prohibited
Gabinetti/Servizi	Toilets
Uomini	Men
Donne	Women

Can I look at it?
Posso dare un'occhiata? — *po*·so *da*·re oo·no·*kya*·ta

How much is this?
Quanto costa questo? — *kwan*·to *kos*·ta *kwe*·sto

It's too expensive.
È troppo caro/a. (m/f) — e *tro*·po *ka*·ro/a

Can you lower the price?
Può farmi lo sconto? — pwo *far*·mee lo *skon*·to

There's a mistake in the bill.
C'è un errore nel conto. — che oo·ne·*ro*·re nel *kon*·to

ATM	*Bancomat*	*ban*·ko·mat
post office	*ufficio postale*	oo·*fee*·cho pos·*ta*·le
tourist office	*ufficio del turismo*	oo·*fee*·cho del too·*reez*·mo

TIME & DATES

What time is it?	*Che ora è?*	ke *o*·ra e
It's one o'clock.	*È l'una.*	e *loo*·na
It's (two) o'clock.	*Sono le (due).*	*so*·no le (*doo*·e)
Half past (one).	*(L'una) e mezza.*	(*loo*·na) e *me*·dza

in the morning	*di mattina*	dee ma·*tee*·na
in the afternoon	*di pomeriggio*	dee po·me·*ree*·jo
in the evening	*di sera*	dee *se*·ra

yesterday	*ieri*	*ye*·ree
today	*oggi*	*o*·jee
tomorrow	*domani*	do·*ma*·nee
Monday	*lunedì*	loo·ne·*dee*
Tuesday	*martedì*	mar·te·*dee*
Wednesday	*mercoledì*	mer·ko·le·*dee*
Thursday	*giovedì*	jo·ve·*dee*
Friday	*venerdì*	ve·ner·*dee*
Saturday	*sabato*	*sa*·ba·to
Sunday	*domenica*	do·*me*·nee·ka

January	*gennaio*	je·*na*·yo
February	*febbraio*	fe·*bra*·yo
March	*marzo*	*mar*·tso
April	*aprile*	a·*pree*·le
May	*maggio*	*ma*·jo
June	*giugno*	*joo*·nyo
July	*luglio*	*loo*·lyo
August	*agosto*	a·*gos*·to
September	*settembre*	se·*tem*·bre
October	*ottobre*	o·*to*·bre
November	*novembre*	no·*vem*·bre
December	*dicembre*	dee·*chem*·bre

TRANSPORT

At what time does the ... leave/arrive?	*A che ora parte/ arriva ...?*	a ke o·ra *par*·te/ a·*ree*·va ...
boat	*la nave*	la *na*·ve
bus	*l'autobus*	*low*·to·boos
city ferry	*il vaporetto*	eel va·po·*re*·to
ferry	*il traghetto*	eel tra·*ge*·to
plane	*l'aereo*	la·e·re·o
train	*il treno*	eel *tre*·no

bus stop	*fermata dell'autobus*	fer·*ma*·ta del *ow*·to·boos
one-way	*di sola andata*	dee *so*·la an·*da*·ta
platform	*binario*	bee·*na*·ryo
return	*di andata e ritorno*	dee an·*da*·ta e ree·*tor*·no
ticket	*biglietto*	bee·*lye*·to
ticket office	*biglietteria*	bee·lye·te·*ree*·a
timetable	*orario*	o·*ra*·ryo
train station	*stazione ferroviaria*	sta·*tsyo*·ne fe·ro·*vyar*·ya

Does it stop at ...?
Si ferma a ...? see *fer*·ma a ...

Please tell me when we get to ...
Mi dica per favore quando arriviamo a ... mee *dee*·ka per fa·*vo*·re *kwan*·do a·ree·*vya*·mo a ...

I want to get off here.
Voglio scendere qui. *vo*·lyo *shen*·de·re kwee

I'd like to hire a/an ...	*Vorrei noleggiare un/una ...* (m/f)	vo·*ray* no·le·*ja*·re oon/*oo*·na ...
bicycle	*bicicletta* (f)	bee·chee·*kle*·ta
car	*macchina* (f)	*ma*·kee·na
motorbike	*moto* (f)	*mo*·to

bicycle pump	*pompa della bicicletta*	*pom*·pa de·la bee·chee·*kle*·ta
helmet	*casco*	*kas*·ko
mechanic	*meccanico*	me·*ka*·nee·ko
petrol/gas	*benzina*	ben·*dzee*·na
service station	*stazione di servizio*	sta·*tsyo*·ne dee ser·*vee*·tsyo

Is this the road to ...?
Questa strada porta a ...? kwe·sta *stra*·da *por*·ta a ...

(How long) Can I park here?
(Per quanto tempo) Posso parcheggiare qui? (per *kwan*·to *tem*·po) *po*·so par·ke·*ja*·re kwee

I have a flat tyre.
Ho una gomma bucata. o *oo*·na *go*·ma boo·*ka*·ta

I've run out of petrol.
Ho esaurito la benzina. o e·zow·*ree*·to la ben·*dzee*·na

VENEXIAN

A few choice words in Venexian will endear you to your hosts, especially at happy hour. To keep up with the *bacaro* banter, try mixing them with your Italian:

Yes, sir!	*Siorsì!*
Oh, no!	*Simènteve!*
You bet!	*Figuràrse!*
How lucky!	*Bénpo!*
Perfect.	*In bròca.*
Welcome!	*Benvegnù!*
Cheers!	*Sanacapàna!*
Watch out!	*Òcio!*

cheap wine	*brunbrùn*
glass of wine	*ombra* (lit: a shade)
happy hour	*giro di ombra* (lit: round of shade)
to become Venetian	*Venexianàrse*
Venetian	*venexiano/a* (m/f)
you guys	*voàltri*

GLOSSARY

alla busara Venetian prawn sauce
anatra wild lagoon duck
baccala mantecato creamed cod
bigoli Venetian whole-wheat pasta
branzino sea bass
bruscandoli wild hop buds
canoce mantis prawn
capasanta/canastrelo large/small scallops
carpaccio finely sliced raw beef
castraure baby artichokes from St Erasmo Island
cicheti Venetian taps
contorni vegetable dishes
crostini open-faced sandwiches
crudi Venetian sushi
curasan croissant
dolci sweets
dolci tipici venexiani typical Venetian sweets
fatto in casa house-made
fegato alla veneziana liver lightly pan-roasted in strips with browned onion and a splash of red wine
filetto di San Pietro fish with artichokes or radicchio trevisano
fritole sweet fritters
fritto misto e pattatine lightly fried lagoon seafood and potatoes
frittura seafood fry
gnochetti mini-gnocchi
granseola spider crab
krapfen doughnuts
latte di soia soy milk
lingue di suocere biscuit; 'mother-in-law's tongues'
macchiatone espresso liberally 'stained' with milk
margherite ripiene all'astice com sugo di pesce ravioli stuffed with lobster in fish sauce
moeche soft-shell crabs
moscardini baby octopus
mozzarella di bufala fresh buffalo-milk mozzarella
orechiette 'little ear' pasta
pan dei dogi 'doges' bread'; hazelnut-studded biscuits
panino sandwich
pastine pastry
peoci mussels
pizza margherita pizza with basil mozzarella and tomato
pizzette mini pizzas
polpette meatballs
radicchio trevisano feathery red radicchio
risotto di pesce fish risotto
saor Venice's tangy marinade
sarde sardines
sarde in saor sardines fried in tangy onion marinade with pine nuts and sultanas
senza limone without lemon
seppie cuttlefish
seppie in nero squid in its own ink
sfogio sole
sopressa Venetian soft salami
sopressa crostini soft salami on toast
sorbetto sorbet
spaghetti alla búsera spaghetti with shrimp sauce
surgelati frozen
tramezzini sandwiches on soft bread often with mayo-based condiments
verdure vegetables
zaletti cornmeal biscuits with sultanas
zuppa di pesce thick seafood soup

Behind the Scenes

SEND US YOUR FEEDBACK

We love to hear from travellers – your comments keep us on our toes and help make our books better. Our well-travelled team reads every word on what you loved or loathed about this book. Although we cannot reply individually to postal submissions, we always guarantee that your feedback goes straight to the appropriate authors, in time for the next edition. Each person who sends us information is thanked in the next edition – and the most useful submissions are rewarded with a free book.

Visit **lonelyplanet.com/contact** to submit your updates and suggestions or to ask for help. Our award-winning website also features inspirational travel stories, news and discussions.

Note: We may edit, reproduce and incorporate your comments in Lonely Planet products such as guidebooks, websites and digital products, so let us know if you don't want your comments reproduced or your name acknowledged. For a copy of our privacy policy visit lonelyplanet.com/privacy.

OUR READERS

Many thanks to the travellers who used the last edition and wrote to us with helpful hints, useful advice and interesting anecdotes:

Bernadette Davis-McGreal, Fredo Donnelly, Damien Hatcher, Bruce Grice, Edith Hornick, Sarah Lowney, Fabian Schreiber and Georg Sengstschmid

AUTHOR THANKS

Alison Bing

Mille grazie e tanti baci alla mia famiglia a Roma and stateside, the Bings, Ferrys and Marinuccis; to superstar co-author and fellow traveller Robert Landon; to editorial masterminds Joe Bindloss and Sasha Baskett; and *bravi* to Venezia intelligentsia Cristina Bottero, Alberto Toso Fei, Francesca Forni, Rosanna Corrò, Giantantonio De Vincenzo, Giovanni d'Este, Francesco e Matteo Pinto, Jane and Luigi Caporal and Jamie Pearson; and to the food and wine vanguard at Cook Here & Now, Slow Food and Vinitaly. Thanks also to dauntless cartographer Amanda Sierp, who navigates canal bends with grace; to Susie Ashworth, whose editorial savvy anchors Venice's otherwise illimitable narrative; *ma sopra tutto:* to Marco Flavio Marinucci, for making *la bea vita* possible, even outside Venice.

Robert Landon

Grazie mille for: 1) the on-the-road companionship of Caterina Enni, Marco Mazzoni, Neri Torrigiani and Fernanda Drummond; 2) the insights and hospitality of Stefano Piovesan, Donata Grimani, Pamela Berry and Stefano, and Filippo Barusco; 3) the long-distance connections made by Nancy Pietrafesa and Susan Filter; and 5) the patient forbearance of Thiago Fico. Special thanks to Alison Bing for too many things. And Mom: Venice was our last international destination. I felt you with me this time, too, each step of the way.

ACKNOWLEDGMENTS

Illustrations p54, p57, pp66-7 by Javier Martinez Zarracina.
Cover photograph: Grand Canal, Venice. HP Huber/4Corners
Many of the images in this guide are available for licensing from Lonely Planet Images: www.lonelyplanetimages.com.

THIS BOOK

This 7th edition of Lonely Planet's *Venice & the Veneto* was researched and written by Alison Bing and Robert Landon. The previous edition was written by Alison Bing, and the preceding edition by Damien Simonis. This guidebook was commissioned in Lonely Planet's London office, and produced by the following:

Commissioning Editor Joe Bindloss

Coordinating Editors Susie Ashworth, Victoria Harrison

Coordinating Cartographer Csanad Csutoros

Coordinating Layout Designer Jessica Rose

Managing Editor Anna Metcalfe

Senior Editor Angela Tinson

Managing Cartographer Amanda Sierp

Managing Layout Designer Chris Girdler

Assisting Editors Elizabeth Anglin, Jackey Coyle, Bruce Evans

Assisting Cartographers Xavier Di Toro, Joelene Kowalski

Cover Research Naomi Parker

Internal Image Research Aude Vauconsant

Language Content Laura Crawford, Annelies Mertens

Thanks to Sasha Baskett, Helen Christinis, Brendan Dempsey, Janine Eberle, Ryan Evans, Jane Hart, Liz Heynes, Laura Jane, David Kemp, Alana Mahony, Wayne Murphy, Trent Paton, Piers Pickard, Lachlan Ross, Michael Ruff, Julie Sheridan, Kerrianne Southway, Sophie Splatt, Laura Stansfeld, John Taufa, Tasmin Waby McNaughtan, Gerard Walker, Clifton Wilkinson

See also separate subindexes for:
EATING P280
DRINKING & NIGHTLIFE P280
ENTERTAINMENT P281
SHOPPING P281
SLEEPING P282

Index

Sights p000
Map Pages **p000**
Photo Pages **p000**

Sights p000
Map Pages **p000**
Photo Pages **p000**

Sights p000
Map Pages **p000**
Photo Pages **p000**

Sights p000
Map Pages **p000**
Photo Pages **p000**

DRINKING & NIGHTLIFE

EATING

ENTERTAINMENT

SHOPPING

SLEEPING

Venice & the Veneto Maps

Map Legend

Sights
- Beach
- Buddhist
- Castle
- Christian
- Hindu
- Islamic
- Jewish
- Monument
- Museum/Gallery
- Ruin
- Winery/Vineyard
- Zoo
- Other Sight

Eating
- Eating

Drinking & Nightlife
- Drinking & Nightlife
- Cafe

Entertainment
- Entertainment

Shopping
- Shopping

Sleeping
- Sleeping
- Camping

Sports & Activities
- Diving/Snorkelling
- Canoeing/Kayaking
- Skiing
- Surfing
- Swimming/Pool
- Walking
- Windsurfing
- Other Sports & Activities

Information
- Post Office
- Tourist Information

Transport
- Airport
- Border Crossing
- Bus
- Cable Car/ Funicular
- Cycling
- Ferry
- Metro
- Monorail
- Parking
- S-Bahn
- Taxi
- Train/Railway
- Tram
- Tube Station
- U-Bahn
- Other Transport

Routes
- Tollway
- Freeway
- Primary
- Secondary
- Tertiary
- Lane
- Unsealed Road
- Plaza/Mall
- Steps
- Tunnel
- Pedestrian Overpass
- Walking Tour
- Walking Tour Detour
- Path

Boundaries
- International
- State/Province
- Disputed
- Regional/Suburb
- Marine Park
- Cliff
- Wall

Geographic
- Hut/Shelter
- Lighthouse
- Lookout
- Mountain/Volcano
- Oasis
- Park
- Pass
- Picnic Area
- Waterfall

Hydrography
- River/Creek
- Intermittent River
- Swamp/Mangrove
- Reef
- Canal
- Water
- Dry/Salt/ Intermittent Lake
- Glacier

Areas
- Beach/Desert
- Cemetery (Christian)
- Cemetery (Other)
- Park/Forest
- Sportsground
- Sight (Building)
- Top Sight (Building)

MAP INDEX

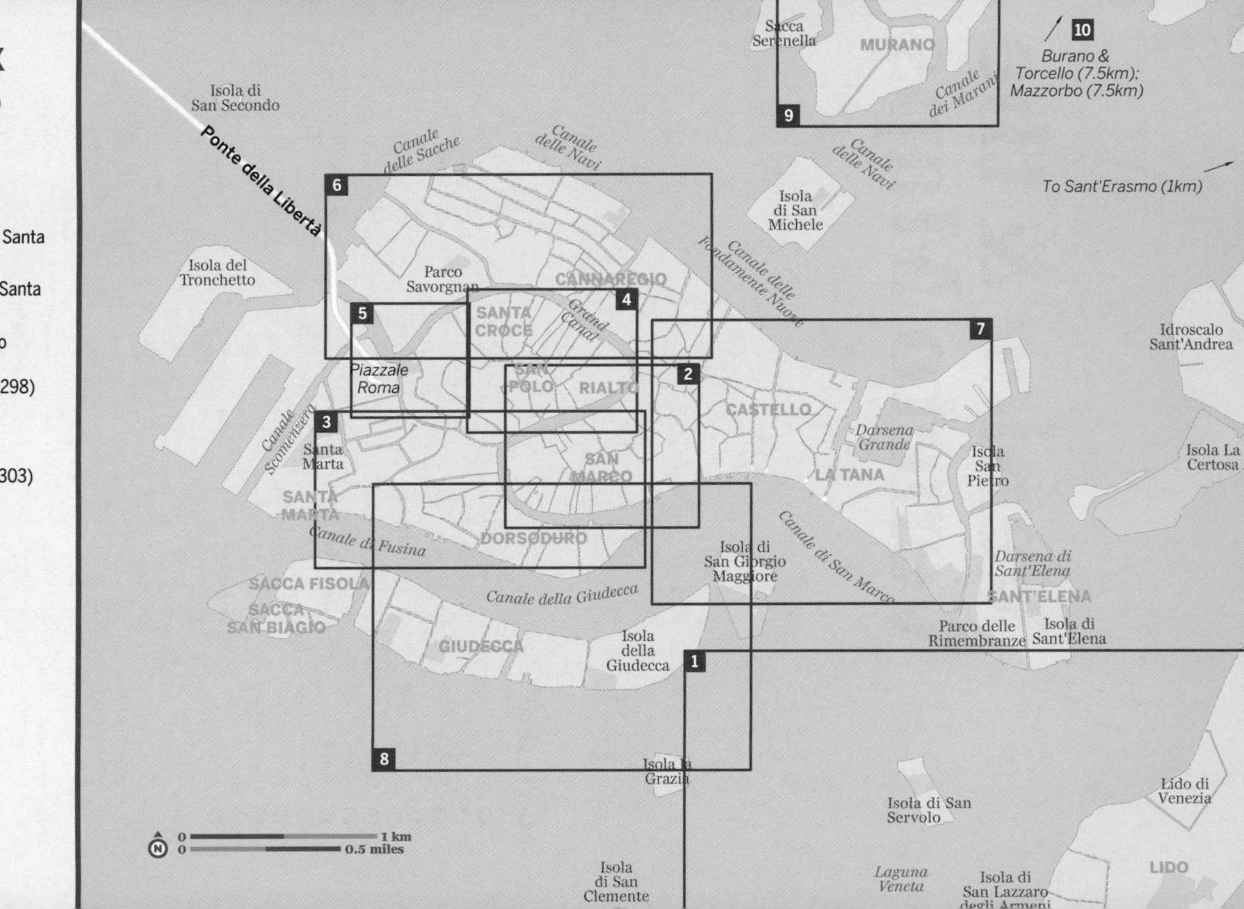

Sacca Serenella
MURANO
Canale dei Marani
Burano & Torcello (7.5km); Mazzorbo (7.5km)
Isola di San Secondo
Ponte della Libertà
Canale delle Sacche
Canale delle Navi
Canale delle Navi
To Sant'Erasmo (1km)
Isola di San Michele
Isola del Tronchetto
Parco Savorgnan
CANNAREGIO
Canale delle Fondamente Nuove
SANTA CROCE
Grand Canal
Idroscalo Sant'Andrea
Piazzale Roma
SAN POLO
RIALTO
CASTELLO
Canale Scomenzera
Santa Marta
Darsena Grande
Isola San Pietro
Isola La Certosa
LA TANA
SAN MARCO
SANTA MARTA
Canale di Fusina
DORSODURO
Isola di San Giorgio Maggiore
Canale di San Marco
Darsena di Sant'Elena
SACCA FISOLA
SANT'ELENA
Canale della Giudecca
SACCA SAN BIAGIO
Parco delle Rimembranze
Isola di Sant'Elena
GIUDECCA
Isola della Giudecca
Isola la Grazia
Lido di Venezia
Isola di San Servolo
0 1 km
0 0.5 miles
Isola di San Clemente
Laguna Veneta
Isola di San Lazzaro degli Armeni
LIDO

LIDO DI VENEZIA

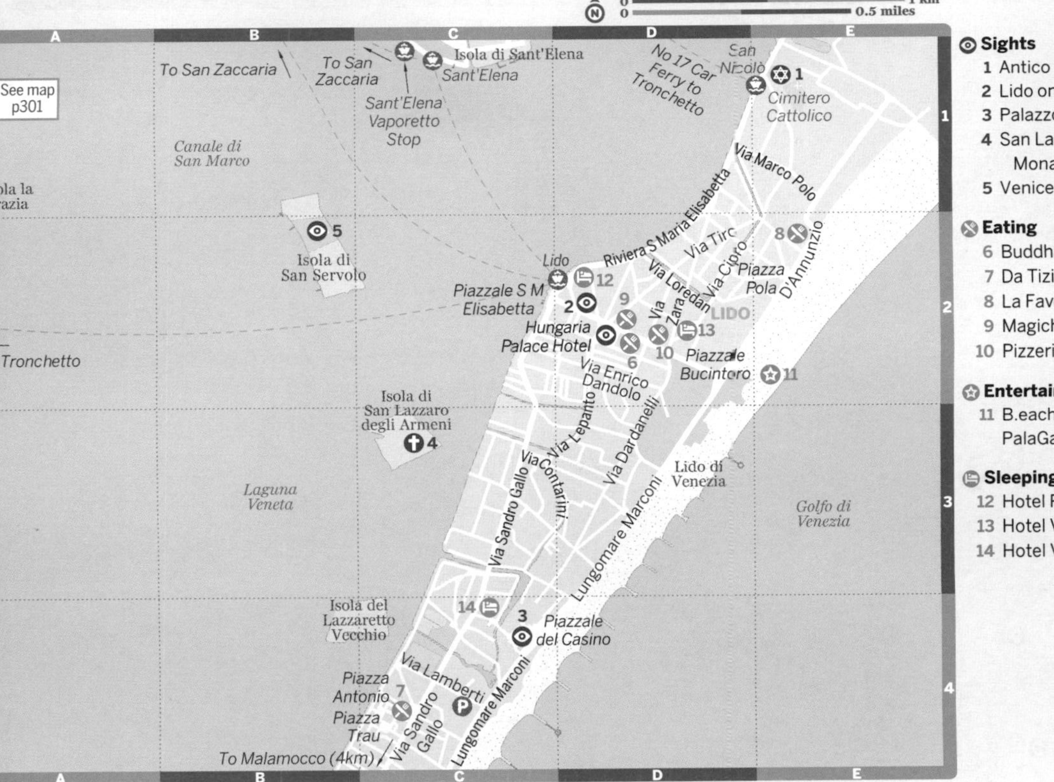

Sights (p149)
- 1 Antico Cimitero Israelitico E1
- 2 Lido on Bike D2
- 3 Palazzo della Mostra del Cinema C4
- 4 San Lazzaro degli Armeni Monastery C3
- 5 Venice International University B2

Eating (p153)
- 6 Buddha D2
- 7 Da Tiziano C4
- 8 La Favorita E2
- 9 Magiche Voglie D2
- 10 Pizzeria alla Botte D2

Entertainment (p153)
- 11 B.each E2
- PalaGalileo concert hall .... (see 3)

Sleeping (p201)
- 12 Hotel Panorama D2
- 13 Hotel Villa Cipro D2
- 14 Hotel Villa Stella C4

Key on p288

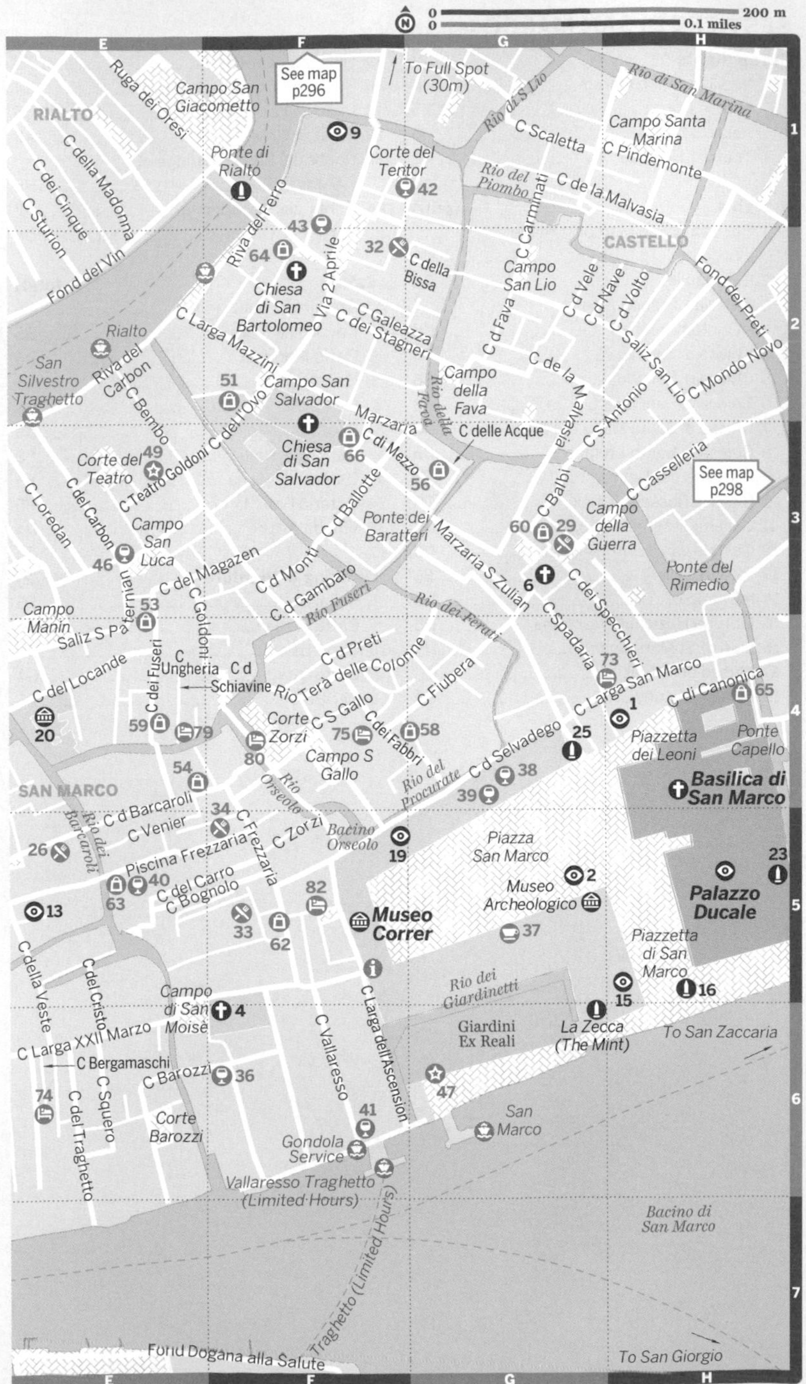

200 m
0.1 miles
RIALTO
CASTELLO
SAN MARCO
Campo San Giacometto
See map p296
See map p298
To Full Spot (30m)
Ruga dei Oresi
Ponte di Rialto
Riva del Ferro
Corte del Tentor
Campo Santa Marina
C Scaletta
C Pindemonte
C de la Malvasia
Rio di San Marina
Rio di S Lio
Rio del Piombo
C Carminati
C della Madonna
C dei Cinque
C Sturion
Fond del Vin
Chiesa di San Bartolomeo
Via 2 Aprile
C della Bissa
Campo San Lio
C d Fava
C d Vele
C d Nave
C d Volto
Fond dei Preti
C Galeazza
C dei Stagneri
Salz San Lio
C Mondo Novo
C S Antonio
C Larga Mazzini
Rialto
San Silvestro Traghetto
Riva del Carbon
C Bembo
Campo San Salvador
Campo della Fava
C de la Malvasia
Rio della Fava
Chiesa di San Salvador
Marzaria
C di Mezzo
C delle Acque
C Casselleria
C Teatro Goldoni
C del l'Ovo
Corte del Teatro
C Loredan
C del Carbon
C d Ballotte
C Balbi
Campo della Guerra
Campo San Luca
Ponte dei Baratteri
Marzaria S Zulian
Ponte del Rimedio
C d Monti
C del Magazen
C d Gambaro
Rio Fuseri
Rio dei Ferai
C dei Specchieri
C Spadaria
Campo Manin
Saliz S Paternian
C Goldoni
C Ungheria
C d Schiavine
C d Preti
C del Locande
C dei Fuseri
Rio Terà delle Colonne
C Fiubera
C Larga San Marco
C di Canonica
Corte Zorzi
C S Gallo
C dei Fabbri
Campo S Gallo
Piazzetta dei Leoni
Ponte Capello
C d Selvadego
Rio del Procurate
Basilica di San Marco
Rio Orseolo
C d Barcaroli
C Venier
Rio dei Barcaroli
C Frezzaria
C Zorzi
Bacino Orseolo
Piscina Frezzaria
Piazza San Marco
Museo Archeologico
Palazzo Ducale
C del Carro
C Bognolo
Museo Correr
Piazzetta di San Marco
C della Veste
C del Cristo
Campo di San Moisè
C Larga dell'Ascension
C Vallaresso
Rio dei Giardinetti
Giardini Ex Reali
La Zecca (The Mint)
To San Zaccaria
C Larga XXII Marzo
C Bergamaschi
C Barozzi
C Squero
C del Traghetto
Corte Barozzi
San Marco
Gondola Service
Vallaresso Traghetto (Limited Hours)
Traghetto (Limited Hours)
Bacino di San Marco
Fond Dogana alla Salute
To San Giorgio
E
F
G
H
1
2
3
4
5
6
7
9
42
43
32
64
51
66
49
56
60
29
46
6
53
73
1
65
20
59
79
75
58
25
80
54
38
39
34
26
19
2
23
40
13
63
82
33
62
37
16
15
4
36
74
47
41

SESTIERE DI SAN MARCO *Map on p286*

41 Harry's Bar ... F6
42 I Rusteghi ... G1
43 Osteria all'Alba ... F1
44 Palazzo Franchetti Caffè ... B6
45 Teamo ... C4
46 Torino@Notte ... E3

Entertainment (p74)

47 HelloVenezia Ticket Office (ACTV) ... G6
Interpreti Veneziani ... (see 5)
48 Musica a Palazzo ... C6
49 Teatro Goldoni ... E3
50 Teatro La Fenice ... D5

Shopping (p74)

51 Antica Modisteria Giuliana Longo ... F2
52 Arcobaleno ... B5
53 Arnoldo & Battois ... E4
54 ArtigianCarta di Massimo Doretto ... E4
55 Bevilacqua ... D6
56 Camuffo ... G3
57 Carpe Diem ... D6
58 Charta ... G4
59 Daniela Ghezzo ... E4
60 Esperienze ... G3
61 Fiorella Gallery ... B6
62 Gloria Astolfo ... F5
63 La Pietra Filosofale ... E5
64 Le Botteghe ... F2
65 Libreria Studium ... H4
66 Materialmente ... F3
67 Ottica Carraro ... D4
Paolo Olbi ... (see 28)
68 Venetia Studium ... D6

Sleeping (p193)

69 AD Place Venice ... D5
70 Bloom/7 Cielo ... B5
71 Giò & Giò ... D6
72 Gritti Palace ... D7
73 Hotel ai do Mori ... H4
74 Hotel Flora ... E6
75 Hotel Noemi ... F4
76 Locanda Antico Fiore ... B4
77 Locanda Art Deco ... B5
78 Locanda Barbarigo ... C7
79 Locanda Casa Petrarca ... E4
80 Locanda Orseolo ... F4
81 Novecento ... C6
82 Palazzo Selvadego ... F5

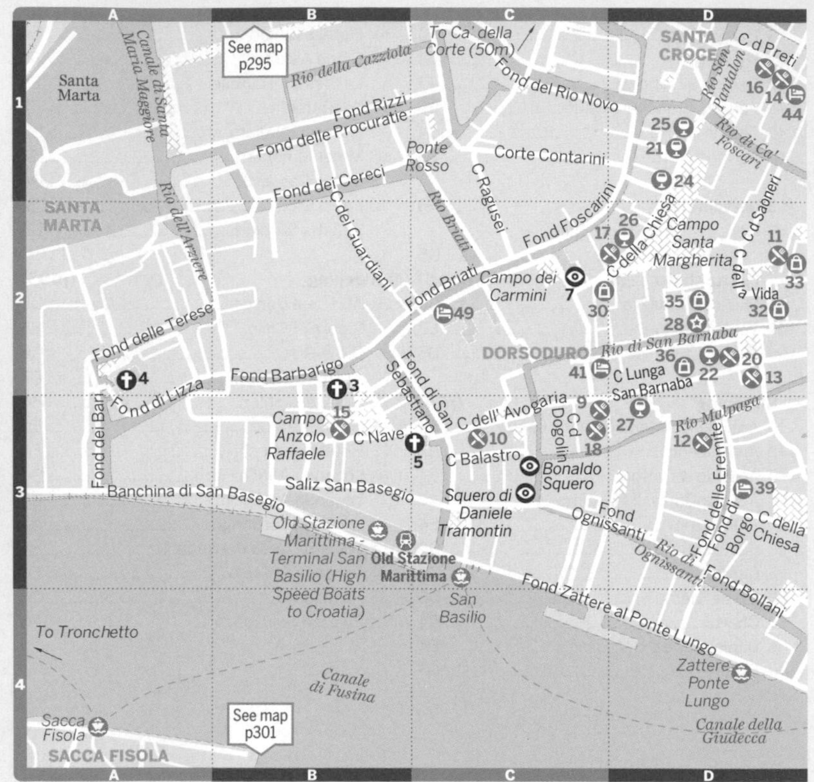

Top Sights (p79)
Ca' Rezzonico ... E2
Gallerie dell'Accademia ... E3
Peggy Guggenheim Collection ... F3
Punta della Dogana ... H3

Sights (p82)
1 Ca' Dario ... G3
2 Chiesa dei Gesuati ... E4
3 Chiesa dell'Arcangelo Raffaele ... B2
4 Chiesa di San Nicolò dei Mendicoli ... A2
5 Chiesa di San Sebastian ... C3
6 Chiesa di Santa Maria della Salute ... H4
7 Scuola Grande dei Carmini ... C2
8 Squero di San Trovaso ... E4

Eating (p85)
9 Al Profeta ... C3
10 Avogaria ... C3
11 Do Farai ... D2
12 Enoteca Ai Artisti ... D3
13 Grom ... D2
14 Impronta Café ... D1
15 Pane Vino e San Daniele ... B3
16 Pasticceria Tonolo ... D1
17 Pizza al Volo ... D2
18 Ristorante La Bitta ... C3
19 Ristorante San Trovaso ... E4
20 Ristoteca Oniga ... D2

Drinking & Nightlife (p87)
21 Ai Do Draghi ... D1
22 Ai Pugni ... D2
Cantina di Millevini ... (see 26)
23 Cantinone Già Schiavi ... E4
24 Il Caffè Rosso ... D1
25 Imagina Café ... D1
26 Osteria alla Bifora ... D2
27 Tea Room Beatrice ... D3

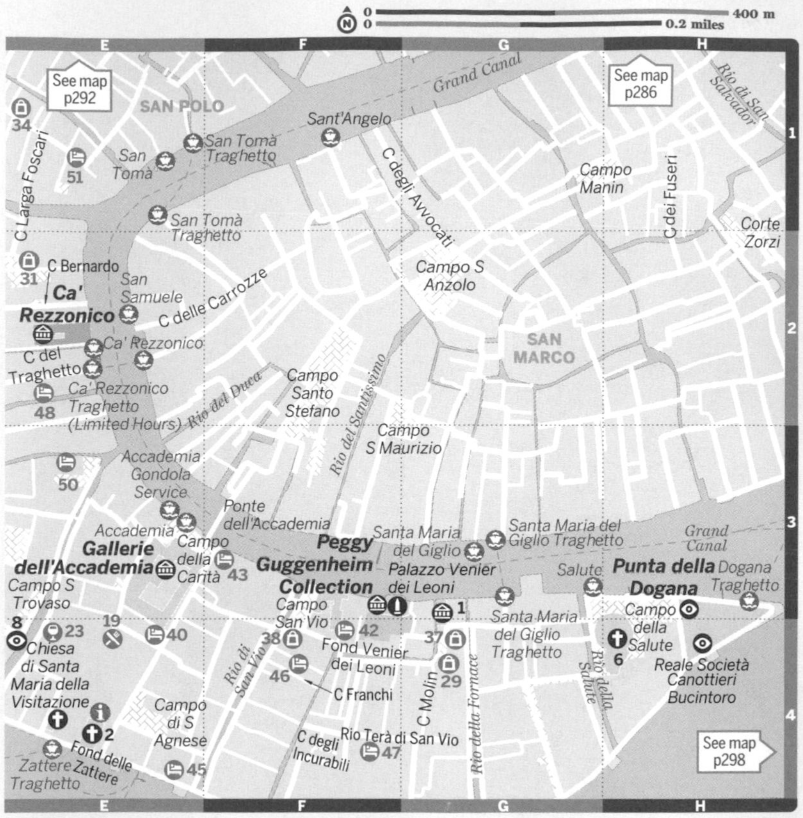

Entertainment (p88)
28 Venice Jazz Club ... D2

Shopping (p88)
29 Antiquariato Claudia Canestrelli ... G4
30 Aqua Altra ... C2
31 Arras ... E2
32 Ca' Macana ... D2
33 Danghyra ... D2
34 Elitre ... E1
35 Gualti ... D2
36 Lauretta Vistosi ... D2
37 Le Forcole di Saverio Pastor ... G4
Madera ... (see 13)
38 Marina e Susanna Sent ... F4
Signor Bloom ... (see 20)

Sleeping (p194)
39 Antica Locanda Montin ... D3
40 Ca' Pisani ... E4
41 Casa Rezzonico ... C2
42 Charming House DD.724 ... F4
43 Hotel Galleria ... F3
44 Hotel Tivoli ... D1
45 La Calcina ... E4
46 La Chicca ... F4
47 Locanda Ca' del Brocchi ... F4
48 Locanda San Barnaba ... E2
49 Palazzo Zenobio ... C2
50 Pensione Accademia Villa Maravege ... E3
51 Università Ca' Foscari Notice Boards ... E1

Key on p294

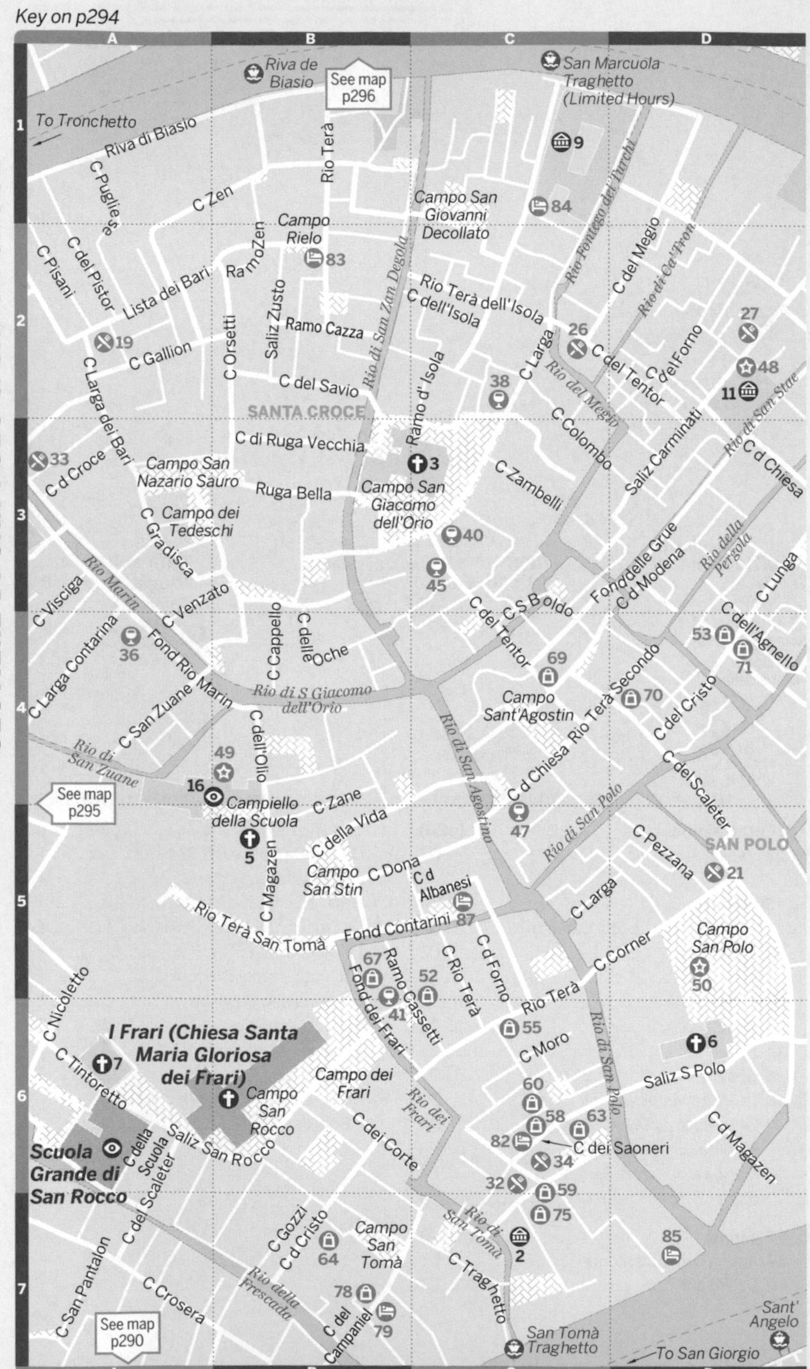
SESTIERE DI SAN POLO & SANTA CROCE
See map p296
See map p295
See map p290
San Marcuola Traghetto (Limited Hours)
Riva de Biasio
To Tronchetto
Riva di Biasio
C Zen
Campo San Giovanni Decollato
Campo Rielo
Rio Terà dell'Isola
C dell'Isola
Ramo Cazza
C del Savio
SANTA CROCE
C di Ruga Vecchia
Campo San Nazario Sauro
Ruga Bella
Campo San Giacomo dell'Orio
Campo dei Tedeschi
Campo Sant'Agostin
Campiello della Scuola
Campo San Stin
Fond Contarini
Rio Terà San Tomà
SAN POLO
Campo San Polo
I Frari (Chiesa Santa Maria Gloriosa dei Frari)
Campo dei Frari
Campo San Rocco
Scuola Grande di San Rocco
Saliz San Rocco
Campo San Tomà
San Tomà Traghetto
Sant' Angelo
To San Giorgio
C dei Saoneri
Saliz S Polo

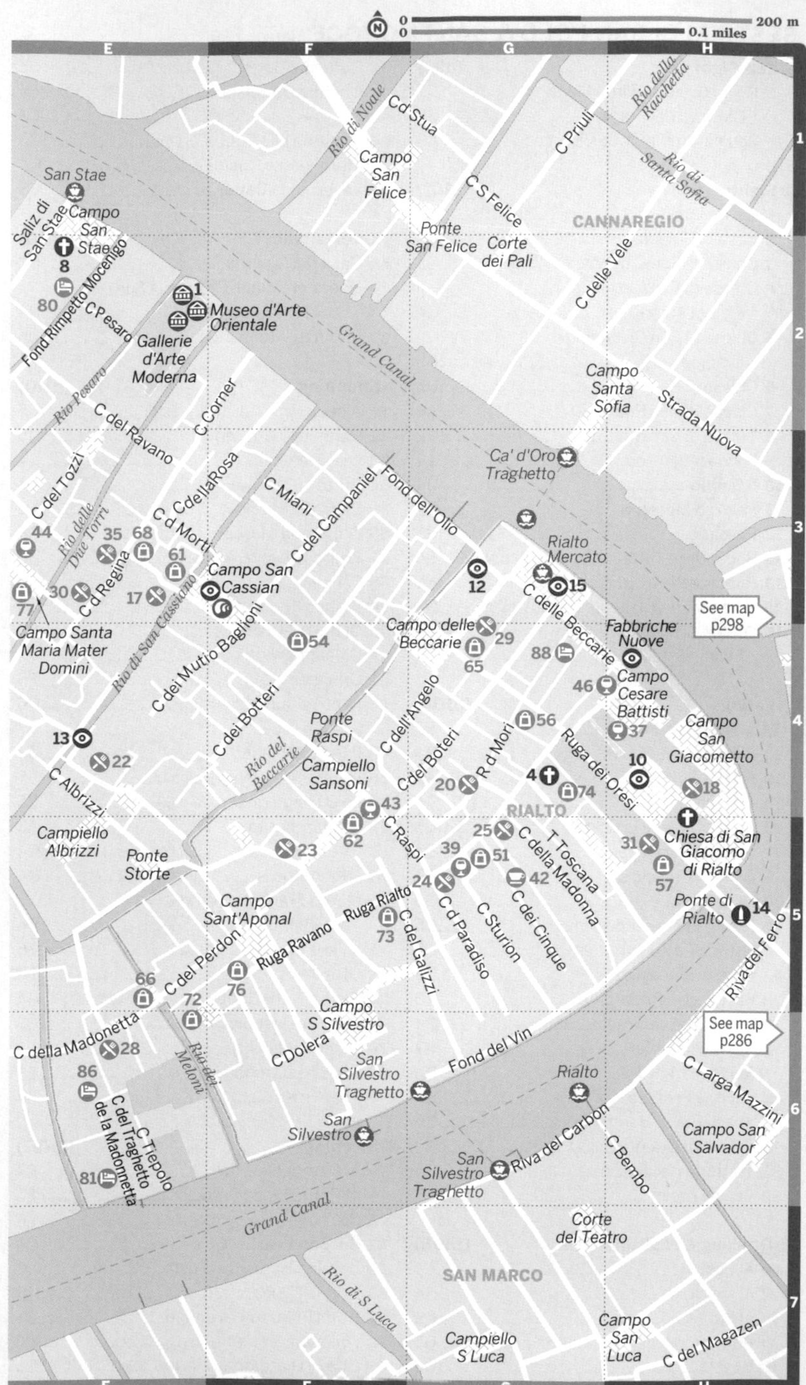

SESTIERE DI SAN POLO & SANTA CROCE
0 200 m
0 0.1 miles
CANNAREGIO
RIALTO
SAN MARCO
Grand Canal
San Stae
Campo San Stae
Saliz di San Stae
Fond Rimpetto Mocenigo
C Pesaro
Museo d'Arte Orientale
Gallerie d'Arte Moderna
Rio Pesaro
C del Ravano
C Corner
C del Tozzi
Rio delle Due Torri
C della Rosa
C d Morti
C d Regina
Campo San Cassian
Rio di San Cassiano
Campo Santa Maria Mater Domini
C dei Mutio Baglioni
C Miani
C del Campaniel
Fond dell'Olio
C dei Botteri
Rio del Beccarie
Ponte Raspi
Campiello Sansoni
C Albrizzi
Campiello Albrizzi
Ponte Storte
Campo Sant'Aponal
C del Perdon
Ruga Ravano
Ruga Rialto
C del Galizzi
C d Paradiso
C Sturion
C dei Cinque
C della Madonna
T Toscana
C Raspi
C dell'Angelo
C del Boteri
R d Mori
Ruga dei Oresi
Campo delle Beccarie
C delle Beccarie
Rialto Mercato
Fabbriche Nuove
Campo Cesare Battisti
Campo San Giacometto
Chiesa di San Giacomo di Rialto
Ponte di Rialto
Riva del Ferro
See map p298
See map p286
C della Madonetta
Rio dei Meloni
C del Traghetto de la Madonnetta
C Tiepolo
Campo S Silvestro
C Dolera
San Silvestro Traghetto
San Silvestro
Fond del Vin
Rialto
Riva del Carbon
C Bembo
C Larga Mazzini
Campo San Salvador
Corte del Teatro
Rio di S Luca
Campiello S Luca
Campo San Luca
C del Magazen
Rio di Noale
Cd Stua
Campo San Felice
C S Felice
Ponte San Felice
Corte dei Pali
C Priuli
Rio della Racchetta
Rio di Santa Sofia
C delle Vele
Campo Santa Sofia
Strada Nuova
Ca' d'Oro Traghetto
E
F
G
H
1
2
3
4
5
6
7
1 8 80 44 35 68 61 30 17 77 13 22 12 15 29 65 88 54 46 37 56 20 4 74 10 18 43 62 23 25 39 51 42 24 31 57 14 73 66 72 76 28 86 81

SESTIERI DI SAN POLO & SANTA CROCE *Map on p292*

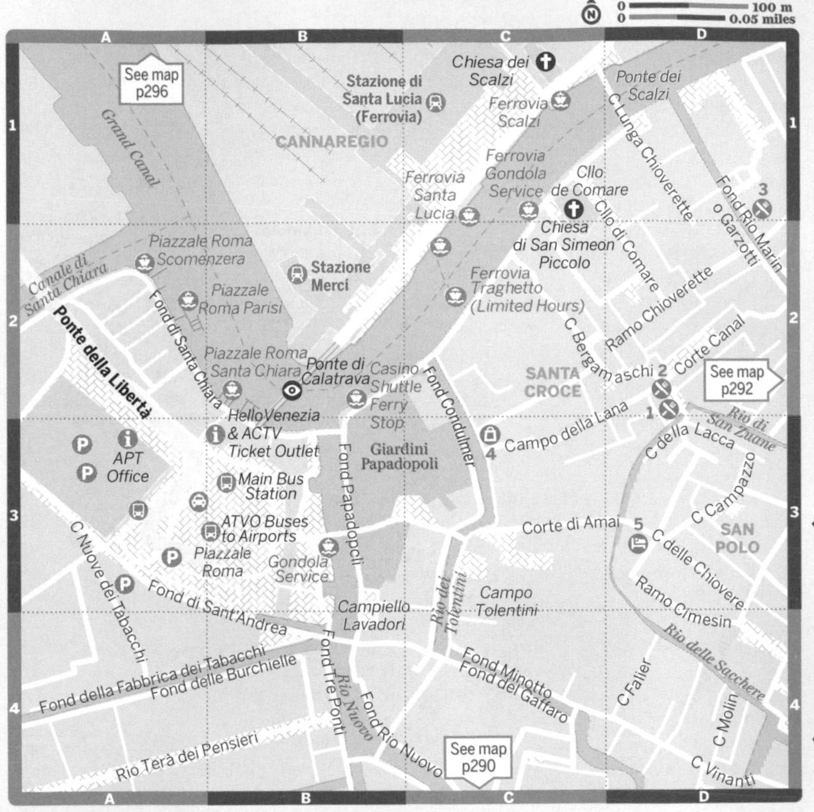

Eating (p106)
1 La Rivetta D2
2 Pasticceria Trevisan D2
3 Tearoom Caffè Orientale D1

Shopping (p112)
4 Mare di Carta C3

Sleeping (p198)
5 Hostel Domus Civica D3

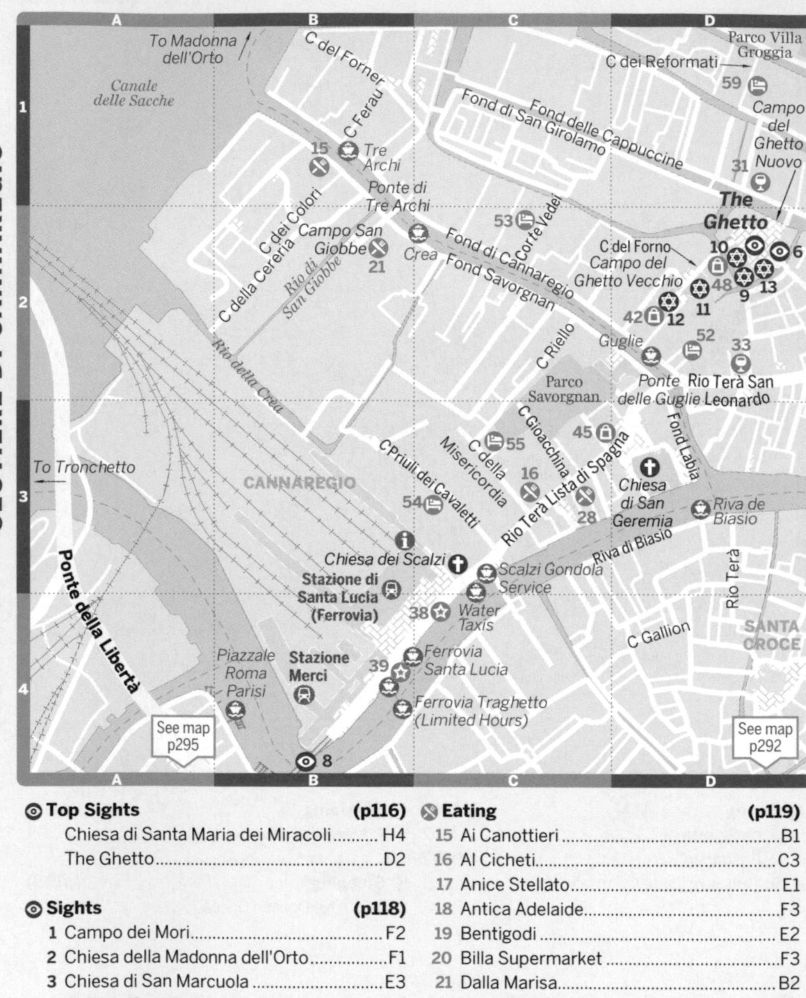

Top Sights (p116)

Chiesa di Santa Maria dei Miracoli H4
The Ghetto D2

Sights (p118)

1 Campo dei Mori F2
2 Chiesa della Madonna dell'Orto F1
3 Chiesa di San Marcuola E3
4 Galleria Franchetti F4
5 I Gesuiti H3
6 Ikona Gallery D2
Museo Ebraico .... (see 13)
7 Palazzo Vendramin-Calergi E3
8 Ponte di Calatrava B4
9 Schola Canton D2
10 Schola Italiana D2
11 Schola Levantina D2
12 Schola Spagnola D2
13 Schola Tedesca D2
14 Spezeria Antica Santa Fosca E3

Eating (p119)

15 Ai Canottieri B1
16 Al Cicheti C3
17 Anice Stellato E1
18 Antica Adelaide F3
19 Bentigodi E2
20 Billa Supermarket F3
21 Dalla Marisa B2
22 La Cantina F3
23 Osteria al Ponte H4
24 Osteria alla Vedova F3
25 Osteria Boccadoro H4
26 Osteria da Alberto H4
27 Osteria L'Orto dei Mori F2
28 Pasticceria dal Mas C3
29 Taverna del Campiello Remer G4

Drinking & Nightlife (p121)

30 Agli Ormesini E2
31 Al Timon D1

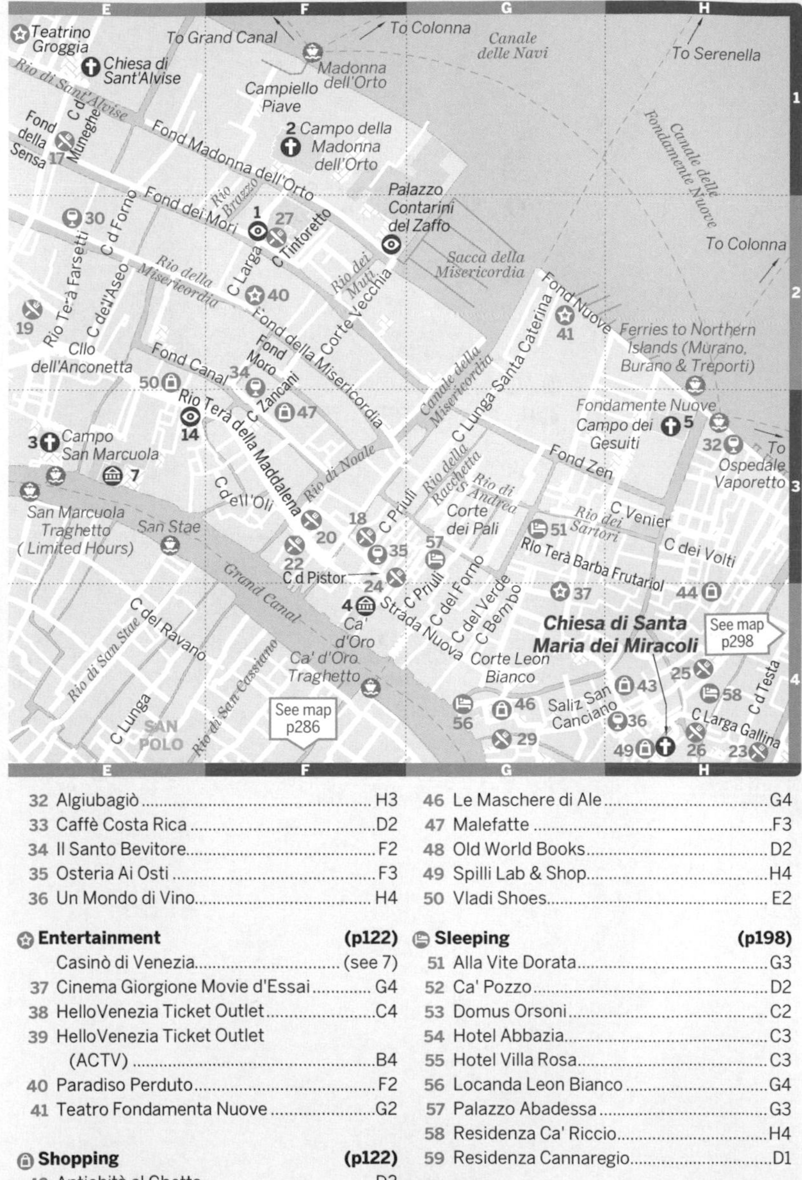

Teatrino Groggia
Chiesa di Sant'Alvise
To Grand Canal
To Colonna
Canale delle Navi
To Serenella
Madonna dell'Orto
Campiello Piave
2 Campo della Madonna dell'Orto
Fond Madonna dell'Orto
Fond dei Mori
Palazzo Contarini del Zaffo
Sacca della Misericordia
To Colonna
Ferries to Northern Islands (Murano, Burano & Treporti)
Fondamente Nuove
Campo dei Gesuiti
To Ospedale Vaporetto
Campo San Marcuola
San Marcuola Traghetto (Limited Hours)
San Stae
Grand Canal
Ca' d'Oro
Ca' d'Oro Traghetto
Chiesa di Santa Maria dei Miracoli
See map p298
See map p286
SAN POLO
Corte Leon Bianco
Corte dei Pali
Strada Nuova
Rio Terà della Maddalena
Fond della Misericordia
Fond Nuove
C Lunga Santa Caterina
Fond Zen
C Venier
C dei Volti
Rio Terà Barba Frutariol
Saliz San Canciano
C Larga Gallina

Key on p300

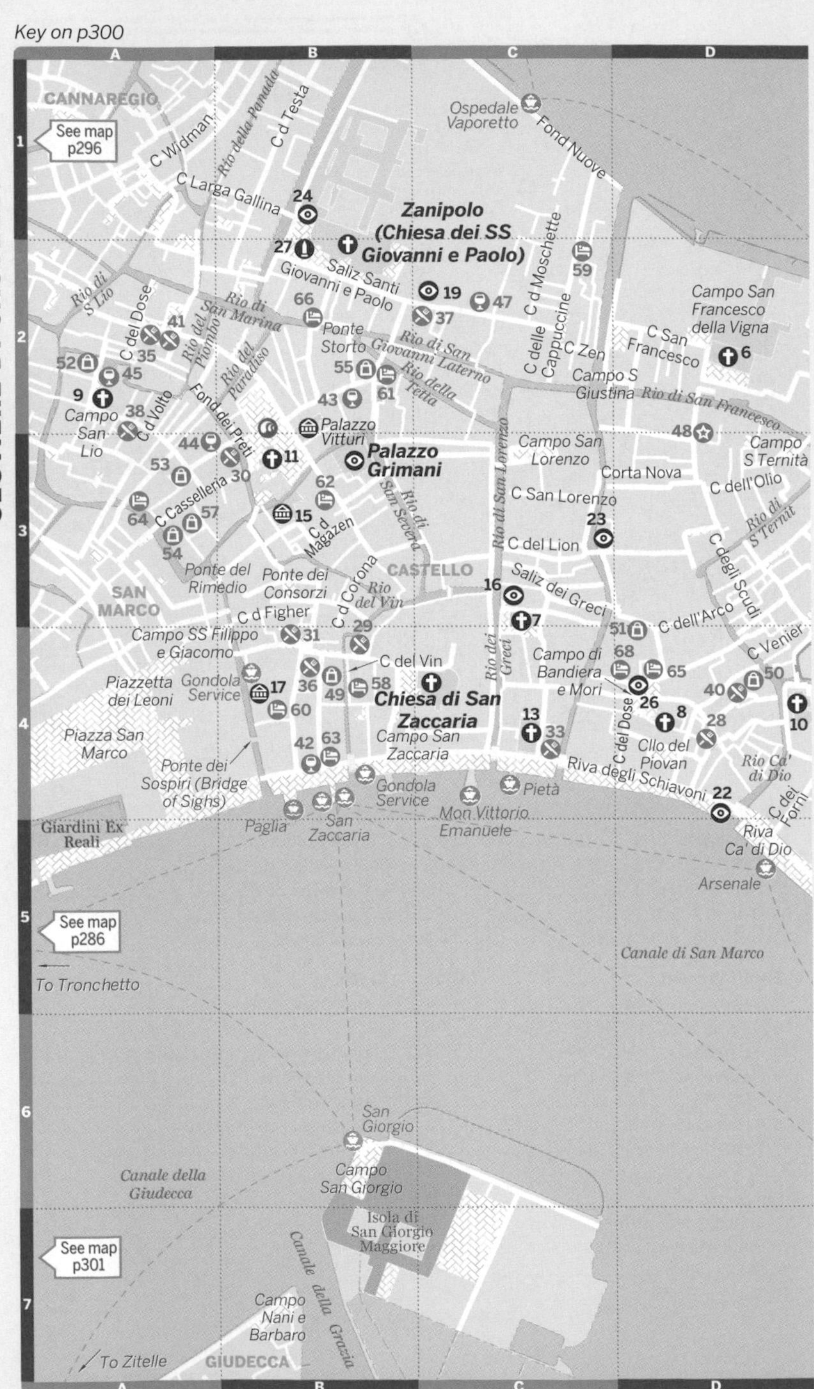
SESTIERE DI CASTELLO
CANNAREGIO
See map p296
C Widman
Rio della Panada
C d Testa
C Larga Gallina
Ospedale Vaporetto
Fond Nuove
Zanipolo (Chiesa dei SS Giovanni e Paolo)
Saliz Santi Giovanni e Paolo
Rio di S Lio
C del Dose
Rio del San Piombo
Rio di San Marina
Rio del Paradiso
Ponte Storto
Rio di San Giovanni Laterno
Rio della Tetta
C d Moschette
C delle Cappuccine
C Zen
Campo S Giustina
Rio di San Francesco
C San Francesco
Campo San Francesco della Vigna
Campo San Lio
C d Volto
Fond dei Preti
Palazzo Vitturi
Palazzo Grimani
Rio di San Severo
Rio di San Lorenzo
Campo San Lorenzo
Corta Nova
C San Lorenzo
Campo S Ternità
C dell'Olio
Rio di S Ternit
C Casselleria
C d Magazen
C del Lion
C degli Scudi
Ponte del Rimedio
Ponte dei Consorzi
C d Corona
Rio del Vin
CASTELLO
Saliz dei Greci
SAN MARCO
C d Figher
Campo SS Filippo e Giacomo
C dell'Arco
C Venier
C del Vin
Rio dei Greci
Campo di Bandiera e Mori
Piazzetta dei Leoni
Gondola Service
Chiesa di San Zaccaria
Campo San Zaccaria
Piazza San Marco
Ponte dei Sospiri (Bridge of Sighs)
C del Dose
Cllo del Piovan
Riva degli Schiavoni
Rio Ca' di Dio
C dei Forni
Gondola Service
Pietà
Paglia
San Zaccaria
Mon Vittorio Emanuele
Giardini Ex Reali
Riva Ca' di Dio
Arsenale
See map p286
To Tronchetto
Canale di San Marco
San Giorgio
Canale della Giudecca
Campo San Giorgio
Isola di San Giorgio Maggiore
See map p301
Canale della Grazia
Campo Nani e Barbaro
To Zitelle
GIUDECCA

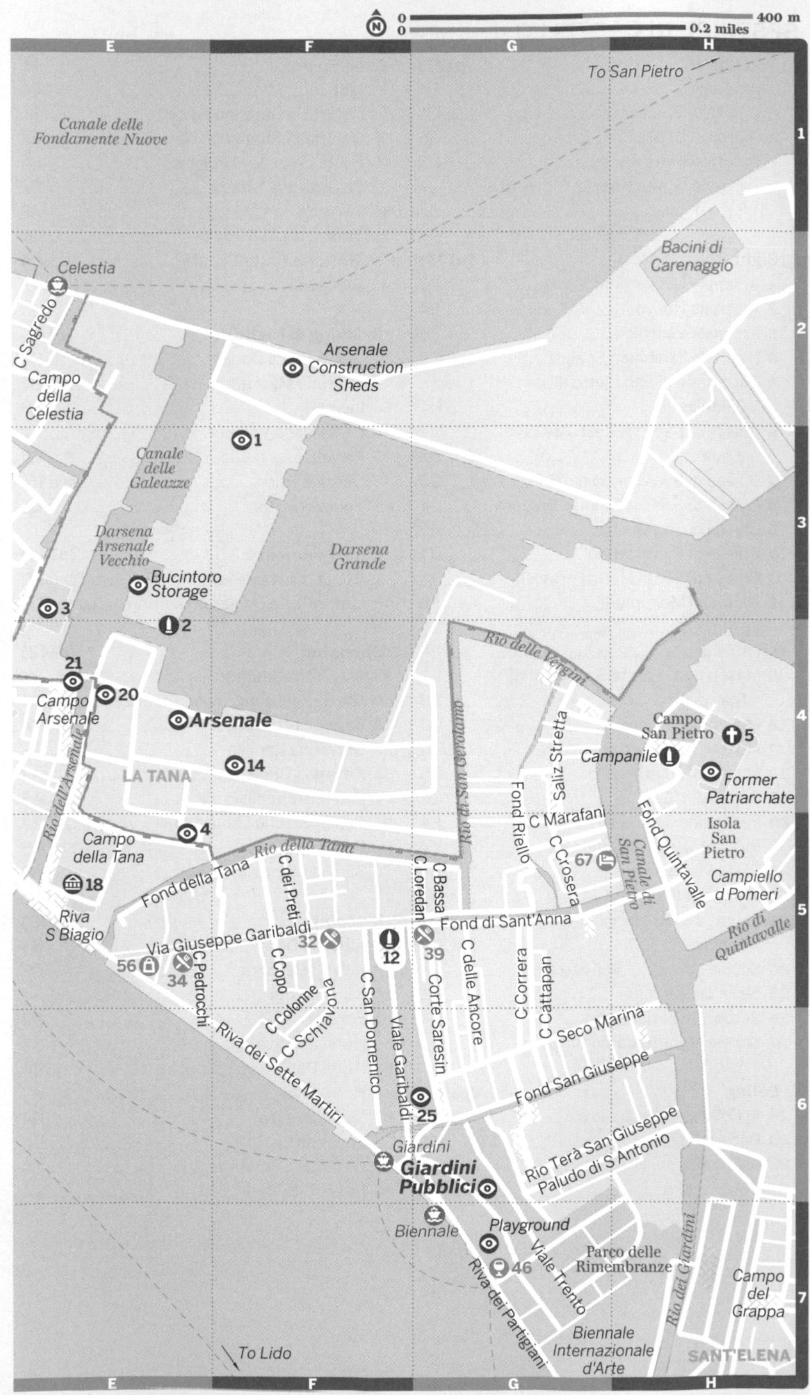

SESTIERE DI CASTELLO
0 400 m
0 0.2 miles
To San Pietro
Canale delle Fondamente Nuove
Bacini di Carenaggio
Celestia
C Sagredo
Campo della Celestia
Arsenale Construction Sheds
Canale delle Galeazze
Darsena Arsenale Vecchio
Darsena Grande
Bucintoro Storage
Campo Arsenale
Arsenale
LA TANA
Rio dell'Arsenale
Rio delle Vergini
Rio di San Gerolamo
Campo San Pietro
Campanile
Former Patriarchate
Saliz Stretta
Fond Riello
C Marafani
C Crosera
Canale di San Pietro
Fond Quintavalle
Isola San Pietro
Campiello d Pomeri
Rio di Quintavalle
Campo della Tana
Rio della Tana
Fond della Tana
C dei Preti
C Loredan
C Bassa
Fond di Sant'Anna
Riva S Biagio
Via Giuseppe Garibaldi
C Pedrocchi
C Copo
C Colonne
C Schiavona
C San Domenico
Viale Garibaldi
Corte Saresin
C delle Ancore
C Correra
C Cattapan
Seco Marina
Fond San Giuseppe
Riva dei Sette Martiri
Rio Terà San Giuseppe
Paludo di S Antonio
Giardini
Giardini Pubblici
Biennale
Playground
Viale Trento
Parco delle Rimembranze
Riva dei Partigiani
Rio dei Giardini
Campo del Grappa
Biennale Internazionale d'Arte
SANT'ELENA
To Lido

SESTIERE DI CASTELLO *Map on p298*

Top Sights (p127)

- Arsenale E4
- Chiesa di San Zaccaria C4
- Giardini Pubblici G6
- Palazzo Grimani B3
- Zanipolo (Chiesa dei SS Giovanni e Paolo) B2

Sights (p133)

1 Arsenale Nuovissimo F3
2 Arsenale Nuovo E4
3 Arsenale Vecchio E3
4 Biennale Exhibition Spaces E5
5 Cattedrale di San Pietro di Castello H4
6 Chiesa di San Francesco della Vigna D2
7 Chiesa di San Giorgio dei Greci C3
8 Chiesa di San Giovanni in Bragora D4
9 Chiesa di San Lio A2
10 Chiesa di San Martino D4
11 Chiesa di Santa Maria Formosa B3
12 Garibaldi Monument F5
13 La Pietà C4
14 La Tana F4
15 Museo della Fondazione Querini Stampalia B3
16 Museo delle Icone C3
17 Museo Diocesano di Venezia B4
18 Museo Storico Navale E5
19 Ospedaletto C2
20 Padiglione delle Navi E4
Palazzo Querini Stampalia (see 15)
21 Porta Magna E4
22 Riva degli Schiavoni D4
23 Scuola di San Giorgio degli Schiavoni C3
24 Scuola Grande di San Marco B1
25 Serra dei Giardini G6
26 Sotoportego dei Preti D4
27 Statue of Bartolomeo Colleoni B2

Eating (p138)

28 Al Covo D4
29 Bacaro Risorto B4
30 Cip Ciap B3
31 Conca d'Oro B4
32 Le Spighe F5
33 Met C4
34 Osteria al Garanghelo E5
35 Osteria di Santa Marina A2
36 Pasticceria da Bonifacio B4
37 Pizzeria alla Strega C2
38 Taverna San Lio A2
39 Trattoria alla Rampa G5
40 Trattoria Corte Sconta D4
41 Zenzero A2

Drinking & Nightlife (p141)

42 Bar Terazza Danieli B4
43 Enoteca Mascareta B2
44 Inishark A3
45 L'Olandese Volante A2
46 Paradiso G7
Qcoffee Bar (see 15)
47 Venezia Caffé C2

Entertainment (p142)

Concerts at La Pietà (see 13)
48 Laboratorio Occupato Morion D2

Shopping (p142)

49 Arte Vetro Murano B4
50 Atelier Alessandro Merlin D4
51 Banco Lotto 10 D4
52 Giovanna Zanella A2
53 Kalimala Cuoieria A3
54 Paolo Brandolisio A3
55 Papier Mâché Laboratorio B2
56 Profili E5
57 Sigfrido Cipolato A3

Sleeping (p199)

58 Albergo Doni B4
59 Alloggi Barbaria C2
60 Ca' dei Dogi B4
61 Foresteria Valdese B2
62 Hotel al Piave B3
63 Hotel Danieli B4
64 Hotel Riva A3
65 La Residenza D4
66 Locanda La Corte B2
67 Locanda Sant'Anna G5
68 Palazzo Soderini D4

GIUDECCA

Top Sights (p147)

Chiesa di San Giorgio Maggiore E2

Sights (p148)

1 Chiesa del SS Redentore C3
2 Chiesa delle Zitelle D2
3 Chiesa di Sant'Eufemia A2
4 Fondazione Giorgio Cini E2
5 Fortuny Tessuti Artistici A2
6 Galleria Santa Eufemia B2
7 Giudecca 795 .... A2

Eating (p151)

8 Al Pontil dea Giudecca C3
9 ESU B3
10 Harry's Dolci A2
11 I Figli delle Stelle D2
La Palanca .... (see 17)
12 Mistrà D3
13 Thursday Organic Market A2

Drinking & Nightlife (p153)

14 Skyline Molino Stucky A2

Entertainment (p153)

15 Teatro Junghans B3

Sleeping (p201)

16 Bauer Palladio Hotel & Spa D2
17 Casa Genoveffa B2
18 Ostello Venezia D3

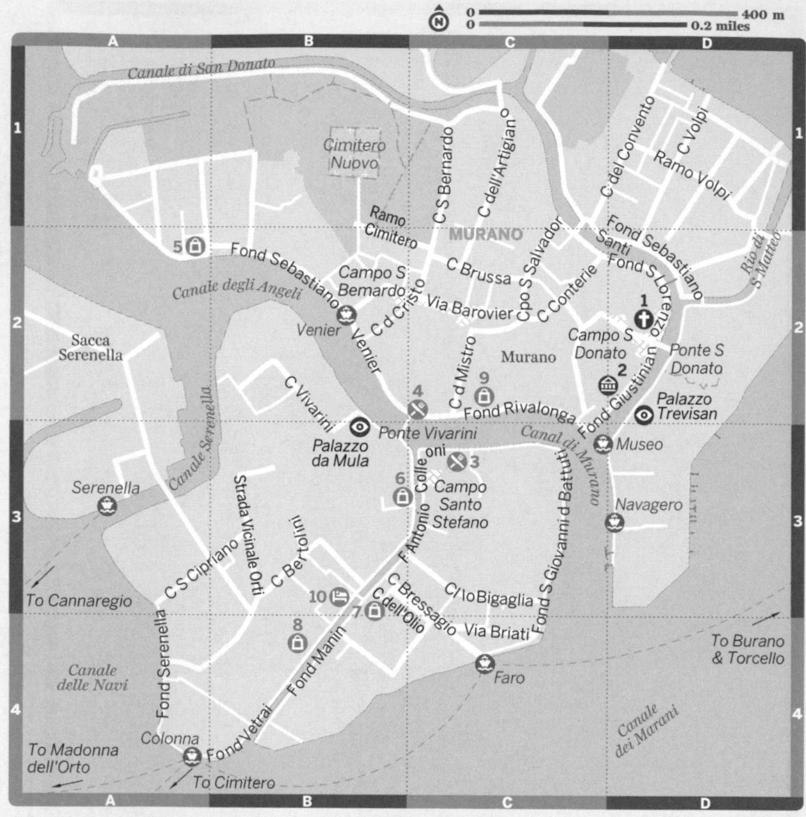

Sights (p157)

Eating (p100)

Shopping (p101)

Sleeping (p202)

BURANO & TORCELLO

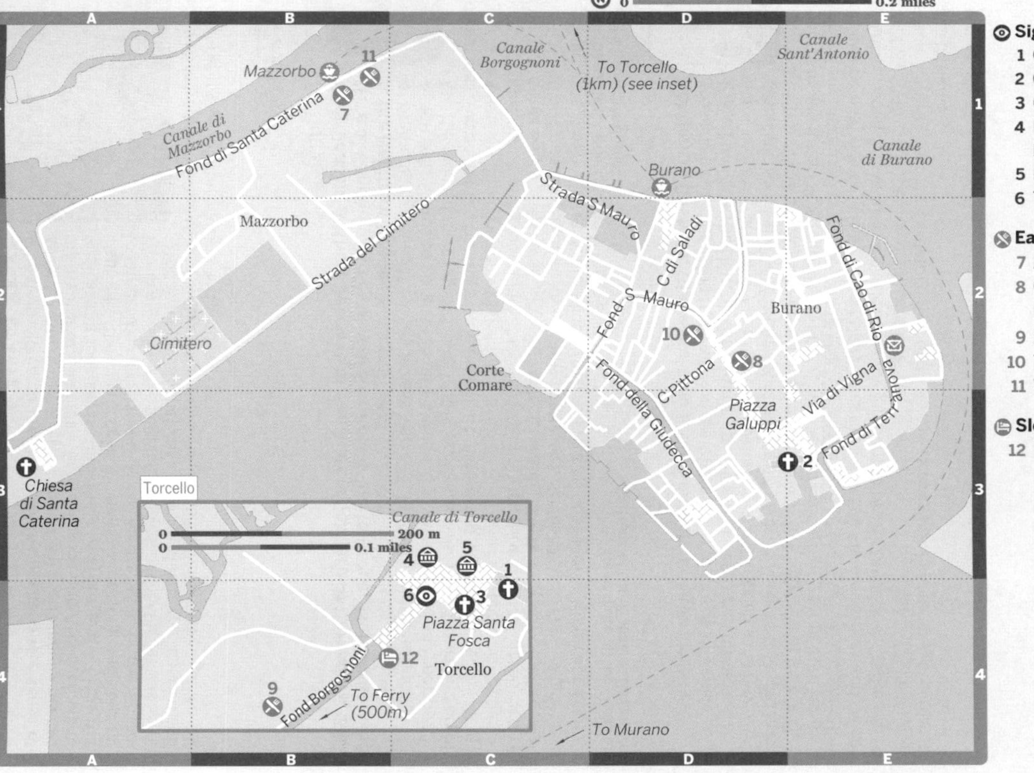

Sights (p157)

Eating (p101)

Sleeping (p202)

Our Story

A beat-up old car, a few dollars in the pocket and a sense of adventure. In 1972 that's all Tony and Maureen Wheeler needed for the trip of a lifetime – across Europe and Asia overland to Australia. It took several months, and at the end – broke but inspired – they sat at their kitchen table writing and stapling together their first travel guide, *Across Asia on the Cheap*. Within a week they'd sold 1500 copies. Lonely Planet was born.

Today, Lonely Planet has offices in Melbourne, London and Oakland, with more than 600 staff and writers. We share Tony's belief that 'a great guidebook should do three things: inform, educate and amuse'.

Our Writers

Alison Bing

Coordinating Author, Sestiere di San Marco, Sestiere di Dorsoduro, Sestiere di Cannaregio, Sestieri di San Polo & Santa Croce, Murano, Burano & the Northern Islands When she's not scribbling notes in church pews or methodically eating her way across Venice's *sestieri* (neighbourhoods), Alison contributes to Lonely Planet's *Venice, USA, Morocco, San Francisco, Marrakesh, California* and *Discover Italy* guides, as well as food, art and architecture magazines. Alison holds a bachelor's degree in art history and a master's degree from the Fletcher School of Law and Diplomacy, a joint program of Tufts and Harvard Universities – perfectly respectable diplomatic credentials she regularly undermines with opinionated culture commentary for newspapers, magazines, TV and radio. Currently she divides her time between San Francisco and an Etruscan hilltop town in central Italy with partner Marco Flavio Marinucci, and tweets her finds at www.twitter.com/AlisonBing. Alison also contributed Plan Your Trip, Sleeping, Understand Venice & the Veneto and the colour sections in this guide.

Read more about Alison at:
lonelyplanet.com/members/alisonbing

Robert Landon

Sestiere di Castello, Giudecca, Lido & the Southern Islands Since first crossing from congested Piazzale Roma into the car-free canals of Venice, Robert has been hooked on the watery city. He's returned many times and in every season, from snowy February to sweltering August; its charms never diminish. However, it was albino asparagus and Valpolicella reds that had him writing home on his most recent trip to the Veneto. Before working for Lonely Planet, Robert studied Italian at Stanford University, and he also lived a half-year in both Rome and Florence. Currently based in Rio de Janeiro, he has written about travel, arts and culture for a range of publications, including the London *Daily Telegraph*, the *Los Angeles Times* and *Dwell* magazine. Other Lonely Planet titles include *Florence Encounter, Brazil, Colombia, California, Portugal* and *West Africa*. Robert also contributed Day Trips from Venice, Sleeping, Directory A–Z and Transport in this guide.

Read more about Robert at:
lonelyplanet.com/members/robertlandon

Published by Lonely Planet Publications Pty Ltd
ABN 36 005 607 983
7th edition – Feb 2012
ISBN 978 1 74179 852 4

10 9 8 7 6 5 4 3 2 1
Printed in China